The Tree of Visions

Visionary Traditions Of The Western World

The Tree of Visions
Visionary Traditions Of The Western World

Copyright © 2018 by David Nez

David Nez has asserted his right to be identified as the author of this Work. All rights are reserved, including the right to reproduce this book, or portions thereof, in any form. Reviewers may quote brief passages.

Cover and Interior art supplied by David Nez
Book design by Jeremy Berg

Published by Starseed Books
(an imprint of Lorian Press LLC)
6592 Peninsula Dr
Traverse City MI 49686

ISBN: 978-1-939790-20-0

Nez, David
The Tree of Visions:
Visionary Traditions Of The Western World/David Nez

Library of Congress Control Number: 2018940642

First Edition: April 2018

Printed in the United States of America

www.lorianpress.com

The Tree of Visions

Visionary Traditions Of The Western World

Shamanism, Magic & Myth
From Prehistory To The Present

David Nez

Acknowledgements

To my father George Nez for his encouragement,
to my wife Kirsten for her patience,
to my friends Milenko Matanovic and Marko Pogacnik
for their inspiration,
to Maria Brignola and Darcy Scholtz
for commenting on the manuscript,
and all my fellow travelers on the path of return...

Dedication

To the ancestors whose wisdom has guided us down through the ages... we stand on the shoulders of giants.

Contents

Introduction   1

    Introduction Notes   7

Chapter I: The World of the Shaman   8

    Defining Shamanism   9
    The Roles of the Shaman   11
    Trance Techniques   13
    Multiple Souls and Reincarnation   15
    Shamanic Cosmology   16
    The Lowerworld   17
    The Upperworld   20
    Sacred Geography of the Middle World   21
    Shamanic Skywatchers   23
    The Great Bear & The Cosmic Hunt   24
    Chapter 1 Notes   27

Chapter 2: The Shaman's Craft   30

    The World Tree   30
    The Eagle & the Serpent   33
    Helping- Spirits   34
    Animal Spirits in Shamanism & Ancient Magic   36
    Otherworldly Partners   38
    Black & White Shamans   39
    Tools of the Shaman   41
    The Sacred Circle & Four Directions in Shamanism   44
    Divination   44
    Shamanic Initiation   45
    Death & Rebirth of Shamans & Gods   46
    Chapter 2 Notes   48

Chapter 3: Shamans of The Paleolithic & Neolithic   51

    Cave Art & Shamanic Trance   51
    Did the Shaman's Trance—Make Us Human? Scientific Views   55
    Paleo-Writing   56
    Ice Age Astronomers of Lascaux Cave   56
    Paleolithic Mal'ta   58
    Genetic Links Between—Ancient Europeans & Native Americans   59

The Oldest Grave of a Shaman	60
Magic & Astro Ceremonialism of the Mesolithic	60
Gobekli Tepe—Temple of Animal Spirits	61
The Neolithic Revolution	63
Catalhoyuk and Ancestor Worship	64
The Woman & The Bull	65
Chapter 3 Notes	**67**

Chapter 4: Mesopotamian Magic — 71

Heavenly Writing & Magic Circles	71
The Rise of the First City-States	72
The Sacred Tree in Ancient Mesopotamia	73
Divining the Will of the Gods	75
Oracles of Ishtar	76
Inanna's Descent to the Underworld	77
Mesopotamian Cosmology	80
The Birth of Astronomy & Astrology	81
Planets and Pantheons	82
The Zodiac- Circle of Animals	83
The Shamanic Flight of Etana & the Eagle	84
Akitu Festival—Renewal of the King & Land	86
Temples & Ziggurats—Homes of the Gods	86
Demons of Mesopotamia	87
Talismans to Repel Demons	88
Babylonian Magic Circle	89
Celestial & Infernal Magic	90
Necromancy—Working with the Dead	91
Books of Stars & Stones	92
Herbal Magic	93
Astrology in Babylon	93
Chapter 4 Notes	**94**

Chapter 5: Ancient Egypt — 98

Magicians of the House of Life	98
Prehistoric Egypt	98
Nabta Playa- The Earliest Astronomical Monument	100
Gods & Cosmologies of Egypt	101
The Calendar/ Decans & Month Gods	103
Heka- God of Magic	104
Summoning Heka	104
Pharaoh As Arch-Magician & Shaman	106
Priests & Priestesses	108

Temples of Heaven	110
Magicians of the House of Life	111
The Magician's Box	112
Magical Medicine	112
Wise Women	113
Letters to the Dead	113
Demons of Egypt	114
Shamanic Elements in Egyptian Magic	114
The Opening of the Mouth Ceremony	115
The Soul in Ancient Egypt	116
Training for the Afterlife	116
The Books of the Dead	117
The Myth of Osiris	121
The Death & Resurrection of Osiris/Orion	123
Mysteries of Osiris & Isis	123
Chapter 5 Notes	**125**

Chapter 6: Megalithic Tombs & Sun Chariots — 128

European Magic in the Neolithic & Bronze Ages	128
Old Europe and the Goddess Civilization	129
Kurgan Warriors	130
Steppe Hypothesis	131
Anatolian Farmers	132
Paleolithic Continuity Paradigm	132
Newgrange—Gateway to the Otherworld	133
Stonehenge & Durrington Walls—Temples of Life & Death	135
The Megalith Builders	137
Enter the Proto-Indo-Europeans	138
The Sky Gods	139
Shamanic Influences	141
Metal Smiths & Magicians	142
Crete & the Goddess Religion	143
Cave, Mountain & Tree Sanctuaries	144
Sacred Dance & Drama	145
The End of the Minoans	146
Journey into the Labyrinth	146
The Mycenaeans	147
Smiths, shamans & magicians of the Iron Age	148
Rise of the Greeks	149
Altaic Origins of Apollo & Artemis?	151
Hermes—God of Magic	152
Divination & Oracles of Ancient Greece	153
Delphi	155

Dream Incubation of Asklepios	156
Oracles of The Underworld	157
The Goetes—Greek Magicians or Shamans?	158
Chapter 6 Notes	**160**

Chapter 7: Druids & Volvas   165

Celtic & Germanic Magic of the Iron Age	165
The Celts	165
Bards, Ovates & Druids	166
Druid Magic—Celtic Shamans	167
Otherworldy Journeys of the Bards	168
Gods of the Celts	169
Survival of Celtic Culture	170
The Germans & Scandinavians	172
Yggdrasil—the Tree of Worlds	172
Aesir & Vanir—Gods of Sky & Earth	173
Odin the Shamanic God	175
Volvas & Seidr—Nordic Magic	176
Berserkirs & Werewolves—Shamanic warriors	177
Christianity at Sword-Point—Conversion Of the Germans	178
Chapter 7 Notes	**179**

Chapter 8: Indigenous European Shamanism   182

The Sami Noaide—Shamans of Scandanavia	182
The Scythians & Huns—Shamans of the Eurasian Steppes	184
Was Attila the Hun A Shaman?	187
The Taltos: Hungarian Shamans	188
Chapter 8 Notes	**190**

Chapter 9: The Mystery Religions   192

Personal Encounter With The Gods	192
Samothracian Mysteries	194
Isis—The First Universal Goddess	195
The Myth of Persephone	196
The Eleusinian Mysteries	198
The Lesser & Greater Mysteries	200
Nine Days of Eleusis	200
To Live in Joy & to Die with Hope	202
The Orphic Mysteries	203
Orpheus as Shaman—The Legend of Orpheus & Eurydice	204
Orpheus—Bringer of Immortality	206

Orphism—Spirituality of the Individual	206
Orphic Initiation	207
The Golden Tablets	208
Chapter 9 Notes	**211**

Chapter 10: The Quest for Immortality — 213

The Axial Age Awakening	213
The Presocratic Greeks—Philosophers & Shamans	214
Pythagoras—Lover of Wisdom	217
The Pythagorean Brotherhood	219
The Music of the Spheres	221
Empedocles & the Four Elements	223
The Four Roots & The Theory of Love & Strife	224
Empedocles As Shaman & Wonder Worker	225
Zoroastrianism	226
Jewish Monotheism	227
Heaven & Hell/ Angels & Devils	228
The Vision of Wiraz	230
The Magi & Magic	231
Origins of Reincarnation	233
Plato & Askesis—The Practice of Living & Dying	234
The Immortal Soul as Heavenly Star	238
Plato's Allegory of the "Soul's Chariot"	238
The Spirit Vehicles of Neoplatonism	240
Chapter 10 Notes	**242**

Chapter 11: Hellenism & Religion of the Stars — 246

The Rise of Alexandria	246
The Religion of the Stars	247
The Heavens as the New Underworld	249
The Myth of Er	250
Hellenistic Astrology	253
Chains of Sympathy	253
The Hellenistic Zodiac	254
Astrology of the Individual	254
The Age of Pisces & The Fishers of Men	256
Hellenistic Magic—The Goes, Magus & Divine Man	257
The Ritual for Summoning a Divine Assistant	258
Divination by Lamps & Bowls	260
The Stigmatization of Magic	260
From Daimons to Demons	262
Chapter 11 Notes	**265**

Chapter 12: 268

Ascent Through the Celestial Spheres — 268
Hermeticism — 269
Hermetic Initiation — 270
Poimandres & Ascent to the Ogdoad — 270
The Technical Hermetica — 271
Hermetic Cosmology — 272
Greco-Egyptian Alchemy — 272
The Greek Magical Papyri — 274
The Mithras Liturgy — 274
Gnosticism & Early Christian Magic — 276
The Afterlife Journey of the Gnostic Mandeans — 280
Mithraism/ The Astrological Religion — 280
Neoplatonism — 282
Theurgy of Iamblichus — 283
Legends of the Divine Iamblichus — 286
The Legacy of Theurgy — 287
The Lyre of Orpheus—Music in the Mysteries & Shamanism — 288
Merkabah--Riders of the Chariot — 289
The Four Holy Creatures & The Zodiac — 291
The Sefer Yetsira — 292
Tree of Life / Shaman's World Tree — 293
Chapter 12 Notes — **294**

Chapter 13: The Magical Grimoires — 298

Testament of Solomon — 299
The Hygromanteia — 301
The Key of Solomon the King & the Lemegeton — 301
Who Wrote the Magical Grimoires? — 303
The Astrological Magic of the Picatrix — 304
The Sacred Magic of Abramelin the Mage — 306
The Magician's Practice & Use of Magical Tools — 307
Chapter 13 Notes — **309**

Chapter 14: Renaissance & Enlightenment Esotericism: Arranging Life According to the Heavens — 311

Marsilio Ficino—the Second Orpheus — 311
Pico & The Angels — 315
Hermetic Kabbalah & The Modern Tree of Life — 317
Spiritual Alchemy — 318
The "Philosophical Tree" in Alchemy — 319

Divination by Crystals in Renaissance Magic	320
The Art of Drawing Sprits into Crystals	320
The Enochian Magic of Dee & Kelly	321
The Travels of Paracelsus	324
Agrippa's "Three Books"	326
Rosicrucianism	328
The Chymical Wedding of Christian Rosenkreutz	329
Hermeticism & the Rise of Modern Science	330
Freemasonry—Carving the Rough Ashlar	332
Swedenborg—The Man Who Talked with Angels	333
Chapter 14 Notes	**337**

Chapter 15:   341

Survival of Pagan Magic in Modern Europe	341
Celtic Folklore & Magical Traditions	341
Survival of Nordic Pagan Traditions	342
Shamanic Traditions of Europe	343
The Dragon Men—Wizards of the Balkans	344
Grimoires & Folk-magic	346
Cunning Folk & Witches: The Shamanic Connection	346
Chapter 15 Notes	**349**

Chapter 16: The 19th Century Occult Revival   351

Spiritualism—Mediums & Shamans	352
Theosophy—Madame Blavatsky & the Astral Letters	354
Levi & the Tarot	357
The Rise of the Golden Dawn	358
Chapter 16 Notes	**360**

Chapter 17:   361

Visionary Journeys in the Modern World	361
Psychoanalysis- Making the Unconscious Conscious	364
Carl Jung's Descent into the Unconscious Underworld	366
Jung's Nekiya Experience	367
Near-Death Visions	369
Jungian Active Imagination	370
"Directed Daydreams" of Robert Desoille	371
Psychology & Healing in Modern Magic	372
Shamanism, Ancient Healing & Modern Medicine	374
Chapter 17 Notes	**375**

Chapter 18: Science & Altered States — 378

- Hypnagogia—Visions Between Waking & Sleep — 378
- The Neuropsychological Stages of Shamanic Trance — 379
- Robert Monroe's Out-of-Body Journeys — 381
- Raymond Moody–Near-Death-Experience, Apparitions & Visions — 384
- Shamanism as a Universal Experience — 385
- **Chapter 18 Notes** — 387

Chapter 19: Neopaganism Today — 388

- Alternative Spirituality & Earth Religions — 388
- Neopaganism & Shamanism — 390
- Megalithomania — 391
- Western Esotericism Today — 391
- **Chapter 19 Notes** — 393

Chapter 20: Neoshamanism — 394

- Resurgence of Shamanism Worldwide — 394
- "Plastic Shamans" — 395
- Commercial Threats to Native American Religion — 395
- Ayahuasca Tourism — 396
- Core Shamanism & Neoshamanism—What's the Difference? — 397
- **Chapter 20 Notes** — 399

Chapter 21: From Root to Branch — 400

- The Revival of Animism — 400
- Thinking Like an Animist — 402
- Revisioning The Future... — 402
- **Chapter 21 Notes** — 404

Bibliography — 405

The Tree of Visions

"Up above there is a certain tree where the souls of the shamans are reared, before they attain their powers. And on the boughs of this tree are nests in which the souls lie and are attended...The higher the nest in this tree, the stronger will the shaman be who is raised in it, the more will he know, and the farther will he see."

—Tungus Shaman Semyonov Semyon

"...we are a plant not of earthly but of heavenly growth...for the divine power suspended the head and root of us from that place where the generation of the soul first began..."

—Plato, Timaeus 90 a-d

"Step by step the aspirant slowly climbs the Tree of himself. In this way he continually balances and perfects each stage, passing from sefirah to sefirah...In this way the ascent is safely made from Earth to Heaven while the man is still in the flesh."

—Z'ev ben Shimon Halevi

Introduction

Petroglyphs of Shamans – Tamgaly Kazahkstan.

This book is about shamans, magicians and mystics whose visionary experiences gave rise to mankind's earliest spiritual beliefs, myths and religious traditions. It is a historical overview of over 40,000 years of human spirituality—beginning with the shamans of Paleolithic Europe who recorded their visions on cave walls, concluding with scientific studies of altered states of consciousness. Although its primary focus is on visionary traditions of the western world, these will be compared to shamanic and magical-religious practices world-wide, revealing their many similarities. We will discover that the "family tree" of western spirituality is rooted in the prehistory of Europe as well as the ancient civilizations of Eurasia, the Near-East, Asia and Africa.

Some may be surprised to learn the Occident has its own visionary traditions surviving to the present day, comparable to those of eastern mysticism or indigenous shamanism. These traditions have been termed "western esotericism" by historians and described as our culture's "alternative" or "underground" spirituality. In contrast to mainstream religions which rely on the authority of clergy, dogma and scripture, western esotericism provides a non-institutionalized approach to spirituality. It encourages individual initiative and self-transformation in the quest for illumination, offering direct knowledge of spiritual reality to its adepts, an experience known as *gnosis*.

Scholars trace the origins of western esotericism to the magical-religious traditions of ancient Egypt, the Near-East, and Greece. These will be considered in this book, as well as the less familiar native spiritual heritage of Europe including Celtic and Germanic paganism, witchcraft, folk-magic and shamanism. Beyond a doubt all these traditions contributed to the contemporary revival of "alternative spirituality" with its diverse paths of Hermeticism, Ritual Magic, Alchemy, Wicca, Druidry, Neopaganism and Neoshamanism.

The term "esotericism" is derived from the Greek word *esoterikos*, meaning "within". This originally referred to secret teachings taught to inner circles of students of the ancient Greek philosopher Pythagoras. Legend has it neophyte students were not allowed to see Pythagoras in person, instead having to listen to him speak from behind a linen curtain. Only after a trial period of five years were they literally permitted within the veil to see the master face to face, earning the title of "esoterics". Perhaps the long period of silence and introspection taught them to turn their minds inward to awaken to their own experience of gnosis?

Pythagoras, one of the first philosophers and scientists of the western world, was also a mystic and visionary said to be able to hear the "music of the spheres"—the sounds of the planets and stars whirling across the heavens. According to legends he also exercised many of the powers of the shaman: it was said he could predict earthquakes, calm storms, charm wild beasts, as well as "bi-locate" or separate his soul from his body and send it to distant places. Most significantly, he introduced ideas of the immortality of the soul and its transmigration—or reincarnation—to the Greeks.

The ideas and teachings of Pythagoras did not develop in isolation however. According to ancient writers he learned his mystical doctrines of mathematics, divine rites, and worship of the gods in the temples of Egypt and Babylon. He was also initiated into the mystery religion of the Idean Dactyls in Crete, retreating into a cave for a month during which time he saw visions of the god Zeus. From the Dactyls he may have gained his knowledge of music as a means of soothing the passions of body and soul through rhythm, song and incantation. It is also possible he learned from the peoples who inhabited the northern borders of Greece—the Thracians and Scythians—as well as the nomadic peoples of the Central Asian steppes—all of whom practiced their own forms of shamanism.

The first shamans were Paleolithic (Stone Age) hunter-gatherers who lived in small bands scattered across Africa, the Near-East, Eurasia and Europe. We find evidence of their beliefs in the form of awe-inspiring cave paintings depicting men shapeshifting into animals and stylized carvings of corpulent women, perhaps representing pregnant fertility goddesses. Artifacts such as lunar calendars carved on bone as well as markings on cave walls depicting constellations of stars attest to their knowledge of astronomy as well. The communal ceremonies led by prehistoric shamans were arguably a seminal force behind the invention of human culture, laying the foundations of mythology, religion and magic. Neuropsychologists suggest that cognitive skills such as imaging, symbolic thinking and recall of dreams acquired through early shamanic practices may have served as catalysts for neurological advances of *Homo sapiens*. The trance experiences of shamans may have even "made us human" in the words of archaeologist and neoshaman Mike Williams.[1]

Anthropologist Holger Kalweit writes about the visionary flight of the shaman: "the experience of leaving one's body and of undertaking journeys of consciousness is probably one of the oldest underlying principles of religion and magic".[2] Scientific research into out-of-body experiences, near-death-experiences, and hypnagogic imagery, which will be explored in these pages, focuses on altered states of consciousness. Mastery of these mental states was not exclusive to shamans however—they were also familiar to ancient esoteric initiates—the mystics, magicians, priests and oracles of Europe and the Near-East.

Ancient funerary texts such as the *Egyptian Book of the Dead* and the Greek *Orphic Tablets* narrated visionary journeys to the "otherworld" undertaken in altered states. Psychologist Stanislav Grof argues these books were written not only for the dead, but also to guide living initiates. He insists they are not products of superstition and primitive imagination but accurate descriptions of the experiential territories traversed in non-ordinary states of consciousness, based on countless personal experiences and many centuries of careful observation.[3] These "books of the dead" will be examined as guidebooks to the afterlife experience and compared to shamanic narratives of visits to the land of the dead.

Echoing the tales of otherworldly journeys of tribal shamans are myths from ancient Mesopotamia, Egypt and Greece that tell of descents of gods, goddesses and heroes to the dark underworld. Similar to the initiation experiences of shamans, the Sumerian goddess Inanna descends to the land of the dead where she undergoes ordeals culminating in her death and magical resurrection. In another Sumerian myth, the *Epic of Etana*, a king ascends to the sky on the back of an eagle to attain the "plant of life", similar to shamans who journey in vision to the upperworld with their spirit-helpers.

Myth and magic are at the heart of western esotericism. Since these terms will be used often in the following pages, a brief definition is in order. *Myths* are those stories passed down through the generations that explain human experience on collective as well as individual levels. They speak in the language of symbols, providing metaphorical answers to the big questions of human existence: where did we come from, why are we here, where we are going? Stories of the birth, life, death, and rebirth of the universe and the gods, as told by myths, reflect the human life cycle. They explain our connection to the universe, bringing meaning and order to our lives.[4] Myths are closely related to *religion* and provide the creation stories, cosmologies, and tales of the gods upon which religions are based. Both mythology and religion are concerned with the experience of the sacred and numinous. Joseph Campbell wrote that the function of myth is to: "...evoke in the individual a sense of grateful, affirmative awe before the monstrous mystery that is existence".[5]

In ancient societies magic, myth, and religion were closely related and often inseparable. In Egypt there was no word for "religion", there was only *heka*, roughly translated as "magical power". The Egyptian priest's performance of the magical liturgy praising the sun-god Ra in his daily journey across the sky was the practical expression of his religious faith. Magic was the means by which the cosmos was believed to be sustained. Through the power of universal sympathy, the idea that all things are interconnected, ancient magicians sought to influence the supernatural forces of the cosmos and their manifestations—gods, goddesses, angels, daemons and spirits—to act in their favor. Egyptologist Robert Kreich Ritner defines *magic* as "any activity which seeks to obtain its goals by methods outside the simple laws of cause and effect".[6] He insists that any expression of magic has to be understood in respect to its specific cultural contexts and belief systems. Accordingly we will look at the various forms magical practices have assumed from their beginnings in prehistoric cultures and ancient civilizations to the present day.

The Tree of Visions is based on the thesis that widespread shamanic beliefs and practices such as visionary journeying to the otherworld, shapeshifting, use of helping-spirits, asceticism, initiation ordeals, divination, astro-ceremonialism, mythic symbolism, magical rituals and paraphernalia, also occurred in the magical-religious practices of the ancient Near-East and Europe. Archaic shamanism formed the deepest stratum of human culture, myth, and spiritual practices worldwide. Through cross-cultural comparisons of the visionary traditions of western magic and indigenous shamanism we will attempt to gain new insights into our spiritual origins.

Chapter One looks at the role of shamans in indigenous cultures and their use of trance techniques for accessing altered states of consciousness. The shamanic cosmology of the three worlds: lowerworld, middle and upperworld will be introduced, and parallels drawn with the cosmologies of early civilizations of the Near-East and Europe. We will also compare traditions of skywatching and astro-ceremonialism found in shamanic cultures across the northern hemisphere from Scandinavia to North America.

Chapter Two presents myths of the World Tree from around the world, the role of helping-spirits in shamanism and magic and the working tools of the shaman such as the drum, staff and costume. The initiation experiences of shamans will be examined and compared to ancient Near-Eastern and Greek myths of *catabasis* or underworld descents.

Chapter Three explores Paleolithic shamanism, viewing cave art as the record of altered states of consciousness from a neuroscience perspective. Recent discoveries into the prehistoric origins of writing and astronomy will also be revealed. We will explore archaeological research which connects the Paleolithic cultures of Europe with those of the Siberian Altai, along with genetic research into the shared prehistoric ancestry of Europeans, Siberians and Native Americans. The cultures of the Mesolithic and Neolithic Near-East who built the world's first temple of Gobekli Tepe, and early settlements such as Catal Huyuk and Jericho will also be discussed.

Chapter Four focuses on the magico-religious traditions of ancient Mesopotamia. Parallels will be drawn between the powers and duties of the sacred king of Mesopotamia and the tribal shaman. Likewise the myth of the goddess Inanna's descent to the land of the dead will be compared to the shaman's initiatory death and rebirth in the underworld. Mesopotamian cosmology, astronomy and astrology, its pantheons of astral deities, demons, magical practices, divination and oracles will be explored.

Chapter Five looks at ancient Egypt beginning with Nabta Playa, a prehistoric megalithic monument based on astronomical alignments, as the precursor of later pharaonic temples. The Egyptian pharaoh's role as mediator between the gods and mankind will be compared to the role of the tribal shaman. The pantheon of Egyptian deities will be discussed along with the theory of Egyptian magic—*heka*—and its practice by the king and priesthood. We will look at *The Egyptian Book of the Dead* as a guidebook for living initiates, and compare it with shamanic narratives of journeys to the land of the dead.

Chapter Six explores the Neolithic civilization of "Old Europe" and its goddess cultures. Recent genetic research and historical theories will be presented suggesting the ancestry of modern Europeans is the mixture of three ancient populations: hunter-gathers, farmers, and pastoralists. We will discuss the function of megalithic monuments of Newgrange and Stonehenge from the perspective of Neolithic ancestor worship and shamanic ceremonies for contacting the dead. The origins, migrations and magical-religious beliefs of the Proto-Indo-Europeans will be discussed in regard to their seminal influence on European civilization. We will look at the "goddess civilization" of Minoan Crete and its ritualistic uses of the labyrinth. The Mycenaean origins of the Greek gods, divination and oracles, and the necromantic magic of early Greek magicians, the *goetes,* will be compared to the practices of shamans.

Chapter Seven looks at the myths and deities of the Celtic and Germanic peoples and the magic of the Druids and Volvas, comparing them with similar Eurasian shamanic practices. We will encounter the Scythians, Huns, and Sami peoples, emphasizing their contribution to European shamanism and folk-magic. The Sami *noaide* and Hungarian *taltos* are presented as examples of indigenous European shamans.

Subsequent chapters will survey the mystery religions of ancient Greece, focusing on the Eleusinian mysteries and Orphism. Possible shamanistic influences on the Greek Presocratic philosophers Pythagoras and Empedocles will be considered, and their important legacy in the ideas of Plato and the Neoplatonists. The visionary allegories of Plato as well as the ascetic exercises of Greek philosophers will be examined, along with their exercises in the "practice of living" which are relevant to this day. We will look at the influence of the Magians of Persia and their magical practices. Zoroastrian angelology, demonology, and eschatological doctrines—beliefs concerning the soul's destiny, final judgement and afterlife—so influential to Judaism, Christianity and Islam—will also be discussed.

We move on from there to an overview of Greco-Egyptian magic, alchemy, astrology, and mysticism of late-antiquity. This includes the philosophies and mystical practices of the Hermeticists, Gnostics, and Jewish Merkabah mystics whose visionary ascents through the heavens will be explored and compared to the shaman's magical flight to the upperworld.

The following chapters trace Hermeticism's rebirth in the Italian Renaissance, as well as the contribution of the Kabbalah to western esotericism. The "grimoire tradition" of magic books will be surveyed, emphasizing the continuity of magical practices from the ancient world to modern Europe. Hermeticism's influence on the birth of modern science, as well as the rise of Rosicrucianism and Freemasonry in the Age of Enlightenment will also be discussed.

Existing alongside Renaissance Hermeticism were the folk-magical traditions of rural Europe, remnants of pre-Christian paganism and Eurasian shamanism. We will look at the role of the cunning-folk, witches, and wizards in early modern Europe whose magical practices share striking similarities with those of Eurasian shamans. These two currents, the classical and native folk traditions, laid the foundation of the diverse paths of western esotericism which continue to thrive to this day.

The final chapters bring us up to the present with a survey of modern visionary techniques including magical pathworking, Jungian active imagination, scientific research into hynagogia, neurological models of altered states of consciousness, out-of-body-experiences, and near-death-experiences—shedding light on the visionary journeys of shamans, magicians and mystics.

We finish with an overview of the 19th century "Occult Revival" in the western world, including modern esoteric traditions such as Spiritualism, Theosophy, the Hermetic Order of the Golden Dawn and a look at contemporary Neopaganism, Neoshamanism and Neo-animism, and their contributions to the evolving spirituality of the 21st century.

We begin our descent into the labyrinth of history with a look at shamanism...

Introduction Notes

Tuvan petroglyphs of shaman's masks.

1. Williams, Mike. *Prehistoric belief: shamans, trance and the afterlife*. 2010: 30-31.
2. Kalweit, Holger. *Dreamtime & Inner Space: the world of the shaman*. 1988:32.
3. Grof, Stanislav. *Books of the Dead -Manuals for Living and Dying*. 1994.
4. Witzel, E.J. Michael. *The Origins of the World's Mythologies*. 2012: 423.
5. Campbell, Joseph; Kudler, David. *Pathways to Bliss: Mythology and Personal Transformation*. 2009: 6-10.
6. Ritner, Robert Kriech. *The Mechanics of Ancient Egyptian Magical Practice*. 1993: 237.

Chapter I: The World of the Shaman

"Shaman" by David Nez.

"The shaman begins to beat his drum. He murmurs a song. The song and the drumming rise in crescendo. Soon the shaman is bellowing...The music grows louder to the point of paroxysm, then stops abruptly, so that nothing is heard but the hum of mosquitoes...The music resumes furiously and reaches its highest intensity. The shaman then invokes the help of the *amagat* and his familiar spirits. They do not accede at once; the shaman implores them, they equivocate. Sometimes they arrive so suddenly and violently that the shaman falls over backward...On the arrival of the *amagat* the shaman begins leaping, makes swift, violent gestures. Finally he takes his place in the center of the yurt, the fire is rekindled, and he begins to drum and dance again. He flings himself in the air, sometimes as high as four feet. He cries out wildly. This is followed by another pause; then in a low, serious voice he intones a solemn hymn...Finally he goes to the patient and summons the cause of the illness to depart; or he lays hold of the trouble, carries it to the middle of the room and, never stopping his imprecations, chases it away, spits it from his mouth, kicks it, drives it with his hands and breath".[1]

-Sieroszewski "The Yakut"- 1896.

Defining Shamanism

The word "Shaman" derives from the Siberian Tungus word *saman*, formed from the verb *sa*— "to know"—therefore a shaman is "one who knows". Alternatively the word means to "heat oneself", probably referring to the feverish inspiration of the trance state.[2] Originally the term referred to magical healers of the indigenous cultures of Siberia, Mongolia, and neighboring areas of Inner Asia.

One of the earliest European encounters with these shamans was recorded by Venetian explorer Marco Polo in the thirteenth century. During his travels in Asia, Polo witnessed a shamanic healing ceremony in which the participants danced, sang, and played instruments. After awhile one of the shamans was possessed by an "evil spirit", in the words of Polo. The shaman's companions then asked him, or his possessing spirit, to diagnose the sick person's illness.[3]

Another eyewitness account of a Siberian shamanistic ceremony was recorded by an Englishman named Richard Johnson in 1557. Like Marco Polo before him, Johnson describes "devilish rites" among the Samoyedic speaking natives.[4]

Throughout the modern era western attitudes towards Siberian shamans have been widely ambivalent. Catherine the Great (1729-1796) Empress of Russia, whose opinions reflect the prevailing rationalistic views of the Age of Enlightenment, denounced shamans as "mystic impostures". On the other hand, European intellectuals embracing the philosophy of Romanticism idealized shamans as "creative personalities" and "unspoiled noble savages". Russian Orthodox missionaries in Siberia showed a certain degree of tolerance towards indigenous religious beliefs. Their Protestant counterparts were downright hostile to them however, viewing shamanism as the "worship of evil spirits", according to anthropologist Jeroen Boekhoven.[5] As the mysterious "other", shamans seem to have served as a sort of "rorschach test" for psychological projections for those westerners who encountered them.

Russian ethnologists and anthropologists during the 19th century studied and documented shamanic performances in Siberia. Some like Sieroszewski, whose account we read above, were sympathetic toward the natives and their culture. Soviet Communists in the 20th century, however, viewed traditional Siberian culture as "backward" and "primitive", requiring "modernization." Shamans as keepers of local religious traditions were seen as obstacles to progress. Under the genocidal rule of Stalin in the 1930's shamans were arrested, deported to labor camps, tortured and executed. Later in the 20th century, field studies of Siberian shamans were again undertaken—based on interviewing the few remaining shamans who had survived the purges. Vilmos Dioszegi, a Hungarian ethnographer who participated in these studies ironically declared: "it is important that shamanism should disappear as soon as possible, but it is just as important that this should not happen without records." [6]

The renowned 20th century historian of religion Mircea Eliade, using the ethnological fieldwork of the Russians and other researchers, constructed his influential theory of shamanism. He writes that shamanism is "at once mysticism, magic, and "religion" in the broadest sense of the term."[7] Eliade saw Siberian shamanism as a pure example of a magico-religious practice that once existed worldwide. He argues in his book *Shamanism-Archaic Techniques of Ecstasy* that traditional societies in many parts of the world have figures similar to shamans. He finds examples of them in South-East Asia, Polynesia, Australia, North and South America and Africa. Eliade's theory of shamanism has been influential among academia as well as the practitioners of modern Neoshamanism. Some contemporary scholars propose that shamanism was the earliest religious practice of mankind, originating during the Paleolithic era. Others claim it influenced the development of ancient European magical-religious practices, and elements of it have survived in folk-magic practices until recent times. We will explore both these theories later.

In order to distinguish the shaman from other magical-religious practitioners, Eliade proposes several criteria which define the "shamanic complex": first, the shaman masters the technique of ecstasy, specializing in trance during which his soul is believed to leave his body in magical flight. In this state he journeyed to the sky to gain useful information from spirits, or descended to the underworld to guide the souls of the dead. Another distinguishing trait of shamans is their intimate relationship with the spirit world, allowing them to become mediators between the spirits and the community. In this regard Eliade insists the shaman remains in control of the spirits, rather than becoming possessed by them. Finally, shamans suffer an initiatory illness along with initiation ordeals involving visions of dismemberment and rebirth.[8]

Critics have pointed out that Eliade's definition of shamanism tends to "universalize" the practices of indigenous peoples which are complex and culturally specific.[9] Some researchers find his criteria too limited to be applied cross-culturally or in modern urban contexts. Psychologist Stanley Krippner provides a more general definition: "Shamans can be defined as community-assigned magico-religious professionals who deliberately alter their consciousness in order to obtain information from the spirit world. They use this knowledge and power to help and to heal members of their community, as well as the community as a whole".[10]

Anthropologist Piers Vitebsky notes that the word "shaman" has been used interchangeably with "medicine man", "sorcerer", "magician" and "witch-doctor", especially when these operate outside mainstream religions.[10] Eliade insists however "though the shaman is, among other things, a magician, not every magician can be termed a shaman."[11] Admittedly in only two traditional European societies is the "shamanic complex" as defined by Eliade found intact: among the shamanic practitioners known as the *noiade* in Scandinavia, and the *taltos* in Hungary. On the other hand, Eliade acknowledges that the myths and magical practices of ancient Indo-European peoples display many shamanic elements: ecstatic techniques, shapeshifting into animal helping spirits, communication with the dead, oracular seances, myths of descent to the underworld, etc.[12] Likewise It can be argued that contemporary western esoteric paths such as neopaganism and ritual magic share similar cosmologies, beliefs and practices as shamanism, which will be later be discussed.

Shamanism, mankind's earliest spirituality, continues to be practiced and is in fact undergoing a revival in traditional as well as modern cultures around the world. It continues to thrive not only among among tribal hunter-gatherers, but in pastoral, agricultural, and modern industrial societies as well.

The Roles of the Shaman

Shamans are mediators between the extraordinary reality of the spirit-world and ordinary reality. In the words of Eliade, they are the "technicians of the sacred" who communicate with the spirits on behalf of the community, mediating between this world and the otherworld, maintaining balance between mankind and the forces of nature[13]. Shamans serve a wide range of needs in their communities, assuming many roles: They are healers who retrieve the souls of their patients which have strayed from their bodies, as well as exorcists who combat demons believed to cause physical and psychological illness. They are "psychopomps" who lead souls of the recently dead to their new home in the lowerworld, and likewise assist souls there to be reborn among the living.

In some cultures shamans are "weather wizards", rainmakers who also protect crops from hail. Most shamans practice divination, determining the causes of illness as well as predicting future events. The shaman is the tribal religious specialist who leads communal ceremonies, assisting in the annual regeneration of life through negotiations with the spirit world.

Shamans played the role of "culture heroes", and many of mankind's oldest epic tales and myths may have originated in their dramatic narratives of otherworldly journeys. Joseph Campbell writes: "The realm of myth...and the realm of shamanic trance are one and the same."[14] The shaman was wisdom keeper and storyteller who preserved tribal religious traditions, myths, and cosmology. They were also entertainers who during their spiritual seances used ventriloquism to imitate animals, gods, and spirits, singing songs and reciting poetry to entertain their audiences. Historian Ronald Hutton writes: "If shamanism was partly a craft and partly a spiritual vocation, it was also an aspect of theatre, and often a spectacularly effective one."[15] Audience participation is considered essential in shamanic performances. Viewers respond by chanting, singing refrains, and often entering trance states themselves, vicariously participating in the shaman's journeys. These experiences are often transformative, leading to catharsis, healing and increased self-confidence of participants.[16]

Neoshamanic practitioner and anthropologist Michael Harner defines the shaman as "a man or woman who enters an altered state of consciousness at will—to contact and utilize an ordinarily hidden reality in order to acquire knowledge, power, and help other persons."[17] Anthropologist Emma Wilby defines them as magical practitioners who enter altered states of consciousness characterized by visionary experiences, during which they travel to other realms at will, bringing back information about the spirit worlds and the desires and intentions of the beings who inhabit them. According to her, the shaman serves the community through propitiation, battling or negotiating with spirits to facilitate physical survival.[18]

The shamanic profession in many traditional societies was hereditary and passed down through family lineages. Often shamans were individuals chosen by the spirits against their will, for the shamanic vocation could be difficult and demanding. There are also examples of individuals freely choosing to become shamans. Most shamans after their initiations study with other shamans to learn their craft. In some societies shamans were distinguished by their unusual characteristics often visible from an early age like being born with a caul (the placenta covering the face), possessing six fingers, or suffering epileptic seizures. Future shamans in some cultures experienced the "shamanic illness", exhibiting unusual behaviors such as seeing visions, singing in their sleep, or wandering in solitude. Mircea Eliade writes:

> "One destined to shamanship begins by becoming frenzied, then suddenly loses consciousness, withdraws to the forests, feeds on tree bark, flings himself into water and fire, wounds himself with knives. The family then appeals to an old shaman, who undertakes to teach the distraught young man the various kinds of spirits and how to summon and control them..." [19]

The "shamanic illness" may appear similar to psychosis, depression, or other mental disorders as defined by modern western medicine; in fact Eliade and other researchers have compared it to hysteria and epilepsy. However, psychological testing administered to shamans as well as non-shamans in several Native American tribes found that shamans demonstrated the same high degree of reality testing as non-shamans, contradicting the assumption they were schizophrenic.[20] Anthropologist Ruth-Inge Heinze insists the majority of shamans she studied over many years never went through a psychotic state or showed any sign of pathology, but were instead high-functioning individuals living productive, altruistic lives.[21]

Shamans in traditional societies around the world were sometimes distinguished by their unconventional gender orientation, practicing transvestism; they were men who assumed women's behavior and married another man. In the Cheyenne tribe of North America the *hemaneh*, meaning "half-man, half-woman" symbolically represented the union of blue-sky with the deep-earth.[22] In indigenous societies shamans are generally male, but females past the childbearing years are considered to be among the most powerful shamans. The robe of Siberian shamans is always cut in the characteristic design of a woman's garment. The Siberians believed *women* were the first shamans, whom later male shamans imitated.

Although shamans are often exceptional individuals in their communities, there is reason to suspect they may have been far more prevalent in prehistoric cultures. Among the !Kung Bushmen of the Kalahari Desert it is estimated that half the men and a third of the women in the tribe are, or were in the past, shamans.

Trance Techniques

Shamans specialize in trance during which the soul is believed to leave the body and journey to the otherworld, a state which Michael Harner terms the "Shamanic State of Consciousness".[23] They possess the power of "magical flight" by which they traverse vast distances instantaneously. Although this technique is widely practiced by Siberian shamans, other approaches are also used, such as "possession" during which the shaman invites a helping-spirit to speak through them. Among some Siberian groups, shamans summon spirits and carry on dialogues with them, similar to the ritual magician's evocation of spirits. Studies of shamans in many cultures suggest they practice *both* soul flight as well as possession; while journeying to the spirit-world an entity such as an ancestral spirit or deity is believed to enter into their body and shamanize in their absence.[24]

Anthropologist Neville Drury notes that shamanic experiences involve altered states of consciousness brought about by techniques which induce a degree of psychic dissociation, resulting in trance. Such techniques include: isolation, fasting, celibacy, fatigue, chanting, breath control, sensory deprivation, monotonous drumming and dancing, staring into flames or darkness, ingestion of entheogens, etc. Trance brings about the withdrawal of consciousness from everyday reality and a shift to the inner, subjective world of reverie, thoughts and images. Drury writes: "the shaman awakes from the trance with with conscious memory of the journey to the gods or ancestral spirits, and full knowledge of magical cures or healing procedures".[25] Heinze however insists that some shamans who experience possession retain little or no memory of the experience. She proposes shamans experience a continuum of states ranging from "full possession" and "dissociation" to "increasing control" and "mind-expansion"; she observes that with practice shamans tend to progress from full possession to more consciously controlled forms of trance. A range of altered states are experienced by shamans. At one end of the spectrum is mild waking trance in which they are in control of their bodies, engaging in the visionary state while being aware of the external world. On the other extreme is deep trance accompanied by ecstasy. In this state bodily control is absent and awareness of the environment is drastically reduced—as in cataleptic trance in which the body becomes rigid and immobile.[27]

The milder version of trance described above is similar to states of "hypnagogia" accessed through techniques such as Active Imagination used in Jungian psychology and other forms of psychotherapy, which we will return to later.

Shamans in some cultures ingest hallucinogens to induce altered states. South American shamans are among the few whose practice depends on such substances, however. In the past, some Siberian shamans used the psychoactive mushroom Amanita Muscaria, as well as cannabis to facilitate trance, though vodka is more commonly used by them today.[28] Most shamans do not rely on psychoactive substances at all, having mastered trance states through prolonged training.

Multiple Souls and Reincarnation

Shamanic cultures developed notions about the soul which are surprisingly similar to those of ancient mystics of Europe and Asia. The arctic explorer Rasmussen discusses beliefs about the soul held by Innuits of Greenland:

> "They believe that a human being has a soul, or a spirit, which is immortal. The soul is outside a person, but follows it, as his shadow follows a man in the sunshine. Although the soul is thus not inside the body, the body and the soul are nevertheless inseparable as long as the person is to continue alive; for when the soul leaves the body, the body pines away and dies.... after death of the body, the soul ascends to heaven or goes down into the sea. It is good to be in either place".[29]

Siberian Shamans believe a man has *multiple souls,* three or as many as seven of them.[30] The Yukagir people believe in three souls. At death they separate— one soul stays with the corpse, another descends to the lowerworld while the third ascends to the sky finding its way to the Supreme God.[31] The Khants and Mansis of Siberia conceive of four souls.[32] The first one is known as the "soul shadow", a material soul which remains with the physical body as long as it exists. The second soul is called "the soul that goes down the river". It leaves a person regularly during sleep and travels widely, and shamans are able to send it out for special purposes. After death it travels to the lowerworld in the form of a bird such as a swallow, magpie, or cuckoo. The third soul called the "dreaming soul" lives outside a person, coming to them only during sleep. If it perishes and a shaman cannot quickly retrieve it, the person dies. The fourth soul is known as the "reincarnation soul" or "little soul" which stays with a person but moves with the speed of thought, traveling during sleep. It dwells in a person's head and often appears as a soul-bird, defending its owner. This soul is inherited down the generations since each child is believed to be the reincarnation of a deceased ancestor.

The ancient Egyptians likewise believed in multiple souls, even picturing one of them—the *ba* soul—as a bird, like the Siberians. The Hindus and Buddhists developed the notion of several "subtle bodies" comprising the soul. The Hermetic philosophers of antiquity also conceived of the soul's multiple envelopes or garments which we will explore later.

Beliefs similar to *reincarnation*, that the soul is reborn in a succession of physical bodies, are widely held by indigenous peoples around the world, including the ancient Celts who believed in the soul's *transmigration*, including rebirth into animal existences. Reincarnation was a doctrine first held in the Greek world by Pythagoras and the Orphic philosophers, and later inherited by Plato and the Neoplatonists.

The notion that one's actions and ethical choices effect the the soul and its afterlife state is also widespread. The Ojibway tribe of North America believe the body contains an immortal substance that continues to grow while it resides in the physical body. It is a man's duty to nurture and develop this spirit-soul by living a life of harmony between heart and spirit. Living life in a state of "goodness" guarantees the person will go to the "land of souls" after death.[32] It is remarkable how similar this Native American prescription for "care of the soul" is to the practices of ancient Greek Orphic and Pythagorean mystics. They also stressed the need for personal integrity and virtuous actions in one's life—leading to the soul's reward of a blessed afterlife.

Anthropologist Holger Kalweit insists that the universal belief in the soul and its nature has been confirmed by the living experience of all cultures during all epochs. He writes: "The belief in a soul is therefore not a tradition but a living reality." [33]

Shamanic Cosmology

Shamanic cosmologies in traditional cultures generally divide the universe into three levels: sky, earth and beneath the earth or *upperworld, middleworld* and *lowerworld*. These are perceived as being connected by a central vertical axis—the *axis mundi*—or "world axis" often envisioned as a colossal tree, pillar, tree or tent-pole which supports the canopy of the sky. Other versions of the axis-mundi consist of a cosmic mountain reaching through the lowerworld, earth and heavens, or a ladder by which the shaman ascends or descends between the worlds.

This basic idea of three cosmic zones, according to astronomer E.C. Krupp, can be found from Siberia to Mesoamerica, and Africa to Mediterranean Europe. In one variation or another it occurs worldwide.[34] The creation myths of Egypt and Mesopotamia began with the separation of earth and sky by the gods, thereby creating the the world and making life possible for mankind. The Mesopotamians believed gods reigned above in heaven, mortal humans lived on earth to serve the gods, while the dead descended to dwell in the underworld. The writers of the Old Testament envisioned a tripartite universe with heaven, earth, and the underworld of Sheol surrounded by the waters of chaos. The Homeric Greeks also divided their cosmos into three parts: the heavens of Olympus, the flat earth surrounded by Oceanus, and the underworld of Tartarus. The cosmology of the Celts presented a world of three levels or circles. The Germans believed in a cosmos of three worlds which in turn were divided into nine worlds, joined together by Yggdrasil the World Tree. The cosmology of tripartite worlds was inherited by the Abrahamic religions and developed into heaven, earth and hell.

The Lowerworld

The lowerworld, also referred to as the "underworld", is the land of the dead as well as a place of ancestral wisdom and power, rarely entered by the living. The Kets of Siberia view the lowerworld as an immense cavern of seven successive layers associated with seven *pudak* or "obstacles" which shamans must overcome in their journeys there.[35] The Mongols believe it is ruled over by the god Erleg Khan and his seven sons and daughters. The souls of the dead dwell there, some of them awaiting rebirth to this world. Shamans are sometimes called to retrieve the souls of the living who have strayed there due to illness, or who have been stolen and taken there by spirits or evil sorcerers. Many shamanic cultures believe the souls of animals killed in the hunt also live in the lowerworld, guarded by a female deity, the "mistress of animals". The shaman travels there to ask her to release them, assuring their rebirth in the world and successful future hunts.

The Yugakir people of Siberia believe the souls in the lowerworld live as they did on earth, except in a shadow world, as shadow souls living in shadow tents and hunting shadow animals. The world of the dead is thought to be a sort of "upside down world", not that different from this world but with things reversed. The Yugakir say that in the world of the living we look towards the outside, while the dead direct their gaze *inwards*. The Samoyed of Siberia believe the rivers in the lowerworld run backward, trees grow downward, the sun rises in the west, and life begins with old age and one grows younger and younger.[36]

Travel to this realm by the Siberian shaman can take place by way of the World River which flows from south to north. The journey along it is hazardous and full of perilous rapids. Caverns, springs, whirlpools, and tunnels are also used by shamans as entry points to the lowerworld. It can also be entered through a tunnel or opening in the earth. Rasmussen writes about a classic shamanic method for entering this realm given to him by an Iglulik Innuit shaman of Hudson Bay:

"For the very greatest shamans a way opens right from the house whence they invoke their helping spirits; a road down through the earth...and by this route the shaman is led down without encountering any obstacle. He almost glides as if falling through a tube so fitted to his body that he can check his progress by pressing against all sides, and need not actually fall down with a rush. This tube is kept open for him...until he returns on his way back to earth".[37]

The belief in the underworld was widespread among ancient cultures, and perhaps the earliest conception of a land of the dead. It may have originated in the vision quests of Paleolithic shamans in caves.[38] Archaeologist Jean Clottes writes: "Everywhere and at all times, the underground has been perceived as being a supernatural world, the realm of spirits or of the dead, a forbidding gate to the beyond..." [39] By venturing deep into caves, Paleolithic shamans may have ritually enacted a descent to the underworld. This dark realm was likely believed to be the dwelling place of the spirits of the ancestors as well as animals who could be communed with in trance states. Kalweit describes the paradoxical enlightenment experienced in the lowerworld by the shaman: "Having descended to the center of the earth, into darkness, he is illumined. Having been blinded, he comes to see".[40]

Dianne Wolkstein discusses myths of descent into the earth in tribal initiation rites: "In many traditional societies, initiatory tribal rites are often characterized by a symbolic descent into and ascent from the labyrinthian Earth Mother. These rituals give women and men the experience of being reborn on a spiritual plane".[41] Eliade notes that *rituals of descent* follow a universal pattern: separation from family, regression to the pre-natal state of the cosmic night, death, dismemberment, suffering and rebirth.[42] As we will see, this pattern of *death* and *dismemberment* followed by *rebirth* is characteristic of the shaman's initiation.

In myths of the ancient Mediterranean world deities and heroes descended to the underworld to undergo initiatory ordeals. These stories were re-enacted by initiates of the mystery religions as part of their sacred rites. In ancient Egypt, visionary journeys to the underworld similar to the shaman's were practiced, according to philosopher Jeremy Naydler. He insists that familiarity with the underworld was essential knowledge of the Egyptian priest-magician, and mastery of its psychic energies was necessary on the path toward spiritual attainment.[43]

The peoples of ancient Egypt, Mesopotamia, and Europe developed their own mythic narratives of the underworld journey which have many parallels in the lore of indigenous shamanic cultures. The underworld was imagined as a place of darkness where all familiar sights and memories of one's former life were left behind. The journey through that realm by shamans or souls of the dead often consisted of trials during which they faced dangerous obstacles.

The location of the underworld was often believed to be towards the western horizon where the sun, moon and stars set. The Egyptians, Greeks, and Semites associated dying with going towards the sunset. In Celtic mythology the islands of the Otherworld were believed to be in the western sea. In many Native American cultures it was also believed the soul's initial journey after death was towards the west.

Rivers or similar bodies of water served as liminal boundaries which were crossed by the dead in their journey. For the Chumash tribe of California, upon entering the land of the dead the soul first crossed a river. In Siberian shamanic narratives the soul travels along the World River to find the entrance to the underworld. The Finno-Ugrians believed the dead crossed a river, lake or sea in the form of an aquatic animal.[44] In Homer's *Odyssey* the hero Odysseus sailed across Oceanus, the ocean at the edge of the world, to reach the entrance of Hades. The realm of Hades includes several rivers, including Acheron meaning "woe", Phlegeton the river of fire, Lethe the river of forgetfulness and the Styx the river of unbreakable oaths. In the *Egyptian Book of the Dead* the underworld was imagined as a region of bogs and swamps, containing a lake of fire similar to the fiery river in the Hades. The Babylonians also believed a river was crossed by the dead as part of their postmortem journey.

The dog is commonly associated with the underworld and sometimes guards its entrance in shamanic tales. In Greek myths, Cerberus the fierce three-headed dog guards the palace of his master Hades, god of the underworld.[45] In Egyptian myths, the jackal-headed god Anubis is the psychopomp who guides the dead through the underworld. In the Welsh *Mabinogian* otherworldly hounds accompany Arawn, lord of the underworld, in his hunt.

Siberian shamans often shape-shifted into birds in their travels to the land of the dead; the Finno-Ugrians believed souls reached the otherworld by flying like birds along the Milky Way.[46] The Egyptians depicted the *ba* or soul of the deceased as a bird with a human head. Similarly, Homer described the dead in the *Odyssey* as "twittering like bats in a cave" with a noise like "the screaming of birds." In the Babylonian myth of Nergal and Erishkegal, the dead are clothed in a garment of feathers like birds.

Often monsters inhabit the land of the dead. In the lore of the Chumash tribe of California, the fearsome "Woman-who-stings-with-her-Tail" threatens the wandering soul. In the Egyptian underworld, souls sailed across a marsh in which monsters lurked, such as the giant serpent Apep as well as various wild beasts and demons.

The soul's transitional journey through the underworld sometimes involved crossing over bridges and arriving at crossroads. The Chumash believe the dead arrive at two roads, one straight and one to the left. In Greek myths, souls come to a junction of three roads in Hades leading to paradise, purgatory, or hell. The Chumash, as well as the Persians, Germans, Finns and Hungarians envisioned the soul crossing over perilously narrow bridges during the afterlife journey.

The Upperworld

In shamanic myths worldwide, the heavens or "upperworld" is believed to be the abode of the Supreme Being. It is the bright realm of the gods and celestial spirits who grant gifts of spiritual inspiration, prophecy and healing. Northern Siberians envision the heavens as the roof of a vast tent held up by the Pole Star, representing the navel of the sky on which the supreme being rests. The Pole Star which crowns the celestial axis is passed through by shamans, who thereby enter into the highest heaven to gain audience with the celestial spirits.

Central to the cosmological myths of the Altaic cultures of Siberia and Inner Asia is the constellation Ursa Major—commonly known as the Big Dipper. The Altaic peoples derive their mystical number *seven* from it, based on its seven stars, according to historian Geoffrey Ashe. The seven stars of Ursa Major are believed to also represent "seven wise shamans" in Mongolian lore.[47]

The heavens are often divided into three, seven, nine, or more levels. The Evenks of Siberia believe the upperworld consists of several heavens: the highest is the region of the Supreme Being known as Amaka Sheveki; the second heaven is the region of Esheri Shevek, protector of birds, animals, fishes and plants. In the other heavens abide other spiritual beings: the sun, moon, thunder, stars, clouds, etc. The Chuckchi of Siberia also envision several levels in their heavenly realm. The floor of one heaven is the roof of another—a concept that is uncannily similar to the ancient Babylonian and Greek cosmological models of the "celestial spheres" which will later be discussed.

Siberian shamans ascend in vision to the sky to visit Bai Ulgan, the supreme god, to gain information from him about the weather and harvest, as well as to converse with celestial spirits to gain prophecy and healing remedies.[48] They escort the souls of the dead to the upperworld to the top branches of the World Tree to live there as little birds near the Supreme Being, and from there bring them back to rebirth in the human community.[49] The upperworld of the Siberian shaman, though similar to this world, is brighter and some say it has seven suns. It is unspoiled and its inhabitants live in a manner similar to the ancestors.

Traveling to the upperworld requires the power of "magical flight". Shamans shape-shift into the forms of their animal spirit-helpers to journey there. Shamanic practitioner and author Sarangerel writes that Mongolian shamans often transform themselves into birds, or may ride upon a flying deer or horse during their celestial journeys.[50] This ascent was sometimes accomplished by climbing the "world axis", imagined as the World Tree which spanned the earth and heavens. Often a ladder of seven steps or a stairway was climbed into the sky.[51] The Cosmic Mountain which had seven or more levels representing the seven planetary heavens, was also traversed.

Shamans in other cultures around the world possess similar means of ascent. The medicine men of the Australian Kurnai, along with their helping-spirits, climb a rope or staircase to heaven through a hole created for them by a spirit of the dead. The Tsimshian of the Canadian pacific coast often have holes in their totem poles through which they can ceremonially enter the house of the Creator, and the shaman commences his journey through this "hole through the sky".[52]

Sacred Geography of the Middle World

The "middle world" in shamanism refers to the earth, the physical realm in which we exist along with other living creatures. Indigenous people believe in an *animistic* world-view in which all natural phenomena—forests, springs, plants, sky, wind, water and fire—are thought to possess spirits or souls. According to the Altaic peoples of Siberia, mountains, lakes, or rivers had their own "spirit owners", master spirits who controlled the animals and birds living there. One could obtain their goodwill and protection through offerings, sacrifices and prayers. Ethnologist Mihaly Hoppal insists that since everything was believed to have a soul, humans were encouraged to maintain a respectful attitude towards the natural environment. He writes: "...the deepest meaning or message of Siberian animism was to balance man and nature."[53]

The earth was revered by many ancient cultures as a goddess—mother earth—who was paired with a sky-god, their union bringing about all creation. Among Central Asian cultures the fertile earth-mother, Eje, is paired with the sky-god Tengri, or Blue Sky. The Lakota tribe of North America calls the primal couple "grandmother earth" and "grandfather sky". In ancient Mesopotamian myths the earth goddess Ki is married to the sky god An. Indo-European myths likewise tell of an earth-mother and sky-god. There are exceptions to these gender associations though; the ancient Egyptians represented the earth as the god Geb whose intercourse with the sky goddess Nut gave birth to the other deities.

The Tree of Visions

Many indigenous societies saw the the earth as mirroring the heavens, basing their religious and ceremonial life on the cycles of the heavenly bodies. The Lakota people of North America have a saying: "...what is on earth is in the stars, and what is in the stars is on the earth".[54] The Lakota saw the land forms of their sacred homeland in the Black Hills of South Dakota mirroring the constellations in the sky; they performed special ceremonies at these locations, timed by the yearly movement of the sun through the constellations. Beginning in the spring when the sun entered the constellation known to them as the "Seven Little Girls" (the Pleiades or seven sisters), tribal bands journeyed to Harney Peak, performing a ceremony there. This peak with its seven small hills was associated with the seven dim stars of that constellation. The ceremonial cycle culminated in midsummer as the sun moved into the constellation known as the "Bear's Lodge", represented in the landscape by the volcanic butte commonly known as Devil's Tower. There they performed their most important ceremony, the Sun Dance. By synchronizing their ceremonies with the seasonal movement of the sun through the constellations the Lakota believed they followed the sun's path on the earth, drawing down the sacred power of *Wakan Tanka*, the Great Spirit.[55]

The ancient peoples of the Near East and Europe likewise inhabited their own sacred landscapes. The Egyptians conceived of their land as "the image of heaven", its features mirroring the sky above. They saw the "celestial river" of the Milky Way replicated in the winding course of the Nile River. According to authors Bauval and Gilbert, the three prominent stars in the belt of the constellation Orion determined the placement of the three pyramids on the Giza plateau.[56] The entire land of Egypt was believed to be the body of the god Osiris. Each province or "nome" constituting one of his body parts, also ruled over by local gods.

The Babylonians built their ziggurat temples with seven steps to mirror the seven sacred planets in the heavens. The temple or *ziggurat* was thought to be a "cosmic-mountain" or "mooring-pole" enabling communication between heaven and earth, similar to the shamanic notion of the *axis-mundi*, the symbolic center of the earth which connects the worlds together. Similarly is the notion of the *omphalos*, meaning "navel", the mythic center of geography in ancient Greece associated with the oracle of Delphi. Historian M.L. West draws parallels between the cosmology of Asiatic shamanism and the sacred geography of the Greeks:

> "Delphi was at the centre of the world, as Zeus established by setting two eagles to fly in from the ends of the earth until they met. Earth's Navel

was there, presumably marking the place where there was once a physical link with heaven; and there was also direct access from the sanctuary to the great krater in the underworld according to an Orphic poem. This concept of a cosmic centre point where sky, earth and the underworld are all connected is important to Asiatic shamans, who regularly journey there so that they can pass from one world to another and obtain knowledge, conduct souls, etc. The centre is marked by a mountain and a tree and a pillar. At the top of the tree, in the highest heaven, sits the supreme deity, who may take the form of an eagle. It is not surprising that Delphi, being the centre of the cosmos, is a capital for divination. The Pythia resembles a shamaness at least to the extent that she communicates with her god while in a state of trance"...[57]

The landscapes of ancient cultures became the subject of myths and storytelling. In Ireland these "stories of place", were called the *Dindsenchas*.[58] One such story tells of the mythic origin of the river Boyne, named after the goddess Boand who walked around the source of the river three times *widdershins*, against the circuit of the sun, a foolhardy and dangerous act which upset the cosmic order. Yet by doing so, she released the river's waters for all people. The Celts revered springs, lakes, bogs, mountains, stones, islands and trees as liminal places where contact with the otherworld was possible. Nigel Pennick considers such places to be the *"anima loci"* or the place-soul of the Celt's sacred landscape, writing: "there is no feature of the landscape that is not associated in local tradition with some event or legend..." [59]

Shamanic Skywatchers

Cosmological and astronomical knowledge was held by skywatchers and calendar keepers in some native american cultures, who tracked the annual motions of the stars and constellations, according to archeoastronomer E.C. Krupp. Among the Chumash tribe of California, the *'alchuklash* was a shamanic ritual specialist who watched the sky, counting the cycles of the moon and determining the times of the solstices and seasonal appearances of the stars. They also participated in the naming of newborns, reading their destinies in the sky, similar to astrologers. The 'achuklash presided over communal ceremonies, instructing and initiating the youth, kept the calendar and coordinated most aspects of village life.[60] In other tribes skywatchers were consulted before any important undertaking such as the spring hunt, early summer fishing, gathering food and harvesting crops as well as timing religious ceremonies. A member of the Cahuilla tribe of Southern California explains:

"The old men used to study the stars very carefully and in this way could tell when each season began...After several nights of careful watching, when a certain star finally appeared, the old men would rush out, cry and shout, and often dance....for it meant that they could now find certain plants in the mountains. They never went to the mountains until they saw a certain star, for they knew they would not find food there previously." [61]

The heavens provided an ordering principle for tribal peoples of North America, according to archaeoastronomer Ray Williamson. He writes that these various groups based their cosmology and ceremonial life on the cycle of the seasons related to the motions of the sun, moon, and stars: "Virtually every Native American tribe or social group developed models of the celestial realm that were part of their everyday patterns of life." [62]

Ancient Native Americans built monumental structures for observing the heavenly bodies that had ritual and calendrical uses as well. One such example is the Bighorn Medicine Wheel in Wyoming, originally built by the Cheyenne people. It consists of rocks placed on a mountain side arranged in the pattern of a wheel of twenty-eight spokes, which probably marked the days of the month. Surveys of the site have also shown alignments to sunrise at summer solstice as well as the risings of the stars Aldeberan, Sirius, and Rigel, which were used for timing the tribe's ceremonial cycle.[63] The site continues to be used to this day by native peoples for fasting, prayers and vision quests.

The Great Bear & The Cosmic Hunt

One of the most widely distributed astronomical myths of the northern hemisphere is the "Cosmic Hunt", associated with the constellation Ursa Major (the Big Dipper) and its neighboring stars. It is found in different versions across Scandinavia, Eurasia, Asia and North America.

Evenk tribes of Siberia called Ursa Major *kheglun* the moose, and its neighboring constellation Bootes *mangi* the bear. Legends tell of the bear who pursued the moose in the skies through the seasons, eventually killing it. Similarly some ancient Scandinavian peoples perceived Ursa Major as a moose. Curiously a few Siberian groups identified the constellation as a mammoth, suggesting it was named as such during the Mesolithic period (Middle Stone Age) or perhaps earlier since the creature likely became extinct around 10,000 years ago.

Many of the myths concerning Ursa Major refer to the hunt of a *female* animal associated with the shamanic "Mistress of Animals", the deity believed to provide animals for the hunt. She was seen as the life giver of the universe and mother of all animals, according to archaeoastronomer Elio Antonello. Imagined as both woman and animal, the Mistress of Animals was considered the "first ancestress" of many shamanic cultures, reflecting their matrilineal beliefs.[64] Geoffrey Ashe points out the curious etymology of the Siberian word *etugen*, a name for the earth goddess, which also means "female shaman" as well as "bear" in one dialect. Significantly, all of these were associated with Ursa Major as well.[65]

Native American tribes such as the Mahicans and Munsee of the Algonquin nation interpreted the four stars of the quadrangle of Ursa Major as a *cosmic bear*. Revolving around the North Star, the bear was thought to leave its den in the spring, pursued by seven hunters—associated with the three stars in the handle of Ursa Major, the star Arcturus, and three stars of the neighboring constellation Bootes. These star-hunters followed the bear around the heavens through the summer, slaying it in the fall. The reddening of the forest leaves was attributed to the spilling of its blood. The celestial bear came to life again though, emerging next spring from its den to re-enact the same drama all over again.[66]

The Munsee-Mahicans celebrated this yearly sky-hunt as part of their New Years renewal ceremonies every January with a bear sacrifice. The sacrificed animal was highly revered and believed to serve as a cosmic messenger between the sky and earth. The ceremony first required that a woman of the tribe dreamed about the bear, revealing its location and signaling the beginning of the ceremony. The ceremonial Big House was laid out to mirror the heavens on earth—the interior furnishings and the positions occupied by the ceremonial officials corresponded to the position of the stars in the constellation. The acts and movements of the ritualists repeated the movements of Ursa Major. They enacted the myth of the celestial bear telling of the annual life cycle of the sacrificial bear which was sacrificed by the chief beneath the center post of the lodge, symbolic of the World Tree. The ceremonies were performed at night, possibly because Ursa Major was visible in the sky above the lodge at this time.

Bear ceremonialism was widespread among other indigenous northern cultures such as the Sami of Finland, The Gilyaks of Siberia, and the Ainu of Japan. It is probable Siberian peoples brought the bear-cult with them during their migrations across the Bering Straight, spreading it to North America. Bear ceremonialism may have originated as early as 26,000 BCE among the Paleolithic inhabitants of Europe, according to Antonello. He cites discoveries in Belgian caves of bear remains with traces of red ochre pigment on them, usually found in Paleolithic human burials, and notes that peoples of the circumpolar region also color bear skulls and paws red and black during rituals.[67] Antonello refers to the drawing of a bear with bleeding mouth, nose, ears and dart marks in the Trois-Freres cave in France, dating to the Magdalenian period, which may depict a bear sacrifice. Archaeologist Marija Gimbutas likewise speculates that bear cults date back to the Paleolithic, insisting this would explain the widespread distribution of bear ceremonialism.[68]

Among many shamanic cultures the bear was thought to be half-animal and half-human, perhaps based on its uncanny ability to walk on its hind legs and use its paws like human hands. Its death-like hibernation through the winter and seeming rebirth in the spring reminded them of the shaman's powers of transformation. Bears are revered by native americans as a culture-hero from whom humans first received the gifts of fire and stone tools.[69] Among the Sioux, Chippewa, Pueblo and Iroquois peoples of North America, bear-gods are seen as benevolent healers. Siberian tribes held bear festivals in which people dressed as bears and a ceremonial bear was respectfully killed—sacrificed and "sent home" to the spirit world—where it was believed to serve as an intermediary between humans and the gods, similar to the Mahican-Munsee ritual mentioned previously.

Remarkably, similar symbolism occurs among the Indo-European peoples as well. The ancient Greeks named the constellation Ursa Major "The Great Bear", and in Vedic India it was known as *Rksah* or "the bears".[70] The Greeks associated it with Artemis, the goddess of the hunt, whose totem animal was a bear.[71] In the myth of Callisto, Artemis transforms her maiden follower Callisto into a bear as punishment for betraying her vow of virginity, then places her in the heavens as Ursa Major. Artemis was believed to be the protector of the young of all species, and when Athenian girls reached puberty they undertook an initiation rite in which they were dedicated to her, called "young bears" and dressed in bear skins mimicking the behavior and motions of bears with ritual dances.

According to ethnologist Roslyn Frank, bear ceremonialism was widely practiced across ancient Europe, and can be traced back to the shamanistic beliefs of hunter-gatherers of the Paleolithic and Mesolithic periods. The last traces of these traditions only recently died out among the Basques in the Pyrenees, as well as in parts of the Balkans, where trained bears were taken around on visits to households to bring healing and to drive away evil spirits.[72] Frank notes that the Basques, along with the Finns and Siberians, tell stories of the bear's origin in the heavens near the constellation Ursa Major.

Chapter 1 Notes

Shaman's drum design showing three worlds – Altai Kizi.

1. Eliade, Mircea. *Shamanism- Archaic Techniques of Ecstasy*. 1964: 231-232.
2. Pratt, Christina. *An Encyclopedia of Shamanism. Vol. 1.* 2007:xxi.
3. Flaherty, Gloria. *Shamanism and the Eighteenth Century.*1992:27.
4. Hutton, Ronald. *Shamans-Siberian Spirituality and the Western Imagination.* 2001:30-31.
5. Boekhoven 2012: 34-45.
6. Hutton. *Shamans-Siberian Spirituality and the Western Imagination.*2001: 43.
7. Eliade. *Shamanism- Archaic Techniques of Ecstasy.*1964: xxv.
8. Ibid., 3-6.
9. Even in the home of "classic" shamanism in Siberia and Mongolia there are several types of magico-religious specialists comparable to shamans: curers, bone-setters, mid-wives, sorcerers, etc. who enter altered states and work with spirits to heal, as do shamans. Among individual shamans there are also highly individualized approaches to shamanizing. (Humphrey & Onon 1996:55)
10. Heinze, Ruth-Inge. *Shamans Of The 20th Century.* 1991:xi.
11. Vitebsky, Piers. *Shamanism.* 2001: 6.
12. Eliade. *Shamanism- Archaic Techniques of Ecstasy.*1964: 3.
13. Ibid., 375.
14. Campbell *The Masks of God: Oriental Mythology*. New York: Penguin Books, 1987: 250.
15. Hutton. *Shamans-Siberian Spirituality and the Western Imagination.*2001: 85.
16. Heinze. *Shamans Of The 20th Century.*1991:190.

17. Harner, Michael. *The Way of the Shaman*. 1980:25.
18. Wilby, Emma. *The Visions of Isobel Gowdie: Magic, Witchcraft and Dark Shamanism in Seventeenth-Century Scotland*.2011: 252-254.
19. Eliade. *Shamanism- Archaic Techniques of Ecstasy*.1964 :16
20. Heinze *Shamans Of The 20th Century*.1991:xvi. Some psychologists propose shamans are "fantasy-prone" individuals. Surveys among the general American population found that around four percent are found to have "fantasy- prone personality". These people are easy to hypnotize and have imaginary playmates as children. In adult life they spontaneously experience paranormal and mystical experiences: telepathy, clairvoyance, precognition, and out-of- body experiences. Two thirds of these individuals claim to be able to heal, and three out of four have encountered apparitions, ghosts and spirits.
21. Heinze. *Shamans Of The 20th Century*.1991:173.
22. Schleiser, Karl H. *The Wolves of Heaven*. 1987. Similarly the *basir* shamans of Borneo dress and behave like women and are considered intermediaries between the feminine (earth) and masculine (sky). See Heinze 1991: 174.
23. Harner. *The Way of the Shaman*. 1980:26.
24. Heinze. *Shamans Of The 20th Century*.1991:158.
25. Drury, Nevill. *The Shaman and the Magician: journeys between the worlds*. 1982:14,18.
26. Heinze. *Shamans Of The 20th Century*.1991:159-64. For a description of the three levels of possession of Umbanistas of Argentina see Heinze pp. 161-162.
27. Sarangarel *Chosen by the Spirits: following your shamanic calling*.2001: 184-188. For the use of Vodka by Mongolian shamans for spells (serjim), and offerings to the spirits.
28. Wilby *The Visions of Isobel Gowdie*: 2011.
29. Rasmussen, Knud. *Across Arctic America: Narrative of the Fifth Thule Expedition*.1908:106.
30. Eliade. *Shamanism- Archaic Techniques of Ecstasy*.1972:216.
31. Ibid., 246.
32. Schleiser. *The Wolves of Heaven*. 1987: 28-29.
33. Kalweit. *Dreamtime & Inner Space: the world of the shaman*.1988: 25.
34. Krupp, E.C. *Beyond the Blue Horizon: Myths and Legends of the Sun, Moon, Stars, and Planets*.1991: 279.
35. Schlesier. *The Wolves of Heaven*. 1987: 20.
36. Kalweit. *Dreamtime & Inner Space: the world of the shaman*. 1988: 59.
37. Harner, Michael. The Way of the Shaman. 1982: 32.
38. West, M.L. *Early Greek Philosophy and the Orient*. 1971:152.
39. Clottes, Jean."Paleolithic Cave Art Painting and Rock Art in France". *Adorant Magazine*- 2002. 2002.
40. Kalweit. *Dreamtime & Inner Space: the world of the shaman*.1988:199.
41. Wolkstein, Diane and Kramer, Samuel Noah. *Inanna Queen of Heaven and Earth*.1983:156.
42. Eliade, Mircea. *Myths, Dreams & Mysteries*.1975:197-200.
43. Naydler, Jeremy. *Temple of the Cosmos- The Ancient Egyptian Experience of the Sacred*. 1996: 216.

44. Walter, Mariko Namba; Fridman Eva Jane Neumann, eds. Shamanism: An Encyclopedia of World Beliefs, Practices *and Culture*, Vol.1. 2004:489.
45. See p.102 of *The Tree of Visions* for the underworld in Indo-European myths.
46. Walter; Fridman. eds. *Shamanism: An Encyclopedia of World Beliefs, Practices and Culture,* Vol.1. 2004:489.

47. Ashe, Geoffrey. *Dawn Behind The Dawn: A Search for the Earthly Paradise*.1992: 34.
48. Krupp. *Beyond the Blue Horizon: Myths and Legends of the Sun, Moon, Stars, and Planets.* 1991: 29.
49. Schlesier. *The Wolves of Heaven.*1987:21.
50. Sarangerel. *Riding Windhorses: A Journey into the Heart of Mongolian Shamanism.* 2000:13.
51. Eliade. *Shamanism- Archaic Techniques of Ecstasy.*1964: 267.
52. Kalweit. *Dreamtime & Inner Space: the world of the shaman.* 1988: 213.
53. Hoppal, Mihaly. *Nature Worship in Siberian Shamanism.* Folklore, Electronic Journal of Folklore. Vol. 4 1997:1.
54. Goodman, Ronald. *Lakota Star Knowledge.*1992:1-15.
55. Ibid. 50-51.
56. Bauval, Robert and Gilbert, Adrian. *The Orion Mystery- Unlocking the Secrets of the Pyramids.*1994:119.
57. West, M.L. *The Orphic Poems.*1983:147.
58. Matthews, Caitlín; John, Matthews.*The Encyclopedia of Celtic Wisdom.*1994:16-17.
59. Pennick, Nigel. *Celtic Sacred Landscapes.* 1996:11-14.
60. Krupp, E.C. *Skywatchers, Shamans & Kings: Astronomy and the Archaeology of Power.* 1997:156.
61. Hooper, Lucille, Kroeber, Alfred. *Studies in Cahuilla Culture.*1978: 315-80.
62. Williamson, Ray, A. *Living the Sky: the Cosmos of the American Indian.*1987: 311.
63. Ibid. 217.
64. Antonello, Elio. *The Myths of the Bear.* World Wide Web 2011:11.
65. Ashe: *Dawn Behind The Dawn: A Search for the Earthly Paradise. 1992:166.*
66. Schleiser. *The Wolves of Heaven.*1987:175-176.
67. Antonello. *The Myths of the Bear.* 2011:11.
68. Gimbutas, Marija. *The Language of the Goddess: Unearthing the Hidden Symbols of Western Civilization.* 2001:116.
69. Jacobson, Esther. *The Deer Goddess of Ancient Siberia: A Study in the Ecology of Belief.* 1993:182.
70. West, M.L. *Indo-European Poetry and Myth.* 2007: 351.
71. Ashe. *Dawn Behind The Dawn: A Search for the Earthly Paradise.* 1992:158-159.
72. Frank, Roslyn M. *Hunting the European Sky Bears: German"Straw Bears"and their Relatives as Transformers.*World-Wide Web 2004:5.

Chapter 2: The Shaman's Craft

Sacred Mayan Yaxche Tree with bird as spirit messenger.

The World Tree

In the previous chapter we discussed the three worlds through which the shaman journeys: middleworld, lowerworld and upperworld. These are thought to be joined together by the *axis-mundi* or world axis, often envisioned in the form of the "World Tree" extending through the worlds and connecting them together. With roots deep in the lowerworld, its branches reach up to support the sky. Shamans attain prophetic visions ascending it's trunk into the heavens to commune with celestial spirits—and descend its roots to the underworld, visiting the land of the dead. Sometimes the ascent was physically acted out by shamans during initiation ceremonies by climbing an actual tree, or notched pole or ladder. In northern Siberia, a young tree with seven branches left on the top representing the seven levels of the heavens was placed inside of tents, jutting through the smoke hole. The Cheyenne of Wyoming also placed a tree with seven branches in the middle of a ceremonial tepee as part of their yearly renewal ceremony.[1]

Myths of the World Tree are distributed world-wide, found in the Americas, Asia, Micronesia, the Middle-East, Europe, and Africa. It appears as the "Mes Tree" in a Babylonian myth, described as the "flesh of the gods...whose base reaches the bottom of the underworld and whose summit reaches into the heaven of Anu". In Persian myths the "Tree of All Seeds" grows in Paradise, and from its scattered seeds all plants grew. In the Greek myth of the Garden of Hesperides a tree growing apples of immortality is guarded by a serpent. Serpents or dragons guarding cosmic trees are also found in Thracian and Persian myths. The *Book of Genesis* tells of the Tree of Life in the Garden of Eden, and next to it the Tree of Knowledge of Good and Evil. Here Eve encounters the serpent who offers her a taste of its alluring fruit resulting in their expulsion from Paradise. Similar to the biblical account, a myth from Micronesia tells of a paradisiacal garden in which two trees grow under which men and women live, eating their fruits. By mingling together, however, they eat of the Tree of Death and become mortal.

The World Tree is a common motif in Indo-European myths, appearing in the lore of Greek, Thracian, Latvian, and other European cultures. In India it is known as the Asvattha Tree, an aspect of the god of creation, Brahman. It is inverted however, with its roots in the heavens and branches growing down to the earth below. In Nordic myths the Yggdrasil Tree connects the worlds together, its fruit and nectar feeding gods, humans and animals alike. Beneath it flows a prophetic spring at which sit the Three Norns, oracular goddesses of Past, Present and Future. The god of wisdom and magic, Odin, sacrifices himself by hanging for nine nights upon the tree to learn magic spells and runes. Yggdrasil means "horse of the terrible one", referring to Odin, as the tree was his mount for supernatural journeys between the nine worlds.[2]

In the mythology of Pre-Columbian cultures—the Olmecs, Mayans, Aztecs, Mixtecs and others—the World Tree was associated with a cross and four directions. The Maya believed the giant Yaxche Tree stood at the center of the world connecting heaven, earth and underworld. They associated this mythic tree with the Milky Way, which at certain times of the year appears to extend vertically from the horizon into the sky like a vast tree with starry leaves, according to Linda Schele.[3] Souls of the ancestors were believed to ascend through the roots and trunk to the celestial realm. Similar to the Siberians who believed the souls of shamans rested in the heavenly World Tree awaiting rebirth, the Mayans envisoned souls growing as flowers on its branches. In an Iroquois myth a tree grows in the sky-world at the entrance to the world below. The tree is uprooted and a woman falls through the hole into the lower world, bringing about the creation of the earth. A similar Polynesian myth tells of a tree rooted in the heavens which produces bright and nimble sons.[4]

In an Egyptian myth, the sibling deities Isis and Osiris emerged from an acacia tree. Some Siberian groups traced their origin to trees, believing that in the beginning a tree split in two, out of which came a man and woman. Likewise in an ancient Persian myth the trunk of a primordial tree separated into a man and woman, its fruit becoming the different races of mankind. Similarly in Germanic myth the first man and woman also emerged from a tree.

Ancient cultures revered trees as symbols of the life force as well as localized versions of the *axis-mundi*—the sacred center of the universe. The early Greeks fenced off groves of sacred trees which became places of worship. Deities were associated with certain trees: Zeus ruled the oak, Aphrodite the myrtle, Hera the willow, Athena the olive and Dionysus the vine.[5] Often worship was simply conducted on an altar beneath a tree. No temple was considered dedicated unless it had a sacred tree nearby, sometimes revered more than the temple itself. At the famous Oak of Dodona, sacred to Zeus and the oldest oracle in Greece, prophecies were received from the rustling of the tree's branches and interpreted by three elderly priestesses named "doves". The Celtic Druids worshipped in groves of oak trees. The pagan Norwegians built their temple at Uppsala next to a large evergreen tree representing Yggdrasil, hanging sacrifices of men and animals from its branches.

The World Tree has endured as an archetypal symbol throughout the history of western esotericism. Plato the classical Greek philosopher compared man to a tree with roots in the heavens and branches on the earth. The Jewish Kabbalists of the Middle Ages meditated on the cosmological diagram of the "Tree of Life" upon which they juxtaposed the body of the cosmic man, Adam Kadmon. The Hermetic alchemists of the Renaissance conceived of the Arbor Philosophica or "Philosophical Tree" symbolizing the stages of alchemical transformation. The kabbalistic Tree of Life continues to be used today by modern ritual magicians for meditation and visionary work, which will be explored later.

The Eagle & the Serpent

Myths of the World Tree often feature an eagle that nests in its upper branches and a serpent or similar reptile dwelling in its roots. The eagle is usually associated with the heavenly realm, and the serpent with the underworld. This pair can be found in myths of the ancient Mesopotamians, Norse, Siberians, Persians, Chinese, Mesoamericans and other peoples. They appear in the Sumerian *Epic of Etana* in which the eagle and serpent are neighbors dwelling in the same tree. In the Germanic myth of the Yggdrasil Tree a wise eagle lives in the tree's upper branches fending off the serpent Niohoggr, continually gnawing at its roots, threatening to destroy it.

The eagle is also a frequent spirit-helper of shamans, assisting them in their visionary journeys to the upperworld. According to a Siberian Buryat legend, the first shaman was born from the sexual intercourse between an eagle and a woman, and it is believed the eagle first taught men shamanism. The eagle served as the totemic bird of ancient kings as well, who displayed some of the magical charisma of shamans. Etana, an early Mesopotamian king, flew to the heavens on the back of an eagle. Similarly the souls of deceased Roman emperors were believed to be borne to the heavens by eagles to their patron the sun-god.

Serpents likewise play an important role as shamanic helping spirits. The *Kalevala* epic of ancient Finland tells of Sami shamans who shapeshift into serpents during their travels. Siberian shamans use a drumstick made of snake skin and wear tassels resembling serpents on their costumes. Australian aboriginal medicine men believe that during their initiations a snake is placed in their head, giving them healing powers. Andamanese and San shamans ascended in vision to the heavens on the back of a "rainbow serpent".[6]

The Hopi people of Arizona perform a Snake Dance to pray for rain as well as honor their ancestors. In preparation, snake priests go out into the desert to capture whip-snakes, bull snakes and poisonous rattlesnakes. During the ceremonies they dance with the serpents, first holding them in their hands then clenching them between their teeth. They finally release them back in the desert with the belief they will carry their prayers to the Rainmakers which dwell in the lowerworld along with the ancestors and gods.[7]

Images of serpents are engraved on a panel of mammoth ivory dating back to the Upper Paleolithic culture of Mal'ta in Siberia circa 23,000 BCE.[8] Archaeologist Marija Gimbutas conjectures that serpents engraved on antlers and stones from the Mesolithic and Neolithic eras in Europe may be related to timekeeping. According to her the wavy serpentine lines appear to measure time, each wave used as a counting unit of days in the lunar calendar. She insists serpents are associated not only with the passage of time, but also with funerary monuments and the belief in regeneration from death. Gimbutas writes: "The serpent's life force is at the heart of this symbolism. It influences the renewal of nature by moving time from the point of death to life, from the dark moon to full moon, from winter to spring".[9]

In the matrifocal civilization of Minoan Crete, figurines have been found of bare breasted women with their arms entwined by serpents, likely associated with fertility cults. The goddess Wadjet, protector of lower Egypt and the pharaoh, was depicted as a single serpent wrapped around a papyrus reed. Heka, the Egyptian god of magic, was depicted as a man holding two serpents crossed over his chest. The early Babylonian god of the underworld, Ningishzida, was symbolized by two copulating serpents intertwined around a rod—perhaps the prototype of the serpentine "caduceus wand" of Hermes, Greek god of magic. Snakes were also associated with male Greek gods: Dionysus, Hermes, Zeus, Asklepios, and Agathos Daimon.[10] It is remarkable that live snakes continue to be venerated as house guardians in the rural Balkans and Greece to the present day.

Joseph Campbell writes that the serpent appears commonly in the myths of Bronze Age matriarchal cultures as a symbol of fertility and life but was subjected to "mythic defamation" by their Iron Age patriarchal conquerers, turned into a symbol of primordial chaos and evil.[11] Though Indo-European myths feature heroes who battle and slay evil dragons, the serpent continued to be venerated as a symbol of wisdom as well.[12] In many cultures it has a dual symbolism, associated with death as well as fertility and healing. By shedding its skin, it symbolizes rebirth and immortality.

Helping- Spirits

The concept of "helping-spirits", fundamental to shamanism as well as magic, may seem credulous and even naïve to modern thinkers. In a world dominated by rationalism and logical "left-brained" thinking, those who hear voices or see visions of spirits may be diagnosed as mentally ill. Psychiatrists until recently labelled the visionary experiences of shamans as "pathological", associating them with schizophrenia, hysteria, epilepsy or magical thinking.

Over the past few decades however there has been a paradigm shift in science—an increasing number of psychologists and scientists have begun to study shamanism as a means of gaining insight into non-ordinary states of consciousness. Transpersonal psychologist Roger Walsh acknowledges that the shaman's interactions with "spirits" may even be beneficial as they provide them with information and guidance. He notes that Jungian and Gestalt schools of psychology use guided imagery or fantasy to access the inner wisdom of the patient, including techniques such as dialogue with a sage or "inner teacher".[13] Through this technique insightful information can be accessed, similar in some aspects to the shaman's use of helping-spirits.

The renowned psychologist Carl Jung, who studied thousands of his patient's dreams as well as the myths of ancient cultures, possessed unusual insight into helping-spirits based on personal experience. Following a prolonged period of introspection during which he examined his own fantasies and dreams, Jung concluded: "I came to the realization there are things in the psyche which I do not produce, but which produce themselves and have their own life..."[14] In fact Jung had several "inner teachers" with whom he dialogued using his technique of Active Imagination. Dr. Michael Winkelman writes about spirits from the perspective of neuropsychology: "whatever they are ultimately and ontologically, spirits are experientially real."[15]

Anthropologist Emma Wilby explains that tribal shamans hold an *animistic* belief system based on the assumption that the cosmos and all phenomena are animated by an immaterial force. This can be conceived of as essence, consciousness, spiritual energy, or soul, or alternately as autonomous "spirits". It is these spirits which shamans communicate with to influence the world around them.[16]

For the shaman, spirits serve as teachers and helpers in the otherworld. Spirits in the form of gods, nature spirits, animal-helpers and ancestors play an essential role in maintaining the secular and religious life of indigenous communities. They are believed to be ever-present, helpful or malevolent, influencing fertility, abundance, and the successful hunt or harvest.

Peoples of the ancient Near East and Europe were animists as well, living in a world ensouled by spirit beings. The Greeks believed in a spirit-world populated by *daimons* who protected the living, but could also cause harm. The early Greek philosopher Thales expressed this sentiment when he said "The universe is alive and full of daimons". Daimons were associated with the celestial Muses and gods, as well as various nature spirits or the spirits of the dead. We will return to the subject of daimons later, as they share many characteristics with the helping-spirits of shamans.

Among tribal peoples it is the shaman who specializes in working with spirits, since contact with them is considered risky for ordinary people. Evil spirits are believed to cause maladies such as depression, accidents and destruction of crops and animals.[17] Illness is often seen as the result of offending the spirits, or unpaid debts to the spirit world. It can also occur when the patient's soul strays from their body or is stolen by spirits or malevolent shamans.[18] Treatment consists of the shaman finding and restoring the lost soul. The shaman "calls back" the soul to the patient's body, and if it refuses to return they undertake a visionary journey to retrieve it. Eliade provides an account of a Finnish shaman who journeys to the underworld to search for his patient's soul: "He persuades the dead to let him bring it back to earth by promising them the gift of a shirt or other things; sometimes, however, he is obliged to use more forceful means. When he wakes from his ecstasy the shaman has the patient's soul in his closed right hand and replaces it in the body through the right ear".[19]

Possession by spirits is also believed to sometimes cause illness or insanity, requiring exorcism by shamans.[20] In Mongolia, newborn children and their mothers are isolated from the community for a certain amount of time following birth to protect the newly entered soul of the child, and also to protect the mother who is more otherworldly and susceptible to spiritual influences at this time. Similarly, the household as well as the name of a recently deceased person may become taboo for a period. It is believed that speaking their name could call them back to the world of the living where they might cause problems.[21]

For these reasons and others, the shaman's expertise in dealing with the spirit world is of crucial importance to the health and well being of the community. Eliade writes:

> "A shaman is a man who has immediate, concrete experiences with gods and spirits, he sees them face to face, he talks with them, prays to them, implores them..." [22]

Animal Spirits in Shamanism & Ancient Magic

In hunter-gatherer societies, people's mundane and religious experience is dominated by the animals upon which they depend for survival. All creatures are believed to possess souls, personalities, language, and psychic abilities similar to humans as well as unique magical powers which can be accessed by shamans to help them in their work. Shamans cultivate an intimate relationship with their animal-helper spirits, transforming themselves into them while journeying in trance between the worlds.

Shamans may have originally developed this skill through hunting, learning to mimic the behavior of their prey while stalking, leading them to identify with the souls of animals as guardian spirits.[23] During his séance the shaman imitates his animal-helper's cries and movements, writhing like a snake or imitating the flight of a bird. Eliade writes that though it may appear as if he is being possessed, in actuality the shaman "takes possession of his helping spirits" as if "putting on an animal mask". The animal-helper becomes the shaman's alter-ego or another of their "souls" who assists him in his work. A shaman of the Paviotso tribe of western North America discusses how he initially contacted his animal spirits and gained his skills from them:

> "A man dreams that a deer, eagle, or bear comes after him. The animal tells him that he is to be a doctor. The first time a man dreams this way he does not believe it. Then he dreams that way some more and he gets the things the spirit told him to get (eagle feathers, wild tobacco, stone pipe, rattle made from the ear of a deer or from the deer's dew claws). Then he learns to be a doctor. He learns his songs when the spirit comes and sings to him." [24]

According to Karl Schleiser, there were three categories of Siberian shamans related to animals of the three regions of the universe. He writes: "The bird shaman generally was associated with sky space, the bear shaman with the deep earth, whereas reindeer and deer shamans could be associated with either region or the middle world." [25]

The earliest artistic record of what appears to be a masked reindeer shaman is preserved as a wall painting in Trois Freres Cave, in southern France, dated to the Late Paleolithic. Cave paintings display humans with animal features, thought by researchers to depict shamans in the process of transforming into their animal-allies. Animals such as bulls, deer, horses, bears, lions, snakes and birds are represented in artwork of the Upper Paleolithic, and may have been associated with shamanic animal helping spirits.

Likewise, art of the early Neolithic Near-East and Europe depicts spirits in the form of anthropomorphized human-animal hybrids. The Greek god of the forest, Pan, was represented as a horned man with the legs of a goat. Archaeologist Marija Gimbutas suggests Pan's associations with wild nature and hunting imply his origins in prehistory.[26] Pan is indeed eerily similar in appearance to the horned men depicted in Paleolithic cave paintings. In Egyptian art, deities were often represented as bird or animal headed humans such as the ibis-headed Thoth, or cow headed Hathor.

While Paleolithic art depicts men with the heads of bulls, stags, and birds, during the following Neolithic period representations of human-headed animals begin to appear, according to archaeologist Klaus Schmidt.[27] In the artwork of the ancient Mediterranean, genii with human heads juxtaposed on the bodies of lions, bulls, horses, or serpents are commonplace. Goddesses such as Isis and Ishtar are sometimes depicted with wings, and likely influenced Christian and Islamic religious iconography of angels depicted as winged humans.

In ancient Egypt, animals symbolized the qualities of different deities. For example, the goddess Hathor was sometimes represented as a cow since she was the archetype of feminine fertility. Likewise the predatory nature of the hawk was associated with Horus, the god of war. In the *Egyptian Book of the Dead*, spells are provided for transformation into the forms of animals sacred to the gods, such as the swallow of Isis or the crocodile of Sobek. The following spell is for transforming into a hawk: "I ascend from the balcony as a hawk of gold coming forth from its egg. I have flown; I have alighted as a hawk of gold" [28]. Similar to the shaman's use of animal helping-spirits, Egyptian magicians used the powers of animals for magical purposes.

Celtic myths are also full of examples of humans shapeshifting into animal forms. In the Welsh story of *Gwion Bach*, the hero escapes the wrath of the goddess Ceridwen by transforming himself successively into a hare, a fish, a bird and finally a grain of wheat. Ceridwen in turn pursues him by shapeshifting into a greyhound, an otter, a falcon and a finally a hen. In that form she eats the grain of wheat and becomes pregnant—giving birth to the bard Taliesin.

In ancient Greek myths, the god Zeus is a master shapeshifter changing his appearance into different animals, such as a bull, swan, and eagle, in whose forms he seduces his lovers. In Teutonic lore, Odin is the master shapeshifter, who in a state of trance could assume the shape of a "fish, or dragon, or bird or beast and travel to distant lands". The Nordic goddess Freyja who taught her magic to Odin possessed a feathered cloak and shapeshifted into a hawk, traveling great distances in her raptor form.

Otherworldly Partners

Along with their animal spirit-helpers, shamans can access a broad range of other spirit-allies without definite form. These are believed to dwell in rocks, lakes and other natural phenomena such as: "blue sky, night, mist, ghosts, graves, bones, and hair and teeth of the dead", according to Eliade.[29] Medicine men of the American West worked with "the little green man", a guardian spirit who was described as standing two feet tall, carrying a bow and arrow, who shot arrows into those who spoke ill of him. Dwarves who granted supernatural power were also encountered.[30] Native american legends also tell of the "little people" who inhabit rivers and forests.

Similar kinds of nature spirits populate the myths of Indo-Europeans as well. Faery-folk, nymphs, satyrs, elves, dwarves, gnomes, giants and dragons are found in folklore from Ireland to India.[31] Numerous legends tell of the intimate involvement of these spirits with mankind. The poet Orpheus, for example, married Eurydice, a beautiful wood nymph. Other Greek myths speak of love affairs between the *nereides*, the water spirits, and humans, and the offspring that were born from their unions. Celtic folklore includes marriages between humans and mermaid-like *selkies*, or other faery folk. Merlin, the great wizard of Arthurian legend was said to be born of a human mother and demon father, from whom he inherited his supernatural powers.

In Near-Eastern folklore the Queen of Sheba, who married King Solomon the great magician, was described in some legends as being a demoness with the left-foot of a goat. Myths in southern Africa tell of the python god who marries a human wife and drags her down with him to his watery home in the lowerworld.[32] Similarly the renaissance era alchemist Paracelsus writes of marriages between humans and "undines"—elemental spirits of water—claiming that through entering into this union they are able to obtain a soul.[33]

In many indigenous cultures, shamans enter into alliances including marriages with spirit beings. These otherworldly wives or husbands become powerful "tutelary spirits" who form a working partnership with the shaman, without whom they would be unable to heal or exercise their magical powers. Eliade discusses this in relation to the shamans of the Goldi people of Siberia, writing that they "...clearly distinguish between the tutelary spirit (ayami) which chooses the shaman, and the helping spirits (syven) which are subordinate to and are granted to the shaman by the ayami itself".[34] The shaman's tutelary spirit often manages and directs the lesser spirits which are used for specific magical tasks. A Siberian Nanay shaman discussed such a spirit who lived with him like a wife. He revealed his ayami was a beautiful small woman, with one half her face painted red and the other half black. She could appear in the form of an old woman, a wolf, or a winged tiger. She provided him with three spirit helpers—a leopard, a bear and a tiger. He confided: "When I am shamanizing, the ayami and the assistant spirits...penetrate me, as smoke, or vapour would. When the ayami is within me, it is she who speaks through my mouth, and she does everything herself".[35]

The tutelary spirit of shamans is similar to the guardian angel or "familiar spirits" of Near-Eastern and European magicians, witches and cunning-folk who will be discussed later.

Black & White Shamans

Shamans were often viewed ambivalently in their communities—respected for their healing powers but feared for their powers to curse. In Mongolia there were traditionally two types of shamans—"black" and "white", which referred to the types of spirits they worked with.[36] The black shamans got their power from the northern direction, and were warrior shamans. During the Mongol

Empire they performed magic to influence the outcome of battles, such as causing heavy rainstorms to disorient and overpower the enemy.[37] They also bolstered the morale of warriors and served as political advisers. In times of peace, black shamans engaged in hunting rituals, divination, healing, protection and cursing.

In contrast, white shamans derived their power from the western direction. They engaged in blessings and divination, and their focus was on calming angry spirits and helping people to live in balance with nature. White shamans did not use tools like drums, but instead a wooden staff and bells. Neither did they use the antlered headdress of the black shaman, but wore a cape called a *nemerge* and a bare breastplate, in contrast to black shamans who wore metal effigies sewn onto their robes that represented their helping spirits.

According to Valentina Kharitonova, in most aspects Siberian black shamans resemble white shamans but their status reflects the mythological duality of the universe—seen as divided into moral realms of "good" and "evil". Thus black shamans gained their powers from demonic spirits and had power to penetrate far into the lower worlds. They appealed primarily to the spirits of the earth and the god of the lowerworld, Erlik. They were sometimes associated with sorcery and described as acting in immoral ways.[38] Attacks by shamans on other shamans were more common in the past when clans and tribes were often fighting among themselves—shamans would spiritually attack the enemy, or their shamans, causing illness or soul loss.[39]

Eliade concurs that among the Yakut of Siberia white shamans had relations with the celestial gods, while black shamans were associated with evil spirits of the underworld.[40] He insists these categories of spirits are not necessarily seen as in opposition to each other, writing: "the Altains appear to know three groups of shamans—those who concern themselves with the celestial gods and powers, those who specialize in the (ecstatic) cult of the gods of the underworld, and finally, those who have mystical relations with both classes of gods." Benevolent as the heavenly spirits are, they are seen to be more passive and of less help in the human drama than the spirits of "below" who are vindictive, closer to the earth, and more interested in the affairs of men.

Black shamans tended to be poorer and lower in social status than white shamans, according to Kharitonova.[41] She notes that since women in the past were considered impure, they were not allowed to become white shamans who appealed to the heavenly gods, and by default became black shamans. Kharitonova notes this restriction no longer exists in present day society. According to her, Siberian Buryat white shamans originally may have belonged to aristocratic clans and the ruling elite, or may have been priests of ancient tribal cults. As an example she cites the court shamans employed in the court of Genghis Khan, who wore white robes and rode white horses.

In Near-Eastern and European cultures so-called "black" and "white" magic and magicians are also found. Like Siberian shamans, western magicians sometimes specialize in working with either celestial or chthonic spirits. During antiquity this duality expressed itself in the contrasting figures of the popular *goes* and the aristocratic *theurgist* which we will look at later.

Tools of the Shaman

The shaman's performance involves certain paraphernalia and magical tools considered essential to their craft. Each piece of the shaman's equipment is believed to be alive, having its own "master spirit" which enters into it at its moment of creation.

The drum is widely used by Eurasian shamans who call it the shaman's "horse", as they ride its driving beat while journeying in vision to the otherworlds. Scientific studies have proven that monotonous drum beats at certain frequencies induce altered states of consciousness in listeners, similar to shamanic trance. Drums were also used to invoke the gods and helping spirits by Sami shamans. In many shamanic traditions they are believed to be a dwelling place for the shaman's helping spirits and a place to hold spirits captured during travels in the otherworlds. The frame of the shaman's drum was believed to be cut from a branch of the World Tree, thus enabling the shaman to climb it to the realm of the sky, according to Eliade.[42] The drum is usually oval in shape with the skin of a reindeer, elk, or horse stretched over it. Siberian shamans would often hunt a specially consecrated deer and use its skin for the drum, believing the deer's spirit inhabited the drum and became the helping spirit of its owner. The parts of the drum such as its edges, handle and frame were named its "ears", "lungs" and "artery", and believed to be parts of a living body according to Veikko Anttonen.[43] The surface is often decorated with cosmological diagrams including imagery of the sun, moon, and stars. Lapp shamans paint their drums on both sides of the skin with cosmic symbols such as the World Tree, sun and moon, the rainbow, etc., representing the shaman's journeys and adventures. Eliade writes that the iconography of the drum depicts a microcosm with the three zones—sky, earth and underworld—through which the shaman ecstatically journeys.[44] Tungus shaman's drums are painted with representations of birds, snakes and other animals.

The shaman's mirror, known as the *toli* in Inner Asia, was used to help the shaman "see the world". It served a number of purposes, such as concentration, trance induction, and divination. Shamans gazed into their mirrors for divining the source of illness in a patient's body, for seeing a dead person's soul, as well as for clairvoyant "far seeing". The mirrors were circular pieces of metal often made of bronze and were sometimes hundreds of years old, handed down through many generations of shamans. The concave side was worn against the shaman's body and was believed to be the home for their familiar spirits. The convex side facing outwards was believed to protect by reflecting or repelling evil spirits. Often several toli mirrors were attached to the shaman's costumes, and the number of them indicated her or his level of spiritual power.[45] Magic mirrors were also widely used in the ancient Near-East and Europe and are used to this day for divination by modern western magicians.

Siberian and Mongolian shamans often carry one or two staffs carved of wood or made from iron. These are used during their journeys in the spirit world to cross icy or rocky paths or stave off demons.[46] The head of the staff is usually carved into a horse's head or occasionally a dragon or human head. These symbolically represent the flying horse or other helping-spirits the shaman rides during his visionary travels. The staffs measure from 15 inches to over a yard and a half in length and resemble the horse-headed prayer sticks made by North American plains tribes according to Sarangerel.[47] They are also adorned with bells or metal rings that jingle when the shaman dances, and can be used as a type of rattle. As mentioned previously, "white shamans" in Mongolia do not use drums, but only staffs. Among the Tungus, the staff is used for dealing with the spirits of the upperworld.[48] In some Siberian tribes the novice shaman will use the staffs before graduating to a drum. The staff is used in initiation rites, and is also ridden like a horse during journeys to the other worlds. In Mongolian myths, shaman's staffs possess magical powers like calming stormy waters, subduing evil spirits and bringing sleep to people—similar to the magic wands of European folklore.

Other commonly used tools of Central Asian shamans are swords and knives which are used to frighten away evil spirits. In Inner Mongolia a sword may be used rather than a staff or drum as an aid to visionary journeying and merging with helping-spirits.[49] Interestingly, swords are also used for protecting the magician and subduing evil spirits in European "grimoire" magic, which we will later discuss. The belief that iron repels spirits seems to be universal, occurring in Celtic folklore as well as many other ancient traditions where fairies and similar spirits are thought to be repelled by iron.

Magical fetishes called *ongons* are made by Siberian and Central Asian shamans and used as dwelling places or "houses" for their spirit helpers including ancestors, spirits of deceased shamans, animals or nature spirits. The term ongon also refers to the helping-spirits themselves. They serve as protectors of households or flocks, and bring good luck in hunting and travel, protection from floods, etc.[50] Ongons are made from a wide range of materials including bone, wood, leather, feathers, cloth, paper and metal. They can be abstract, pictorial, or figurative, taking the form of dolls, fetish figures or paintings. While ordinary people can make an ongon, it is enlivened only after a shaman summons a spirit to dwell in it. They are honored by being placed in sacred places of the ger, the Mongolian yurt, where they are fed daily offerings of milk, liquor, blood or fat.

The Buryats of Siberia place ongons carved from posts on hilltops to watch over the land and animals. If they fail in their duties of bringing prosperity or protection a household may "punish" them by withholding offerings; likewise, they may have decorations added to them to express thanks for their help. Ongons of some shamanic helping spirits are passed down through generations, and the residing spirits are believed to become hostile if neglected. Sarangerel writes that ongons are placed out in nature or ritually burned when no longer needed so its indwelling spirit can return to the natural world.[51]

The shaman may create ongons which are given to the patient to protect them and aid the healing process, and temporary ongons are made to hold the spirit of the disease which is later discarded. Some tribes have traditions of "living ongons" such as "prayer trees" with special qualities which link them to the spirit world. Similar to these are special animals such as reindeer or horses marked by a ribbon passed through the ear or tied to the mane, which may not be killed.[52]

The shaman's costume allows them to transform their identity from the mundane to the sacred—by putting it on they enter into contact with the spirit world. It is a storehouse of spiritual power which provides protection to the body while the soul journeys to the spirit world. Costumes are made of the skin, feathers, claws and bones of respective animal guardians, and by wearing them shamans are able to transform into those animals and assume their powers. Mongolian and Siberian shamans attach feathers on the back of their robes below the shoulders to represent the power of magical flight, and in some dances they extend their arms to imitate the flight of eagles. Ribbons are sewn on frocks to represent snakes, and shaped into snake's heads with open jaws.[53] Some of the symbols attached to the costumes include bones and skeletons to represent the shaman's initiation and rebirth as one of the "living dead", as well as cosmological symbols such as disks symbolizing the sun and lunar crescent.[54] A number of metallic objects are attached to them such as figurines of helping spirits, as well as chains and bells; these serve to frighten away evil spirits, resulting in costumes weighing as much as forty pounds or

The Tree of Visions

more! Shamans also wear headdresses of deer antlers forged from metal, as well as bonnets made from the feathers of owls, eagles, cranes, etc.

The Sacred Circle & Four Directions in Shamanism

In Mongolian shamanism the cosmos is symbolized as a circle which encompasses space and the cycles of time, the sun, moon and stars. The traditional dwellings of Mongolians and other steppe nomads—the *ger*, or *yurt*—as it is called in Russian, is based on this circular symbolism. Its floor plan is arranged according to the symbolism of the four directions. The entrance of the *ger* is always in the south, while the north is the place of honor where altars are kept and elders and shamans sit. The western side is where men sit and store their tools. The eastern side is for women and storage of cooking utensils and women's objects.[55]

The center of the *ger*, the fireplace, represents the center of the cosmos, and the vertical column of smoke rising from it symbolizes the World Tree which shamans ascend in vision to the upperworld. In some instances an actual tree is set up inside the dwelling which shamans climb during their initiations. Movement in the *ger* is always "clockwise", following the movement of the sun.

Sarangerel notes that the circular pattern and alignment to the four directions in maintained in outdoor ceremonies by shamans, in walking and dancing around sacred *oobo* cairns, or in the *yohor* dance around a *turge* tree; by doing this shamans raise a spiral of energy to carry them to the heavens in visionary flights. Sunwise movement is used in blessing and in all types of shamanic dances.[56]

The four directions in Mongolian shamanism are likewise associated with colors and elements: the south with red and fire, the west with white and earth, north with black and water, and the east with blue and air, according to Sarangerel. She notes similarities between the *ger* and the Native American "medicine wheel", as both are physical representations of the cosmos and four directions.[57] We will later explore the parallels between the sacred circle of these shamanic cultures and the *magic circle* used in European magic.

Divination

Shamans practice divination by which they contact the spirit world for answers about the future. Siberian Tungus shamans throw a drumstick into the air and its position upon falling to the ground is interpreted to answer questions. Mirror gazing is another common divination technique, and Mongolian shamans gaze into reflective surfaces of bowls of water or other clear liquids.[58] Pyromancy or fire gazing is also used for divination, and images are seen in flames or embers; the crackling noises of a fire are also interpreted as signs of unseen spirits in the vicinity. One of the most widely practiced divination techniques, scapulimancy, uses the shoulder blade of a sheep or deer which is briefly placed in a fire and removed, its burns and cracks examined and interpreted.

Yukagir shamans in the past divined with the skulls of ancestral shamans, based on the belief that the spirits of the dead know the future and reveal hidden things.[132] The flight of birds, especially raptors such as hawks, eagles, ravens and vultures are studied. Predatory birds are considered a good omen while carrion-eaters are believed to be unfortunate. Meteorological phenomena are also interpreted as omens in Mongolia: lightning striking a house, tree, or livestock is seen as the anger of the sky god towards the owner; if clouds open and a ray of sunlight falls upon a particular object it has a fortuitous meaning.[59]

Dreams are also considered important omens of the future. Shamans interpret dreams for others, as well as engaging in lucid dreaming themselves to obtain information from the spirits. In some cases, the initiation vision of a shaman will take place in a dream rather than during waking trance.

Shamanic Initiation

Shamans in many traditional societies undergo an initiation ceremony at the beginning of their training which prepares them for their future practice. This often involves a sequence of suffering, ritualized death and resurrection in which the candidate's former life and identity are abandoned and transformed — leading to their rebirth as a shaman. The traditional shamanic initiation was usually a prolonged ordeal of isolation, asceticism, and sensory deprivation during which the apprentice withdrew from fellow human beings and sought the loneliness of the mountains, tundra, or forest. Fasting, sleep deprivation and sometimes the use of entheogens resulted in hallucinations and altered states of consciousness revealing the spiritual dimensions of reality. The Innuit shaman Igjugarjuk was placed in a remote hut where he fasted for thirty days. He declared after the ordeal was over that he "sometimes died a little". He endeavored to keep his mind only on the Great Spirit, and free from all memory of human beings and everyday things. Towards the end of his initiation his helping-spirit in the shape of a woman came to him.[60]

Eliade writes that during their initiations, shamans had ecstatic experiences involving one or more of the following themes: "dismemberment of the body, followed by a renewal of the internal organs and viscera; ascent to the sky and dialogue with the gods or spirits; descent to the underworld and conversations with spirits and the souls of dead shamans; various revelations, both religious and shamanic." [61]

In Siberian Yakut shamanism, the initiate undergoes an experience of "dying" and lies in a yurt without eating or drinking for three days, undergoing frightening visions of death and dismemberment. Eliade continues: "The candidate's limbs are removed and disjointed with an iron hook; the bones are cleaned, the fresh scraped, the body fluids thrown away, and the eyes torn from their sockets".[62] In some accounts the soul of the shaman is carried by a mythical bird to the underworld, where it ripens on the branch of a tree, before being brought back to earth where the candidates body is torn to bits and fed to the evil spirits of death and disease. Through this process the shaman gains healing powers. The gruesome visions of death and dismemberment could be understood as part of the dissolution of the former ego-identity, necessary before gaining a new spiritual identity. Holger Kalweit writes:

> "Exposed to wild animals and the stormy elements, deprived of sleep and food, his thoughts constantly directed towards the spirits and the sacred, the shamanic apprentice-once his ego identity has collapsed-experiences himself to be one with the world, the universe, nature, animals and plants. The experience of the transpersonal self is the reward." [63]

Newly initiated shamans often envision themselves as reborn into a spiritual body composed of imperishable materials such as crystals or light. They are given new eyes with which they can see the spirits, and ears that allow them to hear the conversations of plants. They gain magical powers such as healing and clairvoyance by which they are able to shamanize.

Death & Rebirth of Shamans & Gods

The initiation experiences of shamans have remarkable parallels to the mythic ordeals of heroes, gods, and goddesses of ancient Europe and the Near-East who descended to the underworld land of the dead. This descent was called *katabasis* by the Greeks, meaning "to go down". In the Sumerian myth *The Descent of Inanna*, the goddess Inanna decides to journey to the underworld. There she is stripped of her garments, killed and hung on a hook, then magically resurrected.

In some myths the god's suffering is a voluntary sacrifice—similar to the shaman's. In a Nordic myth, the god Odin willingly subjects himself to torture. He pierces himself with a spear and undergoes fasting, hanging upside down on the Yggdrasil Tree for nine days and nights to learn the magical secrets of the runes. The Titan Prometheus in Greek mythology is chained to a rock in the underworld where an eagle gnaws on his liver as punishment for stealing fire from the gods and giving it to mankind.

The myths of death, dismemberment, and rebirth of gods and shamans likely originated from rituals of sacrifice in Stone Age hunter-gatherer societies, according to E.J. Michael Witzel. He argues that the myths of shamans are based on the life cycle of their prey, the animals which are killed and then believed to be reborn. Witzel writes: "The process is seen as paralleling that of the fate of humans—as well as that of the reconstituted and reborn shaman—and the world at large".[64] In later agricultural societies, however, it was *plants* and their deities which were sacrificed, dismembered, and consumed, according to Witzel. Vegetation gods such as Osiris, Tammuz, and Dionysus were *dying gods* associated with the yearly growth and decay of the crops.

The earliest evidence of shamanic initiations can be found in the cave paintings of Late Paleolithic Europe in the deepest recesses of the caves of Cougnac and Pech Merle in France, according to archaeologist David Lewis-Williams. Here human figures which he calls "wounded men" are depicted with bodies bent forward, impaled with many darts or spears. Lewis-Williams hypothesizes the artists who painted these figures experienced hallucinations involving painful piercing sensations of their bodies, perceived as multiple stabbings with sharp spears.[65] He writes:

> "The "wounded men" may, I argue, represent a form of shamanic suffering, "death" and initiation that was closely associated with somatic hallucinations...That experience comprised isolation from other people, sensory deprivation by entrance into the underground realm, possible ingestion of psychotropic substances, "death" by a painful ordeal of multiple piercing, and emergence from those dark regions into the light".[66]

This mythic pattern of descent into darkness, suffering, and death, followed by rebirth and ascent to the light was also ritually enacted in the initiation rites of the mystery religions of antiquity, which we will later explore.

Chapter 2 Notes

Siberian shaman in costume.

1. Schlesier. *The Wolves of Heaven*.1987: 21.
2. Krupp. *Beyond the Blue Horizon: Myths and Legends of the Sun, Moon, Stars, and Planets*.1991: 287.
3. Freidel, David, Schele, Linda & Parker, Joy. *Maya Cosmos*. 2005:183.
4. Witzel, E.J. Michael. *The Origins of the World's Mythologies*. 2012:134.
5. Jones & Pennick. *A History of Pagan Europe*.1995: 6.
6. Witzel. *The Origins of the World's Mythologies*.2012: 387.
7. Waters, Frank. *The Book of the Hopi*.1977: 229.
8. Ashe. *Dawn Behind The Dawn: A Search for the Earthly Paradise*. 1992:16.
9. Gimbutas. *The Language of the Goddess: Unearthing the Hidden Symbols of Western Civilization*. 2001: 286-288.
10. Burkert, Walter. *Greek Religion*.1985.
11. Campbell, Joseph. *The Masks of God vol. 2: Oriental Mythology*. 1991: 81.
12. Ibid. :21.

13. Walsh, Roger N., M.D., Ph.D. *The Spirit of Shamanism.* 1990.
14. Jung, C.G. *Memories, Dreams, Reflections.*1963:183.
15. Winkelman, Dr. Michael. *Shamanism A Biopsychosocial Pardigm of Consciousness and Healing—Second Edition.* 2010:12.
16. Wilby, Emma. *Cunning Folk and Familiar Spirits: Shamanistic Traditions in Early Modern British Witchcraft and Magic.* 2006 :128.
17. Stutley, Margaret. *Shamanism: An Introduction.* 2003:67.
18. Soul theft, in which a "black shaman" stole the soul of a child to help a patient recover from an illness was once common among the Khakass people of Siberia, according to Valentina Kharitonova (Walter & Fridman 2004: 578).
19. Eliade. *Shamanism- Archaic Techniques of Ecstasy.*1964: 220.
20. Ibid. 216-217.
21. Sarangerel. *Riding Windhorses: A Journey into the Heart of Mongolian Shamanism.* 2000: 59.
22. Eliade. *Shamanism- Archaic Techniques of Ecstasy.*11964: 88.
23. Winkelman. *Shamanism A Biopsychosocial Pardigm of Consciousness and Healing.* 2010: 80.
24. Kalweit. *Dreamtime & Inner Space: the world of the shaman.* 1988: 21.
25. Schleiser. *The Wolves of Heaven.* 1987: 40.
26. Gimbutas, Marija. *The Living Goddess.*1999:162.
27. Schmidt, Klaus. *Gobekli Tepi, A Stone Age Sanctuary in South-Eastern Anatolia.* 2007:202.
28. Naydler, Jeremy.*Temple of the Cosmos- The Ancient Egyptian Experience of the Sacred.*1996:154.
29. Eliade. *Shamanism- Archaic Techniques of Ecstasy.* 1964:106.
30. Ibid,:102.
31. West. *Indo-European Poetry and Myth.* 2007: 280.
32. Willis, Roy G. *World Mythology.*1993: 31.
33. See page 227 of *Tree of Visions* for Paracelsus's notion of marriages between elemental spirts and humans.
34. Eliade. *Shamanism- Archaic Techniques of Ecstasy.* 1978: 437.
35. Ibid.: 71-73.
36. Circle of Tengerism. "The Different Types of Shamans". www.tengerism.org.
37. Kingsley, Peter. *A Story Waiting to Pierce You: Mongolia, Tibet and the destiny of the Western world.* 2010:101.
38. Karitonova, V. Walter, Fridman, (ed.) *Shamanism: An Encyclopedia of World Beliefs, Practices and Culture,* Vol.1. 2004: 536.
39. Sarangerel. Riding Windhorses: A Journey into the Heart of Mongolian Shamanism.2000:108.
40. Eliade. *Shamanism- Archaic Techniques of Ecstasy.*1964:184-189.
41. Kharitonova, V. Walter & Fridman (ed.) *Shamanism: An Encyclopedia of World Beliefs,* 2004:537.
42. Eliade. *Shamanism- Archaic Techniques of Ecstasy.*1964:168.
43. Anttonen, Veikko. Walter, Fridman, (ed.). *Shamanism: An Encyclopedia of World Beliefs,* 2004: 5010.
44. Eliade. *Shamanism- Archaic Techniques of Ecstasy.* 1964:173.

45. Edson, Gary. *Shamanism: A Cross-cultural Study of Beliefs and Practices.* 2009:135.
46. Walter & Fridman. *Shamanism: An Encyclopedia of World Beliefs, Practices and Culture,* 2004: 549. in essay by Esther Jacobon-Tepfer.
47. Sarangerel. *Riding Windhorses: A Journey into the Heart of Mongolian Shamanism.* 2000: 89.
48. Stutley. *Shamanism: An Introduction.* 2003:47.
49. Sarangerel *Riding Windhorses: A Journey into the Heart of Mongolian Shamanism* 2000: 168.
50. Ibid., 2001:168.
51. Sarangarel *Riding Windhorses: A Journey into the Heart of Mongolian Shamanism* 2000: 61.
52. Ibid., 2000: 62.
53. Eliade. *Shamanism- Archaic Techniques of Ecstasy.*1964:149.
54. Ibid.:148.
55. Sarangerel. *Riding Windhorses: A Journey into the Heart of Mongolian Shamanism.* 2000:10.
56. Ibid., 2000:11.
57. Sarangerel. *Riding Windhorses: A Journey into the Heart of Mongolian Shamanism.* 2000:120.
58. Eliade. *Shamanism- Archaic Techniques of Ecstasy.*1964: 382.
59. Sarangerel. *Chosen by the Spirits: following your shamanic calling.* 2001:120.
60. Rasmussen. *Across Arctic America: Narrative of the Fifth Thule Expedition.* 1999.
61. Eliade. *Shamanism- Archaic Techniques of Ecstasy.*1964: 34.
62. Ibid., 1972: 36.
63. Kalweit. *Dreamtime & Inner Space: the world of the shaman.* 1988: 75-110.
64. Witzel. *The Origins of the World's Mythologies.* 2012: 393-4.
65. Lewis-Williams derives his theory from comparisons of the images of Paleolithic "wounded men" with modern rock paintingsby South African San shamans which also depict men with bodies pierced by multiple lines, concluding they refer to similar experiences.
66. Lewis-Williams, David. *The Mind in the Cave.* 2002: 278-283.

Chapter 3:
Shamans of The Paleolithic & Neolithic

Bison Man engraving—Les Trois Freres cave, France 13,000 BCE.

Cave Art & Shamanic Trance

To gain a deeper understanding of shamanism we must look back to its beginnings during the Paleolithic period (early Stone Age) between 65,000-10,000 BCE. During this period *Homo sapiens sapiens*—modern humans—lived in small bands, surviving as nomadic hunter-gatherers. They originally left their land of origin in Africa, via the Near East, following the coast lines of Asia. By 35,000-40,000 BCE humans had spread across the Old World from Australia and Eurasia all the way to Europe.[1]

These people arrived in Europe around 45,000 BCE, surviving by hunting migratory herds of bison, reindeer, mammoths and horses. During the Upper Paleolithic, new and sophisticated stone tools and weapons were developed along with embryonic forms of mathematics and writing.[2] These and other technological and cultural advancements led to a population explosion, possibly linked to the extinction of the Neanderthals, *Homo sapien's* closest relatives. Paleolithic humans were such effective hunters they may have also contributed to the extinction of wooly mammoths, mastodons, and other large mammals as well.

While men engaged in hunting, women likely foraged foods and communally cared for the young. Relationships between the sexes were probably more equal during this period than any time since, since women contributed to the food supply as much, or more so, than men, according to historian L.S. Stavrianos.[3] Archaeologists speculate Paleolithic clans may have been *matrilineal*, like many modern hunter gatherer societies. In those groups ancestral descent is traced through the mother and power is shared equally between the sexes.

Anthropologist Marshall Sahlins calls prehistoric hunter-gatherers "the original affluent society", due to their mode of subsistence which was less time consuming than that of the farmers peoples who came later.[4] Similar to modern hunter-gatherers, Paleolithic people likely enjoyed an abundance of leisure time—unequalled in agricultural or modern industrial societies. This would have allowed them time to develop shamanism, storytelling, art, music, and communal rituals. In fact shamanism likely contributed to the "cultural explosion" that generated early forms of culture and religion. According to Witzel, the first myths were told by shamans and concerned the life cycle of their prey, the hunt, and death and rebirth of animals. Their story-lines based on common human experiences laid the foundations for the mythologies and religions of all later societies, and still have deep resonance and meaning today.[5]

Some of the world's oldest artworks in the form of figurines carved from mammoth ivory were probably used for shamanistic and religious purposes. The so-called "Lion-Man" figurine found in a cave in the Swabian Alps in Germany dates to the Aurignacian period around 40,000 BCE. Skillfully carved from mammoth ivory it depicts a lion-headed human figure—possibly a shaman—transforming into a lion. Around this same period the "Venus of

Schelkingen" was also produced, a small ivory carving of a corpulent female figure. She is the earliest of many such Venus figures that would be produced by Paleolithic peoples all across Eurasia. Archaeologists speculate these figurines which seem to depict pregnant women were fertility figures or perhaps goddess images. Some form of shamanism and the worship of the generative power of a universal mother represent the earliest forms of mankind's religious life, according to Witzel.[6]

During the Cro-Magnon period around 30,000 BCE, wall paintings of aurochs, bison, mammoths and other large game animals began to be produced in the caves of western Europe. The cave artists displayed uncanny powers of observation, accurately depicting the anatomy and motion of their animal subjects. Paintings of "therianthropes" — composite human-animal figures — have also been found, such as the bison headed man in the cave of Gabillon, or the horned Sorcerer of Les Trois Frere. Similar to the Lion-Man figurine, these images appear to depict shamans in the act of transforming or shape-shifting into their animal spirit-helpers.

In the cave of Lascaux in France a wall painting depicts a bird-headed man lying prone with an erect penis, and next to him planted a staff with a bird perched on top of it. Above the figure looms the figure of a huge bison impaled through its body with a spear. Andrew Collins proposes this image is based on cosmological symbolism. He claims the staff represents the vertical axis or sky pole around which the heavens turn, and the bird perched on it symbolizes the constellation Cygnus the swan, which was located close to the celestial pole at the time of its painting around 16,500-15,000 BCE. He conjectures that the prone figure represents a shaman in trance, ascending the sky pole in the form of his avian familiar-spirit to enter the heavens.[7] Collins proposes a bird cult was practiced by the Paleolithic Solutrean peoples of Ice Age Europe, writing: "Maybe it was believed that a mask-wearing shaman could project his or her soul into a soaring bird to observe the herd animals below, providing vital information in advance of the chase".[8]

Authorities on cave art such as Jean Clottes and David Lewis-Williams also propose that cave paintings, sculptures, and other artifacts are records of shamanic trance journeys to the spirit-world. They argue that the widespread occurrence of shamanism results from "...the inescapable need to make sense within a hunting-gathering community of the universal propensity for the human nervous system to enter altered states."[9] These authors hypothesize that many of the abstract designs painted on cave walls—zig-zags, hatched lines, and starbursts were painted by shamans during their rituals and likely represent "phosphenes" or entopic images, the psychedelic patterns that appear before the eyes while entering trance states.

Clottes and Lewis-Williams propose the neuropsychological stages experienced during trance led Late Paleolithic people to believe in the underworld as part of a multi-leveled cosmos.[10] They saw caves as literal entrances to the underworld. A long journey to the caverns may have been part of a ritual sequence according to these authors. This involved entering larger communal chambers where paintings of animals covered the walls, preparing the "vision quester" for solitary experiences in deeper and more constricted recesses of the caves. The dark journey into the innermost depths of the caves, illuminated with fat burning lamps, would have involved considerable risk and was likely undertaken only by a select few for important ritual purposes. The experience itself would have been trance inducing; modern cave spelunkers have reported auditory and visual hallucinations while caving due to the prolonged conditions of darkness and silence.

According to Clottes and Lewis-Williams the walls, ceilings, and floors of the caves were seen as permeable membranes between the shaman and the spirit creatures of the underworld. Often the shapes of the rocks suggested the forms of animals. Through isolation, sensory deprivation, ritual activities, and possibly the use of entheogens, shamans experienced hallucinations of spirit creatures. According to these authors, shamans recreated their visions as *art*—"fixing" them as paintings and carvings on the rock faces to record their experiences, thereby gaining control over them. Some of the animals depicted were likely similar to the "spirit-allies" of modern shamans. The artists may have also been engaged in hunting magic, believing that by depicting animals they were magically influencing them to bring a successful hunt. Shamanic practitioner Harold Alden writes that in the caves shamans would have encountered the spirits of the painted animals, and made offerings and requests to them to ensure their return to another cycle of life.[11] Since some of the paintings are of creatures that were not commonly hunted such as rhinoceroses and large felines, they may have also had symbolic and religious significance.

As well as paintings, carved stone friezes have been found such as the collapsed rock shelter of Roc-de-Sers in southwest France which perhaps served as a religious sanctuary. Here, a number of large limestone blocks originally placed in a semi-circle are carved with images of deer, ibexes, bisons, boars, as well as bird-headed human figures. In the opinion of Andrew Collins the site may have been used for ceremonial and ritual activities by the people of the Upper Paleolithic Solutrean culture around 17,000 BCE.[12]

Musical instruments such as bone flutes have also been found in the caves, as well as conch shells, whistles, rattles and rasps.[13] Nearby heel prints in the cave floors suggest ritual music and dance were used to induce trance states in religious ceremonies. Lewis-Williams notes that research into the acoustic properties of different chambers and passages in the caves suggests that resonant areas are more likely to have images painted on the walls than non-resonant ones.[14] He also points out that certain types of stalactites in the caves emit deep booming sounds when struck, and may have been used for percussive effects. Curiously, some rock formations in caves were intentionally broken off at different heights as if to vary the sound, and are worn along the edges, suggesting they may have been used as huge percussion instruments.[15]

Did the Shaman's Trance—Make Us Human? Scientific Views

Shamanism played a central role in the evolution of human consciousness during the Upper Paleolithic "explosion" of human cognitive advances around 40,000 years ago, according to anthropologist Dr. Michael Winkelman.[16] These advances manifested as cave paintings, carved figurines, jewelry, flint and bone tools and other refinements in material culture. He argues this revolution was *not* based on anatomical evolution or increases in brain size. Instead it consisted of cultural breakthroughs, and these in turn seem to have been the result of shamanic practices.

Winkelman writes: "the shaman's visionary journey involved a special and intense kind of imaging; that imaging manifested in cave art production was central to cognitive advances associated with the Middle/Upper Paleolithic transition". He proposes that shamanic practices enhanced cognitive abilities such as *analogical* and *symbolic thinking* leading to integration of the brain hemispheres, frontal-limbic integration, brain-stem-limbic-frontal integration, and integration across the neuraxis. With their enhanced cognitive abilities shamans assumed leadership of the group, directing communal religious rituals and planning the hunt. These activities in turn led to advances of tribal culture in general—increased social bonding, development of personal and social identities, and technical ability. Winkelman's theory suggests the prehistoric shaman was a leader, culture-hero, innovator, and explorer of consciousness who introduced dramatic advancements to early societies.

Psychologist Matt J. Rossano argues based on clinical research into meditation that the deep focus achieved during archaic shamanic healing rituals strengthened parts of the brain involved in memory. This in turn led to sharpened mental focus and the ability of the mind to connect symbols and meanings.[17] He writes: "Consciousness altering rituals, often taking the form of shamanistic healing rituals...targeted those areas of the brain involved in focused attention and working memory, and, in time, facilitated the genetic mutation or mutations that ultimately enhanced working memory and symbolic formation in the human population." [18]

Archaeologist and shamanic practitioner Mike Williams proposes that the prehistoric shaman's trance states may have created the conditions for a gradual genetic shift from primary to higher order traits of consciousness, asserting: "it was trance that made us human". He conjectures trance experiences of ancient shamans enhanced problem-solving, working memory, and recall of dreams, leading to the notion of the "otherworld".[19]

Paleo-Writing

Researchers have long been intrigued by mysterious geometric markings found along with the paintings of animals on cave walls. Some of these marks may be "entopic images", depicting the hypnogogic imagery experienced during shamanic trance states. But this doesn't explain their sheer quantity, repetition and wide-spread occurrence as they are found in prehistoric sites across Europe and around the world. Researchers such as Andre Leroi-Gourhan and Marija Gimbutas have conjectured that these markings are *signs*, and may have carried symbolic messages.[20]

Recently, anthropologist Genevieve von Petzinger has compiled a computer database of thousands of signs from 146 French rock art sites, and was able to identify twenty-six distinct shapes that commonly occurred. She found the signs were repeated and continuously used—for over 20,000 years in some instances—and they were widely distributed. Von Petzinger concludes : "I do think that the geometrics probably represent abstract ideas or concepts that were important to those who created them".[21] She doesn't believe this was a full-blown system of writing such as a phonetic alphabet as we know it, but a "first step" towards writing, similar to ideograms and pictographic language.

Historian Richard Flavin insists prehistoric writing was a "sacred art" connected with divination and oracles, comparing them to the Celtic Ogham alphabet which was used for such purposes. He proposes that early writing may have developed from calendrical, constellation and zodiacal symbols.[22] From this we may conjecture that the mysterious Paleolithic signs, often juxtaposed on or near paintings of animals on cave walls, may have had magical as well as astronomical significance.

Ice Age Astronomers of Lascaux Cave

Supporting the theories of Late Paleolithic cognitive and cultural advances, archaeoastronomers conclude that the people of the Cro-Magnon Age of Europe (30,00-10,00 BCE) had a surprisingly sophisticated understanding of astronomy and timekeeping. French paleo-astronomer Chantal Jegues-Wolkiewiez insists there was a long cultural tradition of skywatching in the Ice Age.[23] She proposes that the famous cave paintings of Lascaux recorded the constellations of a prehistoric version of the zodiac which included solstice points and major stars. Jegues-Wolkiewiez bases her theory on the discovery of numerous circular marks and tracings superimposed on the paintings of animals. She claims these correspond to the patterns of stellar constellations, most notably the constellation of Taurus and the stars Aldeberan, the Pleiades and Antares. She has shown that most of the constellations in the sky are represented by animals in the murals, accurately depicting their coloring and coats during the corresponding seasons of the year.

Jegues-Wolkiewiez visited 130 cave sites over a period of seven years, identifying solar alignments throughout the seasons. Using computer modeling she found that 122 of the sites had optimal orientations to the solsticial horizons. She concludes that Paleolithic cave painting sites in South-west France were mainly selected because their interiors were illuminated by the setting sun on the day of the winter solstice. She also determined that the sun's setting rays illuminated the painting of the Red Bull on the back wall of the Hall of Bulls in Lascaux 17,000 years ago, during the summer solstice.

German scientist Dr. Michael Rappenglueck believes the paintings of the Lascaux caves not only represent constellations, but also depict the cosmology of Paleolithic shamans. He points to what he claims is a "sky map" in the area of the caves known as the Shaft of the Dead Man. Here is found the enigmatic painting of the prone man, bull, and bird on a staff, which we previously discussed. According to Rappenglueck, these figures form a map of the heavens with the eyes of the bull, birdman, and bird representing the three prominent stars Vega, Deneb and Altair. These stars form the constellation of the "summer triangle" which can be seen overhead during the summer months in the northern hemisphere. Around 17,000 years ago this group of stars would have never set in the sky and would have been prominent during the early spring; significantly Deneb served as the Pole Star at the time. Rappenglueck notes: "It is a map of the prehistoric cosmos...It was their sky, full of animals and spirit guides." [24] Like Jegues-Wolkiewiez, Rappenglueck proposes that the dots painted inside the image of a bull at Lascaux confirms that the constellation Taurus was known during the earliest times. The Pleiades, or Seven Sisters constellation, is depicted over the bull's shoulder, leading him to propose that Taurus and the Pleiades were used as seasonal markers of the autumn and spring equinoxes.

In the cave of La Marche in western France, Rappenglueck found a series of pits carved in the floor arranged in the pattern of the constellation of the Pleiades.

He speculates these small holes could have been filled with animal fat and set ablaze to imitate the constellation in the sky.[25] The cave is believed to have been used by the Paleolithic Magdalenian peoples around 15,000 years ago.

The earliest known depiction of the Orion constellation was carved on a piece of mammoth tusk, according to Rappenglueck.[26] This 32,000 year old artifact of the paleolithic Aurignacian people represents a male figure with arms and legs outstretched in the same pose as the constellation. The tablet also has markings on its sides and back, which Rappenglueck proposes could have served as a "pregnancy calendar" designed to estimate when a pregnant woman would give birth. The tablet also has 86 markings on its sides and back. Rappenglueck notes these are the number of days which when subtracted from a year equal the average number of days of human gestation. That number also matches the days that one of Orion's brightest stars, Betelgeuse, is visible yearly, suggesting early skywatchers may have connected women's pregnancy with the cycles of the celestial gods.

Another scientist, Alexander Marshack, found what appears to be the worlds oldest calendars— small bone plates dated around 30,000-32,000 years old, engraved or painted with dots or lines. After extensive analysis Marshack concluded these correspond to lunar or solar motions. One tablet from Dordogne, France apparently represents the waxing and waning lunar positions in serpentine form.[27]

These discoveries suggest that Upper Paleolithic peoples were sophisticated observers of the sky who tracked the motions of the sun, moon, and stars by calendars and recorded their observations in cave paintings. Undoubtedly that knowledge would have enhanced their chances of survival, allowing them to predict seasonal animal migrations and weather. The paintings of Lascaux, embellished with the markings of the constellations, as well as the engraving of the Pleiades on the floor of the cave of La Marche, offer intriguing clues about religious beliefs and ritual practices as well. They suggest these cultures possessed their own celestial myths and performed ceremonies associated with the solstices and annual cycles of the stars. This raises the intriguing possibility that some of the star-lore of Paleolithic skywatchers may have been passed down to the astronomers of the early Near-Eastern civilizations. In Mesopotamia and Egypt the constellations Taurus, Pleiades, and Ursa Major also played significant roles in celestial myths.[28]

Paleolithic Mal'ta

The region of the Altai Mountains on the borders of Russia, China, and Mongolia has been the home of populations practicing shamanism for millennia.

Archaeologists have discovered the remains of an Upper Paleolithic culture at Mal'ta in the Siberian Altai area near Lake Baikal, dated to around 24,000 BCE. Significantly, Mal'ta shares many similarities with the Paleolithic cultures of Europe.

A number of figurines believed to be fertility symbols with stylized and exaggerated breasts and buttocks have also been found there, carved from mammoth ivory—curiously similar to the Paleolithic European "Venus" statuettes. Along with these are aesthetically refined carvings of stylized birds, as well as beads and necklaces made from tusks and antler. Joseph Campbell discusses the Mal'ta iconography which combines the themes of both shaman and goddess:

> "We are clearly in a paleolithic province where the serpent, labyrinth, and rebirth themes already constitute a symbolic constellation, joined with the imagery of the sunbird and shaman flight, with the goddess in her classic role of protectress of the hearth, mother of man's second birth, and lady of wild things and of the food supply." [29]

One of the most intriguing discoveries at Mal'ta is an oblong panel of mammoth ivory. On it a design of seven spirals is carved, consisting of a large central spiral with seven coils. On the reverse side are etched three meandering forms which appear to represent serpents. According to historian Geoffry Ashe, the spiral design represents the earliest known version of a *labyrinth* pattern, as well as the symbolic use of the *number seven*—occuring frequently in later Altaic shamanic lore, which he claims originated in the seven stars of Ursa Major.[30] Discussing the worldwide distribution of the labyrinth pattern, Ashe writes: "...the starting point could hardly have been anywhere but in northern Asia. There is nowhere else from which people or motifs could have spread both across the Eurasian landmass and to a North America that received its settlers from Siberia, when the continents still were connected." [31]

Genetic Links Between—Ancient Europeans & Native Americans

Ashe's theory is supported by recent genetic studies of ancient human remains unearthed at Mal'ta. A grave was found there by researchers, containing the body of a boy aged three to four years who died around 24,000 years ago. Scientists were amazed to discover his mitochondrial DNA belonged to the same lineage as that found among the populations who settled Europe around 44,000 years ago. Equally exciting was the discovery that it matches a large proportion of the DNA of modern Native Americans.[32] The testing of another skeleton, dating to 17,000 years ago, found the same genetic markers of European origin. These findings, as well as previous genetic testing suggest that the Paleolithic people who settled Europe spread much further east across Eurasia than previously thought—all the way to Siberia during the Last Global Maximum, when glaciers were at their thickest.[33] The scientists claim that the people who crossed the Bering Straight to settle North America over 15,000 years ago were genetically related to ancient Europeans. Dr. Eske Willerslev, who led the team of researchers, stated: "We estimate that 14 to 38 percent of Native American ancestry may originate through gene flow from this ancient population".[34]

The research suggests there is an ancient genetic heritage shared by Europeans, Siberians, and Native Americans. It supports the theory of prehistoric migrations and the diffusion of shamanic myths and practices across the northern hemisphere, from Northern Europe and Eurasia to North America. Astronomical myths of Ursa Major as the Great Bear were spread around the northern hemisphere, as well as other myths found from Lithuania to North America, including the Milky Way as the "Path of Birds" traversed by the dead in the afterlife, and myths of the "Girl in the Moon". [35]

The Oldest Grave of a Shaman

Dramatic evidence of shamanism from the "Mesolithic" Period—the Middle Stone Age—was discovered in Israel, where archaeologists excavated a grave of what appears to have been a female shaman, dating to 12,000 BCE. In a cave they found a mud-plastered rock lined pit covered by a large stone slab. Inside was the skeleton of a female aged about forty-five years, buried with leopard and boar bones, the wing of an eagle, and a human foot. She was surrounded by some fifty tortoise shells, arranged deliberately around her body. Her elaborate burial, along with the animal remains, strongly suggests she was a shamaness as well as a person of high social status. She belonged to the Natufian culture which existed between 15,000 and 11,500 years ago in the eastern Mediterranean region of the Levant. This culture was transitional between earlier nomadic hunter-gatherers and the more complex Neolithic farming cultures that would follow.[36]

Magic & Astro Ceremonialism of the Mesolithic

A recent archaeological discovery in North-Western Poland seems to provide evidence of shamanism during the Mesolithic period in Europe as well. During excavations in a peat bog near Lake Swidnie, the remains of a wooden structure dating back 9,000 years or more were uncovered. Inside this artifacts were found appearing to be ritual objects: a so-called "magic wand" made of an antler decorated with geometric motifs, an "amulet", and a meteorite fragment. Professor Tadeusz Galinski, head of the research project, speculates the meteor was "an object of belief, and maybe even shamanic magic". In addition to these artifacts, seven perfectly preserved yew stakes set in the pattern of the constellation Ursa Major were found driven into the floor of the structure.[37] This discovery, along with the previously discussed findings from the Paleolithic, adds weight to the theory that astro-ceremonialism involving the constellation Ursa Major continued to be practiced in Mesolithic Europe.

Gobekli Tepe—Temple of Animal Spirits

Archaeological discoveries at Gobekli Tepe in southeast Turkey reveal the world's oldest known stone ceremonial structure dating from around 9,600 BCE. In the Turkish language Gobekli Tepe means "belly hill", an oddly appropriate name for what is undoubtedly a birth place of civilization. German archaeologist Klaus Schmidt, who fortuitously discovered the site in 1994 and later excavated it, calls Gobekli Tepe "the first temple", as well as "a sanctuary of the Stone Age hunter". He proposes it was a place for religious gathering where shamanic rituals were performed.[38]

Gobekli Tepe is a complex of huge smoothly finished standing stones arranged in circles, of which only four have been excavated so far from an estimated twenty. Amazingly, the people who built these impressive monuments were Mesolithic hunter-gatherers and not members of a highly organized agricultural society. They were able to transport sixteen-ton stones, despite the fact they lacked beasts of burden or the wheel.

The bas-relief carvings on the stone pillars depict gazelles, snakes, scorpions, foxes and wild boars. All the animals in the carvings are male in gender and many are depicted in aggressive postures. Schmidt concludes Gobekli Tepe was a ritual center—a cult of the dead—and its carved animals were placed there to protect the dead.[39] He suggests the "T" shaped pillars may represent mythical creatures, deities or ancestral figures that illustrate the other world.[40]

Other researchers have speculated that the stone pillars of the complex were oriented in *astronomical alignments,* and the animal carvings were associated with specific stars and constellations. Andrew Collins presents astronomical evidence that the stones of Gobekli Tepe are aligned with the constellation of the Northern Cross, also known as Cygnus the Swan.[41] He notes that Cygnus is located on the "Great Rift" of the Milky Way, the dark area in the sky where the stream of the Milky Way divides in two. This was associated with the womb of the heavens as well as the entrance to the sky-world by some ancient peoples.[42]

The Tree of Visions

Both Collins and Schmidt point to a carving on one of the pillars depicting a vulture with wings seemingly articulated like human arms, as well as anthropomorphized feet, suggesting it may represent a shaman. Above the vulture's right wing is the carving of a circle, which in the opinion of Collins represents a human soul being carried by a shaman to its afterlife destination in the Milky Way and the constellation Cygnus. Supporting this theory he shows that the pattern of the constellation Cygnus when overlaid on the vulture-shaman carving matches it closely. Remarkably, the Sumerians of the 5th millennium BCE knew the constellation Cygnus as the "Anzu Bird" whose function was to lead discarnate souls to the afterlife, which supports this assumption.[43] Below the vulture is carved the image of a scorpion, which several experts have proposed represents the constellation Scorpius positioned below Cygnus in the sky. Evidence of vulture related shamanism has been found at other sites in the region dated to the same period as Gobekli Tepe; archaeologists discovered the wings of vultures and large predatory birds which appear to have been worn as part of ritualistic costumes, thought to have been used in a cult of the dead.[44]

Collins proposes other structures at Gobekli Tepe such as a stone pillar with a hole in it may have been used in celebrating birthing rituals. He notes that the constellation Cygnus is traditionally identified with the swan and stork throughout Eurasia, a bird associated with the bringing of souls from the sky-world into birth in this world. As well as a temple of death, Collins proposes Gobekli Tepe was "...a place where the rites of birth, death and rebirth were celebrated both in its architectural design and in the highly symbolic carved art left behind by its builders".[45]

It is likely that communal religious worship at Gobekli-Tepi led by shamanic ritual-specialists brought groups of widely dispersed nomadic peoples together, catalyzing cultural changes and technological breakthroughs. Schmidt proposes the need to sustain the community of builders at Gobekli Tepe led to the earliest cultivation of wild cereals, and in turn the discovery of agriculture. Through their innovations in stone masonry, carving, and cultivation of wild grains, the religious leaders of Gobekli Tepe likely laid the foundations for the Neolithic revolution to come, characterized by agriculture and monumental building. Schmidt speculates these people inspired Sumerian myths of the Annunaki gods who were believed to have first brought the gifts of civilization to mankind. Collins proposes they are the source of myths of the "Watchers" of the Hebrew Book of Enoch—the fallen angels who intermarried with the daughters of men—teaching them the forbidden arts and sciences of heaven.[46]

Archaeologist Ian Hodder writes: "Gobekli Tepe changes everything". Its revolutionary implication is that organized religion *preceded* civilization as we know it by centuries. In the words of Klaus Schmidt "first came the temple, then the city". Historians and archaeologists previously assumed the discovery of agriculture led to the rise of cities, followed by art and religion. Gobekli Tepe turns this widely accepted theory on its head. Instead it appears the urge of humans to gather together to worship led to civilization.[47]

The Neolithic Revolution

Around 13,000 BCE at the same time as the Ice Age in Europe was drawing to a close, small bands of hunter-gatherers began to settle in the lands of the Levant, the areas of modern day Israel, Palestine, Jordan, Lebanon and Syria. Here archaeologists have discovered remains of the earliest villages. Beginning around 10,000 BCE during the period known as the Neolithic (New Stone Age) nomadic groups began to settle in the lands of the Fertile Crescent in Mesopotamia, and the Nile Valley in Egypt. This occurred during the same period as the building of Gobekli Tepe.

Some experts theorize that the move from hunter-gatherer to agricultural societies may have been forced by climate change and rising populations. Archaeologist Jacques Cauvin offers a different hypothesis—a "symbolic revolution" took place first—bringing about changes in religion and symbolism *prior* to the invention of agriculture, similar to what we saw occurring at Gobekli Tepe. He writes "the great civilizing changes of the Neolithic were first anticipated and played out within religious and ritual contexts".[48] Cauvin insists the development of the human imagination and its expression in symbols, myths, and religion were decisive in awakening the peoples of the early Neolithic to a "new type of expansiveness", enabling them to live in a "self-regulating world".[49] Archaeologist Trevor Watkins contends that the Neolithic Revolution led to the rapid development of the first "comprehensive world-view" involving religious ideas, ideology, cosmology, and symbolic representations in the arts.[50] For the first time humans were able to conceive of controlling nature, rather than being at its mercy, resulting in innovations such as agriculture, domestication of animals and permanent settlements.

These cultural and technological advances resulted in organized societies with stratified social classes. Neolithic shamans were likely absorbed into a new class of religious specialists—priests and priestesses. These ritual-specialists provided the symbols and myths by which an ordered cosmos and spirit-world populated by gods and supernatural beings could be envisioned, whose assistance could be sought in sustaining the spiritual and material needs of the community.

Catalhoyuk and Ancestor Worship

During the period between 8,000 BCE- 5500 BCE, people of the Near-East began widespread planting of cereal crops and domestication of animals. The earliest settlements of Jericho in the Levant and Catalhoyuk in central Turkey were built during this time of transition between hunter-gatherer and agricultural societies.[51] These cultures were the first to master pottery, weaving, carpentry, polished stone tools, as well as religious architecture. As the result of agricultural practices, surpluses increased, resulting in increased populations and larger settlements. Along with these changes came social stratification and organized religion. Elders in these societies assumed the roles of family and community leadership, gaining high social status. Burial practices of the time suggest belief in the continuing spiritual presence and authority of elders after death, resulting in the religious practice of ancestor worship.

At the settlement of Catalhoyuk, ancestor worship is implied by the discovery of human remains buried in houses beneath floors, hearths and beds. In fact, underneath the floor of one building sixty-two bodies were found interred. Often the corpses were flexed into a fetal position, as if awaiting rebirth in the womb of the earth. In some cases skulls were removed from skeletons, plastered, and painted with ochre. At Jericho and other nearby Neolithic settlements, human skulls were plastered over and cowry shells placed in the eye sockets. It is likely souls were believed to inhabit skulls, which were used by shamans for communing with the spirits of the ancestors.[52] Discussing these burials, archaeologist Ian Hodder who excavated the site writes: "The ability of the shaman or ritual leader to go beyond death and return...would be especially important in a society in which the ancestors had so much social importance. By going down into a deep room in which the dead were buried, the ritual leaders could travel to the ancestors through the walls, niches and floors".[53]

Animals continue to exert a powerful mythic presence in the artwork of the Neolithic. Murals of hunting scenes with wild animals such as bulls and deer are prevalent at Catalhoyuk. The skulls of vultures and bulls are found plastered into the walls of rooms which appear to be shrines. Lewis-Williams proposes these can be understood in shamanic terms as the movement of animal spirits from the underworld through the walls and into the house.[54] The first excavator of Catalhoyuk, archaeologist James Mellart, found many remnants of stalactites and stalagmites, leading him to propose that the shrines may have been the home of underworld deities.[55]

Paintings of crane dancers, and remains of crane wings cranes have been found at Catalhoyuk. The wings may have been part of costumes used in "crane dances", according to Hodder.[56] Cranes with their dramatic mating dances were likely associated with fertility. Vultures also played a prominent role in the religious symbolism of Catalhoyuk. Murals found there show vultures with human legs, similar to the carving of the "vulture-shaman" at Gobekli Tepi. Other paintings at Catalhoyuk show vultures devouring human corpses placed on towers. This is an early example of the process of excarnation, or "sky-burial", in which corpses were placed on platforms and the flesh was stripped from the bones by vultures prior to burial. Vultures seem to have been associated not only with death, but also rebirth. They are depicted with human infants inside their bellies, suggesting they might have been seen as bringers of life as well, similar to storks in European folklore.

Sculptures of women found at Catalhoyuk may be connected to fertility magic, such as the statue of a corpulent and possibly pregnant woman enthroned between two leopards. The motif of pregnant woman is reminiscent of the Venus figurines of the Upper Paleolithic. Historian Walter Burkert argues that such images may also be the origin of later goddess iconography. He writes that the statue is "...overwhelmingly clear proof of religious continuity over more than five millennia...the association with the Asia Minor great mother with her leopards or lions is irresistible." [57]

Archaeologists insist that at Catalhoyuk all evidence points to equal social status of women and men. In Neolithic societies the role of women was enhanced both socially and symbolically according to Joseph Campbell, for they participated in, and even dominated the planting and harvesting of crops.[58]

The Woman & The Bull

Cauvin notes the first appearance of the symbolism of the primordial couple of woman and the bull during the early Neolithic era, which would later spread throughout the Mediterranean world. He proposes the woman was associated with fertility and the birth of human infants as well as beasts. She became the "mistress of animals"—the universal mother goddess—who brought life, as well as death. The bull, on the other hand, symbolized brute instinctual force and violence. By braving the dangerous wild bull, males could prove their courage and prowess in combat. Cauvin writes: "The goddess flanked by a male partner assimilated by the bull, will be the keystone of a whole religious system organized around her".[59] Archaeologist Marija Gimbutas argues the goddess was primary to the cultures of the Neolithic, reflecting a matrilineal social order in which women served as heads of clans or as queen-priestesses, worshipping a great goddess who symbolized the natural cycles of birth, death and rebirth. She believes women and men shared equal authority in these societies, with neither sex dominating.

According to Gimbutas the various aspects of the great goddess were symbolized by animals. As *birth-goddess,* she was represented as a woman with a bird's head, or wearing a bird-mask; migratory water-birds such as swans, geese or cranes were associated with her, symbolizing life-giving moisture and the annual return of life. As *mother-goddess* she was sometimes depicted as a female bear or doe nurturing her young. As *death-goddess* she commonly appeared in the forms of vultures, ravens, owls and poisonous snakes. As *goddess of regeneration* she was associated with creatures such as bees, fish, frogs, sows and serpents.[60]

Gimbutas contends the male god descended from Paleolithic images of half-human, half-animal men found in cave art. She writes "...the male god's epiphany was in the form of a bull". Gimbutas claims that in the Neolithic period from the 7th millennium onward, phallic masked-men, bull-men and goat-men represent a male stimulating principle in nature without whose influence nothing would grow or thrive. Sculptures of hybrid figures combining the features of man and bull appear in the Neolithic Vinca culture of the Balkans from the 5th-4th millennia BCE. The sacrifice of the bull, widespread in ancient cultures, was symbolic of the renewal of life.[61]

The iconography of Neolithic art shows a gradual shift from the animal spirits of Paleolithic shamanism to spirits which appear more *human-like*. These changes reflect the transition from hunter-gatherer to more complex agricultural societies in which human ancestors and mythical rulers became sources of transcendent power, according to ethnologist Roberte N. Hamayon.[62] The evolution from animal to anthropomorphic deities took millennia to complete, and the earlier animal "totemic" forms often persisted in later historical cultures, for example in the animal-headed gods and goddesses of Egypt and the totemic bird mascots associated with the Greek gods and goddesses—the eagle with Zeus, the owl with Athena, etc.

Although the Neolithic Revolution brought innovations in symbolism and mythology, the basic outlines of older creation myths and story-lines were preserved, according to Witzel.[63] He claims that many of the mythic themes such as the magical power of the shaman, the fertility of the universal mother, and the interdependence of animals and humans were inherited by Neolithic cultures from earlier Mesolithic and Paleolithic cultures. Witzel notes the worldwide distribution of myths from this period such as: father heaven and mother earth, the world tree, the world mountain, dragon slaying, trickster gods, hero myths, the theft of fire, the flood, creation of mankind, etc.[64] Gimbutas writes: "Indeed, what is striking is not the metamorphosis of the symbols over the millennia, but rather the continuity from Paleolithic times on". She insists that aspects of the goddess of the Neolithic such as birth-giver, nourisher, protector, and death-wielder, can all be traced back to 25,000 BCE and earlier.[65]

Chapter 3 Notes

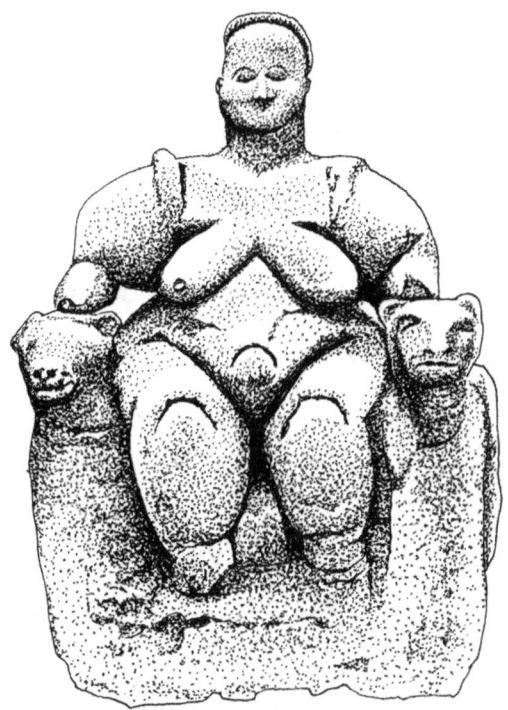

"Seated Woman" of Catalhoyuk baked clay sculpture, 6000 BCE.

1. Witzel. *The Origins of the World's Mythologies.*
2. Rudgely, Richard. *The Lost Civilizations of the Stone Age.* 1999:74-89.
3. Stavrianos, Stavros, Leften. *A Global History From Prehistory to the Present.* 1991: 9.
4. Pearson, Mike Parker. *Stonehenge A New Understanding.* 2012: 20.
5. Witzel. *The Origins of the World's Mythologies.* 2012: 422.
6. Ibid. 2012: 377.
7. Collins, Andrew. *Gobekli Tepe Genesis of the Gods.* 2014:71.
8. Ibid. 2014:185.
9. Clottes, Jean and Lewis-Williams, David. *The Shamans of Prehistory.* 1998: 81.
10. Ibid., 1998: 85.
11. Alden, Harold. "Shamanism and Sacred Arts in Finland- Part 2." *Spirit Boat- exploring Finnish shamanism and its relevance for today.* 2014.
12. Collins. *Gobekli Tepe Genesis of the Gods.* 2014:184.
13. Rudgely, Richard. *The Lost Civilizations of the Stone Age.* 1999:204.
14. Lewis Williams. *The Mind in the Cave.* 2002:25.

15. Rudgely. *The Lost Civilizations of the Stone Age.* 1999:205.
16. Winkelman, Dr. Michael. *Shamanism A Biopsychosocial Pardigm of Consciousness and Healing—Second Edition.* 2010: 76-79.
17. Jaffe, Eric. "Meditate on It- Could ancient campfire rituals have seperated us from Neanderthals?" *Smithsonian.com /Anthropology and Behavior section.* Feb. 1, 2007.
18. Winkelman. *Shamanism A Biopsychosocial Pardigm of Consciousness and Healing.* 2012: 47.
19. Williams. *Prehistoric belief: shamans, trance and the afterlife.* 2010: 30-31.
20. Gimbutas. The Living Goddess. 1999: 44.
21. von Petzinger, Genevieve. "Initial findings from the study of 146 French rock art sites". *Bradshaw Foundation* 2011:2.
22. Flavin, Richard D. *The Karanovo Zodiac and Old European Linear. Epigraphic Society Occasional Papers.* Vol. 23; pp. 86-92. 1998:1-7.
23. Thompson, Gary D. "Paleolithic European Constellations- Ice-Age star maps?" *Members.westnet.com.au.* 2013.
24. "Ice Age star map discovered". BBC *News/ Sci/Tech* Wednesday, 9 August, 2000."Ice Age star map discovered".
25. Whitehouse, Dr. David. "Faces from the Ice Age".*BBC News-world edition. Science/Nature.* Tue. 28 May, 2002.
26. "Oldest star chart found." *BBC News-world edition. Science/Nature.* Tue. 21 January, 2003. Whitehouse, 2003.
27. Krupp, E.C., *Echoes of Ancient Skies: The Astronomy of Lost Civilizations.* 2003: 157-165.
28. Joseph, Frank. *Before Atlantis: 20 Million Years of Human and Pre-human Cultures.* 2013: 73-74.
29. Campbell, Joseph. *The Masks of God vol. 1: Primitive Mythology.* 1987: 331.
30. Ashe. *Dawn Behind The Dawn: A Search for the Earthly Paradise.*1992: 16.
31. Ibid., 1987: 17.
32. Wade, Nicholas. "24,000 Year-Old Body Shows Kinship to Europeans and American Indians". *The New York Times. Science.* Nov. 13, 2013.
33. Ibid. 2013:2. Genetic testing of modern Mansi populations of northwest Siberia has shown that 29% of their mitochondrial DNA are of ancient European origin. (Derbeneva, Starikovskaya, Wallace, Sukernik 2002:3)
34. Wade. "24,000 Year-Old Body Shows Kinship to Europeans and American Indians". Ibid. 2013:2.
35. Berezkin, Yuri. "The Pleiades as Openings, the Milky Way as Path of Birds, and the Girl on the Moon: Cultural Links Across Northern Eurasia". *Folklore Journal*. 2010.
36. Milstein, Mati. "Oldest Shaman Grave Found; Includes Foot, Animal Parts". *National Geographic News.* Nov. 4, 2008.
37. PAP-Science and Scholarship in Poland. "Mesolithic sanctuary reveals constellation riddle". Www.naukawpolsce.pap.pl. "Past Horizons". September 23, 2014.
38. Coppens, Phillip. "Gobekli Tepe: the world's oldest temple". *Nexus Magazine.* Vol. 16, Number 4 (June-July 2009).

39. Lewis-Williams, J. David; Pearce, D.G.. *Inside the Neolithic Mind.*
40. Schmidt, Klaus. *Gobekli Tepi, A Stone Age Sanctuary in South-Eastern Anatolia.* 2007:113.
41. Collins, Andrew. "Gobekli Tepe: its cosmic blueprint revealed". *www.andrewcollins.com.* 2013: 5.
42. Collins 2014:88-89. Collins notes that the ancient Egyptians saw the Great Rift as the womb of the sky-goddess Nut, from which the sun god Ra was reborn every morning. The Mayans saw it as the jaws of a caiman, from which the sun god One Hunaphu was reborn.
43. White, Gavin. *Babylonian Star Lore: an illustrated guide to the star-lore and constellations of ancient Babylonia.* 2008:51.
44. Collins 2013: 9. It is notable that large numbers of bird bones such as those of swans have also been found in Mesolithic burial sites such as the cemetery of Oleni Ostrov at Lake Onega in Russia. Their placement alongside human burials suggests shamanic beliefs in which birds accompany the soul to the otherworld.
45. Collins, "Gobekli Tepe: its cosmic blueprint revealed". *www. andrewcollins.com.* 2013:11.
46. Collins, Andrew. *Gobekli Tepe Genesis of the Gods.* 2014:259.
47. Mann, Charles C. "Gobekli Tepi- The Birth of Religion". *National Geographic,* June 2011.
48. Lewis-Williams, J. David; Pearce, D.G. *Inside the Neolithic Mind.* 2005: 20-23.
49. Cauvin, Jacques.*The Birth of the Gods and the Origins of Agriculture.* 2000: 209.
50. Watkins,Colin. "The Neolithic revolution and the emergence of humanity a cognitive approach to the first comprehensive world-view". *Academia.edu.* 84.
51. Cunliffe, Barry. *Europe Between The Oceans.* 2008: 93.
52. Uyanik 1974 p. 12. This is an early example of the tradition of using skulls for oracles which endured for millennia. As previously mentioned, Siberian shamans used skulls as oracles, and the custom endured in Greek myths of Orpheus, whose severed head was said to utter prophesies, as well as the Nordic god Odin who consulted skulls for divination.
53. Hodder, *The Leopard's Tale- Revealing the Mysteries of Catalhoyuk.* 2006:29.
54. Ibid. 2006:29.
55. Collins, Andrew. *Gobekli Tepe Genesis of the Gods.* 2014:259.
56. Hodder, Ian. *The Leopard's Tale- Revealing the Mysteries of Catalhoyuk.* 2006:49.
57. Burkert, *Greek Religion.* 1985: 12.
58. Campbell, Joseph. *The Masks of God vol.1: Primitive Mythology.* 1987: 139.
59. Cauvin, *The Birth of the Gods and the Origins of Agriculture.* 2000: 25-69. Similarly, Gimbutas notes the pairing of male and female deities as "mistress and master of animals" in Neolithic art and myth. She speculates the male god descended from Paleolithic images of half-human, half animal men found in cave art.
60. Gimbutas, Marija. *The Language of the Goddess: Unearthing the Hidden Symbols of Western Civilization.* 2001.
61. Gimbutas, Marija. *The gods and goddesses of Old Europe: 7000 to 3500 BCE myths, legends and cult images.*1974. These traditions endured in ancient Greece as ithyphallic masked-men who participated in winter and spring festivals

dramatizing the seasonal cycles of death and rebirth, according to Gimbutas. The motif of the woman and bull would persist in Bronze Age Greek myths, in the "The Abduction of Europa", and the myth of the Minotaur, the result of the union between a woman and bull.

62. Krupp, *Skywatchers, Shamans & Kings: Astronomy and the Archaeology of Power*. 1997: 124.
63. Witzel, *The Origins of the World's Mythologies*. 2012: 264.
64. Ibid.: 105-185.
65. Gimbutas, *The Language of the Goddess: Unearthing the Hidden Symbols of Western Civilization*. 2001: xix.

Chapter 4: Mesopotamian Magic Heavenly Writing & Magic Circles

Assyrian Sacred tree from palace of Ashurnasirpal II, Nimrud—bas relief c. 900 BCE.

The word "Mesopotamia" in Greek means "land between the rivers". This referred to the fertile geographical area between the Tigris and Euphrates rivers encompassing present day Iraq and parts of Syria, Turkey, and Iran. The home of the earliest historical civilizations, Mesopotamia was inhabited long before them, however. Paleolithic hunter-gatherers lived in the Zagros mountains and sporadically dwelled in the lowlands until the end of the last Ice Age around 10,000 BCE.

Around 7,000 BCE, Neolithic settlements based on agriculture such as Jarmo, Samarra, and Tell Halaf arose in northern Mesopotamia, roughly during the same time period as the cities of Jericho in the Levant and Catalhoyuk in Anatolia.[1] The first farmers settled in southern Mesopotamia around 5,400 BCE bringing with them the Samarran culture from the north. There they built mud-brick buildings and canals using sophisticated irrigation methods which allowed them to practice agriculture in the marshes of the Euphrates river.

Neolithic Mesopotamians worshipped deities of nature: the celestial gods of sun, moon and venus, as well as earth gods and chthonic deities. Some of these were associated with animals—the sun with the bull, the air with the eagle, and underworld gods with snakes. Cults of dying and resurrected chthonic gods were also practiced which survived into the early historical period, according to historian F.A.M. Wiggerman.[2]

The first city of Eridu was established close to the Persian Gulf and the mouth of the Euphrates River. The people known as the Sumerians are found there around 3,500 BCE during the Uruk period.[3] Eridu in Sumerian means "mighty place", an appropriate name for the seat of the first kings of Mesopotamia. Soon after its founding, other Sumerian cities such as Ur, Uruk, and Larsa were established—the world's earliest "city-states". The origin of the Sumerians is a mystery and most linguists believe their language is unrelated to any other, though some words in Sumerian vocabulary bear similarities to Eurasian languages, possibly the result of contacts between prehistoric cultures.[4]

Following the Sumerians, a series of Semitic civilizations rose to power—the Akkadians, Babylonians, Kassites, Assyrians, and Chaldeans as well as an Indo-European group, the Hittites—each in turn ruling the "land between the rivers". Mesopotamia finally fell to the Persians in 539 BCE. Despite the succession of peoples and empires, the oldest language of Mesopotamia, Sumerian, continued to be used for ceremonial, literary, and scientific purposes until the 1st century CE.

The Rise of the First City-States

Assyriologist Noah Kramer aptly titled one of his books "History Begins at Sumer".[5] The Sumerians are credited with revolutionary inventions such as writing, mathematics, the calendar, kingship, wheeled carts, and metalwork with bronze, which laid the foundations for future civilizations to come.

The earliest towns in Sumer were agricultural settlements which grew up around temples of a local god. These eventually expanded into city-states in which private property, a class system, and governments ruled by elites were established. The earliest ruler was a religious leader—the *en*—who was in charge of the city's temple, a role later assumed by the "sacred king". The king however owed his authority to the patron deity believed to rule the city, whom he served as vice-regent.[6] He needed to continually discern the will of his ruling god or goddess, surrounding himself with priests who specialized in divination, religious ritual and magic to assist him in interpreting their proclamations.

The sacred kings and their supporting priesthoods became the mediators to the divine world—assuming roles similar to those held by shamans in tribal cultures. The shaman's symbols and powers as well as his duties now fell upon the king, according to historian Thomas McEvilley.[7] The stories of otherworldy journeys of shamans of the past were retold as myths of the kings of the city-states, thereby legitimizing their spiritual authority. In the Sumerian *Epic of Gilgamesh* the king of the city of Uruk, Gilgamesh, is given a magical drum made from the Huluppu Tree, reminiscent of the shaman's drum made from the World Tree. In another story Gilgamesh in his quest for immortality undertakes a shamanic-like journey, descending into the underworld traveling through a long, dark tunnel which leads to the garden of the gods. Likewise the goddess Inanna journeys to the underworld where she suffers death and is magically resurrected, recalling the shaman's initiation. In the *Epic of Etana*, an early Mesopotamian king ascends to the heavens on the back of an eagle in search for the "plant of life", similar to the shaman who ascends to the sky with the aid of his avian helping-spirits to gain healing remedies.

The shaman's societal role as visionary who communicated with the spiritual realm was assumed in Mesopotamia by the king. He became responsible for "sacred dreaming" as a means of communicating the intentions of the gods to mankind, his dreams interpreted by priests and diviners. For example, the Sumerian king Gudea (2144-2124 BCE) received the following dream telling him to build a temple for the warrior god Nigirsu :

> *"In the dream there was someone who was as enormous as the heavens, who was as enormous as the earth. His head was like that of a god, his wings were like those of the Anzu bird, his lower body was like a flood storm. Lions were lying at his right and his left. He spoke to me about building his house, but I could not understand exactly what he meant, then daylight rose for me on the horizon. Then there was a woman...She held a stylus of refined silver in her hand, and placed it on a tablet with propitious stars, and was consulting it. There was, furthermore, a warrior. His arm was bent, holding a lapis lazuli tablet in his hand, and he was setting down the plan of the house. The holy basket stood in front of me, the holy brick mold was ready and the fated brick was placed in the mould for me."* [1]

In subsequent dreams king Gudea was even given specifications for the size of bricks to be used. He ritually made the first brick and supervised the building of the temple. According to McEvilley: "he was functioning like a medium or shaman who communicates directly with the deity" [8].

The Sacred Tree in Ancient Mesopotamia

An enduring symbol of the kingship in Mesopotamia was the "sacred tree"—reminiscent of the shaman's World Tree. In the Old Testament *Book of Daniel,* Nebuchadnezzar, king of Babylon, dreams of a huge tree growing in the middle of the earth, its crown reaching to the sky. The Jewish prophet Daniel is summoned to interpret the dream and tells him: "That tree, O king, is you, for you have become great and grown strong, and your majesty has become great and reached the sky and your dominion to the end of the earth." (Daniel 4:10-22)

The Tree of Visions

The Assyrians held their kings to the highest ethical standards and saw kingship as a sacred institution rooted in heaven. Assyrologist Simo Parpola proposes that the king was a model of human perfection and seen as a prerequisite for mankind's personal salvation. According to Parpola, the heavenly origin of kingship is also expressed in the myths of the earlier Mesopotamian cultures of Sumeria and Babylon, allegorized by the image of the tree planted upon earth by the goddess Inanna/Ishtar.[9]

The motif of sacred tree is often represented as a stylized palm tree growing on a mountain, and occurs frequently in Assyrian royal art. The walls of the palace of king Ashurnasirpal II (883-859 BCE) in Nimrud were covered with more than four hundred representations of the sacred tree. The tree's image was engraved in a stone relief on the wall behind the throne of Assyrian kings. According to Parpola, the king was seen as the embodiment of the sacred tree. He writes:

> "The cosmic tree growing in the middle of the world and connecting heaven with earth was the best imaginable visual symbol for the king's pivotal position as the focal point of the imperial system and the sole representative of god upon earth. When seated on his throne, the king, from the viewpoint of the people present in the throne room, merged with the tree, thus becoming, as it were, its human incarnation." [10]

Parpola claims the sacred tree symbolized the divine world order while the king who embodied the tree represented the "perfect man". He compares this with the Jewish kabbalistic notion of Adam Kadmon as the "divine man" juxtaposed upon the kabbalistic Tree of Life. Parpola argues that closer analysis of the kabbalistic Tree of Life symbol reveals it is based on an earlier Assyrian "sacred tree" model dating from the 2nd millennium BCE. He points out that when the divine powers of the *sephiroth* (spheres) of the Tree of Life are replaced by the corresponding Assyrian sacred tree, a similar hierarchy based on three levels of generation is obtained. Parpola writes: " The crown of the tree is the god of heaven, Anu; its foundation is the god of the netherworld, Nergal; in between heaven and earth, connecting them, is the goddess of love, Ishtar". He relates these gods to the central vertical spheres of the kabbalistic Tree of Life: Kether, Malkuth, and Tipareth respectively. Arguably the Assyrian sacred tree with its three levels of generation was derived in turn from a much older cosmological schema—the shaman's World Tree—joining together sky, earth, and underworld.

Parpola concludes that ancient Assyria possessed an esoteric tradition based on the concept of a single transcendent god, in which all the manifest gods converged. He insists this tradition may have provided some of the basic theological concepts of the Jewish Kabbalah, Neoplatonism, Pythagoreanism, and Orphism which were so influential in the development of western esotericism.[11]

Divining the Will of the Gods

Divining the will of the gods was believed essential for survival in the harsh and unpredictable geography of Mesopotamia, subject to droughts, flash floods and sporadic invasions by nomadic peoples. Since the king was believed to be the earthly servant of the true ruler, the patron god or goddess of the city, he needed to constantly consult them about affairs of state.

Based on this need, a priestly class of diviners and seers arose around the king known as *baru* priests whose role was to help him interpret messages from the gods. They studied omens and signs, observed the stars, and explained the calendar with its lucky and unlucky days.[12] They also practiced a form of divination known as "haruspicy" or "extispicy" examining the internal organs of sacrificed sheep for anomalies. Haruspicy was one of the most widely used divination techniques in Mesopotamia and developed into a complex system of interpretation. The same method was later adopted by the Etruscans, Greeks, and Romans. Divination by the flight of birds was also practiced by baru priests. Meteorological conditions such as clouds, thunder, etc., were observed for omens they might provide. Astroscopy, the observation of the planets, stars, moon and sun, eventually developed into astrology, based on the systematic interpretation of the positions of the heavenly bodies in the zodiac.[13] Onieromancy, or divination by dreams was another widely used divination technique, and kings as well as commoners sought diviners to interpret their dreams. Oleography examined and interpreted patterns of oil poured on water. Another Babylonian divination technique involving oil is recorded in Jewish texts of the Talmudic period called "The Princes of the Thumb" in which a young boy was placed within a magic circle and his thumb anointed with olive oil. He was told to gaze at the reflective surface of his thumb-nail and report to the magician any visions of spirits. The magician then communicated with the spirits through the child medium, seeking answers to his questions.[14]

In the holistic worldview of the Mesopotamians, divination developed into an all-encompassing symbolic system by means of which all events in the cosmos could be interpreted. In a Babylonian diviner's manual it is written: "The signs of the earth together with those of the sky produce a signal, heaven and earth both bring us portents, each separately though not different, since sky and earth are interconnected. A sign that is evil in the sky is evil on earth, a sign that is evil on earth is evil in the sky".[15] The gods Shamash and Adad, sons of the Moon god Sin, ruled over divination. Adad was associated with lightning and thunder storms, and shared rulership of the skies and control of nature with his brother Shamash, the sun god. These gods were invoked by the Babylonian diviner, and invited to enter into a magic circle with him to deliver judgement:

> "O Shamash, lord of judgement. Adad, lord of ritual prayers and divination, Who sits on a throne of gold, eats at a table of lapis lazuli, You will descend, you will eat, you will sit...you will render judgement. In the ritual prayer that I perform, In the extispicy that I do, Place the truth".[16]

Oracles of Ishtar

Another form of divination used oracles, often involving spirit possession, an important aspect of the religious life of Mesopotamia, according to historian Johanna Stuckey. An example of this is the "Sacred Marriage" ritual in Sumeria, celebrated yearly between king and high priestess in which the goddess Inanna possessed the priestess, who acted as her oracle while in an entranced state.[17]

Oracular prophecies were often though not exclusively delivered by women, many of whom were devotees of the goddess Ishtar, the Babylonian version of Inanna. It was usually Ishtar who possessed Assyrian mediums who were often associated with her cult.[18] The Mesopotamian word for prophet—*raggimu*, means "shouter". Another kind of prophet was the *muhhutu*, meaning "ecstatic", derived from *mahu*, meaning "to go into a frenzy". Both types of prophetesses were attached to the temple of a deity, who spoke through them while in a state of possession. According to historian Tammi J. Schneider, prophets would often receive messages in a temple, in dreams, or while performing a haruspicy.[19] In one historical account, Ishtar spoke through her human medium, an aristocratic woman named Sinqisha-amar of Arbela: "King of Assyria, have no fear! I will deliver up the enemy of the king of Assyria for slaughter...I am the Great Lady. I am Ishtar of Arbela". In another prophecy delivered through the same oracle, the possessing deity assures the king: "I am your father and mother. I raised you between my wings".

Stuckey notes that cross-dressing was part of the cult of Ishtar, who had the ability to alter a person's sex so a man became a woman, and vice versa. She writes: "Ishtar also confused the lines that separated the sexes, the generations, the classes, and the species, human and animal".[20] Ishtar was believed to manifest in both genders—in her association with the morning star she was female; as evening star she was male and sometimes depicted wearing a beard.

According to Parpola, the devotees of Ishtar emulated her sufferings and saw the world with its temptations as analogous to "prostitution", causing them to practice ascetic denial of the flesh. Sexual abstinence was considered virtuous and self emasculation was common among her male devotees. They saw themselves as "brides" adorning themselves for a final union with the deity in a heavenly wedding. Parpola writes: "The ascetic practices of the cult frequently led to visionary experiences and altered states, including prophecy." [21]

Inanna's Descent to the Underworld

We previously discussed the underworld journeys of shamans during their initiations. The underworld was believed to be a dangerous realm, a place of trial and ordeals, which if survived led to the shaman's transformation and rebirth. In a similar vein, the Sumerian myth *The Descent of Inanna* tells of that goddess's ordeals and resurrection in the underworld. It is the oldest written account of an underworld journey, recorded between 1,900-1,600 BCE.[22]

Inanna's name is derived from the Sumerian *nin-anna* meaning "queen of heaven", and she was associated with venus, the brightest planet in the heavens. Paradoxically, Inanna was a goddess of love as well as war, the alluring goddess of fertility and sexual passion who also delighted in stirring up rage on the battlefield. One of the most popular and beloved goddesses of ancient Mesopotamia, people could identify with her all too human passions and behavior—her promiscuity, jealousy, anger, and hubris, recounted in many myths.

In the *Descent of Inanna*, the goddess decides to journey to the underworld ruled by her sister Erishkegal.[23] Inanna knows full well that none who descend to the land of the dead ever return, but her curiosity gets the better of her. Accordingly she instructs her trusted minister before her departure to go and "weep" before the gods, so they will come to her rescue should she not return after three days.

Arriving at the gate of her sister's palace deep below the earth, Inanna bangs on the door, even threatening to break the bolts, demanding to be let in. Angered by her brashness Erishkegal instructs the doorman of the *kur* —the underworld—to open the gates for her. However, this is only on the condition that she surrenders one of her seven "divine powers" at each of the seven gates—her turban, lapis measuring rod, jewelry and clothes:

"Come Neti, my chief gatekeeper of the *kur*,
Heed my words:

Bolt the seven gates of the underworld.
Then, one by one, open each gate a crack.
Let Inanna enter.
As she enters, remove her royal garments.
Let the holy priestess of heaven enter bowed low." [24]

At the last and seventh gate the goddess is stripped bare. Entering her sister's palace, Inanna brashly attempts to sit on her throne. Enraged by her arrogance, Erishkegal calls for Inanna's death. She is judged by seven judges, struck and killed by Erishkegal, and her corpse hung on a hook to rot:

"Naked and bowed low, Inanna entered the throne room.
 Ereshkigal rose from her throne.
Inanna started toward the throne.
The Anunna, the judges of the underworld, surrounded her.
They passed judgement against her.
Then Ereshkigal fastened on Inanna the eye of death.
She spoke against her the word of wrath.
She uttered against her the cry of guilt.
She struck her.
Inanna was turned into a corpse,
A piece of rotting meat,
And was hung from a hook on the wall.

As previously commanded, Inanna's minister approaches various gods to come to her rescue, including her father Nanna the moon-god. Nanna ignores her pleas, replying that those arrogant enough to crave the divine powers of the underworld must remain there. Finally, Enki the god of wisdom and magic takes pity on Inanna's plight and agrees to help. He creates two figures named Galatur and Kurgarra from the dirt under the fingernails of the gods. They are told to go to the palace of Erishkegal and "enter the door like flies". There they appease Erishkegal who is moaning and crying like a woman ready to give birth, expressing empathy for her suffering. In gratitude, she asks them what they want as a reward.

Without hesitating they ask for Inanna's corpse, which they sprinkle with the water of life and a life-giving plant, given to them by Enki. Inanna is magically revived, and promptly flees from the underworld back to the world of the living. The demons, however, chase after her demanding a replacement. She arrives home to find her husband Dumuzi sitting idly on her throne. In fact, during her absence he hadn't even bothered to mourn her loss. Enraged at his lack of concern, Inanna gives Dumuzi to the demons to take. Dumuzi's sister Geshtinanna selflessly steps forward and volunteers to take his place. Brother and sister alternate, each living in the underworld for half of each year, and on the surface world the other half.

Goeffry Ashe stresses the shamanic motifs in the myth. He points out that the story is similar to the trance descents to the underworld performed by Altaic shamans or shamanesses. He writes: "Inanna dons a septenary outfit with septenary magical gear. On the way she passses through the ordeal of the seven gates, just as the shaman passes through the seven *pudak*, or obstacles."[25] The *pudak* Ashe refers to are the seven levels of the underworld of Altaic myths which bear a resemblance to the labyrinthine underworld visited by Inanna.

The basic structure of the archaic shamanic myth—descent to the underworld followed by the death and rebirth of the shaman—was preserved by the Mesopotamians, yet altered to accommodate their new agricultural mythos. The shaman's role is now played by the fertility deities Inanna and her husband Dumuzi, who becomes the sacrificial victim demanded by the powers of the underworld. Dumuzi as the lover of Inanna was called the "shepherd", whose divine powers helped the sheep multiply and the grain grow. He personified the yearly cycle of natural growth. His mating with Inanna in the spring caused the earth to blossom. During the heat of summer, however, Dumuzi descended to the underworld as the crops withered and died. During his period of confinement there he was mourned by funeral rites as the sacrificial Wild Bull. This practice was so widespread that the Hebrew prophet Ezekiel witnessed it at the temple in Jerusalem, commenting: "...behold, women were sitting there weeping for Tammuz". (Ezekiel 8:14) Tammuz/Dumuzi was reborn after the heat of summer, and his return from the land of the dead was believed to bring life giving rains and fertility to the fields.

Inanna's descent can be seen as an allegory of initiation and spiritual awakening that is as relevant today as in ancient times. Parpola writes: "In the Descent of Ishtar, the goddess plays the role of a fallen but resurrected soul, thus opening the possibility of spiritual rebirth and salvation to anyone ready to tread her path."[26] Innana must relinquish the powers of her ego—her hubris and ambition—and be stripped naked. Erishkegal demands that Inanna is judged then killed; the death of the old personality must occur prior to *rebirth* into a new spiritualized identity. As well as being the realm of death, the underworld, paradoxically, is also the place of regeneration from which new life emerges.

There is an astronomical dimension to the myth as well, which Mesopotamian astronomers were well aware of. The planet venus, the celestial manifestation of Inanna, always travels in close proximity to the sun as seen from the earth. It leads or follows the sun in the sky, and is never more than forty-eight degrees apart from it. Venus sets *after* the sun during certain phases of its orbit as the "evening star", and rises *before* the Sun as the "morning star" during other phases. When venus closely approaches or "transits" the Sun it disappears into its light, vanishing from sight. This period of venus's disappearance was interpreted as Inanna's confinement and death in the underworld. Eventually in its next phase venus would be seen reappearing on the opposite horizon to which it was last sighted, hailed as Inanna's rebirth and return to the land of the living.[27]

Mesopotamian Cosmology

The earliest Mesopotamian creation myth from Sumeria tells how in the beginning a great mountain rose out of the dark chaos of the primeval sea. Its peak reached heaven, and its base was the earth. Enlil, god of air, separated heaven from earth to provide a dwelling place for mankind. The primordial mountain of the Sumerians is reminiscent of the "cosmic mountain" of Altaic shamans which stood at the center of the earth and joined the worlds together.[28]

Of later origin is the Babylonian creation myth known as the *Enuma Elish*, meaning "when on high". It tells of the battle between Marduk, king of the gods, and Tiamat the elder goddess of oceanic waters and her brood of demons. Marduk slays Tiamat, splitting her body in half to create heaven and earth.[29] In the *Enuma Elish* it is written: "He then constructed stations for the great gods, fixing their astral likenesses as the stars of the Zodiac".

The Babylonians conceived of the earth as a flat disk surrounded by the sea, with the bowl of the heavens arching over it. By the second millennium BCE they had developed several models of the cosmos composed of three, or as many as seven heavens. Gavin White writes that the heavens of Mesopotamian cosmology were thought to be formed by concentric spheres or domes, each one nested within the next; the ceiling of the lower sphere forming the floor of the next higher sphere.[30] This concept of concentric heavenly spheres may in fact be the precursor of the "celestial spheres" model of later Greek astronomy, which we'll look into later. The first and highest heaven of Babylonian cosmology was the abode of Anu, god of the sky and most distant of the gods, believed to be made from red stone speckled with patches of black and white colors. The middle heaven was ruled by Marduk, king of the gods, and within this realm the major gods and goddesses dwelled, each associated with one of the seven visible planets including the sun and moon, Marduk's heavenly sphere was made from dark blue stone. The third and lowest heaven was made from translucent stone upon which the gods engraved the figures of the constellations of stars.[31]

Three levels of earth were placed beneath these heavens. The "upper earth" was the familiar world populated by mankind. Beneath the earth's surface was the realm of the *Abzu*—"middle earth"—imagined as an abyss of freshwater which fed all the springs, rivers and lakes of the upper earth. This was ruled by Enki, god of the waters, wisdom and magic. Inhabiting the middle earth were the Seven Sages, the Apkallu, who emerged from the ocean to give civilization to mankind. Dwelling here as well were hosts of mermaids and mermen and other denizens of the deep. Below this was the "lower earth" or underworld ruled by Erishkegal and her husband Nergal, inhabited by the chthonic gods as well as the souls of the dead. The lowest world was connected to the upper worlds by subterranean rivers and stairways placed at the eastern and western horizons. The sun descended and climbed these stairways each day on its nightly journey through the underworld, entering in the west at dusk and emerging at sunrise from the eastern stairway.[32]

In the atmosphere between heaven and earth dwelled a plethora of supernatural beings, hybrid creatures combining the features of both humans and animals born from the union of heaven and earth, who embodied the destructive aspects of storms, thunder and tempest. Demons could be found at all levels of the cosmos, causing eclipses in the heavens, as well as tormenting mankind and the souls of the dead in the underworld.[33]

The Babylonian cosmology integrates astronomy, myth, and geography into a hierarchical scheme, according to White, a cosmic order in which mankind inhabits the central world, while divine, demonic and elemental powers occupy the other realms. Through the practice of divination humans could discover the intentions of the gods. By the power of magic, threatening demons could be exorcised and supernatural powers appeased or appealed to for assistance.[34]

The Birth of Astronomy & Astrology

The Mesopotamians poetically referred to the starry night sky as "the writing of heaven". So closely did they associate the celestial bodies with the ruling deities, the symbol for "star" came to mean "god" in cuneiform writing, according to Assyriologist Erica Reiner.[35] The constellations were thought to be a symbol system created by the gods for communicating with mankind. Astronomer-priests specialized in observing the movement of the sun, moon, and stars, interpreting them as heavenly omens revealing the destiny of the king and land. Systematic observations of the stars and planets developed over the millennia into the science of astronomy.

By studying the heavens the calendar was also established—essential for determining the time to plant crops, observe religious festivals, and perform magical rites. The Mesopotamians used a soli-lunar calendar consisting of lunar months of $29^{1/2}$ days each month and twelve months a year. Since this fell short short 11 days each solar year, they corrected it by adding an extra month into the calendar every three years.[36]

The first written record of the five visible planets as a group comes from a 13th century BCE Babylonian star list. A Babylonian tablet written in 523 BCE predicts the positions of the sun and moon. Here for the first time in history the relative positions of the sun and moon are calculated in advance, along with their eclipses, the precise dates for the conjunctions of the moon with the planets, and the planets with each other, and their position in the zodiac.[37]

Planets and Pantheons

Important Mesopotamian deities were associated with the seven visible planets—the five planets plus sun and moon—based on their brightness, color and speed of orbit. Venus, most luminous of all planets manifested the power of Inanna/Ishtar. When venus appeared as the "morning star" rising before the sun, it was seen as Inanna in her role as goddess of love. When setting after the sun it was seen as the "evening star", the goddess of war—these opposing aspects reflecting Inanna's dual nature[38]. The planet mercury was addressed as "The Leaping One" as it is the fastest moving planet. It was associated with the gods Nabu, Enki, and Ea, and become patron of scholars and merchants. Saturn, associated with Ninib god of the hunt, was called the "Steady One" as its orbit is the slowest of the visible planets. Mars was known as "The Enemy", the blood-red planet that presided over destruction, plague, and pestilence associated with Nergal the god of war; Nergal also ruled over the underworld as husband of Erishkegal queen of the dead. Jupiter was associated with Marduk, king of the gods, and in the *Enuma Elish*, Marduk claimed the luminous planet Jupiter for himself. The sun, the manifestation of the god Shamash, was known as The "God of Justice" as he saw everything occurring on earth, hence his associations with divination.

Of all the planets the moon—associated with the god Sin—was of greatest importance to the Babylonians as it regulated their calendar based on lunar months; this was passed down to the Jews who to this day observe a lunar calendar, and the Hebrew language still retains some of the Babylonian names for the months. In the ancient world it was widely believed that the waxing and waning of the moon influenced the cycles of earthly life: birth, growth, and decay of plants, animals, and humans. The moon was described as "a fruit" constantly renewing himself in growth each month. Sin was depicted as a bearded old man sailing across the heavens in a silver boat, the father of Shamash, Ishtar, and Adad the storm god. Even though male, Sin had an affinity with female magicians and sorceresses since the moon's phases determined the timing of various magical rituals.[39]

The sun, moon, and venus formed the religious trinity of Shamash, Sin, and Ishtar, the most important grouping of gods. Represented respectively by the symbols of solar disk, lunar crescent and eight-pointed star of venus, they were carved on monuments and boundary stones as guardians and witnesses to the signing of deeds and treaties. The pairing of venus and the sun as brother and sister in Babylonian myth may have derived from a primary astronomical phenomenon—the planet venus is the brightest heavenly body after the sun and moon, and never moves more than forty-eight degrees apart from the sun as observed from earth. As morning and evening star, venus heralds the rising and setting of the sun and was therefore seen as his devoted sister. As evening star she was herald of her father, the moon.

The Zodiac- Circle of Animals

The word *zodiac* means "circle of animals" in Greek, appropriately so as the majority of zodiac signs are zoomorphic in form. The custom of naming constellations after animals can be found in many ancient cultures. As previously mentioned, the Paleolithic cave painters of Europe represented the constellation Taurus as a bull, and prehistoric cultures from Europe to the Americas associated constellations with animals. By the 3rd millennium BCE, the Sumerians had already identified and named most of the zodiacal constellations known to us today, likely inheriting some of them from the star-lore of prehistoric peoples.

The Babylonians were the first to mathematically conceptualize the zodiac, dividing it into twelve signs of thirty degrees each, composed of the band of constellations located on the "ecliptic", the path the sun, moon and planets travel across the sky. The constellations were observed in their "heliacal" position—rising above the eastern horizon just before sunrise. Since the sun moves approximately one degree daily in relation to the stars, a different zodiacal sign was seen to rise each month of the year, serving as a practical form of calendar. The season in which a zodiac sign had its annual rising gave it its symbolic meaning.[40] For example, the first sign of the zodiac, Aries, rising at the spring equinox was depicted as a newborn lamb, while the last constellation of Pisces was depicted as two fish, originally symbolizing the Tigris and Euphrates rivers and late winter floods.[41]

As well as the zodiac, the Babylonians identified and named many other constellations. Their constellation the "Goat" was called Lyra by the Greeks. Their "Snake" became the Greek constellation of Hydra, while their "Demon With Gaping Mouth" was known to the Greeks as Cygnus the Swan. The Babylonian constellation called "True Shepherd of Anu" became Orion the Hunter.[42] Ursa Major was known by the Mesopotamians as the heavenly "Wagon" which travelled around the pole star. According to Gavin White it may have been envisioned as a celestial funeral carriage which transported the souls of the dead to the afterlife. This star group was of greatest importance to the Sumerians who associated it with the god Enlil, ruler of the sacred city of Nippur, the central city of Sumer and its oldest city and religious capitol.[43] The Babylonians associated Ursa Major with the goddess Ishtar, believing it emanated her influence even when her planet, venus, was not visible in the sky. Like most ancient peoples, the Mesopotamians attributed special significance to the circumpolar stars and constellations, as they never set in the sky and were visible throughout the year.

The Shamanic Flight of Etana & the Eagle

The earliest written account of a mystical ascent through the heavens is the *Epic of Etana*, recorded around the 3rd millennium BCE. It's hero, Etana, was an early king of the city of Kish in Sumeria, and his adventure to the heavens on the back of an eagle clearly recalls the shaman's flight to the upperworld.

The story begins with an eagle and serpent who are neighbors inhabiting a tall poplar tree—the eagle roosting in the branches and the serpent nesting in its roots. The two become friends, swearing an oath before Shamash, the sun-god, to share their prey with each other and their offspring. However, one day while the serpent is away hunting the eagle betrays their trust and eats the snake's young. The serpent in his grief complains to Shamash, who counsels him to trap the eagle while it is feasting on prey, then cut its feathers and imprison it in a pit.

Meanwhile, king Etana, distraught that he has been unable to produce an heir, approaches Shamash, asking his help to find the magical "plant of birth" so that his barren wife may conceive. The god advises him to search for the eagle who will help him with his quest. Etana finds the trapped bird, feeds it and nurses it back to health. The two develop a friendship and the eagle even interprets Etana's his dreams for him; in one of these dreams Etana journeys to heaven and meets the goddess Ishtar who gives him the plant of birth. The eagle interprets this as meaning the two should attempt the journey, telling him:

> "...Come, let me take you up to heaven,
> Put your chest against my chest, Put your hands against my wing feathers,
> Put your arms against my sides". He put his chest against his chest,
> He put his hands against his wing feathers, He put his arms against his sides,
> Great indeed was the burden upon him. When he bore him aloft one league,
> The eagle said to him, to Etana: "Look my friend, how the land is now
> Examine the sea, look for its boundaries. The land is hills...
> The sea has become a stream". When he had borne him aloft a second league,
> The eagle said to him, said to Etana,"Look my friend, how the land is now!
> The land is a hill."When he had borne him aloft a third league,
> The eagle said to him, said to Etana, "Look my friend, how the land is now!
> The sea has become a gardener's ditch"...[44]

As they soar higher and higher Etana loses heart, begging the eagle to return him to earth. He falls off the eagle's back but is rescued by him in midair. At home in his city, Etana and his wife are sent more of the same dreams. The eagle interprets this as meaning they should attempt the journey again. This time the two succeed in entering the heavens of the gods Anu, Enlil, Ea and the sky gods; they pass through the gates of the moon god Sin, Shamash the sun god and Adad the god of storms. Finally they come to a palace where they find a beautiful young unnamed woman, probably Ishtar, sitting on a throne under which lions crouch. Unfortunately, due to a missing portion at the end of the tablet the tale remains unfinished, leaving us in suspense. Etana apparently *did* obtain the plant of birth from Ishtar, since according to the Sumerian king list he indeed had a male heir.

The *Epic of Etana* has remarkable parallels with shamanistic narratives, with it's theme of "magical flight" through the heavens on the back of an eagle, a well known spirit-helper of shamans. In Siberian myths the "first shaman" was born from an eagle, and eagles figure prominently in shamanic initiations and costumes.[45] As previously mentioned, the motif of eagle and serpent inhabiting the World Tree appears in myths around the world.

The Epic of Etana can also be interpreted as a morality tale according to Parpola, who insists it concerns the conflicting aspects of man's soul—the heavenly and chthonic sides as symbolized by the eagle and serpent. Parpola interprets Etana's befriending of the eagle as a metaphor for spiritual restoration and salvation, followed by the mystical ascension to heaven where Ishtar, Etana's personal goddess, is encountered.[46]

Etana and the eagle's flight through the heavens anticipates by millennia the visionary ascents through the celestial spheres in search of union with the divine by Hermetic, Gnostic, and Merkabah mystics, which we will later explore.

Akitu Festival—Renewal of the King & Land

The "Akitu Festival" was a Mesopotamian New Year's ceremony occurring near the time of the barley harvest after the first new moon of the spring equinox. It celebrated the renewal of nature as well as the kingship, and procured favorable destiny for the coming year. The ceremonies in Babylon centered around the cult of Marduk, king of the gods, the city's patron deity. He was symbolically enthroned for the upcoming year, accompanied by the recital of the *Enuma Elish,* the creation story which told of the birth of the gods and the world's creation.

At the beginning of the festival a somber mood prevailed in the city—the priests and priestesses expressed grief and bereavement and citizens fell into wailing. The king retreated into the shrine of Marduk where he was ritually humiliated by a priest who first stripped him of his royal regalia, then slapped his face so hard he wept—he was expected to express genuine humility before the god. Kneeling before Marduk's statue the king reassured the god of his innocence, that he had not neglected his duties towards city and temple. Following this, the priest re-invested the king, restoring his rule.[47]

During his confinement it was believed Marduk had been taken prisoner in his ziggurat by Tiamat, the goddess of the watery abyss, and her demons. However Marduk's son Nabu, accompanied by an army of gods arrived to liberate him, symbolically represented by their statues which were carried to the temple by faithful townspeople. A ritualized mock battle was enacted in which the supporters of the gods triumphed over the forces of chaos, restoring order to the cosmos. Marduk's statue was carried in a victory procession through the city followed by cheering crowds. The king, as proxy for Marduk, then celebrated the Sacred Marriage ritual, spending a night of sexual intercourse with a high-priestess who impersonated Ishtar. Through his ritualized union with the goddess the continuing fertility of the land was assured.

Temples & Ziggurats—Homes of the Gods

The temple in Mesopotamia served as the *axis-mundi*, the world-axis of the city, believed to be the meeting place of the gods and mankind. It's ground plan was based on the mythic archetype of the central "world mountain", a rectangle with corners oriented to the cardinal directions, symbolizing the four rivers which flow from the center to the four regions of the earth, according to historian John. M. Lundquist.[48]

Ziggurats were huge towers located in temple precincts, built in the form of step-pyramids, named *etemananki* by the Sumerians, meaning "the foundation of heaven and earth". They were believed to be the dwelling places of the patron gods of the city, who according to Greek historian Herodotus, had their shrines at the top. Kramer notes that the Sacred Marriage rite involving the king and high priestess occurred in the top chamber of the ziggurat. Many ziggurats were constructed in *seven terraces* associated with the seven planets and seven heavens. In one example the terraces were painted in different colors from the bottom to the top, corresponding to the planets: black/saturn, orange/jupiter, red/mars, gold/sun, yellow/venus, blue/mercury, and silver/moon.[49]

The temple was literally the house of the patron god or goddess of the city. There in the form of their statues they slept, were fed, bathed and entertained. The kings of city-states who were the deity's representatives on earth considered it their duty to maintain the deity's temple and provide all their daily needs, believed to be similar to those of humans. They required regular meals and were served water and beer. On special days they received offerings such as the first-fruits. They also left their sanctuaries to visit other gods to celebrate the New Year and other events.[50]

While the major deities represented the agendas of kings, priesthoods, and aristocracies, among the rest of society "personal gods" were widely revered. Their function was to take the prayers and petitions of individuals and present them to the greater pantheon of gods. The personal gods were referred to as "my god" or "my goddess" and were believed to provide protection and good fortune. The relationship between worshipper and god is here prescribed: "Every day worship your god. Sacrifice and benediction are the proper accompaniment of incense. Present your free-will offering to your god...Then you will have communion with your god." [51]

Demons of Mesopotamia

Besides the gods whom man was created to serve, evil demons played a significant role in the religious world-view of Mesopotamia and were believed to cause many of the world's ills. The Babylonians knew of two kinds of demons. The most powerful were cosmic in nature and placed in the heavens, known as the seven demons of the "ignited spheres", counterparts to the gods of the seven planets who governed the cosmos. Besides these were the seven spirits of the abyss who dwelled in the depths of the earth, causing earthquakes and tormenting mankind. A Babylonian conjuration provided by historian Francois Lenormant describes the effects of evil demons:

"On high they bring trouble, and below they bring confusion. Falling in rain from the sky, issuing from the earth, they pass from house to house. Doors do not stop them, bolts do not stop them, they glide in at the doors like serpents, they enter by the windows like the wind" [52]

Other kinds of evil demons lived in the uncultivated wilderness and deserts. These were categorized into different groups: the Alal—"destroyers", the Telal—"warriors", and the Maskim—"layers of ambushes". The exorcist-priests of Mesopotamia combated these and other evil spirits which were believed to the cause illnesses of body and soul. Since diseases were thought to be caused by demons, medicine was seen as a branch of magic and practiced by incantations, exorcisms, philters, and potions. Among the worst effects of malefic demons upon mankind was spiritual possession, and it was the work of the exorcist to expel them from their human hosts. Different demons were believed to attack various parts of the body:

"The malevolent Utuq upon the forehead of man,
The malevolent Alal upon the chest of man,
The malevolent Gigim upon the bowels of man,
The malevolent Telal upon the hand of man" [53]

Once the possessing demons were expelled from the body, the only guarantee against their return was to obtain a good demon such as a giant to replace them. An exorcist's litany reads "May the bad demons depart! May they seize upon one another! The propitious demon, the propitious giant, may they penetrate into his body." [54]

Besides demons, the shades of the dead also manifested themselves in frightening apparitions such as phantoms and specters. Vampires were believed to attack the living. The Incubus and Succubus victimized people in their sleep and induced erotic dreams to feed off men's sexual emissions. The Lilitu were demons that killed children. In Hebrew folklore, they became the demoness Lilith who was Adam's first wife—the seducer of men as well as the kidnapper and murderer of children.

Talismans to Repel Demons

Magical talismans made of different materials were used to ward off malevolent demons. Some of these consisted of bands of cloth inscribed with written formulas which were fastened to furniture or garments, similar to the phylacteries of Jews. There were also amulets made from different materials, worn around the neck to safeguard against diseases—often stones engraved with images of protective deities or genii along with written formulas. The following is a magical formula to be recited over an amulet:

"Talisman, talisman, boundary that cannot be taken away, boundary that the gods cannot pass...barrier immovable, which is opposed to malevolence! Whether by a wicked Utuq, a wicked Alal, a wicked Gigim...a phantom, a spectre, a vampire, a succubus, a nightmare...may the (talisman) retake him a prisoner." [55]

Statuettes made from clay, stone, or metal were used for similar apotropaic purposes and placed in locations such as temples, palaces or houses to protect them from demonic influences. An incantation to be recited over such an image instructs the magician: "place the image of the god Nergal, who is without equal, in the enclosure of the house...in order that no evil may happen.." Nergal, as god of war and lord of the underworld was obviously seen as a fierce deity whose protection was valued. The Chaldeans also made statues representing evil demons in hideous forms, believing that if demons were shown their own image they would flee in terror.

Some demons were also recruited for protection against even nastier demons. One of these was Pazuzu who ruled over the south-west wind. He is a fearsome looking creature with the body of a man, the head of a lion, eagle talons and wings, erect penis and scorpion's tail. He was invoked to protect women during childbirth, as well as against plagues and misfortune, and effigies of him were worn as protective amulets.

By placing such images near doors or in windows, it was believed demonic influences could be averted. The enormous winged bulls with human heads which flanked entrance gates of palaces are examples of such talismanic protection, believed to guard the king and prolong his life. These were known as *kuribu* and were the prototypes of the Jewish "cherubim", similarly represented as winged bulls or lions with human faces, whom we will later discuss.[56] The Assyrian king Esarhaddon in one of his inscriptions writes: "May the guardian bull, the guardian genius, who protects the strength of my throne, always preserve my name in joy and honor until his feet move themselves from their place".[57]

Babylonian Magic Circle
The Babylonians were the first to record the use of the "magic circle" for

protection. Assyrian exorcists drew circles on the floor with flour to protect the sick or possessed person, thereby creating a barrier from attack by demons of disease. Below is an incantation for casting a magic circle for such purposes. The healing goddess Bau is invoked at the beginning of the spell:

> "Bau, Bau, Barrier that none can pass,
>   Barrier of the Gods that none can break,
>   Barrier of heaven and earth that none can change,
>   Which no god can annul,
>   Nor god nor man can loose,
> A snare without escape set for evil,
> An net whence none can issue forth, spread for evil,
> Whether it be evil spirit, or evil demon, or evil ghost.
> Or evil devil, or evil god, or evil fiend,
> Or hag demon, or ghoul, or robber-sprite,
> Or phantom, or night wrath, or handmaid of the phantom,
> Or evil plague, or fever sickness, or unclean disease,
> Which hath attacked the shining waters of Ea,
> May the snare catch it...." [58]

Celestial & Infernal Magic

There is an extensive body of Babylonian literature recording "celestial magic"—the use of the planets and stars to influence the world for benevolent or malevolent purposes. Assyriologist Erica Reiner notes that astral magic was practiced by scholars such as professional diviners and exorcists to foretell the future and to avert evil portents. On the other hand sorcerers and sorceresses used the same powers to inflict harm upon an adversary.[59]

Specific stars were invoked to repel the malefic magic of sorcerers, to protect from afflictions, or to achieve desired goals. Magical materials such as herbs and stones were placed outside at night under the stars to irradiate them with their power, rendering them magically potent. The planetary gods were the focus of rituals meant to persuade them to act in the magician's favor. Lovers would turn to venus, the planet of the goddess Ishtar, who was addressed as the "luminary of heaven". A ritual text instructs the magician to set up a reed altar before Ishtar of the Stars and to make offerings and prepare figurines before her. Ishtar was also invoked before administering a potion to the love-sick patient. Witches were also known to carry out their magic spells while facing a star, and sorceresses were thought to have the power to "draw down the moon", a skill also practiced by Thessalian witches.[60]

The Mesopotamians, like other ancient cultures, viewed magic as a cosmic power which could be used for good or evil purposes. If derived from the gods, it could be used to avert misfortune and combat demonic influences, or could be used by the sorcerer or witch for malevolent purposes. The sorcerer in Mesopotamia was known as an "evil-doer", who caused ill fortune, demonic possession, terrible diseases and death by the use of spells and poisons. A Chaldean incantation laments his malefic magic: "He who enchants images has charmed away my life by his image...he has taken the enchanted philter, and has soiled my garment with it, he has torn my garment and dragged it in the dust of my feet. May the god of Fire, the hero, dispel their enchantments..." [61]

Necromancy—Working with the Dead

The term "necromancy" is derived from the Greek words *necros*, meaning "dead body", and *manteia*—"prophecy" or "divination". Necromancy was the magical art of communicating with the spirits of the dead, for prophecy as well as cursing, widely practiced by ancient magicians as well as shamans.

In Mesopotamia the dead were believed to return to persecute the living in the form of ghosts if they died in unhappy circumstances, or had not been given the proper burial or offerings. They might afflict people with a variety of ailments: sleeplessness, nausea, anorexia, cold sweats, miscarriages, or pains in the body which could prove fatal.[62] In order to appease the dead, they were invoked with ceremonies at the new moon of every month and placated with offerings. In exchange, magicians often asked the spirits to perform tasks for them, to remove illnesses or even escort a harmful ghost back to the underworld. They might also be asked to prophesy, and were called up through magical ointments or offerings placed in ditches, similar to the rite the Greek hero Odysseus performed to summon the ghost of Tiresias in the *Odyssey*.

Mesopotamian magicians also used the souls of the dead "offensively"— they were commanded to "seize" victims, according to historian Sarah Iles Johnston.[63] A figurine of the living victim made of wax or clay was placed in a new grave in the lap of a corpse, its ghost intended to carry them to the underworld. Personal effects of the victim such as fingernail clippings, hair, or semen were also placed in graves, linking them with the dead. There was also the macabre practice of "marrying" living victims to ghosts as a form of curse.

Magicians offered antidotes for ghostly attacks such as amulets which could be worn for protection as well as ointments rubbed on the doors of houses. A figurine was used to represent the ghost which was then offered food and drink and "sent down the river" or buried if it represented an unburied dead person. Figurines might also be burnt or melted to drive the offending ghost away. It was the task of "exorcist magicians" to combat sorcerers and protect people from their malefic spells.

Mention of the practice of necromancy first appears in Assyrian texts around 900 BCE, and it played an important role during the reign of Assyrian king Esarhaddon (681-669 BCE) according to Johnston. She claims necromancy originated in Mesopotamia and spread from there to Egypt, Anatolia, the Levant and Greece.[64]

Ethnographer Vilmos Dioszegi argues the art of necromancy has earlier shamanic origins.[65] As previously mentioned, the shaman served as psychopomp who communicated with the souls of the dead for helpful as well as malevolent purposes. Mongolian and Siberian "black shamans" were skilled in working with underworld spirits which could be used for cursing. It was also their duty to combat evil spirits that caused illness and soul loss, sent by shamans from hostile clans.

Books of Stars & Stones

The first books of magical correspondences were created in Mesopotamia.[66] The Babylonians kept "calendar texts" which compiled correspondances of zodiacal signs with trees, stones, herbs, animals, gods, cities, and other things. In a text dating to around 300 BCE from Babylonian Uruk, recipes for ointments corresponding to each of the zodiacal signs are given: for Aries the blood, tallow and wool of sheep; for Taurus the blood, fat and hair of a bull; for Gemini the head, blood and feathers of a rooster, and so on for each sign.[66]

The Babylonians also kept "stone books", the first lapidary manuals. Stones were believed to possess different magical virtues and were used for making amulets. Beads made of semi-precious stones, shells, and colored glass were believed to protect from the evils sent by demons or witches. The stars were thought to imbue stones with their power, therefore amulets were exposed to their rays during nocturnal rituals. The text below invokes Gula, a chthonic healing goddess associated with the "Goat Star", Vega, in the constellation of Lyra. It instructs the magician:

"You string the stones and phylacteries on a (linen thread), you set in place a holy water vessel, you purify the stones....you place the stones before the Goat Star, you set up a censor with aromatics, you libate beer, you recite the incantation: O bright one, let your angry heart be appeased...O Gula , exalted lady....be present at my lawsuit, let me obtain justice through your verdict, because of the sorcerers spittle and spattle, evil machinations of my adversary, let his evil doings turn back against him...I your weary servant will sing your praises". [67]

Herbal Magic

Other innovations of the Mesopotamians included pharmaceutical and medical texts containing herbal lore, providing physicians with knowledge about the medicinal properties of herbs. They advised the best times to harvest particular herbs to maximize their magical healing powers. The texts prescribe doing this in the dark of night, first drawing a magic circle of flour around the herb to protect the herbalist from the wrath of angry plant spirits. Instructions for the preparation of herbal medicines and potions are also provided. One such recipe instructs the physician: "You place the three herbs steeped in beer before the Goat Star, you draw a circle around it, in the morning you strain it, he drinks it without eating". Most important was knowing the correct time to administer herbs to the patient by selecting the astrologically propitious moment.[68]

Astrology in Babylon

The role of Babylonian astrologer-priests was to interpret omens from the stars to predict events effecting the king and realm. One such omen based on the the planet Jupiter and the constellation Taurus reads:

"If Sagmegar (Jupiter) comes near to the Bull of Heaven; the treasures of the land will perish".[69]

When the celestial signs predicted disaster, magical apotropaic rituals— protective spells— were performed to ward off evil and protect the king. An entourage of exorcists and lamentation priests would calm the angry gods and drive off demons. Most dreaded among celestial events was a lunar eclipse, which was calculated with great accuracy. Dire predictions had to be averted by rites such as the crowning of a temporary substitute king, often a sentenced criminal. The surrogate king reigned for only a hundred days and was then put to death, taking upon himself the misfortune and death predicted for the king by the eclipse.

The concept of natal astrology was developed by the Babylonians between the 7th-4th centuries BCE, according to astrologer James Herschel Holden.[70] It consisted of determining the positions of the sun, moon, and planets in the zodiac on the date of birth. Horoscopes were probably first made available to the king and royalty, courtiers, and other prominent persons. With increasing demand, professional astrologers offered their services to the general populace. By the time of the Selucid era in Babylon around 300 BCE, the use of astrology had become widespread. Along with its popularity came books known as *Lunaria* which gave the moon's position, considered to be lucky or unlucky for certain activities.[71] For example, the most auspicious time to go before a king or judge was thought to be when the Moon was in Aries. To give or receive borrowed money, the Moon in the signs of Aries, Cancer, Libra, and Capricorn was deemed most favorable. It was considered fortunate to bring back a fugitive while the Moon was in the region of the star Regulus, or the sign of Libra.

Chapter 4 Notes

"Ishtar Queen of Night"—baked clay relief from Babylon 1500-1750 BCE.
(May represent Ishtar or Erishkegal)

1. "History of Mesopotamia/ Chalcolithic Period. Wikapedia".
2. Wiggerman, F.A.M. "Theologies, Priests, and Worship in Ancient Mesopotamia." *Academia.edu.*:1867.
3. Woolley, C.L. *The Sumerians.* 1965:9. Also see Campbell, *Primitive Mythology.*1959:144.
4. Mircea Eliade mentions that the Sumerian term for divinity, "dingir" meaning "shining" referring to the sky is similar to the Turko-Mongolian word *tengri* meaning "sky" and "God". The sky god Anu may have been imported in prehistoric times from Central Asia into Mesopotamia according to P.A. Barton. Eliade writes that as early as the fourth millennium contacts can be found between the cultures of Elam (pre-Iranian) and the Caspian and Altaic cultures. (Eliade 1958:64). Similarly, the Maikop Culture of the Caucasus (3,700-3,100 BCE) which practiced metallurgy bridged the cultures of Mesopotamia and the European steppe such as the Cucutini Culture. (Manco 2013:109).

5. Kramer, Samuel Noah. *History Begins at Sumer: Thirty Nine Firsts in Recorded History.* 1988: xix-xx.6.
6. Wiggerman. "Theologies, Priests, and Worship in Ancient Mesopotamia". Edited by Sasson, Jack M. *Civilization of the Ancient Near East.* 1995:1868.
7. McEviley, Thomas. *The Shape of Ancient Thought. (Comparative Studies in Greek and Indian Philosophies).*2002.
8. Ibid.:2002:269.
9. Parpola, Simo."Sons of God- The Ideology of Assyrian Kingship". *Gateway to Babylon.*1999.
10. Parpola, Simo."The Assyrian Tree of Life: Tracing the Origins of Jewish Monotheism and Greek Philosophy". *Journal of Near Eastern Studies,* volume 52, No. 3. (July 1993) :161-208.
11. Parpola, Simo. "The Mesopotamian Soul of Western Culture". Lecture on Nov.1, 2000 at Harvard University. 2000:8.
12. Sabourin, Leopold. *Priesthood: A Comparative Study.* 1973: 64.
13. Campbell. *Oriental Mythology.* 1991: 104.
14. Daiches, Samuel. *Babylonian Oil Magic in the Talmud and in Later Jewish Literature.* 1913: 16-17.
15. Koch, Ulla Susanne. *"Mesopotamian Astrology".* 1994:138.
16. Lenzi, Alan. (Ed.). *Reading Babylonian Prayers and Hymns. An Introduction.* 2011:100.
17. Stuckey Johanna."Spirit Possession and the Goddess Ishtar in Ancient Mesopotamia".*Matrifocus Cross*
    -Quarterly. Samhain 2008 v. 8-1. 2008.
18. Ibid.
19. Schneider, Tammi J. *An Introduction to Ancient Mesopotamian Religion.* 2011: 87.
20. Stuckey Johanna.*"Spirit Possession and the Goddess Ishtar in Ancient Mesopotamia".*2008.
21. Parpola, Simo. In *Religions of the Ancient World: A Guide.* Ed. Johnston 2004: 643.
22. "Cuneiform Timeline".*Ancient History Encyclopedia. www.ancient.eu.*
23. Inanna goes there to participate in the funeral rites of Erishkegal's husband, the Bull of Heaven, recently killed by the heroes Gilgamesh and Enkidu. Ironically, it was Inanna who unleashed the destructive bull of heaven upon the earth in revenge for having her amorous advances rejected by Gilgamesh.
24. Wolkstein, Diane & Kramer, Samuel Noah. *Inanna Queen of Heaven and Earth.*1983: 52-73.
25. Ashe. *Dawn Behind The Dawn: A Search for the Earthly Paradise.* 1992: 93-5.
26. Parpola, Simo. In *Religions of the Ancient World: A Guide.* Ed. Johnston 2004: 643.
27. The planet Venus was also revered by the ancient Aztecs as the god *Quetzalcoatl*. In his manifestation as the *Evening Star* he descended closer to the western horizon- closer and closer to the setting sun, there he "died" and was cremated in its fire, disappearing from view. He then wandered in the underworld for eight days before being "reborn"- reappearing as the *Morning Star* on the eastern horizon. (Krupp 1991: 201)

28. Ashe. *Dawn Behind The Dawn: A Search for the Earthly Paradise*. 1992: 54-65.
29. Campbell, Joseph. *The Masks of God: Occidental Mythology*.1964: 79-80. Campbell insists this myth symbolizes the conquest of the pre-existing matriarchal order by patriarchal invaders. Through the process of "mythic defamation" the earlier goddess lore became the subject of demonization.
30. White, Gavin. *Babylonian Star Lore: an illustrated guide to the star-lore and constellations of ancient* Babylonia. 2008.
31. Ibid.:18.
32. Ibid.:19.
33. Ibid.:20.
34. Ibid.:20.
35. Reiner,Erica. *Astral Magic in Babylon*. 1995: 9.
36. White, Gavin. *Babylonian Star Lore: an illustrated guide to the star-lore and constellations of ancient Babylonia*. 2008: :291.
37. Cumont, Franz. "Astrology and Religion Among the Greeks and Romans". *Sacred-texts.com*. 1912: 8.
38. *Venus* was of great importance to many other prehistoric cultures because of it's orbit and precise eight year cycles which could be used for calendrical purposes. It's cycle was observed worldwide—recorded in the Mayan Calendar as well as by the megalithic builders of Newgrange in Ireland.
39. Reiner. *Astral Magic in Babylon*. 1995: 8.
40. White, Gavin. *Babylonian Star Lore: an illustrated guide to the star-lore and constellations of ancient Babylonia*. 2008: White 2008: 10.
41. Ibid.: 8.
42. Reiner. *Astral Magic in Babylon*. Reiner 1995.
43. Ashe. *Dawn Behind The Dawn: A Search for the Earthly Paradise*. 1992:82.
44. Benjamin, Foster. *From Distant Days: Myths, Tales and Poetry from Ancient Mesopotamia*. 1995.
45. Eliade. *Shamanism- Archaic Techniques of Ecstasy*.1964:70.
46. Parpola. "The Assyrian Tree of Life: Tracing the Origins of Jewish Monotheism and Greek Philosophy". *Journal of Near Eastern Studies*, volume 52, No. 3. 1993: 161-208..
47. Roy, Christian. *Traditional Festivals: A Multicultural Encyclopedia, vol. 1*. 2004:6.
48. Parry, Donald N.;Ricks, Stephen E. (eds.) Lundquist, John. *What Is A Temple? A Preliminary Typology. (83-118)* in *Temples of the Ancient World*.1994:83-118.
49. Lethaby, W.R. "Architecture, Mysticism and Myth". *sacred-texts.com*. 1892: 129.
50. Schneider. *An Introduction to Ancient Mesopotamian Religion*. 2001: 72.
51. Ibid.:65.
52. Lenormant, Francois. *Chaldean Magic: Its Origin and Development*.1994: 29.
53. Ibid.:17.
54. Ibid.:11.
55. Ibid.:46.
56. Uzdavinys, Algis. *Philosophy & Theurgy In Late Antiquity*. 2010:152.
57. Lenormant. *Chaldean Magic: Its Origin and Development*.1994: 60.
58. Wedeck, Harry, E. *A Treasury of Witchcraft*.1989.
59. Reiner. *Astral Magic in Babylon*. 1995: 2-3.

60. Ibid.:97.
61. Ibid.
62. Johnston, Sarah Iles. *Restless Dead*. 1999: 87.
63. Ibid.: 89.
64. Ibid.: 88.
65. Stutley, Margaret. *Shamanism: An Introduction*. 2003:22.
66. Reiner. *Astral Magic in Babylon*. 1995: 116.
67. Ibid.:128-129.
68. Ibid.: 58.
69. White. *Babylonian Star Lore: an illustrated guide to the star-lore and constellations of ancient Babylonia*. 2008: 287.
70. Holden, James Herschel. *A History of Horoscopic Astrology*. 1996: 5.
71. Reiner. *Astral Magic in Babylon*. 1995: 108.

Chapter 5: Ancient Egypt
Magicians of the House of Life

Opening of the Mouth Ceremony with mummy of king Tutankhamun.
(1332-1323 BCE)

Prehistoric Egypt

Although the land of Egypt is usually associated with the civilization of the pharaohs, the Nile Valley was inhabited since the earliest times. During the Lower Paleolithic era around 125,000 years ago it served as a passageway for early humans in their migration out of East Africa to the Near East and elsewhere. Modern humans, hunter-gatherers, began living in Egypt around 120,000 years ago. During this period, Egypt had a moister climate and the Sahara consisted of savanna and grasslands, providing food and vegetation.

This lasted until about 30,000 BCE when the climate became warmer and drier.[1] Scientists have recently concluded that climate change may have been gradual in some areas but more rapid in others, driving migrations of populations from North-Central Africa into the Nile Valley seeking its water, game, and arable land.

Writer and researcher Robert Bauval proposes that Egyptian civilization grew out of a sophisticated African civilization that existed for millennia prior to the pharaohs. In his opinion prehistoric peoples from sub-Saharan Africa, originally hunter-gatherers, became pastoral herdsmen as they adapted to the warming climate and vanishing game. They eventually developed a more settled lifestyle based on animal domestication, agriculture, sign writing, and timekeeping using the sun and stars.[2] During the Middle and Later Neolithic periods around 6,600-5,100 BCE they built large organized settlements and structures, the most remarkable of which is the stone monument of Nabta Playa.

Some form of shamanic ceremonialism was practiced by these nomadic peoples according to Bauval who visited numerous caves on the border of Egypt, Libya, and Sudan where he found rock paintings left by Neolithic herders.[3] There he saw images depicting humans merging with or "morphing" into animals, typical of shamanic art. Bauval also found paintings of people with cow-like animal heads eerily reminiscent of the Egyptian goddess Hathor, as well as images he claims bear a striking resemblance to the god Set, an Egyptian god of desert regions.

Likewise, Egyptologist Miroslav Barta has studied the cryptic Neolithic rock art of the remote Cave of the Swimmers and the Cave of the Beasts in Southwest Egypt. He conjectures the paintings there depict deities who are precursors of Egyptian gods. Most strikingly, Barta identifies a painting of a large female figure standing in arched position, and standing beneath her two smaller male figures. He proposes this painting is an archaic version of the familiar motif of Egyptian sky goddess Nut with the male gods Shu and Geb standing beneath her.[4]

The theory of African origins of Egyptian civilization is not new. It was first proposed by 19th century explorers as well as Egyptologist Sir Wallis-Budge in 1911, who argued that the religion of ancient Egypt was derived from the peoples of Northeastern and Central Africa. Budge points to numerous similarities between ancient Egyptian and modern African religion and magic: ancestor worship, funerary customs, veneration of cattle and other animals, similar pantheons of gods, use of magical fetishes, etc. He reasoned that since many African tribes probably never had contacts with the Egyptians, cultural influences must have originated with them, spreading northward along the Nile.⁵

Nabta Playa- The Earliest Astronomical Monument

Nabta Playa in the southwestern desert of Egypt near Abu Simbel is a circle of upright monoliths, or standing stones, arranged according to sophisticated astronomical alignments. Constructed around 4,500-4,000 BCE, it predates Stonehenge in Britain by a thousand years. Astroarchaeologist J. McKim Malville insists Nabta Playa was a ceremonial center, a place where geographically dispersed people gathered periodically to conduct religious ceremonies.⁶ It was originally built on the shoreline of an ancient lake which has long since evaporated and become desert.

The structure consists of ten large stones and a circle of upright slabs, some of which are nine feet tall. There are also two slab covered tumuli, one containing the remains of a long-horned bull, suggesting religious ritual.⁷ The twelve foot diameter stone circle contains four sets of vertical stones—two sets aligned north-south, while the other pair is directed toward the summer solstice horizon. Alignments have also been found to the brightest stars in the night sky during the 5th millennium BCE including Arcturus, Sirius, Alpha Centauri, and Alnilam—one of three stars in the belt of the constellation of Orion. An east-west alignment has also been found between a megalithic structure and two stone megaliths about a mile away. Two other alignments were identified involving about a dozen additional stone monuments sited northeast, and southeast from the central megalithic complex.

Many of the megaliths at Nabta Playa are sculpted, appearing to have anthropomorphic form, suggesting they represented the dead. Elaborate burials have been found nearby, and the site seems to have been a "necropolis" or ancient cemetery. Malville notes the shaped stones and human and cattle burials face the *northern* region of the sky, revealing an early symbolic connection to the heavens. He points out that the northern circumpolar region of the sky was also associated with eternal life in pharaonic Egypt. During the summer and autumn seasons the stones would have been partially submerged in the lake, serving as ritual markers for the onset of the rainy season. Malville concludes these objects created a symbolic geometry that integrated the concepts of death, water, cattle, sun, and stars.⁸

Malville and others propose the Nabta Culture may have influenced the development of the culture of the pharaonic Egypt that built the first pyramids over a millennium later. The Egyptians practiced an astral religion, and like their predecessors from Nabta Playa venerated the constellation Orion and the circumpolar stars in burial rituals. Worship of cattle, first practiced at Nabta Playa would continue in Egypt with deities such as the cow-headed Hathor and the sacred bull Apis.

Nabta Playa was followed by other Neolithic cultures in Egypt, culminating in the Naqada Culture between 4,000-3,000 BCE. These people successfully developed agriculture, accumulating enough surplus wealth to support a class of artisans who perfected stone and metalworking techniques. Elite burials found at this time indicate an increasingly complex and hierarchical society. They contain wooden coffins and mummies with bodies wrapped in linen strips similar to later pharaonic mummies. Larger towns in Upper Egypt were becoming walled settlements and centers of craft production, having trading networks with Palestine, Syria and Mesopotamia. The first hieroglyphic writing began to appear at this time using ideographic and phonetic signs.[9]

The earliest dynasty of Egypt likely began with the reigns of the proto-dynastic king Narmer and his predecessor King Scorpion who united the two lands of Upper and Lower Egypt around 3,100 BCE. During the Early Dynastic period monumental arts and architecture developed to an unprecedented level, the earliest visual expression of the religion and rulership that would unify the land. It is a testament to the achievements of Egyptian civilization that it endured with only occasional interruptions of pharaonic rule for three millennia.

Gods & Cosmologies of Egypt

The religion and mythology of Egypt reflects its unique geography. Egypt is aptly called the "gift of the Nile" as the river is the only reliable source of water and irrigation in a narrow strip of habitable land bordered on either side by deserts. Egypt was named "Khemet" by the ancient Egyptians, literally meaning the "black land", referring to the dark alluvial soil found along the Nile. The Egyptians worshipped the Nile as the god Hapi, pictured as an androgynous figure with male body and female breasts, alluding to his nurturing nature. The river flooded yearly in a fairly predictable and benign manner, bringing rich and fertile silt for farming.

Egypt was also commonly called "The Two Lands" since its topography is distinctly dual. The Nile flows from south to north creating the long narrow valley of Upper Egypt and the broad marshy delta of Lower Egypt which empties into the Mediterranean Sea. The unification of the two lands was symbolized by the crown of the pharaoh which displayed both the vulture goddess Nekhebet of Upper Egypt, and the cobra goddess Edjo of Lower Egypt.

The Egyptians viewed their land as the reflection of the heavens. In the Greco-Egyptian text the *Corpus Hermeticum* it is written: "Egypt is an image of heaven...our land is the temple of the entire cosmos", expressing the belief that the microcosm of earth reflects the order of the heavens above.[10] The Egyptians saw their origins extending back to the mythic *Tep Zepi* or "first time"—the golden age when the gods lived upon the earth. Myths of the deities often had an astronomical dimension, based on observations of the heavenly bodies. The vault of the heavens was personified by the goddess Nut, depicted as a woman arched forward over the sky with hands and feet touching the horizon. Her arms and legs were imagined as the four pillars of the sky, her hands and feet touching the four cardinal directions on the horizon. In some depictions, Nut's body is spangled with stars. Modern astronomers speculate her image may have originated in the phenomenon of the Milky Way galaxy spanning the pre-dawn sky, which can be imagined as a giant figure stretched across the heavens.[11] Nut was the daughter of Shu, god of air, and Tefnut, goddess of moisture. Her grandfather was Ra, the sun-god, the creator of the universe and the first of the gods according to the Heliopolitan cosmogony, one of several Egyptian creation myths.

The earth was believed to be flat and personified by Geb, the god of earth. He laid beneath his wife Nut, goddess of the heavens, with an erect phallus impregnating her. Ra, fearing the usurpation of his own power, was said to have placed a curse on Nut to stop her from giving birth on the 360 days of the Egyptian calendar. Nut's father Shu, stood beneath her, holding the couple apart, interrupting their embrace. By separating heaven and earth, the world was thus created. The god Thoth came to Nut's aid and won five extra days of the year on which she was able to bear the deities Osiris and Isis, Horus the Elder, Set and Nephthys. This myth explains the Egyptian calendar which consisted of twelve months of thirty days—360 days total—onto which five extra "epagomenal" days were added at the end of each year.

In one of his myths, the sun god Ra journeyed each day through the heavens in his solar barque and was swallowed by Nut each evening. He traveled through her body at night—to be reborn from her womb the next morning. In his daily journey across the sky Ra assumed different forms: in the morning upon rising he was Khepri the scarab beetle, at his height at noon he became Ra the hawk, and at his setting he was Atum, often pictured as a feeble old man with the head of a ram leaning on his staff. Ra was thought to transform into twelve different forms during his daily journey—one for each hour of the day. There were also twelve hours of the night, each associated with regions of the *duat* or underworld through which Ra's sun-barque journeyed, before he emerged on the eastern horizon at dawn.[12]

Egyptian astronomical texts mention many gods and goddesses of the night sky, including planetary and stellar deities. The northern circumpolar stars were known as the "imperishable ones", symbolizing the idea of eternity as they were visible each night, never setting. The Egyptians called the constellation Ursa Major the "Leg of Set", and Draco, the "Hippopotamus". The severed leg of the god Set, torn off by Horus in battle with him and flung to the stars, was believed to give life to the dead.

The planets were called "the stars that know no rest", represented as deities who sailed across the heavens in their own barques, moving against the background of the fixed stars. Venus was known as the "god of the morning", and mercury as "Sebegu" possibly a form of Set. Mars was called "Horus the red", jupiter was "Horus who limits the Two Lands", while saturn was known as "Horus bull of the heavens".[13]

The Calendar/ Decans & Month Gods

By the Middle Kingdom (2,000-1,700 BCE) calendars were constructed that divided the sky into 36 decans or star groups, imagined as "star gods". These stars appearred to consecutively rise on the eastern horizon during each daily rotation of the earth, one decan ascending every forty minutes of modern time. Each decan's rising at night marked the beginning of a decan hour and was used as a form of star clock. A different decan star-group rose "heliacally", visible just before sunrise, every ten days throughout the year. This ten day period corresponded to one Egyptian week, with three weeks equalling one month. The Egyptians were the first to establish the length of the solar year which they divided into twelve months. From the time of the New Kingdom, they associated each of these months with a god, celebrating their festivals and making offerings to them on the first day of their month.[14]

Although the Egyptians practiced their own form of astrology based on the decans, the *zodiac* was unknown in early Egypt. It was imported by the Greeks from Mesopotamia during the Ptolemaic era, third century BCE, when the Egyptian twelve month-gods became associated with the zodiacal signs. The Greek historian Herodotus wrote: "each month and each day belongs to one of the gods." The best known Egyptian example of a zodiac is the Dendera Zodiac (50 BCE), carved on the ceiling of the Temple of Hathor in Dendera. It is surrounded by a circle of 36 decans, with the inner circle showing the familiar zodiacal signs imported from Babylonia. Although the zodiac was not native to Egypt, astrology as we know it took root and thrived in the fertile soil of Hellenistic Egypt with the writings of Ptolemy and other Greco-Egyptian astrologers who will be discussed later.

Heka- God of Magic

In ancient Egypt there was no word for "religion"–its closest approximation was the word *heka*, meaning magical power. Heka literally means "the activating of the *ka*", the spiritual "double" or life-force within the human body which survives it after death, as well as the vital force shared by mankind and the gods. It is the universal life energy and creative force circulating through spiritual and physical worlds which makes creation possible, every act of magic continuing this process.[15] Thus magic preceded the creation of the gods and was believed to be even more powerful than them. In the *Pyramid Texts* the power of magic is extolled: "The sky quivers, the earth quakes before me, for I am a magician, I possess magic."

Heka was personified as the god of magic and associated with the power of the written and spoken word, as well as medicine and healing. He accompanied the sun-god Ra on his barque during its daily journey through the heavens, along with the gods Sia (divine perception) and Hu (divine speech). Heka was depicted as a man holding two serpents crossed over his chest. His female equivalent was the goddess Weret Hekau, meaning "great of magic" or the "great enchantress" who was often represented in the form of a cobra. Egyptian magicians in their ceremonies carried bronze staffs, possibly associated with her powers.[16]

Summoning Heka

Egyptian magicians summoned the power of *heka* through the use of sacred words, images, and rituals, according to Jeremy Naydler.[17] Using the principle of sympathy—"like affecting like"—they attempted to influence the course of the cosmos through magic, circumventing ordinary laws of cause and effect. All things on earth were believed to be linked to their divine archetypes, therefore by using the names and images of the gods—the *neters*—they could be persuaded to assist the magician in accomplishing his goals. The spoken word was believed to manifest that which existed on spiritual causal levels, especially when uttered with intention and proper intonation. Words gave life to the things they represented, exemplified by the god Tehuti, or Thoth—who spoke the words which created the heavens and earth.

Hieroglyphs—*medju neter*—meaning "the word of god", were also believed to be inherently magical since they possessed the indwelling presence of the gods they represented.[18] They were used in temple inscriptions, spells on tomb walls, coffins and monuments. The writing of hieroglyphs was considered a magical act. Hieroglyphic signs and images of gods were also used for practical magic, sometimes drawn in ink on the skin of a person for healing or protection.

Written amulets were also used for healing, inscribed on a piece of papyrus then hung around a patient's neck, or worn on the afflicted part of the body. In Graeco-Egyptian magic, some spells were written in myrrh-based ink, which was washed off and the mixture swallowed, a practice which survives in Arabic magic to this day.

Magical statuary was an essential part of the religious and magical practices of ancient Egypt. Cult-images of the gods were placed in the innermost chambers of temples and cared for by "oracle priests" who presented them with food and incense several times a day, clothing them in the morning and sealing their chambers in the evening. This was essential as the *ba* or soul of the patron god was believed to inhabit its statue. During important festivals cult-statues were removed from their shrines and carried in processions where the public consulted them as oracles, and in some cases they were put on boats and sailed along the Nile.

Statues also served as guardian figures, such as those of the dancing dwarf god Bes, placed around temples and households to protect during childbirth and ward off demons and bad luck. Bes can be traced back to pre-dynastic times and his cult is thought to have originated in present day Sudan. Curiously, as recently as the last century, an ugly dancing dwarf was said by the people of Luxor to haunt the ruins of the temple of Karnak, according to Geraldine Pinch.[19] The four sons of Horus were represented in Canopic jars placed in tombs, which guarded the internal organs of the deceased. Tombs contained numerous *ushabti*—magical figurines of otherworldly servants—made from materials such as clay, wax, dough or stone. These were animated by magical spells for the purpose of waiting on the needs of the deceased in the afterlife. Wax figures were frequently used by magicians for spells. The practice of making wax models of enemies of the state and then destroying them, thereby holding the forces of chaos at bay, was common in Egyptian temples.

Egyptian magicians performed spells of magical transformation into the gods, identifying with them for the purpose of acquiring their power—similar to the shaman's practice of shapeshifting into their helping-spirits. In the *Egyptian Book of the Dead*, spells of transformation into hawks, phoenix birds, the Eye of Horus and various deities are recorded. One of these reads: "I am a horned snake, long of years/lying down, born every day..." [20] A similar technique known as the "assumption of god-forms" is practiced by modern ritual magicians. This involves visualizing oneself in the form of a particular deity and assuming its identity and magical power. By doing so, the magician aspires to an altered state of consciousness in which he or she can merge with the deity's power, while still maintaining conscious control. Naydler points out that many of the ritualized poses depicted in Egyptian artwork transformed the priest-magician into a human hieroglyph—an icon of the god—causing the divinity's *heka* to manifest in them.[21]

Deities such as Thoth, Isis, and Sekhmet were considered great magicians, but by the power of *heka* the human magician could coerce even the gods. Egyptian magical spells sometimes plead with or command a god to carry out the magician's desires, even threatening them with punishment if their demands are not met. This was not due to irreverence or disrespect for the gods, but was rather based on an understanding of the symbiotic relationship of the divine and human worlds. The deities were sustained by the worship, rituals, and offerings of the magician, just as his well-being was dependent on their benevolence.

Pharaoh As Arch-Magician & Shaman

The Egyptian king, also known as the pharaoh, served as political and religious leader of the land. He was responsible for maintaining the rule of *ma'at*—cosmic harmony and order—and defeating the powers of chaos. Considered a living god and the incarnation of Horus the divine ruler, he assumed the title of *netjer nefer*—"junior god". Historian Jaromir Malek writes:

> "For the people of Egypt, their king was a guarantor of the continued orderly running of their world: the regular change of the seasons, the return of the annual inundation of the Nile, and the predictable movements of the heavenly bodies, but also the safety from the threatening forces of nature as well as enemies outside Egypt's borders. The king's efficacy in fulfilling these responsibilities was therefore of paramount importance for the well-being of every Egyptian".[22]

The pharaoh was in fact believed to be the greatest magician in the land, serving as mediator between the spiritual world and his people, similar to the tribal shaman. The Egyptian concept of the god-king was derived from the prehistoric African "rain-maker" who kept his people and their animals in good health, in the opinion of Egyptologist Cyril Aldred.[23] Like the rain-making shaman, the pharaoh was believed to sustain the fertility of the land through his magical control of the annual Nile flood, upon which all life depended. Rain-maker kings and queens have existed into modern times in the Sudan as well as in South Africa. They are responsible for bringing rain in times of drought, as well as maintaining social harmony, similar to the role shamans play in indigenous cultures.

The pharaoh was also the high priest of all state sanctioned temples. His duties included the building and maintenance of temples as well as the performance of religious rites. One of the most important of these was the *Heb-Sed Festival*, a kind of jubilee usually celebrated after thirty years of the king's reign, and every three years thereafter. It is thought to have originated in predynastic times and was first recorded during the Old Kingdom. The central episode of the festival was the ritualized death and rebirth of the king, and his revitalization which assured continued harmony between him and the universe.

During this festival, statues of the gods were brought from all over Egypt, representing the diverse energies of the land. The king visited the statues in their shrines, engaging in ritual communion with them. He then went on to perform the "sed dance", demonstrating his vitality by running around a large courtyard between sets of hoops and cairns symbolically representing the boundaries of his kingdom. Following this, a coronation was celebrated in which the king was crowned with the white and red crowns of Upper and Lower Egypt. By doing so, he symbolically united the two lands as well as embodied the energies of the gods Osiris and Horus within his being.

Naydler proposes that by participation in these magical rites the king united not only the physical but the spiritual realms together, assuring the fertility of the entire land.[24] He points out the similarities of the Sed Festival with the Akitu Festival performed by Babylonian kings, also performed to assure the fertility of the kingdom. According to him, the shaman's role was paralleled in ancient Egypt by the king, who similarly acted as mediator between the divine and human worlds. Naydler writes: "Such important shamanic themes as the initiatory death and dismemberment followed by rebirth and renewal, the transformation of the shaman into a power animal, the ecstatic ascent to the sky, and the crossing of the threshold of death in order to commune with the ancestors and gods are all to be found in the Pyramid Texts..." [25]

The *Pyramid texts* date back to the Old Kingdom around 2,400-2,300 BCE. These were inscribed on the walls of pyramids and sarcophagi, and are among the world's oldest religious texts. He insists these so-called "funerary texts" were also used by *living* kings, and chronicle many of the secret magical rites performed by them during the Sed festival. [26]

Following the public ceremonies, the king undertook a solitary initiatory ordeal which some experts have proposed occurred in a chamber inside the pyramids. There, he apparently laid on a bed or in a sarcophagus, entering a state of deep trance. This resulted in the awakening of his *ba* or subtle body by means of which he entered the otherworld or *duat* in visionary consciousness, according to Naydler. The *ba* was depicted as a human-headed bird, and possibly in this form the king ascended in vision to the sun-god Ra in the heavens, where he was reborn as a star. A passage of the *Pyramid Texts* describes the pharaoh's celestial ascent: "...I will ascend to the sky to you, Ra, for my face is that of falcons, my wings are those of ducks...O men, I fly away from you." [27] Needless to say this passage bears a striking resemblance to the shaman's visionary ascent through the heavens, often facilitated by shape-shifting into a helping spirit such as a bird for similar purposes of communing with the Supreme deity and celestial gods.

The last native pharaoh of Egypt, Nectanebo II, ruled from 360-342 BCE. He was reputed to be a great magician who read the stars, interpreted omens, and controlled kings of foreign lands through magic. The ancient Greek writer Pseudo-Callisthenes chronicles Nectanebo's legendary magic which he used to protect his kingdom when threatened by invasion:

> "...he retired into a certain chamber, and having brought forth a bowl which he kept for the purpose, he filled it with water, and then, having made wax figures of the ships and men of the enemy, and also of his own men and ships, he set them upon the water in the bowl, his men on one side, and those of the enemy on the other. He then came out, and having put on the cloak of an Egyptian prophet and taken an ebony rod in his hand, he returned into the chamber, and uttering words of power he invoked the gods who help men to work magic, and the winds, and the subterranean demons, which straightway came to his aid. By their means the figures of the men in wax sprang into life and began to fight, and the ships of wax began to move about likewise; but the figures which represented his own men vanquished those which represented the enemy, and as the figures of the ships and men of the hostile fleet sank through the water to the bottom of the bowl, even so did the real ships and men sink through the waters to the bottom of the sea."

For a few years Nectanebo successfully kept Egypt safe from his enemies. He was ultimately defeated by combined Persian and Greek forces in the Battle of Pelusium in 342 BCE. [28]

Priests & Priestesses

The pharaoh could not be present at all ceremonies around the land, so priests acted as his surrogates, performing ritual functions at the temples. As the priesthood grew in size it became more hierarchical in structure, with priests specializing in various sacerdotal roles. Some of the most important duties were those of the "oracle priests" who cared for the statues of the gods in their shrines. Geraldine Pinch writes: "The daily liturgy was designed to persuade deities to manifest themselves in the statues kept in the holy of holies and to bestow blessings on king, people and country." [29] It was the duty of the "priests of the hour" to calculate the hours of the day and night based on observations of sun and stars, determining the times for temple rituals.[30] The "astrologer priests" were custodians of the mythic calendar. The "lector" priests were scribes who copied magical texts and royal decrees, and recited incantations and hymns during temple rituals.

Except for a few senior resident priests, most priests rotated their duties and were assigned to the temple for one month, three times a year. They lived the rest of their lives as laymen in the community. During their temple service they upheld strict standards of ascetic purity and cleanliness, bathing four times a day, shaving all the hair of their body, and abstaining from eating certain types of meat and fish. They wore only linen clothing as wool was considered unclean. They also practiced sexual abstinence during the period of their temple duties. Neoplatonic philosopher Porphyry describes the daily routine of the Egyptian priests:

> "...they divided the night into observation of the celestial bodies and sometimes devoted a part of it to offices of purification; and they distributed the day into the worship of the gods, according to which they celebrated them with hymns, thrice of four times, viz. in the morning and evening, when the sun is at his meridian altitude, and when he is declining to the west. The rest of their time they devoted to arithmetical and geometrical speculations...In winter nights also they were occupied in the same employments, being vigilantly engaged in literary pursuits..." [31]

During the Old Kingdom, many women served as priestesses in temples. At Thebes, the chief-priestess of Amun had the title of "God's Wife" and served as ceremonial consort of the god, exceeding even the power of the high priest. She led the female musicians who were regarded as the "god's harem", identified with Hathor, goddess of love and music. Beginning with the twenty-third dynasty priestesses gained great power, their worship focusing on Isis and other deities. According to Geraldine Pinch, it is possible some women even played the role of goddesses in temples. For example, in the late first millennium BCE a pair of young twin sisters were paid to perform the roles of the sister goddesses, Isis and Nephthys, in the funerary rites of the sacred Apis bull in Memphis.[32] Hatshepsut (1508-1458 BCE) the daughter of Thutmose I, was a successful and powerful pharaoh who wore a pharaoh's ceremonial beard and impersonated a man during her reign. Egyptologist James Henry Breasted wrote that she was "the first great woman in history of whom we are informed."

Temples of Heaven

The name for "temple" in ancient Egyptian is *hwt-ntr* or "mansion of the gods", and the deities were believed to literally dwell in their temples. These were oriented to the rising and setting of certain heavenly bodies associated with their patron deities. The laying out of the temple axis was performed by the pharaoh himself for more important temples in the "Stretching of the Cord" ceremony. He did this by stretching a string in the direction of the heavenly body to which the temple was dedicated as it ascended on the horizon.

Nineteenth century astronomer Norman Lockyer surveyed a number of Egyptian temples and found their axes aligned to solar, lunar, and stellar risings and settings. He writes that due to their alignment, rays of light from the heavenly bodies on certain days of the year would penetrate down the axis of the temple into the innermost sanctuary in which the statue of the deity was kept, illuminating it.[33] Lockyer notes that due to the gradual shift in the rising position of the stars on the horizon due to the astronomical phenomenon known as the "precession of the equinoxes", temples were rebuilt after a few hundred years—slightly shifting their axes to re-align with the new stellar positions. Lockyer discusses the calendrical uses of the temples: "....a temple oriented in this manner truly to a solstice was a scientific instrument of very high precision, as by it the length of the year could be determined with the greatest possible accuracy..." [34]

Recent statistical surveys by archaeoastronomers M. Shaltout and J. A. Belmonte have confirmed Lockyer's theory that temples were aligned to significant astronomical events. They found many were oriented to *winter solstice sunrise* and a few to the heliacal rising of the stars Sirius and Canopus. As mentioned earlier, the megalithic site of Nabta Playa also had alignments oriented towards Sirius and Canopus, and the orientation of Egyptian temples towards those same stars may point to a continuity of astro-ceremonial traditions. Shaltout and Belmonte also found the majority of Egyptian temples were also sited perpendicularly to the course of the Nile which was visible from the temples entrances; this linked them symbolically to both the Nile and the heavens.[35] The frequent orientation of temples to winter solstice sunrise reveals the centrality of the sun in Egyptian religion which celebrated the rebirth of the sun-god at this time of year.

In ancient Egypt the lay public was not allowed within the temple, but they came to the outer walls to pray, give offerings and seek oracles from the gods. Many temples provided buildings where pilgrims slept in hopes of contacting the gods in dreams through the practice known as "dream incubation", which will be discussed later. Most Egyptian temples had *seven doorways* leading from the exterior courtyard to the inner sanctum.[36] The chambers, each separated by a doorway, became progressively smaller and darker as one entered deeper into the heart of the temple. This would have led to an experience of heightened awareness and awe as one moved from the noisy outside world to the inner silence and cavernous darkness of the innermost shrine where the god dwelled. Naydler points out the parallels between entering the Egyptian temple and the journey through the underworld, in which the soul of the deceased was believed to pass through a number of pylons or doorways before finally arriving in the presence of the god Osiris.[37]

Magicians of the House of Life

Attached to the larger temples was the *Per-Ankh*, the "House of Life", which was the temple's library. Here texts were kept and studied by magician-priests called *kher-heb* or "lector priests". These were learned scribes who determined the texts to be written on temple walls, clarified religious texts, wrote magical spells, and maintained the temple's collection of magical papyri. The lector priests recited incantations and hymns during temple and state rituals and were closely associated with magical practices, as well as being skilled dream interpreters.[38] Laymen would come to the House of Life if they needed a spell or amulet, to have dreams interpreted, to cure illness, or seek protection from malign influences of sorcerers, demons or ghosts.[39] There funerary texts such as the "books of the dead" were composed, as well as medical texts for magically curing diseases. On a wall of the House of Life in the Temple of Edfu the following list of magical books are recorded:

The Book of Appeasing Sekhmet, The Book of Magical Protection of the King in his Place, Spells for Warding Off the Evil Eye, The Book of Repelling Crocodiles, The Book of Knowledge of Secrets of the Laboratory, The Book of Knowing the Secret Forms of the God.[40]

The House of Life was also a center of esoteric training where initiations into "various degrees of symbolic death and rebirth" were experienced, according to Naydler.[41] He insists that by studying the "books of the dead" there, the student could undergo a course of spiritual development involving a visionary journey to the underworld; during this they acquainted themselves with the deities and understood their natures. Familiarity with the underworld was essential knowledge for the magician-priest, and mastery of its energies was necessary on the path of spiritual attainment. The *Egyptian Book of the Dead* will be discussed later as it is essential to understanding the shamanistic dimensions of Egyptian magic.[42]

The Magician's Box

When not serving in the temples, lector priests "moonlighted" as magicians in the community, according to Egyptologist Robert Kriech Ritner. The best evidence of their practices comes from the discovery of a shaft burial known as the Ramasseum Tomb or the "Magician's Tomb" dating from the Late Middle Kingdom (1773-1650 BCE). In it was found a "magician's box" containing twenty-three papyri, reed pens, and broken knives. Along with these are an assortment of beads, amulets, a bronze cobra or *uraeus* serpent as well as several female figurines. The image of a jackal, associated with the god Anubis, is sketched on the lid of the box identifying the owner of the box as an official who had access to cultic mysteries, according to Ritner.[43]

The papyri are mostly magical, consisting of hymns and rituals. Others are magico-medical, as well as literary in nature. The beads and amulets were likely used for healing and protection, while the knives were intended to magically protect infants from demons. The figurines were of protective deities, and one of these is a doll-like figure of a lion-headed woman with articulated arms holding a serpent in each hand. The bronze cobra may have been used as a magic wand.

Ritner proposes the papyri and pens were probably used to write amuletic charms, while the literary texts imply the owner of the box combined the roles of storyteller and entertainer with that of magician.[44] These same arts—magic, storytelling and performance—have been practiced since time immemorial by tribal shamans as part of their communal healing ceremonies.

Magical Medicine

Egyptian magicians served the local community as healers in a manner similar to the Mesopotamian exorcist-magician or the tribal shaman—combating and exorcising the demons of illness. Sickness was believed to be caused by evil spirits, and physicians used rituals and magical spells as part of their cures. In one such spell for curing snakebite the magician created a small sculpture of the god Horus which he placed on the head of the patient, accompanied by this spell:

> "Flow out, poison! Scatter yourself on the ground! Horus curses you, he wipes you out! He grinds you underfoot!... You creep away, And you are not seen again. So speaks Horus the Great Magician!" [45]

There appears to have been more than superstition involved in these ancient healing practices. Modern medicine is rediscovering the power of the so-called "placebo effect" in which the patient's belief in the healing power of the physician has been proven to play a significant role in their recovery. Shamans in healing rituals induce altered states of consciousness in their patients through hypnosis, suggestion and guided imagery. Similar approaches were likely used by ancient Egyptian healer-magicians.

The priests of Sekhmet, the lion-headed goddess, often specialized in medicine. Sekhmet was also believed to bring plague and disease and had to be propitiated by her clergy. Selkhet, the scorpion goddess, also had her own magician-healers who specialized in curing the bites of scorpions and snakes.

Wise Women

The practice of magic in Egypt was not the exclusive right of male priests. Wise women known as *rekhet*, meaning "female knower", were consulted as seers and their clairvoyant abilities were apparently passed down through families. These women exercised powers similar to modern "mediums" and were able to predict the future as well as reveal which of the gods had placed a spell on a person, causing them misfortune. The *rekhet* also determined what the grievances of the dead were against the living and how they might be resolved, and could diagnose which evil spirit or deity was responsible for causing the illness of a sick child.

The goddess Isis, who is portrayed in myths as a great magician with healing powers, may have been a patron deity of the rekhet. On the 30th dynasty Metternich Stela, an inscription identifies Isis as a rekhet: "I am a daughter, a knowing one *(rht)* in her town, who dispels a poisonous snake with her oral powers. My father has taught me knowledge." [46] This suggests the rekhet also cured snakebite and practiced healing with magical incantations.

Letters to the Dead

The soul of the deceased—their *ba*—was believed to journey to the underworld where it faced numerous ordeals. If it survived these it became an *akh*, a transfigured spirit. Families made regular offerings to their ancestors who had become *akhu,* praying to them almost as if they were gods. Later, however, akh became a general term for demon. Another Egyptian word for the dead, *mut,* nearly always seems to refer to jealous and dangerous ghosts. There seems to have been a widespread belief that the dead were jealous of the living.[47] The *mut* was a ghost who could not, or chose not to enter the proper realm of the dead. Perhaps they died violently, or too young, or they may not have received appropriate funeral rites. It was assumed the spirits could cause discord in the home by making people bad tempered and quarrelsome. Many spells promised protection against the dead who might try to inflict harm on the living.

Egyptians also wrote "letters to the dead"—deceased family members—petitioning them to fight on their behalf against living persons as well as ghosts. Sometimes these letters were inscribed on bowls and vases and accompanied by offerings of food and drink. One such letter to a deceased relative reads: "Who then will pour out water for you [if you refuse to help us]."[48] The letters sometimes accused the dead of causing illness as well as emotional, physical, or even legal problems.

Demons of Egypt

Demons with foreign names derived from Semitic languages spoken in Syria and Palestine are common in Egyptian magical texts, and are known as *samana* demons. They were blamed for various kinds of sickness, fevers, and infectious diseases. A technique for dealing with demonic possession was to find a spirit powerful enough to drive the demon out, or negotiate with it. Along with demons are the *bau* of deities—their divine manifestations—which could also inflict harm. A person might offend a god and experience their displeasure as an illness or panic attack. Sometimes the gods might also send lesser deities or demons as their emissaries to carry out their commands on earth.

Magicians invoked bizarre composite entities to combat the bau.[49] One of the most notable of these was the god Tutu, known as "he who keeps enemies at a distance". He had a sphinx-like form consisting of the head of a man on a lion's body, as well as a cobra tail, and is sometimes depicted holding a knife which he brandished against demons. Tutu was considered the chief of the demons who could also harness their power. He was prayed to and given offerings to protect against bad dreams.

Shamanic Elements in Egyptian Magic

In Egyptian artwork, priests are depicted wearing leopard skin robes. According to Egyptologist Wolfgang Helk, the earliest Egyptian magician was the *s(t)m* priest who practiced shamanic trance and wore a leopard skin to facilitate shape-shifting into animals during visionary journeys to the spirit-world.[50] Only as rituals later became codified in writing was the inspired shaman replaced by the literate lector-priest. Pinch supports this idea, writing: "As the written word gained in prestige, the dramatic and intuitive rites of the shamans would have been replaced by standard rituals, whose form and content were fixed in sacred books." [51]

Pinch agrees with Helk that the leopard skin worn by several categories of Egyptian priests could be a relic of earlier shamanistic rites. She refers to a legend in which Set, the brother and murderer of Osiris, turned himself into a panther after attacking Osiris's corpse. Anubis, the jackal headed god, captured and branded the panther, creating the leopard's spots and decreeing leopard skins should be worn by priests in memory of his victory over Set. Real or artificial leopard skins were worn by *sem* priests who officiated at funerals and by the high priest of Ra whose title was "Seer". The spotted coats of leopards were also associated with the starry night sky which was regarded as the realm of the dead in early periods of Egyptian history.

Another fascinating example of Egyptian magical ritual that may have retained elements of predynastic shamanism is presented by Egyptologist Greg Reeder.[52] During the funerary ritual known as the "Opening of the Mouth" a *sem*-priest known as the *tekenu* was shrouded in cloth while kneeling in the fetal position and pulled on a sledge by other priests into the tomb of the deceased. Reeder speculates that while his body was seemingly lifeless the *tekenu* entered a "deep, cataleptic trance-like dream state". During this time he travelled to the spirit-world and located the soul of the deceased before being awakened. Having achieved this, the next stage of the ritual could be performed.

The Opening of the Mouth Ceremony

The "Opening of the Mouth" ritual was based on the Osiris myth and used in funerary rites of the pharaohs, according to authors Robert Bauval and Adrian Gilbert. They propose this ceremony may have taken place within the chambers of the Great Pyramid.[53]

For a few decades researchers have speculated that the so-called "air shafts" leading from the King and Queen's chambers inside the pyramid to its exterior were oriented towards specific stars, and may have functioned symbolically as channels for the soul of the dead king. These stars include Orion and Sirius in the southern sky and the northern constellations of Ursa Major, Ursa Minor and Draco. Most significant are the shafts pointing to the position of Sirius associated with the goddess Isis, and the constellation Orion, linked with Osiris.[54]

Bauval and Gilbert propose the Opening of the Mouth ceremony began in the lower Queen's Chamber of the pyramid where the king's mummy was positioned in front of the shaft pointing towards Sirius. There, the deceased king—identified with the dead god Osiris—was symbolically revived by the goddess Isis, associated with Sirius. The king's son, playing the role of the god Horus, used various tools to touch the eyes and mouth of his father's mummy, magically restoring its sight and speech, enabling it to eat and drink in the afterlife. One of these tools was an adze made of meteoric iron, formed in the shape of the constellation Ursa Major, which linked it with the concept of immortality. Through this ritual act the *ka* or spiritual life force of the dead king was believed to reawaken. The mummy was next taken up to the King's Chamber and placed in front of the shaft oriented to the stars of Orion, associated with the resurrected Osiris.[55] This prepared the king for his magical ascent to the heavens—his destination being the constellation Orion—where it was believed he would dwell as a star throughout eternity. In the *Pyramid Texts* it is written:

> "Behold he has become Orion...O king, the sky conceives you with Orion, the dawn bears you with Orion...you will regularly ascend with Orion from the eastern region of the sky, you will regularly descend with Orion in the western region of the sky".[56]

The Soul in Ancient Egypt

The Egyptians believed in an immortal soul, a complex entity consisting of multiple parts. These included the *khat*—the physical body, the *ab*—or heart, *ren*—the name, *ka*—the life force, *khaibit*—the shadow, *ba*—the soul which inhabits both earthly and heavenly realms, *sahu*—the spirit body, and *akh*—the "shining one" or eternal spirit. The bird shaped ba image by which the deceased journeyed in the afterlife is frequently depicted in Egyptian tombs. As mentioned previously, the shamanic cultures of Siberia also believed humans possessed multiple souls—from three to seven souls in different accounts; like the Egyptians, they pictured one of these as a bird. Similar to Egyptian belief, some of these souls were thought to be immortal, while others perished upon death.

Egyptian esoteric practices seem to have involved the cultivation of these parts of the soul through magical rituals and visionary journeying to the otherworld, known as the *duat*.

Training for the Afterlife

The Book of Coming Forth into Day, commonly called the *Egyptian Book of the*

Dead, as well as other texts such as the *Coffin Texts* and *Pyramid Texts,* served as guidebooks for the soul's afterlife journey. The majority of Egyptologists assume these texts are funerary in nature and only intended to be buried with the dead in their tombs.

Naydler argues they were also meant to aid the *living* in experiencing elevated levels of spiritual consciousness in preparation for the afterlife.[57] He claims the ancient Egyptians practiced highly charged rituals in which the initiate experienced the afterlife state—crossing the threshold of death while still alive—leading to spiritual rebirth. Pinch notes the magical and shamanistic qualities of these texts: "Some of the Pyramid Texts do have a visionary and ecstatic quality, giving an impression that they are records of journeys into a spirit world...when spoken, or more likely, chanted aloud, the many repetitious passages would have had an almost hypnotic effect." [58] It will be recalled that during their initiations, shamans experienced visions of death and the afterlife, and in more severe ordeals may have suffered something similar to the "near-death experience".

Plato, the great Greek philosopher, taught that philosophy is the practice of "learning to die". It is significant that he studied in Egypt, suggesting some of his ideas may have been influenced by the mystery teachings of Egypt.

The Books of the Dead

We previously looked at the *Pyramid Texts* as initiatory narratives. These chronicled the king's visionary journey during which his *ba*-soul ascended to reunite with the sun-god Re. Among the oldest literature in Egypt, the *Pyramid Texts* were originally inscribed on the interior walls of the pyramids of Cheops, Chephren, and Mykerinos and intended exclusively for the use of the pharaoh. Pinch writes that these funerary texts developed from even older shamanistic traditions: "There could have been a long period of oral transmission before this. It has been suggested that the earliest Egyptian rulers were advised by shamans and that some funerary texts could have developed out of their rites".[59] As previously mentioned, the visionary journey of the *tekenu* in the tomb to retrieve the soul of the deceased may have been a survival of an archaic shamanic funerary rite.

In the *Book of Amduat,* dated to the Middle Kingdom, the nightly journey of the sun through the netherworld is recorded. Sailing in his barque, the sun-god Re entered into the western gate of the underworld at dusk. In the midst of his journey during the seventh hour of night he confronted the demonic serpent Apep, who threatened his very existence. Emerging victoriously from the struggle Re merged with Osiris, king of the dead, and was magically reborn.

The Tree of Visions

The sun's daily resurrection and rising at dawn offered the promise of rebirth and immortality to the Egyptian initiate. Historian Edwin F. Wente writes about the use of these texts by the living: "Identification with high deities such as Re allowed the individual to share in divine processes of renewal even before death".[60] Originally the texts were exclusive to the pharaoh, but by the Middle Kingdom they were made available to an elite group of scribes and temple officials. Eventually with the rise of the cult of Osiris, immortality was "democratized" and the promise of eternal life offered to humble followers.

The various books of the dead describe the surreal topography of the underworld—its marshes, lakes of fire, caverns and pylon gates. The journey through that realm was hazardous and filled with obstacles along the way, requiring knowledge of many magical spells to enlist the help of the gods. These included incantations to subdue monsters and demons as well as the names of fearsome gatekeepers who needed to be addressed before they permitted the traveller to continue on their way. The ordeals and trials finally culminated in the soul's judgement and rebirth in the presence of Osiris, god of the dead. There are many parallels here to the shaman's journey to the underworld, with similar themes of dismemberment of the soul, its magical transformations, and rebirth.

The *Papyrus of Ani* is a version of the *Egyptian Book of the Dead* written for Ani, a royal scribe, around 1275 BCE. In this text the underworld journey begins with the "Opening of the Door of the Tomb", during which the *ba* soul of the deceased is released. The soul then sets out towards the horizon through a region known as Re-stau, the place of many paths. It is advised to seek out Anubis, the jackal-headed god known as The Opener of the Ways as a guide. The initial experience of entering into the underworld is one of darkness and hopelessness, in which the soul realizes the familiar sights and comforts of earthly life have vanished. The soul of Ani laments:

> "What manner of land is this into which I have come?
> It hath not water, it hath not air; it is deep unfathomable,
> it is black as the blackest night, and men wander helplessly therein.
> In it a man may not live in quietness of heart; not the longings
> of love be satisfied therein."

In his despair, Ani invokes Atum, god of the First Time, receiving reassurance from him that his spiritual needs will be met, and he shall live eternally:

> "But let the state of the shining ones

be given unto me for water and for air
and for the satisfying of the lovings of love,
and let quietness of heart be given to me
for bread and for ale....
How long then have I to live?
It is decreed that thou shalt live
for millions of millions of years,
a life of millions of years." [61]

The underworld journey was often envisioned as a voyage through a watery region of bogs, swamps and burning rivers. Boats were the preferred means of transport, sometimes rowed by a ferryman named Mahaf whose name means "he who sees behind him", who bears a distinct resemblance to Osiris. The element of *water*, universal to most myths of the underworld, represents purification and the transitional state that has to be crossed by the soul in order to attain a higher level of consciousness. This transition was also symbolized by a rope ladder or staircase by which the soul could ascend to the stars. Themes of crossing over water with boats and climbing ladders also occur in shamanic narratives of the underworld journey, as previously mentioned.

Beneath the waters lurked the dreaded evil serpent Apep, as well as other monsters who threatened to devour the traveler. Naydler explains that the underworld is primarily a psychic experience where the soul exteriorizes its contents, finding itself in environments which reflect its present state:

> "Just as in a dream one finds oneself in situations and contexts that reflect one's own inner state, so in the Underworld what is presented to one as an external environment is but a reflection of one's own psychic energies... Progress through the Underworld consists in a gradual purging of the *ba* of all those elements in it that are spiritually disharmonious. In this way, the "outer" environment in which it finds itself gradually changes and becomes less threatening or ugly, and more beautiful and pacific".[62]

Holger Kalweit similarly interprets the underworld experience described in shamanic narratives:

> "The structure of the Land of the Dead would thus seem to be the structure of our consciousness. Mental discipline and knowledge of the mechanisms of mental projections are the first principle of orientation; otherwise we get lost in the images of pseudo material realities we have conjured up,

and in consequence have to pass through the torments of hell. It therefore depends on the psychic maturity attained during one's lifetime whether the entry into the Beyond causes us pain or transforms us into a blissful state". [63]

Various wild animals such as crocodiles, serpents, and pigs were confronted in this underworld purgatory, in which the soul experienced projections of its own bestial and unregenerate elements as in a dream. The following is a spell recited to repel the serpent Apep, the personification of evil, by identifying oneself with Ra, the god of light:

"Get back! Crawl away!
Depart from me you snake!
Go and be drowned in the Waters of Nun,
at the place where your father
has commanded that you shall be slain.
Depart from the divine birth-place of Ra!
You tremble with fear,
for I am Ra at whom all tremble,
Get back you fiend, before the arrows of his light!
Ra has overthrown your words." [64]

In the *Payrus of Ani* there are twenty-one pylon gates in the underworld that must be passed through by the journeying soul. Each pylon has a doorkeeper who challenges its right to pass, threatening to burn it in fire or cut it into pieces. These guardians have terrifying names such as She Who Repeats Slaughter, Lady of the Knife Who Dances in Blood, and The Purifier of Sinners.[65] Ani is required to recite their names at each gate in order to gain passage. At the last gate he comes to the doorway guarded by Anubis, the guide of souls who initially led him into the underworld.

Ani now arrives at the Hall of Truth where he must recite the "negative confession". He addresses each of forty-two silent assessor gods in turn, denying any wrongdoing during his lifetime on earth, stating: "I have not done anything false...I have not robbed with violence...I have not borne false witness...I have done no harm..." Following this he recites a positive declaration of his good deeds: "I have appeased God by doing his will. I have given bread to the hungry, and water to the thirsty, clothes to the naked, and a boat to the shipwrecked. I have made offerings to the gods, and sacrificial meals to the Shining Ones...I am pure of mouth and pure of hands." [66]

Finally Ani undertakes the most important trial of all, the "balancing of the scales". Here his heart, emblematic of his conscience, is weighed in the balance against the feather of truth. The heart was believed to contain the record of the deceased's actions in life, and without it there was no memory or chance for eternal life. Thoth, the ibis-headed god of wisdom, witnesses this act, recording it on his writing palette, while Anubis tends the scales. If the heart weighs heavier than the feather, it might be devoured by the monster Ammit—part lion, crocodile, and hippopotamus who waits nearby. Thoth announces that Ani's heart has been found true, containing no wickedness, and he has done no harmful deeds. He is led into the presence of Osiris, ruler of the underworld and god of rebirth and regeneration. Osiris welcomes him into his kingdom as one of the "living ones"—the blessed dead.[67]

These pure souls were believed to live for eternity in the paradisiacal Fields of Reeds. This environment was envisioned as a place similar to one's abode during life, except there was no death, sickness or sorrow and all one's needs were provided for. A tomb inscription describes this place: "May I walk every day unceasing on the banks of my water, may my soul rest on the branches of the trees which I have planted, may I refresh myself in the shadow of my sycamore". Other accounts tell of souls joining Ra on his daily journey across the heavens in his Boat of Millions of Years.

The Myth of Osiris

The story of Osiris, focused around themes of death and resurrection, was one of Egypt's oldest and most beloved myths. Osiris's popularity increased through the centuries as he was associated with hopes of the soul's resurrection. As well as being the ruler of the land of the dead, he was also thought to have been the first king of Egypt. Egyptologist E.A.Wallis Budge writes: "Osiris became the great ancestor of all Egypt and was worshipped as such..." His myth is paraphrased as follows:

> Osiris was the son of Ra the sun-god and the sky goddess Nut. He grew up to become a wise and powerful king bringing civilization to his people, teaching them agriculture, animal husbandry, laws to live by and the worship of the gods. Egypt prospered under his wise rule.
>
> Set, the brother of Osiris, and god of desert and chaos was envious of him. He schemed against Osiris, devising a plot in secrecy with seventy-two other conspirators. He invited Osiris to a feast and set out a beautifully decorated box which he had made to fit the exact measurements of his body. Set offered it to anyone whom the box fit. One guest after another

tried to fit in the box until it was Osiris's turn. As he innocently laid in the box the conspirators slammed the lid it on it and nailed it closed, pouring molten lead on it to seal it tightly. Set threw the coffin into the Nile river and Osiris was never seen again.

When Isis heard of this she was grief stricken. She set out to find the body of her husband, knowing the dead could not rest until they had a proper funeral. She searched far and wide, finally learning that the coffin containing the corpse had floated out to sea, coming to shore in the land of Byblos. There it became lodged in a tamarisk tree which had miraculously grown to enclose it within its trunk. The king of Byblos cut down the tree and made it into a pillar in his palace.

Isis travelled there to recover her husband's body. Pretending to be a nurse she was invited to care for the queen's son. In secrecy each night she piled logs on a fire and held the boy over the flames. The queen eventually discovered this and was terrified, jumping up to save her child. Isis scolded her, revealing her true identity. She explained that she was tempering the child to be a god, but now his chances at immortality were lost. Telling the queen the true purpose of her visit, Isis asked to have the pillar in which the corpse of Osiris was hidden.

The queen granted her wish and Isis returned to Egypt with the pillar, cutting it open and exposing the coffin. Isis wept over her dead husband, joined by her sister Nephthys. She hid the coffin but to no avail. That night while out hunting Set found it, and enraged at the sight of Osiris he tore his corpse into fourteen pieces, scattering them throughout the land of Egypt. Isis learned of this and set out once again to find her husband's remains. She recovered all the pieces except for his phallus which had been swallowed by a fish. Instructed by the god Thoth, Isis used magic to reassemble the body of Osiris, resurrecting him briefly to life. She magically reconstituted his phallus, and hovering over his body in the form of a falcon was impregnated by him, giving birth to her son Horus.

Horus grew to manhood, and was it was decided by a tribunal of gods that he was the rightful heir of his father as king of the land. Set was unwilling accept this verdict and surrender the throne. Osiris appeared to Horus and urged him to avenge the evils committed by his brother. Horus challenged Set to a dual and a great battle ensued between the forces of good and evil. During the battle Horus lost his eye and Set lost his testicles. In this story good triumphs over evil, and some day Horus will be victorious and Osiris will return to rule the world of the living.

The Death & Resurrection of Osiris/Orion

The myth of Osiris has an astronomical dimension as well. The ancient Greek historian Plutarch comments that the Egyptians believed the story of Osiris's death and resurrection was enacted yearly in the heavens.[68] Osiris was associated with the constellation *Orion,* and Isis with the brilliant star *Sirius.* These two are in close proximity in the sky, forming a celestial couple.

Orion disappears from view every year from the spring equinox until mid-summer—since the sun transits through the area of the sky occupied by the constellation, causing it to disappear from sight. During this time it was believed Orion/Osiris had died and gone to live in the underworld. His absence coincided with the summer season of hot-dry southern winds which brought drought and sandstorms. These were believed to be caused by the evil god Set, god of the desert and brother and murderer of Osiris. During this season the Nile was also at its low ebb. Set was thought to rule the land until late summer until Isis, represented by the star Sirius, appeared again on the eastern horizon just before sunrise.

Sirius's heliacal rising coincided with the annual Nile floods that restored life and fertility to the land, and the Egyptian New Year was celebrated at this time. It's waters were believed to be caused by the tears of Isis weeping for her dead husband Osiris. Accompanying Sirius, however, the constellation Orion again became visible in the eastern sky before dawn— interpreted as Osiris resurrected and risen from the underworld.

Mysteries of Osiris & Isis

The mysteries of Osiris and Isis were popular annual ceremonies in ancient Egypt. Their mythos was celebrated with passion plays at Abydos, Osiris's cult center. They recalled the life, death, and rebirth of Osiris and lasted for many days. Leading roles were assigned to priests and high ranking members of the community. After the performances a mock battle was staged between the followers of Horus and Set. A procession also took place in which statues of Osiris, made from precious metals, were carried from the temple and set up in public places where people could gaze on the image of Osiris "The Beautiful One".[69]

Osiris was also worshipped in festivals such as the "Fall of the Nile" held when the river's waters receded from flooding. During this time worshippers went to the river bank to give gifts and display their grief over the death of Osiris. When the Nile began to flood again they held another festival honoring him. Priests poured sweet water into the river, declaring "Osiris Is Found!" Osiris as fertility god was connected with the annual flood upon which all life depended. The myth of Osiris, his early association with agriculture, and his death and resurrection symbolized the seasonal cycle of growth of the crops. The fourteen parts that Osiris's corpse was torn into by Set may refer to the days of the moon's waxing, since the moon, like Osiris was associated with growth and moisture.

The living pharaoh of Egypt was identified with Horus, and his deceased father with Osiris. As king of the underworld, Osiris was responsible for the judgement and rebirth of all souls. In fact "Osiris" became a title for all deceased souls. The relationship between Horus and Osiris exemplified the close relationship felt by Egyptians between the living and their departed ancestors, with the understanding that from the invisible realm of death emerges life and renewal. Through the myth of Osiris, the ancient worshipper was able to identify with the immortal god within their own being—the part of their spirit which was resurrected in eternity.

The Osiris myth shares symbolic parallels with the shaman's initiation. Historian Gloria Emeagwali writes: "This motif of death and resurrection resembles elements of shamanic initiation in north Asia and elsewhere: ritual dismemberment of the initiate's body and subsequent rebirth as a fully fledged shaman." [70]

The mysteries of Osiris, Isis, and Horus may have been the model of initiation rites in the ancient Mediterranean world, according to Masonic historian Albert Pike. He notes that ancient writers believed the mystery religions of Attis and Cybele celebrated in Phrygia, Demeter and Persephone at Eleusis and elsewhere, were copies of the mysteries of Osiris and Isis. Pike writes that the deities were also seen as equivalent: "the Ceres of the Greeks was the same as the Isis of the Egyptians and Dionysos or Bacchus was the same as Osiris." [71]

The Osiris myth has endured in traditions of modern western esotericism as well, serving as the prototype of initiation rites where candidates undergo a symbolic death, burial and raising, which we will later explore.

Chapter 5 Notes

Anubis weighing the heart. Papyrus of Ani 1250 BCE.

1. Shaw, Ian. *The Oxford History of Ancient Egypt*. 2000: 17.
2. Bauval, Robert & Brophy, Thomas. *Black Genesis- The Prehistoric Origins of Ancient Egypt*. 2011:167.
3. Ibid.: 2011:97.
4. Barta, Miroslav, Frouz, Martin. *Swimmers in the Sand*. 2010:48.
5. Budge, E.A.Wallis. *Osiris and the Egyptian Resurrection*, vol. 1. 1911: 361-383.
6. Malville J.McK, Wendorf, R., Schild, F. & Brenner, R. *"Astronomy of Nabta Playa"*. African Skies, no. 11. July 2007.
7. Shaw, Ian. *The Oxford History of Ancient Egypt*. 2000: 30.
8. Malville J.McK, Wendorf, R., Schild, F. & Brenner, R. "Astronomy of Nabta Playa." 2007.
9. Shaw. *The Oxford History of Ancient Egypt*. 2000: 50.
10. *Asclepius III, 24 b*.
11. Wilkinson, Richard H. *The Complete Gods and Goddesses of Ancient Egypt*. Wilkinson 2003:161. Curiously the "Great Rift" of the Milky Way, where it divides in two could be seen to resemble the legs and womb of Nut, from which the sun-god emerged every day. (Collins 2014:110)
12. Naydler, Jeremy. *Temple of the Cosmos*. 1996:64-65.
13. Wilkinson. *The Complete Gods and Goddesses of Ancient Egypt*. 2003: 91.
14. The month gods in sequence are: Thy, Ptah, Hathor, Sekhmet, Min, Rkh-Wr, Rkh-Nds, Rnwtt, Khonsu, Khnnt-Khnty, Ipt and Re-Harakhty who finished the year. These included five gods, five goddesses and two hipopotami which sometimes were replaced by jackals.
15. Pinch, Geraldine. *Magic in Ancient Egypt*. 1994: 10.

16. Ibid.: 11.
17. Naydler. *Temple of the Cosmos*.1996: 139-146.
18. Uzdavinys, Algis. *Philosophy & Theurgy In Late Antiquity*. 2010: 215.
19. Pinch. *Magic in Ancient Egypt*. 1994 :171.
20. *Papyrus of Ani,* spell 87.
21. Naydler. *The Future of the Ancient World- Essays on the History of Consciousness*. 2009:144.
22. Malek, Jaromir. Shaw, Ian. (ed) *The Oxford History of Ancient Egypt*. 2000: 92.
23. Aldred, Cyril. *The Egyptians*. 1998: 69.
24. Naydler, Jeremy. *Shamanic Wisdom of the Pyramid Texts- The Mystical Tradition of Ancient Egypt*. 2005: 86-7.
25. Ibid.:15.
26. Ibid.
27. *Philosophy & Theurgy In Late Antiquity*. Uzdavinys 2010: 209.
28. Pinch. *Magic in Ancient Egypt*. 1994: 92.
29. Ibid.:1994: 18. The priests removed the god's statue from their chamber once or several times a year, adorned it with jewelry, then carried to the roof of the temple where it was exposed to the rays of the sun so that the *ba* of Ra could unite with it and energize it. (Uzdavinys 2010:190).
30. Brier, Bob. *Ancient Egyptian Magic*. 1981: 41.
31. Porphyry- *On Abstinence From Animal Food,* Book IV.
32. Pinch. *Magic in Ancient Egypt*. 1994: 57.
33. Lockyer, J. Norman. *The Dawn of Astronomy*. 1973: 155.
34. Ibid.:155.
35. Shaltout, M. & Belmonte, M. "Archeoastronomy of Egyptian Temples". *Academia. edu*. 2005: 9.
36. Johnston, Sarah Iles. (editor) *Religions of the Ancient World: A Guide*. 2004: 246.
37. Naydler. *Shamanic Wisdom of the Pyramid Texts- The Mystical Tradition of Ancient Egypt*. 2005: 252-254. The seven doors and chambers are probably based on cosmological symbolism, which occurs also in the seven steps of Mesopotamian ziggurats, which were associated with the seven sacred planets, as well as the seven gates of the underworld in the myth of Inanna's descent to the underworld.
38. Ritner, Robert Kriech. *The Mechanics of Ancient Egyptian Magical Practice*. 1993: 220.
39. Brier. *Ancient Egyptian Magic*. 1981: 44.
40. Ibid.:45.
41. Naydler. *Shamanic Wisdom of the Pyramid Texts- The Mystical Tradition of Ancient Egypt*. 2005: 131.
42. Ibid.:131.
43. Ritner. *The Mechanics of Ancient Egyptian Magical Practice*. 1993: 232.
44. Ibid.:231.
45. Naydler. *Temple of the Cosmos*. 1996: 160-61.
46. Brown, Carolyn-Graves. *Dancing For Hathor: Women in Ancient Egypt*. 2010:80.
47. Pinch. *Magic in Ancient Egypt*. 1994: 45.
48. Johnston. *Restless Dead*. 1999: 91.

49. Pinch. *Magic in Ancient Egypt*. 1994: 36.
50. Ibid.:103-108.
51. Ibid.: 51.
52. Reeder, Greg. "A Rite of Passage: The Enigmatic Tekenu in Ancient Egyptian Funerary Ritual". in *KMT: A Modern Journal of Ancient Egypt*, Reeder 1994.
53. Bauval, Robert; Gilbert, Adrian. *The Orion Mystery*. 1994:210.
54. Ibid.:267.
55. Ibid.:210.
56. Ibid.:89.
57. Naydler. *Shamanic Wisdom of the Pyramid Texts- The Mystical Tradition of Ancient Egypt*. 2005: 48.
58. Pinch. *Magic in Ancient Egypt*. 1994: 51.
59. Ibid.: 51.
60. Johnston. *Religions of the Ancient World: A Guide*. 2004: 641.
61. Budge, E.A. Wallace. *The Egyptian Book of the Dead (The Papyrus of Ani) Egyptian Text Transliteration and Translation*. 1967: 342.
62. Naydler. *Temple of the Cosmos*. 1996: 228-229.
63. Kalweit. *Dreamtime & Inner Space: the world of the shaman*.1996: 64.
64. Naydler. *Temple of the Cosmos*.1988: 248.
65. Budge. *The Egyptian Book of the Dead*.1967: 298.
66. Ibid.: 205.
67. Ibid.: 183.
68. Plutarch. *Moralia* Vol.V.: 53.
69. Bunson, Margaret. *Encyclopedia of Ancient Egypt*. 2002: 290.
70. Walter, Mariko Namba; Fridman, Eva Jane Neumann, editors. *Shamanism: An Encyclopedia of World Beliefs, Practices and Culture*, Vol.1. 2004:907.
71. Pike. Albert. *Morals and Dogma*. 1949: 377.

Chapter 6: Megalithic Tombs & Sun Chariots
European Magic in the Neolithic & Bronze Ages

Trundholm Sun-Chariot. Bronze with gold. Denmark 1800-1600 BCE.

The earliest human inhabitants of Europe, known to archaeologists as the Aurignacian culture, arrived on the continent around 45,000 BCE during the Paleolithic era.[1] As previously discussed, these people left evidence of what seem to have been shamanistic practices in the form of cave paintings, carvings of figurines and other artifacts. Around 18,000- 9,600 BCE the climate of Europe began to warm, causing the ice-caps and glaciers which had covered most of the continent to melt. This drastically changed its geography, leading to higher sea levels which separated Britain, Ireland and Scandinavia from the mainland.[2] With climate change came the advance of forests and new animal species. Mammoths and wooly rhinos became extinct, replaced by smaller animals such as red deer, elk, reindeer, pigs, horses and aurochs.

The Mesolithic or "Middle Stone-Age" people who inhabited this warmer climate survived by hunting, trapping, and fishing, leading nomadic lifestyles. At Starr Carr in Yorkshire, archaeologists discovered remains of Britain's oldest structure dating from 8,700 BCE, as well as a number of deer skulls with horns attached. In one of these, eye holes were bored in the front of the skull, suggesting it may have been worn as a mask by shamans.[3]

During the following Neolithic period or "New Stone Age", caves continued to be used for communal rite of passage rituals, as well as by secret societies, according to archeologists Miranda and Stephen Alhouse-Green.[4] In caves such as the Grotta di Porto Badisco in Italy, dating from 5,000 BCE, rock paintings have been found depicting horned and bird-headed humans—similar to those found in Paleolithic cave paintings. Burials have been discovered from this period of apparently high status individuals who appear to have been shamans; placed along side them are animal effigies which possibly represent their animal-spirit helpers.[5] These authors note that archaeological evidence suggests a continuous transition of shamanic practices from the Paleolithic to the Neolithic period in Europe.

Old Europe and the Goddess Civilization

The settlement of Sesklo in central Greece, dated to around 6,850 BCE, gave its name to the earliest Neolithic culture in Europe, the first to use farming, domestication of livestock and pottery. A number of statuettes of pregnant women have been found at Sesklo suggesting they may have been used in a fertility cult. In excavations there, archaeologist Marija Gimbutas and colleagues found a temple containing a ceramic workshop and an altar on which were displayed figurines she describes as "bird goddesses" with hybrid human-bird features.[6]

Another early permanent settlement from around the same period was Lepenski Vir in the Iron Gorge in Serbia on the banks of the Danube river, dating from around 6,500 BCE. It consists of a village of well built houses and a larger structure which may have been used for communal religious rites. Fishing was important to the community's survival and carvings found on large boulders seem to represent hybrid human-fish creatures, suggesting shamanic beliefs. Burials were discovered with heads positioned to face downstream, implying the belief that souls traveled down the river to the afterlife.[7]

In the centuries to follow, several highly developed cultures based on agriculture and animal domestication arose in the Balkans and eastern Europe. One of these, the Vinca culture, flourished around 5,300-4,800 BCE in present day Serbia, Bulgaria, Romania, Macedonia and Greece. These people were the first to live in densely populated urban settlements, according to Gimbutas. These consisted of multi-room wooden houses arranged along streets, as well as temples of several stories. They produced ceramics, weaving, and copper metallurgy involving smelting and casting which they traded in networks reaching across southeast Europe.[8] The neighboring Varna Culture in Bulgaria was among the first in the world to produce gold objects. Numerous gold artifacts have been found in burials, probably intended as symbols of royal or spiritual power. The Cucuteni-Tripolye Culture spread from Romania and Moldova to the Ukraine, with settlements containing up to 1,500 dwellings inhabited by as many as 7,700 people.[9] Despite their size there is no sign of social stratification—this was apparently an egalitarian society.[10]

What is remarkable about these cultures is that some of them actually *predated* the Sumerians, challenging widely held theories of the origin of civilization in Mesopotamia. The Vinca culture produced symbols believed by some to be an early form of writing, in which characters may have served as religious and magical symbols, as well as script.[11] The Dispalo Tablet from Northern Greece dates to this period, predating Sumerian pictographic script, considered to be the world's oldest writing, by a thousand years.[12]

Gimbutas uses the term "Old Europe" to describe these Neolithic cultures, claiming they were homogeneous, peaceful and *matrifocal* societies. She argues that the people of Old Europe worshipped a great goddess who symbolized the cycle of birth, death and rebirth. Gimbutas's hypothesis of a matriarchal religion is based on her study of numerous clay and bone artifacts such as vases, statues, and figurines depicting females in different life stages—young, pregnant and old. She believes women headed clans or served as Queen-Priestesses, while men were hunters or builders, but the societies were "equaliterian", with neither gender dominating.

Religious traditions originating in Old European societies such as worship of animal-headed deities including snake and bird goddesses, votive offerings, as well as ritual dramas with masked participants, left a cultural legacy which Gimbutas insists was passed on to later European civilizations such as the Minoans, Myceneans and Greeks.[13]

Kurgan Warriors

According to Gimbutas, the peaceful matriarchal civilization of Old Europe was abruptly brought to an end by invasions of warriors from the Pontic-Caspian steppes north of the Black Sea in today's southern Russia and Ukraine. Gimbutas named her theory the "Kurgan Hypothesis" after these people's typical earthen burial mounds called "kurgans". She argues the Kurgans conquered the cultures of Old Europe, imposing their patriarchal values and Indo-European languages and religion on them.[14]

Recent research suggests however that a period of cold and drought afflicted Europe from 4,200 to 3,800 BCE, likely causing crop failures which could have afflicted Old European settlements, leaving them vulnerable to sporadic raids by the steppe peoples.[15] Some groups of Old Europeans probably assimilated with the newcomers adopting their language and culture, while others may have migrated south to the shores of the Aegean, the Cyclades islands and Crete, preserving elements of their culture there.[16]

The Kurgans, according to Gimbutas, emerged over several millennia from their homeland in the Caucasus. They expanded outward in several waves of migration between the 5th –3rd millennia BCE, establishing themselves across Europe, the Near East, India, and western China. All these groups spoke a *Proto-Indo-European* (PIE) mother tongue, the ancestor of the Celtic, Germanic, Italic, Greek, and Slavic languages.

Steppe Hypothesis

Building on the Kurgan theory is the "Steppe Hypothesis". It proposes there were mass migrations of pastoral nomads—known as the *Yamnaya Culture*—from their homeland in the Pontic-Caspian steppe to Europe around 2,500 BCE. Supporting this theory is recent genetic research revealing these people spread their DNA across a vast area from the Urals in Russia, to Europe as far north as Scandinavia, and eastward to Central Asia and the Altai region between Mongolia, China and Siberia.[17] The Yamnaya people rode horses to manage huge herds of sheep, following them across the steppes with wagons full of food and water. They also built massive funeral mounds, kurgans, in which they buried their dead. They carried with them their genes for pale skin, brown eyes, tall stature, and lactose tolerance which allowed them to consume dairy products. As well, they brought new Bronze Age technologies such as copper smelting, cattle herding and dairy farming and the use of wheeled vehicles. Geneticist Eske Willerslev insists the Yamnaya were a "high-tech culture" bringing new family structures, religion and burial customs, as well as the beginnings of cities to Europe.[18]

Researchers recently compared ancient DNA samples from the Yamnaya people with DNA from skeletons of the *Corded Ware* people who inhabited central and northern Europe from 2,900-2,350 BCE. They found they could trace 75% of Corded Ware ancestry to the Yanmaya newcomers. This suggests that most modern Europeans, who can trace some of their genes to the Corded Ware people, also are related to the Yamnaya people.[19]

Gimbutas identifies the Yamnaya as speakers of PIE languages, and the Corded Ware people are also thought to have disseminated Indo-European languages in Europe. To support this theory, researchers point out that many of these languages share words for objects such as axles, harness poles, and the wheel which were likely introduced by the Yamnaya migrants.[20]

Anatolian Farmers

Another prevailing theory of prehistoric European origins is the "Anatolian Hypothesis" of archaeologist Colin Renfrew, based on linguistic analysis combined with archaeology. Renfrew proposes migrating farmers from Anatolia brought Neolithic culture as well as their language which he calls "Archaic Proto-Indo-European" to Europe. He writes: "It seems likely that the first Indo-European languages came to Europe from Anatolia around 6,000 BC, together with the first domesticated plants and animals, and that they were in fact spoken by the first farmers of Europe." [21] By 3,000 BCE, farming practices had spread all over Europe. Anatolia, as previously discussed, was the location of early Neolithic settlements like Catalhoyuk, where pottery, the domestication of animals, and farming first developed. Renfrew's chronology suggests these early migrant farmers were contemporaneous with, and perhaps the same people as the goddess worshippers of Gimbutas's "Old Europe".

While recent genetic research supports Renfrew's theory of Anatolian origins of Neolithic populations in Europe, some experts dispute his assertion that they spoke a PIE language. Historian David W. Anthony argues they spoke an Afro-Asiatic language similar to those spoken in the Near-East—the same language family that generated Egyptian and Semitic languages.[22]

The migrations of these people to the Balkans may have been forced by over-exploitation of their lands through farming and grazing, as well as abrupt climate changes which brought hyper-arid conditions to Anatolia around 6,200 BCE, according to historian Jean Manco.[23]

Paleolithic Continuity Paradigm

The "Paleolithic Continuity Paradigm" is another current hypothesis based on linguistic and genetic evidence.[24] In contrast to the other theories presented here, it proposes *native European* origins of PIE languages, dating as far back as the Upper Paleolithic.[25] It suggests that at the end of the Late Glacial Maximum around 25,000 years ago, as the climate of Europe warmed the indigenous population expanded out of the Franco-Cantabrian refuge in France and Spain north and eastward, repopulating areas of the continent that were previously abandoned during the Ice Age.[26]

Millennia later, according to this scenario, small pioneering groups of Neolithic farmers from the Near-East moved into areas of Europe from the opposite direction, the southeast. At first the native hunter-gatherers entered into trading relationships with the newcomers, only later adopting practices of farming and livestock herding from them.[27] Based on the rate of genetic assimilation, it appears these two populations lived side by side for centuries.

In the beginning their interactions were probably based on mutually beneficial trading relationships, but with increasing numbers of farmers displacing indigenous groups they may have sporadically engaged in warfare.[28] This hypothesis argues for a gradual assimilation of Neolithic farming culture by the indigenous Europeans, taking centuries or even thousands of years in some areas. The two cultures probably had much in common, in fact Gimbutas insists that the hunter-gatherers and farmers shared the same religious beliefs and symbol systems.[29]

According to this theory there is no evidence of massive migrations displacing native populations—it argues instead that the Celts, Germans, Slavs and Baltic peoples have lived in areas close to their original homelands in Europe since the Paleolithic, speaking Indo-European languages since that time. This assumption is supported by research showing 70% of European genetic lineages date back to the Upper Paleolithic and the recolonization of Europe after the Last Glacial Maximum.[30]

Despite their different and contrasting conclusions, all of the above theories provide pieces of the puzzle of prehistoric European origins. From them we can conclude that three ancient populations: native hunter-gatherers, Anatolian farmers, and Pontic-Caspian pastoralists eventually interbred to create the gene-pool of modern Europeans. It becomes apparent that Europe down through the ages has been a melting pot of diverse peoples, cultures, and religions—the result of prehistoric migrations as well as diffusion of religious beliefs, ideologies and technologies.

Newgrange—Gateway to the Otherworld

The shift from the hunter-gatherer lifestyle to farming, known as the "Neolithic Revolution", was one of the truly momentous changes in history—leading to profound transformations in culture and religion. In Europe, as in the Near-East, the adoption of agriculture led to surpluses of wealth, population growth and increasingly complex societies with stratified social classes. Out of these emerged ruling elites—aristocracies who emphasized their ancestral lineage as a means of maintaining their high social status. This was reflected in religious beliefs such as ancestor worship and the building of monumental megalithic tombs.

In many shamanic cultures it is believed the seat of the soul resides in the bones from which both humans and animals will be resurrected, therefore bones are carefully gathered up and preserved.[31] Similarly in the funerary customs of Neolithic cultures corpses were first exposed to the elements and left to scavengers to remove the flesh. After this process was complete the bones of the ancestors were interred in communal tombs. This practice, known as "excarnation", has been found at Catalhoyuk in Anatolia, and may have occurred even earlier.

Commenting on megalithic funerary temples, Gimbutas writes: "The motivation behind these amazing structures appears to be the satisfaction of an obligation to the ancestors, alignment with the cosmos, and honoring of the goddess of birth, death, and regeneration".[32] She compares the passageway and chamber of these tombs to the symbolic birth canal and womb of the goddess of death and regeneration.

One of the most impressive examples of European megalithic tombs is at Newgrange, in the Boyne Valley of Ireland, built around 3,100 BC—over five hundred years before the construction of the pyramids of Egypt. Such structures may have been used as cave-like environments in which religious specialists such as shamans could contact the spirits of the ancestors in trance states. Archaeologist Mike Williams writes that many traditional peoples believed death has two stages: leaving the world of the living, then joining the world of the dead. Between these stages it was thought the souls of the recent dead were close by and could be communicated with by shamans. The most likely location for this contact would be in or near the megalithic tombs.[33]

It is likely the dark stone tombs, illumined by flickering lamp light, were seen as entrances to the underworld, similar to the caverns used by earlier Paleolithic peoples. David Lewis-Williams and David Pearce write that entering the dark tomb would have been similar to entering an underground cave.[34] They propose that in the chambers people could "experience both the vortex of the mind and the tunnel of the tomb", leading to altered states of consciousness. According to these authors the megalithic passage tombs facilitated a "visual, experiential dramatization of spiritual journeys". In fact, some Neolithic tombs have been found to have acoustic properties which enhance the sound of drumming, producing frequencies optimal for inducing trance states.[35] Supporting this theory are clay drums ranging from small to large in size which have been found in these sites.[36]

The discovery of opium residues and ceramic braziers in some Neolithic tombs also suggests that mind-altering substances may have sometimes been used during mortuary rituals by shamans to enhance communication with the ancestors, according to David Whitley.[37] The complex spiral engravings on stones at Newgrange and other megalithic sites resemble geometric "entopic" patterns of phosphenes seen before the eyes during the early stages of trance, as noted by Lewis-Williams.

Some megalithic tombs incorporate astronomical alignments, similar to the Egyptian temples previously discussed. The passageway of Newgrange is oriented to the direction of the rising sun during winter solstice. Archaeoastronomer C.L. Ruggles insists that rather than using the monument for practical purposes such as determining the calendar, the builders of Newgrange and similar megalithic structures were more interested in their ceremonial and symbolic use. He proposes the tombs expressed a symbolic association between the solstice sunlight and the deceased ancestors.[38] The ray of sunlight that illuminated the innermost chamber of Newgrange for only a few hours a year at winter solstice was perhaps believed to magically assist the ancestors in their rebirth.

Stonehenge & Durrington Walls—Temples of Life & Death

The Salisbury Plain in England, the location of Stonehenge, has been a center of ritual activities for at least 11,000 years according to recent geophysical surveys by archaeologists. During these, they discovered a three kilometer long "cursus", which they speculate may have been used for solar worship, and a massive timber burial structure they describe as a "house of the dead". In fact, Stonehenge is now thought to be among the most recent of a number of ritual structures built in the vicinity.[39]

Archaeological excavations at Stonehenge suggest the structure was built in several stages by successive cultures from 3,000-1,600 BCE, and was used as a funerary monument as well as an astronomical observatory. It was begun in the Neolithic period by the Windmill Hill people, semi-nomadic farmers who dug the surrounding ditch. The monolithic stones were raised in the following centuries by the Bell Beaker people, and the final stages finished by the so-called Wessex people.

Researchers have concluded that Stonehenge is *half* of a larger ceremonial complex—it is connected with the henge of Durrington Walls less than two miles away, situated on the Avon River which flows between it and Stonehenge. Durrington Walls is the largest Neolithic settlement discovered so far in Britain, and was also the largest in all of Europe around 4,500 years ago, according to archaeologist Mike Parker Pearson.[40]

The henge at Durrington Walls consists of a large circle of earthen banks and ditches which enclosed a ring with four concentric circles of huge timber posts known as a "woodhenge". Pearson, who excavated the site, writes that both Stonehenge and the neighboring woodhenge were..."virtually built from the same blueprint, one in wood and the other in stone."[41] The excavations have exposed a roadway paved with stone leading from the woodhenge to the

Avon River, similar to another road at Stonehenge. This suggests the two sites were linked together via the river. The evidence, according to Pearson, shows that the two monuments were complementary in symbolism and astronomical alignment: Stonehenge is aligned to the sunrise at summer solstice, and sunset at winter solstice, while Durrington Walls is its complementary opposite, oriented to sunrise at winter solstice, and the sunset at summer solstice. The *summer solstice sunrise* orientation of Stonehenge suggests a symbolic association with "death" as the sun begins its decline on the longest day of the year and the length of daylight hours begin to shorten. Likewise, the Durrington Walls alignment with *winter solstice sunrise* has a symbolic connection with "life" as the days begin to lengthen at this time as the sun begins its daily ascent higher in the sky, as if being reborn.

Archaeologist Mike Williams proposes the woodhenge may have been meant to be walked like a maze as part of a funerary ritual. He writes: "This was the place where people seasonally gathered at the solstices to feast and remember the dead, and on the morning of the solstice itself, to journey via the river and avenue to visit the stones themselves".[42] Pearson contends that Stonehenge with its durable stones was a memorial to the dead and their final resting place—while the wooden architecture of Durrington Walls symbolized the "transience of life". Bones of pigs and cattle as well as broken pottery are found in abundance at Durrington Walls, suggesting it was a site of ritual feasting. He conjectures that people from all over the region probably came there to celebrate and deposit the remains of their ancestors into the river for transport to the afterlife.

The two circular temples of life and death—Durrington Walls and Stonehenge—incorporated the features of the surrounding landscape into a ritualistic cosmology. They mirrored the circle of the horizon, as well as the paths of the heavenly bodies which circled above, serving as an *axis-mundi*, or center of the world. Gimbutas suggests they replicated a symbolic universe that honored the Old European goddess of death and regeneration.[43] According to her, time was seen in Old European cultures to move in cycles and regeneration immediately followed death. Upon burial, the dead entered the body of the goddess to be reborn.

As previously mentioned, ancient cultures around the world believed the souls of the dead travelled to the underworld along the course of rivers, and myths feature rivers which must be crossed by the dead during their afterlife journey. The builders of Stonehenge may have had a similar understanding of rivers as pathways of the dead to the afterlife, as the Avon river links Durrington Walls with the mortuary temple of Stonehenge.

Among these peoples the sun was seen as the giver of life and fertility, and also associated with death, regeneration and rebirth. During the winter solstice the sun itself was thought to be reborn. Gimbutas writes: "In northern countries, winter solstice marks the turning point between death of the natural world and its return to life." [44] This belief seems to have prevailed across the northern hemisphere. Native American peoples believed celebrations at that time were important for the survival and continuity of all life, and supernatural intervention by shaman-priests was needed to encourage the sun to ascend again in the sky.[45] Among the Chumash tribe of California, mourning ceremonies honoring the ancestors journey to the land of the dead occurred at winter solstice.

Similarly, the ceremonial centers of Stonehenge and Durrington Walls with their orientations to the solstices, celebrated the annual solar cycle which was symbolically associated with the human life cycle of birth, death and rebirth.

The Megalith Builders

The era of megalithic building reached its peak during the European Neolithic and early Bronze Age. There are also literally tens of thousands of megalithic structures such as chamber tombs, dolmens and stone circles which are distributed across the Near East, Eurasia, Asia, Africa, Australia, Micronesia and the Americas as well. Amazingly, many of these structures are so similar in design they are practically indistinguishable, despite being constructed half a world apart. In the opinion of author Frank Joseph, these monuments served as ceremonial centers as well as astronomical observatories for a Neolithic religion focused on the worship of the heavens, spread across the globe by prehistoric seafarers.[46]

So who built the megalithic monuments in Europe? Early *chamber tombs* such as Newgrange were likely constructed by communities of Neolithic farmers, perhaps as centers for ancestral cults as well as solar worship. During the following Bronze Age, there was an emphasis on building *stone-circles* oriented to astronomical alignments. Besides the obvious solar solstice orientations of Stonehenge, archaeoastronomers have discovered alignments to the 18.6 lunar Metonic cycle there and at other stone-circles. In Britain many of the stone-circles were probably raised by the so-called Bell Beaker people, Indo-European migrants from Iberia named after their distinctive bell shaped pottery. They may have used the sites for worshipping their sky-gods as well as determining the calendar. According to archaeologist Aubrey Burl, the large British stone-circles were likely used by local communities as places of worship during the winter and summer solstices, as well as centers for trading goods such as stone axes.[47]

Investigators like Frank Joseph and Paul Devereux point out that megalithic structures are often located over geological fault areas which generate natural "energy zones" of local electrical and magnetic fields. The seismic activity at these places exerts mechanical stress on the megaliths which contain a high percentage of quartz crystal, occasionally causing them to produce clouds of negative ions which glow in the dark, called 'fairy lights". These piezoelectrical phenomena have also been known to induce altered states of consciousness—modern visitors to the sites have reported experiences of euphoria and visions.[48]

The era of megalithic building came to an end during the late Bronze Age, when many of the monuments were abandoned and fell into disrepair. Ronald Hutton speculates about the demise of the cultures that built them in Britain: "...the Bronze Age suffered an ecological disaster profound enough to destroy faith in the traditional deities and rituals".[49] He conjectures this crisis may have been caused by climate change which brought cooler temperatures, as well as soil depleting farming practices and deforestation which turned large areas of land into bog and marsh useless for agriculture.

Enter the Proto-Indo-Europeans

As previously discussed, the Proto-Indo-Europeans migrated out of their homeland in the Caucasus, some spreading southwest into the Balkans to become the ancestors of the Thracians and Greeks, while others migrated north and west to establish the Celtic, Germanic, Baltic and Slavic speaking cultures; those who spread to the south-east founded the cultures of Armenia, Iran, and India, while those in the south became the Mittani of Syria and Hittites of Anatolia.

These various peoples likely did not mount large scale invasions, but originally migrated to new lands as a loose network of tribes, small clan groups and warrior bands. According to historian Christopher Beckwith, they probably first fought for their new neighbors as mercenaries, and only later seized control from them, intermarrying with local wives who spoke non-Indo-European languages. Within a generation or two local "creole" Indo-European daughter languages developed from which modern European languages descended—such as the Latin, German, Celtic and Slavic.[50]

Wherever they settled, Indo-Europeans practiced *patrilineal kinship*—descent through the male line. Their societies developed into *three castes* according to philologist George Dumezil: the ruler and his warriors comprising the aristocracy; a priestly caste involved in religious, legal, and ritual activities such as sacrificial rites; and commoners, the peasant farmers and producers of goods.[51] Each social group worshipped its own gods which represented its activities according to Dumezil. For example, in ancient Germanic cultures Odin was the patron of priests and magicians, Thor the god of warriors, and Freyr of farmers.[52]

The Sky Gods

A Proto-Indo-European myth tells of two brothers named Man and Twin who travelled through the cosmos accompanied by a great cow. In order to create the universe, Man with the help of the sky gods sacrificed his brother Twin, or in other accounts the cow. By doing so they created the wind, sun, moon, sea, earth, fire and finally humans. Man became the first priest whose primal sacrifice to the gods became the basis of the world's order.[53]

All Indo-European cultures worshipped celestial gods believed to dwell in the sky, as evidenced by similar root words related to "gods" or the "divine" such as *deva* in Vedic, *deus* in Latin, *tiwas* in Germanic, *dievas* in Latvian and *dia* in Old Irish. These were derived from the root word *diw/dyu* denoting the bright sky or light of day, according to M.L.West.[54] The majority of gods were male, reflecting the Indo-European patriarchal social structure.

The king of the gods, the all-knowing sky father, was paired with his wife mother earth, and intercourse between them brought forth herds, crops, and all life. Another important deity was the Sun-god, believed to daily travel across the sky in his chariot drawn by fiery steeds, or sometimes a boat; as an "all seeing" god he was associated with justice and oaths. Solar festivals—winter and summer solstices—were celebrated by Indo-European peoples. The Moon was personified as masculine, but played only a minor role in Indo-European myths according to West.[55] Other important celestial deities included the goddess of Dawn, gods of Thunder and Storm, and gods of fire, wind, and waters. The Divine Twins are prominent gods among the Indo-Europeans as seen in the foundation myth of Man and Twin. Paired gods such as the Roman Jupiter-Dius, the Germanic Odinn-Tyr and Indian Varuna-Mitra are expressions of Indo-European dualism, in the opinion of J.P. Mallory.[56] Since the Proto-Indo-Europeans were primarily herders, cattle and horses were revered in myths, as well as ritual sacrifices.

Besides the heavenly deities, the earth was believed to be inhabited by a plethora of nature gods and spirits similar to those found in later Greek, Germanic, Roman and Celtic myths such as nymphs, satyrs, fauns, gnomes, elves, dwarves and giants. Myths tell of liasons and marriages between nymphs and humans which produced royal dynasties. The oldest Indo-European holy places were situated near trees, groves, springs, and rivers. Public religious ceremonies were celebrated in groves of sacred trees.

The Indo-Europeans, like many ancient peoples, believed in an underworld land of the dead. Hades of the Greeks, Hel of the Germans, and Yama of the Indo-Aryans share similar features such as rivers which are crossed by the dead, and a house of the god of death with gates guarded by supernatural dogs. The dead, who were either buried or cremated, were believed to dwell with their fathers in the underworld. Leaders, warlords, and people of high social status were buried in pomp in "kurgans", pit graves covered by large earthen mounds.

The warrior ethos was paramount in Indo-European societies. During their initiation rites into manhood, boys joined a pack and were compared to "wolves", raiding the tribe's enemies or engaging in cattle raids. Warriors aspired to die gloriously in battle with the hopes of attaining post-mortem fame, their name extolled in poetry, epics and sagas. The ancient Indic hero Karna declares: "I choose fame on earth even at the cost of my life. The famous man attains to heaven, the inglorious man perishes". Mythic wars between the gods of heaven and earth appear as battles between the Olympic gods and Titans, the Aesir and Vanir of the Germans, and the Tuatha De Danann and Fomoire of Celtic myths. It is likely these myths reflect the conquests by the Indo-Europeans of the indigenous peoples whose lands they conquered.

Indo-European kings, as well as being war-leaders were remembered for their virtues of justice, liberality, and prosperity of rule. They maintained their prestige and power by sponsoring ostentatious sacrifices and feasts involving praise poetry, animal sacrifice and distribution of meat and mead.[57] The root word for "king" in Latin, *rego*, means "to draw straight, regulate, rule".[58] The king was thought to mediate between the human and divine worlds, and if he offended the divine powers it was believed misfortune would befall his kingdom and he could be deposed.

There are close parallels between the priestly classes in various Indo-European societies—the Celtic *druids*, the Roman *flamen* and Vedic *brahmans*, according to Isaac Bonewits.[59] Priests were the poets, musicians, historians, astronomers, judges and diviners of their societies. They led public ceremonies and were responsible for music, prayers, sacrifices, divination and other ritual duties. The Indo-European root word for magic is *mag(h)*, meaning "ability" or "power". This is likely related to the word *Magi*, the name of the hereditary priesthood of the Persian Medes who were court diviners, astrologers and magicians.

All Indo-European priesthoods specialized in the magical arts. These involved hymns, incantations, poetic invocations of the gods, spells for cursing and binding enemies, as well as healing using incantations and herbs. The number *nine* was believed to possess great magical power and words or actions were often repeated three or nine times in magical rituals.[60] Eliade notes that the myths and magical practices of the Indo-Europeans display numerous shamanic elements: ecstatic techniques, shapeshifting into animal helping spirits, communication with the dead, oracular seances, descent to the underworld, etc.[61] Some of these may have been absorbed by the Indo-Europeans from conquered native cultures who held shamanic beliefs.

Shamanic Influences

During their far-ranging migrations Proto-Indo-European groups spread as far east as the Altai mountains of Siberia, attracted by its rich pastoral land and metal resources. The earliest of these was the Afanasievo culture, late in the fourth millennium BCE, followed by the Andronovo culture in the second millennium. In the Altai region these groups encountered indigenous peoples who had practiced shamanism for millennia, absorbing their myths of a mythical golden "world mountain" as well as reverence for the constellation Ursa Major, according to Geoffrey Ashe. He argues that groups related to the Andronovo later migrated throughout the Near-East, India, and the Mediterranean, carrying these shamanic myths with them. Their descendents, or people who were closely related to them, were the Indo-Aryans who conquered the Indus Valley, as well as the Indo-Iranians who spread into the Near-East and the Levant.[62] Ashe traces the origins of the myth of the "Seven Rishis" or Seven Seers recorded in the *Rig-Vedas* of India, and the Seven Sages or Sebettu of Mesopotamia, to the Altaic myth of the "Seven Old Men" who were wise shamans associated with the seven stars of Ursa Major. He argues that these Proto-Indo-European groups spread the Altaic symbolism of the *number seven*, *Ursa Major*, as well as the *world mountain* motif to India, Mesopotamia, the Levant and Greece.

Eliade notes the similarities between the religious life and mythology of the Indo-Europeans and Proto-Turkic cultures of Central Asia, Mongolia and Siberia who practiced shamanism. Both groups were patriarchal societies, herders and hunter-gatherers who worshipped a sky-god and celestial spirits, revered fire and horses, and practiced ritual horse sacrifices.[63]

M.L.West suggests there was a diffusion of shamanistic motifs from the Finno-Ugric peoples of North Eurasia which influenced Indo-European gods of magic such as Lugh of the Celts, the Germanic god Odin, and Apollo of the the Greeks.[64] Finno-Ugric speakers include today's Hungarians, the Sami of Scandinavia and various Siberian populations. The Finno-Ugrians were neighbors of the Pontic steppe dwelling Proto-Indo-Europeans and in contact with them from the earliest times.

The linguistic roots of Indo-European languages retain references to shamanism according to Michael Winkelman who writes: "the many different meanings associated with the root*"sa"* point to shamanic origins." [65] As examples he notes that in Pali Sanskrit the word for religious specialist is *samana*. In the English language words such as "sacred", "sacrifice", and "saint" also contain the root *sa*, bearing related meanings to the word "shaman".

Metal Smiths & Magicians

The ancient Greek poet Hesiod compared the mythical "Ages of Man" to the metals. In the beginning was the paradisiacal Golden Age, followed by the Age of Silver, the Age of Bronze and finally the Age of Iron. The terms "Copper Age", "Bronze Age" and "Iron Age" are also used by archaeologists to describe the technological and cultural levels of ancient cultures, based on their mastery of metalworking along with advances such as writing, trade networks and urban civilization.

Bronze technology which requires smelting of copper and tin began in Sumeria around 3,500 BCE, and from there spread to Europe and Eurasia. Weapons and tools of bronze were stronger and easier to cast than copper. The rise of the Indo-European warrior societies coincided with the beginning of the Bronze Age (ca. 2,800-1,300 BCE) in Europe. Their aristocracies were dependent on advances such as weaponry, chariots, and luxury items made from bronze and other metals.

The religions of the Bronze Age emphasized feasting and ceremonies— including ostentatious burials of wealthy leaders in earthen barrows. In contrast to the predominantly communal burials of the earlier Neolithic peoples, Bronze Age burials place an emphasis on high status *individuals* and their survival in the otherworld. Interred with kings and warlords were their chariots, weapons, horses, and ritual objects. As a grisly reminder of their power, often their wives, slaves, or warriors were sacrificed and buried with them, meant to accompany them in the afterlife.[66]

Among the ritual objects found in burials are objects in gold and bronze associated with celestial themes and crafted by skilled metal smiths. An example of their refined artistry is the *Trundholm Sun-Chariot* unearthed in Denmark, featuring a golden sun-disk mounted on a bronze horse drawn wagon. Archaeologist Miranda Green speculates that the sculpture is probably a miniature replica of a chariot used in solar-cult processions and ceremonies— perhaps as an attempt to magically "woo the sun in winter".[67] The sun disk is gold-plated on one side and decorated with circles, rays and spirals, and mounted vertically on the wagon. One side is shining and the other side is dull and ungilded, likely representing the day and night aspects of the sun. The entire assembly is pulled by a slender horse. The wagon was deliberately broken before burial, a common practice for offerings to the gods, making them unfit for further secular use. The image of the sun-chariot is commonly found in Indo-European myths, such as the chariot of Helios, the Greek sun-god, who daily drove the sun in his chariot across the sky.

Another curious group of artifacts associated with the sun are Bronze Age "cauldrons on wheels". These vessels have an undercarriage of spoked wheels and often include sculptures of water birds sitting on the axles. Green proposes these were used in *weather magic* as symbolic vessels to attract, collect, or drive away rain and propitiate the sun.[68] The bronze disk known as the *Nebra Sky-Disk*, an instrument possibly used by ritual specialists, dates to 1,600 BCE. It shows the constellation Pleiades, as well as the sun, moon, and horizon, and may have been used to compute seasonal events associated with the farming year.

In Southern Sweden, Bronze Age rock carvings dating from around 1,800 BCE depict humans with bird beaks. The appearance of these half-human, half-animal figures suggests shamans dressed in animal costumes and engaged in performances to contact the spirit-world.[69]

Crete & the Goddess Religion

The Minoan civilization which flourished on the island of Crete from 2,700-1,500 BCE was named after the legendary King Minos of Greek myth by archaeologist Sir Arthur Evans. This remarkable culture was protected by the seas from Indo-European cultural influences spreading on the mainland of Europe at the time.

The Minoans were the first known literate civilization of Europe, though their Cretan hieroglyphic and Linear A scripts have yet to be deciphered. Linear A shares many signs in common with the Vinca script of Old Europe, and Minoan culture seems to have roots in earlier European Neolithic cultures, as well as in Anatolia and the Near-East. Historian Walter Burkert traces Minoan religious symbols such as the double axe and bull horns to Mesopotamia, and even back to the early Neolithic settlement of Catalhoyuk.[70] Gimbutas proposes these symbols originated in the Vinca culture of the Balkans.[71] She argues that the Minoans were the last remaining matrilineal civilization of Old Europe in which women wielded equal power with men and played the dominant role in religion. According to her, the matrifocal society of Minoan Crete flourished for some two thousand years after most other Old European cultures had been changed or destroyed through contact with the patriarchal Indo-Europeans.[72]

The Minoans were skilled mariners and merchants. Crete became a center of trade in tin, copper, gold, silver, and saffron between Egypt, the Near-East, Mycenae and Spain. Monumental structures described by most archaeologists as "palaces" arose on Crete. Gimbutas argues these buildings were more likely temple complexes. Towns and cities grew around them and at Knossos a city of 80,000 or more people thrived. The temples were centers of commerce, religious ceremony, and the arts, supporting specialists such as priests, scribes, painters, stone carvers, potters, bronze workers and jewelers. Archaeologists have unearthed many refined artworks such as murals and figurines—yet evidence of weapons as well as fortifications is lacking—suggesting the Minoans were a peaceful civilization.

The majority of Minoan art represents females, implying a goddess centered religion was practiced by the populace. The best known example of these are the figurines of bare-breasted young women whose arms are entwined with snakes, popularly known as "snake goddesses". They were perhaps associated with the powers of regeneration and used in domestic fertility cults. Frescoes in the palace of Knossos depict bull games in which both young female and male athletes somersault over the horns of bulls, suggesting Crete was a society in which women held equal status to men.

Cave, Mountain & Tree Sanctuaries

Crete contains a number of caves in which evidence of Bronze Age worship has been found including altars, votive offerings of figurines, as well as miniature double axes made from gold. In the Cave of Psychro, axes and swords were hung between stalactites in the lower grotto, while other offerings were thrown into pools of water. In the upper grotto, fragments of libation tables along with animal bones and ash have been found. This was a site of sacrificial feasts where animals were slaughtered and eaten. Homer's *Odyssey* mentions the Cave of Eileithyia, a goddess of childbirth near Knossos, which contains rock formations such as an oval elevation near the entrance reminiscent of a belly with navel. At the center of the cave is a stalagmite resembling a female figure which has been rubbed and polished smooth by hands of worshippers, and near it is an altar. One of these caves on Mt. Dikte was used long before the Greeks arrived to worship the mother goddess. Greek myth has it that in this cave the god Zeus was suckled by the goat-nymph Amaltheia.[73]

As well as caves, more than twenty mountain peak sanctuaries have been identified, such as the grave of Zeus on Mt. Yuktas near Knossos, where worship was performed. The peaks are marked with remains of votive terracotta figurines of animals such as cattle and sheep, as well as statuettes of men and women standing with arms raised as if worshipping. Remains of fires, lamps, and animal bones have been found suggesting night time celebrations where votives were thrown into the fire as offerings. Burkert proposes the peak cult may be associated with Near-Eastern traditions such as fire sacrifices for Canaanite gods such as Baal, which were also celebrated on mountain tops.[74]

Trees were also focal points of worship in Crete. Artwork depicts gatherings around large imposing trees set apart by an enclosure. Often olive and fig trees are shown along with altars and temple-like buildings nearby. A fresco in Knossos shows a large group of people beside a group of trees, including women with hands raised possibly in a gesture of worship.

Sacred Dance & Drama

Large circular tombs, known as *tholoi* appear in the early Minoan period. These served as burial places for entire clans over many generations, similar in function to the collective Neolithic barrow tombs of Northern Europe. Next to the tombs paved dancing grounds are laid out, suggesting these places were possibly cult centers and gathering places. Burkert speculates that a communion between the living and the souls of the dead occurred through dance at these tombs, during which the life force of the community was renewed.[75]

The significance of sacred dance in Crete is implied in Homer's *Illiad*, where a dancing place in Knossos built by king Daedelus for his daughter Ariadne is mentioned. Dancers are depicted in numerous examples of Cretan art, often as bare breasted women and occasionally men. In some images a figure appearing to be a goddess or god hovers in mid-air, prompting Burkert to write: "the most peculiar and characteristic feature of the Minoan experience of the divine is... the epiphany of the deity from above in the dance." [76] From this, one could infer that dance was used in magical rites for invoking the gods. Parallels could be drawn to the ecstatic dances of shamans calling upon their gods and helping-spirits. Along with dance, Gimbutas notes the occurrence of masked figures in Minoan art which imply religious liturgy and rituals with an emphasis on theatrical drama.[77] As previously mentioned, Gimbutas traces the use of masks and ritual dramas back to the Neolithic "goddess cultures" of Old Europe.

Minoan religious statuary usually depicts females, though occasionally a smaller male partner accompanies the goddess, reminiscent of vegetation gods such as Tammuz, found so frequently in the art of the Near-East. Images of a goddess holding a spear or sword, with a lion accompanying her have been found on seals, bearing a likeness to the Mesopotamian goddess Ishtar in her warrior aspect. Sculptures of the well known "snake goddesses" are found frequently in excavated house shrines. Many deities in Crete were probably never given human form, as evidenced by the number of mountain top, cave, and tree shrines. Until the alphabet of Linear A is deciphered, we can only conjecture about the pantheon of Cretan deities.

The End of the Minoans

The Cretan civilization flourished until 1,500 BCE when its palaces and towns were suddenly devastated by fire, earthquakes, or foreign invaders, leaving most of its sites abandoned. There is a strong possibility that the eruption of the volcano of Thera, one of the largest volcanic eruptions in history which destroyed the neighboring island of Santorini, may have also devastated Crete. Some have speculated this disaster was alluded to in Plato's myth of the end of Atlantis, the destruction of Minoan Crete being the inspiration for that fabled sunken civilization.

Crete was finally invaded by the Indo-European Mycenaeans from Greece who administered it for several centuries, absorbing much of its culture which they exported back to the mainland. Cretan culture was a formative influence on the emerging civilization of Greece, and referred to in several myths. In the well known myth of Theseus and the Minotaur, seven youths and seven maids were required to be sent from Athens as annual tribute to King Minos of Crete. There they were sacrificed to the minotaur, a monster with a human body and bull's head which lived in an underground labyrinth. Theseus, the Greek hero, rescues the victims and kills the Minotaur with the help of the king's daughter Ariadne, who gives him a spool of thread to help him retrace his path out of the labyrinth. Ariadne then leaves with Theseus to the island of Delos where they perform the Crane Dance in celebration, its spiraling steps said to re-enact the labyrinth journey. This dance was considered a mating ritual, symbolic of the cultural exchange between the Cretan and Greek cultures. As previously mentioned, evidence of a Crane Dance was found in Catalhoyuk in Anatolia where it also had fertility associations, suggesting a continuity of traditions down through the millennia.

According to author John Kraft, the myth of Theseus and the Minotaur may allegorize the conquest of the Minoan civilization by the Mycenaean Greeks, with Theseus deposing the bull-headed Minotaur, the totemic symbol of Crete.

Journey into the Labyrinth

The word "labyrinth" is derived from the Lydian word *"labrys"*, meaning "double-edged axe", a symbol of royal power used by Minoan priestesses for ceremonial purposes. Gimbutas claims the goddess symbolized by the double ax was worshipped at the Knossos temple complex which was associated with the labyrinth.[78]

Labyrinth patterns appear worldwide and are mentioned in Homer's *Iliad*, the Indian *Ramayana*, the *Old Testament* story of the conquest of Jericho, as well as the Greek myth of Theseus and Ariadne mentioned above. Labyrinths of identical design are found as widespread as Europe, India, and the American Southwest in Hopi and Navaho artwork. As previously mentioned, Geoffrey Ashe speculates the labyrinth pattern may have originally spread from a cultural "seedbed" in Paleolithic Siberia to Europe, Asia and North America.[79]

John Kraft believes the labyrinth and its associated myths originated in an ancient fertility cult rooted in the Bronze Age. He proposes that Ariadne, the Cretan princess who helped Theseus kill the Minotaur, was originally a goddess associated with Persephone, the queen of the dead. Like her, she was a vegetation goddess who died and was reborn yearly. The labyrinth can also be associated with the underworld in myths such as the *Descent of Inanna*, where that goddess enters into *seven* gates of the palace of her sister Erishkegal, queen of the dead. Likewise the classic Cretan Labyrinth pattern is based on seven concentric circuits.

Neolithic stone labyrinths in Sweden have their entrances in the west or north-west—the direction of spring sunset, according to Kraft.[80] He notes that among many ancient peoples *west* was the direction of death. Kraft proposes that a western entrance to the labyrinth would have made it easier for the sky-god to reach the underworld, where the earth-goddess was waiting for him. He presents examples of modern Swedish folk rituals where girls were rescued by boys from the middle of labyrinths. He writes: "every ancient community had a labyrinth which was used as an arena for a religious drama performed every spring, when people tried to imitate the vegetation-goddess standing in the center of the labyrinth and the sky-god trying to force his way through the windings to liberate her in a divine wedding securing fertility for the whole community".[81]

The Mycenaeans

The Mycenaeans were Indo-Europeans, arriving in Greece during the late Bronze Age around 1600-1100 BCE. During this period the Helladic culture of mainland Greece was heavily influenced by Minoan culture, and the Mycenaeans owed much of their culture to Crete including their architecture, art, and their alphabet of Linear B influenced by Cretan Linear A script. Unlike the Cretans, however, the Mycenaean's rise to power was based on military conquest rather than trade.

Historian Barry Cunliffe writes: "Mycenaean society was a world of warrior heroes- a world hauntingly echoed in Homer's Illiad".[82] Warriors are depicted in their wallpaintings, seals, and metalwork. Weapons and armor are prevalent, reflecting the militaristic trends in the rest of Europe at this time. The Mycenaean period was the setting for the epics of Homer and much of ancient Greek literature and myth.

Scholars have differing opinions as to the origins of the Greek gods and goddesses and their mythology. Burkert traces the Greek gods to the Mycenaeans but claims some myths such as the generations of the gods, the opposition of sky gods to earth gods, as well as Olympian sacrifices to the gods, originated in the Near-East.[83] M.L. West sees Zeus, the king of the gods, as the only Mycenaean god with clear Indo-European ancestry.[84] Gimbutas argues that despite their glorification of war and patriarchy, the Mycenaeans retained strong Old European beliefs inherited from the Minoan civilization—including many female deities which outnumber male gods.[85] She insists that formerly independent goddesses of earlier matriarchal cultures, while still fulfilling important roles, became subjected as wives and daughters to the new patriarchal gods of the Indo-European invaders. According to her, the Mycenaean religion was the "mother" of the Greek religion, and their pantheon included many deities later found in classical Greece: Poseidon, Apollo, Dionysos, Zeus, Hera, Hermes, Athena, Demeter and Persephone as well as others.[86]

Reflecting the changes in mythology and religious beliefs of this period, there was a dramatic shift from burials to *cremations* in most areas of Europe, beginning around 1,300 BCE. Bodies were burnt on pyres and ashes collected for burial, usually in cremation urns. These changes may have reflected the religious beliefs of Indo-Europeans who venerated sky gods. Cunliffe writes: "There may have been a major shift in belief systems that separated concepts of earth from concepts of sky".[88] Previously the body and material wealth of the deceased was buried in recognition of the earth's sustaining importance, but now the soul was freed into the heavens—to dwell in the realm of spirits believed to reside there.

Smiths, shamans & magicians of the Iron Age

The Iron Age began around 1,200—500 BCE in various locations around the ancient world. Along with changes in technology and the crafting of iron weapons and tools, the archaeological term "Iron Age" also characterizes changes in religion and the arts.

The craftsmen who forged iron—blacksmiths—earned the reputations of magicians and shamans, as they exercised magical powers of transforming metals and controlling spirits. In ancient cultures animistic beliefs were held—rare metallic objects were believed to possess souls. In Celtic myths special swords were revered as having their own personalities and life stories, and given names. Siberian shamans wear metal effigies crafted by smiths on their robes in which their helping-spirits are believed to reside.

Blacksmith shamans of Siberia known as *darkhan* were believed to associate with evil spirits similar to black shamans. Like them, they had hypnotic powers and performed extraordinary feats—healing, levitating, and magically inflicting injuries, according to Valentina Kharitonova.[89] Through their mastery of fire, smiths were believed to be able to handle molten iron and control demonic spirits. Shamans, like smiths, were also "masters of fire" possessing the power to handle fire, swallow burning coals and generate inner heat that allowed them to resist freezing temperatures. According to a proverb of the Yakuts of Siberia "smiths and shamans are from the same nest".[90]

Around the world from Africa to Europe smiths formed secret initiatory societies and were feared as well as respected for their powers according to Eliade.[91] In ancient Greece, a mysterious group of metalworkers and magicians known as the Dactyls, were credited with the invention of ironworking. It is believed they originated in Crete and Phrygia in central Turkey. They were associated with Hephaistos, the smith-god, and the metallurgical mysteries of Samothrace. Legend has it the Dactyls discovered music and used the ringing sounds of metal to magically influence daimons and spirits. Orpheus the famous musician, poet, and founder of mystery religions, was believed to have been initiated into their mysteries. Pythagoras, who also used music for healing, received initiation from the Dactyls in the Idean Cave in Crete. Along with metalworking, the Dactyls cured with magical formulae, consecrations, and mystery rites. They were also associated with the *goetes*—the necromantic magicians of ancient Greece who will be discussed later.

Rise of the Greeks

During the period between 1250-1150 BCE the entire economy and culture of the Near-East and Mediterranean collapsed, possibly due to climate change leading to a long arid period, as well as by attacks from a confederacy of naval marauders called the "Sea Peoples". These brought the Mycenaean civilization to an end, leading to the Dark Ages during which Greece and Crete reverted to illiteracy for several hundred years. All large-scale building ceased, as did the arts, effectively ending the Bronze Age in Greece. By 1,000 BCE Greece had recovered, emerging as a dominant force in Europe.

Greece of the Iron Age was a collection of separate city-states such as

The Tree of Visions

Athens, Argos, Corinth and others where the civic participation of free male citizens developed into the first democracies. Two literary giants arose around the years of 800-650 BCE—Homer and Hesiod—whose writings would lay the foundation of Greek literature and mythology. Homer wrote the *Illiad and Odyssey* about the abduction of Helen of Troy and the wars between Sparta and Troy which ensued; Homer in fact may have been the pseudonymous name of a group of poets, rather than a single individual. The poet Hesiod in his *Theogony* presented the ancient Greek creation story and myths of the Olympian gods. The works of these poets would serve as the creative source from which later poets would draw inspiration. They created the genealogy of the gods and provided them with their poetic epithets and forms by which they were known, according to Burkert.[92] Despite their brilliant innovations, Homer and Hesiod drew on ancient traditions. According to Gimbutas, Greek mythology and religion inherited many beliefs and cultic practices from the Mycenaeans, Minoans and Old Europeans. She also traces the origins of Greek comedy and tragedy with the use of masked actors to the liturgy and masked ritual dramas of these earlier cultures.[93]

During the 8th and 7th centuries BCE, thousands of Greeks migrated from their homeland and founded colonies, settling around the Black Sea, the west coast of Anatolia, and along the Mediterranean coasts, including Southern Italy.[94] The island of Miletos in the 6th century BCE became the home of a number of brilliant thinkers–including Thales, Anaximander, and Anaximenes who were the first mathematicians and astronomers of the Greek world. Pythagoras, the first man to call himself a philosopher or "lover of wisdom", was a native of the island of Samos, and the philosopher Heraclitus came from nearby Ephesus in Turkey.

The world of these early philosophers was vitalized by cultural contacts with peoples of the Near-East through trade made possible by sea-travel. As historians like Parpola and Burkert argue, the early Greeks were part of the sphere of Mesopotamian and Anatolian culture, and their science, religion, and philosophy during this period reflect those influences. We will discuss Pythagoras and the other early Greek philosophers later in the book, noting their debt to the esoteric traditions of the Near-East and Asia.

Among the most significant and enduring expressions of Greek spirituality, the Eleusinian Mysteries, may contain elements imported from foreign lands. Although this mystery religion arose in Eleusis near Athens, based on an indigenous Neolithic agricultural cult, it seems to have syncretized Minoan, Egyptian, and Thracian influences as well. Orpheus—who was influenced by shamanism—is believed to have brought his mystery religion from Thrace to

Greece.

Altaic Origins of Apollo & Artemis?

Two of the most beloved divinities of ancient Greece—Apollo and his twin sister Artemis—may have also originated in foreign lands where shamanism was practiced, according to Ashe. The ancient Greeks themselves believed Apollo's worship had been brought from Hyperboria, the mystical land beyond Boreas, the North-Wind. The location of Hyperboria was unknown, but several ancient historians placed it beyond the snowy Riphean Mountains in the north, possibly the Ural Mountains of today's Russia.[95]

Apollo displays several traits which are clearly shamanistic: he was associated with oracles and healing, and was said to have descended to the underworld where he received his divine powers. The number *seven* was sacred to him—his lyre had seven strings, he was worshipped on the seventh day of the month, and in his temple the maxims of the Seven Wise Men of Greece were inscribed. The symbolism of the number seven also plays a conspicuous role in the myths of the Siberian Altai, such as the "seven wise shamans" associated with the seven stars of Ursa Major.[96] Ashe conjectures that a northern "proto-Apollo", a shamanic deity, was worshipped in Eurasia, his cult spreading to Asia Minor and eventually Greece.[97] At his shrine in Delphi, Apollo possessed his oracle, who uttered prophecies while in an ecstatic state. He was worshipped by his devotees Orpheus, Pythagoras, Abaris and other mystics, who will later be discussed.

Artemis was the Greek goddess of the hunt, whom Ashe equates with the *mistress of animals*. He argues for her origin among the Indo-European migrants of the Eurasian steppes, who acquired her characteristics from exchanges with Uralic and Altaic peoples who practiced shamanism. They originally revered a mistress of animals associated with bear symbolism, female shamans, and the constellation Ursa Major. As previously mentioned, Artemis is associated with bear symbolism and Ursa Major, having placed her follower Callisto in the heavens as that constellation. Historian Carlo Ginzburg similarly views Artemis as the "lady of animals", tracing her bear cults in Europe back to the gods, myths and rituals of Siberian shamans.[98]

Artemis is often depicted holding two animals, while surrounded by pairs of other beasts, a motif which originated in the Neolithic, according to J.D. Hughes. He writes that she was seen as a defender of wildlife who was believed to punish hunters who killed animals cruelly or for objectionable reasons. Artemis as a goddess of wilderness was also associated with the conservation of nature, and thanks to belief in her, large areas of the ancient Greek landscape were preserved for many years, according to Hughes.[99]

Hermes — God of Magic

Hermes was the messenger of the gods as well as the god of magic. His name has a curious derivation, appropriate for a trickster deity associated with humor. It likely originated from the Greek word *herma* — designating a pile of stones set up to mark a territorial boundary, according to Burkert who writes: "Another form of territorial demarcation, older than man himself, is phallic display, which is then symbolically replaced by erected stones or stakes".[100] Burkert explains that in ancient Greece, phallic wooden figures were placed on top of stone cairns as territorial markers. These developed into square stone pillars with an erect phallus and bearded head carved on them, used to mark midway points between villages. This monument was called a "Hermes" and soon spread to every neighborhood in Athens where sacrifices were held at them. These territorial markers eventually became personified as the god Hermes, associated with boundaries and the founding of civilizations.

True to his character, Hermes became the god of paradoxical transgression of those boundaries as well — the "divine trickster" and thief. In one of his myths, the infant Hermes stole the cattle of his older brother Apollo and concealed all traces of his mischief, backtracking in his footsteps to his cradle. In compensation for his theft, Hermes gave Apollo his lyre which he invented from a tortoise shell.

As a god of boundaries, Hermes crosses between life and death, traveling between Olympus and Hades. He is the *psychopompos* or guide of the dead, leading souls to Hades and back again. It was he who fetched Persephone from the underworld, and escorted Eurydice back to Hades when Orpheus inadvertently turned around to glance at her. The Chthonic Hermes was invoked with libations to the dead, and graves were cared for by him. As divine messenger, Hermes was dispatched by his father Zeus, king of the gods, on various errands. During one of these he aided the hero Odysseus, giving to him the antidote to the bewitching drug Circe the sorceress had given his companions, changing them from animals back into their human form.

Hermes is represented in artwork wearing winged sandals and hat, bearing his magical staff, the *kerykeion* or caduceus which charms men into sleep or wakefulness, as he wills. He may have originally been a a serpent god, according to historian Jane Ellen Harrison, who regarded him as a humanized form of Agathos Daimon, the serpentine daimon of reincarnation.[101] Hermes's wand, consisting of two copulating serpents wrapped around a rod, may have originally derived from the staff of the Babylonian serpent god Ningishzida, a fertility deity with underworld associations. In fact, the goddess Ishtar is often depicted holding a double serpent staff in her right hand.[102]

Hermes was depicted until the 5th century BCE as a mature bearded man. Later he was represented as an athletic youth, the patron of the gymnasium and athletic games and competitions. Under his Roman name, Mercury, he became the god of commerce—the words "merchant" and "mercantile" derive from his name, and he was shown carrying a bulging money bag. The Greek historian Diodorus Siculus describes Hermes as a culture hero:

> "For this god was the first to bring language to perfection; he named many nameless things, invented the alphabet, and ordained ceremonies governing divine worship and sacrifices to the gods. He was the first to perceive order in the stars and to discern the nature and harmony of musical sounds...and he taught the greeks eloquence (hermeneia) which is why he is called Hermes.[103]

Like the shaman, Hermes travels by the power of magical flight through the heavens, earth and underworld. He mediates between the gods and mankind, assuming the role of divine messenger and psychopomp who guides the souls of the dead. Likewise he is the god of healing, magic, divination and oratory who brought the arts of civilization to mankind.

Divination & Oracles of Ancient Greece

Various types of divination arrived in Greece from the Near-East around the 8th -6th centuries BCE. The classical Greeks however attributed the origin of their divination practices to the god Prometheus whose name means "foresight". The myth of Prometheus tells how he stole fire from the gods in heaven to give to mankind, and was punished for his crime by being chained to a rock in Hades where raptors gnawed on his liver every day.

Robert Temple emphasizes the significance of divination in the ancient world:

> "It is not generally realized that divination was an important part of classical life and was practiced on a daily basis. We could even go so far as to say that the whole of classical civilization was based on divination as the foundation of all its actions. No major decision of state, such as going to war, was made without consulting the god through divination. Few undertakings, such a financial investment, getting married or making a journey, were embarked upon without divination. Even the great Socrates

consulted the Oracle at Delphi."[104]

Alexander the Great, who became the world's most powerful ruler during his brief meteoric career based some of his most important decisions on divination. Soon after his conquest of Egypt in 331 BCE, he and his army traveled across formidable deserts to consult the Oracle of Siwa in the Libyan desert. The oracle confirmed that he was indeed the son of the god Zeus-Ammon and the legitimate ruler of Egypt and all the lands he had recently conquered. Alexander was subsequently depicted on coins wearing the horns of Amun—the Egyptian ram-headed deity—confirming his god-like status as ruler of the Hellenistic world. A firm believer in oracles, Alexander relied on the advice of a Syrian medium who uttered prophecies during seizures that later turned out to be true. She accompanied him on his military campaigns and was granted access to him day and night, often standing over him while he slept, even saving his life once by warning him of an assassination attempt.[105] Alexander himself experienced "divine dreams" and his army was apparently saved from destruction when the god Dionysus appeared to him in a dream giving him the antidote to a poison used on the arrows of the enemy.[106]

In 323 BCE during his army's march to Babylon, Alexander was met by Chaldean astrologers who begged him not to enter the city through the western gate. They explained that their god Bel had cautioned them this would be a fatal mistake. According to the Greek historian Arrian of Nicodemia, Alexander took their warning very seriously. He rerouted his army to enter the city from the east but the terrain made it impossible for them to continue and they were forced to use the western gate instead. Arrian wrote: "The truth was that fate was leading him to the spot where it was already written that he should die..." Chaldean diviners performed a *haruspicy* at this time by sacrificing a sheep and examining its liver, finding it was missing a lobe. Upon hearing this omen Alexander became distraught, realizing it was an ominous sign. It proved to be the first of a chain of disastrous events culminating in his death from fever shortly thereafter.[107]

In ancient Greece, seers were consulted for divination. The word for seer in Greek is *mantis*, which historian Michael Flower interprets as "one who speaks from an altered state".[108] In the state of inspiration the *mantis* interpreted dreams, the movement and cries of birds, portents such as thunder, lightning, earthquakes, eclipses and unusual occurrences—similar to the shaman's divination by omens. The God Apollo possessed the sybil of the Oracle of Delphi while she prophesied, as well as the *iatromantes* or "healer prophets" who were similar to shamans, in the opinion of historian I. P. Couliano.[109]

The Greeks also knew of prophets called *oneirokritai*, who uttered prognostications while in a state of trance, induced by the god's presence within them. In the dramas of Sophocles and Euripides, religious visionaries are presented who are in constant rapport with the spirits, similar to shamans. The expertise of Greek seers went beyond divination, and included healing, purification, and understanding of the supernatural.

The blind seer and prophet Tiresias appears in several plays and other literature. Tiresias, a diviner of Zeus's will, was the resident *mantis* of Thebes. He received his gift of "second-sight" as compensation for being blinded by the goddess Hera, who was outraged by his claim that women enjoyed sex more than men. Teresias's opinion on the subject was sought because he himself had experienced a gender change, from male to female then back again. Discussing Tiresias, Miranda and Stephen Aldhouse-Green note that such "gender-bending" is a "shamanic marker" found across many times and cultures.[110] As previously mentioned, the transgender identification of Assyrian oracles, as well as some tribal shamans, set them apart from others as chosen by the gods.

The experience of the numinous was widespread in ancient Greece. Prudence Jones and Nigel Pennick write: "Gods and goddesses appeared to individual people in dreams and on shamanistic flights of inner vision; they appeared to whole armies and crowds in visions; and from earliest times there were established oracles at permanent sanctuaries, staffed by professional seers".[111] The Oracle of Zeus at Dodona was founded by an Egyptian missionary priestess around the eighth century BCE. She selected a single oak tree which stood in a clearing with a spring at its base. Three elderly priestesses known as "doves" entered into a state of ecstasy and prophesied there, listening to the rustling of the leaves and clanging of metal objects hung from the tree's branches. The Oracle of Apollo in Miletus also grew up around a spring where a priestess sat on an *axon* or axle, symbolizing the *axis-mundi* or world center. Sitting with her feet in the waters of the spring she breathed its vapors and fell into a trance before speaking oracles.

Delphi

The famous Oracle of Delphi had origins in prehistoric times as the site of worship of Gaia, the earth mother. Some legends claim it was founded by the Hyperboreans whose associations with Eurasian shamanism, as well as the god Apollo, have been previously mentioned. Delphi became dedicated to Apollo, god of oracles and prophecies, after he killed Python the dragon who lived there protecting the earth's navel or *omphalos*, the symbolic center of Greece. At Delphi the seeress was known as the "Pythia", who called herself "the wife of Apollo".[112] She sat on a tripod over a fissure in the earth into which the body of Python was believed to have fallen after being slain; the fumes that arose there were thought to emanate from the serpent's decaying flesh. Legend has it the Pythia inhaled those vapors and fell into a trance during which Apollo possessed her spirit.

Similar to the shaman's possession by his or her helping spirits, the prophetesses of Apollo were not merely passive to the god, since they never totally lost individual control while in trance.[113] One scientific theory conjectures that the subterranean fumes the Pythia breathed may have contained ethylene, used until recently in surgery as an anesthetic, which could have contributed to their altered stated of mind. In her ecstasy the Pythia uttered enigmatic prophecies which were "translated" by priests of the temple into hexameters of verse and conveyed to the questioner.

The fame of the Delphic Oracle was widespread in the ancient world and the Pythia was consulted before major state decisions such as going to war or founding new colonies. The philosopher Heraclitus discusses the Pythia, who "with raving mouth...reaches over a thousand years...by force of the god".[114]

Dream Incubation of Asklepios

The practice of dream incubation, widely practiced in the ancient world, was also used in ancient Greece for healing. The Asklepion was a temple dedicated to the god of healing Asklepios, the son of Apollo and a mortal woman. After a preliminary period of purification and performance of sacrifices, inquirers would fall asleep in a special cell in the temple called the *abaton*. There they dreamed of a visitation from the god Asklepios himself, or received information in a dream about a cure. Priests would later interpret their dreams for them and recommend healing remedies.

Like his father Apollo, Asklepios was a divine healer. He appeared both in his human form as well as that of his totem animal, the serpent.[115] Like shamans, Asklepios healed through dreams and visions. He could restore the dead to life, and as a result was punished by Zeus who killed him with a lightning bolt, fearing he would upset the cosmic order by defeating death. Subsequently Asklepios was immortalized by being placed in the heavens as the constellation Ophiuchus, "the serpent holder". Non-venomous snakes were kept in his temples and were used in healing rituals, crawling on the floors where patients slept. Indeed, Asklepios is often pictured holding a wand around which a single serpent is entwined, which has endured as a symbol for the medical profession to this day. It is said that the Greek physician Hippocrates (460 BCE- 377 BCE) regarded as the "father of medicine" was descended from Asklepios.

Oracles of The Underworld

While oracular shrines such as Delphi were devoted to the celestial gods, there were also oracles of Hades and Persephone—deities of the underworld. These were believed to be located at the actual entrances to the underworld. Spirits of the dead were consulted there, as it was thought they knew about future events. Consulting with the shades of the dead was deeply ingrained in the Greek psyche. Homer writes in the *Odyssey* about the hero Odysseus who descended to Hades to meet the soul of Tiresias the great seer, to ask about his future.

The Thesprotian Oracle was also known as the Nekromanteion, meaning the "Oracle of the Dead". It was built in the town of Ephyra in a remote region in Greece, and was in use since the 8th century BCE. The oracle was reached by boat on the river Acheron, named after the river in Hades. The Nekromanteion was indeed designed to remind the visitor of Hades. It contained an underground séance crypt reached by ladders or stairs from the surface through a narrow shaft. For a period of time, and in total darkness, the pilgrim ate food associated with the dead such as broad beans, pork, barley bread, and oysters. They purified themselves through washing and prayers to strengthen their defenses against contact with the spirits of the dead.[116] Then, accompanied by a priest who uttered prayers and invocations, a sheep would be sacrificed and the pilgrim would be led through a meandering passage to three arched iron bound doors, the same number as the doors in Hades. The middle and last of these doors led to the central hall where the visitor would leave offerings. There the souls of the dead would finally appear to them to answer their questions.

The excavator of the site, archaeologist Sotirios Dakaris writes: "How the spirits became visible is not known. Undoubtedly faith contributed greatly, aided by the physical and psychological preparation and the vivid suggestions to which the visitors had been exposed during their wanderings in the dark corridors of the sanctuary before coming to the sombre realm of Hades."[117] Dakaris found remnants of an enormous bronze cauldron on the site. He conjectures that the priests who ran the oracle concealed themselves in it and acted out the part of spirits for those who had come to seek their counsel. Dr. Raymond Moody an investigator of near-death-experiences, visited the oracle concluding that the cauldron may have been filled with a liquid and used as a *specula,* a device for mirror-gazing in which apparitions of the dead were seen.[118]

In later and more skeptical times, the priests who ran the oracle used theatrical mechanisms such as cranes which had a human image on one side and a counterweight on the other to create the illusion of spirits. Despite the trickery there is every reason to assume genuine visionary experiences occurred there. A substance similar to hashish was found during excavations, suggesting food and water may have been drugged to induce altered states of consciousness. The experiences of the visitors of the Nekromanteion seem to have been similar to the trance inductions of shamans where isolation, sensory deprivation, fasting, prayer, psychoactive substances, as well as fear, contributed to visionary experiences.

The Goetes—Greek Magicians or Shamans?

The name commonly used by the Greeks for magician was *goes*—or *goetes* plural—derived from the Greek word for "howling". The goetes were originally professional mourners, named for the howling sounds they made at funerals. Historian Morton Smith writes about their magical practices known as *goetia*: "It seems to have been a sort of Greek shamanism, a form of mourning for the dead in which the *goetes* became ecstatic and were thought to accompany the dead on their journey to the underworld."[119] Plato in the *Laws* said that those who practice goetia claim their sacrifices, chants, and prayers can lead up souls from the underworld and persuade the gods. The goetes were experts in the care and control of the disembodied soul and could negotiate a variety of relationships between the living and the dead, as well as the gods of the underworld, according to historian Sarah Iles Johnston.[120]

They were also associated with the performance of initiations for the living that guaranteed them a safe and happy afterlife. During these they used their skills in singing, chanting, and music of all sorts, for it was believed music had the power to enchant souls. The goetes were originally connected to ecstatic mystery-rites such as the Samothracian mysteries and the rites of the Daktyls, the sorcerers and ironworking smiths previously mentioned. Performing purifications for individuals as well as entire city-states, they atoned for wrongs committed against the dead, as well as purifying the souls of the dead.

Along with their skills in necromancy, the goetes were feared for their ability to send ghosts to torment the living. It was believed the souls of the "restless dead" were vulnerable to manipulation by them. These unhappy ghosts were spirits who could not find peace in the underworld due to improper burial, dying at an early age or through violence, or not achieving their purpose in life. A common means of employing these spirits was through "curse tablets", leaden sheets on which curses were inscribed and deposited on graves with the presumption the dead would carry them out. Often the name of Hecate, an underworld goddess, was called upon as she was believed to command the souls of the dead.

The origin of *necromancy*, the magical art by which the goetes communicated with souls of the dead, is traced to Assyria by Johnston.[121] It was first recorded in texts around 900 BCE, and from there it spread to Greece. She notes that the earliest description of the use of goetia is in Aeschylus's play *The Persians* performed in 472 BCE. The scene opens as the Persian queen carries offerings for the dead such as milk, honey, water and wine to the tomb of her deceased husband Darius. She then asks a chorus of Persian men to sing hymns to call up his soul from the underworld.[122] As previously mentioned, the art of necromancy, first recorded in Mesopotamia before spreading to Greece, was likely inherited from archaic shamanic traditions of exorcism and guiding the souls of the dead to the underworld. Besides their powers of communicating with the dead, Herodotus mentions beliefs that the goetes could transform themselves into wolves as well as control the weather, which further links them with shamans.

The performance of goetia was predominantly a male occupation. Women who performed sorcery were known as *pharmakides*—derived from the word *pharmaka*—meaning drugs, medicines, and magical potions. These women worked with drugs and poisons in combination with spoken spells and rituals. By the late fifth century BCE, literary sources portray women receiving magical help from the goddess Hecate, whose importance in magic grew from her role as leader of dead souls. Hecate's alternate role as birth goddess would have brought her into contact with women and folk-medicinal practices, according to Johnston.[123] A legendary magical feat associated with female sorcerers was "drawing down the moon", to bring it closer to earth making it easier for them to gather magical herbs and other substances.

Chapter 6 Notes

Entrance to Newgrange. Boyne Valley, Ireland 3100 BCE.

1. Oppenheimer, Stephen. *The Real Eve.* 2003. According to geneticist Stephen Oppenheimer, the Aurignacians migrated from a homeland in the Zagros mountains of Mesopotamia around 45,000 years ago to become the first *homo sapiens* to settle Europe.
2. Cunliffe, Barry. *Europe Between The Oceans.* 2008: 35 -69.
3. Williams, Mike. *Prehistoric belief: shamans, trance and the afterlife.* 2010: 61.
4. Aldhouse-Green, Miranda J.; Stephen Aldhouse-Green. *The Quest for the Shaman.* 2005: 69.
5. Ibid.: 74.
6. Gimbutas, Marija, *The Living Goddess.* 1999: 77.
7. Williams, Mike. *Prehistoric belief: shamans, trance and the afterlife.* 2010: 67.
8. Anthony, David W. *The Horse, The Wheel, And Language.* 2007 :163.
9. Ibid. 225, 279.
10. Khol, Philip. *Archaeological Transformations. Crossing the Agricultural Pastoral Bridge.* 2002: 37:151-190.
11. Haarman, Harald. *Early Civilization and Literacy in Europe.* 1995: 77.
12. Gimbutas. *The Language of the Goddess: Unearthing the Hidden Symbols of Western Civilization.* 2001: 54. Gimbutas argues the Vinca script developed from the tradition of proto-writing found in the Upper Paleolithic, previously discussed.

She traces the origin of several abstract signs commonly found on Vinca pottery such as chevrons, "X", "V", and "M" marks, to similar signs found on Paleolithic cave paintings, tools and carvings.

13. Gimbutas. *The gods and goddesses of Old Europe: 7000 to 3500 BCE myths, legends and cult images*. 1974: 85.
14. Gimbutas. "Primary and Secondary Homeland of the Indo-Europeans: comments on Gamkrelidze-Ivanov articles", (Spring– Summer 1985), *Journal of Indo-European Studies* 13. (1&2): 185–201
15. Manco, Jean. *Ancestral Journeys*. Manco 2013: 113.
16. Haarman. *Early Civilization and Literacy in Europe*. 1995:52.
17. Zimmer, Carl. "DNA Deciphers Roots of Modern Europeans." *NYT Science*, June 10, 2015.
18. Griffiths, Sarah & Newton, Jennifer. "Modern Europe was formed by milk-drinking Russians: Mass migration brought new genetic make-up to continent 5,000 years ago". *Daily Mail*. June 10, 2015.
19. Balter, Michael. "Mysterious Indo-European homeland may have been in the steppes of Ukraine and Russia." *Science News* 13 Feb. 2015.Balter: Science News 2015.
20. Griffiths & Newton. "Modern Europe was formed by milk-drinking Russians: Mass migration brought new genetic make-up to continent 5,000 years ago". 2015.
21. Renfrew, Colin. *Archaeology & language: the puzzle of Indo-European origins*.1987: 288.
22. Anthony, David W. *The Horse, The Wheel, And Language*. 2007:76.
23. Manco, Jean. *Ancestral Journeys*. 2013: 83.
24. Alinei, Mario. "The Paleolithic Continuity Paradigm for the Origins of Indo European Languages, an Introduction in Progress". May 2012.
25. Cory Panshin conjectures that not only Indo-European, but Uralic and Altaic families of languages are all members of a single ancient language group originating during the Paleolithic—"Eurasiatic". By the end of the Ice Age, the Indo-European languages had already differentiated into Proto-Celtic, Germanic, Baltic and Slavic languages, and all these peoples occupied territories close to their original homelands. Frank, Roslyn M. "Evidence in Favor of the Paleolithic Continuity Refugium Theory (PCRT) "Hamalu" And Its Linguistic and Cultural Relatives". Part 1. *Insula, #4*. 2008: 97.
26. Silva, Fabio. "Cosmologies in Transition Continuity, Innovation and Transformation in Neolithic Europe" *Academia.edu*.. 2012 :21.
27. Ibid.:21.
28. Ibid.
29. Gimbutas. *The Living Goddess*.1999:59.
30. MtDNA testing has confirmed that the percentage of overall genetic makeup in Europe varies, with Southern Europeans sharing more ancestry with the ancient farmers—up to 90% in Sardinia, while the people of Northern Europe, especially in the Baltic states, share 50% of their genes with the hunter-gatherers. This study cites that the s -called North Eurasians—supposedly synonymous with the Yamnaya Culture--contributed up to 20% of the genes of modern

Europeans, (Dunham 2014:2).
31. Stutley, Margaret. *Shamanism: An Introduction.* 2003: 75.
32. Gimbutas. *The Living Goddess.* 1999: 111.
33. Williams, Mike. *Prehistoric belief: shamans, trance and the afterlife.*
34. Lewis-Williams, J. David; Pearce, D.G.. *Inside the Neolithic Mind.* 2005:194-195.
35. Williams. *Prehistoric belief: shamans, trance and the afterlife.* 2010: 111.
36. Rudgely. *Lost Civilizations of the Stone Age.* 1999:207.
37. Walter & Fridman. *Shamanism: An Encyclopedia of World Beliefs, Practices and Culture,* Vol.1. 2004: 17.
38. Ruggles, Clive. *Astronomy in Prehistoric Britain and Ireland.* 1999: 87.
39. Ahlstrom, Dick. "Hundreds of New Discoveries At Stonehenge." *Irish Times,* Wed. Sept. 10, 2014. Using high-tech magnetometers and lasers archaeologists have discovered 17 previously unknown ritual monuments and hundreds of other smaller structures in the surroundings, many dating back before Stonehenge.
40. Pearson, Mike Parker. *Stonehenge A New Understanding.* 2011: 4.
41. Ibid.:90.
42. Williams. *Prehistoric belief: shamans, trance and the afterlife.* 2010:119.
43. Gimbutas. *The Living Goddess.* 1999: 107.
44. Ibid.:1999: 68.
45. Williamson, Ray, A. *Living the Sky: the Cosmos of the American Indian.* 1987: 40.
46. Joseph, Frank. *Before Atlantis: 20 Million Years of Human and Pre-human Cultures.* 2013:209-222. A conservative estimate is approximately 70,000 menhirs and dolmens globally, according to Joseph (Joseph 2013:210).
47. Burl, Aubrey. *Great Stone Circles.* 1999: 44.
48. Joseph. *Before Atlantis: 20 Million Years of Human and Pre-human Cultures.* 2013; 215-221.
49. Hutton, Ronald. *The Pagan Religions of the Ancient British Isles.* Hutton 1991: 134.
50. Beckwith, Christopher, I. *Empires of the Silk Road: A History of Central Eurasia from the Bronze Age to the Present.* 2009: 30.
51. Dumezil, G. *Gods of the Ancient Northmen.* 1973.
52. Ibid.
53. Anthony. *The Horse, The Wheel, And Language.* 2007:134.
54. West, M.L. *Indo-European Poetry and Myth.* 2007:121.
55. Ibid.:214.
56. Ibid.:403.
57. Anthony. *The Horse, The Wheel, And Language.* 2007: 343.
58. West. *Indo-European Poetry and Myth.* 2007: 412.
59. Bonewits, Isaac. "Indo-European Paleopaganism and its Clergy." *Druid's Progress #1,* 1984.
60. West. *Indo-European Poetry and Myth.* 2007:332.
61. Eliade. *Shamanism Archaic Techniques of Ecstasy.* 1964:375-403.
62. Ashe. *Dawn Behind The Dawn: A Search for the Earthly Paradise.* 1992: 215. The

Andronovo culture invented the spoked-chariot, and established metal trading networks with the Near-East making such long-distance migrations entirely possible. One group of Indo-Iranians became the Mitanni, chariot driving warrior aristocracy who conquered Mesopotamia and ruled for several centuries. The Mitanni were Old- Indic speakers whose language and gods are similar to those found in the *Rig-Veda*.

63. Eliade. *Shamanism Archaic Techniques of Ecstasy*.1964: 11.
64. West. *Indo-European Poetry and Myth*. 2007: 149. The borrowing went both ways, and the Uralic languages, which Finno-Ugrian is descended from, borrowed agricultural vocabulary from the Indo-Europeans. (Anthony 2007:95).
65. Winkelman. *Shamanism A Biopsychosocial Pardigm of Consciousness and Healing – Second Edition*.2010: 67.
66. Similar funerary practices occurred in the Bronze Age cultures of early Mesopotamia and Egypt, where entire courts–servants, concubines, soldiers, boats and chariots were buried with the ruler upon their death.
67. Green, Miranda J. *Sun Gods of Ancient Europe*. 1992: 66.
68. Ibid.: 68.
69. Aldhouse-Green.. *The Quest for the Shaman*. 2005: 96.
70. Burkert. *Greek Religion*. 1985: 37-8.
71. Gimbutas. *Goddesses and Gods of Old Europe:7000 to 3500 BCE myths, legends and cult images*. 1974:93.
72. Gimbutas. *The Living Goddess*. 1991.
73. Burkert. *Greek Religion*. 1985:25.
74. Ibid.:28.
75. Ibid.:33.
76. Ibid.: 40.
77. Gimbutas. *Goddesses and Gods of Old Europe:7000 to 3500 BCE myths, legends and cult images*.1974:66.
78. Gimbutas. *The Living Goddess*. 1999: 143.
79. Ashe. *Dawn Behind The Dawn: A Search for the Earthly Paradise*.1992: 27.
80. Kraft, John. *The Goddess in the Labyrinth*. 1985: 38.
81. Ibid.: 15-17.
82. Cunliffe 2008: 196.
83. Burkert. *Greek Religion*.1985: 19.
84. West. *Indo-European Poetry and Myth*. 2007: 24.
85. Gimbutas. *The Living Goddess*.1999: 152.
86. Ibid.:154.
87. Campbell. *The Masks of God. Occidental Mythology*. 1964: 79.
88. Cunliffe, Barry. *Europe Between The Oceans*. 2008: 234.
89. Karitonova, V. in Walter & Fridman. *Shamanism: An Encyclopedia of World Beliefs, Practices and Culture*, Vol.1. 2004: 537.
90. Eliade. *Shamanism Archaic Techniques of Ecstasy*. 1964: 470.
91. Ibid.: 473.
92. Burkert. *Greek Religion*. 1985: 123.
93. Gimbutas. *Goddesses and Gods of Old Europe:7000 to 3500 BCE myths, legends and cult images*. 1974:85.

94. Cunliffe. *Europe Between The Oceans*. 2008: 278.
95. Ashe. *Dawn Behind The Dawn: A Search for the Earthly Paradise*. 1992: 55-66.
96. Ibid.:154.
97. Ibid.:175.
98. Ginzburg, Carlo. *Ecstasies: Deciphering the Witches' Sabbath*. 1991: 127-137.
99. Hughes, J.D. "Artemis: Goddess of Conservation". *Oxford Journals*, vol. 34, issue 4, pp. 191-197) 1990 :191.
100. Burkert. *Greek Religion*.1985: 156.
101. Frothingham, A.L. *Babylonian Origin of Hermes the Snake-God, and of the Caduceus*. American Journal of Archaeology- Second Series. Journal of the Archaeological Institute of America, vol. xx (1916) no.2 1916: 179.
102. Another obvious association to the caduceus is the *kundalini* power of Hindu Yoga, thought to be coiled at the base of the spine like a serpent, and awakened by meditation; Its three "nadis" or subtle nerve channels resemble the stafr and twin serpents of Hermes's staff. When awakened, the kundalini force is directed up the "chakras" of the yogi's spine to the crown chakra at the top of the head, leading to enlightenment.
103. Diodorus Siculus, *Bibliotecha historiae*.
104. Temple, Robert. *Oracles of the Dead- Ancient Techniques for Predicting the Future*. 2002: 71.
105. Dickey, Matthew W. *Magic and Magicians In The Greco-Roman World*. 2001: 112.
106. Clarke, Emma; Dillon, John; Hershbell, Jackson. (trans.) Iamblichus *On the Mysteries*. 2003:127.
107. Lenderling, Jona. "Alexander and the Chaldeans". *Livius Articles on Ancient History*.1995-2013.
108. Flower, Michael. *The Seer in Ancient Greece*. 2008: 22-25.
109. Couliano. *Out of This World*. 1991: 127.
110. Aldhouse-Green. *The Quest for the Shaman*. 2005: 145.
111. Jones, Prudence & Pennick, Nigel. *A History of Pagan Europe*.1995: 19.
112. Burkert. *Greek Religion*. 1985: 117.
113. Ashe. *Dawn Behind The Dawn: A Search for the Earthly Paradise*. 1992: 177.
114. Burkert. *Greek Religion*. 1985: 117.
115. Matthews, Caitlín; John, Matthews. *The Encyclopedia of Celtic Wisdom*. 1996: 337.
116. Sophia, Fotopoulou."The Nekromanteio at Acheron". *Newsfinder*. 2003
117. Temple. *Oracles of the Dead- Ancient Techniques for Predicting the Future*. 2002: 41.
118. Moody, Raymond A.; Perry, Paul. *Reunions*. 1993: 34-6.
119. Smith, Morton. *Jesus The Magician*.1978: 70.
120. Johnston. *Restless Dead*. 1999: 107.
121. Ibid.: 88.
122. Ibid.: 117.
123. Ibid.: 113.

Chapter 7: Druids & Volvas
Celtic & Germanic Magic of the Iron Age

Cernunnos surrounded by beasts. Gundestrup Cauldron, Denmark 200-300 CE.

The Celts

The Greeks and Romans used the words "Celt" and "Gaul" interchangeably to describe the "barbarians" of Western or Central Europe.[1] These peoples were not unified groups but mixtures of different tribes likely descended from Indo-European speaking peoples such as the Bell Beaker Culture (2,700-2,000 BCE) who were in turn related to the Corded Ware and Yamnaya people, previously mentioned. The Celts settled across wide expanses of Europe using horses, wheeled vehicles, the plough and engaging in trade of copper.[2] The earliest evidence of the Celts was the Iron Age Hallstatt Culture of western and central Europe, (ca.750 BCE) whose elite were buried with funerary wagons and a wealth of other objects. Long distance trade in amber from the Baltics and Etruscan luxury objects led to the emergence of the Celtic La Tene culture. Around 500 BCE, tribes of Celts migrated towards Mediterranean lands, driving chariots and wielding bronze weapons. Raiding and the demand for slaves from Greeks and Etruscans gave incentives for them to journey into hostile territory and they even ventured so far as to sack Rome in 390 BCE. Migrating Celts spread across Europe as far as central Turkey and the Iberian peninsula.

Early La Tene burials feature weapons, usually a sword, and one or more spears buried with the dead. In their society prowess in war and raiding was all important. Mike Williams writes: "For the Celts of the Iron Age, the warrior ethic was paramount and to be declared champion, and to receive the hero's portion of meat, was something to fight and even die for".[3] Hospitality and sharing was the basis of Celtic feasts. For the host, largesse on a grand scale was part of maintaining his elevated social status and influence, and the whole population as well as strangers were invited to food and drink.

Celtic men and women adorned their bodies with gold jewelry and wore "torc" neck rings, as well as wrist and arm rings. Celtic women were buried lavishly with their jewelry, suggesting high social status, perhaps due to the fact they administered the settlements while the men-folk were away fighting. Several warrior queens were known among the Celts such as Boudica, Scathach, and Medb. Ancient writers mention Celtic women who fought alone or next to their husbands.

In battle the Celts often fought naked, perhaps to prove their bravery and to terrify their foes with their fearlessness. Some of them "spiked" their hair with lime and drank large quantities of alcohol before fighting, working themselves into a frenzy with dances and blazing trumpets. Strabo, the Greek historian (64 BCE-24 CE) writes that the Celts have the custom of "hanging the heads of their enemies from the neck of their horses when returning from battle, and of nailing them as an exhibition before their doors when they arrive home." This may have been due to their belief that the head is the seat of the soul, and the enemy's head was an object of spiritual power.

Bards, Ovates & Druids

Typical of other Indo-European cultures, Celtic society had three classes: aristocratic warriors, commoners who farmed the land, and their spiritual leaders, the Druids. The word *"druid"* is derived from Old Irish—*drui*—for sorcerer, or possibly from Early Welsh—*druw*—for seer. The Greek historian Strabo writes: "Among the Gauls there are generally three classes to whom special honor is paid...the Bards, the Uatis and the Druids. The Bards composed and sung odes; the Uatis attended to the sacrifices and studied nature; while the Druids studied nature and moral philosophy". The "Uatis" whom Strabo refers to are more familiarly known as Ovates.

Druids were the judges, advisers and peacemakers of their communities and were exempt from military service. Roman writer Dion Chrysotom writes: "without their advice even kings dared not resolve upon nor execute any plan." They were also educators, and twenty-two Druidic colleges are recorded to have existed in the British Isles. Aristocratic youth from as far away as Gaul came to study there. The training of Druids was rigorous, lasting twenty years. They passed on their knowledge orally, and emphasis was on memory rather than writing. In fact the entire history, mythology, and genealogy of their culture was committed to memory.

Celtic Druids started learning Greek writing around 600 BCE, and also acquired knowledge of classical philosophy. Various Greek and Roman writers mention that the Druids practiced the philosophy of Pythagoras, believing like him in immortality of the soul and reincarnation. Julius Caesar wrote about these beliefs among the Druids of Gaul and Britain: "The principle point of their doctrine is that the soul does not die and that after death it passes from one body to another".[4] Whether the Druids acquired these teachings from Pythagoras is debatable, as the belief in the soul's rebirth was apparently common among the early Celts. It can be found in a number of Irish sagas, according to W.Y. Evans-Wentz who insists that great heroes and heroines of Irish literature such as Cuchulainn, Mongan, and Etain were originally regarded as reincarnations of gods and goddesses.[5]

Druid Magic—Celtic Shamans

Ancient writers describe the Druids as seers, diviners, and wizards who could foretell future events. They practiced divination by crystal gazing and observing the patterns of clouds, fire, smoke and the stars. Movements of animals were interpreted as omens, as well as the voices of birds, especially the croaking of ravens and the chirping of the wren. They also consulted the spirits of the dead.

Druids used their supernatural powers to assist their kings in battles, often fighting opposing wizards.[6] The druid Mag Ruith was reputed to be able to create a magical fire in battle, directing it at the enemy whose druid tried in vain to deflect it. The druid Mathgen boasted of being able to throw mountains at the enemy. They made trees, or spears magically appear as armed men, confusing their enemies in this manner. Legends tell of the magical manipulation of weather by druids in battle, during which they raised tempests, snow, thick mists, and sudden darkness. Druidic bards could also use their magic to end fighting. The Roman Diodorus Siculus observed: "Frequently when armies confront one another in line of battle...these men intervene and cause them to stop, just as though they were holding some wild animal spellbound with their chanting". There was a widespread tradition of wizards performing "military magic" in the ancient world. As previously mentioned, the black shamans of Central Asia served as military advisors to warlords and used their magical powers to assist them in battle.

Druidesses were renowned to the Romans for their prophecies. Many magically potent witches and fairy-women also figure in the tales of druids, such as the priestesses of Sena who could rouse the sea and winds by their enchantments. According to tradition, there were "sunset isles" of women where female druids lived apart from their families during times of the year. These included the Ile de Sein off the coast of Brittany where a sisterhood of nine miracle-working healers lived, as well as the Isle of Avalon which the Arthurian legends mention as training places for sorceresses and healers.[7]

The druids served as intermediaries between humans, fairy folk and the invisible realms. As such their role was in many ways similar to that of the tribal shaman. Caitlín and John Matthews write: "There is little doubt that early Celtic peoples had a predominantly shamanic culture. Their shamans were the inspired ones, the gifted people or *aes dana*, who could walk between the worlds with ease—the druids, poets and seers."[8]

Some druids and Celtic poet-seers wore the *tugen,* a cloak of bird feathers, perhaps symbolizing their power of soul-flight. The 9th century *Cormac's Glossary* describes the poet's cloak: "For it is of skins of birds white and many-colored that the poet's toga is made..." Siberian and Finno-Ugrian shamans are recorded to have been attired in similar feathered robes, which may have represented their avian helping spirits.[9]

Otherworldy Journeys of the Bards

Many of the myths and stories of the Celts seem to have been inspired by visionary journeys to the otherworld. Caitlín & John Matthews write about the training of the bardic poet, and the use of storytelling in their visionary practices: "...the soul-journey was a specialist practice, requiring formal tuition by those who had made such journeys, and who could teach from personal experience." These authors note that over three hundred and fifty stories were memorized by bardic initiates, which included knowledge of otherworldly pathways and their inhabitants.[10] During their soul journeys, sacred animals, ancestral spirits or otherworldly beings such as the *sidhe* or fairy folk were encountered.

According to these authors, some ancient visionary practices may have survived in oral traditions. Among Gaelic storytellers, the *echtra,* or adventure story, similar to the shamanic journey, involves a purposeful visit to the otherworld, whose inhabitants provide information, healing or solutions to problems. The *immram* or "voyage quest" features a heroes journey to otherworldly isles where faery folk are visited and supra-human wisdom acquired. The Matthews suggest these stories may be remnants of a once coherent teaching similar to a "book of the dead" which prepared people for states of existence after death.[11]

Different methods for entering the trance state were used by the ancient Celts such as listening to bird-song, harp or timpan music, singing, incantation, darkness, and silence. Incantation was often used by the seer known as the *filidh* to induce the soul journey and to call upon personal spirit allies.[12] The Irish Druids also practiced a form of dream incubation known as *Tarbh feis*. After sacrificing a white bull and making a broth from its flesh, a druid would wrap himself in its flayed hide and fall asleep for the purpose of receiving a dream oracle, usually to answer important questions such as the secession of a king or other queries. The Roman author Tertullian writes that the Celts also had a custom of sleeping on the tombs of their ancestors, by which they received inspiration and wisdom from them.[13]

Evidence of hallucinogens such as opium, henbane and ergot found at Iron Age sites suggests the Druids may have had access to these psychoactive substances as a means of altering consciousness and inducing trance.[14]

Gods of the Celts

The Druids held the oak tree as sacred, meeting in groves of oaks to worship. Cults of the oak and yew tree probably existed in Britain before the coming of the Celts, according to modern druid Ross Nichols, and were adopted by the Celtic Druids from their Neolithic predecessors. Celtic shrines were situated in natural locales such as groves of trees, hilltops and near lakes. It was only later under Roman influence that they built temples.

The Celtic gods were derived from numerous local gods and their names change and blend with one another in a "bewildering way" according to Nichols, bearing only a general similarity with Greek and Roman deities.[15] Many goddesses were local, ruling over natural features such as healing springs or rivers. Although different tribes honored their own local deities, sky-gods, sun-gods and mother goddesses were universal among the Celts, according to Miranda Green.[16] She writes that due to the influence of Greco-Roman religion, the Celts began to represent their gods in anthropomorphic form.[17] Eventually the names and characteristics of some Celtic deities were syncretized with Greco-Roman gods and goddesses.

Lugh was the god of light, identified by the Romans with their god Mercury as guide of the dead. Celtic statuary often depicts him with three faces, as if facing the three worlds of heaven, earth, and underworld. One of the most widespread of Celtic gods, his name appears in place names around Europe and Britain. *Taranis* ruled over lightning and thunder; he was the roaring bull associated with the power of the heavens, identified with the Roman god

Jupiter. *Teutates* was the heroic warrior god, likened by the Romans to Mars, and sometimes Mercury.[18] *Cernunnos* was a god of nature, fertility, prosperity and healing represented as a man with stag horns. He is a "lord of animals", usually depicted in the company of animals such as ram-horned serpents, stags, dogs, bulls or hares. Miranda Green writes that Cernunnos is an example of transformation from anthropomorphic to animal form and a "true blend of man and beast".[19] His shape-shifting and healing attributes suggest he may have been associated with shamanic practices; his totem creature, the serpent, links him to magical gods of other ancient cultures.

Some goddesses were widely popular such as *Brighid*, the goddess of crafts, war, nursing and motherhood. She is a solar and fire goddess who was later transformed into the Christian saint Brighid. In Gaul, the goddess *Epona* ruled over horses and is sometimes depicted as centaur or a woman sitting on a horse, also known by the Welsh as *Rhiannon*. She is identified with the shamanic "mistress of animals" by Carlo Ginzburg. Epona was a popular goddess and the only Celtic deity to be worshipped in Rome.

Many Celtic deities had solar associations according to Miranda Green, who notes there was a continuity of solar worship from the Neolithic megalith builders to the later Celtic and Romano-Celtic cultures. She writes that much of their religion was: "a magical response to the desire to make the sun appear and warm the earth after night and winter".[20] One of these solar gods was *Apollo Belenus*—Bright Apollo—a Gaulish god concerned with healing, who presided over hot-spring healing sanctuaries.[21] Celtic goddesses associated with the sun include the healer goddess *Sulis* at Bath, *Eriu* the patron goddess of Ireland, as well as *Epona* the horse goddess. In ancient Ireland, both *Og* and *Grainne* were deities of the sun. Belinus was associated with the Sun and the fire festival of Beltainne. *Dagda* was a god of the sun as well as the earth, possessing only one eye and a huge cauldron which could feed armies.

The appearance of gods and goddesses in triple form also occurs among the Celts—the number three had symbolic significance for all Indo-Europeans, as previously mentioned. The triple Brigit sisters, the three craftsmen Goibhniu, Luchta and Creidhne, and the three war-mothers, the Morrigna and the Machas, are examples of such triplicities.[22]

Survival of Celtic Culture

The Roman historian Tacitus chronicles the Roman army's battle against the Druids at one of their last strongholds on the Isle of Anglesey off the coast of Wales, in 60 CE:

"On the coastline, a line of warriors of the opposition was stationed, mainly made up of armed men, amongst them women, with their hair blowing in the wind, while they were carrying torches. Druids were amongst them, shouting terrifying spells, their hands raised towards the heavens, which scared our soldiers so much that their limbs became paralyzed. As a result they remained stationary and were injured. At the end of the battle, the Romans were victorious, and the holy oaks of the druids were destroyed."

The transition to Roman rule among the Celts was by no means smooth, however. A bloody uprising led by Boudica, queen of the Celtic Iceni tribe, almost succeeded in driving the Romans out of Britain. Christianity arrived in Britain with the Romans, but it was not until the end of the sixth century CE that Christian missionaries crossed the English Channel to bring their faith to England. Before long, churches were built over earlier Druidic and Neolithic holy sites, and Christian holidays were juxtaposed over older pagan festivals. Modern druid Phillip Carr-Gomm writes that although the Christians replaced the Druids, they also inadvertently preserved some of their beliefs by continuing to use older sacred sites such as holy wells. Christians adapted the festivals and folklore associated with the pagan calendar, as well as co-opting some of the Celtic deities as saints.[23]

As Celtic culture in continental Europe declined due to Roman and Christian rule, the British Isles became the last stronghold of Celtic traditions. Ironically, Christian monks can be credited with preserving remnants of the pagan Irish oral tradition. Beginning in the sixth century they began to transcribe pre-Christian legends in the scriptoria of their monasteries. The *Mabinogion,* the collection of ancient Welsh tales which monks recorded in the 13th and 14th centuries, is an important source of Celtic myth, albeit far removed in time from its sources. The Arthurian legends and other Celtic folk tales also present pre-Christian stories of entering the underworld, shapeshifting into animal forms, divination, and magic—themes which are essentially shamanistic in nature.

In Ireland, which the Romans never conquered, some of the bardic tradition was kept alive through stories of the *Fionn Cycle* of the ancient Irish hero Fionn MacCumhal. In the *Ulster Cycle* the hero Cuchulainn is presented as being possessed by spirits while in trance. Miranda and Stephen Aldhouse Green write: "In relating these Irish and Welsh texts to the quest for ancient shamans, perhaps the most significant issue is that of the way in which earth-world and the otherworld encroach upon each other."[24] According to Gimbutas, the Irish and Welsh oral traditions preserved the myths of the primary Old-European goddesses, especially the life giver Brigid, and the death bringers Danu, Morrigan, Macha, and Badb—with little change from Neolithic times.[25]

The Germans & Scandinavians

The ancient Germans, like the Celts, were Indo-European speaking peoples originally related to the Corded Ware and Yamnaya cultures. The Iron Age Jastorf culture (600-100 BCE) began in northern Germany, influenced by the neighboring Celtic Halstatt culture to the south.[26] Around this period, the Germans began expanding into areas formerly inhabited by the Celts—the Alps, the Netherlands and lowland Britain, absorbing existing populations as they moved. In the beginning they were not a unified group but a mixture of different tribes and clans. However they shared a common Indo-European parent language, Proto-Germanic, which gave rise to Danish, Dutch, English, German, Icelandic, Swedish and Norwegian.[27]

These disparate groups who came to be called the "Germani" by the Romans, were halted by them at the Rhine. With the collapse of the Roman Empire between the 4th- 6th centuries CE, the Germanic tribes moved swiftly across the face of the Western Roman empire conquering its lands and peoples. The Christian bishop of Constantinople described the onslaught: "The barbarians have left their own territory and many times have overrun huge tracts of land, setting fire to the countryside. Instead of returning to their homes, like drunken revelers they mock us."[28]

The religion of the ancient Germans was similar in many respects to those of other Indo-Europeans, emphasizing a pantheon of sky-gods while adapting deities of the native peoples in whose lands they settled. The myths and magical practices of the Norse also share some similarities with those of shamanic cultures of Northern Eurasia, suggesting prehistoric contacts with those peoples.

Yggdrasil—the Tree of Worlds

Our understanding of Germanic mythology is based largely on the *Eddas*, the Icelandic Sagas, a collection of poems, songs, and myths written in the old Norse language in 13th century Iceland. Some scholars believe they could have been composed as early as the 5th or 6th century CE. Ralph Metzner notes that the *Eddas* may have been written down as an attempt to preserve the earlier lore during the Christianization of Nordic lands. Originally the Germans, like the Celts, preferred oral transmission of ancestral wisdom through stories and songs over writing.[29]

Germanic cosmology is structured like other shamanic cosmologies as three worlds joined along the axis of the World Tree, known as the *Yggdrasil Tree*. This was envisioned as a mighty ash tree, so huge that its branches and roots encompassed heaven, earth and the underworld. Three roots supported the trunk, one passing into Aesir, the realm of the sky gods, another root into the land of the frost-giants, and a third into the realm of the dead. Beneath the root in the land of giants was the spring of Mimir, flowing with the waters of wisdom. The god Odin gave one of his eyes for the right to drink a single draught of the spring's waters. Below the tree in the realm of Aesir was the Well of Urd, where the gods assembled for their court of law to discuss problems and settle disputes. Near this spring dwelled three maidens called the Norns who ruled the destinies of men. They watered the tree every day with pure water and whitened it with clay from the spring, preserving its life.

On the top bough of the tree sat an eagle with a hawk perched on its forehead, the same eagle whose flapping wings were said to cause the winds of the earth. At the tree's root lived a great serpent along with many smaller snakes, and these gnawed at its base, threatening to destroy it. The serpent and eagle were constantly at war with each other, while a squirrel ran up and down the trunk relaying insults from the creatures above and below.

Each world spanned by Yggdrasil was envisioned as containing three lesser worlds within it, for a total of *nine* worlds all together. Gods, giants, dwarves, elves, and humans each lived in their own world, though travel between worlds was possible by shamans, seers, and sorcerers like Odin, who by learning nine songs was able to travel through all the worlds.[30]

Aesir & Vanir—Gods of Sky & Earth

The Roman historian Tacitus (56 – 117 CE) writes about the ancient German religion: "They do not think it in keeping with the divine majesty to confine gods within walls or to portray them in the likeness of any human countenance. Like the Celts, their holy places are woods and groves, and they apply the names of deities to that hidden presence which is only seen by the eye of reverence." [31] Similar to the early Celts, the Germans did not depict their deities with anthropomorphic imagery until exposed to the influence of the Greeks and Romans.

The *Aesir* and the *Vanir* were the two groups of Germanic gods. Scholars have proposed the Aesir were sky gods brought by the Indo-European speaking invaders, while the Vanir were fertility gods of the earlier Neolithic inhabitants of the land, associated with the raw powers of nature. *Odin* was the father-god of the Aesir gods whose home was in Asgard located at the crown of the Yggdrasil tree. *Tyr* was an Aesir god of conflict and justice, equated by the Romans with Mars; the weekday of Tuesday was derived from the Old English version of his name, Tiwesdaeg. The god *Thor,* whose name means "thunder", was highly popular among the Nordic-Germanic people as the hero and protector of farmer-warriors. He gave his name to the day of Thursday. He was pictured as a red-haired giant accompanied by two male goats, carrying his magical weapon the throwing hammer. Thor was also associated with weddings and fertility, and his hammer symbol was carried as an amulet.[32] *Balder*, the son of Odin and his wife *Frigg*, is described in the Eddas as "one of whom only good things can be said." He was so fair of face and bright that a radiance emanated from him. He was the wisest of the gods and the most eloquent and kind. His death, caused by the treachery of the god Loki, set in motion the events leading to Ragnarok, the end of the world. Metzner notes there are elements in the myth of Balder that are similar to the death and resurrection of Near-Eastern vegetation gods, as well as the story of Christ. The trickster god *Loki* is a giant who lives nevertheless among the gods, instigating conflict among them, yet also teaching them the magic of the runes. Like the shaman, he is a shapeshifter who changes into male or female, a salmon, mare, otter or eagle. Loki fathers the Fenriswolf which later destroys the world, as well as the Midgard serpent and *Hel* the ruler of the underworld.

While the Aesir were gods of the warrior and aristocratic classes, the Vanir were the deities of farmers and fishermen. Their chief deities, Freyja, Freyr and Njord, were concerned with fertility, sexuality, prosperity and natural growth.[33] The Vanir were also associated with the land spirits and elves, who represent the remnants of the earth-religion of Old Europe, in the opinion of Metzner. As previously discussed, the Indo-Europeans also possessed their own myths of nature spirits. The elves were seen as helpful to mankind and called upon to foretell the future, warn of dangers, and bring prosperous harvests. The *vaettir* of Iceland, and the *trolls* of Norway were considered malevolent beings. The *giants* were the primal forces of nature and generally seen as indifferent to humans. *Freyr* was believed to rule over Alfheim, the land of elves.

Freyr's wife *Freya* was the goddess of love, beauty and sexuality, often associated with Venus and Aphrodite of the Romans and Greeks. Our weekday of Friday is probably named after her. Her name means "lady", and Freyr's name means "lord". They were brother and sister, similar to Isis and Osiris of Egyptian myth, as the sibling-consort rulership was common in ancient matrifocal societies. Freya was renowned for her magical powers. She was a priestess of the Vanir and was said to have taught magic to the Aesir, including Odin, who learned his arts of divination and seership from her. Freya was associated with animals such as birds, and she journeyed through the worlds with an animal or in the shape of one, similar to shamans. Traveling in a chariot drawn by wild cats, she wore a feathered falcon robe which bestowed the magical power of flight upon her. She possessed a magical necklace, the Brisingamen, which was crafted by the four dwarves who were master smiths stationed at the four quarters of the world. In exchange for the gift, Freya agreed to spend one night of love with each of them.

Odin the Shamanic God

Odin was referred to as the "All Father" of the gods who slayed the giant Ymir and created the world from his body. Odin is the god of shamans, sorcerers, singers, poets, storytellers, seers and seeresses, and berserker warriors, all of whom were said to be "seized" by Odin during a state of ecstatic inspiration.[34] The Norse word for magic is *seidr*, which means "boiling" or "seething", which could refer to the state of ecstatic trance where the trembling or shaking of the body sometimes occurred. This state of seizure is sometimes observed among shamans during possession by their helping spirits. Odin, the god of war as well as wisdom, is in many ways the Norse equivalent of a shaman. He voluntarily sacrificed himself by hanging on Yggdrasil, piercing himself with a spear and fasting for nine days and nights to learn the magic of the Runes, recalling the shaman's initiation trials. This passage from the *Eddas* describes his ordeal :

> I know that I hung
> on that wind-swept tree,
> through nine long nights,
> pierced by the spear,
> to Odin sacrificed,
> myself to myself,
> on that great tree
> whose roots
> no one knows
> Neither food nor drink
> did they give me.
> I looked downwards—
> took up the runes,
> took them up with a cry.
> Then I fell down.[35]

Edred Thorsson compares Odin's ordeal to the shaman's quest for wisdom, writing: "This describes an initiatory process of a shamanistic type, in which the initiate passes through nine worlds of the world-tree to the realm of Hel (death) and momentarily enters into her sphere. At that moment the initiate receives the entire body of rune wisdom and it is etched into his being".[36] Like the shaman,

Odin practiced trance, shapeshifting and magical flight. In the *Ynglinga Saga*, the Chronicle of the Kings of Norway, these powers are described: "Odin could change himself. His body then lay as if sleeping or dead, but he became a bird or a wild beast, a fish or a dragon, and journeyed in the twinkling of an eye to far-off lands, on his own errands or those of other men."

Odin travelled to the dark underworld of Hel and back, riding on his eight-legged steed Sleipnir. Curiously, some Siberian shamans are also known to travel on a similar eight-legged horse in their otherworldly journeys. Odin stole the mead of poetic wisdom and flew off in the form of an eagle—a few drops fell to earth, giving humans the gift of poetry. He practiced divination, using a head which spoke, similar to the heads once kept by Siberian shamans for oracles. Like them he was skilled at necromancy, the magical art of summoning and speaking with the dead. In the *Ynglinga Saga* it is written: "Odin carried with him Mime's head, which told him the news of other countries. Sometimes he even called the dead out of the earth, or set himself beside the burial mounds; whence he was called the ghost-sovereign."

The Romans equated Odin with their god Mercury, and the Saxons in England gave his name to the day of Wednesday, derived from the Saxon word Wodanesdaeg. Unlike Mercury who was described as a youth, Odin was pictured as a rugged middle-aged man who wore a dark cloak and brimmed hat to conceal his missing eye, which he lost in exchange for drinking from the Well of Remembrance. He carried a staff inscribed with runes and was accompanied by a pair of wolves and ravens. Both these creatures play prominent roles as helping-spirits among shamans of Siberia and North America as well.

R.A. Davidson suggests there were shamanic influences on the myths of Odin: "Resemblances between the Odin traditions and the shamans might be due to certain tendencies once shared by the Germanic peoples with those of the steppes and tundra, which died out in western Europe with the advent of Christianity." [37]

Volvas & Seidr—Nordic Magic

The ancient Germans believed in the power of prophetesses such as Veleda (69-79 CE) who sang them into battle and was revered as divine. Numerous wise women and sibyls were known who exhibited shamanic talents such as consulting with the shades of the dead, foretelling the future, and working protective and healing spells. Priestesses known as Volvas, followers of the goddess Freya, practiced public seances known as *seidrs*. Since Freya was a fertility goddess, their ceremonies specialized in the prosperity of the community, as well as questions about marriage, fertility and the destiny of children.

The word Volva is derived from the Norse word *vol*—meaning "staff" or "staff carrier"—perhaps due to the carved staff with brass knob set with stones carried by these priestesses. They also wore a cloak with ornamental stones on their shirts and a lambskin hood lined with catskin, as well as catskin boots and gloves. Freya travelled in a chariot drawn by cats, and it is likely cats were familiar spirits of Volvas. They also carried a pouch containing charms and rune stones as well as an ivory handled dagger with a broken point. Volvas conducted oracular ceremonies in which they sat on a high platform and fell into trance as incantations were chanted by a choir of youths and maidens. Metzner notes that similar rhythmic chanting is practiced to this day as a way of inducing trances by shamans among the Sami people of northern Scandinavia.[38]

In their seidrs, the Volvas also divined with the runes and foretold the outcome of battles, success of harvests, expeditions and alliances. Similar to shamans, they communed with spirits to gain hidden knowledge. R. A. Davidson writes that the garb and practices of the Volvas presented remarkable parallels to those of shamans. Not only did they wear elaborate costumes made from animal skins, but in sagas and poems they narrated their supernatural journeys through the darkness, cold, and fire of the otherworld, similar to shamanic narratives in seances.[39] Volvas travelled in groups of nine or thirteen, performing their divinatory rituals. With the coming of Christianity they were demonized and identified with witches, reputed to use their sexual powers to cause harm. Their spirit allies, cats, became reviled as the evil familiar spirits of witches.

Besides the Volvas, the Nordic peoples also had priests and priestesses known respectively as *godi* or *gydjur* in Old Norse. These lived in small temples and occasionally toured the countryside with statues of their patron or matron deities with whom they were considered to be "married", according to Isaac Bonewits.[40]

Berserkirs & Werewolves—Shamanic warriors

The *berserkirs*, meaning "those wearing bearskins" were Nordic warriors dedicated to Odin. Along with them were the *ulfhednar* or "wolfskins" who identified with the wolf to gain it's hunting abilities, inspiring legends of werewolves.[41] In the *Volsunga Saga*, Sigmund and his son, both outlaw warriors, put on wolfskins and were unable to take them off, speaking to each other in wolf-language.[42] Both berserkir and ulfednar warriors were said to enter battle in an ecstatic trance or "holy rage", like Celtic warriors such as Cu Chulainn and Finn, and his Fian warriors. They howled, fought without armor, and terrified their enemies. Snorri in the *Ynglinga Saga* writes: "His (Odin's) men went without armor and were as mad as hounds or wolves. They bit their shields, and were as strong as bears or bulls. They slew men, but neither fire nor iron had effect on them. This is called to run berserk."

In their state of "battle fury" these warriors performed apparently miraculous feats and endured tremendous pain, as well as appearing to change their physical size and shape.[43] It has been conjectured that at times the berserker's trance was a kind of "out of body experience" in which the soul of the warrior shapeshifted into animal form and raged in battle. The celebrated champion of King Hrolf of Denmark was said to fight in the form of a great bear in the ranks of the king's army, while his human body lay at home in sleep.[44] Such spirit-allies were known as *fylgia* in Old Norse, or "fetch" in English, comparable to the spirit animal-helper of shamans. More than likely these Norse warriors were influenced by the shamanic practices of northern Eurasian peoples, in which wolves and bears were common helping-spirits and shamans wore those animal's pelts, believing they endowed them with their powers.

In the cult of Odin, warriors were disciplined with combat training, combined with initiation ordeals such as fighting wild animals. Their lack of fear of death was probably reinforced by the belief that those slain in battle would be taken to Valhalla, the paradise of brave warriors where they would spend their time drinking, feasting and fighting. Only those who died in battle were guaranteed such a fate—all others were condemned to the dark and dreary realm of Hel after death.

The *Valkyries* who were attendants of Odin could also act as guides or spirit wives to their chosen heroes; they were pictured as armed females on horseback, often appearing in groups of nine or thirteen. Women played an important role in warfare of Germanic tribes, who sometimes had female warriors as well as military leaders. According to the Roman writer Tacitus, the wives and womenfolk of the family or clan accompanied men into battle, taking care of the wounded, bringing food and supplies, and rallying the warriors.

Christianity at Sword-Point—Conversion Of the Germans

The southern German tribes were converted to Christianity centuries earlier than those in the north, and by 325 CE, the Goths already had a Christian bishop. The Germans were often reluctant to accept the new faith however. The emperor Charlemagne fought against the Saxons who refused to convert, destroying their sacred symbol the Irminsul, the pillar which was believed to hold up the sky, comparable to the Yggdrasil Tree. He issued a harsh edict in 785 CE declaring that those who "shall have scorned to come to baptism and shall have wished to remain a pagan, let him be punished by death".[45]

Christianity arrived late in the northern lands, and until the 11th century the Swedes maintained a temple in Uppsala to their gods Thor, Odin, and Freyr, next to which grew a huge evergreen tree in imitation of Yggdrasil.[46] From the branches of that tree hung the corpses of dogs, horses and humans—victims sacrificed to the gods. It was only in 1033 CE that Norway was Christianized by force and pagan temples looted and burned. Many pagans refused to convert, dying for their faith. Even after the destruction of the Uppsala temple around 1100 CE, paganism continued openly until the 1120's, when the Christian Norwegian king Sigurd declared a crusade against the pagans, laying waste to the country.[47] The Swedes were the last Germanic people to adopt Christianity, and the Sami were not converted until the 17th century. Like the people of other European countries, the Scandinavians retain traces of pagan traditions in their folklore, which will be discussed later.

Chapter 7 Notes

Odin and bear-headed berserker. Bronze plate, Sweden 5th-8th cent. CE.

1. Cunliffe. *Europe Between The Oceans*. 2008: 354.
2. Manco, Jean. *Ancestral Journeys*. 2013:158.
3. Williams. *Prehistoric belief: shamans, trance and the afterlife*. 2010: 189.
4. Julius Caesar. *De Bello Gallico VI*.
5. Evans-Wentz, W. Y. *Fairy Faith in Celtic Countries*. 1911: 368.
6. MacCulloch, J. A. *The Religion of the Ancient Celts*.1911: 321.

7. Tina Fields (ed) Walter & Fridman. *Shamanism: An Encyclopedia of World Beliefs, Practices and Culture*, Vol.1. 2004:471.
8. Matthews, Caitlín; John, Matthews. *The Encyclopedia of Celtic Wisdom*.1996:2.
9. Aldhouse-Green. *The Quest for the Shaman*. 2005: 196.
10. Matthews. *The Encyclopedia of Celtic Wisdom*. 1996: 352-4.
11. Ibid.:352.
12. Ibid.: 356.
13. Ibid.:334.
14. Williams. *Prehistoric belief: shamans, trance and the afterlife*. 2010:196.
15. Nichols, Ross. *The Book of Druidry: History, Sites and Wisdom*. 1990:124.
16. Green, Miranda J. *Symbol & Image in Celtic Religious Art*. 1989:224.
17. Green, Miranda. *Sun Gods of Ancient Europe*.1992: 86.
18. Matthews, John. *The Druid Source Book: from earliest times to the present day*. 1997: 325.
19. Green. *Symbol & Image in Celtic Religious Art*. 1989:96.
20. Green. *Sun Gods of Ancient Europe*.1992:17.
21. Ibid.:112.
22. Ibid.:170.
23. Carr-Gomm. 2002: 31.
24. Aldhouse-Green. *The Quest for the Shaman*. 2005: 202.
25. Gimbutas. *The Living Goddess.1999*.
26. Schultz., Herbert. *The Prehistory of Germanic Europe*. 1983:309-311
27. Manco. *Ancestral Journeys*. 2013: 202.
28. Cunliffe, *Europe Between The Oceans*. 2008: 416.
29. Metzner, Ralph. *The Well of Remembrance: Rediscovering the Earth Wisdom Myths of Northern Europe*.1994: 92-93.
30. Ibid.: 96, 192.
31. Ibid.: 93.
32. Ibid.: 126.
33. Ibid.:151.
34. Ibid.:112.
35. Ibid.:193-195.
36. Thorsson, Eldred. *Futhark: A Handbook of Rune Magic*. 1984:5.
37. Davidson, H.R.Ellis. *Gods and Myths of Northern Europe*.1964: 149.
38. Metzner. *The Well of Remembrance: Rediscovering the Earth Wisdom Myths of Northern Europe*.1994: 89.
39. Davidson. *Gods and Myths of Northern Europe*. 1964:119.
40. Bonewits, Isaac. "Indo-European Paleopaganism and its Clergy". Published in *Druid' Progress #1*, 1984.
41. Metzner. *The Well of Remembrance: Rediscovering the Earth Wisdom Myths of Northern Europe*. 1994:75
42. Davidson. *Gods and Myths of Northern Europe*. 1964: 68.
43. Metzner. *The Well of Remembrance: Rediscovering the Earth Wisdom Myths of Northern Europe*. 1994:75-77.
44. Davidson. *Gods and Myths of Northern Europe*. 1964 p. 68.
45. Munro, Dana Carelton. *Selections From the Laws of Charles the Great*. 2004.

46. Krupp, E.C. *Beyond the Blue Horizon: Myths and Legends of the Sun, Moon, Stars, and Planets.* 1991: 287
47. Jones, Prudence & Pennick, Nigel. *A History of Pagan Europe.* 1995: 137.

Chapter 8: Indigenous European Shamanism

Scythian elk tattoo found on mummy of Pazyryk chief. 5th cent. BCE.

The Sami Noaide—Shamans of Scandanavia

The Sami people inhabit areas of Finland, Norway, Sweden and the Kola Peninsula of Russia. They were the indigenous inhabitants of those lands before the arrival of Indo-European speaking Germans and Slavs. Although in recent centuries they adopted reindeer herding, they originally were semi-nomadic, living in small bands which survived by hunting, fishing and gathering edible plants.

The religion of the Sami was based on shamanism and nature worship. They followed a pantheon of four main gods: the Mother, Father, Son and Daughter; (Radienacca, Radienacce, Radienkiedde and Radienkieda respectively) as well as the god of fertility, fire, and thunder Horagalles; the sun goddess Beive; the Moon god Manno; and the goddess of death Jabemeahkka. They also honored the ancestors and spirits of the land, including a number of animistic guardian spirits such as the "wind-master", "the water man", and the god of reindeer and hunting.[1] Sacred groves, boulders, and other natural sites were their places of worship. The bear cult played an important role in many Sami tribes, and bears were believed to be mediators between the gods and humans.

The Vikings respected the Sami as miracle workers and experts in magic, including wind magic and raising of storms. The *Saga of Olaf Tryggvason* tells the the story of a great Finnish Sami sorcerer Raud, who prevented the Christian king from entering a fjord in which he lived by raising squalls and a storm. According to another story, two Sami Lapps were sent on a shamanic journey of "remote viewing" to Iceland by the Viking Ingimund the Old, to locate a silver image of the god Freyr. Their description was accurate and Ingimund found it exactly where they predicted he would.

The Sami had their own shamanic practitioners called *noaide*. They passed on their traditions between families, with an aging shaman training a young relative to take their place before dying. Training lasted as long as the noaide lived, and the student had to prove their abilities before a group of other noaidi before becoming a shaman at their mentor's death. One of their shamanistic ceremonies is described by Baron John Abercromby. It corresponds closely to the practices of Siberian shamanism in its use of drumming, handling fire, intoxication, deep trance, and journeying with the aid of spirit-allies to the otherworld to gain information:

> "Striking his drum, and singing as loud as he could, he began to summon his *saivo* followers or helpful spirits. First he summoned the *saivo bird*, and told it to bring from that region some of its inhabitants, but first of all the saivo fish or snake. When all who intended to assist at the ceremony had arrived, the wizard took off his cap, loosened his belt, placed his hands on his knees, and began, drum in hand, to run around on his knees with wonderful rapidity and with curious gestures. Now and then he cried out: harness the reindeer! launch the boat! Then he threw hot ashes from the fire with his naked hands, pretending fire did not hurt him, drank brandy, and struck himself on the knee with an axe. Finally, from the effects of previous fasting and his violent exertions he fell into a swoon, during which no one might touch him, for his spirit was now traveling on the saivo fish...When he came to himself he related what he had seen, what arrangements he had made with the dead, and announced in an oracular manner what ought to be done". [2]

The prehistoric origins of the Sami continue to be debated by scholars. One theory proposes they are descended from the mesolithic Komsa people who settled in Northern Finland around 9,000 BCE. The Komsa in turn may have originated in the Late Paleolithic Ahrensburg cuture of northwest Europe.[3] An alternate theory suggests paleolithic origins in the Franco-Cantabrian refuge of northern Spain and southwestern France in the vicinity of Lascaux, the same area inhabited by the cave painters.[4] Genetic studies suggest mixed Berber/Iberian as well as Northern Eurasian ancestry of the Sami.[5]

To complicate matters, the Sami speak a *Finno-Ugrian* language, similar to that spoken by the Khants and Mansi peoples of Siberia, and their shamanic practices are remarkably similar to them. About one-third of the Sami's vocabulary has no equivalent in Finno-Ugrian, however, and is thought to be the remnant of an ancient European language, possibly related to Basque.[6]

The Scythians & Huns—Shamans of the Eurasian Steppes

Beginning around the 8th century BCE, nomadic populations from the steppes of Central Asia started moving westward toward Iran—and eastward to the borders of Mongolia and China. Although the reason for their migrations is unclear, one possibility is prolonged drought forcing populations to abandon farming and become nomadic shepherds.[7]

The Scythians were among these waves of migrating peoples. They were related to the Iranians and spoke an Indo-European language, though there may have been groups among them with Mongolian ancestry as well. According to some researchers, the Scythians originated in the Siberian steppe lands, the same area where earlier groups of early Indo-Europeans had settled, as previously discussed. The Scythians were nomadic warriors, skilled archers, and horsemen who lived by plundering and trading. Some of them controlled sections of the lucrative Silk Road trade from China to the West.[8] They mastered riding horses and using horse-drawn wagons, allowing them to be highly mobile and far ranging.

The ancient Greek historian Herodotus records that Scythian warriors were so ferocious they drank the blood of their first victims in battle, and made cups from their skulls. He also mentions that their fiercest warriors were not always men—women also fought in battle and female archers would cut off a breast in order to draw their bow strings more efficiently. Archaeologists have uncovered graves in which female bodies have been found dressed like men and buried with weapons, seeming to confirm the reports of Herodotus.

The Scythians mummified and embalmed their dead, burying important individuals in large earthen mounds—called *kurgans,* along with their horses, consorts and servants to accompany them in the afterlife. The dead, which were often mummified, were considered "living corpses", which were not buried for forty days until the soul was finally believed to leave the body, according to archaeologist Jeannine Davis-Kimball.[9] Mummified bodies have been found that are remarkably preserved, displaying full body tattoos with intricate designs of imaginary beasts.

The Scythian pantheon of deities included goddesses such as *Tabiti*, goddess of the hearth and family, *Api*, the Earth goddess and *Argimpasa*, patroness of fertility and marriage. Prominent gods included *Papaios* the sky god and *Oitosyros*, god of crops and herds and defender against disease.[10] Like other steppe nomads, the Scythians worshipped nature gods: the sun and moon, thunder and lightning, mountains, lakes, rain and wind. They also eclectically absorbed elements from the religions of the Greeks, Romans, Persians, Indians, Thracians and Zoroastrians. Their religion was a mixture of polytheism, ancestor worship and animism.

According to historian Yulia Ustinova, female deities dominated the Scythian pantheon, perhaps a reflection of women's former importance in their society.[11] Their religion was presided over by *priestesses*—as the female sex was credited with greater intuitive powers that facilitated communion with the gods. Archaeologist Jeannine Davis-Kimball also asserts that women played a prominent role in Scythian society, serving as tribal leaders, warriors, healers and priestesses. Davis-Kimball excavated burial kurgans in Pokrovka on the border of Russia and Kazakstan dating to 500 BCE. There she discovered graves containing the skeletons of females whom she believes were priestesses, interred with stone and clay altars, seashells, carved bone spoons, and hemp seeds. Amulets were also found embellished with animal-style motifs such as snow leopards. She insists these are significant, since large felines were believed to be the animal-spirit helpers of female shamans, associated with the shamanic "mistress of animals".[12] In these graves bronze mirrors were often found—likely used for divination and perhaps healing. Davis-Kimball insists Scythian priestesses practiced the healing arts and served as oracles for the gods. They appeased the gods through sacrifice and prayer, using cultic spoons to ritually feed them, or their symbolic representations. The few males found buried with religious artifacts seem to have been transvestites or eunuch priests.

Male shamans eventually replaced priestesses, starting in the early Iron Age around 1,000 BCE, according to Davis-Kimball. She writes that the influence of shamanism originated among the forest tribes of Siberia then spread south, first coexisting with, then displacing Scythian priestesses.

Carlo Ginzburg also asserts the Scythians derived shamanic practices from Central Asian and Siberian shamans.[13] He points out that like them, they built sweat lodges in which they burned hemp seeds on heated stones. They also used cannabis to induce trance prior to divination. Herodotus writes about Scythian soothsayers who predicted the future using willow tree rods or the bark of linden trees. They were called *Enares*, meaning "non-men", or "women-men", practicing transexualism, similar to some shamans from Siberia and elsewhere.

First settling in Iran, the Scythians were driven out by the relatives of the Persians, the Medians, then migrated westward. They settled along the shores of the Black Sea where they traded amber, gold and furs with the Greeks. Around the 6th century BCE they moved further to the west, settling along the borders of Thrace in the area of the lower Danube, in present day Bulgaria and Romania. There they mingled with local Celtic and Thracian populations, passing on elements of their culture and shamanic religion to them, according to Ginzburg.[14] He writes that a Scythian goddess—the "mistress of animals"—is echoed in the Celtic horse goddess Epona, as well as the Thracian goddess Bendis. Ginzburg proposes that shamanistic practices such as ecstasy, magical flight, and animal metamorphosis or shapeshifting were known to the Scythians, who shared them with the ancient Celts.

Ginzburg also credits the Scythians with the origins of "Animal Style" art which featured stylized zoomorphic designs on jewelry, weapons, textiles, etc. He argues that from them the style spread to the Thracians, Celts, and Scandinavians in Europe—as well as eastward to the Mongolians, Siberians and Chinese.[15] An example of diffusion of artistic styles is the famous Gundestrup Cauldron found in a Danish bog, assumed to be Celtic but probably made by craftsmen in Thrace.[16] The vessel's "animal-style" imagery suggests an exchange of cultural influences between the Scythians, Thracians and Celts. It's most striking image depicts a cross-legged man with antlers on his head, surrounded by beasts, likely representing the Celtic horned god Cernunnos who may have shamanic associations. Curiously, Altaic shamans wear deer horned headdresses to this day.

Ginzburg proposes that a "nocturnal goddess" surrounded by animals became the center of an "ecstatic cult of the shamanistic variety" spread by the Scythians throughout Europe. He suggests this cult may have endured in the form of various folk-traditions into the Middle Ages, appearing as the *benandanti* in Italy and the *kresniki* in Serbia, who will later be discussed. These people—like shamans—left their bodies in a state of ecstatic trance and engaged in battles with witches to ensure the health of their crops as well as to commune with the dead.

Traditions also persisted in European folklore about witches, followers of the Greek goddess Artemis or Diana, the "mistress of animals" who engaged in ecstatic flight to the realm of the dead in the shape of animals, or riding upon animals. Ginzburg writes: "The folkloric nucleus of the Sabbath—magic flight and metamorphosis—seems to derive from a remote Eurasian shamanism."[17] He points out that similar to Siberian shamans, European witches used hallucinogens including the *amanita muscaria* mushroom, and rye ergot, to induce altered states of consciousness.

Ginzburg concludes there was an underlying "Eurasian mythological unity" of folk traditions, shamanic beliefs, and rituals reaching across Europe to Central Asia.[18] He conjectures this was spread by the peoples of North and Central Asia, the Siberian hunters and nomads of the steppes, to the Scythians—and from them to the Celts, Thracians and other European peoples.

Was Attila the Hun A Shaman?

The Huns were another wave of Central Asian nomads who migrated to the west, appearing in Europe between the 4th -6th centuries CE. They consisted of groups of Turkic, Mongol, and Ugric peoples who had lived a nomadic existence on the vast Eurasian steppes. Like the Scythians before them they were skilled horsemen, fierce warriors and mounted archers.

Under the rulership of their war-lord Attila the Hun (406-453 CE) they conquered and ruled over an empire extending from the Ural River in Russia to the Rhine and Baltic Sea, even plundering Gaul and Italy. The Huns terrorized the newly Christianized Roman empire as well as the Germanic tribes, causing some of the greatest upheaval the European world had ever known. They were much feared by the Christians who believed them to be the demons Gog and Magog, bringers of the apocalypse in allegiance with the devil, calling their leader Attila the "scourge of god".[19]

The Huns, needless to say, never converted to Christianity. They and and other nomadic steppe peoples had their own shamanic religion known as Tengerism. Based on the worship of the eternal blue sky *Tengri,* the Earth, the spirits of nature, and ancestors, it survives in Mongolia, Central Asia and Anatolia to this day. The Huns consulted their shamans called *kams* before going to war. Attila used divination before deciding to go into battle, examining cattle entrails, as well as using the technique of scapulimancy, based on interpreting the cracks in bones to read the future.[20]

Some speculate Attila was himself a shaman due to his divination skills. During the prolonged siege of the Italian city of Aquileia, Attila based his victory on an omen. The early Christian historian Jordanes provides the following account :

"Attila chanced to be walking around the walls, considering whether to break camp or delay longer, and noticed that the white birds, namely the storks, who build their nests in the gables of houses, were bearing their young from the city and, contrary to their custom, were carrying them into the country. Being a very shrewd observer of events, he understood this and said to his soldiers: "You see the birds foresee the future. They are leaving the city sure to perish...Do you think this is a meaningless or uncertain sign?... He inflamed the hearts of the soldiers to attack Aquileia again." [21]

According to legend, the wall on which the storks had nested cracked and collapsed soon after, and Attila and his men entered the city, razing it to the ground. Following this conquest Attila sacked other cities in Italy including Milan, Verona, and Padua, devastating and depopulating the land. The Huns finally reached the gates of Rome where Attila was met by Pope Leo I, who entered into his tent and negotiated with him in person. According to legend, Leo, dressed in his papal robes, implored and threatened Attila with the power of St. Peter if he did not spare Rome and return to his homeland. Atilla agreed to do so, turning his troops back. Later asked by his servants why he had capitulated so easily, Attila replied he had seen a vision of St. Peter hovering above the Pope's head, holding a sword and threatening to kill him if he didn't acquiesce.

Was Attila's decision to spare Rome really based on a vision? Historians conclude it is more likely famine and the inability to feed his troops were the cause of his withdrawal. In any case, the Western Roman Empire was saved that day from destruction, and Atilla and his hoards returned to their homeland in the plains of Hungary.

The Taltos: Hungarian Shamans

Related to the Huns were the *Magyars,* another nomadic tribe from the Central Asian steppes who migrated into south-eastern Europe in the 10th century CE, settling in present day Hungary. Early Hungarian kings, however, traced their lineage to Attila, and he is still a national hero in Hungary, where boys are named after him to this day. Hungarian linguist Andras Rona-Tas insists that the Hungarians between the 6th and 9th centuries CE practiced the shamanic religion of Tengerism. He writes: "Tengerism and shamanism together provided the wider framework into which the conquering Magyar's beliefs can be placed".[22]

Other linguists and ethnologists note that the *Finno-Ugrian* language spoken by Hungarians is related not only to the Sami language of Finland, but also to Siberian. Hungarian ethnologist and linguist Vilmos Dioszegi conducted field research in Siberia on shamanism. He observed that the practices of the Hungarian folk-magicians—the *taltos*—were similar to those of Siberian shamans, concluding the Magyars had originally migrated from Siberia.

According to historian Ronald Hutton, the Siberian shaman and the Hungarian *taltos* share similar characteristics: both undergo an initiatory experience in childhood, acquire powers such as shapeshifting into animals, duel with spirit enemies during magical flight, and use special equipment such as a feathered or horned head-dress and drum or sieve. Hutton writes: "the Magyars represent a southern parallel to the Sami, an isolated example of "classic" shamanism of the Siberian sort..."[23] During their initiations, the taltos dreamed of being cut into pieces, as well as climbing a tree to reach the sky. They communed with ancestors and spirits in the state of ecstasy—experiences also shared by Siberian shamans.

Some ancient Hungarian myths reveal striking similarities with those of Inner Asia. The cosmos was divided into three worlds, linked together by the World Tree. Upon its branches sat an eagle, along with the spirits of unborn children—mythemes found also in Siberian myths.

The conclusions of these scholars and others suggest that the Scythians, Huns, and Magyars who settled in south-eastern Europe brought with them the religion, myths and shamanic practices of the peoples of the Eurasian steppes and Inner Asia. Similar to the Hungarians, the Sami people of Scandinavia also speak a Finno-Ugrian language, and like them practice their own form of shamanism closely related to that of the Siberians.

Chapter 8 Notes

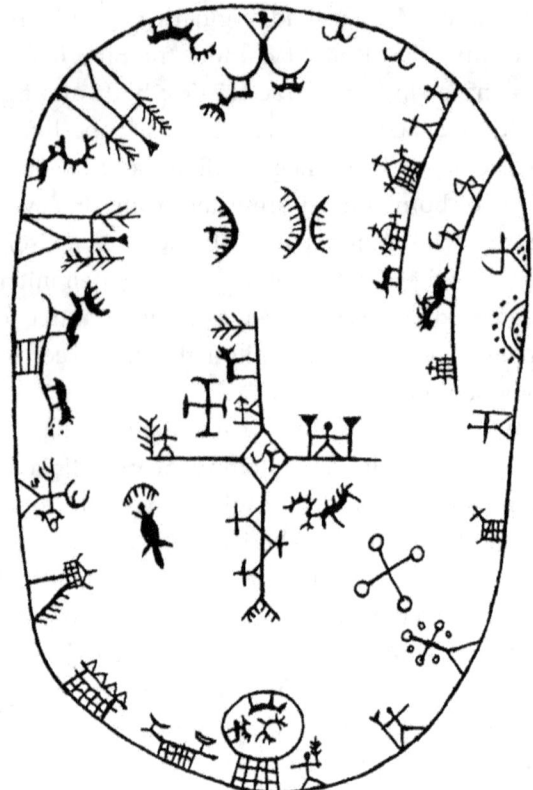

Sami shaman's drum.

1. Jones & Pennick. *A History of Pagan Europe*. 1995: 181-182.
2. Abercromby, John. *The Pre-and Proto-historic Finns, Both Eastern and Western: with the Magic Songs of the West Finns.* 1898: 174-175.
3. "Sami history" Wikapedia.
4. Alden. "Shamanism and Sacred Arts in Finland- Part 2". *Spirit Boat-exploring Finnish shamanism and its relevance for today*. 2014.
5. Manco. *Ancestral Journeys.* 2013:66.
6. Alden. "Shamanism and Sacred Arts in Finland- Part 2". 2014.
7. Ginzburg. *Ecstasies: Deciphering the Witches' Sabbath.* 1991: 208.
8. Manco. *Ancestral Journeys.* 2013:140.
9. Davis-Kimball, Jeannine. Ph.D. *Warrior Women*. 2002: 74.
10. Ibid.: 68. Herodotus mentions the Scythians worshipped Hestia, the Greek goddess of the hearth. Notably, the cult of the hearth is also widespread among the Mongols and Turks.
11. Ustanova, Yulia. *The Supreme Gods of the Bosporan Kingdom: Celestial Aphrodite and the Most High God*. 1998:69.

12. Davis-Kimball. *Warrior Women*. 2002: 72. The Mistress of Animals later became "Great Mother" goddesses such as Cybele in Anatolia, according to Davis-Kimball.
13. Ginzburg. *Ecstasies: Deciphering the Witches' Sabbath*. 1991:210.
14. Ibid.: 214.
15. Ibid.
16. Williams. *Prehistoric belief: shamans, trance and the afterlife*. 2010:196.
17. Ginzburg. *Ecstasies: Deciphering the Witches' Sabbath* 1991: 136.
18. Ibid.: 296.
19. Menchen-Helfen, Otto. *The World of the Huns: Studies in their History and Culture*. 1973: 5.
20. Ibid.: 269.
21. Ibid.:133.
22. Rona-Tas. Andras. *Hungarians and Europe in the Early Middle Ages: An Introduction to Early Hungarian History*. 1999:151.
23. Hutton. *Shamans-Siberian Spirituality and the Western Imagination*. 2001: 143-144.

Chapter 9: The Mystery Religions

Maenad dancing ecstatically for Dionysus, Greek kylix 5th cent. BCE.

Personal Encounter With The Gods

The mystery religions flourished during the Hellenistic era (3rd century BCE) until the end of the Roman Empire, worshipping deities from across the Hellenistic empire: Egypt, Syria, Anatolia, Persia and Greece. They offered deeper and more satisfying religious experiences than the older cults of the Olympic gods of the *polis* or city-state. Rather than showing external allegiance to the gods of the city by participating in public rituals, the mysteries emphasized an inward and personal form of worship. Remarkably egalitarian in nature, they were open to slaves, the rich and poor, all ethnic groups, and men and women alike. As such, they offered a temporary liberation from the restrictions of social class, based on the realization of spiritual equality. In fact they provided an "alternative spirituality" to the mainstream religions of their societies—similar in many ways to the paths of modern western esotericism which will later be explored.

The word "mystery", or *mysterion* in Greek, derives from the Greek verb *myein*—"to close", according to historian Marvin W. Meyer. This refers to the vow of silence taken by initiates, who were required to close their eyes and lips, to not reveal the secret ceremonies they had witnessed.[1] The mystery religions were secret societies based on initiations into the spiritual realities of the gods and goddesses of their cults. They focused on a personal encounter with the divinity and the individual salvation of the participant.

These experiences were sometimes ecstatic in nature, as in the Dionysian rites, where worshippers were led out of the city to roam the countryside. There they engaged in *orgia*—meaning "secret rites" and "worship". Through the use of music, dancing, chanting and drinking of wine, the Maenads were possessed by Dionysus the god of wine and ecstasy. In the opinion of researchers Wasson and Ruck, the wine used in Dionysian ritual was likely a concoction of hallucinogenic ingredients added to the alcohol which induced altered states of consciousness.[2]

While some rituals in the mystery religions were public and celebratory, others were private, devotional, and ascetic in nature. These consisted of purifications and lustrations, as well as sacrifices and prayers to the deities. In the Eleusinian Mysteries of Athens there were three types of observances that may shed some light on the esoteric teachings and practices of the mysteries in general. The *legoma* or "things recited" probably consisted of chantings or recitations of stories of the cult's deities to provide a mythological background for the initiates. The *deiknymena* or "things shown" consisted of the unveiling of sacred cult objects during the height of ceremonies. Finally the *dromena* or "things performed" included mystical dramas enacting the myths of the deities of the cult, and were probably theatrical productions staged by the priestesses and priests. They presented liturgical dramas in which the initiates played the roles of the goddesses and gods—wearing their masks and costumes and re-enacting their sufferings and joys.

Many of the mysteries were rooted in the archaic religions of the Neolithic and Bronze Age, based on agrarian festivals that celebrated the fertility of nature and the yearly seasonal cycle of planting, growing, and harvesting crops. The Eleusinian Mysteries were founded on the myth of Demeter the goddess of the ripe grain, and her search for her daughter Persephone who symbolized the grain sown in the fields. The cult of Dionysus was based on the deity of the grapevine and wine, as well as wild vegetation, celebrating the life force in all nature. Dying gods such as Osiris, Baal, Tammuz, and Adonis were also linked to the seasonal cycle of vegetation. The search for, and reunion with the dying god by his lover the goddess, and his resurrection, provides the mythos of their cults. The agrarian festivals were dominated by goddesses and were connected with the fertility of the earth and the divine mother worshipped as Isis, Cybele, Demeter, and Kore. The sacred marriage or *hieros gamos* between the god and goddess, as well as the birth of the divine child, was also celebrated.

Samothracian Mysteries

In contrast to agrarian mysteries, the chthonic *Samothracian Mysteries* possibly grew out of guilds of craftsmen—blacksmiths—and were associated with the Cabeiri, the mythic dwarf-like sons or grandsons of the god Hephaestus, the divine smith. They were also related to mythical races such as the Cyclopes, Dactyls, and Korbyantes who likewise were connected to the art of metallurgy.

The Cabeiri were pre-Greek in origin, according to Burkert, originating in Thrace or Phyrigia with possible influences from the Hittites and proto-Etruscans.[3] Their cult was centered on the North Aegean islands of Samothrace and Lemnos. The Samothracian mysteries were nearly as popular as the Eleusinian mysteries, and like them endured for centuries. Participation was open to all—men and women, children and adults, Greeks and non-Greeks, slaves or freemen. Among its famous initiates were the historian Herodotus as well as King Philip II of Macedon, father of Alexander the Great, who first met his wife Olympias there.

Although it was taboo to mention the names of the deities honored in the secret rites, ancient sources imply they consisted of two goddesses and a god: Axieros, Axiokersa, and Axiokersos and their servant Cadmilos. One of the goddesses could be identified with Meter or Kybele the Anatolian "mountain mother", another with Hecate, while Cadmilos, a god with phallic associations was probably similar to Hermes. The mysteries of the Cabeiri had a raucous, burlesque character.[4] Scenes of grotesque figures engaged in comical dramas are depicted on pottery associated with them.[5] They were probably celebrated by a bull sacrifice, sacred dances, as well as the drinking of wine. Similar to the mysteries of Eleusis, the abduction of a goddess of fertility by the god of the underworld was probably ritually enacted.

In Homer's Odyssey, the Argonauts were initiated into the mysteries of Samothrace, and it has been suggested that Orpheus was also initiated into their cult. They were believed to protect sailors at sea, as well as confer a happy life in this world and the next.

Isis — The First Universal Goddess

The cult of Isis originated in Egypt and became Hellenized around the 3rd century BCE. Isis was often paired with her husband Sarapis, who was a hybrid of the gods Osiris and Apis—and later syncretized with the Greek gods Zeus, Asclepius, Hades, and Dionysus. The cult of Isis and Serapis was one of the first of the "international" religions. It took hold among the peoples of the Mediterranean at the same time as they were losing their distinct ethnic identities and religions due to the spread of the Hellenistic and Roman empires. At that time Isis arrived, saying "I am Isis, sovereign over all countries". This was a new idea, according to historian Tran Tam Tinh, breaking with the ethnically centered religious traditions of antiquity.[6] Isis was known as "the queen of heaven" and became the first universal goddess, embodying the attributes and powers of all other deities. Her religion spread around the Mediterranean world, with temples in Rome, Pompeii, Athens and elsewhere.

Isis was a savior goddess who was ready to come to the aid of all human suffering. Credited with miraculous healing powers, she was believed to protect and bless her worshipers with good fortune. Her cult was open to all and she was worshipped by the downtrodden as well as the powerful, including a number of Roman emperors.[7] The iconography of Isis suckling the child Horus was likely the prototype of Mary nursing the infant Jesus. The widespread and popular cult of Isis competed with early Christianity which finally abolished her worship upon gaining political power. Nevertheless, some of Isis's traits were assimilated into the Madonna of the new faith. As a universal religion, the cult of Isis prepared the ground for Christianity.

The mysteries of Isis featured initiation rites modeled on her sufferings, and included a symbolic death and resurrection of the initiate and salvation through her grace. During the initiation the candidate spent ten days fasting and in abstinence. Then on an evening chosen by the goddess they underwent secret rites of purification and instruction. The next day the initiate, holding a torch and dressed in magnificent robes, was presented to the public to be adored like the Sun god.[8] Public celebrations and processions accompanied the celebration of Isis's mysteries. Meyer describes them as "carnivals that would rival modern celebrations of Mardi Gras".[9] Apuleius (125-180 CE) was a Roman writer and initiate into several mystery religions, including the cult of Isis. Here he describes a public mystery procession of her initiates in his novel *The Golden Ass or Metamorphoses:*

> "Then came the throng of those initiated in the mysteries, men and women of all ranks and ages in shining robes of pure white linen..Next appeared

the gods who deigned to proceed on human feet. First was the dread messenger between the gods above and the Underworld, his dog's head held high aloft, his face now black, now gold: Anubis, holding a caduceus in his right hand and brandishing a green palm-leaf in his left. Hard on his heels followed a cow standing upright, the fertile image of the All-Mother, proudly borne on the shoulders of one of her blessed priests. Another was carrying a chest containing mystic emblems and securely concealing the secrets of the glorious faith. Another carried in his fortunate embrace the worshipful image of the supreme divinity...." [10]

The purpose of the mystery religions was not so much instruction in doctrine, but to provide a personal experience of the sacred. The philosopher Aristotle writes that the mysteries contain "not a lesson to learn, but an experience to undergo and a condition into which they (the initiates) must be brought while they are becoming fit (for revelation)." In other words they are put into a certain state of mind which allows them to experience the transcendent. Often the initiate was led through cathartic ritual dramas of death and darkness— emerging from them into light and rebirth—similar to the initiation experiences of shamans. Apuleius describes the revelations and visions of the underworld he experienced during his initiation rite:

"I approached the confines of death and having trodden on the threshold of Proserpina returned, having been carried through all the elements, to the depths of midnight I saw the sun glittering with a splendid light, together with the infernal and supernal gods, and to these divinities approaching, I paid the tribute of devout adoration".[11]

The Myth of Persephone

The ancient Greek myth *The Rape of Persephone* is another example of an underworld descent, known as a *katabasis*, meaning "to go down". It echoes many of the motifs of earlier myths including those of Inanna and Osiris, as previously mentioned. Persephone, also known as Kore, was the daughter of Demeter, goddess of grain and harvest, and Zeus, god of the heavens. The story of her abduction and eventual return to her mother became the scenario of the Eleusinian mysteries. The following version of the myth is paraphrased from Homer:

The gods Apollo, Hermes, Ares, and Hephaestos all desired the hand of the beautiful maiden Persephone for marriage. Her mother Demeter rejected their gifts and hid her daughter away from them. Hades, the lord of the underworld was also infatuated with the girl, and approached his brother Zeus about it. Knowing that Demeter would never allow her daughter to be his bride, Zeus advised him to abduct the girl instead.

One day while the innocent Kore was playing with her friends the nymphs in a flowery meadow, she wandered off, attracted to a beautiful narcissus flower. Suddenly she was seized by her uncle Hades who had emerged through a cleft in the earth, who then carried her off to the underworld in his chariot. Demeter searched far and wide for her daughter. For nine days she wandered over the face of the earth, torches ablaze in her hands, looking for her. Her sorrow was so great that not once did she think about eating, drinking, or bathing. The goddess Hekate approached Demeter and told her she had heard the cries of Kore but had not seen the abduction. Demeter and Hekate both approached Helios the sun-god who witnesses all actions. Sure enough, he had seen the deed and told Demeter of Kore's whereabouts.

Angry with Zeus who had betrayed his own daughter, Demeter withdrew from Olympus and wandered the world in disguise, mourning the loss of her daughter. Upon reaching the city of Eleusis she was greeted by the daughters of King Keleos. Demeter agreed to serve as the nursemaid for the son of the king and his wife Metaniera in their palace. In secrecy Demeter anointed the boy named Demophoon with ambrosia and held him over a fire nightly to make him immortal. The horrified parents caught her in the act and begged her to stop. Demeter did so and shed her human disguise, revealing her true nature as a goddess to everyone's astonishment. She demanded they build a temple to her, telling them she would instruct them in her sacred rites. Demeter took up residence in the temple and stayed within it, brooding. That year was terrible for mankind. Demeter abandoned her duties as goddess of grain, and the earth did not send up any seed. The grain refused to grow and hunger afflicted all creatures. Zeus, moved by the cries of the people, sent his messenger Iris, the rainbow, to Demeter asking her to relent. Demeter refused. Following this all the gods visited her, receiving the same reply. No one could persuade her, and she swore she would never send up the harvest of the earth until she saw her daughter again.

Zeus, fearing the extinction of mankind, sent Hermes the divine messenger to the underworld to convince Hades to release Persephone. But before doing so, Hades tricked her by giving her four pomegranate seeds to eat. He knew the Fates had decreed that whoever ate the food of the underworld was condemned to remain there. Having eaten the seeds, Persephone was obliged to spend four months of each year in the land below with her husband Hades during the barren season, but allowed to live the rest of the year with her mother on the surface world. The annual joyful reunion of Kore with Demeter brought growth and fertility back to the land, while her descent to the underworld every year brought death and decay.

According to Plutarch the classical Greek historian, Persephone symbolized the "psyche" or soul, and Demeter the physical body. The myth could be seen as an allegory of the human soul's journey between this world and the afterlife. To the uninitiated, Persephone was the feared queen of the underworld and death, but to initiates of her mysteries she was the merciful goddess who granted immortality. In an Orphic myth, Zeus, god of the heavens, mated with Persephone and she gave birth to Dionysus Zagreus, god of fertility, ecstasy and the immortal spirit.

The Persephone myth repeats motifs of earlier myths such as the Sumerian myth the *Descent of Inanna:* similar to Inanna's lover Dumuzi, Persephone is forced to live in Hades during the barren season, allowed to return to the surface world during the fertile part of the year. It borrows from the Osiris myth as well—the mourning of Isis and her search for Osiris is reiterated in Demeter's grief and search for Persephone. Another borrowing from the Osiris myth occurs when Demeter serves as nursemaid to the son of the king of Eleusis, holding him over a fire to bestow immortality upon him, exactly the same action performed by Isis for the son of the king of Byblos.

Besides their associations with the natural cycles of growth and decay, the myths of Inanna, Osiris, and Persephone also serve as allegories for the search for immortality and the soul's journey between this world and the next. The sequence of *loss, search, and reunion* could be seen as the universal pattern of the spiritual quest.

The Eleusinian Mysteries

The Homeric version of the Persephone myth given above was clearly linked to the mysteries and initiation rites celebrated in the city of Eleusis, near Athens. These mysteries preserved archaic religious rituals and probably remained relatively unchanged from their beginnings during the Mycenean Bronze Age around 1500 BCE. They were based on an agrarian cult much older than the Olympic gods and had strongly matriarchal elements featuring mother and daughter goddesses. The women's festival known as the Thesmorphia which honored Demeter and Persephone originated in the early Neolithic according to Burkert.[12] He notes that pig sacrifices were a feature of this festival, as in Eleusis, and clay statues of pigs studded with grains have been found dating back to this early period. Demeter and her daughter Persephone personified the grain—Demeter the ripe harvested grain, and Kore the newly planted seed.

There are differing opinions as to the origins of the mysteries of Eleusis. Some point to Minoan Crete where the worship of the great goddess dominated, claiming Demeter's name may be derived from the Cretan word for barley, *deai*. Legend has it that Orpheus brought the mysteries of Osiris and Isis from Egypt to Greece where they became the basis for the Eleusinian Mysteries. On the other hand, the cult may have derived from the north of Greece from Thessaly or Thrace, according to archaeologist George E. Mylonas.[13]

Whatever their origins, it is impressive that the Eleusinian mysteries were continuously celebrated until 395 CE when its temples were destroyed by the Visigoths led by Alaric. They were open to women as well as men, and all classes of society from kings to slaves, requiring participants only to be Greek speakers of upright moral standing. Among their initiates were illuminati such as Aristotle, Sophocles, Plato, Cicero, and a number of Roman emperors such as Augustus, Marcus Aurelius, and Hadrian. They were considered to be among the most important mysteries in the ancient world. It was believed Demeter had given grain and the arts of agriculture to mankind at Eleusis, thus civilization was founded there.

Although we know little about the details of the mysteries due to the secrecy to which initiates were sworn, it is known they involved ritual dramas enacted by priestesses and priests as well as the participants. The mystery drama probably consisted of three parts: the enactment of the abduction of Persephone by Hades to the underworld, the search by Demeter for her missing daughter, and Persephone's return to the surface world and joyful reunion with her mother. Karl Kerenyi argues that Dionysus the god of wine, ecstasy, and immortality originally played the role of male protagonist, rather than Hades, and probably fathered a divine child with either Demeter or Persephone. The birth of their child Brimo or Ploutos, meaning "wealth" from the flames of underworld, was possibly enacted through ritual drama by which participants glimpsed the possibility of their own rebirth. Demeter's attempt to immortalize the king's son in the fire, as told in the Homeric myth, may also allude to this mystery, according to Kerenyi.[14]

Just as Demeter searched for her missing daughter Persephone, initiates at Eleusis sought a missing part of themselves, their own souls. To be initiated into the mysteries, one experienced a ritualized death and rebirth, a metaphorical descent to the underworld, and return as one who was "born twice". Initiates gained an experience of Hades while alive, relieving them of the fear of death and promising a happy afterlife. The ancient Greek historian Plutarch wrote:

"Thrice happy are those mortals who see these mystery rites before they depart to Hades. For to them alone it is permitted to have true life of the other side". He also observed: "Thus death and initiation closely correspond" and noted the similarity of the Greek verbs *"teleutan"* — to die, and *"teleishai"* — to be initiated. The sophist Aelius Aristeides tells us that for the initiates of the Eleusinian Mysteries, birth and death no longer had any hold over their lives. One may speak endlessly of the afterlife, he adds, but if he has not descended into Hades he doesn't know what he is talking about.

The Lesser & Greater Mysteries

The Eleusinian mysteries consisted of two parts: the Lesser and Greater mysteries. The Lesser Mysteries were held every year in Athens in the month of February, and were dedicated to Persephone. At this time new initiates or *mystai* prepared by listening to the myth's narration, and purified themselves by bathing in the river Illisos. The Greater Mysteries were also celebrated each year, and every fourth year with special extravagance. They were dedicated to Demeter and took place in Eleusis during the month of Boedromion, at the end of September and early October. Occurring over a nine day period, they commemorated the nine days Demeter wandered the earth searching for Kore. These initiates had completed the previous lesser mysteries and were called *epoptes,* meaning "one who has seen". The nine day duration of the greater mysteries may have symbolically referred to the nine-months of gestation in the womb.

Nine Days of Eleusis

On the *first day* of the Greater Mysteries a herald would invite all who wished to participate, excluding those who "were not clean of hand" or "imprudent of voice", meaning murderers, criminals, as well as gossips. The initiates would walk from Athens to Eleusis along the Sacred Way, illuminated by the full moon, a distance of fifteen miles. On the *second day* they rallied to the cry: "To the Sea, oh Mystai".[15] They purified themselves and a piglet which they carried with them in the sea, then returned to Athens. On the *third day* the entire city of Athens mourned Demeter's loss of Persephone while the "victims" were brought to the altar. Each candidate symbolically sacrificed themselves by offering their piglet as a surrogate sacrifice to the goddess. All citizens then fasted until night. The *fourth day* celebrated the festival honoring Asklepios, god of healing.[16] On the *fifth day* the "sacred articles", probably consisting of Mycenaean clay idols preserved down through the generations, were carried in ceremonial containers along with totems of the Eleusinian deities.[17] Following this was another procession from Athens to Eleusis which crossed a narrow bridge on which men in masks insulted and pilloried the rich and famous, humbling them to the amusement of other participants. To the shouts of "Iacchos! Iacchos!" a wooden statue of the god of the festivities was transported in a carriage at the head of the procession, bearing a torch and crowned with a wreath of myrtle.

The mystai carried rods made of woven branches and wore myrtle wreaths while engaging in a Dionysian frenzy of rapturous dancing throughout the night. Loud music, whirling, and darkness induced a sort of mania or exaltation of spirit leading to a state of ecstasy. The procession arrived in Eleusis, and participants entered the Temple of Demeter. There they spent the night in ritual dancing while female dancers held the *kernos,* which were containers filled with seeds and fruit on their heads.

The *sixth day* commenced the initiation rites proper. Sacrifices were first made to the Eleusinian deities. A herald then announced: *ekas, ekas oi veviloi* or "away, away with the profane". Initiates spent the night fasting and drank *kykeon,* a brew made of barley and mint, in remembrance of the drink offered to Demeter in her mourning. There have been recent theories proposing that kykeon contained a psychoactive substance, the hallucinogenic ergot fungi— *Claviceps purpurea*—which grows on barley[18]. Although consumption of a psychedelic potion by initiates would have induced altered states, the chanting, whirling torches, loud music, and frenzied dancing could also bring about ecstasy through sensory overload, stimulating the sympathetic nervous system to the point of exhaustion. Carrying torches, the mystai wandered through the dark, re-enacting Demeter's search for Persephone. Plutarch alludes to this event: "At first there are wanderings and toilsome running about in circles and journeys through the dark over uncertain roads and culs de sac; then just before the end there are all kinds of terrors with shivering, trembling, sweating and utter amazement."[19] It should be noted that trembling and "frenzy" are also experienced by some shamans during trance states.

A gong would sound and the *mystai* would then gather at the main temple known as the Telesterion, a large square building which could contain up to 3,000 people. In its center was the Anaktoron, a small stone building where the sacred objects of the cult were kept. The rite included three parts, as previously discussed: the dromena—that which was enacted, the deiknymena—the display of sacred objects, and the legomena—the words that were spoken, telling the myth along with its symbolic formulas, perhaps accompanied by invocations.[20]

A mystical drama based on the myth of Demeter and Persephone was apparently presented by the hierophants and priestesses for the crowd. Following this a great light mysteriously appeared before the assembly, perhaps representing the sun in the underworld, accompanied by silence and awe of the participants. According to Plutarch: "the temple shook; terrifying visions and fearful specters depicted the horrors of Hades and the fate awaiting the evil man". After this terrifying and cathartic spectacle, singing as well as the crashing of cymbals were possibly used by the hierophant to summon Persephone from the underworld, producing her "theophany" or divine appearance. Although skeptics have suggested the visions were illusions produced by stagecraft, Iordanis Poulkouras writes:

> "Much speculation surrounds the optical illusion which could have created the impression of the magical appearance of Persephone, though it must have been very impressive in order to trick such a large crowd...As far as archeological evidence goes, findings have shown that there were no hidden spaces in the Telesterium which might have supported special effects to mislead the adepts".[21]

The climax of the ritual occurred as the Hierophant opened the door to the Anaktoron and declared something like :"The Worshipful Mother has given birth to a son" referring to the birth of the infant Brimo. The sacred objects were then displayed to the crowd as they looked to the sky calling *Ie*—rain!, and then bent to the earth crying *Kye*—be fruitful! According to Hippolytus, the Hierophant then presented "the great, miraculous and most perfect mystery... an ear of grain in silence harvested." Plutarch writes: "After this a strange and wonderful light meets the wanderer; he is admitted into clean and verdant meadows, where he discerns gentle voices, and choric dances, and the majesty of holy sounds and sacred visions." The initiates having suffered the ordeal of days of fasting, physical exhaustion, frenzied dance and heightened expectation were at this point susceptible to a mass religious experience including mystical visions.

On the *seventh day* the statue of Iacchos was taken back to Athens. The *eighth day* consisted of libations and rites for the dead, and worship of the chthonic powers of the underworld. Two clay jars were probably filled with wine or water and placed to the East and West, then smashed when the ceremony was finished. On the *ninth day* the initiates returned to Athens completing the rite.

To Live in Joy & to Die with Hope

The Eleusinian Mysteries utilized dramatic paradoxes to provide a transcendent experience for initiates. Burkert notes that the experience is patterned by antithesis, moving between extremes of terror and happiness, darkness and light, and mourning followed by joy. Demeter's grief ends with exaltation and brandishment of torches.[22] Many days of fasting, physical exhaustion, loud music, whirling dance and torchlight processions brought the participants to a state of disorientation, exhaustion, catharsis and heightened awareness leading to a revelation of the mystery. The ancient Athenian statesman Aristides described these rites as being "...the most frightening and the most resplendent of all that is divine for men."

Similar to the shaman's initiation which bestows direct experience of life after death, the *mystai* experienced a catharsis during their visionary descent to the darkness of the underworld which overwhelmed their senses and transformed their identity. They emerged from this experience "reborn" into a new spiritual awareness. The fear of death no longer held sway over their lives and existence was pervaded with a sense of the sacred. Cicero writes on the importance of Eleusis: "We have been given a reason not only to live in joy, but also to die with better hope".

The Orphic Mysteries

"Mythology, like the severed head of Orpheus, goes on singing even in death and from afar." –Carl Kerenyi

Orpheus was the legendary Thracian poet, musician, and magician reputed to have introduced the mystery rites of his homeland to the Greeks. These may have been similar to those of the legendary Thracian priest-king Zalmoxis, said to have founded initiation rites involving a descent or *katabasis* to an underground chamber followed by a ritualized death and rebirth leading to epiphany. According to Herodotus, Zalmoxis taught that "he who perishes... goes to a place where they would live forever and have all good things". In contrast to the pessimistic view of the afterlife held by early Greeks like Homer, the Thracians believed in a blissful afterlife and the immortality of the soul—ideas that would profoundly influence the Hellenic mystery religions. The mystery religion of Orphism had a profound impact on the development of western esotericism and philosophy. Neoplatonic philosopher Proclus writes: "All the Greek's theology is the offspring of the Orphic mystical doctrine".

Several Presocratic philosophers including Pythagoras, Parmenides, and Empedocles were probably initiates of the cult of Orphism and influenced by its doctrines. It is thought Pythagoras may have pseudonymously authored

Orphic books. Many of Plato's philosophical doctrines originated with Orphism. Historian Giovanni Reale insists: "Without Orphism we cannot explain Pythagoras, nor Heraclitus, nor Empedocles, and naturally not Plato and whatever was derived from him."[23]

According to some legends, Orpheus was the son of the Thracian king Oeagrus and the muse Calliope. In other accounts he was said to be the son of the god Apollo who gave him a lyre, while the muses taught him verses and magical incantations. Through the power of his music it is said Orpheus enchanted wild beasts, a power attributed to shamans, and even made the rocks and trees move to follow his songs. Besides his fame as a musician, poet, and magician, he was also an adventurer who travelled the world. He visited Egypt where he learned sacred rites which he brought back to Greece. He was invited to accompany Jason and the argonauts in their journey to find the Golden Fleece. When the Argo sailed past the island of the Sirens, Orpheus saved his crew from shipwreck, drowning out the alluring enchantments of the Sirens with his own musical incantations.

Orpheus as Shaman—The Legend of Orpheus & Eurydice

One of the central myths of Orphism is the story of *Orpheus and Eurydice*. Historian Ake Hultkranz proposes that the Orpheus tale was from the beginning inspired by shamanistic experiences".[24] He proposes the myth narrates the shaman's ecstatic journey to recover a lost soul in the land of the dead, to restore the ailing person to health. According to him, the legend can be found in different versions across the world from Greece, Eurasia, Japan, Polynesia and North America. Hultkranz, as well as Peter Kingsley conjecture the myth originated in Central Asia and spread from there.[25] Here is a paraphrased version of *Orpheus and Eurydice* as told by the Latin poet Virgil:

On their wedding day Eurydice, the young bride of Orpheus, was bitten by a viper and died. Grief stricken, Orpheus resolved to descend to Hades to retrieve her. Arriving there he charmed the guardians of the underworld with his mournful music, moving Persephone the queen of the dead to release the soul of Eurydice to him—on the condition he did not turn back to look at her during the return trip. Almost reaching the surface world, Orpheus forgot and glanced back at his wife. To his dismay she vanished from sight, returning to Hades forever. In his mourning, Orpheus retired to the mountains to devote himself to the worship of Apollo. While there he was approached by a band of wandering Maenads, female worshippers of the god Dionysus. When Orpheus rejected their amorous advances they became enraged and attacked him, him tearing him limb from limb. His head continued even in death to mournfully utter the name of his beloved Eurydice.

Despite Virgil's tragic version of the myth in which Orpheus fails to bring Eurydice back, earlier Greek commentators say that Orpheus actually *succeeded* in rescuing his wife from the land of the dead. Historian M. Owen Lee argues that the story of Orpheus and Eurydice might have originally been a "charter myth" for the cult of Orphism, in which Orpheus brought back secrets of life and death from the underworld.[26] Lee notes that the name "Eurydice" can be translated as "she who gives justice far and wide", a far more fitting epithet for a goddess than a mortal woman. He suggests the name may actually refer to Persephone, queen of the dead, who was revered as the judge of souls by the Orphics. Accordingly, Orpheus may have learned the secrets of life and death from Eurydice/Persephone in the underworld which he revealed to his followers.

The flesh and blood existence of Orpheus is the subject of scholarly debate. Historians like I.M. Linforth find no evidence of him in historical records, concluding "...the reality of Orpheus is to be sought in what men thought and said about him".[27] Others propose Orpheus was an actual person, perhaps a king from ancient Thrace, the birthplace of the cult of Dionysus.

Historian W. K. Guthrie writes: "Orpheus was the founder of mystery religions and the first to reveal to men the meanings of the initiation rites."[28] As well as bringing the Thracian cult of Dionysus to Greece, legend has it Orpheus travelled to Egypt and studied their religious customs. The ancient Greek historian Diodorus writes:

> "Orpheus...brought from Egypt most of his mystic ceremonies, the orgiastic rites that accompanied his wanderings, and his fabulous account of his experiences in Hades. For the rite of Osiris is the same as that of Dionysus and that of Isis very similar to that of Demeter, the names alone having been interchanged; and the punishments of Hades of the unrighteous, the Fields of the Righteous, and the fantastic conceptions...all these were introduced by Orpheus in imitation of the Egyptian funeral customs."

Diodorus's comparison of the rites of Osiris to those of Dionysus refers to their similar myths and mysteries: both were vegetation gods who were slain, dismembered and resurrected. The myths of the goddesses Isis and Demeter share similarities as well, as mentioned previously. The "Fields of the Righteous" referred to by Diodorus may allude to the "Fields of Rushes" described in the *Egyptian Books of the Dead*, the paradise inhabited by souls of the blessed dead.

Orpheus—Bringer of Immortality

Perhaps the most enduring contribution of Egypt to Orphism however was the notion of the *soul's immortality*. Historian of philosophy Algis Uzdavinys insists that the spiritual revolution of Orphism consisted of a "reversal" of the earlier Greek view of the psyche as the mere "simulacrum" or image of the physical body. Instead they now regarded the living body as illusory and transitory—a mere image of the immortal soul. The Orphic initiate needed to undergo purification by a process of separation from the body, involving asceticism and philosophical contemplation.[29]

There are other aspects of Orphism which may have been borrowed from oriental sources, which will be explored later. One of the most intriguing of these was the belief in "transmigration" of the soul, or reincarnation, which was unprecedented in other ancient Mediterranean cultures. Burkert notes that the transmigration of souls is a doctrine that suddenly appeared in the Greek world toward the end of the sixth century BCE and was associated with Pythagoras and Orpheus.[30]

Orphism—Spirituality of the Individual

Orphism was a reform religion that grew out of the cult of Dionysus. It focused on individual spirituality as opposed to collective ecstasies and *orgia*, the wine drinking and blood sacrifices practiced by the followers of Dionysus. Peter Kingsley writes: "Apollo's ecstasy was different from the ecstasy of Dionysus. There was nothing wild or disturbing about it. It was intensely private, for the individual and the individual alone".[31] Like the cult of Dionysus, it attracted many female worshippers as well as priestesses.

The Orphics honored the goddesses Demeter and Persephone, and may have in turn contributed to the later development of the Eleusinian Mysteries in which those two goddesses played a central role. The queen of the underworld, Persephone, was of great importance to them as she was believed to be the soul's judge in the afterlife.

In Orphic myth Dionysus, also referred to as Zagreus the god of ecstasy and immortality, was born from the union of Zeus and Persephone. The Titans, jealous of the infant Dionysus, lured him away from his cradle then cruelly murdered and devoured him in a cannibalistic rite. Enraged by their crime, Zeus hurled a lightning bolt at them, incinerating them. From the ashes of the Titans, according to the Orphics, mankind was created; thus we contain both the divine spirit of Dionysus as well as the primordial sin of the Titans within our souls.

By living an austere and virtuous life, Orphics aspired to purify the soul of its titanic nature, its "original sin". They assumed the body with its appetites and passions is the source of evil, distracting the soul and plunging it into the world of matter, as epitomized by their saying *soma-sema*—"the body is the tomb". The soul was seen as a spiritual being fallen from a higher realm into the cycle of life and death on earth; it was believed to "transmigrate" not only through human lifetimes, but plant and animal existences as well, incarnating on earth to learn certain lessons and undergo purification for past transgressions. In order for it to return to its original state the mystic practiced virtuous actions, asceticism, celibacy and religious rites such as initiations. By living three virtuous lives in a row and being initiated into the mysteries they believed they could earn a blessed afterlife and be released from the cycles of rebirth.

The Orphics were often wandering ascetics who lived a life of voluntary poverty, rejecting religious traditions of the city-state such as animal sacrifice. According to Burkert they lived an "alternative life-style", shunning meat and sex, taking part in ecstatic festivals, and "proclaiming their spiritual authority in their books in which they recorded hymns and sacred rites".[32]

Orphic Initiation

Although there is scant historical evidence of the secret initiations of the Orphics, we do know that *omophagy* was practiced—the sacrifice of a bull and eating of its raw flesh—which was likely borrowed from Dionysian rites. This was a sacramental communion in which initiates nourished their own immortality through eating the bull's flesh, symbolizing the savior god Dionysus. As well, it re-enacted the myth of the tragic death of the infant Dionysus Zagreus whose flesh was devoured by the Titans. Following this, initiates were expected to abstain from meat for the remainder of their lives. During the rite they also apparently daubed themselves with white clay or gypsum in imitation of the Titans, who did this to conceal their identities after murdering Dionysus. This likely gave initiates a ghostly appearance that emphasized the initiatory symbolism of death and resurrection.

Orphic priests also offered various rites, sacrifices and initiations for the general public. These included purifications for "unholy deeds", cures for disease, methods for averting divine wrath, incantations, chants, and setting up of images. In Plato's *Republic,* Orphic priests who peddle their sacerdotal services door to door are mentioned in a disapproving tone:

"Begging priests and prophets frequent the doors of the rich and persuade them that they possess a god-given power founded on sacrifices and incantations...And they persuade not only individuals but whole cities that the unjust deeds can be absolved or purified through ritual sacrifices and pleasant games, whether for the living or when they have died. These initiations, as they call them, free people from punishment hereafter, while a terrible fate awaits those who have not performed the rituals". [33]

The influence of Orphism on another influential mystery religion—Christianity—cannot be denied. Murals depicting Orpheus as the "good shepherd" are found in early Christian catacombs and he was one of the few pagan philosophers honored by the early followers of Christ. Linda Johnsen argues that Christian sacraments were in fact modeled on Orphism and the rites of Dionysus. She points out the Last Supper is not based on the Jewish meal of Passover, in which an animal is sacrificed and eaten, but on the Orphic sacrament in which the savior himself was believed to be consumed.[34] The parallels between Dionysus and Jesus should be noted as well: both were believed to be the "son of god" born of a mortal woman and fathered by a god, both died and were resurrected, and both transformed water into wine.

The Golden Tablets

The *Orphic Tablets* are small gold sheets, found buried in the graves of Orphic initiates, dating from the 5th–3rd century BCE but likely derived from an older oral source. On them are engraved instructions for the soul of the deceased describing their postmortem journey to the underworld, their judgement by Persephone queen of the dead, and the paradise of the Elysian Fields in which they hoped to eventually dwell. On an Orphic Tablet from Petelia, South Italy (4th century BCE), it is written:

> You will find in the halls of Hades a spring on the left,
> and standing by it, a glowing white cypress tree;
> Do not approach this spring at all.
> You will find the other, from the lake of Memory,
> Refreshing water flowing forth. But guardians are nearby.
> Say: "I am the child of Earth and starry Heaven;
> But my race is Heavenly; and this you know yourselves.
> But I am parched with thirst and I perish; but give me quickly
> refreshing water from the lake of Memory.[35]

Of the two springs the initiate is told they will find in Hades the one to the left, the "Fountain of Lethe", contains the waters of forgetfulness. Those that drink of it's waters forget the lessons learned during their life on earth, especially initiatory teachings. The spring to the right is called the Well of Mnemnosyne, named after the goddess of memory and mother of the muses. It's refreshing water enhances the soul's memory of its divine origins and immortality, freeing it from the cycle of transmigration, or reincarnation.

Near this spring are guardians, or in some accounts Persephone, queen of the dead herself, who will challenge the initiate's passage. He is advised to tell them: "I am a son of earth and starry heaven, but my race is of heaven", proving he has renounced the earthly for the spiritual. Another Orphic tablet instructs the initiate to "tell Persephone that Bacchus himself has liberated you". Bacchus, or Dionysus, as previously mentioned, was the son of Persephone and Zeus, and symbolized the spiritual essence liberated during Orphic initiations. In some versions of the tablets the Orphic is directed towards the sacred meadows and groves of Persephone where it was believed he would dwell blissfully throughout eternity.[36]

The otherworldly journey described in the *Orphic Tablets* is reminiscent of passages from the *Egyptian Book of the Dead* in which the soul of the deceased similarly finds itself in the paradisiacal Fields of Reeds. There a tree grows with a goddess perched in it, who offers him a drink from her breasts to quench his thirst. The Orphic initiate similarly rushes to suckle at the breast of Persephone, who is transformed from dreaded queen of the dead into maternal goddess and nurse of the reborn soul. In the *Orphic Tablets* it is written: "I have sunk beneath the breast of the lady, the Chthonian Queen." Similarly in some shamanic narratives a spirit-woman is encountered in the land of the dead who suckles the shaman at her breast like a newborn infant.

In the underworld journey described by the Roman poet Virgil, souls of the dead follow a road that branches into a crossroads. Here they encounter the three infernal judges Rhadamanthes, Minos, and Aiakos, who render a verdict, judging them based on their merits earned during their lives on earth. As a result of this they are directed either to a road on the left or right. In Virgil's *Aeneid* he writes:

"For here the road divides in two directions:
  on the right it runs beneath the ramparts of great Dis,
  this is our highway to Elysium; the wicked are punished on the left-
  that path leads down to godless Tartarus." [37]

Elysium is the paradise of heroes and philosophers, while Tartarus is the feared prison of impious or wicked souls, deep in the pit of the underworld. Here the dead were condemned to lie face down in mud or perform endless futile tasks like carrying water in a leaking sieve. Orphic initiates, however, through their initiations, purifications, and virtuous actions believed they were guaranteed a blissful afterlife in the Elysian Fields, or Groves of Persephone. It is not too far-fetched to imagine that like Egyptian initiates, the Orphics memorized and rehearsed the underworld journey while still alive, in anticipation of their departure to the shores of Hades upon dying.

Like the *Orphic Tablets*, The *Egyptian Book of the Dead* also places great importance on the powers of memory of the soul. In one of its chapters entitled "The Chapter Of Causing The Deceased To Remember His Name In Neter-Khert" it is written:

> "May my name be given unto me in the great Double House, and may I remember my name in the House of Fire on the night of counting the years and of telling the number of the months. I am with the Holy One, and I sit on the eastern side of heaven. If any god advanceth unto me, forthwith I proclaim his name". [38]

The soul must not only remember its name, but also the route of the journey to the underworld, as well as the names of the deities encountered along the way. Most importantly, by remembering its inherently divine nature it is assured a place among the eternal gods. Similar to Egyptian beliefs, the Orphic initiate is offered *deification* in the afterlife. A verse from the Orphic Tablets assures him: "Happy and blessed one, you will be a god instead of a mortal".

Chapter 9 Notes

Orpheus playing his lyre surrounded by animals
Mosaic from Tarsus, 3rd cent. CE.

1. Meyer, Marvin W. *The ancient mysteries: a sourcebook: sacred texts of the mystery religions of the ancient Mediterranean world.* 1999: 9.
2. Wasson & Ruck; Walter & Fridman. (ed.) *Shamanism: An Encyclopedia of World Beliefs, Practices and Culture,* Vol.1. 2004: 506.
3. Burkert. *Greek Religion.* 1985: 281-84. The name Cabeiri was possibly derived from the Semetic word *kabir,* meaning "lord" or "mighty one". (Cosmopoulos 2003: 126)
4. Ibid.:291.
5. Bowden, Hugh. *Mystery Cults of the Ancient World.* 2010: 59-61.
6. Tinh, Tran Tam. Meyer, Ben R. ; Sanders, E.P. editors. *Sarapis and Isis. Jewish and Christian Self -Definition- Vol. Three.* 1982: 105.
7. Witt, R.E. *Isis in the Ancient World.* 1997: 7.
8. Tinh 1982: 113. *Sarapis and Isis. Jewish and Christian Self -Definition- Vol. Three.*
9. Meyer 1999: 11-12. *The ancient mysteries: a sourcebook: sacred texts of the mystery religions of the* ancient Mediterranean world.
10. Apuleius. *The Golden Ass, or Metamorphoses.* Book XI.
11. Ibid.
12. Burkert. *Greek Religion.* 1985: 13.

13. Mylonas, George F. *Eleusis and the Eleusinian Mysteries*. 1961: 19.
14. Kerenyi, Karl. *Eleusis Archetypal Image of Mother and Daughter*. 1960: 30.
15. Mylonas, George F. *Eleusis and the Eleusinian Mysteries*. 1961:249.
16. Bowden. *Mystery Cults of the Ancient World*. 2010 :35.
17. Mylonas. *Eleusis and the Eleusinian Mysteries*. 1961: 273.
18. Wasson, R. Gordon; Hoffman, Albert; Ruck, Carl A.P. *The Road to Eleusis: Unveiling the Secret of the Mysteries*.1978: 33. Written by the chemist Albert Hoffman, discoverer of LSD, mycologist R. Gordon Wasson, and historian Carl Ruck.
19. Plutarch *"On The Soul"*- Stobaeus IV.
20. Mylonas. *Eleusis and the Eleusinian Mysteries*. 1961: 272-5.
21. Poulkouras Iordanis- "The Eleusinian Mysteries". *Iordanis.blogspot.co*. 2008.
22. Burkert. *Greek Religion*. 1986: 75, 93.
23. Reale, Giovanni. Edited & translated by Catan, John R. *From the Origins to Socrates: A History of Ancient Philosophy*. Vol. I. 1987: 15.
24. Hultkranz, Ake. *The North American Indian Orpheus Tradition: A Contribution to Comparative Religion*. 1957:310.
25. Kingsley, Peter, *A Story Waiting to Pierce You: Mongolia, Tibet and the destiny of the Western world*. 2010: 147.
26. Lee, M. Owen. *Virgil as Orpheus: A Study of the Georgics*. 1996:1-19.
27. Ibid.: 3.
28. Guthrie, W.K.C. *Orpheus and Greek Religion*. 1996: 17.
29. Uzdavinys, Algis. *Orpheus and the Roots of Platonism*. 2011: 47-48.
30. Burkert. *Greek Religion*. 1986: 87.
31. Kingsley. *In The Dark Places of Wisdom*. 1999: 112.
32. Burkert. Tinh. (ed) *Sarapis and Isis. Jewish and Christian Self-Definition- Vol. Three*. 1982:11.
33. Plato. *Republic*, 2.364a-365b.
34. Johnsen, Linda. *Lost Masters-Sages of Ancient Greece*. 1996: 26-27.
35. Edmonds, Radcliffe Guest. *The "Orphic" Gold Tablets and Greek Religion: Further Along the Path*. 2011:5-32.
36. Ibid.: 20.
37. Virgil. Trans. Mandelbaum, Allen. *The Aeneid of Virgil*.Virgil. 1981: 150.
38. Budge. *The Egyptian Book of the Dead (The Papyrus of Ani) Egyptian Text Transliteration and Translation*. 1967: 87.

Chapter 10: The Quest for Immortality

Pythagoras.

The Axial Age Awakening

The "Axial Age", a term coined by the modern philosopher Karl Jaspers, refers to the historical period between 800-200 BCE, centering around 500 BCE. This was a time of great transformations in religious thinking worldwide. Jaspers writes: "The spiritual foundations of humanity were laid, simultaneously and independently in China, India, Persia, Palestine and Greece, and these are the foundations upon which humanity still subsists today." [1] It is remarkable that in the period between the sixth and fifth centuries BCE alone, Zoroastrianism spread throughout the Persian empire, Greece saw the rise of the Presocratic philosophers and the later Hebrew prophets emerged in Palestine. In India during the same period Buddhism, Jainism, and the philosophy of the Upanishads developed, while in China, Confucianism and Taoism emerged.

These religions are all characterized by a universal philosophical perspective emphasizing transcendence, dualism between spirit and matter and reflective thinking. The Axial Age was the beginning of a shift away from archaic tribal consciousness and Neolithic religion rooted in nature and the gods, to the consciousness of the *individual* based on self-reflection, freedom and moral responsibility.

A major catalyst for these changes was the rise of the Persian Empire. During the mid-6th century BCE, the Persian king Cyrus the Great founded the largest empire the world had ever known—stretching across three continents from Asia and Europe to Africa. Thinkers from countries as distant as Greece and India met and exchanged artistic, literary, and philosophical ideas in the cosmopolitan court of Cyrus who promoted a policy of religious tolerance and benevolence towards all his subjected nations. Culture, the arts, and sciences thrived during Cyrus's progressive rule and new cities were built throughout his empire. Trade routes were opened uniting Asia, India, the Middle east and Europe into a single cultural sphere—establishing the first global empire.[2]

In Greece during the 6th century BCE, the Presocratic philosophers arose. Exposed to the influx of Near-Eastern ideas, they forged the foundations of western philosophy, astronomy, mathematics, science, as well as esotericism. The earlier Homeric world-view based on mythological thought would soon be displaced by rational philosophy. As previously discussed, the mystery religions replaced the traditional civic religion of the Olympic gods with a new and more personal faith based on individual redemption and mystical experience.

The belief in one all encompassing and transcendent god—monotheism—would be embraced by the religions of Zoroastrianism and Judaism. Philosophical monism, the idea that the multiplicity of things can be explained in terms of a single reality or origin, was espoused by Plato and the Stoics. This was expressed by the Greek philosopher Heraclitus who said "All things are one". At the same time an idea was spreading that would change the face of western philosophy and religion—the soul's immortality.

The Presocratic Greeks—Philosophers & Shamans

The Presocratic Greeks are known as the first philosophers and scientists of the western world. Combining reason and logic with the language of myth, these early philosophers attempted to uncover the *arche* or essential material principles underlying natural phenomena. Empedocles, for example, used poetry to present his theory of the eternal cycles of cosmic attraction and separation, allegorized as the interplay between Aphrodite, goddess of Love, and Ares, god of Strife. Parmenides in his poem *On Nature* wrote a mythopoetic narrative about his chariot ride to the underworld where he received a revelation from the goddess about the unchanging nature of reality.

Philosophers such as Pythagoras, Empedocles, and Parmenides, despite their reputations as founders of rational western science, engaged in practices that can only be described as *shamanistic* in the opinion of a number of modern historians. In the words of I. P. Couliano: "Greek philosophy was an outcome of earlier shamanic speculations on the soul." [3] As well as their exposure to the cultures of the Near-East, the Greeks were known to have travelled to regions far to the east and north of their homeland, passing through the cultures of ancient Iran, even as far as Central Asia and Siberia. Peter Kingsley notes that trade routes reaching from Europe to China were established long before the age of Pythagoras. He insists that objects and inscriptions have been found showing a continuity of shamanic traditions stretching all the way from the boundaries of Greece across Asia to the Himalayas and Tibet, Nepal and India.[4]

Closer to home, the Greeks colonized and traded along the northern and eastern shores of the Black Sea in the areas of Thrace and Scythia and were exposed to various shamanic practices of the natives of those regions. The cults of Orpheus and Dionysus, so influential to the development of Greek spirituality, were believed to have been imported from Thrace to Greece. The followers of the Thracian god Sabazios apparently practiced ecstatic intoxication in their rites, similar to the Dionysian mysteries. As previously mentioned, Ginzburg argues the Scythians practiced shamanism—derived from their contacts with the cultures of Siberia and Central Asia. The Greeks themselves acknowledged that the worship of Apollo was brought from the northern land of Hyperboria, which Geoffrey Ashe locates between the Ural and Altai mountains in Western Siberia—the home of shamans from time immemorial. Kingsley likewise locates Hyperboria in the region of the Altai mountains bordering Siberia and Mongolia.[5] The shamanic traits of Apollo, the patron god of several early Greek philosophers, were previously discussed.

The pre-Socratic philosophers were known in their time as *Iatromantis*, derived from the Greek words *iatros*–healer, and *mantis*—prophet. These healer-prophets were said to be possessed by Apollo of Hyperborea. They were the equivalents of native Greek shamans according to Couliano.[6] Besides possessing powers of healing, they were also magicians and seers, reputed to be miracle workers. The ability to "bi-locate" or instantly appear in two places at the same time was attributed to the philosopher Pythagoras who was seen conversing with groups of friends in different locations at the same time. He predicted earthquakes, chased away pestilence, and suppressed violent winds and hail, as well as calmed storms on rivers and seas for the safe passage of his friends.

The Tree of Visions

Pythagoras was revered as the son of Apollo by his followers who claimed he gleamed with supernatural brightness.

During his meeting with the sage Abaris at Olympia, Pythagoras showed him his golden thigh, announcing he was the Hyperborean Apollo. In a symbolic gesture Abaris in turn gave Pythagoras his golden arrow. According to some accounts Abaris became Pythagoras's student though in others Abaris was *his* teacher. The mysterious Abaris, whose homeland was said to be the land of Hyperborea, was called the "walker in air" for he was "carried in the air on an arrow of the Hyperborean Apollo over rivers, seas and inaccessible places" in the words of Porphyry. Indeed, the power to travel instantaneously and invisibly through the air seems to refer to shamanic "magical flight". According to Kingsley the golden arrow which Abaris carried upon his person was a symbol used by Central Asian shamans for ecstatic trance, as well as a weapon against the spirits of illness.[7] Abaris was an ecstatic who uttered prophecies, purified cities of plagues, and healed with incantations. Kingsley argues that the name Abaris was derived from the Greek word *Avar*—referring to the native peoples of Mongolia, concluding Abaris was an ambassador of his people who travelled to Greece to acknowledge Pythagoras as an incarnation of the god Apollo. While in Greece, Abaris set about to magically purify and balance the land, then empowered Pythagoras for his spiritual mission of transmitting the shamanic wisdom of Asia to Europe, in Kingsley's opinion.[8]

The Greek poet Aristeas, who lived in the 7th century BCE was also believed to have mastered the power of magical flight. The following account describing his "soul travel" sounds akin to the magical flight of shamans: "...his soul emerged from his body and wandered through the air like a bird, observing everything, the earth, sea and rivers and cities and the tribes of men...and then it entered the body again and roused it and using it like a tool relating all that it had seen and heard..."[9] Aristeas was known to be possessed by Apollo, traveling with the god by shapeshifting into the form of his sacred bird the raven. In that guise he flew the vast distance between Greece and Hyperborea and back again, later writing a poem describing his travels called *Arimaspeia*.[10]

Epimenides (700-600 BCE) the most renowned wonder-worker and poet of ancient Greece is said to have slept in a cave of Mt. Dikte in Crete for fifty-seven years and received divine visions there. Regarding him Eliade writes: "He left the cave a master of "enthusiastic wisdom", that is, the technique of ecstasy."[11] Following his time in Crete, Epimenides journeyed through many lands as a magical healer, prophet, ecstatic seer, and exorcist, expelling the demonic evils that arose from past misdeeds. He was reputed to be one of the founders of the mystery religion of Orphism, and it was said his skin was covered with tatoos — unusual for a Greek but typical of Central Asian shamans — suggesting he may have travelled to their lands and was initiated into their practices.

The shamanic belief that the soul can leave the body in trance and journey to other worlds to gain wisdom had a profound influence on the Orphics, Pythagoreans, and Presocratic Greek philosophers. Ecstatic experiences of a Dionysian variety may have also provided the realization that the soul could temporarily leave the body in a state of rapture. The implications of its ability to bi-locate and exist separately from the physical body influenced belief in the soul's transcendence. The Presocratic notion of the soul's immortality would profoundly influence later generations of philosophers such as Plato and the Neoplatonists as well as the entire course of western spirituality. According to Couliano: "...the closer we look at the hard core of Platonism, the more we discover how much the Iatromantes influenced Plato's beliefs in afterlife, reincarnation, and otherworldly journeys." [12] Burkert insists that this was essentially a new philosophical understanding of the soul or *psyche* in which it is was thought to be composed of an aetherial substance, immortal and unaffected by death and transcendent in nature.[13]

Pythagoras — Lover of Wisdom

Pythagoras (580-500 BCE) was born on the Greek island of Samos near Miletus, an early center of Greek philosophy. It was prophesied that his mother would give birth to a man of supreme beauty and wisdom who would benefit mankind. According to the ancient philosopher Aristippus: "...he was named Pythagoras because he uttered the truth as infallibly as did the Pythian oracle", referring to the oracle of Apollo at Delphi. Legend has it Pythagoras was the first man who called himself a "philosopher", meaning a "lover of wisdom". He could be described in modern terms as a truly holistic thinker whose teachings integrated both the intuitive as well as the rational approaches to knowledge. He was a founder of western mathematics, geometry, astronomy, musicology, and medicine as well as philosophy, metaphysics and ethics.

It is often difficult to separate fact from legends when it comes to the life and legacy of Pythagoras, as he committed none of his teachings to writing. Historian Thomas McEvilley writes about the two sides of Pythagoras: "On the one hand, he is reported as an inventor of mathematical philosophy and an innovator in scientific experimentation. On the other hand, he is associated with a variety of mythical motifs that connect him with the realm of the shaman..."[14] Pythagoras was indeed one of the first scientists of the western world but was also renowned as a religious prophet. He was a charismatic teacher who according to legend wore a gold crown, white robe and trousers, and as previously mentioned, was believed by his followers to be the Hyperborean Apollo in person. It was said he descended to the underworld in a subterranean chamber of the sanctuary of Demeter, and his famous golden thigh was a sign of initiation into the cult of the Great Mother.[15]

In his youth, Pythagoras was a student of the early Greek philosopher Anaximander, with whom he shared interests in mathematics and Babylonian astronomy. He also studied with Pherecydes of Syros who according to some was the first Greek to teach about the soul's immortality as well as "metempsychosis" or reincarnation, while others credit Pythagoras with these doctrines.[16] Pythagoras travelled across the world in his earlier years in the pursuit of wisdom, studying with a number of teachers. The Neoplatonic philosopher Porphyry writes:

> "As to his knowledge, it is said that he learned the mathematical sciences from the Egyptians, Chaldeans and Phoenicians; for of old the Egyptians excelled in geometry, the Phoenicians in numbers and proportions, and the Chaldeans in astronomical theorems, divine rites, and worship of the Gods; other secrets concerning the course of life he received and learned from the Magi."[17]

Pythagoras travelled to Egypt in 535 BCE, learning the Egyptian language and hieroglyphic writing. He so impressed the priests of that land by his intelligence and wisdom that he was finally initiated by them into their mysteries. In 525 BCE the Persians under King Cambyses II invaded Egypt, capturing Pythagoras and taking him to Babylon as a slave. There he continued his studies with the Chaldeans, who were skilled in the magical arts as well as astronomy. The Neoplatonic philosopher Iamblichus wrote of Pythagoras's stay in Babylon: "whilst he was there he gladly associated with the *magoi* and was instructed in their sacred rites and learnt about a very mystical worship of the gods. He also reached the acme of perfection in arithmetic and music and the other mathematical sciences taught by the Babylonians".[18]

Pythagoras also travelled to Crete, one of the ancient sources of Greek religion, where he was initiated into the mysteries of Zeus at the Idaean Cave. He descended into the cavern there where he met with initiates of the mystery cult of the Idaean Daktyls. Porphyry writes: " he was purified with the meteoritic thunder-stone. In the morning he lay stretched upon his face by the seaside; at night, he lay beside a river, crowned with a black lamb's woolen wreath. Descending into the Idaean cave, wrapped in black wool, he stayed there twenty-seven days, according to custom; he sacrificed to Zeus, and saw the throne which there is yearly made for him."[19] The Dactyls were not only skilled in performing initiations, but also in music, using chanting and the ringing sounds of metal to magically invoke *daimons*. The legend that Pythagoras discovered the harmonics of music by listening to a blacksmith hammering on his anvil may have in fact been a ruse—concealing the truth that he actually learned his "musical magic" from the Dactyls.

It is likely Pythagoras was also influenced by the mystery rites of Thrace, the lands north of Greece. According to legend he instructed his Thracian slave Zalmoxis in his teachings, who upon returning to his native land introduced them there. Chronologically, myths of a Thracian priest-king named Zalmoxis seem to pre-date Pythagoras, however. As previously mentioned, Zalmoxis's initiation rites involved descent into the underworld during which a ritualized death and mystical rebirth were experienced, as well as belief in a beatific afterlife and the soul's immortality, likely influencing the teachings of Orphism and Pythagoras, as well as the Eleusinian mysteries.

Along with his legendary magical powers of controlling the elements and bi-locating his soul, Pythagoras also displayed a remarkable kinship and rapport with animals, similar to shamans. He befriended wild beasts such as a ferocious bear, as well as a wild bull which was destroying a farmer's crops. Porphyry writes: "While at the Olympic games, he was discoursing with his friends about auguries, omens, and divine signs, and how men of true piety do receive messages from the Gods. Flying over his head was an eagle, who stopped, and came down to Pythagoras. After stroking her awhile, he released her."

Pythagoras also possessed the shaman's knowledge of the soul's postmortem existence. He was reputed to have remembered a number of his own past lives including a previous life as Hermentimus, a prophet who possessed the power of instantaneous "soul travel" to distant locations, as well as Euphorbus, a hero from Homeric times.[20] Similar to the Orphics, Pythagoras taught the doctrine of "metempsychosis" or transmigration of the soul through the forms of plant and animal, as well as human. One legend claims Pythagoras passed a puppy on the street being whipped and taking pity on it said: "Stop, do not beat it; for it is the soul of a friend that I recognized..."

The Pythagorean Brotherhood

Following years of travel and study in foreign lands, Pythagoras settled down to establish a community in the city of Croton in southern Italy, soon attracting a number of followers. Community members were involved in scientific experimentation in medicine, acoustics, mathematics, as well as philosophy and politics.

The Tree of Visions

While ancient Greek society considered women inferior to men and possessing few rights, Pythagoras's students and followers were of both genders, and women in his community were viewed as equal to men. They were in fact encouraged to study philosophy, teach, and assume leadership roles. Theano, the wife of Pythagoras, wrote about mathematics, physics and medicine; her most important treatise was on the mathematical ratio of the golden mean. Pythagoras and his wife raised several children, since celibacy was not required among members; the raising of children was believed necessary to the perpetuation of the community as well as worship of the gods.

The Pythagorean community was a closed society, and the teachings of Pythagoras were not revealed to outsiders. Initiates had to undergo a five-year trial period during which their character and self-discipline was tested. They listened in silence to the voice of the master, hidden from view behind a curtain. Only after successfully completing this trial were they admitted inside the veil, becoming "esoterics" or members of Pythagoras's inner circle, allowed to see the master in person, according to Iamblichus.[21]

The inner circle of "esoterics" were also called *mathematikoi* or "mathematicians". Their study of mathematics and geometry was intended as a form of contemplation that elevated the mind to the abstract realm of perfect harmony. The esoterics owned no personal possessions and were vegetarians. They were encouraged to practice temperance—controlling their passions, and cultivating tranquility of mind. They lived a communal "alternative lifestyle" that differentiated them from normal people, according to Burkert.[22] Their discipline and ascetic practices are reminiscent of the Egyptian priests previously described by Porphyry, who occupied themselves with the study of mathematics and astronomy as well as their sacerdotal duties. Pythagoras, who studied with the priesthood while in Egypt, may have indeed modeled his school after some of their teachings and methods.

Other less advanced students, known as *akousmatikoi* or "listeners" lived outside the community and were allowed to own possessions as well as eat the meat of sacrificed animals.[23] All students were expected to follow a regime of austerities however. Iamblichus writes that the Pythagoreans maintained a routine of meals shared in common, exercise, reading, and philosophical study, as well as religious teachings. Music was an essential activity and they would sing hymns to Apollo together. They used the lyre to cure illness of body and soul and recited poetry before and after sleep to develop memory. Porphyry writes about Pythagoras's use of music: "He soothed the passions of the soul and body by rhythms, songs and incantations." He also practiced a form of dance that was used for healing the body and maintaining health and longevity.

Mysterious sayings known as *acusmata* or "things heard" were exchanged between community members. These encoded esoteric teachings and functioned as passwords by which they could identify each other. They included sayings such as: "An earthquake is a gathering of the dead"; "The rainbow is the bright ray of the sun"; and "The most beautiful figures are the circle and the sphere." [24] The pentagram was also used as a symbol of greeting and recognition between them, as well as a symbol for *hygieia*. or health.

The Music of the Spheres

The Pythagoreans taught a set of disciplines which later became known as the *Quadrivium* or the four ways to knowledge: arithmetic, geometry, music theory and astronomy, all seen as interrelated forms of mathematics.[25] Plato wrote: "...as the eyes are made for astronomy, so the ears are made for harmony, and these are sister sciences, as the Pythagoreans say."[26] Porphyry writes about Pythagoras's mystical perception of the cosmos: "He himself could hear the harmony of the Universe, and understood the universal music of the spheres, and of the stars which move in concert with them, and which we cannot hear because of the limitations of our weak nature".[27] Through his studies of musical harmony, Pythagoras laid the groundwork for the study of cosmology and astronomy by western science.

The Pythagoreans believed there were ten celestial bodies—as *ten* was considered the perfect number. Since fire was thought to be the most precious element they reasoned there was a central fire or "hearth" of the universe, as well as a fiery outer sphere of fixed stars. Between these two extremes they placed the five visible planets, in addition to the sun, moon, and earth, adding up to the number ten. They assumed these bodies sounded the ratios of music in their rotation through the celestial spheres, producing the "music of the spheres". According to Pliny the Elder, Pythagoras conceived of the musical interval between the earth and moon as a tone; from the moon to mercury a semitone; from venus to the sun a minor third, etc.[28] The seven stringed lyre was compared to the cosmos—with the strings tuned to the ratios of the five planets, the sun and moon.

Pythagoras was also credited with the discovery of the mathematical ratios of musical intervals. He taught that numbers were divine and the cosmos was founded on numerical principles. The geometric "Pythagorean Theorem" named for him was in fact known by the earlier Babylonians, and he probably learned it from them. He was also credited with devising the *tetractys* or tetrad, a mystical triangular figure.

The Tree of Visions

```
      •
     • •
    • • •
   • • • •
```

The tectractys is a triangular diagram of ten points arranged in four horizontal rows—adding up to the perfect number of ten. From the four numerical rows of the tetractys the main harmonic ratios of the Pythagorean musical system can be derived: the octave, fifth and fourth. This means a string divided into two parts, or halves (2:1) produces the "octave"; dividing it into the ratio of a third (3:2) produces a perfect "fifth", and into fourths (4:3) produces a perfect "fourth".

The figure also has profound cosmological symbolism: the top row with a single point symbolizes "unity". The next row of two points represents "polarity" or the dyad, the pair from which all things are generated. The third row with three points is the resolution of polarity in "harmony", and the fourth or bottom row symbolizes "cosmos"—the world of the four elements. Likewise, the *tetraktys* can be seen to generate the dimensions of geometrical space: its top point is equivalent to the *point* in geometry, the second row to the *line*, the third row defines the triangle or two dimensional *plane*, and the lowest row of four points forms the tetrahedron, the basic three dimensional *volume*. So sacred was the tetractys among the followers of Pythagoras they would swear oaths by it: "by him that gave us the tetractys, which contains the fount and root of ever-flowing nature".

The followers of Pythagoras were highly influential in the ancient world. Kingsley writes: "Pythagoreans governed whole cities in southern Italy according to their own principles. They managed to bring together the inner and the outer, politics and the love of wisdom, theory and practice".[29] The community at Croton was finally destroyed by the tyrant Cylon who was enraged that his membership into the fellowship was rejected. In revenge he roused the populace to attack and kill the followers of Pythagoras. Following this tragic event Pythagoras's followers spread to other parts of the Greek world but maintained secrecy in their activities, fearing more reprisals.

The teachings of Pythagoras and his students influenced generations of future philosophers including Plato, who visited a community of Pythagoreans in Italy as a youth. Plato's ideal city envisioned in his *Republic* was inhabited by a well organized society of philosophers inspired by the Pythagorean brotherhood of Croton. The Academy founded by Plato was originally a religious community for honoring the muses, similar to Pythagorean schools.

Plato's *Timaeus* describes the cosmos using Pythagorean sacred geometry and harmony. In his *Phaedo* he presents the idea that the study of philosophy is preparation for death and immortality, echoing the teachings of Pythagoras. In the *Myth of Er* he presents an eschatology of the soul's afterlife journey and reincarnation, based on Pythagorean doctrines.

Western science is deeply indebted to the Pythagoreans who laid its mathematical and experimental foundations. They discovered that relationships between natural phenomena can be expressed by mathematics—a discovery that would in fact become the basis of modern science.[30] The Pythagoraeans were among the first astronomers who speculated the earth was a sphere and revolved around a central fire. Their ideas anticipated the modern heliocentric solar system introduced by the 16th century scientists Kepler and Copernicus, who were both inspired by Pythagorean cosmological concepts.[31]

Pythagoras' vision of the harmonious cosmos and its investigation through observation, reason, and mystical intuition has left an indelible imprint on western esotericism as well, inspiring philosophers, magicians, and alchemists down through the ages.

Empedocles & the Four Elements

> *"God is a circle whose center is everywhere,*
> *and its circumference nowhere"*
> -Empedocles

The Presocratic philosopher Empedocles (490-430 BCE) lived in the Greek colony of Sicily. He is remembered as an important early philosopher and scientist who influenced the development of medicine, chemistry, biology, astronomy, cosmology, rhetoric and psychology. He is also credited with the theory of the "four elements" or *Tetrasomia*. Like Pythagoras with whom he may have studied, Empedocles was a mystic as well as a scientist. He was a follower of Orphism and Pythagoreanism, and a priest of the goddess Hekate, practicing her mysteries as well as those of Demeter and Persephone.

Prior to Empedocles, the philosopher Heraclites speculated the primary substance of creation was fire. Anaximenes speculated it was air, while Thales thought it was water. Empedocles was the first Greek philosopher to incorporate all these theories into a balanced scheme of *four elements*. There is the possibility he may have learned the doctrine of the four elements from the Chaldean Magi. According to Greek geographer Strabo, the Chaldeans worshipped "fire and earth and the winds and water". Thomas McEvilley argues there is convincing historical evidence to support the origin of the theory of the elements in India, spreading from there to Greece.[32] Joseph Campbell supports this view, noting that Buddha studied the doctrine of the elements, tracing the theory back to the Indian sage Kapila who may have lived as early as the eighth century BCE.[33]

The Four Roots & The Theory of Love & Strife

In one of his poems, Empedocles provides the earliest reference to his theory of the *four elements,* which he possibly gave to his students as a riddle, according to Kingsley :

"Hear first the four roots of all things:
  Dazzling Zeus, life-bearing Hera, Aidoneus, and
  Nestis who moistens the springs of mortals with her tears" [34]

Empedocles refers to the four elements as *rhizai* or "roots", and may have chosen this term as he was himself a "root cutter" or herbal magician who applied his theories to develop the doctrine of occult sympathies in plants. The "roots" of the four elements were attributed to the gods and goddesses mentioned in his poem, but the exact correspondences of which deity to which element have long been the subject of debate. One of the more persuasive arguments is provided by Kingsley, who equates Zeus with the element air, Hera his wife with earth, Hades with fire, and Nestis with Persephone and water.[35] These deities are related to early Greek cosmology: the heavens of Zeus were thought to be composed of "aether" or air, the fires of Tartaros were believed to be ruled by Hades, and the rivers of the underworld were associated with Persephone, leaving Hera, Zeus's wife, with earth.

The two primary forces of the universe according to Empedocles are *Love* and *Strife,* which bring about all mixing and separation of the root elements, thereby creating motion. He identified these two forces with Aphrodite, goddess of Love, and Ares the god of war, whose tempestuous relationship in Greek myth is well known. Love attracts or mixes together the elements, unifying the many into the one—while Strife separates the one into the many. Their interplay is responsible for the perpetual coming into being and passing away of all things.[36] The fluctuation and balance of these two forces brings about the cycles of time which they alternately rule, similar to the balance of yin and yang in Chinese Taoism. The theory of Love and Strife reconciles the metaphysical ideas of Parmenides who claimed Being is unchanging and eternal, with the notions of Heraclites who held that all things are in constant change and flux. It proposes that all things in their ceaseless alternation between unity and plurality are forever changeless; likewise unity will always form from plurality and vice versa as part of an unending cosmic cycle.[37]

Love and Strife are also fundamental principles in the operations of magic which work with sympathy or antipathy. Commenting on the magic of Empedocles, the Neoplatonic philosopher Plotinus writes:

> "But how do magical spells work? By sympathy and the fact that there is a natural concord of things that are alike and opposition of things that are different...the true magic is the Love and Strife in the All. And this is the primary wizard and enchanted, from observing whom men came to use philtres and spells on each other." [38]

Empedocles As Shaman & Wonder Worker

Like Pythagoras, Empedocles was as much an *Iatromantis*—a divine healer—as he was a philosopher or scientist. As well, he was an herb doctor, seer, and *magos,* or priest-magician. Described as a wonder-worker, he cultivated a flamboyant theatrical appearance wearing stately robes like a priest, bronze shoes and a wreath of laurel. His followers revered him as a "god made flesh".[39] Empedocles's use of theatrical robes is reminiscent of the shaman's costume, worn to cultivate an aura of spiritual charisma and power, enhancing his healing abilities in the eyes of the community.

Like Pythagoras, Empedocles used the "fascination" of music to effect cures. According to legend he prevented a young man from killing his father in a fit of rage by chanting a solemn song while playing his lyre, thereby subduing him. He taught the use of medicines to avert diseases and the evils of old age. Legends about Empedocles also credit him with the wizardry of controlling the winds and weather, earning him the epithet "wind stopper", skills he was said to have learned from Pythagoras. He claimed to be able to teach these magical powers to others. To his friend Pausanias he made these promises:

> "you shall put a stop to the strength of tireless winds, which rush against the land and wither the fields with their blasts; and again, if you wish, you shall bring the winds back again; and you shall make, after dark rain, a drought timely for men, and after summer drought you shall make tree-nourishing streams which dwell in the aither"...[40]

Empedocles was also a "psychopomp" —a guide of the dead—who wrote a treatise entitled *On Near Death*.[41] It was said he could teach how to "bring from Hades the strength of a man who has died", which could perhaps be understood as retrieving his lost soul from the underworld to restore him to life, thereby resuscitating him from a coma—a power also attributed to shamans. One story tells of his revival of a woman who had not drawn a breath for thirty days back to life.

Like his contemporaries, the Orphics and Pythagoreans, Empedocles believed in the doctrine of *metempsychosis*—that the soul progressed through a cycle of transmigration—and was reborn not only in human form, but also as different creatures, before finally being released from the wheel of existence. This belief can still be widely found across India, Asia, and some shamanic cultures where animals, birds and fishes are thought to have individual souls, and human souls can take animal forms in successive lives.[42] In his *Purifications* Empedocles remembers his soul's previous incarnations: "Before now I was born a boy and maid, a bush and a bird, a dumb fish leaping out of the sea."

Through his mystical practices Empedocles believed he had become a divinity. He declared: "I surpass mortal men who are subject to many deaths...I walk among men as a god, no longer mortal—I have been set free". In one of the legends concerning his death it was said he threw himself into the crater of the volcano of Mt. Etna to prove to his disciples he was immortal, believing that after his body was consumed by fire he would return as a god.

Zoroastrianism

Under Cyrus the Great's rule, Persian influence extended throughout Anatolia and the eastern Mediterranean, lands inhabited by the Greeks. The doctrines of Persian Zoroastrianism undoubtedly influenced the thinking of early Greek philosophers. Pythagoras was said to have learned in Babylon the Magian doctrines of dualism and immortality of the soul. Heraclites argued the universe was created from fire, the sacred element of Zoroastrians. Empedocles may have been influenced by Persian dualism when he declared his theory of the cosmic opposites of Love and Strife. Plato's notion of a universal Logos was likely influenced by Ahura Mazda, the "good god" of the Zoroastrians.

The prophet Zoroaster lived some time between the period of 1700 BCE-500 BCE. The religion based on his teachings, Zoroastrianism, was propagated by Persian monarchs. Notably, it was the first international religion, transcending tribal and ethnic boundaries. As well it was one of the earliest *monotheistic* faiths based on a universal and transcendent god, albeit with strong dualistic tendencies. Mankind's purpose, according to Zoroaster, is to sustain truth by actively participating in the world and practicing "good deeds" to insure happiness, thereby keeping the forces of chaos at bay. It views the human condition as the struggle between *asa*—the truth, and *druj*—the lie. Its emphasis on free will and ethics are among its most important contributions. Zoroastrianism continues to be practiced around the world to this day, with its largest communities of worshippers in India and the United States.

The Persians spoke an Indo-European language, and the principles of their religion can be traced back to the prehistoric Indo-Iranian period before the Indo-Aryans separated from their Persian brethren, migrating to the Indus Valley. In fact, Zoroastrianism shares many beliefs with the ancient Vedic religion of India such as the sacramental use of fire and similar names of deities. Like the Indian *Vedas*, Zoroastrianism believes in an immortal soul.

Jewish Monotheism

Judaism was the other major monotheistic faith to emerge during the Axial Age, and like Zoroastrianism would eventually become a world religion. Jewish monotheism was the result of a lengthy historical evolution, however. The Jews of the Iron Age shared many cultural traditions with their neighbors the Canaanites, practicing a polytheistic religion which included cults of the ancestors and worship of family gods. They worshipped deities such as Baal, El, Astarte, Anat and Asherah well into the first millennium BCE, according to biblical historian Mark K. Smith.[43] The Jewish god Jahweh, originally a storm-god, was often conflated with these deities, and the mother goddess Asherah was worshipped alongside him as his consort. She was symbolized as an "asherah pole", a stylized version of a *sacred tree*, placed in temples and holy places.[44] Magical practices such as necromancy, divination, and healing were also widespread among sections of the Jewish population who had their own share of wizards, witches and mediums. This is apparent in the many condemnations of them by the Jewish prophets in the Old Testament, such as in the *Book of Exodus*: "you shall not suffer a witch to live".

Yahweh's rise to prominence as the god of the emerging nation-state Israel was the result of the centralization of religious worship and his cult was associated with the dynasty of king David. Yahweh's growth in prestige reflected the monarchy's increased political power, according to Smith.[45] It was believed that through the king the people received the blessings of Yahweh. Although the monarchy tolerated traditional worship of other gods as well, the prophets attacked the popular devotion to other deities such as Baal and Asherah. Prophetic proclamations spread through the medium of the written word and Yahweh's cult grew in power.

Jewish monotheism became even more pronounced during the time of the Babylonian Exile, (587-538 BCE). During this period the nation of Judah was conquered by the Babylonian king Nebuchadnezzar, the Temple of Jerusalem destroyed, and a large portion of the population deported to Babylonia. The tragedy of the Exile was interpreted by the prophet Ezekial as divine punishment for the Jews disobedience of God's commandments—as well as their unholy pagan practices. Ezekial demanded a more rigorous obedience to Yahweh's commands, promising that it they returned to God and obeyed him he would restore them to the promised land.[46] Historian William McNeill notes that Ezekial was the first to emphasize the *individual's* relationship to god, which he sees as a response to the weakening of local community solidarity among the Jewish exiles.[47] During this period of estrangement from their homeland, Judaism grew beyond a tribal cult to the beginnings of a universal religion. Texts dating to the Exile express the monotheistic ideal that Jahweh was the *only* deity in the cosmos, stressing the exclusive worship of Jahweh and rejection of other gods, who were seen as non-existent deities represented by lifeless idols.[48]

The Exile ended in 538 BCE when king Cyrus of Persia conquered Babylon, liberating the Jews and allowing them to return home to Jerusalem and rebuild their temple. Cyrus was hailed as a messiah by a jewish prophet of the time, and as one who acted in Yahweh's name and authority.[49] Friendly contact continued between the two nations and religions, and Palestine remained under Persian protection for two centuries. During this period Zoroastrian religious doctrines would deeply influence Judaism. Historian Mary Boyce lists the Zoroastrian contributions to Judaism, as well as the other Abrahamic faiths that would follow in its wake:

> "Zoroaster was thus the first to teach the doctrines of an individual judgement, Heaven and Hell, the future resurrection of the body, the general Last Judgement, and life everlasting for the reunited soul and body. These doctrines were to become familiar articles of faith to much of mankind, through borrowings by Judaism, Christianity and Islam." [50]

Heaven & Hell/ Angels & Devils

Along with these theological doctrines, Zoroastrianism also introduced the idea of a "world savior" born of a virgin, called the Sayoshant, the embodiment of righteousness, who would lead mankind into the final battle against evil; similarities with Jewish and Christian doctrines of the messiah are only too evident.

In contrast to the previously held view of time as consisting of eternal cycles, typical of polytheistic religions, the Zoroastrians conceived of time culminating in an *apocalypse*. Joseph Campbell writes: "This is not the old, ever revolving cycle of the archaic Bronze Age mythologies, but a sequence, once and for all, of creation, fall, and progressive redemption, to culminate in a final, decisive.... victory of the One Eternal God of Righteousness and Truth".[51]

The Zoroastrians also introduced their ideas about angelology and demonology which would influence Judaism and the later Abrahamic religions. Their supreme god, Ahura Mazda, has six divine attributes known as the *Amesha Spenta* or Holy Immortals. These six combined with Ahura Mazda to form *seven* entities, or seven creations, envisioned in forms similar to seven *archangels*. The Holy Immortals are associated with virtues as well as primal elemental powers. For example Spenta Aramaiti, "Holy Devotion", rules over the earth; Haurvatat or "Health" rules over water; while Asha Vahista, "Order", rules over fire. The seven postexilic angels of Judaism—Gabriel, Michael, Raphael, Israfil, Israel, Uhiel and Uriel—are clearly reminiscent of the seven Amesha Spenta and may have been influenced by them, according to Zoroastrian scholar Dr. Jaryoush Jahanian.[52]

The Amesha Spenta in turn emanated the *yazatas* or "beings worthy of worship" who are similar to angels. Like the Amesha Spenta the yazatas personify abstract virtues as well as the forces of nature. They are seen as lesser divine powers, teaching men to reject evil and uplift themselves spiritually. They are given anthropomorphic attributes, and days of the month are named after them.

The third category of angels in Zoroastrianism are the *fravashi* which are similar to the guardian angels of the Abrahamic faiths. Each person is believed to be accompanied by one of these angels throughout their life. Besides protecting and guiding the individual they also serve as a spiritual ideal for them to emulate, becoming one with them after death. The *fravashi* was believed to meet the soul in its afterlife journey at the Chinvit Bridge, also known as the Bridge of Judgement. In one text the fravashi is described as a beautiful and virtuous damsel with a brilliant and delightful form. She tells the soul "I am made more exalted through you—through your good thoughts, good words, and good deeds".[53]

The starkly dualistic theology of Zoroastrianism conceives of an adversary to Ahura Mazda—Angra Mainyu, also known as Ahriman—who is believed to be wholly malign and ignorant. Allied with him are evil forces, the warlike and amoral *daevas*—seen as adversaries of the benevolent Amesha Spenta and yazatas. Zoroaster wrote: "Truly there are two primal Spirits, twins, renowned to be in conflict. In thought and word and deed they are two, the good and the bad". Mankind is forced to choose through free will which side of the cosmic struggle to align with.

After their contact with the Persians the Jews developed eschatological doctrines concerning the afterlife destiny of the soul, its reward or punishment in the next world. Satan was originally the name of the spiritual "accuser" or "adversary" in early Judaism, but upon exposure to Persian beliefs he became identified as the evil entity cast out of heaven with the fallen angels. The cosmic struggle between the powers of good and evil, described in the *Dead Sea Scrolls* of the Jewish mystical sect the Essenes, reflects the influence of Zoroastrian dualism and its notion of the war between the powers of light and darkness. The struggle between Satan and God became a central doctrine of faith in the Abrahamic religions as well.

Michael Witzel argues that Zoroastrianism has had a tremendous influence on modern Christianity and Islam with its emphasis on the hope of paradise for their followers as well as the end of the world and final judgment for evildoers. He observes that these religious ideologies make a sharp distinction between good and evil that was not found in earlier polytheistic mythologies which allowed for more ambiguous "gray" areas of thought.[54]

The Vision of Wiraz

Apocalyptic visions of the otherworld are an essential part of Zoroastrianism. These are similar to Jewish and early Christian apocalypses in their descriptions of the "end times"– the final resurrection and dissolution of cosmic order, according to historian Anders Hultgard. He writes: "The tradition of visionary otherworldly journeys performed in a state of trance is characteristic of Iranian culture and is intimately bound up with eschatological and apocalyptic teachings".[55] According to I.P. Couliano the visionary aspect of Zoroastrianism is based on shamanism, and the most ancient parts of the *Avesta*, the primary texts of Zoroastrianism, refer to an ecstatic visionary union with the angelic Amesha Spentas.[56] This state is defined as a special illumination, a form of transcendental knowledge beyond sense perception and language. The Zoroastrian seer is usually described as "righteous" like the "righteous dead", but he can glimpse visions of the afterlife while still alive, similar to the shaman.

In the Persian apocalyptic text *Arda Wiraz Namag*, a righteous man named Wiraz is chosen by his people to journey to the otherworld for the purpose of gaining divine guidance about religious doctrine. To prepare him for this task Wiraz is taken to a fire temple where he is given a drink of wine mixed with henbane, a powerful psychoactive herb. Upon falling asleep, his soul leaves his body, and he meets the guardian angel Sros, as well as Adur, the divinity of fire.

They lead him across the Chinvat Bridge where they are met by the god Rashn who holds a golden balance to weigh the deeds of the deceased. Wiraz is then taken to purgatory where he witnesses souls awaiting the day of bodily resurrection, as their good deeds and sins are equal. Next he enters the "station of the stars" in heaven, corresponding to "good thoughts" where righteous souls dwell who performed good deeds, yet failed to practice the Zoroastrian religion. Following this they rise to the "station of the moon" corresponding to "good words", inhabited by the righteous who failed to recite their prayers and marry their sisters, considered essential duties for devout Zoroastrians. Wiraz and his guides finally enter the third heaven, the "station of the sun", witnessing there the righteous who sit on golden thrones and carpets. These are the souls who exercised "good sovereignty, rulership and authority" in their lives. Beyond the three heavens is the fourth level, the "endless light"—the paradise of Ohrmazd (Ahura Mazda). Here Wiraz is introduced to Ohrmazd himself, who greets him graciously.

Following this Wiraz is taken back over the Chinvat Bridge to visit the three levels of hell. These are dark, narrow, and "in such stench that anyone getting that wind into his nose would struggle and tremble and fall." In this terrible place Wiraz finds the souls of the wicked: thieves, evil rulers, slaughters of cattle, witches, heretics, etc. Here he glimpses the Evil Spirit, Ahriman, who vents his scorn on the souls of the damned.

Finally Wiraz returns to paradise where Ohrmazd instructs him to tell his fellow men what he has seen and remind them to follow the "one way of righteousness." On the seventh day Wiraz awakens to tell his companions of his journey, relaying the messages from on high.[57]

The apocalyptic Vision of Wiraz shares obvious similarities with the visionary journeys of shamans. Like them his journey to the otherworld is motivated by the need to seek spiritual guidance for his community. Similar to the practices of some shamans he ingests a psychoactive drug to induce visions of the heavens and underworld. The difference primarily lies in the theological content of his vision which clearly reflects Zoroastrian religious beliefs and social mores.

The Magi & Magic

Accompanying the Persians in their conquests was a tribe closely related to them, the Medeans, also known as the Magians, who practiced an ancient Indo-Iranian religion, led by a hereditary priesthood called the Magi. After several uprisings against their Persian brethren and attempts at forming their own empire the Magians were conquered by the Persian king Cyrus in 550 BCE.

The Magi's magical-religious practices seem to have included elements of Central Asian shamanism. Eliade notes the similarities of their ecstatic trances induced by singing and breathing hemp smoke to those of shamans.[58] According to Carl Ruck, the sacramental use of the entheogen *haoma* as described in the Persian *Avesta* was equivalent to the *soma* of the Hindu *Rig Veda*, a psychoactive brew used to induce altered states and visions.[59] Like shamans, the Magi were "psychopomps" who were rumored to send men alive into the world of the dead and bring them back again. Eliade compares their mythology of the Chinvat Bridge crossed in the afterlife with otherworldy passages in shamanic narratives. Similar to shamans who worshipped the forces of nature, the early Magi worshipped the *daevas*, who were nature gods. This lead to harsh condemnation and persecution by the Zoroastrians who viewed the *daevas* as "demons" and "false gods" opposed to the angelic *yazatas*.

The Magi were first introduced to the Greeks during the Persian conquest of Hellenic cities of Asia Minor around 540 BCE, where they served as court advisers, dream interpreters, diviners and astrologers to the Persian kings. Herodotus records that when the Persian invasion of Greece was delayed by a storm, the Magi tried to dispel it by offering victims to the dead and singing loud spells to the wind, as well as sacrificing to Thetis the sea goddess and her nymphs. By doing this, they stopped the storm on the fourth day, or according to Herodotus, "it blew itself out".

The Greeks who were in awe of the Magi's occult knowledge, named their occult practices *magia*, or "magic", after them. The Magi were reputed to have taught their magical arts to the Greeks. Pliny the Elder discusses the famous Persian magus Ostanes in this diatribe:

> "The first person, so far as I can ascertain, who wrote upon magic, and whose works are still in existence, was Osthanes, who accompanied Xerxes, the Persian king, in his expedition against Greece. It was he who first disseminated, as it were, the germs of this monstrous art, and tainted therewith all parts of the world through which the Persians passed...." [60]

Ostanes taught different magical techniques including divination by water, air, stars, lamps and other instruments, as well as necromancy. His legend was widespread in the Hellenistic world, and he was revered as an authority on astrology, the manufacture of amulets, and the occult names and magical properties of plants and stones.[61]

Besides being skilled astrologers and diviners, the Magi were ritual specialists who practiced necromancy, the magical art of summoning and communicating with the souls of the dead, as well as the exorcism of demons. In the Orphic text the *Derveni Papyrus* it is recorded that the Magi offered libations of water, milk and cakes to propitiate the dead. They used incantations to "move the demons who come in between as a hindrance", suggesting in this manner they exorcized troublesome spirits.[62]

The Greek historian Strabo writes that the Persians do not erect statues or altars, but offer sacrifices on a high place—to the heavens as Ahura Mazda, the sun as the god Mithras, venus as the goddess Anahita, as well as the elements of fire, earth, wind and water.[63]

Origins of Reincarnation

The origin of the doctrine of reincarnation in the western world poses an enigma. Also known as "metempsychosis" or "transmigration", this idea seems to have appeared suddenly and fully formed among Orphic and Presocratic philosophers, suggesting it was adopted from elsewhere—the Greeks themselves presumed they inherited the idea from a foreign source.[64] If reincarnation had no obvious precedent in the religious beliefs of ancient Greece, Egypt, Mesopotamia or Persia, then where did it come from?

The Neoplatonic philosopher Porphyry offers a plausible clue in one of his writings, noting that the Persian Magi believe in the transmigration of souls.[65] Historian M.L.West proposes the Magi, who inhabited cities on the fringes of the Greek and Indian worlds, introduced the idea of reincarnation to thinkers of both those cultures.[66]

Thomas McEvilley argues instead that the belief in reincarnation originated in the philosophy of the Upanishads of India and spread from there to Greece *via* the Persians. He writes: "The earliest Upanishads were compiled by 500 BCE bringing them not only into the Pre-Socratic period but into that part of it over which the Persian Empire presided." [67] McEvilley's theory, supported by a clear historical timeline, proposes that reincarnation as well as other philosophical doctrines concerning the soul's immortality were originally introduced to the Presocratic Greeks from India during the time of the Persian empire. According to him the works of Pythagoras, Heraclitus, Empedocles, Parmenides and others fall within this period of historical contact and share striking similarities with the Indian philosophy of the Upanishads.

Oriental scholar Alain Danielou holds a similar opinion, speculating that Jain missionaries from India, contemporaries of the Presocratics, reached Greece in their wanderings, spreading their doctrine of reincarnation as well as ascetic practices focused on liberating the soul from its cycle of rebirths.[68] Likewise Joseph Campbell writes that Orpheus taught "...a system both of thought and practice, exactly paralleling that of Indian asceticism." [69]

There is the possibility that the idea of reincarnation may have been introduced to the Greeks from their neighbors, the Thracians, Scythians or Celts, all of whom held similar beliefs of rebirth. As previously mentioned, indigenous cultures practicing shamanism also believe in the soul's rebirth, seeing this as essential for the tribe's survival. The doctrine of reincarnation as held by Indian yogis, Orphics and Presocratic philosophers was markedly different, however. McEvilley argues it is characterized by "the desire for release, the belief in moral evolution from one incarnation to the next, and the attainment of release as a reward for good actions".[70] This view of reincarnation requires a philosophical disengagement from the world by the mystic, and the practice of asceticism to purify the soul—the goal being permanent release from the cycle of birth and death. As we will see in the following pages, these beliefs and resulting practices became a central preoccupation of Greek philosophers as well.

Plato & Askesis—The Practice of Living & Dying

Plato (428-348 BCE) was born to an aristocratic and influential Athenian family, descendents of kings and lawmakers who included the poet Solon, according to Diogenes Laertius.[71] He writes that Plato's birth name was Aristocles but his wrestling coach gave him the nick-name "Platon", meaning "broad" on account of his robust figure. Plato as a youth was a devoted follower of the great Athenian philosopher Socrates. He was among those who offered to pay a fine on his behalf to release him from prison after he was charged with impiety and corrupting the minds of Athenian youth with his philosophy. After the death of Socrates, Plato fled Athens and spent the next twelve years traveling, studying with Euclid of Megara, the Pythagoraeans in Italy, as well as visiting Egypt, where according to some writers he was initiated by the priesthood into their teachings.

The philosophical works of Plato eloquently restate and systematize many of the ideas of his predecessors—particularly Pythagoras and the Orphics. Like Pythagoras, he shared a passion for mathematics and astronomy, a kinship with nature, and used musical terminology to describe the soul. Plato admired Pythagoras's ascetic lifestyle and like him advocated for the right way of living and pursuing one's life path. He was deeply indebted to Orphism as well, adopting its myths and teachings in his philosophy.

According to Naydler, Plato likely learned doctrines of the soul's immortality from the Egyptians, as well as mystical techniques for separating the soul from the body.[72] The immortality of the soul and the problem of its embodiment certainly preoccupied his thinking. In his *Cratylus*, Plato repeats a well known saying of the Orphics and Pythagoraeans: "the body *(soma)* is the tomb *(sema)* of the soul, which may be thought to be buried in our present life".

Plato saw the soul's purpose as returning to heaven from which it originated, to live in enraptured contemplation of the eternal ideas of goodness, truth, and beauty. In his *Phaedrus* which we will soon turn to, Plato describes such a heavenly ascent, reminiscent of the king's ascent to the stars described in the *Pyramid Texts* of Egypt, as well as shamanic ascents to the upperworld. Nicholas Kazanas writes that Plato defined philosophy as "the system of knowledge and practices whereby a man comes to know himself, realizes his divine nature and attains immortality...he returns to the region of the gods, to his native star." [73]

Plato inherited the doctrine of "metempsychosis" or transmigration of the soul from the Orphics and Pythagoreans and refers to it in his *Myth of Er* and *Phaedrus*. This idea was also familiar to other schools of classical philosophers such as the Stoics, as well as the followers of the mystery religions. One of the goals of philosophers was to be released from the wheel of rebirth. In order to achieve this they practiced ascetic exercises to purify the soul, calm the passions, and overcome attachment to the physical body.

Plato's teacher Socrates (469-399 BCE) was a master of such self-control, renowned for his physical fitness and self-discipline, his feats of physical endurance were legendary. He was known for his curious habit of occasionally standing immobile for hours on end, apparently in a cataleptic trance. On one occasion Socrates stood outside for an entire day and night contemplating a philosophical problem. Curious onlookers camped around him to watch if he would remain there all night, which he did, leaving only the next morning.

Contrary to modern popular opinion, the practice of philosophy by the ancient Greeks did *not* emphasize learning abstract theories or the study of books, but was an exercise in the "practice of living", according to modern philosopher Pierre Hadot. Basic to almost every school of Greek philosophy was the practice of asceticism or *askesis*, meaning "training" or "exercise". This was intended to lead to self-mastery and transformation of the self. Hadot compares the mental exercises of the philosopher to athletic training, pointing out that philosophy was often taught in the same gymnasium in which athletes trained: "Exercises of body and soul thus combined to shape the true person: free, strong and independent".[74]

Platonic *askesis* consisted in renouncing the pleasures of the flesh. Plato writes in the *Phaedo* that the philosopher should not concern himself with the "foolishness of the body" — the pleasures of food and drink, sex, clothes or other bodily ornaments.[75] By rejecting these, the philosopher shall gain direct knowledge of all that is pure an uncontaminated. Like the Indian yogi, he believed that by abstaining from the experience of pleasure the soul's attachment to the body would be loosened.

The Neoplatonist philosophers, borrowing from the Orphics, advocated for dietary restrictions like vegetarianism. They believed that by weakening the physical body through fasting and sleep deprivation one could better live the life of the spirit. Cynic and Stoic philosophers endured hunger, cold, insults, the rejection of luxury, and comforts of civilization to cultivate stamina and independence. Asceticism is also practiced by shamans worldwide who withdraw from society, fasting and exposing themselves to the elements and extreme temperatures to develop their spiritual powers. The Inuit shaman Igjhugarjuk stated: "the only true wisdom lives far from mankind, out in the great loneliness, and it can be reached only through suffering. Privation and suffering alone can open the mind of a man to all that is hidden to others".[76]

Even the Epicurian philosophers who saw pleasure as the highest good believed in limiting their desires and living modestly. In all these philosophical schools the goal was to distance the self from its desires and appetites, leading to a universal perspective on life. Hadot writes that Platonic *askesis* consisted in discovering the pure "I", thereby transcending the ego-centered self. By doing this the "I" separates itself from all attachments that prevent self-awareness.[77]

Many philosophers practiced the *askesis* of awareness of the present moment. Roman emperor and Stoic philosopher Marcus Aurelius wrote: "We live only in the present, so infinitely small. The rest has already been lived, or else it is uncertain. The past no longer concerns us, and the future does not concern us yet."[78] The poet Horace praises living in the present as the key to true happiness stating "Let the soul be happy in the present, and refuse to worry about what will come later."[79]

Awareness of the present acknowledges the inevitability of death. Like Plato who believed philosophy is training for dying, Aurelius writes that one must live every moment as if it is one's last: "Let death be before your eyes every day, and you will never have a base thought or an excessive desire"... "Your way of life achieves perfection when you spend each day as if it were your last." [80]

The examination of conscience was widely practiced by philosophers. Epictetus advises: "As soon as you rise in the morning, ask yourself, "What must I still do to attain impassibility and absence of worry? Who am I? A body? A possession? A reputation? None of those things. But what, then?...Go over your actions in your mind: Of the things that lead to happiness, which have I neglected?" [81]

Greek philosophers also practiced exercises of the imagination such as envisioning the soul's flight through cosmic space, a practice that bears uncanny similarities to the magical flight of shamans. This was used as a means of transcending the narrow limits of the egoistic self, to become aware of one's being within the totality of the universe. Plato in *Theaetetus* describes this exercise in which the soul..."flies in every direction...sounding what is beneath the earth, measuring the earth's surface, studying the path of the stars across the vault which overlooks the sky, exploring the whole nature of each of these realities in its totality..." [82] Philo of Alexandria comments on this practice, writing: "To be sure, their bodies remain on earth, but they give wings to their souls, so that they can rise into the ether and observe the powers which dwell there.." [83]

Plato believed dreams reveal the state of the soul, and Zeno advised that philosophers examine their dreams to become aware of the progress their souls had made. Dream incubation was another technique used by the philosophers. As previously mentioned, this technique was widespread in the ancient world, used as a means of prophecy as well as for curing disease. Kingsley writes: "The goal of dream incubation could be a dream of healing or more importantly to enter another world, make contact with the divine, receive knowledge directly from the gods..." [84] He insists that the Presocratic philosopher Parmenides belonged to a tradition that practiced incubation in *hesychia* or "stillness". [85] Hesychia was the Greek *daimon* of silence, the personification of peace and quiet. The meditative practice of shutting out the physical senses and turning inward to attain union with God known as *hesychasm* is still practiced in the Eastern Orthodox church to this day.

As a result of the practice of philosophy, Plato believed man could "become like a god as far as possible". This "divinization", or realization of one's divine self was achieved through ascetic exercises, meditation, temperance, discrimination and reason.[86] Plato writes in the *Phaidon* that there is the outward turning of consciousness through the senses and body, but also the reverse where the soul withdraws from the body and senses to reach pure and unchanging being, declaring "this state of the soul is called wisdom".[87]

When one of Plato's friends asked him on his deathbed to state his philosophy in one sentence, he replied: "Practice to die". Naydler observes:

> "For both Plato and the mystery religions...it is clear that it was regarded as possible for people, *while still alive,* to enter a state of consciousness in which the soul becomes separated from the body for a short period. During this period of separation, people could have profound experiences that they would not otherwise have until they died, the most important of which was an intense realization that there is an element in their nature that is immortal." [88]

The technique of separating the soul from the body during trance may have been learned by Plato during his studies in Egypt, or he may have acquired it from the Pythagoreans or other initiates of the mystery religions. The altered state of consciousness described by Naydler is similar to the experience of shamans who practice techniques for exteriorizing consciousness from the physical body to experience the afterlife state while still alive. Holger Kalweit writes:

> "The intimate relationship of the shaman to dying, death, and life after death, as well as the mental and spiritual techniques by which he projects himself to the very boundary between life and death, make him an excellent proponent of Plato's philosophy." [89]

Next, we will look at Plato's understanding of the soul's journey—from its origin in the stars to its incarnation on earth.

The Immortal Soul as Heavenly Star

Plato in his *Timaeus* presents the allegory of the *Crater* or "mixing bowl". Here the Demiurge, the Creator, sets about creating the universe as well as the souls of mankind. After first mixing up the World-Soul, he then uses the same material, yet of lesser degrees of purity, dividing it into souls equal to the number of stars, assigning a star to each soul. The Creator then places each of these souls into a chariot, showing them the nature of the universe and declaring unto them the laws of destiny.[90]

The belief in the soul's celestial origins may have been inherited by Plato from the Orphics who saw man as "the child of earth and starry heaven." He may have also learned it from the Egyptians. As previously mentioned, In the *Pyramid Texts*, the king' soul upon dying was thought to ascend to the stars where it dwelled throughout eternity. This notion can also be found among indigenous cultures worldwide. Various native american tribes believed the soul travels along the Milky Way, called the "Path of Souls", on its return to the sky world. The Mandan people believed newborns were stars descended to earth, and in the afterlife returned to the sky as stars.[91] The Lakota people believe infants descend from the stars, and souls of the dead journey to the constellation Ursa Major where they begin their journey across the sky to the spirit world.[92]

Plato's Allegory of the "Soul's Chariot"

In his *Phaedrus*, Plato uses the metaphor of the "Chariot of the Soul" to illustrate his theory of the three-fold nature of the soul. He presents the image of a charioteer driving a chariot pulled by two horses—one white and one black. The Charioteer represents the mind, or "logos", the rational part of the soul which discerns the real from unreal, guiding the soul to truth by making wise decisions. The white horse symbolizes the moral impulse, also described as the "spirit", the source of the soul's positive passions of honor, victory and justice. The black horse stands for the "appetitive nature"—the soul's irrational impulses, including hunger, thirst, cravings and sexual desires. The charioteers's task is to steer the chariot towards enlightenment and wisdom, by controlling and guiding the two horses from going their separate ways.

Plato proceeds to create a mythic allegory of the the soul's journey through the heavens prior to its descent into the world:[93] He envisions the gods circling around the heights of heaven in their chariots led by Zeus, king of the gods. Following them is an army of gods and spirits including "twelve great gods", representing the signs of the zodiac placed around the rim of the heavens. The human souls who follow this divine procession in their own chariots proceed steeply to the top of the heavenly vault. The gods advance easily, but many lesser souls progress with difficulty. The immortals reach the zenith and take their place on the outer surface of heaven, where they behold the things even above heaven. Plato alludes to the eternal and transcendent reality behind the cosmos: " the region above heaven was never worthily sung by any earthly poet, nor will it ever be...for the colorless, formless and intangible truly existing essence, with which all the true knowledge is concerned, holds this region, and is visible only to the mind, the pilot of the soul".[94]

The beatific experience of eternity is reserved for the select few, however. Most of the charioteers are troubled souls who rise and sink due to their "unruly horses", seeing some things but failing to see others. Others yearn for the upper regions, but unable to reach them are pulled down. Plato describes them as "trampling and colliding with one another, each striving to pass its neighbor... many wings are broken through incompetence of the drivers".[95] These souls grow heavy, lose their wings, and fall to the earth.

The souls that have "seen the most" in this journey are reborn as philosophers or lovers of beauty, then in descending order as musicians, kings, politicians, gymnasts, ending in the lowest of births as tyrants. Each soul returns to its place of origin in the period of 10,000 years, except for philosophers, who in 3,000 years of time "become winged again and go their way". The *Phaedrus* seems to allude to the doctrine of metempsychosis or reincarnation, in which souls are bound to the wheel of rebirth until they "re-grow their wings", enabling them to return to their heavenly origins.

The Spirit Vehicles of Neoplatonism

The Neoplatonist philosophers of late antiquity (5th Cent. CE) –Porphyry, Plotinus, Iamblichus, Proclus, and others were the heirs of Plato's thought, introducing their own interpretations of his teachings. They used Plato's allegory of the "Chariot of the Soul" as the basis for their ontological theories, proposing the soul acquired an *ochema-pneuma*—or "spirit-vehicle" during its descent from the heavens to earth.[96] During this process, the soul was believed to acquire increasingly material "envelopes" or "mantles" formed from the four elements.[97] The ochema-pneuma was believed to bridge the spiritual and physical worlds, serving as the organ of sense-perception and imagination. It was called the "ethereal" body as it was believed to be composed of the fifth element of "aether", the most subtle of the elements.

Besides the *ochema-pneuma*, the Neoplatonists described yet a higher aspect of the soul, a vehicle that is radiant, starlike, and eternal which they called the *augoeides-ochema*.[98] The *augoeides* was thought to be centered in the head as a spark of radiant light, while the ochema-pneuma enveloped the whole physical body, surrounding it like the "aura". The entire soul was imagined as spherical in shape, since of all forms the sphere was believed to be most perfect. The *ochema-pneuma* is strikingly similar to the modern notion of the "astral body". In fact, it was the Neoplatonic philosopher Proclus who originated the term *astroeides ochema* or "astral body".

In the Hermetic text entitled *The Key*, the spiritual principles of man are arranged as five envelopes of consciousness. Each of these is progressively denser that the previous one: the mind is contained in the reason, the reason is contained in the soul, the soul in the spirit, and the spirit in the physical body. Linda Johnsen provides the following list of these, relating them in turn to the Egyptian scheme of "subtle bodies" from which they may have been derived originally:[99]

Greek	Egyptian	English
soma	khat	physical body
pneuma	ka	vital force or energy body (spirit)
psyche	ba	sensory awareness, everyday mind (soul)
logos	djed	reasoning faculty, intellect (reason)
nous	akh	intuitive awareness, mystical consciousness (mind)

This scheme shares similarities with the series of subtle bodies found in modern Theosophy: the physical, etheric, astral, mental and causal bodies. It also generally corresponds to the vehicles of consciousness of Hindu Yoga and Buddhism. Proclus believed the denser envelope of the pneumatic body (*pneuma*) survived the death of the physical body, but eventually perished. The more subtle envelopes—the *logos* and *nous*—together comprised the "starlike body", perhaps equivalent to the ochema augoeides, and were thought to be immortal. As previously mentioned, similar notions of multiple spiritual bodies, some of which survive physical death, are held by Siberian shamans.

Naydler notes that the *ba* soul can be separated from the physical body during sleep or death, and also during deep relaxation and trance.[100] In Egyptian art the *ba* is often depicted as a human-headed bird flying forth from the tomb. As previously mentioned, the *Pyramid Texts* provided magical spells for the king to awaken his *ba*, by means of which he entered the *duat*, the underworld, then ascended to the sun-god Ra in the sky. Naydler insists the *Egyptian Book of the Dead* describes this process of metamorphosis of the *ba* into the *akh*, during which it becomes united with the source of spiritual light, finally dwelling in the heavens as a "shining one", a star.[101]

The process of separating the soul from the physical body, and its subsequent ascent through the heavens was a goal of initiatory practices. In the accounts of the Egyptians, Plato, and indigenous shamans, the transcendent ascension is likened to "flying with wings" or "climbing a ladder between earth and heaven". The Hermeticists, Gnostics and Merkabah mystics of antiquity similarly aspired to ascend in visionary consciousness through the celestial spheres to achieve the *unio-mystica*—mystical union with divinity.

Chapter 10 Notes

Ahura Mazda, Zoroastrian god of light
Stone relief from Persepolis, 6th cent. BCE.

1. Jaspers, Karl. *The Way To Wisdom*.1951: 98-101.
2. Campbell, Joseph. *The Masks of God. Occidental Mythology*. 1964: 222.
3. Couliano, I.P. *Out of This World*. 1991.
4. Kingsley, Peter. *In The Dark Places of Wisdom*. 1999: 114
5. Kingsley, Peter. *A Story Waiting to Pierce You: Mongolia, Tibet and the destiny of the Western world*. 2010.
6. Couliano. *Out of This World*. 1991: 127.
7. Kingsley. *A Story Waiting to Pierce You: Mongolia, Tibet and the destiny of the Western world*. 2010: 10-47.
8. Ibid.:10-47.
9. Hunter, Richard. *Plato and the Traditions of Ancient Literature: The Silent Stream*. 2012: 57.
10. Couliano. *Out of This World*. 1991: 129.
11. Eliade. *Shamanism- Archaic Techniques of Ecstasy*. 1964: 389.
12. Couliano. *Out of This World*. 1991: 137.
13. Burkert. *Greek Religion*.1985: 300.
14. McEvilley, Thomas. *The Shape of Ancient Thought (Comparative Studies in Greek and Indian Philosophies)* 2002: 45-46.
15. Baukham, Richard. *The Fate of the Dead: Studies on the Jewish and Christian Apocalypses*. 1998: 32.
16. West, M.L. *Early Greek Philosophy and the Orient*. 1971: 25.
17. Porphyry."*Life of Pythagoras.*"
18. Iamblichus. *The Life of Pythagoras*. Trans. Taylor, Thomas. 1905:10.
19. Porphyry."*Life of Pythagoras.*"
20. Guthrie, W.K.C. *A History of Greek Philosophy: vol. 1, The Earlier Presocratics and the Pythagoreans*. 1979: 164.
21. Iamblichus. *The Life of Pythagoras*. 1905:58. Also see Kahn, Charles H. *Pythagoras*

      and the Pythagoreans -A Brief History. 2001: 8.
22. Burkert. Tinh. (ed.) *Sarapis and Isis. Jewish and Christian Self-Definition- Vol. Three*.1982: 19.
23. Iamblichus. *The Life of Pythagoras.*1905:15.
24. Ibid.:63.
25. Pederson, Olaf. *Early Physics and Astronomy: A History.* 1974: 17
26. Guthrie, W.K.C. Chambers, William Keith. *A History of Greek Philosophy: vol. 1, The Earlier Presocratics and the Pythagoreans.*
27. Porphyry.*"Life of Pythagoras."*: 47.
28. Pliny the Elder. *Natural History.* Books I-II. Trans. Rackham, H.
29. Kingsley. *In The Dark Places of Wisdom.* 1999: 208.
30. Pederson. *Early Physics and Astronomy: A History.* 1974: 17.
31. Kahn, Charles H. *Pythagoras and the Pythagoreans -A Brief History.* 2001:160.
32. McEvilley, Thomas. The Shape of Ancient Thought (Comparative Studies in Greek and Indian Philosophies). 2002.
33. Campbell, Joseph. *The Masks of God: Oriental Mythology.* (Campbell 1991: 452) Campbell writes that in ancient India *five* elements were known: the four elements plus *aether*. These elements were associated with the five senses: aether /hearing, air, touch, fire/ sight, water/ taste, and earth/ smell.
34.   Kingsley, Peter. *Ancient Philosophy, Mystery and Magic.* 1995:13.
35. Ibid.:13.
36. Opsopaus, John. "The Ancient Esoteric Doctrine of the Elements: Fire." *Biblioteca Arcana.* 1999: 7.
37. Kirk, G.S., Raven, J.E. & Schofield, Malcolm. *Presocratic Philosophers: a critical history with selection of texts.* 1957: 288.
38. Stamatellos, Giannis. *Plotinus and the Presocratics: A Philosophical Study of Presocratic Influences in Plotinius' Enneads.* 2007: 51.
39. Dodds, E.R. *The Greeks and the Irrational.* 1968: 145.
40. Diogenes Laertus. *Lives of Eminent Philosophers.* Book VIII. 8:59 A1.
41. Ibid. :15/III.
42. Humphrey, Caroline & Onon, Urgunge. *Shamans & Elders.*1996:100.
43. Smith, Mark S. *The Early History of God. Jahweh and the Other Deities in Ancient Israel.* 1987:5.
44. Ibid.:19.
45. Ibid.:148.
46. Dunn, James & Rogerson, John William. *Eerdman's Commentary on the Bible.* 2003:154.
47. McNeill, William, H.; Petheo, Bela. *The Rise of the West: A History of the Human Community.* 2009:163-164.
48. Smith. *The Early History of God. Jahweh and the Other Deities in Ancient Israel.* 1987: 152.
49. Boyce, Mary. *Zoroastrians- Their Religious Beliefs and Practices.* 2001: 52.
50. Ibid.: 29.
51. Campbell. *Occidental Mythology. The Masks of God.* 1964: 192.
52. Jahanian, Dr. Jaryoush."The Zoroastrian-Biblical Connections- Influence of Zoroastrianism in other Religions". *Zarathushtra.com,* 2003. Also *see* Kohler &

Jackson. *Jewish Encyclopedia.* Zoroastrianism".
53. Campbell. *Occidental Mythology. The Masks of God.* 1964: 194.
54. Witzel. *The Origins of the World's Mythologies.* 2012: 409. Witzel notes that the dualistic worldview of Zoroaster not only set the stage for Judaism, Christianity and Islam, and indirectly even influenced the modern ideology of Marxism.
55. Hultgard, A (ed.) McGinn, Bernard; Collins, John J.; Stein, Stephen. *The Continuum History of Apocalypticism.* 2003: 48.
56. Couliano, I.P. *Out of This World.* 1991: 105.
57. Ibid.:110-111.
58. Eliade. *Shamanism- Archaic Techniques of Ecstasy.*Eliade 1972: 395-397.
59. Ruck. Walter & Fridman. (ed.) *Shamanism: An Encyclopedia of World Beliefs, Practices and Culture,* Vol.1 2004:483.
60. Pliny the Elder. *Natural History--Book* 30.2.3.
61. Smith, Morton. "Ostanes: Legendary Mage in Classical and Medieval Literature". *Encyclopaedia Iranic.* 2002.
62. Burkert 2004: 118.
63. Herodotus. *The Histories.* Customs of the Persians 1.131.
64. McEvilley, Thomas.. *The Shape of Ancient Thought.* 2002:118.
65. Porphyry. *On Abstinence from animal food.* Book 4. 110-138.
66. McEvilley. *The Shape of Ancient Thought.* 2002: 121. Also see West, M.L. *Early Greek Philosophy and the Orient.* 1971:67.
67. Ibid.: 60.
68. Danielou, Alain. *Gods of Love and Ecstasy: The Traditions of Shiva and Dionysus.* 1992:28.
69. Campbell 1964:183.
70. McEvilley. *The Shape of Ancient Thought.* 2002: 98-143.
71. Diogenes Laertius. *Life of Plato III.*
72. Naydler, Jeremy. *Shamanic Wisdom of the Pyramid Texts- The Mystical Tradition of Ancient Egypt.* 2005: 56.
73. Kazanas, Nicholas. "Plato and the Upanishads". *Department of Philosophy.* (website) Panjab University. 2004: 2.
74. Hadot, Pierre, *What is Ancient Philosophy?* Translated by Michael Chase. 2002: 89.
75. Plato. *Phaedo* 67a.
76. Walsh, Roger N., M.D., Ph.D. *The Spirit of Shamanism.* 1990: 54.
77. Hadot. *What is Ancient Philosophy?* 2002: 190.
78. Aurelius, Marcus. *Meditations*-III, 10, 1.
79. Horace. *Odes* II, 16, 35.
80. Aurelius. *Meditations* II ; II,5, 2;VII 69.
81. Epictetus, *Discourses.* IV6, 34.
82. Plato.*Theaetetus*-173 e.
83. Philo of Alexandria. *De specialibus legibus,* II, 45.
84. Kingsley. *In The Dark Places of Wisdom.*1999: 102.
85. Ibid.: 82.
86. Kazanas. "Plato and the Upanishads" 2004: 2.
87. Ibid.: 2

88. Naydler, Jeremy. *Shamanic Wisdom of the Pyramid Texts- The Mystical Tradition of Ancient Egypt.* 2005: 56.
89. Kalweit. *Dreamtime & Inner Space: the world of the* 1988: 3. Kalweit discusses NDE's or *near death experiences* of people who have survived *"clinical death"*, noting that most people have profoundly meaningful and transformative experiences, losing their fear of death and gaining a more positive view of life.
90. Plato. *Timaeus.* v.291.
91. Krupp, E.C. *Beyond the Blue Horizon: Myths and Legends of the Sun, Moon, Stars, and Planets.* 1997:58.
92. Goodman, Ronald. *Lakota Star Knowledge.*1992: 37.
93. Plato. *Phaedrus* 246e-248e. Fowler, Harold. Trans. *Plato in Twelve Volumes.* Vol. 9.1925
94. Ibid.: 247c.
95. Ibid.: 248b.
96. Ochema means "vehicle" or "chariot" while pneuma literally translates as "air" which was associated with breath or spirit.
97. Greene, Elizabeth. *The Celestial Ascent of the Soul- The Morphology of an Enduring Idea.* 2006: 29.
98. Mead, G.R.S. *The Doctrine of the Subtle Body in Western Tradition* Mead 2005: 81.
99. Johnsen, Linda. *Lost Masters of Ancient Greece.*Johnsen. 2006: 162
100. Naydler. *Shamanic Wisdom of the Pyramid Texts.* 2005:22.
101. The *ba* is associated with Osiris, and the *akh* with the sun-god Ra; during this apotheosis the center of consciousness transitions from the underworld to the heavenly world, resulting in spiritual illumination.

Chapter 11: Hellenism & Religion of the Stars

"Then may one see heaven's shining temples teeming with minute points of light and the whole firmament sparkle with the dense array of stars"
-Manilius-Astronomica

Alexander the Great with horns of Egyptian god Amun.
Greek coin, early 3rd century BCE.

The Rise of Alexandria

The Hellenistic Age began with Alexander the Great (356-323 BCE) a Macedonian prince, who succeeded his father to the throne at the age of twenty. Alexander spent the next decade in wars of conquest, defeating the Persians and creating his own global empire—rivaling that of Cyrus the Great before him. It united Europe with Africa and the Middle East, extending across Persia to India. Like Cyrus, Alexander was cosmopolitan in his outlook, valuing the cultural and religious heritage of his subject nations.

The place that most characterized the new spirit of cultural syncretism of the Hellenistic Age was the city of Alexandria in Egypt. It was the brainchild of Alexander who envisioned a port city linking the Mediterranean with the riches of Egypt. Under the tolerant rule of Ptolemy I, a lifelong companion of Alexander, and Ptolemy's descendents, Alexandria became a cultural crossroads. Its citizens were drawn from all over the known world and included Greeks, Egyptians, Jews, Babylonians, Phoenicians, Persians, Syrians, Nubians, Romans, Gauls and even Indians.

Diodorus Siculus wrote of his visit to Alexandria in the first century BCE: "The city in general has grown so much in later times that many reckon it to be the first city of the civilized world, and it is certainly far ahead of all the rest in elegance and extent of riches and luxury. The number of its inhabitants surpasses those in other cities..."[1] Alexandria was known for its landmarks such as the Pharos Lighthouse, deemed one of the "Seven Wonders of the World", as well as the famed Library of Alexandria which was reputed to house from 500,000 to a million books.[2] As a personal student of the great philosopher Aristotle, Alexander valued knowledge and collected books from all the nations and peoples he conquered, sending them to the library which became the greatest in the ancient world. Alexandria became a center of science and the arts, its schools gaining an international reputation for studies in mathematics, geometry, astronomy, astrology, medicine and philosophy.

Alexandria was also the center of religious and esoteric teachings of all varieties, home to Neoplatonic, Stoic and Hermetic philosophers, Zoroastrians, Gnostic Christians, Buddhists, Indian Brahmins, as well as initiates of mystery schools, astrologers, alchemists, and magicians. These groups flourished there for several centuries until the late 3rd century CE when the Christian Emperor Theodosius I declared Christianity the state religion and began the persecution of pagans—closing their temples and according to some accounts destroying the remains of the Library of Alexandria.

The Religion of the Stars

"I know that I am mortal, the creature of one day. But when I explore the winding courses of the stars I no longer touch with my feet the earth. I am standing near Zeus himself drinking my fill of ambrosia, the food of the gods."
- Ptolemy

Following Alexander's conquest of Babylon in 331 BCE, a rich cross-fertilization began between the cultures of Mesopotamia and Greece during which scientific and philosophical knowledge was exchanged. Chaldean priests such as Berossus settled on the island of Cos in Greece, spreading his astronomical and astrological knowledge, while centers of Greek science were established in Mesopotamia.[3] Babylonian techniques for observing and recording the motions of the heavenly bodies were combined with the geometric and cosmological models of the Greeks, giving birth to the science of *astronomy*. Hellenistic *astrology* likewise resulted from the synthesis of older traditions of Babylonian astrology with theories of Greek philosophy.

Hellenistic astrology offered not only a philosophical worldview, but a new astral religion as well, replacing the older religions of the city-states. It provided a universal belief that reflected the new political realities of the cosmopolitan Hellenistic Empire, according to historian Franz Cumont who writes:

> "After the conquests of Alexander a great change took place. The ancient ideal of the Greek republic gave way to the conception of universal monarchy. Thenceforth municipal cults disappeared before an international religion. The worship of the stars, common to all the peoples, was strengthened by everything that weakened the particularism of cities. In proportion as the idea of "humanity" spread, men were the more ready to reserve their homage for those celestial powers which extended their blessings to all mankind." [4]

The new science of astronomy was viewed by Plato as a means of teaching the orderliness of the celestial gods, their harmony and number. In his opinion the gods described by astronomy—the stars and planets—were infinitely superior to the Olympian gods of the older popular religion. He believed the heavenly bodies were "visible gods", animated by the creator, the Demiurge, with his own life and power.

Plato in his *Timaeus* based his astronomy on the archetypal forms of geometry, and like Pythagoras before him conceived of the universe as a sphere, proclaiming that of all shapes it is the most perfect. He envisioned the universe as containing the central sphere of the earth around which the greater heavenly sphere revolved, an idea that would be developed into the concept of the "celestial spheres" by his student, the astronomer Eudoxus (408-355 BCE). Plato spoke of a cosmos designed by God in which the sun, moon and five visible planets were placed in seven orbits around the earth for the purpose of "determining and preserving the numbers of Time."[5] Plato's cosmos was alive and endowed with a "World Soul", connected to all living creatures endowed with souls. Possessing a soul, the universe was seen as a "self acting source of motion".

For Plato, the human soul's fiery nature was similar in essence to the stars, and contemplation of the heavens became an act of spiritual communion. In his project for religious reform, Plato emphasized the cult of the celestial gods. In his *Laws,* Plato mused that the stars are the "gods in heaven", and the sun and moon the "great gods" — therefore prayer and sacrifice should be made to them by all people. He proposed the Twelve Gods ruling over the zodiac should be assigned a central role in the ideal city which would be divided into twelve tribes of citizens, each to be named for one of those gods who would serve as their patron deity. The citizens would in turn hold a festival each month honoring one of those twelve deities.[6]

Stoic philosophers such as Zeno studied astronomy along with astrology and professed a type of astral religion. The Stoic philosopher Posidonius was "very much given to astrology" according to Saint Augustine. The Stoics interest in astrology was connected to their belief in an all-pervading fate which determined events, which they attributed to the stars. Cicero writes of the astral doctrines of the Stoics: "When we have seen this divinity of the cosmos, we must attribute the same divinity to the stars...they may most rightly said to be living beings endowed with consciousness".[7]

The Heavens as the New Underworld

The new cosmology introduced by astronomy and astrology brought about a dramatic shift in eschatological beliefs about the soul. David Ulansey writes: "...the growing importance of astrological doctrines in the Hellenistic and Roman periods also encouraged the spread of a new conception of life after death, according to which the soul ascends through the heavenly spheres to return to its new home in the stars."[8]

These doctrines countered traditional Greek myths which placed the paradisiacal Elysian Fields in the *underworld* beneath the earth. They instead proposed that the final abode of the virtuous soul was in a *celestial* paradise. In fact, during the Hellenistic period, even Hades became relocated into the heavens.[9] Franz Cumont writes that theologians doubted where to place the mythical Elysian Fields, locating them in the moon, between the moon and sun, the fixed stars, the Milky Way and even beyond the outer sphere of the heavens. Likewise they placed the rivers of Hades in the sky — assigning the river Acheron to the air, and Pyriphlegethon to the zone of hail.[10]

Mystics now taught that the souls of the dead ascended to dwell in the moon and sun, or to shine as stars among the constellations. In Plato's view, the souls of philosophers returned to inhabit the heavenly bodies which had served as their dwelling-place before birth, to enjoy immortality there. The new celestially oriented cosmology of the Greco-Roman world tended to present a negative view of the earthly realm. Historian John. J. Collins writes: "The soul was weighed down by bodily existence and was liberated to rise up after death."[11] Plato saw philosophy as a way for the soul to "grow wings" and return to it's home in the heavens. The Gnostics, whom we will later discuss, took this view to the extreme, proposing the cosmos was created by an evil demiurge. They saw the material world as an oppressive prison from which the soul needed to free itself, to return to its home in the heavenly aeons.

Reflecting this transformation in eschatological beliefs, an epitaph from a tombstone of the period reads: "My divine soul shall not descend to the shades; heaven and the stars have borne me away; earth holds my body, and this stone an empty name." [12]

The Myth of Er

Plato, in his *Myth of Er* presents a visionary narrative of the soul's afterlife journey, supposedly based on an account of the "near-death" experience of a soldier named Er. Its cosmology blends the archaic mythic geography of Hades with newfound astronomical ideas of the celestial spheres of the sun, moon, planets and stars. Plato conceives of a cosmos revolving around the "Spindle of Necessity", attended by goddesses such as the Sirens and Fate. These various motifs are woven together to create a seemless eschatological narrative—a story of the soul's afterlife trials, judgement, and rebirth. Following is the author's abridged version of Jowett's translation of the *Myth of Er*: [13]

> Er was slain in battle, and ten days later his body was found unaffected by decay and taken home for burial. On the twelfth day, lying on the funeral pyre, Er returns to life and tells what he has seen in the other world. He reports that when his soul left his body he went on a journey with a large company of other souls and came to a mysterious place where there were two openings in the earth, as well as two openings in the heavens above. Between these openings were seated judges who commanded the just among them to ascend by the heavenly way on the right hand, while the unjust were forced to descend by the lower way on the left. Er met with souls who ascended out of the earth or descended from heaven. They held a joyful reunion, telling each other stories about their journeys beneath the earth as well as the delights and visions of heavenly beauty. Er was told that for every wrong committed against anyone, souls suffer tenfold with punishments, and for any good deed the rewards were in the same proportion. He witnessed the punishment of a tyrant who had lived a thousand years before, as

well as other criminals who committed many abominable crimes, as they tried to escape Hades for the upperworld. Demons appeared as "wild men of fiery aspect" who seized and carried off the "incurable sinners" back to hell, binding them, flaying them with scourges and dragging them while carding them on thorns like wool.

Continuing on their journey Er and the company of spirits came to a place where they saw a column of light extending through heaven and earth, resembling a rainbow in color "only brighter and purer". This light is the "belt of heaven" which holds together the circle of the universe. From its ends are extended the "Spindle of Necessity" around which the universe revolves. It consists of one large hollow "whorl" into which smaller whirls are nested into each other, one containing the other. These whorls are the celestial spheres which are fitted together into proportions along the spindle. The outermost whorl is the sphere of the fixed stars followed by smaller spheres of the sun, moon and five planets. The spindle is turned by the Sirens—goddesses of Fate and Necessity. Each of the eight Sirens hymn a single tone or note, creating a celestial harmony. The Fates also join in this chorus: Lachesis sings of the past, Clotho the present, and Atropos of the future, each spinning the whorls of the planets around.

Er and the other spirits were brought before the Siren Lachesis who rules over fate. They were told that they will begin a new cycle of life and mortality. Lots were scattered randomly among them and each soul took up a lot that fell near them. They were told that he who chooses the first lot has the first choice, and the life he chooses will be his destiny. Samples of different lives were placed before them to choose from, including animal as well as human existences of all sorts, lives of every condition including tyrants, the famous, the wealthy, poor, healthy and sick, all mingled together. The souls were cautioned to carefully consider and choose their new lives with utmost care, based on its virtuous nature rather than being "dazzled" by the allure of wealth and evil. Nevertheless, some souls whose minds were darkened by folly and sensuality choose to be tyrants, though they later lamented over their decision, blaming the gods for their own poor choices. Owing to their inexperience as well as the random lots, many of the souls exchanged a good destiny for an evil one, or evil for good. A number of souls who had come from heaven had never been schooled by trial, whereas the pilgrim from earth who had studied philosophy was happy and his journey to another life was smoother and more heavenly.

The Tree of Visions

The most curious spectacle was the choice of souls who based their decisions on experiences from a previous life. For example the soul which had once been Orpheus chose the life of a swan rather than being born of a woman, as he had been murdered by women. Agamemnon chose the life of an eagle, hating human nature due to his sufferings. Not only did men choose the life of animals, but tame and wild animals changed into one another, and into corresponding human natures—the good into the gentle, and the evil into the savage, in all sorts of combinations. All the souls had now chosen their next lives and they went with their choice to Lachesis who sent them away along with their chosen genius, which was to be guardian of their lives and the fulfiller of their choice. This genius then led the souls first to Clotho, who drew them within the revolution of the spindle spun by her hand, ratifying the destiny of each soul. After they were fastened to this, they were carried to Atropos, who spun the threads of fate and made them irreversible, after which they passed beneath the throne of Necessity.

Finally when all this had passed, Er and the company of souls marched on in scorching heat to the Plain of Forgetfulness, a barren waste destitute of trees and vegetation. Towards evening they camped by the River of Unmindfulness, whose water no vessel can hold. Of this water they were all obliged to drink a certain quantity, and those who were not saved by wisdom drank more than was necessary. Each one as he drank forgot all things. After they had gone to rest, about the middle of the night there was a thunderstorm and earthquake, and in an instant they were driven upwards in all manner of ways to their birth, like shooting stars. Er himself was hindered from drinking the water. But in what manner or by what means he returned to the body he could not say. In the morning, awaking suddenly, he found himself lying on the funeral pyre.

Plato introduces an important esoteric teaching in the *Myth of Er*, that of the spiritual "genius" assigned to each soul before birth to guard and assist in fulfilling their destinies. This is similar to the notion of the *fravashi* of Zoroastrianism and the guardian angel of later Judeo-Christian and Islamic doctrine. Other teachings such as metempsychosis of the soul in human and animal forms, as well as the soul's responsibility in choosing its future life are woven into the story.

According to historian Grace Harriet Macurdy, Plato's *Myth of Er* and his other myths such as *Phaedo* which present eschatological visions of the afterlife, influenced Jewish apocalyptic literature such as the *Book of Enoch* as well as the Christian *Book of Revelations*. These in turn effected Christian doctrines of heaven and hell and the soul's judgment and resurrection.[14]

Hellenistic Astrology

The word "planet" derives from the ancient Greek word *planetes* meaning "wanderer", as the planets move against the unchanging background of the stars. The so-called "ancient planets" are those visible to the naked eye: Mercury, Venus, Mars, Jupiter and Saturn. The Sun and Moon, known as the "luminaries", were also considered planets, since they moved as well. Originally the Greeks gave the planets names based on their visual qualities: Mercury was named the "twinkling star", Mars the "Fiery Star" due to his red color, Jupiter the "Luminous Star", and Saturn the "Brilliant Star".[15]

The Mesopotamians had long associated their pantheon of gods with the seven planets, which were believed to manifest their powers. During the Hellenistic era, Greek astrologers looked to the planets and substituted their own Olympian deities for their original Babylonian planetary gods and goddesses. For example, the planet venus, associated by the Babylonians with Ishtar, was replaced with Aphrodite the Greek goddess of love, etc.[16]

Chains of Sympathy

The Stoic philosophers of the Greco-Roman era envisioned the entire cosmos—the stars, planets and earth—as a living organism in which the whole was connected to the parts through *cosmic sympathy*.[17] They established series of sympathetic correspondences, or "chains" of sympathy which connected together the natural realm. Minerals, plants, animals and even human body parts corresponded to planets ruled by a particular god or goddess.[18] For example, the planet mars corresponding with Ares, the god of war, ruled the zodiacal signs Aries and Scorpio, the day of Tuesday, iron, hematite stone, the color red, as well as the affairs of war and warriors. Ptolemy in *Tetrabiblos* cites mars's rulership over the kidneys, veins and private parts, the masculine gender, dryness and heat, the virtue of fortitude, and the vice of anger. Virtually all areas of human experience were believed to be ruled over by the planetary deities.[19]

Astrologers judged human character and fate based on "planetary dignity", the relative strength or weakness of planets placed in horoscopes. Magicians conjured the planetary gods and their subservient angels and daemons, believing they could thereby persuade them to circumvent fate and realize their desires. Alchemists likewise attributed the rulership of metals and herbs to the planets, timing their laboratory operations according to the motions of the heavenly bodies.

The Roman poet and astrologer Manilius (1st century CE) lyrically extols the astrological world-view of antiquity, in which a supreme god reigns over the universe through the power of cosmic sympathy:

> "I shall sing how the life of the whole universe is based on mutual sympathy and how it moves by the force of reason because a single spirit inhabits all its parts and radiates through the whole world, spreading itself through everything and giving it the shape of a living creature...though the stars are very distant and remote he makes us feel their influence, as they give to the peoples their ways of life and destinies and to each person a character of their own. We do not have to look far for proof: this is why the sky effects the farmland, why it gives and takes away various crops, why it moves the sea by ebb and tide." [20]

The Hellenistic Zodiac

Besides the planetary gods and goddesses, the Greeks also named the constellations of the night sky for numerous heroes and heroines, beasts and iconic objects from mythology—a process known as *catasterism* or "placing among the stars". They borrowed many of their constellations from the sky-lore of older Mesopotamian and Near-Eastern cultures. Virtually all the Greek zodiacal constellations were borrowed from the Babylonian zodiac. For example, the constellation Leo, known by the Greeks as the "Nemean Lion", was based on the archaic Babylonian constellation the Lion.[21]

Coinciding with astrology's increasing popularity, the twelve constellations of the *zodiac*, which means "circle of animals" in Greek, became the most familiar asterisms of the sky. Astrological treatises written during the Greco-Roman era discussed the the zodiacal signs and their influence on worldly events and individual destiny. Books describing the character traits of persons born under the different zodiac signs proliferated. The signs of the zodiac even became associated with the ruling "geniuses" of entire nations. Manilius in his *Astronomica* writes that Italy is ruled by the sign of Libra, and Greece by Virgo.[22] Symbols of the zodiac became familiar cultural icons, appearing on monuments of pagan worship, coins and artwork.

Astrology of the Individual

The practice of horoscopic or individual astrology gained increasing importance during the second century BCE. Early astrological texts pseudonymously authored by Hermes were most likely influenced by Babylonian sources. An early horoscope from Babylon of a child born on April 29, 265 BCE reads:

> "At the time of birth the Sun was in 13:30 degrees Aries, the Moon in 10 degrees Aquarius, Jupiter at the beginning of Leo, Venus with the Sun, Saturn in Cancer, Mars at the end of Cancer..His food will not satisfy his hunger. The wealth that he has in youth will not remain. For thirty-six years he will have wealth. His days will be long." [23]

Although astrology was imported to Ptolemaic Egypt from Babylon, there was a native astrological tradition in Egypt based on the *decans* of the zodiac. Precious stones were engraved with images of the decan gods under whom the person was born to protect them from disease. In Egypt astrology found fertile ground, becoming associated with popular occultism and magic, as well as esoteric Hermetic philosophy. Historian George Luck writes that astrologers became accessible to the public and were consulted about affairs of business, love and politics. Some astrologers claimed to be hierophants or seers, impressing their customers with their occult knowledge. Nevertheless, there was also a genuine mysticism associated with astrology.[24]

A number of Roman emperors such as Numa, Tiberius, and Nero consulted astrologers. As a youth, Augustus Caesar went to the astrologer Theogenes who fell on his knees before him — predicting his future as emperor. Augustus was so impressed he later had his horoscope published, and even issued a silver coin with his sun-sign symbol Capricorn stamped on it. The emperor Hadrian was apparently so skilled in astrology he predicted his own hour of death.[25] Later Roman emperors, however, became increasingly wary of astrologer's predictions of their death or downfall, causing them to ban astrology altogether. They imposed brutal punishment on astrologers and those who would consult them. The Roman jurist Paulus wrote: "Anyone who consults astrologers, soothsayers, readers of entrails, or diviners about the life expectancy of the emperor, or the stability of the government, is to be executed, as is the one who gives the response." [26]

One of the earliest existing texts on astrology was the *Tetrabiblos* written in the early second century CE by the Roman-Egyptian Claudius Ptolemy. As well as being an astrologer, Ptolemy was among the greatest scientists of his day, a mathematician, geographer, and astronomer. He perfected the cosmological model of the "celestial spheres" of Greek astronomy, providing a mathematical theory which explained the motions of the sun, moon and planets. Ptolemy also formulated the "Chaldean" order of the planets, based on their relative speed of motion as observed from the earth. His cosmological model provided fairly accurate predictions of the motions of the heavenly bodies. It became the accepted astronomical model of antiquity and the Middle Ages, until it was finally replaced by the Heliocentric model of Kepler and Copernicus in the 16th century. Ptolemy codified the basic doctrines of astrology as well, including the four elemental qualities of cold, hot, dry and moist, and their influence on the planets.

Vettius Valens was a contemporary of Ptolemy who wrote the first systematic textbook of astrology. Firmicus Maternus who lived in the 3rd century CE, was an astrologer as well as a Christian apologist who wrote an introduction to astrology entitled *Libri Matheseos*. It addresses philosophical questions like destiny vs. free will, as well as technical issues like casting a horoscope.

Astrology grew in popularity and spread throughout the ancient world, reaching as far as India where it became the basis of Vedic Astrology. Astrology's influence on western culture was pervasive until the end of the Roman Empire, and it endured though the centuries to the present day. In fact Hellenistic Astrology is presently witnessing a revival of interest among modern astrologers.

The Age of Pisces & The Fishers of Men

During the early years of the first millennium astrology became linked to apocalyptic ideas of the birth of a new age—the Age of Pisces—by early Christians as well as pagans. The transition of "astrological ages" is based on the astronomical phenomenon known as the "precession of the equinoxes", in which the sun's position at spring equinox gradually moves backward relative to the fixed stars at the rate of one astrological sign every 2,160 years.[27] As the previous Age of Aries ended, it was followed by the Age of Pisces, which began approximately around 145 BCE.

The early Christians, well aware of the importance of this cosmic event, likely borrowed their icon of the *fish* from the symbolism of the constellation Pisces—which means the "fishes" in Latin. In fact the Greek word for fish—*icthys*—became a code word for Jesus. The messiah's apostles were called "fishers of men", and the faithful called themselves "little fish". Astrology may have also influenced the symbolism of the Virgin Mary as well. Authors Timothy Freke and Peter Gandy. write: "As the Age of Pisces began, its opposite sign in the zodiac, Virgo the Virgin, was on the western horizon. Pagan mythology, therefore, expected the savior of the Piscean Age to be born of a virgin".[28]

The apocalyptic predictions of early Christianity were in keeping with older pagan traditions regarding the transition of ages, believed to be heralded by natural disasters such as purifying floods and fire. The fact that the astrological Age of Pisces was imminent at this time no doubt was regarded as a celestial omen confirming the ascendancy of the new religion of Christianity.

Hellenistic Magic—The Goes, Magus & Divine Man

Discussing the role of magic in antiquity, Hans Dieter Betz, editor of the *Greek Magical Papyri*, stresses the importance magical beliefs and practices played in the lives of ordinary people. He comments on the practical role of the magician in the ancient world: [29]

> "He knew the code words needed to communicate with the gods, the demons and the dead. He could tap, regulate, and manipulate the invisible energies. He was a problem solver who had remedies for a thousand petty troubles plaguing mankind... the magician served as a power and communications expert, crisis manager, miracle healer and inflicter of damages, and all-purpose therapist and agent of worried, troubled, and troublesome souls."

Magicians practiced widely during antiquity, providing many of the same services as shamans did in tribal societies. In the Hellenistic world magicians were often categorized into several classes, according to historian Morton Smith.

We previously discussed the *goes* of ancient Greece, described by Smith as a sort of "Greek shaman". They accompanied the souls of the dead to the underworld, purified the living as well as the dead, and likewise could send restless ghosts to torment victims. The *goetes* (plural for goes) were originally connected to ecstatic mystery-rites into which they offered initiations. They were wandering mendicants and popular performers who performed illusions and charmed their audiences with tales of their exploits.

In later times they earned a reputation for trickery; Socrates and Euripides came to use the word *goeteia* synonymously with "deceit", equating them with "beggars" and "scoundrels".

Jewish-Roman historian Josephus also uses the word goetes to describe Jewish "false prophets", "magicians" and "wonderworkers" who promised to perform miracles such as dividing the River Jordan, making the walls of Jerusalem fall down, or giving people salvation and rest from their troubles. According to Smith, goeteia had "lower class connotations" and was widely associated with political orators and similar "spellbinders" or "frauds".[30]

A step above the *goes* in social stature was the *magos,* according to Smith. As previously mentioned, the Magi were a clan of priests closely related to the Persians. Herodotus describes them as interpreters of omens, dreams, and portents, who also supervised private and public sacrifices. So revered were they for their wisdom that the nefarious Roman emperor Nero studied with the magus Tiridates and was initiated by him into his magical rites. Not only were the Magi experts in magic, but they also offered initiations into their religious mysteries. They provided moral teachings about Ahura Mazda, the "good god" and Ahriman, his evil counterpart, as well as the end of the world and the destruction of the wicked, followed by an age of peace and happiness for the righteous, familiar Zoroastrian doctrines.[31] The term "magus" became widespread and was used to describe a broad range of magical practitioners. According to Smith it might mean anything from a genuine Magian priest or potentate to a person who peddled amulets or poisons to the superstitious. It became customary to denigrate one's religious opponents with the names "goes", "magos" or "false prophet".[32]

The third category of ancient magical practitioner was the *theos aner* or "divine man", according to Smith. They differed from the *goes* and *magos* through their possession of an indwelling divinity, which allowed them to dispense with magical spells and rituals altogether. It was the power of a divine *daemon* or god that resided within them that set them apart from the ordinary magician. The *Greek Magical Papyri* describe rites by which one can obtain such a spirit as a constant companion, such as the ritual for gaining the *paredros*, which we will discuss next. The papyri also provide rites by which the magician is "deified" either by joining with a god in permanent union, or by transforming his soul to make it divine. The deified magician could then perform miracles by his own power rather than by summoning spirits to assist him.

Examples of such divine men are Orpheus, Pythagoras, Empedocles, Jesus, and his contemporary Apollonius of Tyana, who were able to perform miracles simply by the power of their divine presence. Although the followers of Jesus described him as a "divine man", his critics accused him of working his magic by the power of the spirit of John the Baptist who they claimed dwelled in him.

In the next chapter we will explore the Theurgy or "divine work" of the Neoplatonist philosopher Iamblichus. Theurgists combined the popular magical practices of the *goes* with the religious magic of the *magos* for the purpose of uplifting their souls to divinity and achieving deification.

The Ritual for Summoning a Divine Assistant
The ritual magician of the Hellenistic world drew from a rich heritage of

myths and deities from ancient Egypt, Greece, Persia, Babylon, Syria and Judea. They invoked spirits of the heavens, earth, and underworld including a wide range of gods & goddesses, angels, archons, heroes, daemons, elemental spirits, and souls of the dead. In the *Greek Magical Papyri* a ritual is recorded by which a *paredros* or assistant *daimon* is acquired.[33] The *paredros* is similar to the "tutelary spirit" of shamans, a guiding spirit with whom the magician forms a lifelong relationship, who in turn helps them control other spirits.

After preliminary purifications and fasting, the ritual begins with an all night vigil by the magician on a lofty rooftop. A black Isis band is worn over his eyes, and in his right hand he is told to grasp a falcon[34]. At dawn the magician is instructed to shake the bird as he hails the rising sun, while burning frankincense and rose oil in an earthen censor. As he recites a spell (missing in the text), a miraculous sign will occur:

> "a falcon will fly down and stand in front of you, and after flapping its wings in (mid-air and dropping) an oblong stone, it will immediately take flight and (ascend) to heaven. (You) should pick up the stone; carve it at once (and engrave it later). Once it has been engraved bore a hole in it, pass a thread through it and wear it around your neck".

In the evening the magician is instructed to return to the rooftop and face the moon, burn incense, and salute the moon goddess while shaking a branch of myrtle.

> "At once there will be a sign...(A blazing star) will descend and come to a stop in the middle of the housetop, and when the star (has dissolved) before your eyes, you will behold the angel whom you have summoned and who has been sent (to you) and you will quickly learn the decisions of the gods. But do not be afraid: (approach) the god and taking his right hand, kiss him and say these words to the angel, for he will quickly respond to you about whatever you want."

Following this, the text advises the magician to lead the angel down into his room, offer it food and wine and address it with these words: "I shall have you as a friendly assistant, a beneficent god who serves me whenever I say "Quickly by your power now appear on earth to me, yea verily, god!" [35] From this time forward, the divine assistant accompanies the magician throughout his life, assisting him in performing all sorts of magical tasks including: sending dreams, stirring up winds, causing invisibility, bringing food and drink, carrying one through the air, etc.

Divination by Lamps & Bowls

Visions were induced by Greco-Egyptian magicians by several means including gazing into lamps, or bowls of water or oil. A charm for "direct vision" is listed in the *Greek Magical Papyri* in which the magician is instructed to take a copper vessel, pour rainwater into it, and make an offering of frankincense.[36] He then recites :

> "Let the earth be still, let the air be still, let the sea be still; let the winds also be still, and do not be a hindrance to this my divination...Open my ears so that you may reveal to me/concerning those things I ask you to answer me...Appear to me Anubis, I command you, for I am Ieo Belpheno who considers this matter."

The magician then gazes at the reflective surface of the water, awaiting a vision from the jackal headed god Anubis, guide of souls in the underworld. The art of gazing into luminous or reflective surfaces to induce hypnogogic visions is known as "scrying". This has a long history in magic, dating back to the ancient Babylonians and Egyptians who gazed into bowls or lamps to receive revelations from the gods.

In the *Greek Magical Papyri* and other magical grimoires, a magician directs a passive scrying "medium", usually a young boy, to gaze at a lamp's flame until they fall into a trance. The boy is then questioned by the magus about any communications with the spirits. This is similar to the previously mentioned "Princes of the Thumb" divination ritual of ancient Jewish magicians, in which a child medium gazed at his thumbnail to see visions revealed by the spirits which he related to the magician.

The Stigmatization of Magic

We have seen how the practice of magic in the earliest civilizations was inseparably linked to religion[37]. State sponsored magical rituals performed by kings, such as the Sed Festival of Egypt, and Akidu Festival of Babylon, were deemed essential for the periodic renewal of their rule and the land's fertility. Magician-priests in these societies also performed magic in the community for many of the same practical purposes as the tribal shaman—healing, divination, protection and exorcism of evil spirits, etc.

During the Graeco-Roman period, however, the reputation of magic began to decline— stigmatization occurred in which magicians came to be feared and ostracized. This change of attitude was largely the result of xenophobia, as magicians were often foreigners, according to Egyptologist Robert Kriech Ritner.[38] He writes that the word "magic" is itself the result of xenophobia, since the Greek word *magia* came to signify fraudulent trickery or demonic sorcery performed by foreigners, the Persian Magi. The classical Greeks passed laws against *pharmakeia*, or "poisoners", magicians who used magical potions to harm others, but were generally tolerant of other forms of magic.[39] Plato in his *Laws*, harshly condemned the pharmakeia, recommending the death sentence for them, as well as for him who "causes harm by means of binding spells or conjurations or incantations or anything of this sort..." [40]

The Romans passed the law of the Twelve Tables of 451 BCE, which forbade the curious practice of using magic to remove crops from a neighbor's field to plant in one's own. In 139 BCE the Chaldeans were expelled from Rome and Italy at large, as they were perceived to be "deriving gain from a false art by imposing on feeble minds". Foreign religious cults were also expelled to protect traditional Roman religious observances. The earliest known expulsion of magicians from Rome took place in 33 BCE at the hands of general Marcus Agrippa, which included not only magicians but astrologers as well. The emperor Augustus Caesar ordered the destruction of thousands of magical books on divination and prophecy as these were considered politically threatening.

By the second century CE, the definition of magic had merged with that of *maleficum*, which originally meant "an evil deed or crime" according to historian Derek Collins.[41] The Romans imposed severe punishment for malefic magic. Those who performed "impious" or nocturnal sacrifices to enchant, curse, or bind anyone with a spell were condemned by law to be either crucified or thrown to the beasts. The most famous prosecution of a magician was the trial of Apuleius, the author of the *The Golden Ass or Metamorphoses*, in the Roman city of Sabratha in 158 CE. He was accused of using magic to seduce and marry a wealthy older woman, which he refuted in a brilliant defense.

The Romans during their rule of Egypt came to view not only the Egyptian religion, but all foreign religions with suspicion and hostility, equating them with "magic", "fraudulent trickery" or "demonic sorcery" according to Ritner.[42] The Roman prefect in Egypt passed a harsh decree in 199 CE against oracles:

> "...Therefore, let no man through oracles...nor by means of the procession of cult images or suchlike charlatanry, pretend to have knowledge of the supernatural, or profess to know the obscurity of future events. Nor let any man put himself at the disposal of those who inquire about this nor answer in any way whatsoever. If any person is detected adhering

to this profession, let him be sure that he will be handed over for capital punishment..."

This draconian law had a chilling effect, driving many Egyptian religious and magical activities underground—and turning magic into an illegal and secretive activity. Similar laws against magic were passed all across the Roman empire. The early Christians were believed by the Romans to practice "black magic" and rumored to indulge in sexual orgies or "love feasts" and cannibalism, contributing to their persecution by the authorities. When the Christians finally gained control of the empire under emperor Constantine the tables were dramatically turned on the Romans, however. Morton Smith comments on the irony of these changes, as the Christians proceeded to ban Roman paganism upon assuming political power:

> "...in 423 it is flatly declared that sacrifices to pagan gods are sacrifices to demons. With this the reversal is complete. Christianity which previously, by Roman law, was magic, has become the official religion, and the official religion of ancient Rome has become, by Roman law, magic." [43]

In fact, under the Christians, *all* pagan practices were judged to be in league with the devil and therefore banned. The Roman emperor Constantius, father of Constantine, in 357 CE threatened to behead those who used any kind of magic or divination. Similar legal codes were enacted by later Christian emperors. Even the wearing of magical amulets to ward off disease might result in execution.[44]

However, the Christians had their own magical practices—sacramental rites such as the mass and eucharist—by which bread and wine were magically transmuted into the body and blood of the savior. Historian Stephen Benko notes that the church began to absorb pagan magical practices such as veneration of relics, and the use of bells and incense. He writes: "This particular Christian brand of magic was not merely tolerated but was promoted as long as it was within the ecclesiastical framework." [45]

From Daimons to Demons

Along with the stigmatization of magic and magicians during antiquity, their helping-spirits were subjected to "demonization" as well, becoming feared and relegated to the shadows. As previously discussed, the belief in spirits who mediated between the gods and mankind was shared by all ancient cultures. The *daimons* of the Greeks were thought to be lesser divinities or supernatural beings whose nature lay between humans and gods: deities, muses, nymphs, nature spirits and souls of the dead. They were originally seen as invisible spirits who protected and aided the living. Homer in the *Illiad* wrote that the gods on Mt. Olympus could be considered daimons. Hesiod claimed they were the men of the Golden Age whose race died out and were transformed by the will of Zeus into guardians over mortals, becoming benevolent beings who dispensed riches. The daimons could assume non-human forms as well—the "good daimon" or *agathos daimon* was imagined in the form of a serpent, and the first libation at wine-drinking was poured out in his honor.[46] Not all daimons were good, however. The Greeks also had a tradition of evil daimons or *kakodaimons* such as harpies, sirens, and *aori,* imagined as hybrids between women and birds, believed to inflict disease and misfortune upon mankind.

The daimon was also conceived of as a god-like power of fate or destiny guiding individuals. In such a manner Socrates understood his personal daimon, experienced as a voice warning him against taking the wrong actions, which he always heeded. His daimon became so trusted it was even consulted by Socrates's friends for advice. In Plato's Symposium, the wise woman Diotima discusses the daimons:

> "All that is daemonic lies between the mortal and the immortal. Its functions are to interpret to men communications from the gods—commandments and favors from the gods in return for men's attentions—and to convey prayers and offerings from men to the gods. Being thus between men and gods the daemon fills up the gap and so acts as a link joining up the whole. Through it as intermediary pass all forms of divination and sorcery... the daemonic is the agency through which intercourse and converse take place between men and gods, whether in waking visions or in dreams." [47]

Diotima it seems, understood daimons in a similar manner as magicians and shamans saw their familiar spirits—as helpful intermediaries between them and the gods, contacted through visions and dreams.

The status of daimons was about to undergo a radical change, however. The writings of Xenocrates (396-314 BCE), one of Plato's prominent students, began to emphasize the *malevolent* nature of daimons. He reasoned that since daimons inhabited the realm between the earth and moon, they were *less* than divine, and therefore subject to delight and suffering. This led him to conclude the daimons were evil and filled with greed for blood and sex, bringing about diseases, bareness of the earth, discord among citizens and similar calamities to make men succumb to their will—even to the point of prompting men to sacrifice pure virgins.[48]

This opinion gained credibility in the *Septuagint* translation of the Jewish scriptures into Greek in the second century BCE, which used the Greek word *daimonion* to translate the words "devils" and "idols" from Hebrew. Likewise in the Christian *New Testament*, "daimons" refer to devils and wicked spirits who "possess" humans.[49] With the coming of Christianity the process of "demonization" was completed—the spirit-world became dualistically split between opposing camps of *angels* and *demons* associated with good and evil. Not only were daimons turned into demons, but the entire host of pagan gods and nature spirits were branded as demons and banished into the shadows as well.

If Xenocrates was the first Greek philosopher to view daimons as evil, how did he arrive at this conclusion, so contrary to earlier Greek beliefs? It is known he was influenced by Persian Zoroastrianism, and was likely familiar with its doctrine of demonology in which the angelic *Amesha Spenta* and demonic *daevas* were cast as adversaries in the cosmic battle of good and evil. The daevas were associated with evil vices such as avarice and greed, strife, and lust, similar to demons. As previously mentioned, Zoroastrian religious beliefs, including demonology, profoundly influenced the doctrines of Judaism, Christianity, and Islam.

Chapter 11 Notes

Angel from magical spell for protection.
Rossi Gnostic Tractate, an early Christian magical text.

1. Lachman, Gary. *The Quest for Hermes Trismegistus*. 2001: 76.
2. Ibid.
3. Cumont, Franz. "Astrology and Religion Among the Greeks and Romans". *Sacred-texts.com*. 1912:334.
4. Ibid.:33.
5. Plato, *Timaeus*, 37d-37e.
6. Gilman, Ken. "Twelve Gods & Seven Planets". C.U.R.A. The International Astrology Research Center. 1996.
7. Ulansey, David. *The origins of the Mithraic mysteries: cosmology and salvation in the ancient world*. 1989: 71.
8. Ibid.: 86.
9. John J. Collins. *Religions of the Ancient World: A Guide*. (ed.) Johnston, Sarah Iles. . 2004: 65.
10. Cumont. *Astrology and Religion Among the Greeks and Romans*. 1912: 108.
11. Collins. *Religions of the Ancient World: A Guide*. 2004: 65.
12. Cumont. *Astrology and Religion Among the Greeks and Romans*. 1912: 98.
13. Plato. The Republic- Book X. "The Myth of Er." Trans. Jowett, Benjamin.1960.
14. Macurdy, Grace Harriet. "Traces of the Influence of Plato's Eschatological Myths in Parts of the Book of Revelation and the Book of Enoch". *Transactions and Proceedings of the American Philological Association*, vol. 41.1910: 65 -70.7015.
15. Cumont. *Astrology and Religion Among the Greeks and Romans*. 1912:27.
16. Zeus was substituted for Marduk the king of the gods who ruled the planet Jupiter. Hermes the patron of scholars and merchants replaced Nebo linked

with the planet Mercury, while Chronos the god of time and old age replaced Ninib associated with Saturn, the slowest moving planet.
17. Salles, Ricardo. *God and Cosmos in Stoicism*. 2009: cxxii.
18. Fowden, Garth. *The Egyptian Hermes: a historical approach to the late pagan mind*. 1986: 78.
19. Ptolemy. *Tetrabiblos*. Book III 11-12 "Of Bodily Form and Temperament". 319.
20. Manilius. 2.60-79, 2.80-149.
21. The earliest surviving detailed description of the Greek constellations is from the poem *Phaenomena* by the Greek poet Aratos, (c. 250 BCE) who mentions forty-seven constellations in his poem. His work in turn was derived from the Greek astronomer Eudoxus.
22. Manilius. *Astronomica*. Book IV.
23. Luck, George. *Arcana Mundi -Magic and the Occult in the Greek and Roman Worlds: A Collection of Ancient Texts*. Luck 1985: 372.
24. Ibid.: 373.
25. Hall, Manly P. *The Story of Astrology: The Belief In The Stars As A Factor in Human Progress*. Hall 2005: 59-61.
26. Smith, Morton. *Jesus The Magician*. 1978: 76.
27. This is based on the gradual and continuous shift in the orientation of earth's axis of rotation—similar to the wobble of a top. It takes 26,000 years for a complete cycle of precession to occur—for the sun to move backward 360 degrees through all the signs of the zodiac. This discovery is credited to the Greek astronomer Hipparchus (190-120 BCE) though the earlier Chaldeans and Egyptians may have known about it before him.
28. Freke, Timothy; Gandy, Peter. *The Jesus Mysteries: Was the "Original Jesus" a Pagan God?* 1999:37.
29. Betz, Hans Dieter. (ed.) *The Greek Magical Papyri in Translation including the Demiotic Spells*. 1992 :xlvii.
30. Smith. *Jesus The Magician*. 1978: 70.
31. Dickey, Matthew W. *Magic and Magicians In The Greco-Roman World*. 2001: 430.
32. Smith. *Jesus The Magician*. 1978: 74.
33. Betz. *The Greek Magical Papyri in Translation including the Demiotic Spells* 1992: 4-5.
34. Although not specified in this ritual, the previous text, PGM-1-42, has the magician "deifying" (sacrificing by drowning) a live falcon, then setting it up in a shrine. It is presumed therefore the falcon in this ritual is dead, not living.
35. Ibid.: 4-5.
36. Betz. *The Greek Magical Papyri in Translation including the Demiotic Spells* 1992: VII. 319-34.
37. The word "magic" is notoriously difficult to define, and has been argued over by scholars for centuries. Robert Kriech Ritner writes that the difficulty is that scholars have attempted to define magic using "universal categories" applicable across time and space. (Ritner 1993: 237) He states: "Inherent in the term is the subjectivity of cultural bias, and thus "magic" must be understood with reference to a specific cultural context". Scholars, according to Ritner,

become attached to their own scholarly categories and terminology seeing them as "universal truisms" rather than realizing they are merely "descriptive approximations" applied to foreign cultures. Ritner defines magic as "any activity which seeks to obtain its goals by methods *outside* the simple laws of cause and effect". According to him, magic has to be defined differently in different cultural contexts. The state sponsored magic of the ancient god-kings, was radically different from the secretive and private magic of the medieval grimoires. Although both share certain actions which are believed to accomplish their goals outside of the laws of cause and effect, they are different cultural expressions, embedded in different cultural belief systems. Historian Owen Davies supports this view, writing that there is no "overarching" answer to the definition of the word "magic". "Any useful understanding must be tied to the cultures of the people being studied in specific periods and places". (Davies 2009: 2)

38. Ritner, Robert Kriech. *The Mechanics of Ancient Egyptian Magical Practice.*1993: 217.
39. Collins, Derek. *Magic in the Ancient Greek World.* 2008: 132.
40. Otto, Bernd-Christian; Stausberg, Michael. (eds.) *Defining Magic: A Reader.* 2013: 22.
41. Collins, Derek. *Magic in the Ancient Greek World.* 2008:132.
42. Ritner. *The Mechanics of Ancient Egyptian Magical Practice.* 1993: 218.
43. Smith, Morton. *Jesus The Magician.* Smith 1996: 215.
44. Kieckhefer, Richard. *Magic in the Middle Ages.* 1990: 41.
45. Benko, Stephen. *Pagan Rome and the Early Christians.*1986: 131.
46. Burkert. *Greek Religion.* 1985: 26.
47. Dedds, E.R. *Pagan and Christian in an Age of Anxiety:Some Aspects of Religious Experience from Marcus Aurelius to Constantine.*1991:86-87.
48. Burkert. *Greek Religion.* 1985: 179-181.
49. "What Does the Bible Say About Demons?". *The Bible Pages.* 2001.

Chapter 12:
Ascent Through the Celestial Spheres

"Consider this for yourself: command your soul to travel to India, and it will be there faster than your command. Command it to cross over the ocean, and again it will quickly be there, not as having passed from place to place but simply as being there. Command it even to fly up to heaven, and it will not lack wings. Nothing will hinder it, not the fire of the sun, nor the aether, nor the swirl nor the bodies of the other stars..."
–Corpus Hermeticum

Ezekiel's vision, from woodcut by Hans Holbein the Younger, Zurich Bible 1538.

The shaman's visionary ascent through the heavens is achieved by climbing the "cosmic axis" at the center of the world—symbolized by the World Tree, a cosmic mountain or stairway of seven steps, or a ladder.[1] In Siberian shamanism seven heavens are most common, but nine, twelve, and as many as thirty-three heavens also occur. Eliade writes: "the shaman appears to have direct knowledge of these heavens, and hence, of all the celestial regions one after the other due in part to the help their inhabitants give him." [2] Before he can address the supreme being, the shaman converses with the other celestial inhabitants and asks for their assistance.

The Theurgists, Hermeticists, Gnostics, and Merkabah Mystics of antiquity likewise engaged in visionary ascents through seven or more planetary heavens. During their celestial journeys they encountered the spiritual inhabitants of those realms: angels, archons, and supernatural creatures who challenged or assisted them towards their goal of attaining the *unio mystica*—the mystical union with divinity. In order to understand their visionary practices, however, we will first look at the philosophies that informed them.

Hermeticism

The philosophy of Hermeticism emerged from the cultural melting pot of Graeco-Roman Egypt, reflecting its cosmopolitan nature. It syncretized the philosophies of Platonism, Neoplatonism, Stoicism, and the mystery religions with the religious beliefs of the Egyptians, Greeks, Persians, Chaldeans and Jews. Combining these into a new revelation, it provided a good deal of the theoretical foundation of western esotericism. Hermes-Thoth, also known as Hermes Trismegistus, meaning Hermes "thrice-great", was the patron deity of Hermeticism. He is the synthesis of the Greek god Hermes and the Egyptian god Thoth, both of whom are deities of philosophical wisdom, magic and science.

The Hermetic texts, collectively known as the "Hermetica", are presented as divine revelations pseudonymously authored by Hermes.[3] The *Corpus Hermeticum* is the largest surviving body of Hermetic texts, dating from the second and third centuries CE. These can be generally divided into two classes: philosophical texts concerned with *gnosis*—the direct knowing of God, and technical writings concerned with science, or *episteme*—understood as the study of magic, alchemy, and astrology. The philosophical Hermetica nevertheless contain a good deal of astrological cosmology and magic, while the technical writings were often seen as preliminary knowledge for the philosophical contemplation of the divine realm. As historian Garth Fowden points out, *gnosis* was the goal of *episteme*, and knowledge of God's creation was seen as essential for the knowledge of God himself.[4]

The philosophical Hermetica were wisdom texts—discourses consisting of conversations between a spiritual teacher and his student, such as Thoth-Hermes and his spiritual son Tat, or Isis instructing her son Horus about the true nature of the universe. Historian Brian Copenhaver writes: "they reveal to man knowledge of the origins, nature and moral properties of divine, human and material being so that man can use this knowledge to save himself".[5] The *Corpus Hermeticum* begins with the following dialogue between the spiritual seeker and his teacher Poimandres: " Once when thought came to me of the things that are and my thinking soared high and my bodily senses were restrained..." Here the basic practice of contemplation is introduced by which the physical senses are stilled and the mind is turned inward to become aware of itself—freed to soar to the heights of the spiritual world. Gary Lachman writes that the Hermeticist strived to "raise his individual mind to the level of the Great Mind and to achieve cosmic consciousness." [6] In the discourse entitled *The Mind to Hermes,* the student is told that to understand God, he must imagine himself as immortal and all-encompassing like God:

"So you must think of god in this way, as having everything–the cosmos, himself, the universe—like thoughts in himself. Thus unless you make yourself equal to god, you cannot understand god; like is understood by like. Make yourself grow to immeasurable immensity, out leap all body, outstrip all time, become eternity and you will understand god. Having conceived that nothing is impossible to you, consider yourself immortal and able to understand everything, all art, all learning, the temper of every living thing. Go higher than every height, and lower than every depth. Collect in yourself all the sensations of what has been made, of fire and water, dry and wet; be everywhere at once, on land, in the sea, in heaven; be not yet born, be in the womb, be young, be old, dead, beyond death. And when you have understood all these at once- times, places, things, qualities, quantities-then you can understand god." [7]

Hermetic Initiation

According to esoteric scholar Stephen A. Hoeller, the first stage of Hermetic training consisted in the student's reading of Hermetic literature and listening to public discourse about the teachings.[8] After a probationary period they progressed to the next level where they were initiated by their tutor, undertaking a symbolic ascent through the seven planetary spheres with the goal of liberating themselves from their influences. In the final stage, they were spiritually reborn in the transcendent region beyond the planets in the region known as the "Ogdoad", the eighth sphere of the fixed stars, and beyond.

Hoeller writes that the Hermetic initiation took place in a private setting and the only two persons present were the initiate and initiator, called "son" and "father" in some texts. Initiation brought about the experience of a profound change of consciousness wherein the initiate became one with his deeper self, believed to be a part of God's essence.

Poimandres & Ascent to the Ogdoad

The Hermetic text *Poimandres* describes this initiatory journey upward through the planetary spheres with goal of attaining *gnosis*. During its heavenly ascent the soul of the initiate discards its "garments" of planetary vices acquired during terrestrial life. As it rises to the first sphere of the moon, it surrenders the energy of "growth and waxing"; in the next sphere of mercury it forfeits the "device of evils"; in the sphere of venus it surrenders the "guile of desires"; in the sphere of the sun it parts with "domineering arrogance"; in the sphere of mars, it surrenders its "daring and rashness of audacity"; in the sphere of jupiter "striving for wealth by evil means" is abandoned; and in the seventh and final planetary sphere of saturn "ensnaring falsehood" is left behind.[9]

Having shed its planetary influences the purified soul enters into the eighth sphere of the Ogdoad, the "fixed stars". Here it hears the voices of those who dwell in the ninth sphere, and rises above all earthly and cosmic existence to be reborn into a transcendent level of spiritual being. It surrenders itself to the "Powers", becoming itself a power in God. As stated in the *Poimandres*: "This the good end for those who have gained Gnosis — to be made one with God".

The initiatory ascent was intended to induce ecstasy and gnosis, and a foretaste of the soul's afterlife condition. Through this process the initiate was *divinized* — transformed into a god-like human — and assimilated into the One God. Fowden writes: "The way of Hermes is the "way of immortality", and its end is reached when the purified soul is absorbed into God, so that the reborn man, although still a composite of body and soul, can himself fairly be called a god." [10]

The Technical Hermetica

The technical books of the Hermetica consist of magical, alchemical, and astrological writings, often involving the investigation and classification of natural phenomena, influenced by the observational science of the philosopher Aristotle. Astrology exercised a pervasive influence in these texts. The *Liber Hermetis*, written around the third century BCE, describes the decans of Egyptian astronomy, the division of the zodiac into 36 parts, each with its own attributions. Other books discuss medical correspondences between the microcosm of man and the macrocosm of the universe, as well as astrological botany and mineralogy.[11] The book *Fifteen Stars, Stones, Plants and Images* singles out particular stars, discussing their pharmaceutical powers. Hermeticists perceived a close relationship between the stars, decans, planets and all events occurring on earth — including the fate of mankind. In the text known as the *Stobaei Hermeticum* it is written:

"The overthrow of kings, the insurrection of cities, famines, plagues, the sudden fluctuations of the sea, and earthquakes, none of these things occurs.... without the action of the decans...and we are in our turn beneath the Seven, dost thou not think that some of their activity extends to us as well..." [12]

The Hermetica are based on the notion that all things in the cosmos are linked by *universal sympathy*. The divine powers that bind the world together are understood as "energies" which derive from the sun, stars, and planets and cause growth, decay, and physical sensation. It is these cosmic energies that the technical Hermetica studied, examining the sympathies, antipathies and occult properties of nature.

Hermetic Cosmology

There is no one single Hermetic cosmology, but instead a "mosaic" of cosmologies derived from Neoplatonism, Stoicism, Gnosticism and Egyptian religious traditions, according to Stephen Flowers. He insists there are only "individual cosmologies revealed by individual Hermetic teachers through texts they wrote." [13]

The dominant influence, according to Flowers, is Neoplatonism. Its cosmology presents a three-fold emanation beginning with the One, or God, also known as the "Good" or the "Father". God creates an intermediary, the Demiurge or "Maker", also known as the Word (logos) or "the Son of God". This in turn creates the World Soul. A hierarchical "chain of being" is thus formed, in which each level receives from that which is above it, and emanates an image of itself to the level below it, creating the universe.

Flowers notes the similarities of this cosmology to the Hebrew Kabbalah as presented in the seminal texts the *Sefer Yetzirah* and the *Zohar*. The "One" of Neoplatonism could be equated with the first sphere of Kether in the Kabbalah, from which the lower sephirah emanate, creating the manifest cosmos.

Greco-Egyptian Alchemy

Alchemy was another popular subject for Hermetic writers. The word alchemy is derived from the Arabic word *Al-Khemiya*. This is turn is derived from the ancient Egyptian name for Egypt—*Khem*—meaning "black earth", referring to the rich, dark soil of the Nile Delta. The Egyptians were skilled metal workers who knew how to manufacture metallic alloys, imitation gold and silver, and artificial gemstones. Eliade writes that the sudden appearance of alchemical texts around the beginning of the Christian era in Egypt was the result of the encounter of esoteric currents such as Neo-pythagoreanism, Neo-Orphism, Gnosticism, astrology, and the mystery religions, with popular traditions preserving the trade secrets of metalworking and magic.[14]

Hermetic philosophy established that the heavenly cycles of stars, sun, moon and planets were linked to the life of all things on earth: animals, plants, and minerals. Hermetic alchemists timed their operations according to *kairos,* the opportune astrological moment, to assist alchemical processes in their perfection.

The Greek philosopher Bolos of Mendes in 200 BCE wrote about metallurgical processes involving gold, silver, gems and dyes that became the basic ingredients of alchemy. The alchemists thought the metals were composed of a physical base or "body" as well as a vitalizing "soul". By purifying and manipulating the soul of metals they believed they could transmute the actual metals themselves into gold. Some alchemists extended this analogy to the purification of the human soul and its ascent to its divine source.[15]

Zosimus of Panopolis who lived in Alexandria around 300 CE, blended Hermetic philosophy with the practical techniques of alchemy, emphasizing the spiritually transformative nature of the alchemical quest. Here Zosimus relates his dream which serves as an allegory of the alchemical process. In it, he sees fifteen (elsewhere he says seven) steps leading up to a bowl-shaped altar where he encounters a priest who tells him:

"I have accomplished the descent of these fifteen steps of darkness and the ascent of the steps of light, and he who sacrifices is himself the sacrificial victim. Casting away the coarseness of the body, and consecrated priest by necessity, I am made perfect as a spirit...and I have submitted myself to an unendurable torment. For there came one in haste at early morning, who overpowered me and pierced me through with the sword, and dismembered me in accordance with the rule of harmony. And he drew off the skin of my head with the sword which he was holding, and mingled the bones with the pieces of flesh, and caused them to be burned with the fire that he held in his hand, till I perceived by the transformation of the body that I had become spirit".[16]

The priest in Zosimus's dream undergoes what could be described as an *initiatory experience,* an "unendurable torment", in which his body is dismembered and transformed by fire into spirit. The alchemical work was understood symbolically, and metals were subjected to similar "torments" in their furnaces. During the initial *nigredo* or blackening stage of the alchemical operation, the base materials were "sacrificed" by being subjected to processes of dissolution and heat. The alchemist believed the transformation of metals was accompanied by a parallel transformation of his soul; through the process of "perfecting" the metals, he in turn perfected himself. The dream bears striking similarities to the shaman's initiation ordeal, as well as myths in which deities are slain and dismembered prior to being resurrected, as previously discussed.

The Greek Magical Papyri

The *Greek Magical Papyri* is the largest surviving collection of magical spells and writings from Greco-Roman Egypt, dating from the period of 200 BCE-500 CE. It draws from Egyptian, Greek, Jewish, Persian, Chaldean, and Christian sources. Interestingly, it includes spells using the name of Jesus for exorcising demons, suggesting his reputation as a powerful magician was well established. Some of the spells in the papyri are theurgic and initiatory in nature, focused on attaining visions, revelations, and oracles of the gods. Others are intended for more mundane goals: increasing business, coercing lovers, enhancing memory, winning in chariot races, detecting thieves, relieving migraines, etc. The spells appear to be collected from the workbooks of itinerant magicians, catering to the various needs of their clients.

Brian Copenhaver notes that similar to the technical Hermetica, the *Greek Magical Papyri* provide an occult technology by which the divine and natural worlds can be manipulated for more or less concrete and immediate purposes.[17] Hermeticism viewed magic as valid as any other form of knowledge, and useful in the quest for gnostic salvation. In the Hermetic text the *Kore Kosmou* it is written : "no prophet about to raise his hands to the gods has ever ignored any of the things that are, so that philosophy and magic may nourish the soul and medicine heal the body".

The Mithras Liturgy

The "Mithras Liturgy", found in the *Greek Magical Papyri*, narrates a magical ascent through the heavens and encounters with the celestial gods, culminating with an oracular revelation. Marvin Meyer notes the text is arranged in seven progressive stages of ascent—beginning with the four elements, the powers of air, the god Aion, Helios the sun-god, the seven fates, the seven pole-lords, and finally a vision of Mithras, the highest god.[18] Although some scholars have associated the text with the religion of Mithraism, occult scholar Stephen Skinner argues it is an example of a solitary mystery-rite performed by an individual, or in the company of his daughter.[19] The Mithras Liturgy provides a tantalizing glimpse into the visionary practices and trance techniques of Greco-Egyptian magicians, including visualizations, invocations, and *voces magicae* or "words of power". Following is my abridged version of the original text (in italics), and commentary, focusing on its visionary content.[20]

The rite begins with this prayer: *"Be gracious to me, O Providence and Psyche, as I write these mysteries handed down (not) for gain but for instruction..."* The author requests immortality by means of an ascent through heaven. This is followed by an invocation of the four elements, spirit, and Aion, the Demiurge. The text then instructs the magician to focus on his breathing, and visualize himself rising on the rays of the sun: *"Draw in breath from the rays, drawing up three times as much as you can, and you will see yourself being lifted up and ascending to the height, so that you seem to be in midair....you will see all immortal things. For in that day and hour you will see the divine order of the skies: the presiding gods rising into heaven, and others setting."*

The magician is warned that he will see the gods staring intently and rushing at him. He is advised to put his right finger on his mouth and say: *"Silence! Silence! Silence!"*..then make a long hissing sound followed by a popping sound. He then intones a long string of *voces magicae* or words of power. Propitiated by these, the gods now look graciously upon him, and the doors of the sun-disk swing open to reveal their world to him.

The narrative continues with a vision of Helios the sun-god: *"...you will see a youthful god, beautiful in appearance, with fiery hair, and in a white tunic and a scarlet cloak, and wearing a fiery crown. At once greet him..."Hail O lord, Great Power, Great Might, King, Greatest of gods, Helios, the Lord of heaven and earth, God of gods: mighty is your breath; mighty is your strength, O lord. If it be your will, announce me to the supreme god, the one who has begotten and made you"*. After this greeting, Helios leads the magus on a road towards the celestial pole.

Next a vision unfolds of the Seven Fates and Seven Pole Lords: *"...you will see doors thrown open, and seven virgins coming from deep within, dressed in linen garments, and with the faces of asps. They are called the Fates of heaven, and wield golden wands. When you see them, greet them in this manner: "Hail O seven Fates of heaven, O noble and good virgins...O most holy guardians of the four pillars!...There also come forth another seven gods, who have the faces of black bulls, in linen loincloths, and in possession of seven golden diadems. They are the so-called Pole Lords of heaven, whom you must greet in the same manner, each of them with his own name: "Hail O guardians of the pivot, O sacred and brave youths, who turn at one command the revolving axis of the vault of the heaven, who send out thunder and lightning and jolts of earthquakes and thunderbolts against the nations of impious people, but to me, who am pious and god-fearing, you send health and soundness of body and acuteness of hearing and seeing, and calmness.."*

The narrative culminates with the revelation of the great deity himself: *"... look in the air and you will see lightning bolts going down, and lights flashing, and the earth shaking, and a god descending, a god immensely great, having a bright appearance, youthful, golden-haired, with a white tunic and a golden crown and trousers, and holding in his right hand a golden shoulder of a young bull: this is the Bear which moves and turns heaven around, moving upward and downward in accordance with the hour. Then you will see lightning bolts leaping from his eyes and stars from his body."*

The magus is then instructed to make a long bellowing sound until he is out of breath, and say: *life of me stay! Dwell in my soul! Do not abandon me!"* He is told to gaze upon the god and greet him with these words: ": *"Hail O Lord, O Master of the water! Hail, O Founder of the earth! Hail O Ruler of the wind! O Bright Lightener...Give revelation, O Lord, concerning the NN matter".* The text assures the magus that the god will immediately provide a spoken oracle in verse in response to his question, and after this will depart. He is advised to remain silent and remember all the things spoken to him by the deity.

The youthful golden-haired god described at the end of the narrative is none other than Mithras, the Persian savior god. He carries the "shoulder" of a bull, referring to the constellation Ursa Major which moves around the pole star. It is composed of seven stars and represented in the vision as seven gods with faces of bulls. The ancient Egyptians knew Ursa Major as the Bull's Thigh or Leg of Set, associated with immortality as it never sets in the sky.

The scenario of the Mithras Liturgy, in which the magician ascends through the heavens with the goal of encountering the highest deity is similar to the visionary ascents of other mystics of antiquity. It also has remarkable parallels to the magical flights of tribal shamans who journeyed in magical flight through the upper world, past the sun, moon and constellations, to commune with the supreme being, receiving prophecies and revelations.

Gnosticism & Early Christian Magic

"Gnosticism" is a modern scholarly term used to describe the religious philosophy that emerged in Egypt alongside Hermeticism in the early centuries of the first millennium. The word is derived from the Greek word *gnosis* — meaning "knowledge". The Gnostics were predominantly Christians, but were influenced by numerous other sources including Judaism, Zoroastrianism, Greek philosophy, as well as astrology, magic, and the mystery religions. Historian Elaine Plagels proposes that the Gnostics may have also been exposed to the ideas of oriental philosophies such as Buddhism and Brahmanism.[21]

Many Gnostics sought salvation through a personal revelation of the divine. They invented elaborate cosmologies and myths concerning the origin of the universe and the soul's salvation, as well as texts detailing mystical practice. In contrast to the doctrines of mainstream Christianity, the Gnostics believed that Jesus, instead of coming to save them from sin, was a guide who opened access to spiritual understanding. According to Plagels, when the Gnostic attained enlightenment Jesus no longer served as his spiritual master—the two became equal, even identical. In the Gnostic *Gospel of Thomas* Jesus says:

> "I am not your master. Because you have drunk, you have become drunk from the bubbling stream which I have measured out...He who will drink from my mouth will become as I am: I myself shall become he, and the things that are hidden will be revealed to him". [22]

The Gnostics produced a number of gospels such as the *Gospel of Thomas, Gospel of Phillip, Gospel of Mary* and others which were later rejected by the church fathers as heretical. In contrast to the exoteric Christianity of the church which was accessible to the masses, gnosticism was secret and *esoteric* in nature. The gnostics viewed their teachings as "mysteries" taught in closed circles, like the pagan mystery religions. Like them, they were concerned with the soul's liberation from the body. According to Morton Smith, there are several references to Jesus performing secret initiations similar to those practiced in the mystery religions of the time. In Gnostic circles secret teachings were passed down from master to disciple and practiced through rituals such as baptisms, anointing and eucharists.[23] Although Gnostics revered Jesus, they also looked to redeemers such as Adam, Eve, Melchizedek, Enoch, Sophia, Spirit and the angels Baruch, Eleleth, and others.[24]

In response to the problem of sexuality many Gnostics went to extremes. Although sexual abstinence was widely practiced, some sects engaged in orgiastic rites as a means of attaining spiritual liberation.[25] The Naasenes, also know as the Ophites, were a sect that revered the serpent as the revealer of gnosis; they were accused of all kinds of sexual misconduct by the church fathers. The Valentinian Gnostics were not as ascetic as other sects, permitting marriage as a necessary evil. In the *Gospel of Philip* some sensible advice is given: "Be not fearful of the flesh, nor love it. If you fear it, it will become master over you. If you love it, it will swallow and paralyze you." [26]

It may strike modern Christians as sacrilegious to associate the name of Jesus with "magic", but some Gnostic writings describe him teaching magical spells for purification and heavenly ascent to his disciples. In his book *Jesus The Magician,* Morton Smith argues that some of the early followers of Jesus revered him as a great magician.[27] In fact, early Christians practiced magical spells, and wrote magical amulets in Greek and Coptic. There are many spells written by pagan magicians of the time which invoke the authority of Jesus alongside the pagan gods, attesting to his fame as a magician. In a Greek exorcism the name of Jesus is listed alongside Thoth, the Egyptian god of magic: "I conjure you by the name of the god of the Hebrews, Jesus, Iaba, Iae, Abraoth, Thoth." [28]

Smith compares historical evidence of Jesus's magical practices with the spells of Greco- Egyptian magicians recorded in the *Greek Magical Papyri*, concluding Jesus likely learned his magic in Egypt. He notes that Jesus's critics at the time dismissed him as a mere magician and necromancer. Jesus was recorded in the *New Testament* performing miracles, healing, and exorcisms of demons—feats which were part of the standard repertoire of magicians of antiquity. Both historians Owen Davies and Morton Smith agree that care was taken by the compilers of the *New Testament* as to which of Jesus's miracles would be included in the gospels; they wanted to avoid drawing comparisons with the magic performed by the other healing magicians of the times, fearing it would invite ridicule.[29] [30]

Besides his magical talents, Jesus also displays characteristics of the *shaman*. His retreat in the wilderness and his temptation by Satan are similar to initiations in which shamans retreat into the solitude of nature, practice ascetic self-discipline, and confront demons.[31] Jesus's ascent to heaven and harrowing of hell, his exorcism of demons and display of healing powers are also feats comparable to those of shamans.

In contrast to the optimistic worldview of Hermeticism and Neoplatonism, Gnosticism viewed the cosmos as inherently evil and hostile, created by an arrogant and ignorant demiurge or creator god. The physical world of matter was considered "fallen", and man was trapped in this lower world of time and change. Through *gnosis* however, the soul escaped the world by ascending through the *aeons* or heavens, though they had to overcome the hostile opposition of the *archons* along the way.[32] Each of the aeons were believed to be ruled by one of these evil archons who were seen as cosmic jailers, associated with the planetary powers. They were considered adversarial and oppressive because of the astrological fate they imposed on the suffering soul. In the Gnostic book *The Apocryphon of John* the archons are described as having the faces of animals, reminiscent of the animal-headed gods and demons of ancient Egypt, and each of the seven aeons seems to be associated with a day of the week:

"The first is Atoth, and he has a sheep's face; the second is Eleaiou, he has a donkey's face; the third is Astaphiaios; he has a hyena'a face; the fourth is Yao, he has a serpent's face with seven heads; the fifth is Sabaoth, he has a dragon's face; the sixth is Adonin, he had a monkey's face; the seventh is Sabbede, he has a shining fire-face. This is the sevenness of the week". [33]

The eternal world of God, on the other hand, consists of the heavenly hierarchy of archangels, cherubim, seraphim, amens, voices, virtues, guardians and splendors. These are grouped into the angelic ranks of principalities, powers, thrones, dominions, and authorities.[34] Ascent through the heavens for the Gnostics was equivalent to spiritual resurrection and divine union, and by this process they believed their souls became immortalized while still dwelling in the flesh. In the gnostic text *The Exegesis of the Soul* it is written: "Now it is fitting that the soul regenerate herself and become again as she formerly was... This is the resurrection that is from the dead...This is the upward journey of ascent to heaven. This is the way of ascent to the father".[35]

Like the Hermeticists, the Gnostics in their visionary ascents aspired to reach the Ogdoad, the eighth heaven—though as many as fourteen or thirty-three heavens existed in other cosmological schemes—culminating with the experience of mystical union with the divine. The attainment of the Ogdoad was believed to "divinize" and transform the gnostic into an *angel*. In his heavenly ascent the gnostic Zostrianos experienced seven baptisms, declaring: "I became a holy angel"..."I became a perfect angel"..."I became divine".[36]

The gnostic's salvation from fate by ascending into heaven was an imitation of the descending and ascending redeemer, who was often but not always identified with Jesus, according to religious historian Dan Merkur.[37] The Coptic Gnostic text the *Books of Jeu* teaches initiates the heavenly ascent. In the following passage Jesus instructs his disciples in the magical seals and numbers as well as *voce magicae*, or magical words of power for entering and ascending through the first aeon:

"When you come forth from the body and reach the first Aeon and the archons of that aeon appear before you, seal yourselves with this seal; this is its name: Zozeze, say it but once, seize this number: 1119, with your two hands... then vindicate yourself with this recitation: "fall back...you archons of the first aeon, because I challenge eaza zeozas zozeoz. Now when the archons of the first aeon draw back and flee in the direction of the west on the left and you will be able to ascend." [38]

This procedure is repeated in each aeon with different seals and magical formulae, up through the eleventh aeon. In the twelfth aeon the gnostic enters the region of the "pleroma", the fullness of the light, and continues to display the seals and numbers until reaching the fourteenth aeon, the holiest of them all in which he or she must perform the "mystery of the forgiveness of sins".

Historian Kurt Rudolph notes the similarities of the gnostic ascent to the journey of the soul through the Egyptian afterlife realm, writing: "This is a picture of the underworld as the ancient Egyptians depicted it in their description of the journey of the dead, which has been transfigured by gnosis to the supernatural intermediate world".[39]

The Afterlife Journey of the Gnostic Mandeans

The Mandeans are the only surviving sect of Gnostics, living in present day southern Iraq. In their funeral rites, the soul of the dead is believed to journey for forty-two days during which time it is accompanied by prayers and rites of the community. The ritual narrative leads the deceased through the "watch-stations" of the planets and the zodiac, which the pure and sinless soul passes through. Magical "names" and "signs" also assist in the journey which culminates in the weighing of the soul in the scales. Here the soul's piety and good works determine its entry into the Kingdom of Light.[40]

The similarities between the Mandean journey of the soul through the heavens, and the journey through the underworld as described in the *Egyptian Book of the Dead*, are striking. These include the weighing of the soul to determine its purity, as well as the use of magical names to guarantee its safe passage.

Mithraism/ The Astrological Religion

Another version of mystical ascension can be found in the initiation rites of Mithraism, the mystery religion named after Mithras, the Persian savior-god, who we encountered in the Mithras Liturgy. Mithraism was probably imported into Rome from Persia or the Near-East. It was spread throughout the Roman Empire in the first century CE by the soldiers of the Roman Legions who were among its most devoted followers. Although initiates were believed to be exclusively male, some evidence points to special grades for female initiates, according to Payam Nabarz.[41]

Mithraic cosmology was explicitly *astrological* and based on the symbolism of the signs of the zodiac, the planets, and the emblems of the four elements. These appear in bas-reliefs, mosaics, and paintings in subterranean temples known as Mithraeums. Walter Burkert writes that these resembled caves mirroring the cosmos, covered by the vault of heaven with the zodiac and the seven planets. Ceremonies were determined by the solar cycle, and some Mithraeums had openings through which a ray of sun would shine on certain days, illuminating the deity's head.[42]

The Neoplatonic philosopher Porphyry writes that the Mithraeum was a place of initiation into the "descent and exit of souls". He discusses the two "soul gates" of the summer and winter solstices: souls enter the world in the Tropic of Cancer and exit it during the Tropic of Capricorn, returning back to the heavenly realm.[43] The Mithraic celestial journey is described by the Greek philosopher Celsus in the second century CE as "a seven-gated ladder with an eighth at the top", suggesting they used the same cosmological scheme of the seven heavens and Ogdoad as the Hermeticists and Gnostics.

Mithraic initiations were based on the symbolism of the four elements and seven planets as well. They involved purifications and ordeals at each stage, according to Nabarz.[44] The first degree of initiation was called the *Corax* (Raven), under the rule of the planet Mercury, symbolizing the death of the candidate to their old way of life and rebirth onto the spiritual path. The second degree was called the *Nymphus* (Male Bride), under the rulership of Venus; at this stage the neophyte wore a veil and offered a cup of water to Mithras, vowing himself to the cult. The third degree was that of *Miles* (Soldier) under Mars, during which the initiate kneeled, naked and blindfolded with hands tied, and was offered a crown on the point of a sword; after the ropes were cut, the initiate removed the crown from his head proclaiming "Mithras is my crown", rejecting his ego and pledging loyalty to a higher power. The fourth degree was called *Leo* (Lion), ruled by Jupiter and the element of fire; the initiate of this grade was not allowed to touch water during the initiation, and was instead given honey to wash his hands and anoint his tongue. Duties at this stage included tending the altar flame. The fifth degree *Perses*, (Persian) was ruled by the Moon. Perses in Greek myth was the son of Perseus, so the initiate was symbolically the son of Mithras; the symbol at this stage was the *harpe*, a curved sword similar to the one used by Perseus to cut off the head of Medusa, symbolic of the destruction of the animal instincts of the initiate. The next degree was the *Heliodromus* (Sun Runner) ruled by the Sun; at this stage the initiate would sit next to the "Father" during ritual banquets, dressed in red robes, the color of fire, blood and life. The highest grade was that of *Pater* (Father), ruled by Saturn, and the initiate at this level became the representative of Mithras upon earth, serving as the teacher of the congregation; his symbols were the libation bowl and sickle.

Ascending up the ladder of initiation—symbolized by the seven planets—Mithraic initiates returned to their divine origin. Nabarz writes: "seven degrees of initiation enabled the neophyte to proceed through the seven celestial bodies, allowing a reversal of the descent of the human soul into the world at birth." [45] The similarities to Hermetic and Gnostic initiations, also involving heavenly ascents through the seven heavens, are only too obvious.

The central mystery of Mithraism, the *tauroctony*, or slaying of the bull by Mithras, suggests the task of the initiate was to sacrifice his animal nature—his ego and its passions—symbolized by the bull, to attain spiritual liberation. It could be understood as a reenactment of the archaic mythic drama of the hero confronting the wild bull which we first witnessed in the religious symbolism of the early Neolithic.

With its hierarchical grades, Mithraism anticipated the modern esoteric brotherhood of Freemasonry, which also follows a scheme of graded initiations. Nabarz writes that Mithraic grades also bear a relationship to shamanism: "The ordeals of fire, water, heating and cooling all point to the shamanistic nature of the mysteries". Mircea Eliade draws parallels between the shamanic initiation ceremonies of the Buryats of Siberia, where the candidate was drenched in the blood of a sacrificial goat, and the initiation rite of the *taurobolion,* the bull sacrifice of the Mithraic mysteries, in which the candidate may have been immersed in bull's blood. In addition he notes the parallel symbolism of the *ladder* with seven rungs in Mithraism by which the candidate symbolically ascended through the heavens, and Siberian initiation rituals where shamans climbed a tree, representing the World Tree.[46]

Neoplatonism

The philosophy of Neoplatonism developed in late antiquity from the ideas of Plato and his followers, most notably the mystical philosopher Plotinus. Like other schools of philosophy which we have already explored such as Hermeticism and Gnosticism, Neoplatonism was the product of Hellenistic syncretism which melded together various religions and philosophies of the ancient world.

Plotinus (205-270 CE) studied under Ammonius Saccas, called "the porter", who was supposedly an Alexandrian dock worker who also happened to be a brilliant philosopher as well. Some scholars have speculated Saccas was of Indian descent, and his teachings may have been influenced by Indian philosophy. This may explain Plotinus's fascination with eastern wisdom. In his youth he joined emperor Gordian's military campaign against the Persians with the intention of traveling to the East to meet Persian Magi and Indian sages to study their philosophies. After the campaign's failure Plotinus returned to live in Rome where he attracted numerous disciples including Porphyry who published his works as the *Enneads.*

Plotinus conceived of god as an absolute transcendent One, whose thoughts emanated three levels of being: the "intellect", the "higher soul" (including the world soul and individual soul), and the "lower soul" which includes nature. His cosmology was related to Ptolemy's astronomical model of the cosmos, conceived as a hierarchy of nine concentric spheres extending from the outermost sphere of god as "prime mover" down through the seven planetary spheres, to the lowest sphere of earth. Plotinus saw the cosmos as a "single living being embracing all living things within it". All its parts: stars, planets, animals, plants, minerals and humans were linked by "sympathy" to the whole.

Although Plotinus believed in the power of magic, prayer, and astrology, there is no evidence he practiced any of them. Instead he engaged in philosophical contemplation, by which the soul separated from the body to apprehend eternal things in the intelligible world of "Forms" or Platonic ideas.[47]

Theurgy of Iamblichus

One of the greatest Neoplatonist philosophers was Iamblichus of Chalcis (245-325 CE), a Syrian by birth, son of a wealthy and illustrious family and a descendent of priest-kings. Iamblichus reacted to what he perceived as the sterile intellectualism and elitism of his fellow philosophers. He rejected the approach of his teacher, Porphyry, who taught the practice of philosophy and contemplation—insisting that a purely cerebral approach was not enough. Instead he advocated the practice of *theurgy*, meaning "god working". Theurgy combined Platonic philosophy with magical rites and rituals directed towards the goal of raising the soul to divinity.[48] Iamblichus writes that theurgy is: "the power of the unutterable symbols, understood solely by the gods, which establishes theurgic union. Hence, we do not bring about these things by intellection alone..." [49]

Iamblichus drew his inspiration from the ancient religions of Egypt and Chaldea, claiming the Egyptians worshipped the true gods of Platonism. He established his own influential school of philosophy, combining ritual magical practices with the Greek philosophical tradition of Pythagoras and Plato, the magical cosmology of Stoicism, and elements of Graeco-Egyptian Hermeticism. Religious scholar Gregory Shaw explains that in theurgy the highest thought of Platonic philosophy was integrated with common magical and religious practices, and heaven and earth were joined through the mathematical structures of Pythagorean science. [50]

The essence of Neoplatonism is the concept of the *embodied soul*, and uniting the soul to divinity, according to Shaw. Rather than rejecting the world as "evil" like the Christian Gnostics, theurgy embraced creation—believing salvation could only be obtained through the magical use of matter. Iamblichus taught that material objects such as stones, herbs, animals, statues and aromatics contained the signatures, or *sunthemata* of the gods, their symbolic essences, and could become their "receptacles".

Besides material objects, the theurgist also used symbols, incantations, music, and numbers which were thought to contain "divine signatures" by which the gods could be invoked. The highest form of theurgy incorporated Pythagorean number mysticism and astrology. In fact, the *sunthemata* were seen as similar to the Platonic "Forms"—the universal essences underlying the cosmos. Examples of these are the Heliotrope or sun-flower, the cock, the lion, and the number sixty, all bearing the signatures of the sun-god Helios and showing affinity with the sun. The concept of the *sunthemata* is similar to the theory of "magical correspondences", as magic and theurgy share similar theories and techniques.

Borrowing from the practices of popular magicians, theurgists used *voces magicae* which were chants of vowels and incomprehensible "barbarous words" from ancient languages, stood on mystical figures, burned aromatics, etc. However, Iamblichus insisted his theurgy was distinctly different than common sorcery. Rather than attempting to manipulate the gods, theurgy served the highest spiritual purpose of elevating the soul to the divine. By performing the appropriate magical rites, Iamblichus believed the theurgist's soul could harmonize with the universe, aligning itself with the world soul and raising itself to unite with the gods.[51] The theurgist became man and god at the same time, a co-creator of the cosmos. The highest form of theurgy was *henosis*—mystical union with God.

Iamblichus drew from the *Chaldean Oracles*, a mystical-poem influenced by Neoplatonist as well as Persian sources, attributed to Julian the Theurgist, a Chaldean mystic who lived in the second century CE. The poem was believed to have been derived from an oracle, and some claim Julian himself dictated it while possessed by the soul of Plato during a séance. The Chaldean Oracles introduced a trinity of archetypal highest principles: the Lynges representing the thoughts of god, also translated as the "wheels" or "whirlings" which initiate the impulse of creation; the Synoches, the connecting powers which bind all things together, maintaining the cosmos; and the Teletarchs, the "perfecters"or "masters of initiation", an order of divine beings associated with the virtues of Faith, Truth and Love.

Theurgy adopted many deities from the mystery religions: Isis, Serapis, Mithra, Hecate and others were syncretized with Hellenistic gods. The leading god of this eclectic pantheon was Helios-Apollo who embodied the sun, the noetic fire and demiurge who initiated human souls, drawing them up towards the divine on his rays. Hermes and Aphrodite produced through their union the god Attis. As the Phrygian vegetation god and son and consort of the goddess Kybele, his drama allegorized the human soul's descent into generation through passionate attraction to the material world.[52] Worship of the Phyrigian Mother of Gods was performed, as well as that of Hecate, goddess of magic, who was used to symbolize the Platonic World Soul.[53]

Iamblichus established a hierarchical ladder, ranking spiritual beings from most exalted to lowest. In descending order they are: the gods, archangels, angels, daemons, heroes, sublunary & material archons, and finally human souls. In contrast to Judaism and Christianity where human souls are placed above the angels because of their power of free will, they are placed at the bottom rung of the hierarchy in Theurgy. Above humans on the ladder are the *daemons* who are responsible for binding souls to physical bodies, producing growth in plants and preserving animal species, including humanity, through the sex drive and other instincts. Iamblichus insisted the theurgist should be on good terms with the daemons as they maintain the physical world which is a manifestation of divinity. The *heroes* on the other hand guide human souls towards spiritual development. They are "leaders" of souls, liberating them from "generation" or worldly attachment and desires. Iamblichus wrote in detail describing the subtle differences in the hierarchies of spirits as they revealed themselves to theurgists during their magical rites:

"The images of the gods flash forth brighter than light, while those of the archangels are full of supernatural light, and those of the angels are bright. But the daemons glow with smoldering fire. The heroes have a fire blended of diverse elements, and of the archons those that are cosmic reveal a comparatively pure fire, while those that are material show a fire mixed from disparate and opposed elements. Souls produce a fitfully visible light, soiled by the many compounds in the realm of generation." [54]

By invoking the "superior races" of gods and angels in their sacred rites, their virtues were believed to be acquired by theurgists. Through the *gods* the theurgist realized "transcendent perfection", "divine love", and "tranquillity of mind". The *archangels* bestowed "spiritual insight and stable power". From *angels* the theurgist received an "allotment of wisdom and truth and likewise pure excellence, sure knowledge and order." The *daemons*, on the other hand brought "eager desire incident to the generated nature", in other words, attraction to things of the material world. Iamblichus taught that each person's soul has a *guardian daemon* assigned to it before birth. This daemon governed their life, until by means of theurgy they could be entrusted with a god for its guardian and "leader of the soul", though this privilege was reserved for only the exalted few.

Through the practice of theurgy the soul was purified and immortalized. First the *ochema pneuma* or "soul vehicle", similar to the modern conception of the astral body, was purified and perfected. It become established in the *ochema augoeides* or "starry vehicle", understood as the luminous body by which the theurgist received visions and was joined to the gods. Iamblichus advocates the use of "exalted imagination", writing that it is "divinely inspired, since it is awakened into modes of imagination that come from the Gods, not from itself, and it is utterly removed from what is ordinarily human".[55] It is likely Iamblichus is referring to the theurgist's visionary practices which induced transcendent visions of the gods. This is perhaps comparable to the modern ritual magician's use of visualization techniques such as "pathworking" and the "assumption of god-forms" which utilize the imagination as a means of accessing states of consciousness which could be considered transcendental or "exalted".

It is likely theurgists also employed breathing techniques similar to those used by yogis which stimulated the "inner heat" and illumination, analogous to the "mastery of inner fire" by the shaman. The Neo-Platonists believed the *ochema augoeides* was solar in origin and returned to the sun when purified. The philosopher Damascius explains the theurgist is made divine "when the radiant vehicle journeys upward to the sun...when we are established in the soul of the sun". Visualizations of rising on sunbeams and uniting with the deity were probably practiced, similar to those found in the Mithras Liturgy. According to the *Chaldean Oracles* each soul has a "leader god" which is identified with one of the solar rays; the soul must discover its "ray" and perform the proper ritual to make its return ascent to the sun.

This solar ascent was likely accomplished during a theurgic initiation rite according to historian Hans Lewy. He conjectures this consisted of a symbolic funeral of the initiate during which they lay on the ground as if dead. His body, with the exception of the head, was covered with a shroud and libations were poured out. Following this, the officiant of the rite would conjure the soul of the initiate and "elevate" it, leading it towards a solar ray where it would ascend to the heavens and experience luminous visions of eternal life.[56] Lewy notes the similarities of this rite with the necromantic rituals of the *goetes* who poured libations into the grave while magically invoking the soul of the deceased.

The visionary technique of scrying was practiced by theurgists to communicate with the gods and gain mystical revelations. Magical statuary was used in a similar manner to that of the Egyptians and Mesopotamians. Theurgists invoked deities into statues, placing herbs, drugs, charms, and various symbols in hollow cavities in their interiors, thereby "animating" or awakening their powers. Gods were also invoked directly into the soul of the theurgist in a kind of temporary "possession" ritual, similar to those experienced by oracles and shamans.

Legends of the Divine Iamblichus

Iamblichus was revered by his students who called him the "Divine Iamblichus". Like previous great philosophers before him such as Pythagoras and Empedocles, legends arose about the master's mystical powers. He was reported by his servants to levitate into the air and take on a golden hue when praying—rumors which he laughed at and tried to dispel. Eunapius records an account of a miracle performed by Iamblichus when which he took his students to the hot springs of Gadara in Syria:

"He at once touched the water with his hand...and uttering a brief summons he called forth a boy from the depth of the spring. He was white skinned and of medium height, his locks were golden and his back and breast shone...His disciples were overwhelmed with amazement, but Iamblichus said, "Let us go to the next spring", and he rose and led the way, with a thoughtful air. Then he went through the same performance there also, and summoned another... like the first in all respects, except that his hair was darker and fell loose in the sun. Both the boys embraced Iamblichus and clung closely to him as though he were a real father. He restored them to their proper places and went away after his bath, reverenced by his pupils." [57]

The Legacy of Theurgy

The writings of Iamblichus were a dominant influence on the Neoplatonism of late antiquity, influencing philosophers such as Proclus who practiced theurgy as well. Iamblichus was even seen by some as the "savior" of the late Hellenic world. The last pagan Roman Emperor, Julian the Apostate, attempted to reform the pagan priesthoods during his brief rule by introducing the teachings of Iamblichus, but his efforts could not stem the tide of history. The end was near for the "old religion" and Christian rulers gained power, destroyed the remaining vestiges of paganism, closing its temples and ending a millennium of Greek philosophy.

Ironically, Theurgy and Neoplatonism influenced the new religion of Christianity through the writings of the philosopher Pseudo-Dionysus the Ageropagite (late 5th or early 6th century CE) who viewed the holy sacraments of the Church as a kind of theurgy, with the eucharist as the highest theurgic rite.[58, 59] The legacy of Theurgy and Neoplatonism on western esotericism has been profound—influencing Christian mysticism, Jewish Kabbalah, and Sufism. The writings of Iamblichus would re-emerge a thousand years later during the Italian Renaissance, influencing the philosophies of Pletho, Ficino and Pico della Mirandolla, who will later be discussed. In the modern era, Theurgy has influenced the teachings of esoteric orders which use similar magical theories and practices with the goal of uniting the soul of the initiate with the divine.

The Lyre of Orpheus—Music in the Mysteries & Shamanism

Neoplatonists such as Iamblichus also used music as an aid to mystical ascension. Musical theurgy was seen as a form of *anamnesis* or "remembering" by which the soul was awakened to its identity with the gods. Earlier philosophers such as Pythagoras, Empedocles and Orpheus used music for purposes of healing and magical enchantment. As previously mentioned, Pythagoras may have learned his musical magic from the Dactyls, the ancient Greek magicians who practiced singing and chanting during ecstatic initiation rites. According to Sarah Iles Johnston, the musician was essential to mystery religions, and their sacred teachings were conveyed through poetry composed and sung by men such as Orpheus. She insists that the talented singer became an excellent initiator because his music communicated with souls and the powers of the underworld.[60]

In the lost Orphic book entitled *The Lyre,* Orpheus apparently taught how to invoke souls through the power of music. Historian Algis Uzdavinys notes that among the late Pythagoreans, the seven strings of the lyre were associated with the seven circles of heaven. They played the lyre during rites of ascension, along with mantric intonation of the seven vowels. By these means they encouraged the soul to escape the darkness of irrational lower existence for the divine realm from which it originally descended.[61]

Uzdavinys proposes theories of the seven vowels and the seven-stringed lyre associated with planets, colors, sounds, and the seasons of the year probably originated in Babylon. In his opinion it was also related to Egyptian esotericism, the ultimate source of Orphic lore. Egyptian priests used the seven vowels, uttering them in succession when singing hymns.[62] Iamblichus believed the *seven vowels* corresponded to the seven planetary gods and the celestial spheres. He cited the authority of Zoroaster to explain their connection with the seven planetary angels who were seen as guardians of the universe.[63] The Gnostic teacher Marcus (2nd century CE) associated the seven vowels of the Greek alphabet with the heavenly spheres as follows: [64]

Alpha / first heaven (Moon),
Epsilon / second heaven (Mercury),
Eta / third heaven (Venus),
Iota / fourth heaven (Sun),
Omicron / fifth heaven (Mars),
Upsilon / sixth heaven (Jupiter),
Omega / seventh heaven (Saturn).

The chanting of vowels was used extensively by ancient magicians, and can be found in the spells of the *Greek Magical Papyri*, where long strings of vowels were vocalized, similar to the use of mantras by eastern mystics. These so-called *voces magicae,* consisting of god-names and incomprehensible words of power in archaic foreign languages, along with sounds such as bellowing, whistling and popping, were probably used to induce trance states as well as invoke gods and spirits.

Music and singing as a means of altering consciousness is essential to the practice of shamanism as well. Songs are taught to shamans by their spirit-helpers and also used by them to call the spirits. In a similar manner some shamans use incomprehensible magical language, chanting, and a wide range of animal sounds in their ceremonies. As well as drumming, they also use instruments such as jaw harps, stringed instruments, and bows to induce trance states.

Similar to the use of the lyre in Orphic tradition, Celtic bards played harps during their recitations to entertain and enchant audiences. Incantation was used by them to heal, harm, or effect the emotions—provoking laughter, tears, or bringing deep sleep to listeners.[65] Mongolian bards to this day sing long epic poems which take several nights to perform. They are considered magicians in their own right, with powers to heal, divine, and influence the weather, and their performances are believed to bring rain or promote a good hunt, according to musicologist Carole Pegg.[66]

Merkabah--Riders of the Chariot

Jewish mystical lore describes the heavenly ascents of prophets who possessed powers similar to shamans. The prophet Elijah was lifted to heaven in a whirlwind, and Enoch ascended to the skies in a storm chariot where he was transformed into the archangel Metatron. In the *Book of Enoch* the prophet describes his fiery transfiguration:

"...at once my flesh was changed into flame, my tendons into a fire of glowing heat, my bones to glowing juniper coals, my eyelids to radiance of lightning, my eyeballs to torches of fire, the hair of my head to glowing heat and flame, all my limbs to wings of burning fire, and my bodily frame to scorching fire. On my right were hewers of fiery flames, on my left torches were burning. There blew around me wind, storm, and tempest, and the noise of earthquake upon earthquake was in front of me and behind me." [67]

The Jewish Merkabah mystics emerged in Palestine between the 3rd –8th centuries CE who practiced ecstatic visionary ascents through the heavens similar to those of the earlier Gnostics, according to the scholar of Jewish

The Tree of Visions

mysticism, Gershem Scholem.[68] "Merkabah" is the Hebrew term for chariot, and *ma'aseh merkavah* means "works of the chariot". The mystics who practiced these works were accordingly known as "riders of the chariot". Their visionary journeys were inspired by the prophet Ezekial's vision in the *Old Testament*, as well as the *hekhalot* literature which told of mystical ascents to the heavenly palaces. In his vision, Ezekial witnesses the throne-chariot of God, as well as the "four living creatures", also called the *cherubim*:

"And I looked, and, behold, a whirlwind came out of the north, a great cloud, and a fire infolding itself, and a brightness was about it, and out of the midst thereof...came the likeness of four living creatures. And this was their appearance; they had the likeness of a man. And every one had four faces, and every one had four wings...As for the likeness of their faces, they four had the face of a man, and the face of a lion, and they four had the face of an ox on the left side; they four also had the face of an eagle..." [69]

Merkabah mystics ascended in vision through the *hekalot* or palaces of the seven heavens to reach the divine throne of God. Scholem writes: "The Merkabah mystics occupy themselves with all the details of the upper world, which extends throughout the seven palaces in the firmament of aravot (the uppermost of the seven firmaments); with the angelic hosts which fill the palaces (heikhalot); the rivers of fire ofan and hashmal; and with all the other details of the Chariot described by Ezekial. But the main purpose of the ascent is the vision of the One Who sits on The Throne..." [70]

Similar to the gnostic's ascent, the Merkabah mystic needed to know the names of the angelic guardians of each palace encountered along the way in order to gain entrance. Scholem notes that similar to Gnostic literature, there is a theurgic and magical aspect to the technique of the ascent.[71] Magical incantations, recitations of names of angels, words of power, as well as charms and magical seals were used to assure their safe passage. In the text *Hekhalot Rabbati*, the mystic's vision of the "seventh palace" is described in surreal detail:

"This man enters and stands at the threshold of the gate of the seventh palace, and the holy living creatures lift up five hundred and twelve eyes on him. And every single eye of the holy living creatures is split open like a great winnowers' sieve. And the appearance of their eyes is as if "they dart like lightning". Besides, there are eyes of the mighty cherubim and ophannim of the Shekhinah, which resemble torches of light and of flames of glowing juniper coals. And this man is in a cold sweat, and he shrinks back and shakes. He is confounded, confused, and overcome, and he falls backward. But Anaphiel the prince supports him, he and the sixty-three guardians of the gates of the seven palaces. All of them help him and say to him "Do not fear, son of the beloved seed! Enter and see "the King in his beauty". You shall not be destroyed, nor shall you be burned...At once (God?) blows the horn "from above the firmament over their heads" and the holy living creatures cover their faces, and the cherubim and the ophanim turn their faces, and he enters and stands before the throne of glory." [72]

The ascent was considered dangerous for the mystic, and judging from the text could be terrifying. Only those who had undergone long and arduous training and ascetic purifications could safely undertake the journey. Scholem describes the trance inducing techniques practiced by the Merkabah rider such as placing his head between his knees, a physical position which can induce self-hypnosis and altered states of consciousness. While doing this, he recited hymns of an ecstatic character, the songs of the holy creatures who bear the Throne of Glory.[73]

Historian James Davila compares the ascetic practices of the Merkabah mystic and the shaman, finding they have much in common: fasting and dietary restrictions, celibacy, purification rites, isolation, sensory deprivation, recitation of songs of power, singing of hymns, repetition of divine names, as well as initiatory disintegration and reintegration—similar to the death/rebirth experience of shamans. Ecstatic ascents through the heavens and the control of angels or spirits are also practiced by both.[74]

The Four Holy Creatures & The Zodiac

The symbolism of the "four living creatures" of Ezekial's vision is central to Merkabah as well as later Kabbalistic mysticism. Aspects of his visionary narrative could have been influenced by Mesopotamian literature which Ezekial was familiar with, according to biblical scholar Daniel Bodi.[75] The iconography of the *four living creatures* may have likewise been inspired by the mythical creatures featured in Babylonian artwork, in particular the large sphinx-like guardian statues found in Babylonian palaces in the form of winged bulls with human heads.

Moreover, the symbolic meaning of Ezekial's four creatures may be based on the astrological symbolism of the "Four Royal Stars of Persia"—four prominent stars in the zodiac which mark the quarters of the heavens and four seasons. When it is understood that the constellation "Aquila the Eagle" was substituted for the astrological sign of Scorpio by the Jews, the Four Royal Stars match the creatures of Ezekial's vision exactly. This suggests it may encode cosmological and calendrical knowledge:

The Tree of Visions

Aldeberan
prominent star of Taurus the *bull*/ spring equinox/ east
Regulus
prominent star of Leo the *lion*/ summer solstice/ south
Antares
prominent star of Scorpio-Aquila the *eagle*/ autumn equinox/ west
Fomalhaut
prominent star of Aquarius the *man*/ winter solstice/ north

The four living creatures, also known as the *tetramorph,* appear in Christian literature in the *Revelation of St. John:* "And the first beast was like a lion, and the second beast like a calf, and the third beast had a face as a man, and the fourth beast was like a flying eagle." These became associated with the four Christian evangelists: Matthew the winged man, Mark the winged lion, Luke the winged bull, and John the eagle. These saints along with their totemic creatures are often depicted in Christian art, architecture and manuscript illuminations. The four living creatures also play an important role in the symbolism of Kabbalah, alchemy and ritual magic, corresponding to the four cardinal directions and four elements.

The Sefer Yetsira

The *Sefer Yetsira* or "Book of Creation", written between the 2nd- 6th century CE, is a Jewish mystical text originating during the same period as the Merkabah literature. It establishes a mystical cosmology of "thirty-two paths of wisdom", composed of the ten primordial numbers or *sephiroth*, plus the twenty-two letters of the Hebrew alphabet,

According to Scholem, The *Sefer Yetsira* was influenced by Greek cosmology and Neopythagorean conceptions.[76] Aryeh Kaplan writes that the text may have been preserved by the Essenes, the mystical Jewish sect who were likened to the Pythagoreans.[77] The first three "primal letters" of the Hebrew alphabet: Aleph, Mem, and Shin, correspond to the elements air, water, and fire, respectively. The second group of seven "double consonants" correspond to the seven planets, seven heavens, seven days of the week, as well as the seven directions: east, south, west, north, above, below and center. The twelve remaining "simple consonants" correspond to the signs of the zodiac, and the twelve months. Scholem writes: "The cosmogony and cosmology, based on language-mysticism, betray their relationship with astrological ideas".[78]

The text was not merely theoretical but was used for meditative as well as magical purposes as well. This is illustrated by the story of Rabbi Hanina and Rabbi Oshayah, who every Friday studied the book, and by means of it magically created a calf, which they proceeded to eat.[79] Kaplan writes that the *Sepher Yetsira* was also used by kabbalists to create the fabled "Golem", a magical android creature intended to serve its master. He writes the text was primarily used for its meditative exercises: "...these exercises were meant to strengthen the initiate's concentration, and were primarily helpful in the development of telekinetic and telepathic powers. It was with these powers that one would then be able to perform feats that outwardly appeared to be magical." [80] So revered were its powers, the Jewish sage Rava (299-353 CE) who studied the *Sefer Yetsira*, claimed: "If the righteous desired, they could create a world."

The *Sefer Yetsira* was a primary source of medieval Jewish Kabbalah and provided the basic elements that would later be incorporated into the kabbalistic Tree of Life diagram, composed of sephiroth and paths associated with the Hebrew letters and their elemental and astrological correspondences.

Tree of Life / Shaman's World Tree

The earliest version of the "Tree of Life" was described in the biblical *Book of Genesis*. It grew in the Garden of Eden, its fruit giving everlasting life. Scholem writes that the literature of Merkabah and later medieval Jewish mysticism refers to the Tree of Life as a "cosmic tree" growing between the celestial Garden of Eden and the terrestrial paradise, on which souls of the righteous ascend and descend as on a ladder.[81] This has striking parallels to the World Tree of shamanic cultures — which grows between heaven and earth — on which shamans climb in their journeys between the worlds. We will later explore the kabbalistic Tree of Life, a cosmological diagram widely used by modern ritual magicians.

Chapter 12 Notes

Mithras slaying the cosmic bull. Marble statue, Rome 3rd century CE.
The bull, snake, dog and scorpion likely symbolize astronomical constellations,
while Mithras is associated with the sun.

1. Eliade. *Shamanism- Archaic Techniques of Ecstasy*. 1964:1972: 267.
2. Ibid.: 272-278.
3. Fowden, Garth. *The Egyptian Hermes: a historical approach to the late pagan mind.* 1986: 32.
4. Ibid.: 101.
5. Copenhaver, Brian. *Hermetica, the Greek Corpus Hermeticum and the Latin Asclepius in a new English translation with notes and introduction.*1992: xxxii.
6. Lachman, Gary. *The Quest for Hermes Trismegistus.* 2001: 89.
7. Copenhaver. *Hermetica, the Greek Corpus Hermeticum and the Latin Asclepius in a new English translation with notes and introduction.* 1992: 41.
8. Hoeller, Stephen A. "On the Trail of the Winged God — Hermes & Hermeticism Throughout the Ages". Gnosis: A Journal of Western Inner Traditions (Vol. 40, Summer 1996) *The Gnosis Archive. Gnosis.org.*
9. Poemandres. *The Shepherd of Men*, I. Trans. Mead, G.R.S. *Gnosis.org.*
10. Fowden. *The Egyptian Hermes: a historical approach to the late pagan mind.* 1986: 111.
11. Copenhaver. *Hermetica, the Greek Corpus Hermeticum and the Latin Asclepius in a new English translation with notes and introduction.* 1992: xxxiv.
12. "Stobaei Hermeticum, Libellus VI Of the Decans and the Stars". Trans. Mead, G.R.S. *The Hermetic Fellowship.*1999.
13. Flowers, Stephen Edred. *Hermetic Magic: the Postmodern Magical Papyrus of Abaris.* 1995: 64.

14. Eliade, Mircea. *The Forge and the Crucible.* Eliade 1956: 146.
15. Fowden. *The Egyptian Hermes: a historical approach to the late pagan mind.* 1986: 89.
16. Ibid.:121.
17. Copenhaver. *Hermetica, the Greek Corpus Hermeticum and the Latin Asclepius in a new English translation with notes and introduction.* 1992: xxxvi.
18. Betz. *The Greek Magical Papyri in Translation including the Demiotic Spells.* 1992: 48-52.
19. Skinner. Stephen. *Techniques of Graeco-Egyptian Magic.* 2014:26-27.
20. Betz. *The Greek Magical Papyri in Translation including the Demiotic Spells.* 1992: 48-52.
21. Plagels, Elaine H. *The Gnostic Gospels.* 1989: xxi.
22. Ibid.: xx.
23. Smith. *Jesus The Magician.* 1978: 132.
24. Merkur, Dan. *Gnosis: an Esoteric Tradition of Mystical Visions and Unions.* 1993: 125.
25. Fowden. *The Egyptian Hermes: a historical approach to the late pagan mind.* 1986: 191.
26. Merillat, Herbert Christian. "The Gnostic Apostle Thomas". Chapter 4--"Beyond the Law". *The Gnostic Society Library.* 1997.
27. Smith. *Jesus The Magician.* 1978: 94.
28. Betz. *The Greek Magical Papyri in Translation including the Demiotic Spells.* 1992: 96.
29. Davies, Owen. *Grimoires: A History of Magic Books.* 2009:16.
30. Smith. *Jesus The Magician.* 1976: 145.
31. Ibid.:104.
32. Goodrick-Clarke, Nicholas. 2008: 27.
33. Wisse, Frederick. Trans. "Online Text for Apocryphon of John". *Early Christian Writings.* Kirby, Peter. 2014.
34. Goodrick-Clarke. *The Western Esoteric Traditions.* 2008: 27.
35. Merkur. *Gnosis: an Esoteric Tradition of Mystical Visions and Unions.* 1993: 138-142.
36. Ibid:120.
37. Ibid:125.
38. Rudolph, Kurt; Wilson, R. McL., *Gnosis: The Nature and History of Gnosticism.* 1983: 173.
39. Ibid.:173.
40. Ibid.:176.
41. Nabarz, Payam. *The Mysteries of Mithras.* 2005: 43.
42. Burkert, Walter. *Ancient Mystery Cults.* 1986: 83.
43. Ulansey, David. *The origins of the Mithraic mysteries: cosmology and salvation in the ancient world.* 1989: 61.
44. Nabarz. *The Mysteries of Mithras.* 2005: 30-38.
45. Ibid.:30.
46. Eliade. *Shamanism- Archaic Techniques of Ecstasy.* 1964: 121.
47. Goodrick-Clarke. *The Western Esoteric Traditions.* 2008: 23.

48. Shaw, Gregory. *Theurgy and the Soul: the Neoplatonism of Iamblichus*.1995 :241.
49. Clarke, Emma C., Dillon, John M., and Hershbell, Jackson P. -trans. and intro. Iamblichus On the Mysteries. 2003: 115.
50. Shaw, Gregory. *Theurgy and the Soul: the Neoplatonism of Iamblichus*.1995 :241.
51. Scholars such as McEvilley have noted the similarities between the Theurgy of Iamblichus and Tantric Buddhism. It is curious that the tantric schools were emerging in India at the same time as Iamblichus was teaching in the West. Both schools utilized magical techniques involving magical rituals, visualizations, invocation of deities, magical symbols, etc.
52. McEvilley. *The Shape of Ancient Thought (Comparative Studies in Greek and Indian Philosophies)* 2002: 591.
53. Hekate, in her role as patroness of theurgy and magic in the system of Iamblichus, played a similar role to that of the Egyptian god Heka, from whom she may have originally derived her name, according to Uzdavinys. (Uzdavinys 2010:106).
54. Clarke, *Iamblichus On the Mysteries*. 2003: 95.
55. Shaw, Gregory. "Containing Ecstasy: The Strategies of Iambichean Theurgy". Academia.edu. Dionysius Vol XXI. Dec. 2003, 53 -88.
56. Lewy, Hans. *Chaldean Oracles and Theurgy*. 2011: 204-210.
57. Eunapius. *Lives of the Philosophers*. Trans. Wright, W.C. *Philostratus and Eunapius: The Lives of the Sophists*.Eunapius;1922: 368-374.
58. Burns, Dylan. "Proclus and the Theurgic Liturgy of Pseudo-Dionysus". Dionysus, Vol. XXII. 111-32. www. Academia.edu. 2004: 368-374.
59. Gregory Shaw writes: "Indeed the Church, with its ecclesiastical embodiment of the divine hierarchy, its initiations and its belief in salvation through sacramental acts, may have fulfilled the theurgical program of Iamblichus in a manner that was never concretely realized by Platonists". Shaw. *Theurgy and the Soul: the Neoplatonism of Iamblichus*.1995
60. Johnston, Sarah Iles. *Restless Dead*. 1999: 114.
61. Uzdavinys, Algis. *Orpheus and the Roots of Platonism*. 2011: 46.
62. Uzdavinys. *Philosophy & Theurgy In Late Antiquity*. 2010:118.
63. Iamblichus. *Theology of Arithmetic*. (trans.) Waterfield, Robin. 1988: 87-88.
64. Mead, G.R.S. *Fragments of a Faith Forgotten*. 1900: 373.
65. Walter, Mariko Namba; Fridman, Eva Jane Neumann, editors. *Shamanism: An Encyclopedia of World Beliefs, Practices and Culture*, Vol.1. 2004: 472.
66. Pegg, Carole. *Mongolian Music, Dance, & Oral Narrative*. 2001:112-115.
67. Davila, James R. *Descenders to the Chariot*. 2011: 152.
68. Scholem, Werblowsky, R.J. Zwi. *Origins of Kabbalah*. 1987: 23.
69. Ezekiel 1-15. *Old Testament*.
70. Scholem, Gershom. *Kabbalah*. 1978: 16.
71. Ibid.:15.
72. Davila. *Descenders to the Chariot*. 2011: 146.
73. Scholem. *Kabbalah*.1978: 15.
74. Davila. *Descenders to the Chariot*. 2011: 124-5.
75. Bodi, Daniel. *The Book of Ezekiel and the Poem of Erra*. 1991: 44.
76. Scholem. *Origins of Kabbalah*. 1987: 27-28.

77. Kaplan, Aryeh. *Sepher Yetzirah*. 1977: xvii.
78. Scholem. *Origins of Kabbalah*. 1987: 31.
79. Kaplan. *Sepher Yetzirah*. 1997: x.
80. Ibid.: xi.
81. Scholem. *Origins of Kabbalah*. 1987: 72.

Chapter 13: The Magical Grimoires

Dr. Faustus in magic circle invoking demon
from The Magical History of Dr. Faustus. 1631.

    The earliest magical texts of Egypt, the *Pyramid Texts,* may have codified prehistoric shamanistic rituals, in the opinion of Egyptologist Geraldine Pinch.[1] Shamanism is predominantly an oral tradition passed down by word of mouth. In contrast, many ancient magical traditions were transmitted through literature. Besides the Egyptian funerary texts, much of the archaeological evidence of Egyptian magic is in the form of written spells on tomb walls, coffins, and inscriptions on monuments, statues and amulets.
    The Akkadians and Babylonians recorded their magical spells in cuneiform writing on clay tablets, and we previously discussed their lapidary, herbal, and astrology books. Excavations of the city of Uruk dating from the 4th--5th centuries BCE have uncovered clay tablets containing magical rituals and incantations.[2] The Orphics of ancient Greece, according to Plato, produced a "hubbub of books". Their use of magic books revolutionized Greek religion, according to Burkert, which prior to writing had been dominated by ritual and the spoken

word of myth. The revolutionary medium of books introduced a new form of authority to which individuals had access—provided they could read.[3]

The Hermetic philosophers of Ptolemaic Egypt recorded their knowledge of astrology, alchemy, and magic—the technical Hermetica—in books as well. The richest source of Greco-Egyptian magic is found in the *Greek Magical Papyri* written in Greek, Demotic Egyptian, and Coptic, as previously discussed. These represent the earliest phase of the "grimoire tradition" of magical manuals that would become the basis of magical practice down through the centuries in the western world.

The books of the *Old Testament* chronicle the miracles performed by Jewish prophets, such as Elijah's contest with the priests of Baal to produce instantaneous fire by praying to god, and his production of a rainstorm by praying with his head between his knees. Moses, who may have learned magic in Egypt, earned the reputation of being a powerful magician. During his contest with pharaoh's magicians, staffs were magically transformed into snakes, and water into blood. In the *New Testament* it is written: "Moses was learned in all the wisdom of the Egyptians and was mighty in words and deeds".

In the *Greek Magical Papyri* the name of Moses is recorded along with Hebrew god-names and angels, suggesting Jewish magic was indeed considered powerful. By the early Christian era the reputation of the Jews as magicians rivaled even that of the Egyptians, according to Owen Davies. He writes that during Roman rule there is evidence of Jewish magicians being sought out, and they could be found in the entourage of high Roman officials.[4] A number of early Jewish magical texts from around the 4th century CE were pseudonymously credited to Moses such as *The Hidden Book of Moses*, *The Key of Moses*, and the *Tenth Hidden Book of Moses*.[5] These contained elements of astrology, herbalism, and magical spells similar to those found in the *Greek Magical Papyri*.

Another legendary Jewish magician mentioned in the *Greek Magical Papyri* is King Solomon, and his name would be linked to an entire genre of magical books attributed to his authorship. Although Solomon was known as a wise king with knowledge of the secrets of plants and animals, he was not associated with magic in the Bible. Nevertheless, legends grew around him as a great astrologer and magician. The first century Jewish historian Josephus wrote that Solomon penned 3,000 books, including books on magical incantation and exorcism of demons.

Testament of Solomon

The Testament of Solomon is one of the earliest examples of the genre of the magical grimoire. Although attributed to King Solomon, it was pseudonymously written in Greek between the 1st-5th century CE in Egypt or Babylon. Based on Judeo-Hellenistic magic, it also contains references to Christian prophecies, suggesting it may have been redacted by a Christian.

The book is a compendium of sixty demons, including thirty-six associated with the astrological decans.[6] Many of the decan spirits are described as having the heads of animals, while others appear in the form of a dog, lion, dragon, and a three-headed woman, reminiscent of the Greek goddess Hecate.[7] Along with the demons, names of the "opposing angels" by which they are controlled are also given, as well as the zodiacal signs they are subject to.

The book begins with the story of Solomon's building of the Temple of Jerusalem, which is delayed by demons who are busy tormenting the workers. In answer to Solomon's prayers, the angel Michael delivers him a magic ring inscribed with a pentagram by which he exorcises the demons, binding them to his service. Starting with the prince of demons, Beelzebul, Solomon summons them one by one, questioning them about their magical powers. Following this, the demons of various diseases are summoned and interrogated along with the angels who command and control them. Here Solomon questions the demon Ornias:

And he said to him: "Who art thou?" And the demon answered: "I am called Ornias". And Solomon said to him: "Tell me, O demon, to what zodiacal sign thou art subject." And he answered: "To the Water-pourer. And those who are consumed with desire for the noble virgins upon earth....these I strangle... Whenever men come to be enamoured of women, I metamorphose myself into a comely female; and I take hold of the men in their sleep, and play with them. And after a while I again take my wings and hie me to the heavenly regions. I also appear as a lion, and I am commanded by all the demons. I am offspring of the archangel Uriel, the power of God." [8]

Upon learning of their supernatural powers, Solomon sets the demons to work building his temple, transporting, cutting, and laying its stones. Despite the king's magical mastery of demons, the book ends with a cautionary tale. Solomon becomes enamored with a foreign woman and is told by pagan priests that if he would possess her he must first sacrifice to Moloch, Baal, and other foreign gods, then build temples to them. In his weakness he does so, and the glory of God departs from him and he becomes the "sport of idols and demons".

The *Testament of Solomon* is the first in a long line of magical grimoires attributed to the authorship of King Solomon. The word "grimoire" derives from the French word *grammaire* which originally meant a book written in Latin. By the 18th century the term was used to refer to magic books in general. Writing was considered a magical act in itself at a time when most people were illiterate. Magic books were believed to be powerful talismans in their own right, and it was believed the act of merely opening a magician's grimoire would summon the spirits whose seals and invocations were recorded therein.

The Hygromanteia

Another important early Solomonic grimoire is the *The Magical Treatise of Solomon or Hygromanteia*. Written in Greek, probably in the 15th century, some of its material appears to be derived from much older Egyptian and Babylonian sources. For example, it contains divination rituals similar to the Babylonian "Prince of the Thumb" ritual, previously mentioned, in which the magician uses a child medium for scrying spirits. It also contains a curious spell from Greek folklore, the conjuration of Kale' the Lady of the Mountains, who may have originally been one of the Charites or Three Graces, the daughters of Zeus. The names of many of the book's spirits are derived from the decan demons of the earlier *Testament of Solomon* according to historian Ioannis Marathakis.[9]

The *Hygromanteia* introduces tables of planetary hours for determining the best times to perform magic, symbols of the planets and their angels and demons, as well as their corresponding incenses and herbs. Preliminary prayers, invocations and conjurations are also provided, as well as instructions for fasting and bathing in preparation for rituals. The book also conatins some of the earliest drawings of magical tools such as the black hilted knife and magic circle. According to magical scholars Stephen Skinner and David Rankine, the word "hygromanteia" refers to the practice of constraining demons in *hydriai*, which are urns or water vessels.[10] Accordingly the book contains several divination rituals involving scrying in pots of water.

The *Hygromanteia* with its drawings of magical tools, magic circles, lists of planetary hours, and talismanic seals became the source of many traditions of European magic.

The Key of Solomon the King & the Lemegeton

The Key of Solomon, dating sometime between the 15th--18th centuries, is the generic name for a group of grimoires which continue in the tradition of the *Hygromanteia*.[11] In the Solomonic grimoires the complete art of invoking and conjuring angels and spirits is presented, along with instructions for the preparation of the magical circle and magical paraphernalia such as the wand, sword, and staff, as well as incense. The texts also provide preliminary prayers, directions for the magical retreat, and conjurations of the spirits as well as favorable astrological times for summoning them. For example, the "days and hours of Mercury" (Wednesday at sunrise) are listed as appropriate for "scientific projects, divination, eloquence, and also intelligence, swiftness in business matters, glamour, apparitions & responses to [questions about] things that will come."[12] A number of designs for "pentacles" or talismans of the seven planets are included. Various spells are given for seeking love and favor, making a magic carpet for interrogating spirits, mastering the spirits who guard treasures, rendering oneself invisible and other curious magical experiments.

The Lemegeton or the Lesser Key of Solomon dates from the 17th century, though parts of it can be traced back to the 14th century or earlier, according to Joseph Peterson.[13] Like other grimoires, it provides the seals of spirits, describes their magical powers and best times for their conjuring, as well as instructions for preparing the magic circle. It is a handbook for evoking so-called "evil spirits", lumped together under the misnomer of *"goetia"*. As previously mentioned, this term originally referred to a type of ancient Greek magic practiced by the *goetes*, rather than a class of infernal spirits, as commonly assumed.

The preface of the *The Lesser Key of Solomon* reads: "This Booke contains all the names, Orders, and Offices of all the spirits Salomon ever conversed with".[14] It explains how King Solomon commanded the demons into a brass vessel which he sealed up and cast into a lake or deep hole in Babylon. The vessel was eventually dug up and opened, whereupon the Legions of demons were "restored to their former places" — in other words, turned loose upon the world again. Despite their wicked reputation, only a minority of the "fallen angels" listed in the *Lemegeton* could be classified as downright evil. Many of them are described as being of "good nature", providing useful services to the magician such as teaching the arts & sciences, alchemy, astronomy, astrology, working with gems and herbs, divination, etc. In fact, some of the spirits teach distinctly shamanistic skills: to understand the speech of birds and other animals, to heal, and to "pass over the the whole earth in the twinkling of an eye".

Based on the descriptions provided for each of the seventy-two demons in the grimoire, many seem to be similar to the helping-spirits of shamans, appearing as animals such as birds, lions, horses, etc. Some of them are also "therianthropes" — human/animal hybrids — or bizarre amalgamations of several different creatures, reminiscent of ancient Egyptian and Mesopotamian demons. One such example is the demon Bune, who..."appeareth in the form of a Dragon with three heads, one like a Dog, one like a Gryphon, and one like a Man..."[15]

Some of the spirits when summoned appear as animals at first, later putting on a human shape at the request of the magus. The following is a description of one such demon:

"The 36th spirit is called Stolas, or Stolos. He is a Great and powerful Prince, appearing in the Shape of Mighty Raven at first before the Exorcist; but after he taketh the form of a Man. He teacheth the Art of Astronomy, and the Virtues of Herbs & Precious Stones..." [16]

Other spirits in the *Lemegeton* may have been assimilated from ancient pagan pantheons of deities. The names of the demons Bael, Astoreth and Haures in particular bear resemblances to Canaanite and Egyptian gods—respectively Bel, Astarte, and Horus.

The medieval grimoires appear to have preserved fragments of ancient pagan religion, astrology and magical practices hidden beneath a veneer of Judeo-Christianity. In fact they may represent the oldest continuous tradition of western magic. Magician and author Jake Stratton-Kent writes: "...the grimoire tradition has its roots not in a mythical Solomon, but a very real background in ancient Greece and the later Hellenistic world".[17] He argues that western magic originated with the *goetes,* the chthonic magicians of early Greece, and was passed down through the *Greek Magical Papyri* and the medieval and renaissance magical grimoires. Aaron Leitch, writer and grimoire magician, asserts "the grimoires reflected nothing less than a survival of shamanism during even the darkest age of medieval Europe".[18]

Who Wrote the Magical Grimoires?

Although the Solomonic grimoires are commonly assumed to be authored by Jewish magicians, Owen Davies writes: "there is no substantive evidence for a Hebrew version before the seventeenth century." [19] If the Jews did not write the Solomonic books, then who did? Ironically, they were probably penned by Christian monks, since they were among the few literate people of the time and had an interest in the supernatural, exorcism, and healing. Leitch writes: "It is obvious enough that the grimoires are clerical in nature, besides the borrowing from Judaism. The rites of the Church are mirrored in the texts, such as techniques of exorcism, recitation of Psalms, the Litany of Saints, and other established Catholic prayers and sacraments."[20] According to Davies, monasteries were important repositories of magic books often donated by monks. Many friars served as parish priests and shared their privileged access to magic grimoires with educated laity.[21] Historian Claude Lecouteux writes that there are many accounts from the Middle Ages castigating priests who practiced magic, referring to a manuscript from 1387 where it is written: "monks and clerics prepare amulets and write magic words (caracteres) on communion wafers, apple quarters, debt certificates, and phylacteries".[22]

Famous Christian clerics such as Michael Scot, Albertus Magnus, and Trithemius studied the esoteric arts of magic, alchemy and astrology. Several popes including Sylvester II, Benedict IX, and Gregory VI were rumored to have practiced magic, and the *Grimoire of Pope Honorius* was even pseudonymously named for a pope. Pope Boniface VIII was tried posthumously for practicing demonic magic. A witness at the trial testified to seeing him draw a magic circle in his garden and sacrificing a cockerel while reading from a grimoire.[23]

The Astrological Magic of the Picatrix

While Europe was in the midst of the Dark Ages, the Islamic world was experiencing a Golden Age of learning. Hermetic scholars such as Thabit ibn Qurra (826-901 CE), kept the scientific and philosophical knowledge of the ancient Greeks alive—translating the Hellenistic philosophers, the Hermetica, and books on alchemy, astrology, and magic into Arabic. He also made his own significant contributions to science and occultism. He boldly writes: "We are the heirs and propagators of paganism...who else have civilized the world... and who else have taught the hidden wisdom?". [24]

The city of Harran in today's south-central Turkey became an oasis of medieval Hermeticism during this period.[25] The word Harran means "crossroads" and the city was indeed the nexus of ancient civilizations and religions. It was founded in the early Bronze Age and mentioned in the *Old Testament* as a home of the Jewish patriarch Abraham. It was also a center of worship of the Mesopotamian moon god, Sin. Curiously, the plain of Harran is overlooked by Gobekli Tepi, the oldest ceremonial monument ever built, which we discussed previously.

Philosophers sought refuge in Harran, fleeing from Christian persecution in Alexandria, as well as from Athens upon the closure of the Platonic Academy in 529 CE. Harranian scholars translated many Hermetic books into Arabic. The so-called "Sabians" of Harran were star worshippers who built planetary temples, performed rituals to the deities of the seven planets, and refined the techniques of astrological magic, continuing to practice their pagan siderial religion until the 11th century CE.[26] They revered the Hermetica as their holy scriptures. By convincing the Muslim Caliph they were "people of the book", similar to Muslims, Christians and Jews, they were allowed to continue practicing their religion, rather than being forced to convert to Islam.

On the northwestern edge of the Islamic empire, in Andalusia, another center of esoteric learning was established in the 11th century by the Moors.

They conquered Spain, ruling in a tolerant fashion over Christian, Jewish, and Muslim populations. The city of Toledo became a center of translation of texts from Arabic into Latin and a mecca of learning, attracting scholars from all over Europe. Toledo was also notorious as a center of black magic and sorcery where forbidden knowledge was taught. It was there, in the court of the Christian king Alfonso the Wise, that the book known as the *Picatrix*, or *Ghayat al- Hakim* — "The Aim of the Sage", was translated from Arabic into Castilian, in the year 1256 CE.[27] The book is a collection of over two hundred short works combining Hermetic philosophy, Neoplatonism, astrology and alchemy, drawn from Arabic, Greek, Jewish, Syrian and Indian sources. It is believed to have originated from the Sabian school of Harran.

The *Picatrix* presents a system of astral magic based on the Hermetic theory of "chains of sympathy" which unite the cosmos, by means of which the influences of the heavens can be drawn down into the material world.[28] Through the power of magic it proposes the *spiritus*, or spiritual rays of the celestial bodies can be "captured" in talismans. The method consists of using complex astrological calculations to determine when the planets and stars are at their peak of influence, during which time talismans are created. The *Picatrix* also provides invocations of the seven planets and their associated angels, as well as their respective symbols, incenses[29], sacrifices, and propitious astrological timing for making astrological talismans.

In the chapter entitled "Attracting the virtues of the planets, and how we may speak with them...", an invocation of the planet Mercury, the divine scribe, is given. The magician is instructed to first dress in the garments of a notary and scribe, and when the Moon is conjunct Mercury in the heavens, to proceed in all his actions as though he is a scribe. He should wear a ring made of "fixed mercury" (solidified mercury) and sit on a chair like schoolmasters use, while turning to face the planet Mercury in the heavens, holding a piece of paper in his hands as though intending to write on it. A proper fumigation of Mercurial herbs is burned, and as the smoke rises the magus recites the following invocation:

> "May God bless you, good lord Mercury, you who are truthful, perceptive, intelligent, and the sage and instructor of every kind of writing, arithmetic, computation, and science of heaven and earth!...Therefore I call on you and invoke you by all your names, that is, in Arabic, Hotarit, in Latin, Mercurius; in Roman, Haruz; in Persian, Tyr; in Indian, Meda; I conjure you above all by the high Lord God...that you will receive my petition, and grant to me that which I ask, and pour out the powers of your spirit

upon me...make me exalted and honored by all peoples and kings, that I may be given secrets, that they may receive my words effectually and have need of me, and seek from me knowledge and wisdom in writing, arithmetic, astrology and divination...dispose me that by all these things I may receive profit and wealth, honors and exaltations before kings and exalted persons, and all that I am able to receive." [30]

Upon its translation from Arabic into Latin, the *Picatrix* spread from Spain to the rest of Europe. It became an important primary source of medieval and renaissance magic, influencing astrological magicians such as Marsilio Ficino, Cornelius Agrippa, Elias Ashmole, William Lilly and others.[31]

The Sacred Magic of Abramelin the Mage

The Book of The Sacred Magic of Abramelin the Mage is apparently of Jewish origin, likely written by Abraham von Worms, a German jewish scholar of the 15th century CE. In the beginning of the book, Abraham provides a fascinating chronicle of his adventures across Europe and the Near-East in search of the "true" magic. In his travels through Greece, Turkey, Arabia, and Palestine he tells how he met many magicians and sorcerers but was unimpressed with their displays of magic. At last he arrived in Egypt where met an elderly sage named Abramelin, writing: "Finally, guided by the mercy of God, through the Holy Angel, I was led to Abramelin. He was the first and only person who showed me the source of all the holy secrets and the true old magic- as it was used by our forefathers; he unlocked and opened these for me and showed me how to use them".[32]

The "Abramelin", like other magical grimoires, provides instructions for preparing the working space and crafting various ritual paraphernalia such as the wand, magic squares and incense. It differs from them in its emphasis on a lengthy and strenuous retreat lasting up to a year and a half, during which time the magician is instructed to live an ascetic lifestyle of devotion, fasting, celibacy and prayer. The Abramelin ritual culminates with a theurgic vision of the magician's "Holy Guardian Angel". Magician and author Lon Milo DuQuette writes: "The lengthy and (increasingly intense) preparation ceremony is a serious and arduous regimen that ruthlessly pushes the magician month-by-month toward a single-pointed passion for the Angel. The operation is crowned by a supreme invocation and ecstatic consummation of the divine marriage".[33] Abraham describes his own encounter with his angel: "I experienced this vision in humility and bliss for three continuous days. I was addressed lovingly and with friendship by my guardian angel. He explained the godly wisdom and

Kabbalah and later completely explained the complete truth about this magic".[34] After gaining mystical knowledge and conversation with the angel who serves as a guide and tutelary spirit, the magician is instructed to evoke the twelve kings and dukes of Hell, commanding them to deliver their "familiar spirits" to him. These lesser demons serve the magus by providing their magical powers of healing, magical flight, control of weather, exorcism, visions, divination, etc.

The Abramelin rite can be compared to the initiation experience of shamans. It culminates with the magician meeting his holy guardian angel—similar to the shaman's *tutelary spirit*—who helps him control other "lesser spirits". As mentioned previously, the shaman enters into an intimate and lifelong relationship with his tutelary spirit, comparable to the "divine marriage" with the holy guardian angel, as described by DuQuette.

The Book of the Sacred Magic of Abramelin the Mage was first translated into English by Golden Dawn magus S.L. MacGregor Mathers,[35] and popularized by Aleister Crowley who attempted the Abramelin rite himself but was never able to complete it. Abramelin offers the modern magician a program of self-initiation leading to the "knowledge and conversation" of the Holy Guardian Angel and discovery of their true "magical will", considered by some to be among the highest attainments of the magical path.

The Magician's Practice & Use of Magical Tools

The strenuous ascetic practices prescribed in the magical grimoires bring to mind similar practices of shamans during their initiations during which they retreat to the wilderness for prolonged periods. During their retreats, magicians isolate themselves, subjecting themselves to various austerities. In *The Key of Solomon the King*, the magician is advised to undertake a nine day retreat—to go to a chamber or secret place where he can free his mind from all "business and all extraneous ideas of whatever nature". He must strip himself naked and bathe in exorcised water, then put on fresh garments. He must abstain from all "idle, vain, and impure reasonings, and from every kind of impurity and sin".[36] He should then maintain a vigil, praying numerous times a day. On the last three days of the vigil before the conjuration of the spirits, he must partake of only bread and water once a day, and on the final day he should fast.

During this time the magician is instructed to prepare his magical tools and robe. *The Key of Solomon the King* describes the *robe* which is to be made of linen or silk: "If they be of linen the thread of which they are made should have been spun by a young maiden", to guarantee its purity.[37] Various magical characters are shown in the grimoire, which should be embroidered on the robe and shoes with red silk. Besides these, he should have a crown made of virgin paper on which the names of god are written in ink. In the *Lesser Key of Solomon* the magician is advised to procure a belt made of lion skin. Like the shaman's costume, the magician's robe is worn to assist in changing identity and focus from the mundane to the sacred, and he is advised to pray as he puts it on.

    The magician's *sword* is an important magical tool in many grimoires. It should be polished on the day of Jupiter (Thursday) and divine names engraved on one side. It is then perfumed and consecrated with the following formula: "I conjure you, sword, by these names of Imabrok, Abrac, Abracadra, so that you will give me strength in all of my Workings, to stand firm against all my enemies, visible and invisible." [38] As previously mentioned, swords are also used by Central Asian shamans to protect from evil spirits.

    The *staff* or *wand* is a symbol of the magician's authority and magical power. It must be made from a branch cut from a hazelnut tree of one year's growth, with a single stroke on the planetary day and hour of Mercury, (Wednesday at sunrise), and inscribed with magical characters. As previously mentioned, Mongolian and Siberian shamans also use staffs for similar purposes of summoning and controlling spirits, as well as journeying between the worlds. The magician's *pentacles* are usually circular pieces of metal on which magical names, figures and sigils are engraved. They are used for protection as well as for attracting benevolent influences of the spirits, similar in some respects to the shaman's *toli* mirrors, and like them are often worn over the breast.

    In the grimoires the *magic circle* is used to create sacred space, as well as for protection. The magus "circumambulates" the circle,[39] treading it in a clockwise direction. In the 17th century grimoire the *Fourth Book of Occult Philosophy*, the magician's treading of the circle is described as a means of inducing trance and ecstasy during which the spirits may be summoned: "...let him arise, and let him begin to walk about in a circuit within the said Circle from the east to the west, until he is wearied with a dizziness of his brain: let him fall down in the Circle, and there he may rest; and forthwith he shall be wrapt up in an ecstasie, and a spirit will appear unto him, which will inform him of all things." [40] The magician associates the cardinal directions of the magic circle to particular angelic, daemonic and elemental spirits. Mongolian shamans tread their own sacred circle in rituals, also in a clockwise direction, associating the four directions with different groups of heavenly Tenger spirits.

    Likewise, *fire* is an important element in the practices of both grimoire magicians and Inner Asian shamans. The magician places candles on the central altar, and censors with burning coals around the perimeter of the circle to ignite clouds of incense by which the spirits are made visible. The hearth fire is the symbolic center of the Mongolian shaman's yurt, and he gazes into it to induce visions, and ascends in magical flight on its smoke as it rises to the sky.

As previously mentioned, grimoire magic is predominantly a literate tradition. Accordingly, the magician reads from his or her handwritten *book of spirits* containing conjurations and spells as well as the signatures, symbols and images of the spirits.

Chapter 13 Notes

1. Pinch. *Magic in Ancient Egypt*.1994: 51.
2. Davies, Owen. *Grimoires: A History of Magic Books*. 2009: 8.
3. Burkert. *Greek Religion*.1985: 297.
4. Davies. *Grimoires: A History of Magic Books*. 2009: 10.
5. Ibid.:10.
6. Skinner, Stephen; Rankine, David. *The Veritable Key of Solomon: three different texts from those translated by S.L. MacGregor Mathers*. 2008: 17.
7. James, M.R. "The Testament of Solomon". Guardian Church Newspaper. March 15, 1899:369.
8. Peterson. "The Testament of Solomon". Trans. Conybeare, F.C. From Jewish Quarterly Review, Oct. 1898. Digital edition. Twilit Grotto-Esoteric Archives. 1997.
9. Marathakis, Ioannis. (trans.) The Magical Treatise of Solomon or Hygromanteia. Forward by Stephen Skinner. Marthakis 2011.
10. Ibid:35.
11. Skinner, Stephen; Rankine, David. The Veritable Key of Solomon: three different texts from those translated by S.L. MacGregor Mathers. 2008: 32.
12. Ibid.: 281.
13. Peterson, Joseph, H. (trans.) The Lesser Key of Solomon—Lemegeton Clavicula Salomonis.2001: xi.
14. Ibid.:5.
15. Mathers, MacGregor, S.L. The Lesser Key of Solomon the King Clavicula Saolmonis Regis.1995: 39.
16. Ibid.:47.
17. Stratton-Kent, Jake. Necromancy. Hermetic Tablet Journal of Western Ritual Magic. Winter Solstice, 2015:14. Stratton-Kent points to the underworld associations of goetia: working with the spirits of the dead, necromancy, divination and guiding souls in the underworld, insisting that in its original social context goetia was not considered anti-social. He explains that goetia only became demonized after the rise of the celestial focus of later Greek religion, as well as its association with foreigners and lower class practices. (Stratton-Kent 2010: vii)
18. Leitch, Aaron. Secrets of the Magical Grimoires.2005: 38.
19. Davies. *A History of Magic Books*. 2009: 15.
20. Leitch. Secrets of the Magical Grimoires. 2005: 9. Leitch writes that pseudepigrapha or attribution of authorship of a text to a famous historical

personality, such as Solomon, was a common Christian literary convention and was used in the New Testament gospels as well as the Apocrypha. It was a way of giving one's writing an air of authority and avoiding persecution by church authorities—especially in the case of magic books.

21. Davies. *A History of Magic Books*. 2009: 36.
22. Lecouteux, Claude. The Book of Grimoires. Trans. by Jon E. Graham. 2013:21.
23. Davies. *A History of Magic Books*. 2009:35.
24. Greer, John Michael, Warnock, Christopher. De Imaginibus of Thabit Ibn Qurra. 2013:9.
25. Lachman, Gary. The Quest of Hermes Trismegistus. 2001.
26. Green, Tamara, M. The City of the Moon God.1992:162-191.
27. Warnock; Greer. Picatrix. Translated by John Michael Greer & Christopher Warnock. 2010:11.
28. Ibid.:55.
29. Some of the incense recipes in the Picatrix contain psychoactive drugs such as opium and henbane, also used by European witches for flying ointments.
30. Greer & Warnock. Picatrix. 2010: 177.
31. Ibid.: 11.
32. Worms, Abraham von, compiled by Dehn, Georg. (trans.) Guth, Steven. The Book of Abramelin- A New Translation.Worms 2006: 21.
33. Ibid.: xv.
34. Ibid.: 28.
35. Mathers, MacGregor, S.L. The Book of the Sacred Magic of Abramelin the Mage. 1972.
36. Mathers, MacGregor, S.L.The Key of Solomon the King (Clivicula Salomonis). 1972:15.
37. Skinner & Rankine. The Veritable Key of Solomon: three different texts from those translated by S.L. MacGregor Mathers. 2008: 349.
38. Mathers, MacGregor, S.L.The Key of Solomon the King (Clivicula Salomonis). 1972:97.
39. The ritual act of "circumambulation", or walking in a clockwise circle is universal. It was practiced by the ancient Greeks, and is still observed in rituals by Brahmans, Buddhists, and Muslims.
40. Agrippa, Henry Cornelius. "Of Occult Philosophy or Magical Ceremonies: The Fourth Book". www. Hermetics.org.
41. Gimbutas suggests that the ritual importance of the cardinal directions can be traced back to the alignments of circular megalithic sites of Old Europe. (Gimbutas 1999:102)

Chapter 14:
Renaissance & Enlightenment Esotericism: Arranging Life According to the Heavens

Philosophical Tree of alchemy with seven planets and triangle of alchemical principles—sulphur, salt and mercury—from Azoth by Basilius Valentius, 1659.

Marsilio Ficino—the Second Orpheus

"...song is a most powerful imitator of all things...when it imitates the celestials, it also wonderfully arouses our spirit upwards to the celestial influence and the celestial influence downwards to our spirit".
-Marsilio Ficino

During the 15th century the books of the Hermetica made their way via a circuitous route from Harran in Mesopotamia to Italy. There they found fertile ground, and along with the writings of the pagan philosophers became seminal influences on the Italian Renaissance.

The rebirth of classical learning began in 1438 with the visit to Florence of a scholar and high ranking official of the Byzantine empire named George Gemistos Plethon. He brought with him a voluminous knowledge of the *Chaldean Oracles* as well as the writings of Plato, Plotinus, Orpheus, Pythagoras, Zoroaster and other pagan thinkers.[1] Plethon was an enigmatic figure, a scholar of Neoplatonism with a pagan streak who practiced "magical music" by singing hymns to the Greek gods. His brilliant lectures on Platonism earned him the nickname "The New Plato".

Pletho so impressed Cosimo de Medici, the wealthy Florentine merchant prince and patron of the arts, that he was inspired to create a new Platonic Academy for the translation of the works of Plato and other ancient philosophers. Medici appointed a promising young scholar, Marsilio Ficino for the task. Ficino, (1433-1499) the son of a Florentine physician, was educated in philosophy, medicine and theology. Only twenty-six years old at the time, he was nevertheless a scholar of Greek, a good writer, and devoted to Plato. Ficino set to work translating the writings of Plato, Plotinus, Proclus, Iamblichus and others which had never before been circulated in Europe. Two years later, Medici obtained a manuscript from a Byzantine monk, an incomplete copy of the *Corpus Hermeticum*. So excited was he by this discovery he had Ficino interrupt his translation of Plato so he could read the work of the fabled Hermes Trismegistus before he died.

An ardent astrologer, Ficino lamented that he was born with the sign of Aquarius, ruled by the malefic planet Saturn, ascending in his horoscope, bestowing upon him a melancholic temperament. He spent much of his time developing magical means to cope with his saturnine melancholy. Ficino was a gentle and charismatic soul, and his Platonic Academy located in a villa outside of Florence soon became a gathering place for philosophers, poets, and some of the most talented artists of the Italian Renaissance. Historian Frances Yates notes that Ficino directed the artist Sandro Botticelli's famous painting, "Primavera". According to her, he envisioned it as a complex magical talisman which would transmit healthy, rejuvenating and anti-Saturnian influences to the viewer. Yeats writes that Ficino introduced an artistic and imaginative magic to the Renaissance: "The operative Magi of the Renaissance were the artists and it was a Donatello or a Michelangelo who knew how to infuse the divine life into statues through their art".[2]

Ficino also performed a kind of astrological music which was probably inspired by the magical music of Plethon.[3] Hermetic scholar Nicholas Goodrick-

Clarke writes: "Ficino laid great emphasis on music in his magic. As the strings of a lyre could resonate with the cosmic tones of the planets and stars, so the magus could communicate with these celestial powers through music." [4] Ficino translated the ancient *Orphic Hymns,* and would sing these invocations to the Greek gods while playing his lyre, for the purpose of healing and uplifting the souls of listeners. Hence he was nicknamed "The Second Orpheus" and dubbed the "doctor of souls" by Cosimo Medici.

Ficino writes about ways of tempering the melancholic influence of Saturn by using the influences of more benign planets like Jupiter, Venus, Mercury, and above all the Sun. Here he explains his theory of astrological magic for attracting the heavenly rays of astral deities:

> "Our spirit is consonant with the heavenly rays, which, occult or manifest, penetrate everything. We can make it still more consonant, if we vehemently direct with our affections towards the star from which we wish to receive a certain benefit...above all, if we apply the song and light suitable to the astral deity and also the odour, as in the hymns of Orpheus addressed to cosmic deities." [5]

The odors to which Ficino refers are the specific incenses prescribed with each Orphic hymn. He provides a list of magical correspondences of the planets—including their colors, metals, gems, plants, animals, as well as astrological timing for receiving their powers. His writings reveal the influences of the astrological magic of the *Picatrix,* as well as the theurgy of Iamblichus on his thinking. In his book *De Triplici Vita* or "Three Books on Life", Ficino discusses the magical correspondences of the Sun:

> "..If you want your body and spirit to receive power from some member of the cosmos, say from the Sun, seek the things which above all are most Solar among metals and gems, still more among plants, and more yet among animals, especially human beings...Solar things are: all those gems and flowers which are called heliotrope because they turn towards the Sun, likewise gold, orpiment and golden colors...amber, balsam, yellow honey... the swan, the lion, the scarab beetle, the crocodile, and people who are blond, curly-haired, prone to baldness, and magnanimous..." [6]

Ficino's disciple Francesco Cattani da Diacceto avidly embraced Ficino's teachings and was a keen practitioner of astrological magic. Here he discusses how symbolic correspondences are used practically in a magical rite for invoking the powers of the Sun, elaborating on many of the same correspondences as given above by Ficino.

> "If for example he wishes to acquire solarian gifts, first he sees that the sun is ascending in Leo or Aries, on the day and in the hour of the sun. Then, robed in a solarian mantle of a solarian colour, such as gold, and crowned with a mitre of laurel, on the altar, itself made of solarian material, he burns myrhh and frankincense, the sun's own fumigations, having strewn the ground with heliotrope and suchlike flowers. Also, he has an image of the sun in gold or chrysolite or carbuncle...then anointed with unguents made, under the same celestial aspect, from saffron, balsam, yellow honey... he sings the sun's own hymn, such as Orpheus thought should be sung...to all these he adds what he believes is most important; a strongly emotional disposition of the imagination." [7]

The astrological magic of Ficino and Diacceto is clearly influenced by the theurgical practices of Iamblichus. Similar to Iamblichus's use of *sunthemata*, they use material substances as magical correspondences for attracting the benevolent "rays" of the planetary gods. Like him, they advocate the elevation of the spirit through the practice of "exalted imagination" to receive the deity's power.

In his commentary on the *Phaedrus* of Plato, Ficino discusses the soul's divine frenzy: "On recovery of these wings, the soul is separated from the body by their power. Filled with God, its strives with all its might to reach the heavens, and thither it is drawn". Ficino believed Orpheus had experienced the "four frenzies" by which the human soul is ecstatically lifted beyond its earthly condition to achieve "spiritual possession", according to hermetic scholar Angela Voss.[8] Like Orpheus, Pythagoras, Empedocles, and shamans before them, Ficino used the power of music to induce divine frenzy or ecstasy, for the purpose of healing.

As musical healer, magician and astrologer, Ficino was a guiding light to his generation as well as future generations of Hermeticists. Due to his influence, magic became part of the intellectual mainstream in the 15th and 16th centuries. Historian John S. Mebane summarizes his greater contribution to western culture: "Ficino helped to provide a philosophical rationale for the growing conviction that the human mind could comprehend the inner workings of nature and for the renewed affirmation of human creative power." [9]

Pico & The Angels

"As the farmer weds his elms to the vines,
 so the ``magus'' unites earth to heaven, that is,
 the lower orders to the endowments and powers of the higher."
-Pico della Mirandola

Count Giovanni Pico della Mirandola was born into a wealthy aristocratic family which excelled in scholarly and artistic pursuits, near Modena, Italy in 1463. As a child he displayed a prodigious memory, and at fourteen he studied law at universities in France and Italy where he mastered Greek, Latin, Hebrew, Chaldee and Arabic.[10]

Abandoning his study of law, Pico settled in Florence in 1484. There on an astrologically fortuitous day, the charismatic young aristocrat met Marsilio Ficino who was to become his teacher, as well as Lorenzo de Medici the grandson of Cosimo, who would serve as his lifelong protector and patron. Soon thereafter the impetuous Pico became involved in a love affair with the wife of one of Medici's cousins, attempting to elope with her. He was caught, wounded, and imprisoned by her husband, but finally released through the intervention of Lorenzo. Convalescing in nearby Perugia, Pico discovered the writings of the ancient Chaldeans, Hermeticists, and the Hebrew Kabbalists.

So inspired was Pico by the Kabbalah he commissioned his Hebrew teacher, a jewish convert named Flavius Mithridates, to translate an entire library of kabbalistic works from Hebrew into Latin, a task which took years. By studying the Kabbalah, Pico believed he could in turn better understand Christianity. He attempted to find correlations between Kabbalistic and Christian doctrines, arranging the names of the Father, Son, and Holy Ghost, as well as Jesus on the *sephirah* or spheres of the kabbalistic Tree of Life.[11] He also identified the ten *sephiroth* of the Tree with the ten angelic hierarchies established by the early Christian writer Pseudo-Dionysus.

Pico's magic operated directly with the *angels*, rather than the lower celestial and planetary powers of "natural magic", as used by Ficino. Through use of the Kabbalah, Pico believed man could ascend to an angelic status and acquire godlike powers.The kabbalistic sephiroth, which existed in the higher intelligible world, were seen to govern the lower spheres of the cosmos, and by learning the names and symbols of these "prime agents" Pico believed the magician could perform miracles.[12] By practicing Kabbalah, Pico believed man could be purged of matter and transformed into an angel, in preparation for *henosis* or mystical union with God. Continuing in the tradition of Hermetic,

Neoplatonic and Gnostic mystics of antiquity, Pico writes:

> "..Let us disdain earthly things; let us struggle toward the heavenly. Let us put in last place whatever is of the world; and let us fly beyond the chambers of the world to the chamber nearest the most lofty divinity. There, as the sacred mysteries reveal, the seraphim, cherubim, and thrones occupy the first places.." [13]

Pico espoused the *prisca theologica*—the "pristine theology"—an idea introduced by Ficino that there was one single true theology which underlies all religion, first revealed by God to man in antiquity. His overarching goal was to synthesize the pagan, Christian, and Hebrew traditions which he believed were rooted in a universal revelation.

As an audacious twenty-three year old Pico proposed to publicly defend his revolutionary ideas on religion, philosophy, Kabbalah and magic in his famous *Oration on the Dignity of Man* in 1486.[14] The debate never occurred, but he nevertheless aroused the suspicion of Pope Innocent the VIII, who condemned Pico's theses, declaring they "reproduced the errors of the pagan philosophers" and seemed to endorse magic, which was heretical. Pico defiantly replied: "there is no science which gives us more assurance of Christ's divinity than magic and the Kabbalah." His bold vision of the freedom and spiritual dignity of man was clearly at odds with the orthodox theologians of the Church and their pessimistic doctrine of the Fall of Man. Pico fled Italy to France to escape the pope's condemnation, only to be thrown in prison there. Through the appeals of his friend Lorenzo de Medici, Pico was released to live in Florence. There he joined the Platonic Academy, attempting to formulate a doctrine of the soul that reconciled Platonic and Christian beliefs.

In 1490, Pico was visited by Johann Reuchlin (1455-1522), a German Hebrew language scholar who became the heir to his kabbalistic doctrines, spreading them north of the Alps. Together the two aroused an interest in Kabbalah that spread throughout the European intellectual community. Reuchlin's agenda for promoting the Kabbalah was in part evangelical; through the Christian Cabala he hoped to prove to the Jews, using their own religious literature, that Jesus was the true messiah.

Towards the end of his short life Pico renewed his friendship with Savonarola, the firebrand Dominican friar and reformer. Savonarola zealously preached sermons against tyrants and corrupt clergy, as well as the corrupt liberal morals of Florence. This resulted in the original "bonfire of the vanities" in which thousands of books, artworks, musical instruments and other such "vanities" were publicly burned. Under the dark friar's influence Pico renounced his past, destroying his youthful poetry and giving away his fortune with the intention of becoming a monk. Pico tragically met his end under mysterious circumstances in 1494, allegedly poisoned by his own secretary due to his closeness to Savonarola, a man whom Ficino had condemned as the "antichrist".

Like a meteor streaking brilliantly but all too briefly across the sky, the life of Pico della Mirandola embodied the renaissance ideal of the dignity of mankind and the individual's freedom to choose his or her own place in the universe. His introduction of the Kabbalah to renaissance esotericism assured a place for himself in posterity.

Hermetic Kabbalah & The Modern Tree of Life

The kabbalistic ideas introduced by Pico della Mirandola and Reuchlin became the basis of the "Hermetic Kabbalah"—an eclectic blend of Jewish Kabbalah, Hermeticism, Neoplatonism, Christianity, and Renaissance Humanism. Kabbalistic ideas soon became accepted as part of the *priscia theologica*, the tradition of perennial wisdom believed to be handed down by the ancients.[15] The Kabbalah provided a conceptual framework for integrating the Hermetic arts of alchemy, astrology, and magic. Its cosmological glyph—the Tree of Life—provided the roadmap for the magus's journey through the spiritual worlds. This diagram, inherited by modern western esotericism, has become one of its most familiar icons.

The earliest depiction of the Tree of Life glyph was published in 1516 in the book *Portae Lucis* by Paolo Riccio, a latin translation of the *Gates of Light* by Joseph ben Abraham Gikatilla (1248-1325), a Spanish Jewish kabbalist.[16] The familiar modern version of the Tree of Life diagram was published by Jesuit priest Athanasius Kircher, in his book *Oedipus Aegyptiacus*, published in 1652, which combined Kabbala, Hermeticism, and Egyptian mythology.[17] In Kircher's Tree of Life diagram, the ten *sephiroth* described in the *Sepher Yetsira* are linked together by twenty-two "paths"–each assigned a letter of the Hebrew alphabet.

Jewish Kabbalists prior to Kircher had invented many versions of the Tree schema, ranging from linear to circular diagrams. However, they never settled on one definitive form, perhaps observing the biblical commandment to avoid graven images, or preferring not to limit their speculative options? Modern kabbalist Colin Low writes: "It is useful to think of the tree as a higher dimensional construct that cannot be described from a single viewpoint".[18]

The ascent of the Tree of Life is compared to an inner spiritual journey by modern Jewish kabbalist Z'ev ben Shimon Halevi who writes: "Step by step the aspirant slowly climbs the Tree of himself. In this way he continually balances and perfects each stage, passing from sefirah to sefirah...In this way the ascent is safely made from Earth to Heaven while the man is still in the flesh."[19]

Spiritual Alchemy

"Spiritual Alchemy" was another innovative contribution of renaissance Hermeticism. It emphasized the metaphorical language of alchemy in which material substances came to symbolize elements within the constitution of man, and alchemical procedures were seen as taking place within the soul.

Historian of esotericism Joscelyn Godwin explains that in spiritual alchemy the term "crucible" symbolizes the human psycho-physical complex, while "laboratory" refers to the *mundus imaginalis,* the real but non-physical universe in which spiritual transmutations occur. The "fire" of the spiritual alchemist symbolizes his deliberate effort of meditation, and the "bellows" that regulate it, his control of the breath. The "purification of substances" requires control of the wandering mind. At every stage, the alchemist is met with opposing forces that must be dominated, otherwise there is danger of the vessel exploding. The final product of spiritual alchemy is the gold of the transformed self of the alchemist.[20]

The alchemist's work of purifying and refining his soul from its initial state of darkness to its final perfection can be compared to the shaman's initiation—beginning with visions of dismemberment of body and soul, and eventually leading to rebirth and illumination. Psychologist Ralph Metzner insists that *animal spirits* play an important role in alchemy as metaphors for the transformation of consciousness, reminiscent of the shaman's work with their animal spirit-helpers.[21] Each stage of the alchemist's labor was symbolized by specific birds or other animals.

The first stage of alchemy, known as the *Nigredo* or "blackening", is associated with the *raven* and the *toad*. It occurs as the substance is decomposed within the vessel, reduced to the prima materia (prime matter) of dark ashes or formless substance. This stage is destructive in nature and evokes corresponding emotions of sorrow, despair, and depression within the soul of the alchemist—similar to the shaman's experience of death and dismemberment during their initiation. It is also associated with the melancholic planet Saturn and the element of earth.

The next stage, known as the *Albedo* or "whitening" is symbolized by the *white swan*, as well as the element of water and the Moon. At this point the purified matter in the alchemical vessel dissolves into whiteness. It is compared to the dawn after a long, dark night, and the cause for rejoicing and return of hope.

Following this is the *Citrinatis* stage, meaning the "yellowing", also called the *"peacock's tail"*. It is accompanied by a display of rainbow and iridescent hues occurring on the surface of the matter within the vessel, experienced by the alchemist as beautiful luminescent visions; it is associated with the planet Mercury and the element of air.

The final stage, called the *Rubedo* or "reddening", is associated with the *phoenix bird*, the Sun, and the element of fire. It results in the congealing of the matter into a transparent red "philosopher's stone", believed to have the power to transmute base metals into gold. This is the completion of the alchemist's labors, experienced as a rebirth of consciousness.[22] Alchemical scholar Adam McLean writes: "the creation of the Philosopher's stone, was the formation of solid inner ground upon which the alchemical philosophers could build their personalities, and experience the full potentiality of being human".[23]

The alchemist, like the shaman, suffers through stages of psycho-spiritual development or initiation. Both experience cathartic visions of death and rebirth as their souls are purified, transmuted and perfected. The final stage of alchemy, the creation of the philosopher's stone which brings spiritual grounding as well as illumination, has similarities with the transformed spiritual body of the shaman—described as being composed of imperishable materials such as crystals and light. Metzner writes: "alchemy shares with shamanism the goal of consciousness transformation, the quest for healing, knowledge and power".[24]

The "Philosophical Tree" in Alchemy

The symbol of the World Tree appears in renaissance alchemy as the "Arbor Philosophica" or Philosophical Tree. The 16th century Belgian alchemist Gerhard Dorn writes: "...the philosophers compare their material to a golden tree with seven branches, thinking that it encloses in its seed the seven metals, and that these are hidden in it, for which reason they call it a living thing." [25]

In a typical illustration of the Philosophical Tree, the planets, sun, and moon grow in its upper branches as fruit, connected by an upward pointing triangle—the alchemical symbol of the element of fire. The downward pointing "water triangle" shows the three alchemical principles of sulphur-mercury-salt, reflecting in the lower elemental realm the heavenly powers above. The Philosophical Tree with its shining fruit of seven planets also relates to stages of alchemical initiation and transformation, suggested by the youth and old man standing on opposite sides of the tree.

In alchemy, the tree is a symbol of the living cosmos, embodying complementary forces of heaven and earth, sun and moon, fire and water, etc. As well as its obvious similarities to the kabbalistic Tree of Life, the Arbor Philosophica also has parallels to the shaman's World Tree. In some Finno-Ugrian cultures the cosmic tree was depicted with the sun and moon in its branches and located in the center of the world where the sun does not set and the moon always appears full.[26] Similarly, in many illustrations of the Philosophical Tree in alchemical texts, the sun and moon are shown perched symmetrically in its branches.

Divination by Crystals in Renaissance Magic

In the Renaissance era the preferred medium for inducing visions was the crystal ball or magic mirror. Several prominent magicians of the period used crystal gazing to establish contact with angels and other spirits. This method is known as "scrying" derived from the Middle English word *descry* meaning to "see something unclear or distant". Scrying is performed by staring into a luminous, reflective, or translucent surface or focal point until hypnogogic visions seem to appear on its surface or in the "mind's eye". These are similar to the images which spontaneously arise during the state between wakefulness and sleep, which we will later explore.

As previously mentioned, ancient Egyptian, Babylonian and Jewish magicians practiced scrying by gazing into bowls of water, oil, or the flames of lamps. Similarly, Siberian shamans gazed into crystals and circular metal *toli* mirrors to induce trance and clairvoyance.

The Art of Drawing Sprits into Crystals

Johannes Trithemius (1462-1516) was a Benedictine abbot, cryptographer, occultist, and mentor of the renowned occultists Cornelius Agrippa and Paracelsus. He possessed a large collection of magical books and manuscripts and published elements of the magical grimoires in his writings. Trithemius's most well known work is the *Steganographia*, a system of cryptography using magical seals to send messages at a distance by means of angels.

The following experiment in scrying entitled *The Art of Drawing Spirits into Crystals* is attributed to Trithemius. It presents a technique for conjuring planetary angels into a crystal ball for the purpose of providing information to the magician.[27] The text first instructs the magus to procure a clear crystal ball and mount it in a pedestal of pure gold around which the names of the principle angels Michael, Uriel, Raphael and Uriel are inscribed. He must then determine the proper planetary hour of the day corresponding to the specific angel he desires to summon. Then commencing work at this hour, he is advised to pray that his "spiritual eye" may be opened that he may converse with the angelic spirits. The particular angel is then conjured into the crystal ball with the following invocation:

> "...In the name of the blessed and holy Trinity, I do desire thee, thou strong mighty angel, Michael, (Or any other angel or spirit) that if it be the divine will of him who is called Tetragammaton & the Holy God, the Father, that thou take upon thee some shape as best becometh thy celestial nature, and appear to us visibly here in this crystal, and answer our demands in as far as we shall not transgress the bounds of the divine mercy and goodness"....[28]

When the angels finally appear in the crystal, the magus is instructed to take careful notes as to their office, sign, character, and times most agreeable to "hold conference" with them in the future. They must be asked to swear in truth that they are angels, and not deceptive spirits masquerading as them. Assuming they pass the test, the magician then writes down any teachings concerning "life or death, arts or sciences or any other thing" that the divine messengers may reveal. Finally they are dismissed in the names of Jesus Christ, God, the Son, and the Holy Ghost.

The Enochian Magic of Dee & Kelly

"Behold, Lord, how shall I ascend into the heavens?
The air will not carry me, but resisteth my folly.
I fall down, for I am of the earth."
-John Dee

Undoubtedly one of the most fascinating episodes in the history of Renaissance magic resulted from the partnership of Dr. John Dee and Edward Kelly. John Dee (1527-1608) was an Elizabethan scientist and mage, one of the most brilliant men of his age, a true polymath and "renaissance man". His knowledge included mathematics, geometry, astronomy, mechanics, cartography, and navigation, as well as the occult arts of astrology, alchemy and magic.

Dee served as an adviser and tutor to Queen Elizabeth I, even casting the horoscope determining the time of her inauguration ceremony. He devoted his life to the quest for knowledge and possessed one of the largest libraries in Europe. Despairing that his intellectual search left many of his questions unanswered, Dee eventually turned to the practice of magic, believing he could learn the "radical truths" which he sought there. He was inspired by biblical prophets such as Enoch, Moses, Abraham, Solomon and others who were instructed by angels. Dee wrote: "I would never attain wisdom by man's hand or by human power, but only from God, directly or indirectly." [29]

Dee's interest in scrying began in 1581, and during this time he recorded paranormal events such as rapping and knocking in his chamber, and a voice like an owl's shriek. He found his scrying abilities were limited however, and he was unable to perceive spirits on his own. Dee began employing various scrying mediums, finally meeting Edward Kelly. Kelly was a vagabond magician and alchemist of questionable character who had been pilloried for forgery, his ears cropped as punishment. It seems his motive for working with Dee was to use divine aid to discover the philosopher's stone by which he could transmute lead to gold. Dee was initially hesitant about working with Kelly, but the results of their first scrying session were so spectacular he forged a magical partnership with him that would continue for seven years.

The couple's seances would begin with Dee fervently praying while Kelly sat gazing into a crystal ball placed on a central table. Kelly would describe his visions while Dee acted as secretary, meticulously recording them word for word. A remarkably talented psychic, Kelly saw detailed visions of angels and various spirits, as well as complex tables with letters and numbers which he dictated to Dee. The following excerpt is an example of one of Kelly's visions in which an angel is seen pointing out letters from a table :

> "(The angel) hath a rod or wand in his hand...it is of Gold...He standeth upon his round table of cristal or rather Mother of Pearl: There appear an infinite number of letters on the same, as thick as can stand by another...He standeth and pointeth with his rod to the letters of his Table..." [30]

The angels dictated detailed instructions for making a scrying table and a large wax pentacle to be placed in its middle, known as the "Seal of Truth". They also provided specifications for making a magic ring and revealed mystical symbols, seals, and tables of letters from which numerous angelic names were derived. Over time, Kelly and Dee received an entire system of magic from the angels, including the planetary magic of the Mystical Heptarchy, the Thirty Ayres or Aethyrs which concentrically surround the earth, and the Great Table of Watchtowers containing the names of the angels presiding over the four directions of the world.

Forty-eight Angelic Keys or "calls" were also dictated to them by the spirits in the language of angels—popularly known as "Enochian". This constitutes an entire language with its own syntax and vocabulary of several hundred words which have been translated into English. Dee was told it was the primeval language by which God spoke to Adam. The angelic calls are weirdly apocalyptic in style, containing passages of evocative poetic imagery, some of them reminiscent of the biblical *Book of Revelation*.

Many have questioned Kelly's integrity, claiming he was a charlatan, psychotic, and plagiarist who fabricated his visions to please his employer Dee. Enochian scholar Geoffrey James addresses these doubts, pointing out that the information dictated to Kelly was far too complex for him to have memorized it from other sources:

> "A serious objection to the theory that Kelly plagiarized visions is the way that the keys were revealed. The first five keys were dictated, letter by letter, backwards, while the rest were dictated forwards, without any significant errors. The bulk of the keys (over 1,000 words) were dictated on a single day during a single session. Most of the English glosses were dictated on a single day, well after the Angelical, yet they match their Angelical counterparts almost perfectly. Kelly would have had to be capable of extraordinary feats of mnemonic virtuosity, if he utilized another magical text as source material for the keys." [31]

As well as the visions, paranormal events would sometimes occur during the duo's seances. Dee records one such occasion during which he witnessed a telekinetic phenomenon—a crystal stone floating in mid air: "There appeared a great flame of fire in the principal Stone...Suddenly one seemed to come in at the fourth window of the Chappel...the stone was heaved up a handful high and set down again."

Following the advice of the angels, Dee and Kelly embarked on travels around Europe, visiting the courts of royalty including the Holy Roman Emperor Rudolph II in Prague. Rudolph (1552-1612) was an eccentric ruler, a patron of the arts, science, and the occult, and a firm believer in astrology and alchemy. Rudolph's lifelong quest was to discover the alchemist's Philosopher's Stone, and with this goal in mind he performed his own experiments in a private alchemical laboratory.[32] The emperor's court became a mecca for alchemical, astrological, and magico-scientific studies, and he spared no expenses bringing alchemists such as Dee and Kelly to it. Dee was told by the angels that he had to personally deliver a message to Rudolph, the most powerful man in Europe, "rebuking" him for his sins. The Emperor calmly received this angelical chastisement, but later at the prompting of a papal envoy expelled Dee and

Kelly from Prague.

Perhaps the most bizarre spiritual communication received by Kelly and Dee was from the angel Madimi, who commanded them to engage in sexual relations with each other's wives. None of the parties in this divinely inspired wife-swap were pleased with the arrangement, but obeyed the angel's orders nevertheless. Following this escapade, Dee ended the spiritual conferences with the angels. Some have speculated the incident may have been a ruse used by Kelly to break up his partnership with Dee, since Kelly was becoming increasingly famous as an alchemist, finding Dee's company a hindrance. The two parted ways in 1589 and Kelly went on to become wealthy through his alchemical work, and was even knighted by Rudoph II. Kelly fell out of favor however, and was eventually accused of murder and imprisoned in a castle in Bohemia. It is suspected the emperor may have jailed him to prevent him from leaving the kingdom with his valuable alchemical knowledge. Kelly apparently died jumping out of his prison window attempting to escape.

Dee did not fare much better. He returned to England where he found his house ransacked and his library burnt by a mob who accused him of being a necromancer. Soon after he was devastated by the loss of his wife and five of his eight children to the plague. Despite his appointment to a position as warden at a college, he received no support from the currently reigning monarch King James I. Dee died in poverty at the age of eighty-one. Although he failed to accomplish his mission of bringing about the moral and spiritual transformation Europe through his magic and alchemy, Dee nevertheless planted the seeds of the Rosicrucian movement during his travels there, in the opinion of historian Frances Yates.[33]

Ironically, there are no records of Dee or Kelly ever practicing the system of magic they labored so diligently to receive from the angels. Many of Dee's magical manuscripts survived however, and were used by the founders of the nineteenth century Hermetic Order of the Golden Dawn, who incorporated parts of them into their syncretic system of magic. Later, the notorious magician Aleister Crowley scryed the thirty Aethyrs of the Enochian tablets, and popularized other aspects of the system. Enochian magic continues to be used by practitioners of ritual magic in this day and age.

The Travels of Paracelsus

"Bomabastus kept a devil's bird
Shut in the pommel of his sword,
That taught him all the cunning pranks

Of past and future mountebanks"
-Samuel Butler 1664

One of the most influential occultists of the late Renaissance period was Phillipus Aureolus Theophrastus Bombastus von Hohenheim, (1493-1541) otherwise known as Paracelsus. He was a Swiss-German physician, alchemist, botanist, astrologer, magician and lay preacher, a genius and reformer whose revolutionary ideas were ahead of his time. Unfortunately he lacked patience for those who questioned his ideas, and his legendary "bombastic" tirades against his opponents alienated everyone around him, including his supporters. Paracelsus was often contemptuous of the medical practices of his day, burning the writings of esteemed physicians such as Avicenna and Galen. He insisted medicine be based on observation and experimentation rather than dogma.

In his youth Paracelsus traveled widely throughout Europe, Central Asia, the Holy Land and Egypt, seeking to expand his knowledge of medicine and healing. He writes: "I went not only to the doctors but also to the barbers, bath keepers, learned physicians, women, and magicians who pursue the art of healing; I went to alchemists, to monasteries, to noble and common folk, to the experts and the simple".[34] While in Russia, Paracelsus was taken prisoner by the Tartars, where he became a favorite at the court of their leader, the Grand Cham. There he demonstrated his skills in surgery and medicine, while at the same time observing the shamanic medicine of his hosts. He admiringly writes that their healing was rooted in "faith and imagination" as well as herbal remedies. It is even rumored that he undertook a shamanistic initiation rite while among the Tartars.[35] Paracelsus later travelled to Constantinople where it is claimed he witnessed the making of the alchemical philosopher's stone. Following this he travelled to Egypt where he cryptically writes he received "magical instructions".

Paracelsus spent his later years wandering through small villages and towns of Central Europe working as an itinerant healer. So remarkable were his healing abilities he developed the reputation of being a wonder-worker. Often impoverished, he occasionally relied on his alchemical knowledge of manufacturing gold to survive. His assistant witnessed Paracelsus transmuting a pound of mercury bought at an apothecary into gold. It was later tested by a goldsmith to be genuine and exchanged for a purse full of Rhenish guilders.[36]

In his book *On Nymphs, Sylphs, Pygmies and Salamanders,* Paracelsus was the first to write about the "elemental spirits", the spiritual inhabitants of the four elements of fire, air, water and earth. He insisted that these spirits of nature are *not* demons and agents of the devil, as believed by the church. Instead, he reasoned, they could be good or bad, similar to man. According to Paracelsus these beings differed in one aspect from humans—they have no souls—and thus no prospect for eternal life, and because of this they crave the company of mankind. Paracelsus writes: "When they enter into a union with man, then the union gives them soul." [37] Some of these spirits such as the nymphs resemble humans, thus marriages between them and men are not uncommon, claims Paracelsus. As discussed previously, such "marriages" between spirits and humans are widely mentioned in folklore around the world; they are intentionally consummated by some tribal shamans who rely on their spirit spouses as "tutelary spirits". The elemental spirits which Paracelsus introduced figure prominently in the theory and practice of modern western magic.

Paracelsus also introduced the notion of the healing power of imagination—which he may have learned from Tartar shamans. He was the first to use the word "unconscious" in his writings, and to espouse the idea of the psychological origin of some diseases.[38] His original ideas regarding medicine, psychology, alchemy, astrology and magic were highly influential, spreading throughout Europe. He anticipated many ideas of modern medicine and toxicology as well as alternative healing practices such as homeopathy.

Paracelsus also published a book *The Archidoxes of Magic,* containing designs for a number of magical talismans for medical purposes. However he denounced magicians who conjured spirits as "arch-Fools, and ignorant men of no worth!", insisting conjurations are "against God, and are contrary to his word".

Agrippa's "Three Books"
Paracelsus's contemporary, Heinrich Cornelius Agrippa von Nettlesheim (1486-1535), was perhaps the most renowned magician of his day. Agrippa travelled widely during his lifetime, serving as a court physician and astrologer in several royal courts around Europe. While in Italy he studied the works of Ficino and Pico. His writings are influenced by classical writers and the philosophies of Neoplatonism and Hermeticism, the Italian Renaissance thinkers, Jewish Kabbalah, and the Arabic astrological magic of the *Picatrix*. Agrippa was mentored in the magical arts by abbot Trithemius, from whom he inherited a large collection of magical books. In turn he dedicated his influential masterpiece *Three Books of Occult Philosophy* to Trithemius. Agrippa writes in the introduction: "Magic is a faculty of wonderful virtue, full of most high mysteries, containing the most profound contemplation of most secret things..." [39] The book's stated purpose is to "redeem ancient magic and the learning of all wise men from impious error". It is aptly described by author Donald Tyson as "the single most important text in the history of western occultism".

Each book in the *Three Books of Occult Philosophy* concerns a different "world": Book One addresses the magic of the "Elementary World" of stones, herbs, trees, metals, etc.; Book Two examines the "Celestial World" of mathematics, geometry and the influence of the planets and stars in magic; Book Three concerns the "Intellectual World" of pagan gods, angels, spirits, devils, and the magical methods for contacting these beings.

In Book Three, Agrippa devotes four chapters to different kinds of "divine phrensy", describing the rapture that occurs when the soul "flyeth forth of the body to the supercelestial habitations..filled with divine light and oracles." [40] He reveals his familiarity with the trance journeys of Sami shamans, writing: "... there are even to this day in Norway and Lapland very many who can abstract themselves three whole days from their body, and being returned declare many things which are afar off..."

By the time he had published his massive tome in 1533 Agrippa had already distanced himself from it, blaming the book on the "vanities" of his "curious youth", perhaps in a preemptive attempt to deflect attacks by the Church. His name nevertheless became associated with diabolical legends which rivaled even those of Paracelsus.

Despite the denunciations by both Agrippa and Paracelsus against demonic magic, they became reviled by the superstitious public as "black magicians". Rumors circulated that Agrippa kept a demonic familiar in the form of a black dog, said to inform him of events in distant lands. Likewise the followers of Paracelsus had to fend off accusations that he trafficked with demons. Their lives offer intriguing parallels, according to Phillip Ball. Both were descended from noble German families and studied medicine. They both travelled widely in search of learning. They were iconoclasts who challenged the authorities with their original ideas influenced by Hermeticism, and were condemned by them in return. Both were also apparently mentored in the magical and alchemical arts by Abbot Trithemius. Clearly they knew of each other—though there is no record of them ever meeting.[41]

The writings of Paracelsus and Agrippa appealed to a Protestant public interested in prophecy and personal revelation, as they promised "direct celestial communication" by providing the keys to the angelic and spiritual hierarchies, according to Owen Davies.[42] Their books spread the philosophy of Hermeticism throughout Northern Europe, influencing future generations of magicians and alchemists.

Rosicrucianism

By the early 17th century, as the enlightenment of the Italian Renaissance had faded, Rosicrucianism appeared in Northern Europe, reviving Hermeticism and laying the groundwork for future esoteric movements. This began suddenly in Cassel, Germany in 1614, with the public posting of a pamphlet written in obscure hermetic and astrological language entitled the *Fama Fraternitas* or "The Fame of the Brotherhood". It announced the existence of a formerly secret society, "The Fraternity of the Rosy Cross" — also known as Rosicrucianism — claiming it promoted the religious, social, and scientific reformation of Europe.

The *Fama Fraternitas* told the story of Christian Rosenkreutz, who travelled in his youth to the mystic east, to Arabia, Morocco, and the fabled city of Damcar in search of hidden knowledge, returning to Europe with the hope of reforming Christendom. In his travels he was joined by followers, but finding his efforts scorned, Rosenkreutz decided to build a temple to preserve his knowledge. He died in 1484 according to the pamphlet, which claimed his uncorrupted body was rediscovered in a seven-sided vault in 1604, a year heralded by celestial omens. Within the tomb were allegedly found a number of mechanical marvels as well as alchemical works by Paracelsus. The tomb's discovery signaled the renewal of Rosenkreutz's mission to reform the world.

The apparent discovery of Paracelsus's works in the vault is intriguing and has led some to speculate that the mythical founder of the movement, Christian Rosenkreutz, was none other than Paracelsus himself.[43] The parallels between their lives are obvious: both engaged in youthful journeys to the mystic east in quest of spiritual knowledge, and upon returning home were met with scorn. Both were alchemists and healers. On the other hand, Francis Yates sees John Dee as the possible progenitor of the movement, writing: "influences from Dee's mission in Bohemia may have percolated to the German Rosicrucian movement." [44]

The posting of the *Fama Fraternitas* set off a "Rosicrucian furore" of people searching for the society to join its ranks. It was so difficult to locate the Rosicrucians they soon came to be called the "Invisibles", and many concluded they were a hoax.[45] Johann Valentin Andreae, a Lutheran pastor, finally confessed he had authored one of the pamphlets, *The Chemical Wedding of Christian Rosenkreutz*, in 1616, which he called a "ludibrium" which translates as a "serious joke". Tobias Churton describes the pamphlets as "the greatest publicity stunt of all time" and the "first multi-national conspiracy theory in Europe". He insists that the purpose of the Rosicrucian manifestoes was to provoke debate on fundamental issues regarding the nature and orientation of science and religion, reviving the spirit of the Renaissance by introducing a second reformation of learning and religion.[46]

The Chymical Wedding of Christian Rosenkreutz

The Chymical Wedding of Christian Rosenkreutz is an adventure story as well as an allegory of the soul's journey of spiritual transformation. Based on alchemical and astrological symbolism, it has seven chapters and takes place over a period of seven days—utilizing the symbolism of the seven planets and seven stages of alchemical transformation.

The story begins as Christian Rosenkreutz, the protagonist of the story, is visited by an angel who delivers him an invitation to a royal wedding. In answer to his doubts as to his worthiness to attend the event, Christian has a dream of being imprisoned in a dark dungeon with other suffering souls; a rope is thrown down and he is freed, which he takes as a sign from providence that he should accept the invitation. He sets out on his journey, finally arriving at the king's castle where he witnesses many marvels. In one of these, he is led up a staircase and given a glimpse of the king and queen, in a vision reminiscent of the heavenly ascents of mystics:

> "There the Virgin led us together with the music, up three hundred and sixty five stairs...at the top we came under a painted arch, where the sixty virgins attended us, all richly apparelled....Meanwhile a curtain was drawn up, where I saw the King and Queen as they sat there in their majesty...I should have forgotten myself, and have equalled this unspeakable glory to Heaven. For besides that the room glistered of mere gold and precious stones; the Queen's robes were moreover so made that I was not able to behold them...here all things so much surpassed the rest, as the stars in heaven are elevated." [47]

Within the castle Christian undergoes various trials, including an initiation ordeal. Later he witnesses a morbid drama in which three kings and their queens, as well as a black "moor" are beheaded. He assists in the work of dissolving their corpses and regenerating them in new bodies in the alchemical laboratory of the seven floored Tower of Olympus. This bizarre alchemical operation has uncanny parallels to the shaman's initiation with its themes of death, dismemberment and rebirth. On another day while exploring the king's castle, Christian's page leads him "down certain steps underground" to a cellar and a mysterious chamber:

> "Herewith I espied a rich bed ready made, hung about with curious curtains,

one of which he drew, where I saw the Lady Venus stark-naked...lying there in such beauty, and a fashion so surprising, that I was almost besides myself, neither do I know whether it was a piece thus carved, or a human corpse that lay dead there. For she was altogether immovable, and yet I durst not touch her...." [48]

Lady Venus was much beloved by Renaissance alchemists as "Dame Nature" whose secrets they hoped to unveil. The greatest of these was the mystery of resurrection and eternal life, for nature continually dies and is reborn. Laying corpse-like in her underground sepulcher, Lady Venus is eerily reminiscent of the goddesses Inanna or Ishtar, also associated with the planet venus, who were reduced to corpses in the underworld before being magically resurrected to life. The iconic symbol of Venus, the *rose,* was combined with the *cross* to create the emblem of Rosicrucianism—the "rosy-cross"—symbolizing the merging of pagan and Christian mysteries into a new Hermetic revelation.

Although the Rosicrucian manifestoes were eventually exposed as fictions, the power of myths to shape history should not be underestimated. The legend of Christian Rosencreutz and his mystical brotherhood helped spread the teachings of Hermeticism, inspiring the works of alchemists and scholars such as Michael Maier, Robert Fludd, and Isaac Newton. From the 17th century to the present day, various esoteric orders have incorporated Rosicrucian symbolism into their grade rituals and teachings. Many Freemasons became Rosicrucians, and Rosicrucianism in turn inspired groups such as the Hermetic Order of the Golden Dawn and other occult organizations of the nineteenth and twentieth century, which will later be discussed.

Hermeticism & the Rise of Modern Science

The philosophy of Hermeticism which championed the dignity of man, freedom of thought, and the study of nature went hand in hand with the development of modern science. Historian Frances Yates insists the Renaissance magus exemplified the new attitude of mankind to the cosmos, necessary for the rise of modern science.[49] Early scientists such as Paracelsus, Dee, Bruno, Campanella, Boyle, Fludd, Kepler, and Newton engaged in Hermetic pursuits as well. Isaac Newton was a passionate alchemist in his earlier years and wrote voluminously on his alchemical work—a fact which historians of science have chosen to ignore until recently. His theory of universal gravity was in fact inspired by discoveries made during his alchemical experiments. Historian B. Y.T. Dobbs writes: "Newton strove to integrate alchemical and hermetic ideas with the mechanical philosophies of the day".[50]

The Hermetic philosophers who pioneered modern science through their investigations of the mysteries of nature were driven primarily by a spiritual quest. In the *Corpus Hermeticum* the world is seen as the body of god, and man's role is to govern and actively participate in god's creation through the performance of magic. The magician experimented to discover the magical signatures and symbols linking together heaven and earth through occult sympathy.[51] Alchemists such as Paracelsus stressed the importance of the observation of nature and performed experiments on plants and minerals. For Paracelsus and his followers science became the search for God.[52]

The Hermeticists believed the universe was an organism, and nature was seen as alive. The Italian Renaissance artist and inventor Leonardo Di Vinci voiced this animistic understanding: "We can say that the earth has a vegetative soul, and that its flesh is the land, its bones are the structure of the rocks...its breathing and its pulse are the ebb and flow of the sea".[53] Biologist Rupert Sheldrake insists that such animistic views persisted in Christianity as well. He notes that although the Judeo-Christian traditions emphasized the male god, mother earth still retained some of her old autonomy throughout the Middle Ages. Medieval Christians continued to regard nature as "animate and motherlike".[54]

Sheldrake argues that the complete suppression of the holy mother's cult occurred during the Protestant Reformation. The "desacralization" of nature occurred later in the seventeenth century with the rise of mechanistic science. He writes:

"Nature became nothing but inanimate matter in motion, created by god and mechanically obedient to his eternal laws. Nature was no longer acknowledged as mother, and no longer considered alive. She became the world-machine, and god the all-powerful engineer. Ironically, the idea that nature functioned mechanically and automatically rendered god increasingly superfluous, and by the late 18th century, he was fading away from the scientific worldview..." [55]

With the ascent of *scientific materialism*, Hermeticism fell out of fashion along with the age-old animistic worldview. The ancient notion of the World Soul was replaced with the scientific view of nature as a machine, operating by the laws of mechanics. The Reformation led to a "contraction of the spiritual realm", according to Sheldrake, and the "withdrawal of spirit from the operations of nature". Spirituality became concentrated within human beings exclusively, as nature was "de-animated". The human soul was finally eliminated all together from the equation as modern secular humanists ceased to believe in its existence all together.

The Enlightenment era, characterized by revolutions in science, philosophy, politics and society, also challenged the authority of the Church. The modern age which it ushered in led to the decline of orthodox religion, yet ironically brought about a resurgence of esoteric spirituality.

Freemasonry—Carving the Rough Ashlar

Gaining popularity during the enlightenment era and scientific revolution, Freemasonry kept the ancient ideals of western esotericism alive. Joscelyn Godwin writes that Freemasonry "was the most lasting creation of the Hermetic tradition of the West, carrying it through the era of skepticism and scientism." [56] Because Hermeticism is cosmological and practical in emphasis rather than theological, it could co-exist with any religion. The teachings of Freemasonry reflect the tolerance of a diversity of religious beliefs of its members, requiring of them only to believe in God. It should not be forgotten that many of the signers of the constitution of the United States, including George Washington, were high ranking Freemasons. Their masonic ideals of freedom of religion and separation of church and state became guiding principles of the new American democracy.

The origins of Freemasonry are obscure, but clearly based on Hermetic philosophy and Pythagorean number mysticism and sacred geometry. Some historians claim it developed as an offshoot of Rosicrucianism. Others see its origins in the stonemason's guilds of the medieval cathedrals. Some trace it to the Knight's Templar, the mysterious order of Christian knights stationed in Jerusalem during the Second Crusade in the 12th century CE, who claim they discovered the ruins of Solomon's Temple and its secrets. In the founding myth of Freemasonry, Hiram Abif, the first grand master and architect of King Solomon's temple, was murdered by lower grade masons when he refused to reveal the secret "Mason's Word" to them. Others place Freemasonry's origins in antediluvian times, before the flood, claiming Hermes Trismegistus learned his knowledge from the first masons.[57] Manly P. Hall claims there is a "definite correspondence between the Hiramic legend of Freemasonry and the Osiris myth as expounded in the initiation rituals of the Egyptians." [58]

Freemasonic lodges are structured in three degrees—Entered Apprentice, Fellowcraft, and and Master Mason—emphasizing the theme of advancement or ascent through the grades. These correspond to the progressive moral perfection of the initiate, symbolized as the carving of the rough ashlar stone into the perfect ashlar.

The *first degree* initiation ceremony consists of leading the candidate blindfolded, with a rope around his neck and left arm and shirt opened, into the temple. There he circumambulates three times, after which he is given basic teachings about the order. The central symbol of the *second degree* of Masonry is the "winding staircase" consisting of three, five, or seven steps which ascend to the middle chamber of the temple. These steps are seen as the "theological ladder" of seven steps. They represent the virtues of faith, hope and charity, as well as the four cardinal virtues of temperance, fortitude, prudence and justice. Masonic historian H. L. Haywood writes: "this ladder was made to stand for the progress of the soul from the earthly to the heavenly".[59] It is compared to the ladder in Jacob's dream in the Bible on which angels ascended and descended. In ancient mystery religions like Mithraism, the ladder was also a symbol of initiation and the descent and ascent of the soul. *The Egyptian Book of the Dead* describes a ladder on which souls climbed to heaven from the underworld. In the initiations of shamans they climbed ladder-like poles representing the World Tree, experiencing visionary ascents to the heavens. During the final *third degree* initiation, the Freemason undergoes a symbolic death, burial, and raising, impersonating Hiram Abif the Master Mason, who like Osiris was murdered and resurrected.

The initiate in Freemasonry experiences symbolic ordeals as he moves through the grades, beginning with being bound and blindfolded, then climbing a staircase or ladder—and finally a ritualized death and resurrection. The progression from darkness, followed by ascent, resurrection, and emergence into the light follows the mythical pattern of initiations in the ancient mystery schools, as well as shamanic initiations.

Swedenborg—The Man Who Talked with Angels

"...it has been granted me to associate with angels and to converse with them as one man with another, and also to see things which are in the heavens as well as those which are in the hells..."
-Emmanuel Swedenborg

Emmanuel Swedenborg (1688-1772), was a Swedish scientist and visionary whose life story epitomized the struggle between science and religion during the Age of Enlightenment. He was a polymath, a scientist, biblical scholar, statesman, poet, and inventor in his youth who became a mystic in his later years, a clairvoyant whose writings describe his visions of heaven and hell, conversations with angels, demons, and spirits of the dead as well as visionary travels to other planets.

As a young man Swedenborg ambitiously pursued the study of science, making important contributions to the natural sciences as well as psychology. Among his many ingenious inventions were plans for a flying machine, a submarine, and water clocks. Although he was a devout Christian, he maintained a lifelong interest in esotericism, studying subjects such as Rosicrucianism, Freemasonry, and Christian Cabala.[60]

At the age of fifty-six, Swedenborg experienced a religious crisis that radically changed the direction of his life, a spontaneous spiritual awakening which he believed was brought about by the "spirit of God", accompanied by inner purification and illumination. For weeks he suffered fainting fits, trembling, and shivering from head to feet, accompanied by feelings of "wonderful and indescribable upheavals" and "indescribable delight". These fluctuated with feelings of feelings of torment, unworthiness, and guilt, and were accompanied by vivid dreams and visions.[61]

Swedenborg's intense experiences are curiously similar to the transformational crisis known as the "dark night of the soul" by western mystics, or the "kundalini awakening" of yoga practitioners. Psychologists Stansilav and Christina Grof have coined the phrase "spiritual emergency" to describe such experiences in which the *kundalini* force, the primal energy at the base of the spine, suddenly arouses in an individual. This unexpected awakening often brings about a spiritual crisis — along with intense emotions, sensory and physical changes, visions, etc. The spiritual emergency is also strikingly similar to the initiation experiences of shamans in which they suffer torments as well as ecstasy. The Grofs describe the effects of the "shamanic crisis": "In most cases the experience of being resurrected after terrible torments, sickness, and near-death is accompanied a feeling of euphoria, because the suffering has annihilated all former characteristics of the personality. The sickness is a cleansing process that washes away all that is bad, pitiful, and weak".[62]

Similarly, Swedenborg described his spiritual crisis as one of inner struggle, exhilaration and purification during which egotism, ambition, arrogance, and selfish pride were purged from his personality. The dramatic climax of Swedenborg's ordeal occurred one evening when he tumbled out of bed and experienced a vision of lying on Christ's bosom "face to face". Goodricke-Clarke writes: "This vision brought about the decisive turning point of his life. Until now Swedenborg had striven for scientific knowledge...but now it was plain to him; one cannot achieve fulfillment and bliss through the understanding of science but only through the understanding of salvation." [63]

During his crisis Swedenborg had dreams and visions of the spiritual realms which he believed were sent to him from God, preparing for the advent of a spiritual community that would supersede the dogmatic teachings of the Church. His new spiritual mission aroused the scorn of his scientific colleagues however, and the great Enlightenment philosopher Emmanuel Kant ridiculed Swedenborg in his book *Dreams of a Prophet Seer*. Other opponents, including clerics, tried unsuccessfully to declare him insane and have him committed to a mental institution.

Following his spiritual awakening, Swedenborg's "interior faculties" were opened and he developed remarkable clairvoyant and precognitive abilities. Once at a dinner party he announced that a fire had broken out in a town 300 miles away, and then reported it had been extinguished—events which were later confirmed to have occurred exactly as he described.

Visions were often revealed to Swedenborg while studying the Bible, during which time angels and spirits elucidated the holy scriptures for him. Swedenborg explains that his writings were inspired by the spirits, to the extent that he became their "instrument" in the delivery of spiritual truths to mankind. He writes: "Yes, I have written whole pages, and the spirits did not just dictate the words, but wholly guided my hand and thus wrote themselves.." He claimed to converse with biblical personalities such as Abraham, Moses, Solomon, and the saints. Visions frequently occurred to Swedenborg in the morning during the state between sleeping and waking which displayed vivid hypnogogic characteristics. He describes one such vision:

> "When I awoke from sleep, I sank into a deep reflection about God; and as I looked up, I saw above me in the sky a blinding light, it withdrew to the sides and dissolved in circles of light. And, lo, heaven stood open to me, and I beheld marvelous things. Angels stood in a circular formation at the zenith of the opening. They conversed with each other; and because I was burning with a desire to know what they were saying, I was permitted to hear the sound of their voices, which was full of heavenly love..." [64]

In his book *Heaven and Hell*, Swedenborg describes in detail the soul's afterlife existence. He writes that there are three heavens and three hells—and between them an intermediate world of newly deceased spirits who have not yet transitioned to either realm. He writes: "after death we enjoy every sense, memory, thought and affection we had in the world. We leave nothing behind except our earthly body".[65] Swedenborg writes about the stages the soul goes through while dying. Dr. Raymond Moody, who recorded many accounts of near-death experiences of modern people, insists that Swedenborg's descriptions are remarkably similar to theirs, including "out-of-body experiences", encounters with angels, meetings with spirits of departed friends, life reviews, etc.[66] Swedenborg explains that a person's afterlife existence reflects their innermost intentions, thoughts and affections: "....our nature after death depends on the kind of life we led in the world." Virtuous persons who cultivated selflessness, love of goodness, and truth during their lives become angels after death, while people involved in self-love, contempt of others, and deceit become demons.

The spirit world envisioned by Swedenborg was comprised of seven concentric spheres inhabited by beings of increasing spiritual advancement.[67] The geographies of the different levels of heaven and hell reflect the inner spiritual states of their inhabitants. In heaven people live in communities similar to those they inhabited on earth, yet more beautiful, complete with city streets, public squares, flower beds and courtyards, suites and chambers. They pursue similar activities as during life and continually learn and grow in perfection. The spirits of hell, on the other hand inhabit the ruins of burnt out cities, crude huts with alleyways, and streets full of thieves and robbers where they are subject to constant quarreling, hostility, beatings and violence.

In his book *Earths in the Universe,* Swedenborg recounts his visionary voyages to other planets within and beyond our solar system, and his conversations with spirits who dwell there.[68] The belief that other planets than our own were inhabited was not unique to him, it was also held by great intellects of the time including Emmanuel Kant and William Herschel. Their notions were likely inherited from the older cosmology of Hermeticism in which deities, angels, and spirits were associated with particular planets and stars. Indeed, Swedenborg's descriptions of the spirits of other planets may have been influenced by astrological character types: the spirits of Mercury excel in knowledge, the spirits of Jupiter are distinguished by their exceeding cheerfulness and inner happiness, while those of Saturn are described as self-effacing and restrained.

Rather than limiting his imaginal travels to the planets of our solar system, Swedenborg writes how he travelled for hours on end through the "starry sky" to visit the spirits who inhabit the worlds which orbit other stars, providing a travelogue of their beliefs and customs, habitations, flora and fauna. Swedenborg in his visionary travels anticipated the modern literary genre of science fiction as well as New-Age channeling of extraterrestrials. All of the spirits inhabiting the universe were seen by him as constituting parts in the body of the "Grand Man", a notion strikingly similar to the kabbalistic concept of Adam Kadmon, the primordial archetype of humanity.

Swedenborg the visionary, like mystics and shamans before him, explored the otherworld and the soul's afterlife existence. His work which combines natural philosophy with revelation profoundly influenced generations of modern spiritualists and occultists who followed in his footsteps. Before we explore their work, however, we return to an often overlooked yet essential thread in the tapestry of western esotericism—the enduring pagan magical traditions of rural Europe.

Chapter 14 Notes

Rose-cross—the symbol of Rosicrucianism—showing rose combined with symbol of Venus, from Summom Bonum, Robert Fludd 1629.

1. Lachman. The Quest of Hermes Trismegistus. 2001: 132.
2. Yates, Frances, Amelia. Giordano Bruno and the Hermetic Tradition. Yeats 1991: 104.
3. Walker, D.P. Spiritual and demonic magic from Ficino to Campanella. 2000: 60.
4. Goodrick-Clarke. *The Western Esoteric Traditions*. 2008: 41.
5. Walker. Spiritual and demonic magic from Ficino to Campanella. 2000:12-23.
6. Ficino, Marsilio. Three Books on Life: A Critical Edition and Translation with Introduction and Notes, by   Kaske, Carol V. and Clark, John R. Binghamton. 1989.

7. Walker. Spiritual and demonic magic from Ficino to Campanella. 2000: 32-33.
8. Voss, Angela. Allen, Michael J.B.; Rees, Valery; Davies, Martin; (eds.) Marsilio Ficino: His Theology, His Philosophy, His Legacy. 2001:230.
9. Mebane, John S. Renaissance Magic & the Return of the Golden Age. 1989: 35.
10. Lachman. The Quest of Hermes Trismegistus. 2001: 139.
11. Pico placed the Father on Kether, the Son on Chockmah and the Holy Ghost on Binah on the kabbalistic Tree of Life—as well as the name of Jesus on the central sphere of Tipareth.
12. Copenhaver, Brian, "Giovanni Pico della Mirandola", The Stanford Encyclopedia of Philosophy (Summer 2012 Edition), Edward N. Zalta (ed.)
13. Mirandola, Pico della. On The Dignity of Man.(trans. Wallis, Charles Glenn; Miller, Paul J.W.; Carmichael, Douglas.1965: 7.
14. Copenhaver, Brian, "Giovanni Pico della Mirandola", The Stanford Encyclopedia of Philosophy.
15. The compatibility of kabbalah and Hermeticism is not at all surprising since Jewish mystics of antiquity absorbed elements of Pythagoreanism, Gnosticism, and Neoplatonism which are reflected in texts such as the Sepher Yetsirah, Bahir, and Zohar, from which the Kabbalah later developed.
16. Colin Low. "The Tree if life." Hermetic Kabbalah. http://www.digital-brilliance.com/
17. Hedrick, Bill. "Athanasius Kircher's Oedipus Aegyptiacus".Bill Hedrick''s "Cross References".
18. Colin Low. "The Tree of Life". Hermetic Kabbalah.
19. Halevi, Z'ev ben Shimon. Adam and the Kabbalistic Tree. 1989: 223.
20. Godwin, Joscelyn. The Golden Thread. 2007: 118.
21. Metzner, Ralph. "Shamanism, Alchemy & Yoga:Traditional Technologies of Transformation". Green Earth Foundation.1987.
22. It should be noted that different alchemical texts and authors categorize the stages differently, ranging from 3 stages to as many as seven stages of transformation, corresponding to the seven planets.
23. McLean, Adam. "Animal Symbolism in the Alchemical Tradition". The Alchemy Website.
24. Metzner. "Shamanism, Alchemy & Yoga:Traditional Technologies of Transformation". 1987.
25. Jung, C.G. Alchemical Studies. Vol. 13. 1983:289.
26. Walter & Fridman. *Shamanism: An Encyclopedia of World Beliefs, Practices and Culture*, Vol.1. 2004: 488.
27. Peterson 1997. "Johannes Trithemius: the art of drawing spirits into crystals." Twilit Grotto-Esoteric Archives. Originally published in"The Magus" by Francis Barrett, (1801).
28. Ibid.
29. James, Geoffrey. (ed. & trans.) The Enochian Magic of Dr. John Dee. 2009: xiv.
30. Ibid.: xxiii.

31. Ibid.: xxi.
32. Marshall, Peter. The Mercurial Emperor: The Magic Circle of Rudolph II in Renaissance Prague. 2007: 129.
33. Yates, Frances Amelia. The Rosicrucian Enlightenment. 1972: 135.
34. Ball, Phillip. The Devil's Doctor- Paracelus and the World of Renaissance Magic and Science. 2006: 78.
35. Ibid.:96.
36. Ibid.:138.
37. Ibid.:306.
38. Ehrenwald, Jan. The History of Psychotherapy: From Healing Magic to Encounter. 1976: 200.
39. Agrippa von Nettlesheim, Heinrich Cornelius; (ed.) Tyson, Donald; Freake, James. Three Books of Occult Philosophy.
40. Ibid.:629.
41. Ball. The Devil's Doctor- Paracelus and the World of Renaissance Magic and Science. 2006: 83.
42. Davies. Grimoires: A History of Magic Books. 2009: 53.
43. Ball. The Devil's Doctor- Paracelus and the World of Renaissance Magic and Science. 2006: 373.
44. Yates. The Rosicrucian Enlightenment. 1972: 135.
45. Lachman. The Quest for Hermes Trismegistus. 2001: 178.
46. Churton, Tobias. The Golden Builders- Alchemists, Rosicrucians and the First Freemasons. Chap. 9: 2005.
47. Andreae, Johann Valentin. (1616) "The Chymical Wedding of Christian Rosenkreutz". The Alchemy Website on Levity.com. (ed.) Adam McLean; Deirdre Green, 1984.
48. Ibid.
49. Frances Yates, *Giordano Bruno and the Hermetic Tradition*, Routledge, London and New York, 1964.
50. Dobbs, Beth Jo Teeter. The Foundation of Newton's Alchemy: or,"The hunting of the green lyon". 1986: xii.
51. Hall, A.R. The Revolution in Science 1500-1750. 1983: 4.
52. Debus, Allen, G. Man & Nature in the Renaissance. 1978: 50-51.
53. Sheldrake, Rupert. The Rebirth of Nature: the greening of science and God. 1991:20-28.
54. Ibid.:20-28.
55. Ibid:20.
56. Godwin, Joscelyn. The Golden Thread. 2007: 15.
57. Lachman. The Quest for Hermes Trismegistus. 2001: 191.
58. Hall, Manly P. The Secret Teachings of All Ages. 2006: 91.
59. Haywood, H.L. "Symbolical Masonry". Sacredtexts.com. Haywood 1923.
60. Goodrick-Clarke, Nicholas. The Western Esoteric Traditions. 2008: xvii.
61. Ibid.:166-167.
62. Grof, Stanislav & Christina. "Spiritual Emergency: Understanding and Treatment of Psychospiritual crises". Reality sandwich.com. 2008.
63. Goodricke-Clarke. The Western Esoteric Traditions. 2008: 172.

64. Ibid.:262-299.
65. Swedenborg, Emmanuel. Heaven and its wonders and hell: drawn from things heard and seen. (trans.) Dole, George F.; Lang, Bernhard, and others. 2000: 348-358.
66. Moody, Raymond A. Life After Life: the investigation of a phenomenon—survival of bodily death. 1975: 118.
67. Cox, Robert S. Body and Soul A Sympathetic History of American Spiritualism. 2003:10.
68. Swedenborg, Emanuel. "Earths in the Universe". Swedenborg.com. 2006.

Chapter 15:
Survival of Pagan Magic in Modern Europe

Witches and devil in flight. Woodcut from
Wonders of the Invisible World, chapbook by Mathers 1689

Celtic Folklore & Magical Traditions

While Hermeticism spread among the literate classes of early modern Europe, the people of the rural areas continued to practice pagan folk-traditions inherited from their forebears. These took the form of seasonal festivals, folk-magic, and belief in the fairy folk. Authors Jones and Pennick comment on the survival of these ancient traditions: "A few of them have continued directly, others have been amalgamated with Christianity, and yet more have turned into folklore and undeciphered tradition."[1]

With the coming of Christianity in Wales, Scotland, Ireland, and Brittany, the old Celtic gods continued to be worshipped in the guise of christian saints, such as the goddess Brighde who was venerated as St. Bridget. In pre-Christian times in County Kildare, Ireland, Brighde had a shrine in which a sacred flame was kept and tended by a college of women, similar to the Vestal Virgins of Rome. Although the temple eventually became a Christian nunnery, the flame was continuously tended until finally extinguished in 1220 by the orders of an archbishop. Goddess worship continued until the 17th century in Brittany, according to Jones and Pennick. Shrines were kept there by old women who taught the "rites of Venus" to young women known as *fatidicae*, or *bonnes filles* who were apparently seeresses instructed in shamanistic practices such as shape-shifting and the raising of storms.[2]

After the breakup of the Catholic church in Scotland during the 16th century Protestant Reformation, some pagan traditions were actually revived, according to Jones and Pennick.[3] The "old rites" of the god Mhor-Ri, the "Great King", also known as St. Maree, were observed with bull sacrifices, pouring of libations of milk, and "adoring of wells and other superstitious monuments and stones" according to Presbytery records. Attempts by the church to suppress the rites failed and they continued until the 19th century.[4]

The four ancient Celtic cross-quarter festivals of Beltaine, Imbolc, Lughnasadh and Samhain were celebrated in Ireland, Wales, Cornwall, the Highlands, the Western Isles as well as the Isle of Man. In contrast, the equinoxes and solstices were observed in areas formerly inhabited by the Anglo-Saxons, according to Ronald Hutton.[5] The tradition of lighting bonfires on Midsummer's Eve and dancing and leaping through the flames, a remnant of pagan sun worship, continued in Britain until modern times. Testifying to the longevity of such traditions, the custom of rolling burning wheels down a hill during Midsummer-Eve celebrations, first chronicled in 4th century Gaul, was last recorded in England in 1950, according to Hutton.[6] He also points to Mummer's plays, Hobby horse dances, and Horn Dances involving the wearing of stag horns, as survivals of ancient pagan folk traditions.

A clergyman in the late 16th century wrote that in Wales the fairies were held in "astonishing reverence" and that the people dare not "name them without honour". The fairy goddesses Aine and Fennel were honored at two hills near Lough Gur in Ireland, according to Jones and Pennick. In fact, belief in the supernatural "fairy-folk" is still alive and well in rural parts of Ireland. As recently as 1999 In County Clare, the route of a highway was diverted so as not to uproot a white thorn bush believed to be sacred to the fairies, after protests were led by a local *seanachai,* a traditional storyteller.[7] It is still considered unsafe in parts of Ireland to build a house on a "fairy path", since to do so is believed to provoke the wrath of the "little people", bringing misfortunes such as illness and accidents.

Survival of Nordic Pagan Traditions

Like the Celtic peoples, the Scandinavians have also retained traces of ancient pagan traditions in their folklore. Pagan deities became Christian saints: Freya became Maria, Baldur was transformed into St. Michael, and Thor became St. Olaf, while older demons were equated with the Christian devil.[8] Jacob Grimm reported that as late as the 17th century in Scandinavia, offerings continued to be made to the god Thor against toothache, and oaths were still sworn in his name.

Midsummer bonfires and sun wheels persist to this day in Denmark and Norway. Most towns and villages still have Maypoles or May trees, and in many Germanic-speaking countries May-Pole festivals are still celebrated. E.J. Witzel explains that these originated from the veneration of the Irminsul, the pagan German version of the World Tree.[9] Labyrinth dances were celebrated until recently in parts of Sweden as games among the young people, and in the opinion of John Kraft are remnants of Neolithic fertility rites.[10]

In Finland as late as the 19th century, folk-magicians known as *tietaja*, meaning "sage" or "knower" practiced their craft. The tietaja were healers, diviners, judges, name-givers, as well as workers of protective magic who recited or sang invocations to the spirits. They fell into trances before their clients, sending out spirit-allies in the form of dogs to battle evil spirits.[11] Rather than relying solely on shamanic trance journeys to the otherworld they also used the singing of runes to achieve altered states, perform healing, and for other purposes.[12] Along with the runes, the tietaja also memorized and recited large numbers of epic poems based on the exploits of shamanic figures from prehistory, which were compiled in the 18th century as the national epic of Finland, the *Kalevala*.

The Sami people of Finland, Norway and Sweden were Christianized during the 16th and 17th centuries, though their shamanic practices remained relatively unchanged until the 19th century when the last of their sacred drums were confiscated by the Christians. Following the recent overturning of laws banning their shamanic practices, the *noiade* are again openly practicing their craft.

Many Icelanders still believe in the elves or "hidden people" which inhabit their land. On occasion, highways have been re-routed around elf habitats, since building on them has apparently resulted in breakdowns of machinery. Polls consistently show the majority of modern Icelanders believe in elves, thought to be invisible humanlike creatures who are fiercely protective of their homes.[13]

Shamanic Traditions of Europe

Some European folk traditions preserve remnants of ancient shamanistic beliefs and rituals, in the opinion of ethnologist Rosalyn Frank. She describes the curious custom of "Good Luck Visits" which occur to this day in parts of Europe. During these performances, actors dressed in costumes of animal fur, horns and bells travel door to door to bring good health and prosperity.[14] Similar to these are "Straw Bear" performances, in which the lead performer wears a straw costume resembling a bear, accompanied by actors dressed as a white mare and stork.

According to Frank, these folk-traditions are remnants of archaic pan-European shamanistic healing practices in which trained bears were taken door to door for the purpose of healing and frightening away evil spirits. House calls of "bear healers" continued among the Basque people of the Pyrenees in Northern Spain, as well as in parts of the Balkans until the 20th century. Frank conjectures this custom harkens back to Paleolithic bear ceremonialism in which bears were believed to possess healing powers. As previously discussed, bear ceremonialism was practiced by shamanic cultures across the northern hemisphere which revered bears as healers and messengers to the spirit world.

The origins of the Basque people, who speak a language unrelated to any other, continues to be the subject of debate. Some historians argue they are descended from the original Paleolithic inhabitants of Western Europe who survived the Ice Age in the Franco-Cantabrian Refuge in the Pyrenees. Others point to the existence of farming vocabulary in the Basque language, claiming this implies Neolithic origins. Genetic research suggests the Basques may have originated in the Balkans and migrated from there after the collapse of Copper Age cultures around 4,000 BCE, according to historian Jean Marco.[15] The Basques were not Christianized until the 17th century in rural areas, and oral traditions of their native pagan religion still survive, as well as winter and summer solstice celebrations. According to Gimbutas, the goddess Mari is worshipped to this day among the Basques. Mari embodies many features of a "prehistoric magician goddess of death and regeneration", according to her, and is associated with caves and oracles.[16]

The Dragon Men—Wizards of the Balkans

The Balkans has its own ancient and enduring history of magic and shamanism. As previously mentioned, the cults of Orpheus as well as Dionysus originated in ancient Thrace, in present day Bulgaria. Native Hungarian shamans, the *taltos*, practiced their own shamanic traditions. The Southern Slavs who migrated to the Balkans around the 6th century CE may have absorbed some of these traditions.

The Slavs also brought their own mythology and magical traditions with them. They had their own wizards, witches, and folk-magicians with practices similar to those of shamans. Like shamans, they journeyed in trance to the otherworld in the forms of their familiar spirits, where they combated demons and conducted healing. Their role was to guarantee agricultural fertility for their communities by acting as mediators between the world of the living and the dead. Similar to some Siberian shamans, Balkan wizards were born with a placenta or caul which was believed to give them supernatural abilities.

In Slovenia and Croatia these people were known as *kresnici* and *zduhaci*, according to anthropologist Eva Pocs.[17] In Bulgaria and East Serbia, wizards with shamanic abilities were called *zmej*, meaning snake, dragon, or winged man, believed to be sons of fiery dragons and eagles, the mythical animal ancestors of their clans. Bulgarian and Rumanian wizards also had helping spirits—often birds, snakes, reptiles or fish—which enabled them to fall into trance and shapeshift into animal forms. The spirits aided them in healing, love magic, divining the future, seeing the dead, regaining stolen objects and finding buried treasure.

Wizards fell into trances during storms, their souls believed to be carried away by heavenly eagles or dragons, the animal forms of the Slavic god Perun who rules the heavens. These were however, "dual faith" wizards, who also fought as assistants of the Christian saint Elijah. In their otherworldly battles their souls appeared as snakes, dragons, lizards, eagles, or cocks. They fought to bring good weather and abundant harvest by killing and expelling the evil infernal dragons responsible for hail. In such battles wizards shot lightning and threw stones at the dragons, using torn out tree trunks as weapons.

According to Serbian author Radomir Ristic, the *kresnici* and *zduhaci* were actually male witches and part of an ancient tradition of witchcraft which still exists in the Balkans. Called "Dragon Men" in Eastern Serbia, they were clairvoyants as well as prophets.[18] Known for their their powers to heal with herbs or magic, to communicate with supernatural creatures and foretell the future, they fell into trance while asleep or awake, and shapeshifted into the forms of male goats, bulls or horses.

The role of the Dragon Men was to defend their communities from demons and other supernatural creatures. In their struggles they would use wooden rods or animal horns and other objects as weapons. Their main enemies were believed to be werewolves, which they fought in mid-air or at crossroads. Their female counterparts—witches—also practiced clairvoyance, healing and divination.

Ristic provides an example of a collective trance-seance by the Serbian *rusalje* or "fallen women" that bears similarities to shamanic trance and possession:

"..the people gathered in front of a deep cave at the source of the Dubocka river. Before gathering, rites dedicated to the dead were performed, and they walked to the "wooden cross" (most often an oak) where sacrifices were offered in the form of food and drink....After gathering around the cave, people started to dance in "kolo" (a circle) with deafening music. That lasted until some of the dancers, most often women, started to fade, shivering, and falling to the ground with a piercing shriek. That condition represents entry into a trance. On the ground, those persons would clench muscles, scream, and sing or speak. As they were talking, the spirits of the dead would get into them and communicated with them, or they were pulled out of their bodies by fairies who took them away..." [19]

Grimoires & Folk-magic

Most charms, spells and rituals practiced by European folk-magicians were transmitted *orally* down through the generations and only recorded by folklorists in the nineteenth century. Literature such as the magical grimoires contained only a fraction of the magical lore of the ancient world, according to Owen Davies.[20]

Nevertheless, literate and oral traditions of magic were not mutually exclusive—cross-fertilization was ongoing between them. Historian Richard Kieckhefer insists there was a "common tradition" of medieval magic that was not limited to one particular social group, but shared among monks, physicians and lay persons alike.[21] The introduction of the printing press in renaissance Europe made the Solomonic grimoires and magical literature such as Agrippa's *Three Books of Occult Philosophy* available to a wide public. Literate folk-magic practitioners borrowed elements from the grimoires such as astrology, magic circles and talismans, using them to construct written charms and protective talismans for popular consumption.[22] On the other hand, the grimoire tradition from its beginning drew from elements of folk-magic such as herbalism, folk-medicine and the conjuring of nature spirits and fairies. These can be found in the *Hygromanteia*, the *Key of Solomon* as well as Elizabethan magic books such as Scott's *Discoverie of Witchcraft* from the 16th century. For example, Scot provides a conjuration for summoning the three fairy sisters Milia, Achilia, and Sibylia for the purpose of bringing the magician a "ring of invisibility" by means of which he can travel invisibly at his will and pleasure.[23]

Cunning Folk & Witches: The Shamanic Connection

Underlying European folk-magic is the archaic undercurrent of shamanism. Archeologists Miranda and Stephen Aldhouse-Green write: "...shamanism, in its broadest sense, is and has been endemic to rural communities in much of the ancient and modern world."[24] Carlo Ginzburg traces folkloric myths, rituals and beliefs back through European history, concluding they are evidence of the survival of pre-Christian, Eurasian shamanistic visionary traditions. He claims these were widespread on a popular level throughout early modern Europe.

Ginzburg writes about the *benandanti*—the "good walkers"—a tradition of visionaries from agrarian communities in the Friuli district of northern Italy during 16th and 17th centuries. The benandanti claimed to travel out of their bodies during trance to combat malevolent witches believed to be threatening the health of their crops. Male benandanti usually reported flying into the clouds to combat witches, while the women reported attending great feasts—similar to witches' sabbaths. Like the wizards of the neighboring Balkans, the benandanti were born with a caul; similar to them the goal of their otherworldly battles was to insure good weather for the crops and to battle malefic witches from neighboring territories.

The benandanti are compared by Ginsburg to Eurasian shamans who also battle with each other while in a state of catalepsy: "men fight men, and women fight women: their souls collide in animal form...until one of them succumbs..."[25] He insists they performed similar tasks as shamans: ecstatic trance journeying, contact with the world of the dead, and magical control of natural powers to ensure the survival of the community.[26]

Anthropologist Eva Pocs studies Hungarian folk magicians—the *taltos*—whose shamanic traditions were recorded as recently as the 1940's in Hungary.[27] The taltos specialized in healing, fortune-telling, finding lost objects, communicating messages from the dead, bringing rain, and warding off hail. She writes: "beyond their manipulation of supernatural powers as magicians, these village specialists were also mediators who contacted the other world through the technique of trance". We previously compared the initiation experiences of Hungarian and Siberian shamans, showing their many similarities. Like the benandanti of Italy and Dragon Men of Serbia, the taltos fought supernatural battles to assure abundant harvests for their communities.

According to anthropologist Emma Wilby, practitioners of folk-magic—witches and cunning-folk—were widespread in rural Great Britain.[28] She cites an early nineteenth century commentator who writes: "Sorcerers are all too common; cunning men, wizards, and white witches, as they call them, in every village". Although there is no evidence they belonged to organized witch-cults or practiced a pagan religion, these people undoubtably inherited fragments of archaic animistic beliefs passed down through folkloric traditions. The cunning folk and shamans were "startlingly similar" according to Wilby. Both came to their profession either by heredity or were called to it by their helping spirits, and employed their skills for healing as well as divination.

Shamans and witches also shared many characteristics. Witches entered trance states and journeyed out of their bodies to attend their sabbaths—similar to the magical flight of shamans. Both shamans and witches rode on the backs of their "familiars" such as stags, goats, birds or other animals. Anthropologist Michael Harner insists witches were part of the shamanic tradition, noting their imaginary journeys to the upperworld performed by riding broomsticks on chimney smoke.[29]

Wilby argues that indigenous pre-Christian beliefs which could be only be described as "animistic" were widely held in Britain through the 16th and 17th centuries. She writes: "...the fairy realm described by popular magical practitioners and represented in folk tales of the period, bore far more resemblance to the underworld (and less frequently the upper world) of the tribal shaman than it did to the lower worlds of the Christian cosmology." [30]

In 16th and 17th century England, cunning-folk formed alliances with familiar spirits who often took animal forms, as well as appearing as angels, deceased humans, and fairy folk. The cunning-man or woman's relationships with spirit beings often involved close companionships with them. Wilby writes: "like relationships between cunning folk or witches and their familiars, relationships between shamans and their helping spirits can continue for many years; exhibiting a complex tension between numinous intensity and down-to- earth mundanity and embracing the full gamut of human emotions." [31] Similar to the initiation experiences of shamans, the familiar spirits of cunning-folk often appeared to them during times of crisis to offer their otherworldly assistance. In the following account, the first meeting of John Webster, a 17th century cunning-man, with his familiar spirit is described:

> "One night before the day was gone, as he was going home from his labour, being very sad and full of heavy thoughts, not knowing how to get meat and drink for his Wife and Children, he met a fair Woman in fine clothes, who asked him why he was so sad, and he told her that it was by reason of his poverty, to which she said, that if he would follow her counsel she would help him." [32]

Similar to shamans, cunning-folk performed magical tasks such as healing, divination, finding lost goods, and contacting the dead, as well as bestowing the gift of the second sight with the help of their familiar spirits. Before the era of doctors and psychologists, rural folk turned to the local cunning person for help, just as tribal societies relied on shamans for meeting similar needs.

According to Wilby, the cunning folk continued to practice their craft until the end of the 19th century in England. However, there is anecdotal evidence suggesting a few of them may have survived into the 20th century in isolated rural areas of Britain. In her autobiographical novel *Seal Morning*, English writer Rowena Farre chronicles her life in the Scottish highlands in the 1930's. There she claims she befriended a traditional Scottish "fairy doctor" who used magical spells for healing animals.[33]

Chapter 15 Notes

1. Jones, Prudence & Pennick, Nigel. A History of Pagan Europe.1995:110.
2. Ibid.:104.
3. Ibid.:107.
4. On the island of Maelrubha in Loch Maree, the sacred oak of Mhor- Ri was studded with nails to which ribbons were tied; the tree was associated with a healing well reputed to cure insanity. The officiating priests of the island were called derilans, a title which may derive from the Gaelic word deireoil, meaning "afflicted", suggesting they were possessed of "divine madness" like shamans the world over, according to Jones and Pennick. (Jones & Pennick 1995: 107).
5. Hutton, Ronald. The Pagan Religions of the Ancient British Isles.1991:183.
6. Ibid.: 327-29.
7. Walsh, John. "John Walsh on Monday: Irish road side-tracked by the fairie's right of way". The Independent, Sept. 20, 1999.Walsh 1999.
8. Jones; Pennick. A History of Pagan Europe. 1995:160.
9. Witzel. The Origins of the World's Mythologies. 2012: 135.
10. Kraft. The Goddess in the Labyrinth. 1985: 15-17.
11. Hutton. Shamans-Siberian Spirituality and the Western Imagination. 2001: 138.
12. Alden, Harold. "Shamanism and Sacred Arts in Finland- Part 2". Spirit Boat- exploring Finnish shamanism and its relevance for today. June 16, 2014.
13. Lyall, Sarah. Building in Iceland? Better Clear It With the Elves First. NY Times. com. July 13, 2005.14.
14. Frank, Roslyn M. "Hunting the European Sky Bears: German "Straw Bears" and their Relatives as Transformers". Academia.edu. 2010: 6.
15. Manco. Ancestral Journeys. 2013: 121.
16. Gimbutas, Marija. The Living Goddess. 1999:173.
17. Pocs, Eva. Traces of Indo-European Shamanism in South East Europe. Tartu: Folk Belief Today. 1995.
18. Ristic, Radomir. translated by Carter, Michael C. Jr. Balkan Traditional Witchcraft. 2009: 39.
19. Ibid.: 33.
20. Davies. Grimoires: A History of Magic Books. 2009:2.
21. Kieckhefer, Richard. Magic in the Middle Ages. 1990:57.

22. Davies. Grimoires: A History of Magic Books. 2009: 67.
23. Scot, Reginald. The Discoverie of Witchcraft. 1972: 234-235.
24. Aldhouse-Green. The Quest for the Shaman. 2005: 8.
25. Ginzburg. Ecstasies: Deciphering the Witches' Sabbath. 1991: 170.
26. Ibid.:1991:14.
27. Pocs, Eva. Traces of Indo-European Shamanism in South East Europe. 1995: 8.
28. Wilby, Emma. Cunning Folk and Familiar Spirits: Shamanistic Traditions in Early Modern British Witchcraft and Magic. 2006.
29. Achterberg, Jeanne. Imagery in Healing: Shamanism and Modern Medicine. 1985: 62. The dress of European witches may have originally been influenced by Eurasian shamans according to archaeologists A.P. Okladnikov and Jeaninne Davis-Kimball. They point out that Central Asian womenfolk, priestesses, and shamans traditionally wore tall conical headgear, and curiously, this distinctive headdress later appeared as the pointed witches hat in medieval Europe. (Davis-Kimball 2002:77.)
30. Wilby. Cunning Folk and Familiar Spirits: Shamanistic Traditions in Early Modern British Witchcraft and Magic. 2006: 146.
31. Ibid.:142.
32. Ibid.: 66.
33. Farre, Rowena. Seal Morning. 1956. Besides practicing healing and spellbinding, Farre's " fairy doctor" knew 376 traditional Celtic stories which he had learned by word of mouth—some of which took over an hour to recite. This is reminiscent of medieval Celtic bards who also learned a vast repertoire of magical stories about the otherworld which they used to induce trance states and visionary journeys, according to John and Caitlín Matthews. (Matthews 1996: 354)

Chapter 16: The 19th Century Occult Revival

Helena Petrovna Blavatsky — founder of Theosophy.

During the nineteenth century, America and Europe witnessed a renewal of interest in esotericism not seen since the Italian Renaissance — the so-called "Occult Revival". In response to the spiritual vacuum left by modern science, secularism, and the decline of organized religion, alternative forms of spirituality emerged, enjoying unprecedented popularity, according to historian James Webb. Groups like the Freemasons, Rosicrucians, Humanists, Swedenborgians, Mesmerists, Transcendentalists, Spiritualists, Theosophists, and others offered egalitarian approaches to spirituality and inspiration for the masses.

There were several key figures whose work laid the foundations of the Occult Revival. Foremost among these was Emanuel Swedenborg, who we looked at previously, whose writings promoted the idea of the "spirit world" and predicted the end of established Christianity.[1] The ideas of Anton Mesmer (1734-1815) a German physician, were also important. Inspired by the idea of "subtle fluids" of Paracelsus, Mesmer developed the theory of "animal magnetism"—the transference of energy between animate and inanimate objects—which could be used for healing. He popularized the idea of the hypnotic trance and "mesmeric sleep", anticipating modern hypnotherapy.[2] Mesmer's ideas were investigated by Benjamin Franklin, who concluded there was no scientific proof for animal magnetism. Nevertheless his ideas gained wide exposure.

The American clairvoyant Andrew Jackson Davis (1826-1910), dubbed the "Seer of Poughkeepsie", became the first theoretician of the Spiritualist movement. Influenced by the teaching of Mesmer, he opened "clairvoyant clinics" where he diagnosed the illness of patients while he himself was in a "mesmerized" state. Although he proudly claimed he had little education and had only read one book in his life, Davis was in fact inspired by the writings of Swedenborg, according to Webb.[3] He used his psychic powers to explore the "Summer-Land", the otherworld from which spirits of the dead were believed to communicate with the living. Davis railed against the corruption of the clergy and prophesied the coming of the Golden Age, promoting progressive social reforms. He published over thirty books, dictated to him while in trance. Davis's work inspired modern clairvoyants such as Edgar Cayce who adopted the technique of "trance diagnosis" from him.

Spiritualism—Mediums & Shamans

Spiritualism was the most popular expression of 19th century alternative spirituality, and a product of the cultural melting pot of America. Influential to its development were Swedenborg's ideas of the spirit world and his rejection of the institutionalized church, as well as the writings of Andrew Jackson Davis. Historian John J. Kucich writes that Spiritualism was a reflection of American multi-culturalism, combining European occultism with African and Native American religious traditions which mingled on the continent.[4] Also influential were the beliefs and practices of the Shakers, utopian Christians active during the late 18th and early 19th century. The Shakers communed with the souls of the dead in ceremonies involving ecstatic dancing, shaking, and visions of the spirit-world that were oddly shamanistic. There was in fact a cultural exchange between them and Native Americans. This apparently resulted in the Shakers incorporating elements of native ceremonial practices into their worship.[5] Geoffrey K. Nelson suggests that early Spiritualists who settled in areas inhabited by Native Americans may have been stimulated by their shamanistic practices and beliefs in guardian-spirits.[6]

The phenomenon of Spiritualism began in the small village of Hydesville in upstate New York, in 1848. There, two teenage sisters, *Margaret* and *Kate Fox*, began their mediumistic adventures with a spirit who made knocking sounds in their house. The girls addressed it as "Mr. Splitfoot", a nickname for the devil. Communicating with the spirit through rapping sounds they worked out a code of raps which signified "yes" or "no", as well as letters of the alphabet. The spirit revealed itself to be the ghost of a peddler who had been murdered and buried in the house's cellar. The word spread, and Hydesville soon became besieged by visitors curious to see that "life did not end at death" in the words of historian Robert S. Cox.[7] To satisfy the public's demand, the Fox sisters took their "spirit rappers" on the road, performing seances for audiences of hundreds of people.

Spreading like wildfire, Spiritualism quickly became a mass movement, reaching its peak of popularity by the late 1800's when it was said to have over twelve million followers and 35,000 practicing mediums in the Americas and a large following in Europe. Luminaries like Queen Victoria and Charles Dickens as well as a number of respected scientists such as Pierre and Marie Curie were interested in Spiritualism. Mary Todd Lincoln, grieving over the death of her son Willie, held spiritualist seances in the White House attended by her husband, president Lincoln. She believed she had contacted her son's spirit, writing: "Willie lives. He comes to me every night and stands at the foot of the bed with the same adorable smile he always has had".[8]

Spiritualists communicated with the spirits of discarnate humans, including deceased relatives and famous personalities from the past. Gifted mediums provided knowledge of the afterlife, healing, and guidance—both spiritual and worldly. During spiritualist seances, paranormal phenomena sometimes occurred such as levitations, table tipping, musical instruments playing themselves, cold winds, "apports" or objects materializing in mid-air, as well as luminous displays of "ectoplasm". Some mediums exhibited the "direct voice", or ghostly voices which later were proven to be produced by ventriloquism.[9] Perhaps the most famous Spiritualist medium was Daniel Dunglus Home, an American who travelled widely demonstrating his clairvoyant and mediumistic powers, healing the sick and communicating with the dead. His most spectacular performances were his levitations which were observed on several different occasions. Although many of the phenomena produced by Home were proven by investigators to be fake, some notable scientists such as William Crookes remained convinced of his abilities.[10]

There are a number of intriguing parallels between Spiritualism and shamanistic seances. Spiritualist mediums fell into trance and become possessed by spirits, relaying their messages to the audience, as did shamans. The séances of spiritualists and shamans provided therapy and emotional catharsis for participants, while confirming their belief in the spirit world and the soul's survival after death. Both held their sessions in the dark, and were known on occasion to use ventriloquism to imitate spirit voices, as well as other staged effects to convince their audiences of the presence of paranormal powers. It is notable that American Indian spirits were among those most frequently contacted during Spiritualist seances.

Spiritualism claimed mediumship was available to all who earnestly inquired, while acknowledging some had more innate psychic abilities than others. It was non-dogmatic in approach, emphasizing individual spiritual guidance and religious egalitarianism, as opposed to the authority of orthodox religion with its scriptures and clergy. Many women were attracted to the movement, and Spiritualists became social reformers and early champions of progressive political movements like women's suffrage, the abolition of slavery, and Native American rights.

Owen Davies argues that Spiritualism galvanized the public's interest in the supernatural and occult—providing a focal point for esoteric groups and ideas circulating in literate society of the nineteenth century. It formed the social milieu from which Theosophy, New Age, and other modern esoteric groups would later emerge.[11] Spiritualism continues to be practiced around the world in Brazil, India, Nigeria, and Europe, but is found predominantly in North America and Britain.

Theosophy—Madame Blavatsky & the Astral Letters

*"The path that leadeth on is lighted by one fire—
the light of daring burning in the heart.
The more one dares the more he shall obtain."*
-Helena Petrovna Blavatsky

In 1875 the Theosophical Society was founded in New York City with the objective of studying occultism and the esoteric traditions of the western and eastern world. The Theosophists were dedicated to similar progressive social reforms as the Spiritualists. Among their goals was "to form a nucleus of the Universal Brotherhood of Humanity, without distinction of race, creed, sex, caste or color".

Visionary Traditions Of The Western World

Helene Petrovna Blavatsky, (1831-1891) also known by the acronym of H.P.B., was the charismatic founder and leader of the movement. A world traveller and aristocratic Russian emigre, her father, Baron von Hahn, was a Russian horse artillery officer, and her mother a romantic novelist descended from royalty. In her biography, "myth and reality begin to merge seamlessly", in the words of Peter Washington.[12] From childhood, H.P.B. was an imaginative and compelling story-teller.

At the age of seventeen Blavatsky married a man many years her senior, the Vice-Governor of Yerevan, and soon fled from the marriage. According to one account, she boarded a steamer on the Black Sea and sailed to Constantinople where she joined the circus as an equestrienne, before being picked up by a Hungarian opera singer. In Paris, the story continues, she was an assistant to the spiritualist Daniel Dunglas Home and later directed the Serbian Royal Choir. On a trip to Africa her boat sank and she was abandoned in Cairo "in a wet skirt and without a penny to her name" in the words of Webb.[13] Other stories were told of her travels, such as meetings with Red Indians in Canada, a covered wagon journey across the American Rocky Mountains, her dealings with voodoo magicians in New Orleans, and kabbalists in Egypt.

Perhaps Blavatsky's most extraordinary adventures were her alleged travels in Tibet where she claims she spent seven years studying with the *mahatmas*—spiritual masters of the so-called "Great White Brotherhood". She insisted she also met these same masters in European capitols on several occasions where they continued to guide her work.[14] Although her Tibetan travels and knowledge of Buddhism are assumed to be fictitious by critics, the foremost authority on Zen Buddhism, D.T. Suzuki, also an avid Theosophist, writes: "Undoubtedly Ms. Blavatsky somehow or other was initiated into deeper propositions of the Mahayana teaching".[15]

During her travels Blavatsky ended up at a farm in Vermont, at the home of the Eddy's who were famous spirit mediums. There she met Colonel Henry Steel Olcott with whom she shared similar interests in occultism and investigations of spiritualistic phenomena. Out of their partnership grew the Theosophical Society. Although she began her career as a spiritualist medium, Blavatsky later denounced Spiritualism, though she continued to produce spiritualist phenomena like "astral bells" and "apports" such as pulling brooches out of flower beds. H.P.B. possessed formidable powers of hypnotic suggestion as well, and was not above demonstrating her psychic powers to exert influence over those around her, according to Rene Guenon.[16] One of her favorite tricks was to point to a person's knee on which they would be startled to see a huge spider crawling; she would smile and say: "that spider does not exist, I made you see it". She complained to confidants that her display of "phenomena" was the only way to attract westerners to her true mission which was revealing the spiritual wisdom of her unseen masters.

Early in her writings, Blavatsky was influenced by Rosicrucian and kabbalistic ideas but later her interest shifted to the philosophies of India and Tibet. She claimed to be in direct psychic contact with the mysterious eastern masters who dictated *Isis Unveiled* to her, the founding text of Theosophy. The book discusses the similarities of religions—western and eastern—claiming they descend from a common source. In an introductory statement that could have been penned by Ficino or Pico, Blavatsky writes that *Isis Unveiled* is "a plea for the recognition of the Hermetic philosophy, the anciently universal Wisdom-Religion, as the only possible key to the Absolute in science and theology".[17] Theosophy's mission, according to Blavatsky, was to reveal a spiritual science which offered an alternative to the false ideals of scientific progress as well as the myths of salvation offered by Christianity.

Along with Theosophy's growing popularity came scandals related to the psychic phenomena H.P.B. had a knack for producing. It was claimed the "masters" or *mahatmas* delivered their teachings in the form of "astral letters" produced out of thin air that floated down from the ceiling. Upon scientific investigation the letters were found to be in Blavatsky's handwriting and declared fraudulent. Rene Guenon writes: "Faith in the "masters" as defined by Blavatsky and her followers is the very basis of Theosophy—either their teachings were acquired and communicated by them or they are a mass of worthless fantasies".[18] Peter Washington speculates that H.P.B's Brotherhood of Himalayan Masters who had supposedly chosen her to communicate their message to the world were probably the result of her extensive readings in Asian scriptures, Rosicrucian, Masonic, and Templar mythology, as well as the writings of nineteenth century occultist Eliphas Levi, and novelist Bulwer Lytton.[19]

Despite accusations by critics that H.P.B. was a plagiarist, charlatan, hashish addict and Russian spy, the Theosophical Society she founded continued to grow over the decades. During the height of its popularity in 1928 it opened branches around Europe, America, and India, claiming a membership of 45,000 people worldwide. Blavatsky was undoubtably a powerful and controversial woman who has drawn criticism as well as praise. Theodore Roszak writes: "Helena Petrovna Blavatsky is surely among the most original and perceptive minds of her time. She is among the modern world's trailblazing psychologists of the visionary mind." [20]

Theosophy can be credited with introducing eastern metaphysical teachings and Buddhism to the western world, as well as campaigning for Indian independence. It also popularized many of the ideas of New Age spirituality such as reincarnation, ascended masters, astral travel, Atlantis etc. Theosophical centers can still be found worldwide, and its contribution to modern esotericism cannot be underestimated. At one time or another, most 19th or early 20th century occultists belonged to the society or read its literature.

Levi & the Tarot

Another seminal figure in the revival of ritual magic and occultism was Eliphas Levi—the pseudonym of French writer and illustrator Alphonse Louis Constant (1810-75). Levi trained as a Catholic priest but left the seminary after apparently falling in love, rejecting the priesthood as "a cold and egotistical cult". Nevertheless, he remained a faithful Catholic his entire life. He wrote a series of books on magic, one of the most notable being *Dogme et Ritual de la Haute Magic* in which Kabbala and Tarot are combined with theories of mesmerism and animal magnetism.

Levi promoted the idea of the Tarot as an esoteric system. He insists: "Without the Tarot the Magic of the ancients is a closed book, and it is impossible to penetrate any of the great mysteries of the Kabbalah." [21] Revealing his Catholic biases, he viewed many of the grimoires as "black magic" and diabolical, labeling them as "unhappy aberrations of the human mind". This did not however prevent him from engaging in a necromantic rite similar to those described in the grimoires—in which he claims to have evoked the phantom of the ancient Greek philosopher Apollonius of Tyana to visible appearance. Levi describes the climax of the rite:

> "Closing my eyes, I called three times on Apollonius, and, when I reopened them, a man stood before me wholly enveloped in a winding sheet...his form was lean, melancholy, and beardless, which did not quite recall the picture I had formed to myself of Apollonius. I experienced a feeling of intense cold, and when I opened my lips to interrogate the apparition, I found it impossible to make a sound."[22]

Levi later swore that he had seen and touched Apollonius, or his apparition, which was sufficient grounds for believing in the "absolute efficacy" of magical ceremonies.

Levi's books would prove to be inspirational for the magicians of the *fin de siecle* and early twentieth century, and his work on the Tarot would influence generations of Hermeticists to follow.

The Rise of the Golden Dawn

The Hermetic Order of the Golden Dawn was founded in 1888 in London by Samuel Liddell McGregor Mathers, William Wynn Wescott, and William Robert Woodman. All three men were high ranking Freemasons and Rosicrucians and members of the Societas Rosicruciana in Anglia. Although the Golden Dawn was associated with Theosophy in the beginning it soon distinguished itself from it, focusing exclusively on western esotericism, termed by Mathers "The Western Mystery Tradition".

Mathers, the "Supreme Magus" of the order, also translated several important magical grimoires: *The Sacred Magic of Abra-Melin, The Key of Solomon the King*, as well as *The Goetia or Lesser Key of Solomon* which were previously mentioned. The Golden Dawn's unique contribution consisted of its synthesis of the many traditional branches of western esotericism: hermeticism, kabbalah, theurgy, alchemy, astrology, renaissance grimoires, enochian magic, Egyptian god-forms etc. into a single coherent system which has since become the source of much modern magical practice.

The Golden Dawn used magic as a means of spiritual advancement of its initiates—similar the theurgy practiced by Iamblichus. Like masonic lodges, it was based on a hierarchical structure and progression through grades marked by a series of initiations.[23] The candidate progressed through initiations associated with the four classical elements of earth, air, water, and fire. Unlike masonry, women were accepted as members of the lodge and equal to men in status. Personal development was taught through study of Qabalah (Christian and Hermetic Kabbalah) as well as astrology, tarot and geomancy.

Having progressed through the outer order of the Golden Dawn, aspirants progressed to the Second Order—the "Rosae Rubeae et Aureae Crucis"—the Ruby Rose and Cross of Gold.[24] This was the "inner order" in which an initiation drama of death and rebirth of the candidate in the "vault of the adepts" was enacted, inspired by Rosicrucian symbolism. Here, initiates were taught a curriculum of practical magic including scrying, astral travel, alchemy, enochian magic and evocation of spirits.

The Golden Dawn was successful in attracting membership from all social classes, and among them were celebrities such as the Irish poet William Butler Yeats, and authors Arthur Conan Doyle and Evelyn Underhill. It spawned several other temples in England and Scotland, as well as America. The notorious magician, poet, and mountaineer Aleister Crowley was initiated into the order in 1898. After advancing rapidly through the ranks, Crowley, who was disliked by the other members, was refused initiation by them into the Second Order. He turned instead to Mathers, living in absentia in Paris, who offered to initiate him. Crowley allied with Mathers in his dispute with the London lodge members over his autocratic leadership style. The two eventually fell out however, and Crowley accused Mathers of using "black magic" against him. Mathers indeed sent "astral vampires" to attack Crowley—who returned the favor by sending an army of demons against his former ally. Following this escapade both men were expelled from the Second Order. Crowley retaliated by publishing several of the Golden Dawn initiation rituals and aspects of its system in his journal *The Equinox*, from 1909-1913, though its small circulation would have limited impact on the occult world.

In 1934 Crowley's former secretary, a young man named Israel Regardie, joined the Stella Matutina, a magical lodge descended from the original Hermetic Order of the Golden Dawn. He soon left the order and published its documents in his famous book *The Golden Dawn*. This caused an uproar among occultists who accused him of violating his initiation oaths by revealing the order's secrets. Regardie justified his action, writing in his book *My Rosicrucian Adventure*: (1936) "...it is essential that the whole system should be publicly exhibited so that it may not be lost to mankind. For it is the heritage of every man and woman—their spiritual birthright." Due to Crowley's and Regardie's books, and those of other occultists who followed in their footsteps such as A.E.Waite, Paul Foster Case, Dion Fortune, William Gray, William Butler, Gareth Knight, Dolores Aschcroft-Nowicki and others, modern western ceremonial magic was made available to the general public—influencing generations of aspiring magicians to come.

The breakup of the Golden Dawn has been compared to the explosion of a seed pod, scattering its seeds in all directions. It led to the formation of other magical orders around the world such as the Ordo Templis Orientalis, the Builders of the Adytum, the Society of The Inner Light, the Servants of the Light, the Ordo Aurum Solis and numerous others which have arisen in the last few decades, perpetuating the Hermetic mysteries.

Chapter 16 Notes

1. Webb, James. *The Occult Underground*. 1974: 22.
2. Ibid.: 24.
3. Ibid.: 28.
4. Kucich, John J. "Ghostly Communion Cross-Cultural Spiritualism in Nineteenth Century American Literature". *Dartmouth.edu*. Hanover & London, University Press, 2004.
5. The name "Shakers" was given to the followers of this religion by non-believers to describe their ceremonies, during which they trembled to shake off the sins of the world, danced, whirled around, and rolled on the ground in ecstatic trance, similar to the practices of shamans. While in this state, the "chosen instruments", usually children or young women, experienced visions of the spirit world and conversed with spirits of the dead. Indian spirits were often contacted during the Shakers ceremonies, and writers such as James Mavor and Byron Dix insist there was a vigorous cultural exchange between Native American groups and Shakers during which they incorporated indian rituals in their ceremonies. (Dix & Mavor 1989:186-212) As well, the Shakers used many of the sacred sites of Native Americans for their worship, according to Daniel Boudillion. (Boudillion 2002-2007).
6. Nelson, Geoffrey K. *Spiritualism and Society*. Nelson 1969: 58.
7. Cox, Robert S. *Body and Soul A Sympathetic History of American Spiritualism*. 2003: 6.
8. Baker, Jean H. *Mary Todd Lincoln: A Biography*. 1989: 220.
9. Webb. *The Occult Underground*. *1974*: 20.
10. Doyle, Arthur, C. *The History of Spiritualism*. 1975: 196.
11. Davies. *Grimoires: A History of Magic Books*. 2009: 174.
12. Washington, Peter. *Madame Blavatsky's Baboon*. Washington 1995: 30.
13. Webb. *The Occult Underground*. 1974: 80-81.
14. Washington. *Madame Blavatsky's Baboon*. 1995: 32.
15. Suzuki, D.T. *Essays in Zen Buddhism*. 1-3 series. 2000: xiii.
16. Guenon, Rene. *Theosophy: History of a Pseudo-Religion*. 2004: 70.
17. Blavatsky, Helena Petrovna. *Isis Unveiled: A Masterkey to the Mysteries of Ancient and Modern Science*. 1919:vii.
18. Guenon, Rene. *Theosophy: History of a Pseudo-Religion*. 2004:49.
19. Washington. *Madame Blavatsky's Baboon*. 1995: 40.
20. Roszak, Theodore. *Unfinished Animal: Aquarian Frontier and the Evolution of Consciousness*. 1977.
21. Levi, Eliphas. *Transcendental Magic*. (trans. A.E. Waite)Levi 1970: 383.
22. Waite, Arthur Edward. *The Mysteries of Magic*. 1986:311.
23. Regardie, Israel. *The Golden Dawn*. Vol. 1 & 2. 1978:41-74.
24. Ibid.: 80-96.

Chapter 17:
Visionary Journeys in the Modern World

Kabbalist contemplating Tree of Life diagram. Paulus Ricius, Portae Lucis, 1516.

The initiates of the inner order of the Golden Dawn were taught a visionary technique for exploring the Qabalistic Tree of Life, called "scrying in spirit vision". This practice later became known as "pathworking", similar in many ways to the visionary ascents of the Hermetic, Gnostic, and Merkabah mystics, and indigenous shamans.

Pathworking is described by Neville Drury as a "trance meditation technique" involving transfer of one's consciousness to the visionary world of symbols through an act of "willed imagination".[1] Francis King describes the technique as "auto-hypnosis by means of a symbol". He explains that the seer begins by visualizing a symbol in their imagination and concentrating on it to the exclusion of everything else. Then in their mind's eye they transform the symbol into a vast door or curtain and pass through it in imagination, allowing the day dream to begin.[2]

Although scrying techniques have been practiced by magicians for millennia, pathworking involving the Tree of Life is the result of modern innovations. Nineteenth century French occultist Eliphas Levi was the first to associate the Major Arcana of the Tarot with the letters of the Hebrew alphabet. The founders of the Golden Dawn took Levi's innovation a step further by assigning the Tarot trumps to the paths of the Qabalistic Tree of Life. They also assigned planets, colors, angels, geometric forms, deities, etc., to its numerous spheres and paths, turning the Tree into a veritable "filing cabinet" for Qabalistic concepts. As well, they transformed the Tree of Life diagram into a road-map for exploring the "astral realms", similar to the "seven heavens" model of the mystics of antiquity, or the shaman's World Tree. Influenced by the writings of early twentieth century magical adepts Israel Regardie and Dion Fortune, pathworkings were elevated into a form of "self-initiation" for the aspiring magician, involving an imaginary journey up the paths of the Tree for the purpose of developing one's psychic and spiritual powers.

The magician begins his or her visionary ascent of the Tree of Life at the *sephirah* of Malkuth, the tenth or bottom most sphere of the Tree, associated with the physical universe. This is the gateway into the *32nd path* which ends in the ninth sphere of Yesod, corresponding to the moon. The tarot trump assigned to the 32nd path is "The World", corresponding to the planet Saturn. The path is also associated with the Greek goddess Persephone, queen of the underworld. Journeying on this path, magicians often experience it as a place of darkness and foreboding where they are forced to confront their own fears—similar to the shaman's initiation in the underworld.

Likewise the paths on either side of the 32nd path, the 31st and 29th paths, also have strong underworld associations. The *31st path*, corresponding to the Hebrew letter Shin and the element of fire, is assigned the tarot card of "Judgement". The experience here could be likened to trial by fire. Drury notes the path's associations with Hephaestos, the blacksmith god of Greek myth, and his resemblance to the Siberian blacksmith deity who forges a new body for the shaman during his initiation in the underworld.[3] The adjacent *29th path*, corresponding to the sign of Pisces, is a watery path of astral illusion and self-deception that the magician must overcome in order to proceed forward. The tarot trump "The Moon" is assigned to it, on which a dog and wolf are depicted—the dog is sacred to Hecate, an underworld goddess with lunar associations.

As adepts further ascend paths of the Tree of Life, they are confronted with different challenges of an initiatory nature. The vertical journey up the the 25th *path* of "Temperance" connecting the lunar sphere of Yesod with the higher solar sphere of Tipareth is associated with a "rainbow bridge" uncannily similar to "Bifrost", the rainbow bridge of Norse myth, as well as the Chinvit bridge connecting purgatory with heaven in Persian apocalyptic lore. Other challenges are met on the adjacent paths corresponding to the tarot trumps of "The Lightning Struck Tower", "Death", "The Devil" and the "Hanged Man"—each presenting its unique trials and initiations.

During their visionary ascents upon the Tree, magicians are advised to call upon the angels assigned to each sphere for assistance—reminiscent of the Gnostic's invocations of the archons, the guardians of the heavenly realms. Arriving at their final goal, the crown of the Tree of Life, the adept's visions become increasingly luminous and transcendent as they approach the source of all being in the tree's first emanation, the sphere of Kether.

The following is a first hand account of a pathworking of the 14th path by Florence Farr, an adept of the Golden Dawn and an exceptionally talented scryer, which illustrates the process:

> "The Tarot Trump, the Empress was taken; placed before the persons and contemplated upon...In vibratory manner pronounced Daleth. Then in spirit, saw a greenish blue landscape, suggestive of mediaeval tapestry. Effort to ascend was then made; rising on the planes; seemed to pass up through clouds and then appeared a pale green landscape and in its midst a Gothic Temple of ghostly outlines marked with light. Approached it and found the temple gained in definiteness and was concrete, and seemed a solid structure....Opposite the entrance perceived a Cross with three bars and a dove upon it; and beside this, were steps leading downwards into the dark, by a dark passage. Here was met a beautiful green dragon, who moved aside, meaning no harm, and the spirit vision passed on. Turning a corner and still passing on in the dark emerged from the darkness on to a marble terrace brilliantly white, and a garden beyond, with flowers, whose foliage was of a delicate green kind and the leaves seemed to have a white velvety surface beneath. Here, there appeared a woman of heroic proportions, clothed in green with a jeweled girdle, a crown of stars on her head, in her hand a scepter of gold, having at one apex a lustrously white closed lotus flower; in her left hand an orb bearing a cross. She

smiled proudly, and as the human spirit sought her name, replied: I am the mighty Mother Isis; most powerful of all the world, I am she who fights not, but is always victorious. I am that Sleeping Beauty who men have sought, for all time...I am the worlds desire, but few find me. When my secret is told, it is the secret of the Holy Grail." [4]

In the above pathworking, Farr used the tarot trump "The Empress", associated with the 14th path of the Tree of Life as an "astral doorway" to her vision. She visualized the trump and intoned *daleth*, the Hebrew letter associated with the path, entering into it by an act of willed imagination. The spontaneous images of her vision—landscapes, gardens, flowers, green dragon, etc., were all related to the symbolism of Venus, the goddess ruling the path. Farr's pathworking culminates with a vision and epiphany of the Empress who converses face to face with her, revealing her secrets.

The visionary dimension explored in magical pathworking is known by modern occultists as the "astral plane", a concept popularized by 19th century occultists like Levi and Blavatsky. The astral plane is believed to be the spiritual realm in which the soul exists prior to its incarnation in the physical body, and during its afterlife. It is experienced by shamans, magicians and mystics as the habitation of gods and goddesses, angels, daemons, nature spirits, and souls of the dead.

The concept of the astral plane is universal, appearing as the Egyptian *duat*, the *anima mundi* or "world soul" of alchemists, as well as the underworld and upperworld realms of shamans. It could also be understood as the dimension of myths, fairy tales, and dreams among all cultures, described by Carl Jung as the "collective unconscious" or "objective psyche". Gary Lachman uses the term "imaginal world", coined by Henri Corbin, to describe this subtle dimension of existence. He writes: "...the Imaginal World is not the world of make believe or fantasy. It is an objective world perceived inwardly, with the mind's eye." [5] Accordingly, an essential part of the training of the magician, shaman, or mystic is the opening of the "mind's eye"—development of the inner vision—by which the astral world is perceived.

Psychoanalysis- Making the Unconscious Conscious

"The mind is like an iceberg, it floats with one-seventh of its bulk above water".
    -Sigmund Freud

The late 19th century witnessed the emergence of the new science of psychology which would become a dominant influence on modern esotericism. Psychoanalysis was developed by Viennese physician Sigmund Freud who realized the *unconscious mind* was the new frontier to be explored by science. As previously mentioned, the 16th century alchemist Paracelsus had originally coined the term "unconscious mind", but Freud popularized it, defining it as the reservoir of feelings, urges, thoughts and memories outside the normal range of conscious awareness.

The goal of psychoanalysis was to bring insight into repressed motivations, emotions, dreams, and fantasies—making the unconscious conscious. Freud's psychoanalysis became a major influence on psychology, defining modern attitudes to personality and sexuality. It even inspired new art movements such as Surrealism, based on dreams and fantasies. Peter D. Kramer writes: "It is impossible to imagine the modern without Freud". His theories have influenced pop culture and modern language with words like like "ego" and "defensiveness".[6]

Freud sought to legitimize psychoanalysis as a "science", distancing his theories from anything resembling the occult, though he nevertheless was fascinated with many of the same paranormal phenomena that preoccupied occultists. Although he was a skeptic he was open minded enough to investigate psychic phenomena, once allowing his study to be used for a spiritualist séance.[7] Freud's relationship with occultism vacillated between attraction and repulsion, and he published on such occult subjects as premonitory and telepathic dreams, *deja vu*, the occult significance of dreams, and the fatal influence of numbers.[8]

Despite the revolutionary nature of psychoanalysis, Freud acknowledged his debt to ancient history. He was fascinated with archaeology and collected ancient artifacts and Egyptian art which filled his consulting room. Freud wrote: "The poets and philosophers before me discovered the unconscious; what I discovered was the scientific method by which the unconscious can be studied." He was deeply influenced by Greek myths, naming his own psychoanalytic concepts and hypotheses after them, such as the "oedipus complex", "narcissism", and the instincts of "Eros and Thanatos".

Although he was a lifelong and uncompromising atheist, in his last book *Moses and Monotheism* written shortly before his death, Freud examined his ancestral religion of Judaism. He concluded Judaism was instrumental to the development of western thought in its commitment to an invisible god—leading to "a triumph of intellectuality over sensuality", preparing the way for abstract thinking.[9]

According to psychologist David Bakan, Freud either consciously or unconsciously used Jewish mystical ideas drawn from the Kabbalah in formulating psychoanalysis.[10] Psychologist Sanford L.Drob insists that Freud was familiar with kabbalistic literature. He tells the story of the time Freud was shown a German translation of the writings of 17th century Jewish kabbalist Chayyim Vital and exclaimed in excitement: "this is gold!" Drob points out the similarity between kabbalistic ideas such as *tikkun haolom*—the mystic's work of restoring the world—and the psychoanalytic process of making the unconscious conscious and restoring the "libido" to the service of the individual, as well as other parallels.[11]

Carl Jung's Descent into the Unconscious Underworld

"Your vision will become clear only when you can look into your own heart. Who looks outside, dreams; who looks inside, awakes."
-C.J.Jung

Swiss psychologist Carl Jung was Freud's foremost disciple, sharing his interests in archaeology, myths, dreams, and paranormal phenomena. In his later years Jung developed a fascination with alchemy, acquiring a large collection of ancient alchemical manuscripts. He perceived many parallels between alchemical ideas and his own psychological theories of the unconscious. Like Freud, Jung borrowed psychological ideas and vocabulary from ancient myths and philosophy, such as the "anima and animus", "archetypes", as well as his "four psychological types" which he adapted from the four humors of ancient Greek medicine. Jung also on occasion resorted to occult techniques in his therapeutic practice—such as casting astrology charts of patients, as well as using the Chinese oracle the I-Ching.

Jung had a number of personal experiences throughout his lifetime which convinced him of the reality of the spiritual dimension. His family on his mother's side displayed clairvoyant abilities, according to his biographer Aniela Jaffe. Jung's maternal grandmother at the age of twenty fell into a trance for three days, uttering prophecies and seeing apparitions of persons unknown to her, but whose historical existence was later confirmed.[12] Jung's maternal grandfather, a preacher, believed himself to be surrounded by ghosts. He would dedicate one day every week to conversing with the spirit of his first wife who was deceased. Psychic abilities were also possessed by Jung's mother. In her diary she writes that she was called upon to protect her father from being distracted by ghosts while he was writing his sermons.[13] Jung apparently inherited some of these mediumistic talents, experiencing clairvoyant dreams and precognitions as well as hauntings, poltergeists, and other paranormal phenomena throughout his lifetime. Despite his fascination with the supernatural, Jung was always careful to publicly identify himself as a scientist rather than a mystic, fearing such associations would jeopardize his professional reputation.

Jung acquainted himself with spiritualist literature at an early age and it became his favorite topic of discussion among college friends, according to psychologist Nandor Fodor.[14] In his university years between 1899 and 1900 Jung became involved with spiritualist seances held with his cousin, whom he describes as "a young woman with marked mediumistic faculties", eventually writing his doctoral thesis on them. During these seances she would fall into trance, breathe deeply, and on occasion speak in the voice of Jung's dead grandfather and other deceased relatives. She delivered predictions about family members that often came to pass.[15] Jung recorded his cousin's fantastic visions, diagrams of the cosmos, descriptions of star-dwellers, and reincarnation fantasies. He later argued that her spiritualist phenomena were produced by her unconscious mind—and her spirit-guides were splinters of her own personality. The experience was a turning point for Jung, who wrote that it allowed him to discover "objective facts about the human psyche." [16]

Display of such paranormal phenomena occurred during Jung's visit to Freud in Vienna in 1909, which he records in his biography *Memories, Dreams, Reflections*. While meeting in Freud's study, Jung asked Freud about his views on precognition and parapsychology, which Freud promptly dismissed as "nonsensical".[17] Jung describes his emotional reaction to Freud, feeling suddenly as if his diaphragm was becoming "red hot". At that moment there was a loud noise in the book case next to them which startled them, as they feared it would topple over onto them. Jung explained that the noise was an example of a "catalytic exteriorization phenomenon", which Freud promptly rejected as "sheer bosh". Jung insisted he was mistaken and predicted another such noise. No sooner had he said this, there was another explosion in the bookcase.

In a following meeting in 1910, Freud warned Jung against succumbing to the "the black tide of mud" of occultism, fearing he was embracing occult ideas and abandoning Freud's "sexual theory" as the basis of psychoanalysis. Jung viewed Freud's attempts to reduce all psychological experiences including spirituality, to sex, as dogmatic and narrow minded. Because of their disagreements, the two eventually had a painful falling-out, ending their relationship.

Jung's Nekiya Experience

Following his traumatic breakup with his mentor Freud, Jung fell into a prolonged period of depression and introspection, later describing this time of his life as a "confrontation with the unconscious". Beginning in 1912, he went

The Tree of Visions

through a period of lengthy self-exploration during which he recorded his dreams and fantasies in his *Red Book*. Jung later described this episode of his life as his "Nekiya", named after the ritual performed by the Greek hero Odysseus in which he summoned the shades from the netherworld to receive guidance for the future. During this period he intentionally engaged in experiments of "mythopoetic imagination", discovering a mythical world beneath the threshold of his conscious ego.[18]

Jung's treated his fantasies as "real" and they were charged with intense emotions ranging from disgust, shame and nausea, to bliss—causing him at times to doubt his sanity. These experiences were so intense Jung had to grip the table with both his hands to steady himself. In order to "seize hold" of his fantasies he imagined descending to a great depth, to the edge of a cosmic abyss to an otherworldly "land of the dead". Indeed, his experience bears uncanny similarities to that of the shaman's underworld initiation. Jung writes about his first experience in which he encountered his unconscious mind by allowing his fantasies to spontaneously emerge.

> "I was sitting at my desk once more, thinking about my fears. Then I let myself drop. Suddenly it was as though the ground literally gave way beneath my feet, and I plunged down into the dark depths. I could not fend off the feeling of panic. But then, abruptly, at not too great a depth, I landed on my feet in a soft, sticky mass. I felt great relief, although I was in complete darkness. After awhile my eyes grew accustomed to the gloom, which was rather like deep twilight. Before me was the entrance to a dark cave, in which stood a dwarf with leathery skin, as if he were mummified. I squeezed past him through the narrow entrance of the cave where, on a projecting rock, I saw a glowing red crystal. I grasped the stone, lifted it, and discovered a hollow underneath. At first I could make out nothing, but then I saw that there was running water. In it a corpse floated by, a youth with blond hair and a wound in the head. He was followed by a gigantic black scarab and then by a red, newborn sun, rising out of the depths of the water. Dazzled by the light, I wanted to replace the stone upon the opening, but then a fluid welled out. It was blood. A thick jet of it leaped up, and I felt nauseated. It seemed to me that the blood continued to spurt for an unendurably long time. At last it ceased, and the vision came to and end." [19]

During his journeys to his unconscious underworld, Jung encountered fantasy figures with whom he conversed as though they were "autonomous" spirits, possessing a life of their own. He met imaginal characters such as a beautiful young blind girl named Salome, a serpent, and a wise old man named "Philemon", described by Jung as his "ghostly guru" in the underworld who acted as his "superior insight". Philemon appeared as an old man with the horns of a bull and the colorful wings of a kingfisher, holding four keys, one of which he clutched as if he were about to open a lock. Soon after his vision of Philemon, Jung was "thunderstruck" by a startling synchronistic event—finding a rare kingfisher bird dead in his garden.[20]

As a result of these encounters Jung writes: "I came to the realization there are things in the psyche which I do not produce, but which produce themselves and have their own life....Philemon represented a force which was not myself...he taught me psychic objectivity, the reality of the psyche." [21] Jung acknowledged that his "conversations with the dead", his imaginal guides in the underworld, and the fantasies and dreams experienced during this period, led to remarkable insights which were critical to developing his own unique approach to psychology.[22]

Near-Death Visions

At the age of sixty-nine, Jung suffered a heart attack, and poised at the edge of death he suffered delirium. His "near-death-experience" was complete with otherworldly visions, eerily reminiscent of the initiatory flights of shamans and mystics to the heavenly realm. In his biography he narrates one of these visions:

"It seemed to me that I was high up in space. Far below I saw the globe of the earth, bathed in a gloriously blue light. I saw the deep blue sea and the continents...Later I discovered how high in space one would have to be to have so extensive a view—approximately a thousand miles! The sight of the earth from this height was the most glorious thing I had ever seen." [23]

As Jung's vision continues he sees a dark block of stone like a meteorite floating in space before him. It reminded him of temples he had seen during his travels in India, hollowed out of granite:

"My stone was one such gigantic dark block. An entrance led into a small antechamber. To the right of the entrance, a black Hindu sat silently in lotus posture upon a stone bench. He wore a white gown, and I knew that he expected me. Two steps led up to this antechamber, and inside, on the left, was the gate to the temple. Innumerable tiny niches, each with a saucer-like concavity filled with coconut oil and small burning wicks, surrounded the door with a wreath of bright flames."

As he approached the steps leading to the entrance of the meteorite temple, Jung felt as if the "phantasmagoria of earthly existence" was being painfully stripped away from him. At the same time he experienced a great fullness and sense of relief. He anticipated entering the temple where he hoped to meet those people who could answer his questions about the past and future. To his disappointment, he next experienced a vision of his doctor telling him he had no right to leave the earth yet, and must return. At this moment the vision ceased.

Jung slowly recuperated, three weeks passing before he made up his mind to live again. He vacillated between depression during the daylight hours and nocturnal ecstasies of floating in space and "filled with the highest possible feeling of happiness." Jung writes:

> "All these experiences were glorious. Night after night I floated in a state of purest bliss, "thronged round with images of all creation….by the time morning drew near, I would feel: Now gray morning is coming again; now comes the gray world with its boxes! What idiocy, what hideous nonsense! Those inner states were so fantastically beautiful that by comparison this world appeared downright ridiculous. As I approached closer to life again, they grew fainter, and scarcely three weeks after the first vision they ceased altogether." [24]

In the above passage, Jung's likening of his waking world to a hideous "gray world with its boxes" is strangely reminiscent of the world rejecting views of ancient Gnostic mystics with whom he felt a deep spiritual kinship. His visions could be compared to the initiation experiences of shamans and mystics, who are subjected to a painful purging of their ego-identities prior to spiritual illumination and rebirth. Upon recovery from his illness, however, Jung's attitude toward life fundamentally changed. He experienced an affirmation of "things as they are" and an "unconditional "yes" to that which is—a sentiment shared by many other survivors of "near-death experiences", which we will later discuss.

Jungian Active Imagination

As a result of his direct encounter with his fantasies and dreams during his *Nekiya* experience, Jung discovered a method of exploring the unconscious mind which he later termed "Active Imagination". He advised his patients to begin by relaxing, then concentrating on a starting point: a mental image such as a fantasy or a dream which they wished to further explore. They focused on this until it began to stir into life, developing into a series of images which eventually created a complete story. Jung states that one of the greatest obstacles to this process is doubt that we have merely "made it up". He insists there is actually little we can do in terms of conscious invention, and that our unconscious mind, if allowed to do so, will "dream the dream onward" and reveal further insights.[25]

Jung used active imagination in his own creative writing and artwork, and encouraged his patients to practice it to explore their dreams and fantasies, not only using journaling, but art, dance, or other forms of creative expression. Through this process they could eventually become independent of him as a therapist and actively engage in their own "individuation process" of psychological growth.

"Directed Daydreams" of Robert Desoille

The modern era has seen a proliferation of psychological therapies using imagery techniques similar to Jung's Active Imagination. In the early years of the 20th century a French engineer, Robert Desoille, developed the "Directed Daydream" technique which is still practiced by psychotherapists. Desoille learned the technique from the occultist Eugene Caslant who published it in a book entitled *Method of Development of Supernormal Faculties* in 1927. Similar imagery techniques were used by the Hermetic Order of the Golden Dawn at the end of the 19th century, in particular the "rising on the planes" technique, by which the magician imagined a vertical ascent up the middle pillar of the Tree of Life.[26]

Desoille's technique explores "waking dreams" which he claims occur during the liminal state between waking and sleep. He used imagery techniques to help his patients confront, understand, and transform their neurotic anxieties and fears. Initially he directed them to close their eyes and relax, then visualize a series of scenes described as "imaginative happenings, as a rule characterized by unexpected adventure...." By entering into and encountering such imaginary scenes, Desoille believed the anxiety of the patient would be aroused and then diminished. He guided his patients to "descend to the deepest depths and ascend to the greatest heights."[27] He found that during their imaginary *ascent* a patient could connect with their higher potential as well as spiritual tendencies, while visualizations of *descent* explored their primitive drives and instincts. Desoille describes the continuum of psychic imagery which his patients spontaneously experienced in therapy sessions:

> "from the bottom to the top these forms were, roughly speaking the following: goblins, dwarves, dragons, giants and strong male figures; female figures, angels and spirits, and in the highest region, god...going upwards the image grows light, more transparent, more volatile, more euphorious, milder, more all embracing. In harmony with this the feelings of the ascender become better, more sublime. On the highest level, the light becomes inexpressibly white, colorless, all images lose their outline as they dissolve into an all- conquering light..." [28]

The experiences of Desoille's patients seem to confirm the visionary experiences of shamans, magicians, and mystics as previously discussed. Ascent through the "inner worlds" is generally associated with increasingly transcendent and blissful experiences involving encounter with beings of light. Descent on the other hand brings confrontation with one's fears and anxieties as well as dark gods and demons—which can bestow their own gifts of spiritual transformation, healing and psychological insight as well. Commenting on his patients' responses to their unexpected experiences, Desoille writes: "The unbelieving patient is somewhat painfully surprised to find himself so immediately confronted with heaven and hell, god and the angels. One of my patients could not refrain from uttering again and again..."but I don't believe in any heaven" and "I don't believe in angels".[29]

Psychology & Healing in Modern Magic

While psychologists borrowed concepts and techniques from ancient esoteric traditions, modern ritual magicians likewise are indebted to the psychological theories of Freud and Jung—psychoanalysts and occultists make "strange bedfellows" so to speak. Historian of esotericism Wouter J.Hanegraaff writes that between the 19th and 20th centuries, occultists transformed magic in order to make sense of it in the context of a secularized scientific world: "Magic became increasingly psychologized in contemporary occultism". [30] The psychologizing of magic served to: "...insulate magical practice from rational critique, thereby legitimizing it." Hanegraaff argues that magic has been re-interpreted by modern magicians as "...a series of psychological techniques for exalting individual consciousness." He contrasts the renaissance magician's focus on using the hidden forces of the natural world with the modern magician's goal of learning to use the hidden forces of the *psyche*.

The notorious Edwardian ritual magician Aleister Crowley was the first to use scientific jargon derived from psychology and neurology, boldly declaring: "The spirits of the Goetia are portions of the human brain".[31] In the same work Crowley writes that magic "brings up facts from the sub-conscious" and consists of "empirical, physiological experiments". This seems to imply he viewed the evocation of demons as a form of psychological self-exploration. Crowley's former secretary Israel Regardie, who became a professional Reichian therapist, took the comparison of magic and psychology a step further, writing: "... psychology and magic comprise a single system whose goal is the integration of the human personality." [32] Dion Fortune, the most well known female magical initiate of the modern era studied psychology and practiced briefly as a psychoanalyst. She acknowledged the ideas of Freud and Jung often in her writings, and in her novel *The Goat Foot God* writes that the old gods are "the same thing as the Freudian subconscious".[33]

Despite their enthusiasm for the new science of psychology it seems highly unlikely that the pioneering mages of the early 20th century saw their interactions with otherworldly beings as existing "all in their heads", or as some sort of magical psychotherapy. Crowley himself contradicts his earlier statement that spirits are portions of the human brain in his description of a superhuman entity named Aiwaz, whom he claims dictated the *Book of the Law* to him. Crowley writes: "Aiwaz is an intelligence possessed of power and knowledge absolutely beyond human experience; and therefore...a god".[34] Fortune likewise seems to repudiate her assertion that the Old Gods are one and the same as the Freudian subconscious, and later in the same novel she attributes an objective and even material existence to them. Writing about the ancient Greek god Pan she insists: "He's elemental force—that's all he is. He comes up from the earth under the feet..." [35]

In fact, Dion Fortune was underwhelmed by the practical therapeutic results of psychoanalysis, writing: "Psychoanalysis may take a mind to pieces expertly enough, but it does not very frequently succeed in putting it together again and making it work....it is a method of diagnosis rather than of treatment". [36] She advocates instead for the method of the spiritual healer who possesses the knowledge of the synthetic nature of man and "the divine spark which is the nucleus of his being". Fortune wrote presciently that the day will come when the medical profession will "recognize the part played by the emotions and imagination in our physical states in both health and disease..."[37] Her prediction has come true with the current focus on imagery in healing in modern medicine.

Shamanism, Ancient Healing & Modern Medicine

Healing with the power of imagination has been practiced by shamans and folk-healers for millennia—a fact that is not lost on modern medical researchers such as Dr. Jeanne Achterberg. She writes: "Shamanism *is* the medicine of the imagination...Shamanism is and and has been the most widely practiced type of medicine on the planet, particularly for serious illness." [38] Achterberg writes that the shaman's rituals have a a direct therapeutic effect on their patients by "creating vivid images, and by inducing altered states of consciousness conducive to self-healing". Guided imagery, suggestion, and the placebo effect—often used by shamans for healing—are also being explored by modern medical practitioners for diagnosis, therapy, and pain relief. They are being used for healing a wide range of illnesses such as cancer, asthma, headaches, diabetes, gastritis, etc. Imagery has been found effective for pain relief, decreasing fears and anxieties, strengthening the immune system, and promoting a sense of well being.[39]

Western medicine has a long history of healing with the imagination, according to Achterberg.[40] The temples of the Greek healing god Asclepius, mentioned previously, used dream incubation practices which often resulted in cures of all sorts of ailments. Ancient Greek physicians Galen and Hippocrates used imagery for diagnoses and therapy. Renaissance physicians such as Ficino used astrological, magical, and mythical imagery, as well as music for healing. Paracelsus belonged to this tradition, acknowledging the power of imagination on the "unconscious mind" of his patients—a concept he may have learned from Tartar shamans. He wrote : "The power of the imagination is a great factor in medicine. It may produce diseases...and it may cure them..." [41] Wise-women, midwives, folk healers, as well as Christian monks served as healers in rural communities of Europe. They were known to practice herbal medicine combined with magical spells, incantations and prayers, and some of their success in healing was probably based on the "placebo effect" that is being acknowledged by modern medical practitioners.

Dr. Michael Winkelman insists that the *placebo* seems to facilitate recovery from a wide range of diseases through symbolically inducing psycho-physiological responses that facilitate healing.[42] Expectations of healing and belief in the healer by the patient are an important element of the placebo. They are derived from any interaction with an individual—usually an authority figure of high status—who encourages expectations of alleviation of one's problems. In tribal societies, the shaman was such an authority figure who was endowed with a supernatural aura of healing power. In modern societies a respected doctor fulfills much of the same role, eliciting the placebo response in patients.[43]

Margaret Stutley writes that shamans use many different methods of healing based on logic, hypnosis, intuition, telepathy, autosuggestion, and the interpretation of dreams. They also use approaches similar to modern psychotherapy, encouraging the patient and giving them hope of recovery.[44] Ethnologist Mihaly Hoppal proposes that communal healing rituals led by shamans may gain their power through the combined collective energy of the participants. He writes: "It is an ancient technique in which each person concentrates and directs their energy to the same spot. Modern medicine has nothing of the kind".[45]

Irving Oyle, an osteopathic physician writes: "All healing is magic. The Indian healer and the western healer have a common denominator. The trust and confidence of both the patient and the healer". Oyle insists that neither the shaman or doctor may understand exactly how healing works, "but if they both believe, it often does".[46]

Chapter 17 Notes

Carl Gustav Jung.

1. Drury, Nevill. *The Shaman and the Magician: journeys between the worlds.* 1987: 64.

2. Mathers, MacGregor, S.L.; King, Francis. *Astral Projection, Ritual Magic and Alchemy*. 1972: 51.
3. Drury, Nevill. *The Shaman and the Magician: journeys between the worlds*. 1987:64.
4. Mathers, MacGregor, S.L.; King, Francis. *Astral Projection, Ritual Magic and Alchemy*. 1972:57-58.
5. Lachman. *The Quest for Hermes Trismegistus*. 2001: 203.
6. Kramer, Peter D. *Freud: Inventor of the Modern Mind*. 2006: 14.
7. Fodor, Nandor. *Freud, Jung, and Occultism*. 1971: 81.
8. Devereux, George. Editor. *Psychoanalysis and the Occult*. 1953: 49-109.
9. Freud, Sigmund. Moses and Monotheism. Trans. Jones, Katherine. 1939:180.
10. Bakan, David. *Sigmund Freud and the Jewish Mystical Tradition*. 2004.
11. Drob, Sanford L., Ph.D. "This Is Gold": Freud, Psychotherapy and the Lurianic Kabbalah". *newkabbalah.com*. Sanford L. Drob. 2001-04.
12. Fodor, Nandor. *Freud, Jung, and Occultism*. 1971: 87.
13. Jaffe, Aniela. "Details About C.G. Jung's Family". *Spring* (1984): 35-43. 1984.
14. Fodor. *Freud, Jung, and Occultism*.1971: 88.
15. Lachman, Gary. *Jung The Mystic*. 2010: 48.
16. Jung, C.G. *Memories, Dreams, Reflections*. edited by Jaffe', Aniela. 1963: 107.
17. Ibid,:155.
18. Jung, C. G. *The Red Book*, Liber Novus. (Ed,& trans.) Shamdasani, Donu, Kyburz, Mark, Peck, John. 2009: 208.
19. Jung. *Memories, Dreams, Reflections*.:179-181.
20. Ibid.:183.
21. Ibid.:183.
22. Ibid:192.
23. Ibid:290.
24. Ibid.:293.
25. *The Symbolic Life: Miscellaneous Writing* (The Collected Works of C.G.Jung, vol. 18.) 1977: 171-172.
26. Mathers; King. *Astral Projection, Ritual Magic and Alchemy*. 1972: 138.
27. Merkur, Dan. *Gnosis: an Esoteric Tradition of Mystical Visions and Unions*. 1993: 44.
28. Desoille, Robert. Trans. Haronian, Frank. *The Directed Daydream*. 1965.
29. Merkur. *Gnosis: an Esoteric Tradition of Mystical Visions and Unions*. 1993: 45.
30. Hanegraff, Wouter. "How Magic Survived the Disenchantment of the World". *Academia.edu*.
31. Mathers, MacGregor. (trans.); Crowley, Aleister. (ed.) *The Goetia: The Lesser Key of Solomon the King: Lemegeton—Clavicula Salomonis Regis*.1995:18.
32. Regardie, Israel; Cicero, Chic; Cicero Sandra Tabatha. *The Middle Pillar: The Balance Between Mind and Magic*. 2002: 5.
33. Fortune, Dion. *The Goat Foot God*. 1989 : 85.
34. Crowley, Aleister. *Book of the Law*. 2011: chap. 7, II.
35. Fortune. *The Goat Foot God*. 1989: 152.
36. Fortune, Dion. *Applied Magic and Aspects of Occultism*. 1987: 157.
37. Ibid.:157.

38. Achterberg, Jeanne. *Imagery in Healing: Shamanism and Modern Medicine*.1985: 6.
39. Ibid.: 88-89.
40. Ibid: 7.
41. Achterberg. *Imagery in Healing: Shamanism and Modern Medicine*. 1985: 72.
42. Winkelman, Dr. Michael. *Shamanism A Biopsychosocial Pardigm of Consciousness and Healing — Second Edition*. 2010:187.
43. According to Winkelman, placebos have been found to treat conditions with major psychosomatic components, mental health problems, and physical conditions such as cardiovascular problems, multiple sclerosis, Parkinsons disease, and rheumatoid arthritis. They are particularly effective for neurotic and hysteric conditions, gynecological problems, gastrointestinal and respiratory disorders, chronic pain, and interpersonal problems. (Winkelman 2010: 245). He writes placebos produce measurable physiological and/or psychological changes; they exert effects on a number of biological mechanisms, including activation of endogenous opioids, release of dopamine in striatum, effects on the subthalamic nucleus, conditioning of immune mediators and reducing excitability in limbic regions. (Winkelman 2010: 188).
44. Stutley, Margaret. *Shamanism: An Introduction*. 2003 :85.
45. Kuznetsov, Nikolay. "Interview with Hungarian Folklorist and Ethnologist Mihaly Hoppal on the Occasion of his 70th Jubilee." *Folklore, Electronic Journal of Folklore*. Vol. 53, 2013:169.
46. Achterberg. *Imagery in Healing: Shamanism and Modern Medicine*. 1985: 97.

Chapter 18: Science & Altered States

Hypnagogia—Visions Between Waking & Sleep

The innate human ability to experience visions is the subject of recent scientific research. Using a multi-disciplinary approach combining neurology, psychology, and clinical studies, the state between waking and sleep known as "hypnagogia" is being explored. The term was coined by the nineteenth century psychologist Alfred Maury who derived it from the Greek *hypnos* (sleep) and *agogeus* (guide).

Dr. Andreas Mavromatis has extensively researched hynagogia. He links it to dreams, daydreams, schizophrenia, meditation and creativity, as well as mystical and paranormal experiences such as psi and telepathy. In fact, the hypnagogic state of being "awake while dreaming" has been known to mystics for ages.[1] The philosopher Iamblichus wrote of "voices" and "bright and tranquil light" that came to him in the condition between sleeping and waking" believing they were a "god-sent" experience. Emmanuel Swedenborg reported his hypnagogic experiences, as well as a method for producing them.

Jung's technique of Active Imagination combines visualization techniques with hypnagogia, according to Dan Merkur who insists that by practicing techniques similar to Active Imagination, mystics experienced visions and mystical unions.[2] He insists that the visions and fantastic imagery of the alchemists may have resulted from hypnagogic experiences while working in their laboratories.

Artists have used hypnagogia to explore imagination and enhance creativity. The surrealist painter Rene Magritte referred to his paintings as "the representations of half sleep". Salvador Dali trained himself to doze in a chair while his chin rested on a spoon which he held in one hand propped by his elbow resting on a table; when his muscles relaxed on the verge of falling asleep his chin would drop and he would awaken, often in the midst of a hypnagogic dream or vision, which he would then proceed to paint.[3]

Mavromatis theorizes that hypnagogic phenomena arise from all three parts of the brain: the central core (reptilian brain), the limbic system (mammalian brain), and the cerebral cortex (neomammalian brain). What is "conscious" and "logical" to one brain may be "unconscious" to another, which would explain the strange quality of hypnagogic experiences which may be the result of what he terms "old brain" activity. He writes that hynagogia is brought about by the activation of the thalamus and other old brain structures which cause the cortex to "idle" as at the brink of sleep, where a minimum of cortex activity occurs.[4]

Cortical brain activity is associated with the "new brain" and our conscious ego. Its inhibition allows for the activation of the "old brain"—the brainstem core, the hippocampus, medulla oblongata and thalamas—which operate through *imagery and symbols* associated with mythological consciousness, according to Gary Lachman. He explains that the "new brain" shuts down enough for the old brain to "turn on"—staying on just enough to observe the old brain's consciousness. He writes: "We can say in hypnagogia one brain "watches" another." [5]

Hypnagogia is characterized by physiological responses such as relaxation and reduced respiration leading to increased carbon dioxide in the blood, similar to the state achieved in meditation, according to Mavromatis. He also points out that hynagogia activates the pineal gland in the thalamus located in the area known as the "third eye"—associated with spiritual visions and enlightenment and described as "the seat of the soul". The pineal gland is the only organ in the body which produces the hormone of melatonin; this in turn affects the synthesis and release of serotonin and other neurotransmitters in the brain, which have a tranquilizing effect on the central nervous system. Interestingly, melatonin is believed to increase with meditation exercises such as relaxation and visualization which are related to hypnagogia.[6]

Mavromatis argues that from an evolutionary perspective, hypnagogia may offer new potentials such as being able to retain consciousness of one's surroundings while sleeping or exploring the internal world. It could provide the ability to dream without losing consciousness—the same state that yogi's aspire to when learning to sustain continuity of consciousness unaffected by sleep. He sees hypnagogia as a state in which "rationality and nonrationality are brought to a synergetic relationship", which could be explored to enhance artistic and scientific insights, awareness of dreams, psychic development, and personal problem solving. Ultimately the hypnagogic state enhances the integration of the unconscious and conscious mind and could be used to access visionary consciousness.[7]

The Neuropsychological Stages of Shamanic Trance

Cognitive archeologists David Lewis-Williams and David Pearce use neuropsychological research into altered states experienced by shamans as a means of gaining insight into the minds of prehistoric people. They propose that shamanistic as well as religious experiences which appear universally can be explained by the functioning of the human nervous system and consciousness, writing: "all religions have an ecstatic component, and, less dramatically, all involve altering consciousness..."

The authors describe a wide range of catalysts used for inducing altered states of consciousness: prayer, chanting, prolonged rhythmic dancing, hypnagogia, psychotropic substances, near-death experiences, sensory deprivation, meditation, schizophrenia and various pathological conditions.[8] They insist however that altered states are *similar* despite the different means of inducing them. They are often characterized by seeing bright geometric patterns, sensations of floating or flying, passage through a tunnel, transformations of one thing into another including humans into animal forms, and the ability to "see vividly". Lewis-Williams and Pearce provide the following neuropsychological model which breaks down the sequence of movement into deeper levels of altered consciousness into three generalized stages:

Stage 1 - Altered states often begin with geometric mental imagery described by researchers as *entopic imagery* or "phosphenes", which appear as grids or lattices of expanding patterns, sets of parallel lines, bright dots and flecks, zig-zag lines, or filigrees of thin meandering lines and spirals. These forms are rapidly changing and pulsate with bright light which expands and rotates, and they "morph" into each other. The authors note that entopic imagery is found commonly in cave art, rock painting, and other shamanic art worldwide, and conjecture these patterns were painted by shamans as a result of their trance states.[9]

Stage 2 - When people move into the next deeper stage of altered consciousness they try to make sense of the entopic images they are seeing by construing them as objects with emotional or religious significance. The mind organizes the chaotic flow of images into *recognizable forms or icons*. Thus, for example a bright pulsating light becomes a "large green eye opening and closing". As subjects move into more profoundly altered states of consciousness they often experience a vortex or *tunnel* at the end of which is a bright light. This appears in experiences of shamans world-wide, who associate it with the tunnel that leads to the underworld in their visions. The authors note this tunnel is often associated with the "near-death-experience" in our culture.

Stage 3 - During the deepest level of the altered state people emerge from the previous vortex experience, and..."enter a bizarre, ever-changing world of hallucinations" in the words of Lewis-Williams and Pearce. In this stage they experience *somatic hallucinations* related to distorted awareness of one's body, as well as *zoopsia*, which involves seeing animals, and changing into animals and other transformations. Awareness of entopic forms (stage 1) persists, along with iconic hallucinations (stage 2). Hallucinations are experienced in all the senses and one may experience *synesthesia*—where the senses become confused and one may "smell a sound" or "hear a color". After-images may recur unexpectedly for some time after the hallucinations.[10]

This neuropsychological model of three stages of altered consciousness could be seen to generally correspond to the visionary experiences of shamans. It describes the entopic geometrical patterns painted on rocks and cave walls by indigenous and Paleolithic shamans, the tunnel leading to the underworld, as well as visions of transformation into animal spirits.

The authors insist consciousness should be thought of as a *spectrum*. At one end is alert consciousness by which we rationally relate to our environment. Further along the spectrum are more introverted states in which we engage in problem solving through thinking. A step further brings relaxation and daydreaming unaffected by the environment. Gradually we slip into the hypnagogic state with hallucinations as described above. From there we drift into dreaming.[11] Surveys show more than 70 percent of the population experiences vivid mental imagery, or hypnagogia prior to sleeping. Lewis-Williams and Pearce write:

> "Many people experience hypnagogia, but dismiss the condition as mere dreaming. But hypnagogic experiences are not the same as dreams. Importantly, attending to hypnagogic experiences increases their duration and frequency. People can learn to engage, control and prolong both their hypnagogic experiences and dreams."

Robert Monroe's Out-of-Body Journeys

Some of the most fascinating research into altered states has involved the study of "out of body experiences" (OOBE). This term was coined by American radio broadcasting executive Robert Monroe (1915-1995), along with his friend, psychologist Charles Tart. While practicing sleep learning techniques in 1958, Monroe began to spontaneously experience his consciousness exteriorizing from his physical body. Fearing for his sanity, he decided to research this phenomenon, discovering that his experiences of OOBE's were not unique. He cites surveys showing some 25 percent of the population remembers at least one such event. Monroe rejected the term "astral projection" as "occult", and "nonscientific" and attempted to study OOBE's in an objective and scientific manner.

Monroe explains: "an out-of-body-experience (OOBE) is a condition where you find yourself outside of your physical body, fully conscious and able to perceive and act as if you were functioning physically...you can move through space (and time?) slowly or apparently somewhere beyond the speed of light. You can observe, participate in events, make willful decisions based upon what you perceive and do. You can move through physical matter such as walls, steel plates, concrete, earth, oceans, air, even atomic radiation without effort or effect." [12]

Monroe found that while in his "second body", which he describes as a mentally created duplicate of his physical body, he could explore several different dimensions of reality. He names the most basic dimension "Locale I", consisting of the physical world and the everyday reality of people and places that exist in the material world at the time of the OOBE. During his visits to Locale I, Monroe was able to provide detailed information about events occurring in distant locations. On numerous occasions he visited distant friends and acquaintances in an out-of-body state to observe their activities at the time, and was later able to confirm with them that they actually occurred.[13]

"Locale II" is a non-physical environment where "thought" is the driving force—you become what you imagine there, according to Monroe.[14] It encompasses the dimension of consciousness known as the "afterlife", including the heavens and hells as described by world religions. It is timeless and inhabited by entities of different degrees of intelligence and evolution. Monroe was able to visit deceased friends, family, and strangers and gain personal assurance that life continues after death. His experiences there, contrary to popular opinion, were not always pleasant or comforting. In "Locale III", he experienced a parallel universe where he lived the life of another person in a world similar to the physical world, yet oddly different.[15]

Monroe eventually founded a research institute with the goal of understanding OOBE's scientifically. Test subjects were isolated in darkened booths that were acoustically and electrically shielded; electrodes for monitoring physiological states were glued to their heads, fingers and bodies and they were monitored by a team of medical, psychiatric and scientific experts. The team found that various audio and electromagnetic sound patterns transmitted through headphones could induce brain-wave frequencies to help the subjects relax, stay awake, or sleep. They discovered a state of consciousness which they labelled "Focus 10" where the mind is awake and the body asleep, which appears to be similar to hypnagogic states previously discussed. The team next developed higher frequency beta signals that enhanced perception. Subjects began to perceive light and color patterns as well as hear voices, music, and sometimes loud explosions which were found to precede the onset of OOBE's. Often they perceived a pinpoint of light, which when approached became larger and larger. Monroe writes: "it felt as though one were going through a tunnel to get to the light"—a common description by those who experience near-death-experiences, as well as shamans who enter the "vortex", or second stage of trance—as discussed above by Lewis-Williams and Pearce.

Monroe's clinical experiments led to workshops where participants were trained in techniques for inducing OOBE's. They were taught to achieve the Focus 10 state and from there they learned how to move on to "Focus 12", where all physical-data input is shut off and consciousness can perceive in ways other than through the five senses.[16] Monroe writes: "The action really begins here, where perspectives and overviews change drastically. It is here where the participant truly understands that he is "more than his physical body"".[17] He insists that the individual begins to *know*, not just believe, that he or she survives physical death.

During their OOBE's, many of Monroe's "explorers" experienced reunions with deceased friends and family, as well as encounters with other forms of intelligent energy. They began to spontaneously make "friends" with benign beings or entities who guided them to explore new levels of consciousness and locales of inner space. Explorers visited other planetary systems and life forms, and many encountered friendly beings who possessed technologies that were far beyond anything known to humans. Monroe found these beings communicated using non-verbal communication or direct thought.

Surprisingly about thirty percent of explorers reported that the friendly entities took over their physical bodies and spoke through them using their vocal cords—a condition which sounds eerily similar to the shaman's conscious possession by their helping-spirits who speak through them in seances. Monroe noted that during such "visits" there was a change in the body voltage and other bio-monitoring of the test subjects.

Robert Monroe's work is remarkable in that it is based entirely on his own experience and research, since he decided from the beginning not to be influenced by prior religious beliefs or occult theories. He spent decades methodically observing his own OOBE's and those of many others. Nevertheless, it is intriguing how his scientific research seems to corroborate ancient accounts of astral projection, visionary journeys, and altered states of consciousness. Monroe concludes that his experiences "...seem to be a continuation of a line of thought that has persisted for thousands of years".[18] They ultimately confirm the experiences of shamans, magicians, and mystics—who also journeyed "out-of-body"—to visit other "locales" of consciousness.

Raymond Moody–Near-Death-Experience, Apparitions & Visions

The term "near-death experience" (NDE) was popularized with the publication in 1975 of Dr. Raymond Moody's influential book *Life After Life*. It is based on his interviews of survivors of physical death through accidents, injury, or illness, as well as those who were resuscitated after having been judged clinically dead by doctors.

Moody writes that his subjects often reported phenomena during NDE's such as "out-of-body experiences" and viewing their physical body from above. They also experienced sensations of being pulled through dark tunnels and inhabiting an invisible spiritual body that could pass easily through physical objects—similar to Monroe's "second body". Feelings of peace and quiet as well as buzzing and ringing sounds often occurred. Encounters with a being of light, meeting dead relatives and friends, and review of one's lifetime memories were also common.

Many of Moody's subjects reported their lives were permanently changed and deepened by the experience. Some experienced enhanced intuition and psychic sensitivity. It was common for them to lose their fear of death. They even compared death to "awakening", "graduating" and "escape from jail", a liberating release from the physical body. Jung's near-death experience mentioned earlier involved many of these same experiences and responses. Moody discusses the parallels with Plato's writings such as *Phaedo, The Republic,* and the *Myth of Er* which contain similar descriptions of death and separation of the soul from the body, as well as descriptions of dimensions of reality other than the physical world. He also mentions Emanuel Swedenborg's writings, claiming they are remarkably similar to the experiences reported by his subjects—including out-of-body experiences, encounters with angels, meeting with spirits of departed friends, life reviews, etc.[19]

In his recent work, Moody has expanded his exploration of near-death-experiences into the study of apparitions of the dead, asking himself whether mirror-gazing could be used to facilitate apparitions in a controlled setting "where scientists could actually watch a person seeing a ghost?" [20] Moody began researching the history of visionary experiences, dream incubation, hypnagogia and mirror gazing. He even visited the Oracle of The Dead in Greece, the ancient *psychomanteum* which people visited to communicate with the dead, which we previously discussed. Moody began to experiment with mirror gazing himself, and was startled to see an apparition of his maternal grandmother who had died some years previously. He conversed with her for an extended period of time and writes:

"I want to emphasize how completely natural this meeting was. As with other subjects who had experienced an apparitional facilitation, my meeting was in no way eerie or bizarre. In fact this was the most normal and satisfying interaction I have ever had with her." [21]

Moody went on to develop his own *psychomanteum*, converting an old mill house into a facility he calls the "Theater of the Mind", in memory of the scrying work of the Elizabethan magician and scientist John Dee. There he created an environment conducive for experiencing visionary encounters. In preparation for a scrying session Moody asks the participant to bring photos or objects which belonged to their deceased relative, and spends time with them discussing their memories of them. They are then directed to enter a darkened booth where they recline on a couch while gazing at a large mirror before them. Moody writes that a number of individuals actually experienced apparitions of deceased family members—around fifty percent reported complex communications. In approximately fifteen percent of the cases, subjects said they actually heard the voice of the deceased.[22] Many saw a different relative than the one intended. Apparitions were not merely confined to the mirror, but occasionally seemed to step out of the mirror into the surrounding environment. Often encounters did not occur in the booth but a few hours later in other locations.

Moody writes in his book *Reunions* that he has observed more than three hundred individuals as they were mirror gazing, interviewing them afterward about their experiences. Many of these sessions were intended as a form of grief therapy to allow emotional closure with departed relatives. Others were done to pursue self-understanding as part of an innovative process of psychotherapy, as well as for exploring altered states of consciousness, relaxation, and creativity.

Dr. Raymond Moody's research into life-after-death experiences, scrying, and facilitated apparitions has pioneered a new approach to consciousness research and psychotherapy. He explores in a modern clinical context aspects of the shaman's age-old work as *psychopomp*—the guide of souls to the otherworld.

Shamanism as a Universal Experience

The scientific research presented in this chapter suggests shamanism can be seen as a universal experience common to all humans. The existence of a "universal drive" to alter consciousness, and procedures for ritually doing so, have been found in virtually all societies, according to anthropologist Michael Winkelman.[23] Neuropsychology proposes that shamanic altered states of consciousness are "hardwired" into the human species and experienced similarly by all peoples—as they are spontaneously produced by our brains and nervous systems. In fact, as Lewis-Williams and Pearce argue, trance states experienced by modern humans are probably similar to those experienced by our Paleolithic ancestors who painted their visions on cave walls—since the human neurological system has not changed for over 35,000 years.

Likewise, our basic instincts, drives, and psychic experiences are likely similar to those of our early forbearers as well. As Jung points out, the human mind has its own history, and the psyche retains traces left from previous stages of its development which it spontaneously reveals in dreams and fantasies.[24] According to Jung, individual visionary experiences draw from the reservoir of myths and archetypes of the "collective unconscious" shared by all mankind. In his study of thousands of dreams of his patients, Jung discovered they often contained symbols similar to those found in ancient myths. His theory of the collective unconscious may account for some of the striking parallels between myths as well as magical and shamanic practices occurring worldwide.

Humans have an innate tendency to access altered states of consciousness, according to psychologist Roger Walsh. He notes the spontaneous occurrences of lucid dreaming, out-of body-experiences, near-death experiences, and hypnosis throughout history. Walsh proposes shamanism emerged spontaneously and independently around the world because of a "common innate human tendency and recurrent social need"–claiming it could have been discovered and rediscovered in different eras and cultures.[25]

The research of Jung, Monroe, Moody, Desoille, Mavromatis, Lewis-Williams and others presented here confirms that hypnogogic imagery, out-of-body experiences, and visionary states familiar to ancient shamans, magicians, and mystics continue to be experienced by people in today's world—and with practice can be developed.

Chapter 18 Notes

1. Mavromantis, Andrea. Hypnagogia. 1987: 3-4.
2. Merkur. Gnosis: an Esoteric Tradition of Mystical Visions and Unions. 1993: ix.
3. Lewis-Williams, David. The Mind in the Cave. 2002: 45.
4. Mavromatis. Hypnagogia. 1987: 258.
5. Lachman, Gary. "Hypnogogia". Fortean Times, Oct. 2002.
6. Mavromatis. Hypnagogia. 1987: 263.
7. Ibid.:278.
8. Lewis-Williams, J. David; Pearce, D.G.. Inside the Neolithic Mind. 2005: 40.
9. Ibid.:48.
10. Ibid.:55.
11. Ibid.: 56.
12. Monroe, Robert A. Far Journeys. 1985: 3.
13. Monroe, Robert. Journeys Out of the Body. 1971:46-59.
14. Ibid.:73-85.
15. Ibid.:86-100.
16. Monroe. Far Journeys. 29-30.
17. Ibid.:29.
18. Monroe, Robert A. Journeys Out of the Body. : 263.
19. Moody, Raymond A. Life After Life: the investigation of a phenomenon—survival of bodily death. 1975: 118.
20. Moody, Raymond A.; Perry, Paul. Reunions. 1993: xv.
21. Ibid.:26.
22. Ibid.:118.
23. Winkelman. Shamanism A Biopsychosocial Pardigm of Consciousness and Healing—Second Edition. 2010: 4.
24. Jung. C.G. Man and His Symbols. 1964: 98.
25. Walsh, Roger N., M.D., Ph.D. The Spirit of Shamanism. 1990: 13-14.

Chapter 19: Neopaganism Today

Alternative Spirituality & Earth Religions

Neopaganism gained popularity as part of the 1960's counterculture, offering alternative spiritual paths to the mainstream religions. Espousing individualistic and non-authoritarian approaches to spirituality, neopagans focus on self-realization and a renewed sense of connection with nature. The word "pagan" literally means "rustic" or "country dweller" in Latin, and refers to the ancient polytheistic religions of ancient Britain, Europe and the Near-East. The term "neopaganism" refers to the contemporary "nature religions" which are inspired by elements of those ancient religions.[1] Margot Adler in her book *Drawing Down the Moon* writes:

> "Most Neo-Pagans look to the old Pre-Christian nature religions of Europe, the ecstatic religions and the mystery traditions as a source of inspiration and nourishment. They gravitate to ancient symbols and ancient myths, to the old polytheistic religions of the Greeks, the Egyptians, the Celts, and the Sumerians. They are reclaiming these sources, transforming them into something new..."[2]

Although it could be argued that neopaganism is not a single religion but a collection of diverse spiritual groups, neopagans share similar values and beliefs.[3] These include polytheism, goddess worship, respect for the earth, celebration of seasonal festivals based on the wheel of the year, and the practice of magic.

The various paths of neopaganism encompass a spectrum of religious philosophies. Wicca and Neodruidry eclectically combine elements of different ancient cultures and religions. While their followers may borrow from pagan religious traditions, they also adapt them to their own needs, as personal freedom is considered a primary goal of their spirituality. In contrast, pagan reconstructionist movements draw from culturally specific traditions of ancient Celtic, Germanic, Egyptian and Greek paganism. They may take a stricter approach, recognizing only certain historical texts and sources.[3]

The repeal of the British Witchcraft Law in 1951 contributed to the revival of western esotericism, making it possible for occultists to "come out of the closet" without fear of legal persecution. In 1954 Gerald Gardner published his book *Witchcraft Today* which led to the phenomenal rise in popularity of Wicca, the most widely practiced form of contemporary neopaganism. Ethan Doyle White writes that Wicca is influenced by various historical sources: the ancient witch-cult, folk-magic, western esotericism, as well as romanticism and paganism.[4] It was also inspired by the writings of 20th century anthropologist Margaret Murray and poet Robert Graves. Wicca has morphed into different traditions such as Gardnerian, Alexandrian, Dianic, Faery, Celtic, and others. Like other forms of neopaganism, it is highly decentralized, with numerous solitary practitioners. Many wiccans develop their own beliefs, rituals and other practices. Others form small groups or covens which offer structured grades and initiations into their craft.

Neodruidry which began in the 18th century as an antiquarian revival of ancient Celtic Druidism metamorphosed into its present form in the 1950's. Contemporary druid Phillip Carr-Gom argues that the "Earth Religions" have emerged in response to the profound sense of alienation from the natural world in modern Western civilization, and "the growing awareness of the necessity to combine our spirituality with a reverence and care for the Earth." [5] He points out that Druidry, based on Celtic traditions, offers a spirituality that is close to the ancestral roots of most Europeans, and therefore many North Americans as well.

The religions of the Northern Tradition such as Asatru, which translates as "faith in the Aesir/gods", is a form of Germanic neopaganism which emerged simultaneously in Iceland, Britain and the United States in the early 1970's.[6] Also known as Heathenry, it focuses on Norse paganism of the Viking Age as described in the ancient *Eddas*.

The Greek religion of Hellenismos which appeared in the 1990's is based on the Olympian gods and the mythology, philosophy, and religion of ancient Greece. Its members celebrate the festivals of their ancestors — the *anthesteria* — based on the cycles of mother nature, which honor the gods and heroes through recitals, hymns, bloodless sacrifice, and offerings and libations.[7] In its homeland of Greece, Hellenismos originally met with condemnation from the Greek Orthodox Church and press, yet its followers have persevered and grown in number over recent years.

In the Baltic countries of Lithuania and Latvia the folk-religion of Romuva, a revival of the indigenous pagan religion, is thriving again, emerging from centuries of suppression by the Catholic Church and more recently Communism.[8] Lithuania was the last country in Europe to practice a pagan faith until forced to convert to Christianity in 1387. As well as celebrating the traditional pagan holidays, folklore, and music, the followers of Romuva are environmental activists and stewards of sacred sites.

In the former Communist countries of Russia, Ukraine and eastern Europe, pagan revivals are also occurring based on local pre-Christian traditions, attesting to the widespread appeal of neopaganism as a means of recovering ethnic nature-based spirituality.

Neopaganism's growth across Europe and North America over the past few decades has been impressive. Isaac Bonewitz estimates the number of self-identified practicing neopagans in the U.S. and Canada at between 500,000 to several million with the numbers increasing rapidly.[9] The 2011 census in England and Wales showed that over 80,000 people described themselves as pagans.[10]

Neopaganism & Shamanism

Many forms of neopaganism share similar beliefs and practices with shamanism, including animism, the reverence for nature, magic and divination, and a spirit world which can be accessed through altered states of consciousness. Because of these commonalities the word "neopaganism" is often used interchangeably with "animism" and "shamanism". Neopagans sense an affinity with the teachings of shamanism and have incorporated shamanic practices into their religions.

Wiccan author Scott Cunningham writes: "many of the techniques of Wicca are shamanic in origin...Wicca can be described as a shamanic religion..."[11] The early founders of Wicca claimed an unbroken lineage originating in prehistoric European shamanism, an idea which has since been refuted by historians such as Ronald Hutton. Nevertheless, wiccan practices such as trance induction, working with animal familiar spirits, divination, and magic clearly bear similarities to those of shamanism. Although the religion of Wicca is a modern reconstruction, its primal deities, the goddess and horned-god, are nevertheless inspired by authentic prehistoric precedents. As previously discussed, the religious beliefs of Late Paleolithic Europe seem to have been dominated by the figures of a pregnant fertility goddess and horned shaman. Likewise, we looked at the early Neolithic societies of the Mid-East in which the mother goddess and her consort the bull-god were worshipped.[12]

John and Caitlín Matthews who have authored numerous books on Celtic mythology and traditions espouse a form of "Celtic Shamanism", presenting workshops which teach techniques similar to shamanic journeying. Some Neodruids in Great Britain use sweat-lodges, derived from the spiritual practices of Native Americans. Practitioners of Nordic Seidr have studied shamanism and adapted its methods in their spiritual seances, according to Robert J. Wallis.[13] Similar to the ancient oracular rites of the Germanic Volvas which were discussed earlier, the modern "seeress" during the Seidr enters a state of trance in which she journeys in vision to the otherworld. There she communicates with the spirits of the ancestors and other spirits for the benefit of the community, similar to the work of indigenous shamans.

Megalithomania

Along with neopaganism's exponential growth have come the inevitable growing pains. In Great Britain, megalithic monuments such as Stonehenge and Avebury have become the destination of religious pilgrimages of Wiccans, Druids, Heathens and goddess worshippers. Heavily used by them for their ceremonies, these ancient archaeological sites have on occasion been damaged by fires, candles and litter left by worshippers. Julian Cope, punk musician and "modern antiquarian", gives this advice to visitors of the sites: "megalithic adventurers should always leave with more rubbish than they came in with".[14] Stonehenge has been the center of political controversy, with skirmishes between police and worshippers over public access to the monument. The conflict has been resolved however, and English Heritage now allows neopagans as well as the general public to use the site for Solstice and Equinox celebrations. During a recent summer solstice, the BBC News reported an estimated crowd of 21,000 people at Stonehenge, a mixture of serious druids, party-goers as well as ordinary visitors.[15]

Western Esotericism Today

Once available only to initiates, esoteric literature has become increasingly accessible to the public over the past few decades. Many large bookstores stock dozens of titles on occult subjects which were all but impossible to find a few years ago. Any quick internet search will reveal numerous websites and blogs providing information on ritual magic, occultism, neopaganism and neoshamanism.

Recently there has also been a notable interest by the academic community in esotericism, past and present. Graduate programs and courses in Western Esotericism are being offered at several universities in North America and Europe. Historians, ethnologists, and anthropologists are researching magic and ancient religions, providing a wealth of published information that was unavailable in the past. Studies of the ancient Hermetic arts of astrological magic, laboratory alchemy, and grimoire magic, as well as traditional witchcraft are being published by scholar-practitioners, which will undoubtedly inspire the next generation of occultists.

Aaron Leitch's book *Secrets of the Magical Grimoires* looks at traditional magical practices of the grimoires.[16] Jake Stratton-Kent's *Encylopaedia Goetica* explores the historical roots of European spirit-based magic.[17] Both books emphasize the shamanic origins of magic. The authors are spokespersons for the "grimoire movement", advocating historical research and practice of traditional approaches to magic, as well as adapting them to modern circumstances.

In the cultural melting pot of North America, local traditions of folk-magic such as southern Hoodoo "Rootwork", Pennsylvania Dutch "Pow-Wow", and hispanic Curanderismo are gaining popularity and recognition. The Caribbean spiritist religions of Santeria, Voudon, and Palo Mayombe, as well as Afro-Brazilian Kimbanda are growing in influence in the western hemisphere. They provide examples of living magical traditions that may help "fill in the gaps" in the practice of traditional western magic according to Stratton-Kent and Leitch. These indigenous magical currents are cross-fertilizing and enriching western esotericism, which like all cultural movements is diverse, dynamic, and changing with the times.

In the words of Nicholas Goodrick-Clarke: "...the historical evidence suggests that esotericism...involves a return to sources, to some archetypal forms of thought and energy which generate a fresh round of cultural and spiritual development."[18] Perhaps in our present era of multi-culturalism spurred on by globalization, esotericism will again contribute to the regeneration of ancient spiritual traditions, allowing us to perceive the commonalities of worldwide magico-religious beliefs and practices.

Chapter 19 Notes

1. Hanegraff, Wouter. *New Age Religion and Western Culture. Esotericism in the Mirror of Secular Thought.*1996: 84.
2. Adler, Margot. *Drawing Down the Moon: Witches, Druids, Goddess-Worshippers, and other Pagans in America.* 2006:1-4.
3. Ibid.: 4.
4. White, Ethan Doyle. *Wicca: History, Belief, and Community In Modern Pagan Witchcraft.* 2015.
5. Nichols, Ross. *The Book of Druidry: History, Sites and Wisdom.* 1990:13.
6. Strmiska, Michael F. (ed.) *Modern Paganism in World Cultures.* 2005:127.
7. Supreme Council of Ethikoi Hellenes. (Official Website) *FAQ's.*
8. Strmiska, Michael F. (ed.) *Modern Paganism in World Cultures.* 2005: 242.
9. Bonewitz, Isaac. "How Many "Pagans" Are There?" *www.neopagan.net.* 2005.
10. "Modern Paganism" *Wikapedia.*
11. Cunningham, Scott. *Wicca: A Guide for the Solitary Practitioner.* 2004: 4.
12. Cauvin, Jacques.*The Birth of the Gods and the Origins of Agriculture.* 2000: 69.
13. Wallis, Robert J. *Shamans/Neo-Shamans: Ecstasies, Alternative Archaeologies & Contemporary Pagans.* 2003: 94-96.
14. Ibid.:152.
15. "Summer Solstice Draws Thousands to Stonehenge". *BBC News, Wiltshire.* 21 June, 2013.
16. Leitch, Aaron. *Secrets of the Magical Grimoires.* 2005.
17. Stratton-Kent, Jake. *Geosophia: the argo of magic: from the Greeks to the Grimoires.* 2010.
18. Goodrick-Clarke, Nicholas. *The Western Esoteric Traditions.* 2008: 14.

Chapter 20: Neoshamanism

Resurgence of Shamanism Worldwide

Beginning with the final decades of the 20th century and continuing to the present, traditional shamanism and animistic religions have witnessed a dramatic revival around the world. The people of Siberia and Central Asia are now recovering their indigenous spiritual traditions following decades of suppression by the Soviets. Since the collapse of Communism, shamans have re-emerged, resuming their healing practices and regaining the respect of their local communities. The ancient Eurasian shamanic religion of Tengrism, an animistic faith based on honoring the deities and spirits of sky, earth, and ancestors, is experiencing a revival in areas of Central Asia such as Mongolia, Kazakhstan, and Turkey.[1]

According to shamanic practitioner Sarangerel, there are hundreds of shamans in Mongolia who have inherited spirits from old lineages, and in Buryatia and other parts of Siberia similar numbers are occurring.[2] Along with shamanism's rise in popularity, however, have come the challenges of commercialization. In Ulan Bator, the capitol of Mongolia, shamanism has become a booming business as hundreds of neoshamans have set up shop, cashing in on the trend. According to a recent New York Times article by Dan Levin: "a steady stream of clients suffering from unemployment, illness or heartbreak are just a phone call or taxi ride away".[3] In Siberia a new generation of shamans are also practicing their craft as well as attempting to preserve and pass on their traditional culture to future generations. In neighboring areas like the Altai, Tuva, and Yakutia, shamanism is also thriving once again.

In Finland and Lapland, Christianity has lessened its hold on the indigenous populations, leading to the resurgence of the practice of shamanism among the Sami people. The *noaidi*, the shamans of the Sami, are reviving their traditions. Reflecting these changes the government of Norway recently officially recognized shamanism as a religion.[4]

In South Korea traditional shamanism has endured centuries of suppression by Christian missionaries and military governments, and is presently experiencing a dramatic revival in one of the most technologically advanced countries in the world. According to a New York Times article there are over 300 shamanistic temples less than an hour from Seoul and an estimated 300,000 shamans—one for every 160 Koreans, according to the Korean Worshippers Association which represents shamans. When traditionally minded Koreans are inexplicably sick, have a bad run of luck in business, or a daughter who can't find a husband, they consult a shaman.[5] In South Korea schools for training in the shamanic performing arts can be found. Some shamans are revered as Human Cultural Treasures and have become media stars and entertainers, regularly appearing on television and performing on stage for elite audiences.[6]

Shamanism and folk-religion are still widely practiced in Asian countries including Japan, Vietnam, China, Malaysia, Thailand and Nepal. In modern Asia people visit urban shamans seeking spiritual help with professional concerns, the blessing of new houses and businesses, and for help with matters of fertility, wealth and longevity, as well as to consult the souls of their ancestors.[7] In Tibet, the indigenous shamanistic Bon religion was recognized by the Dalai Lama in 1978 as the sixth school of Tibetan spirituality alongside Buddhist sects, officially ending centuries of sporadic Buddhist suppression of Bonpo shamans.

In China, shamanism was a taboo subject a generation ago. Recently however the government has changed its policy, and shamanism is again being practiced in parts of China—in fact some Tungus speaking shamans are valued as "cultural treasures". A museum of shamanic culture, as well as a shamanic "theme park" focused on public education about traditional shamanic practices opened recently at Changchun.[8]

"Plastic Shamans"
Commercial Threats to Native American Religion

Native American religions are again being openly practiced by tribal peoples of North America after centuries of suppression by the American government and Christian missionaries. The American Indian Religious Freedom Act of 1978 was enacted to protect and preserve traditional sacred sites and religious ceremonies, but has only slowed rather than halted the destruction of native sacred lands and culture. Native Americans are also struggling to protect their traditional culture and religion from commercial exploitation.

The spiritual traditions of Native Americans were popularized and glamorized for a wide audience by non-natives like Carlos Castaneda, Lynn Andrews, Mary Summer Rain and others, who have written novels based on themes of native spirituality. It has been revealed that Castaneda, whose novels introduced the 60's generation to shamanism, based his books and teachings on research in the UCLA library rather than genuine contact with Toltec shamans as he claimed. Richard De Mille writes: "logical or chronological errors in the narrative constitute the best evidence that Castaneda's books are works of fiction".[9]

Some shamanic workshops feature a grab-bag of themes, mixing Native American religion with the channeling of "space aliens", Atlantis, Tibetan

Buddhism and crystal skulls. These teachers have been labelled "plastic shamans" or "shake and bake shamans" by Native American activists who are outraged at the appropriation and commercialization of their religion. The National Congress of American Indians issued a "declaration of war" against "wannabees, hucksters, cultists, commercial profiteers, and self-styled new age shamans".[10] Natives ironically observe that outsiders profit from selling versions of their traditional culture such as vision quests, sweat lodges, and sacred articles such as pipes and feathers while many of them live below poverty level.

Ayahuasca Tourism

In South America, indigenous Amazonian peoples continue to practice shamanism while facing similar challenges as Native Americans of preserving their traditions from commercial exploitation. They are increasingly catering to eco-tourists and "shaman tours", advertised on internet sites, which offer spiritual retreats and "advanced shamanic trainings" in the rainforest. "Ayahuasca Tourism" is a recent phenomenon in which americans and europeans visit the Amazon for the purpose of ingesting the potent hallucinogen ayahuasca, extracted from jungle vines under the guidance of native shamans. Those who take the tours seek exotic experiences as well as genuine spiritual breakthroughs.[11] Anthropologist Marlene Dobkin De Rios cautions that growing numbers of so-called "ayahuasca shamans" are not tribal natives at all, but middle-class mestizos cashing in on the trend. They provide tourists with mixtures of ten or more different hallucinogens which have never been used traditionally, leading to what she describes as "numerous psychological casualties".[12] Ayahuasca Tourism has been a mixed blessing to the people of the Amazonian rainforest, bringing needed income to local economies but also threatening stocks of the plant with exhaustion.

Despite the many challenges, indigenous shamans around the world are preserving their traditional shamanic healing practices which are increasingly valued as complimentary to modern medicine. In many third-world cultures shamans fulfill the roles of herbal doctors, psychotherapists and counsellors. Shamanism is a practical form of spirituality that has always served the "real life" needs of communities, and shamans are skillfully adjusting to the changes of working in modern industrialized societies. Because of its fluid and innovative nature, shamanism down through history has demonstrated its ability to adapt to any environment.[13]

Core Shamanism & Neoshamanism — What's the Difference?

Anthropologist Michael Harner can be credited with bringing the awareness of traditional shamanism to the westerners. He first encountered shamans while doing fieldwork in Peru among the Conibo and Shuar tribes. There he consumed the psychoactive brew produced from the ayahuasca vine used by Amazonian shamans to induce visions. He also studied with shamans in Mexico, western North America, the Canadian arctic, and Lapland.

In 1979 Harner founded the Center for Shamanic Studies which preserves, studies, and transmits shamanistic knowledge. He claims his organization has helped indigenous peoples recover and preserve their shamanic healing traditions. As the result of his studies with indigenous shamans he developed his teachings of "Core Shamanism". Harner explains that the western world lost its shamanic knowledge centuries ago due to religious oppression. Core shamanism, according to him, is intended to help Westerners reacquire their rightful spiritual heritage so they can discover their own hidden spiritual resources, transform their lives and help others. He writes: "Core shamanism consists of the universal, near-universal and common features of shamanism... not bound to any specific cultural group or perspective".[14] His organization teaches traditional shamanic techniques such as soul retrieval, shamanic extraction healing, divination, and receiving information from visionary sources. It uses "sonic driving" of drums to induce trance states, rather than relying on entheogens. Core Shamanism has developed a large following internationally with trainings in the United States, Great Britain and Europe.

Another form of modern shamanism, Neoshamanism, has become widespread over the past few decades in Europe as well as America. Like Core Shamanism, it is inspired by indigenous shamanism. Neoshamans, however, are less "traditional" than their Core Shamanic counterparts, eclectically combining elements of shamanism with New Age and Neopagan teachings. In Europe there is a tendency to combine Neoshamanism with Nordic or "Celtic Shamanism", as well as Neopaganism.[15] Neoshamans lead pilgrimages to native villages and power spots where "shamanic rituals" are performed for spiritual empowerment and wisdom. Destinations include the American Southwest, Mexico, Hawaii, China, Tibet, Nepal and other exotic locations.

Along with their rise in popularity, both Core Shamanism and Neoshamanism have come under critical scrutiny. Anthropologist Robert J. Wallis argues that by attempting to universalize shamanism and make it accessible to westerners, these modern forms tend to "homogenize" the practices of indigenous shamans, often ignoring the peoples whose techniques have been "borrowed" or "appropriated". He sees them as western constructs removed from their original indigenous cultural contexts while at the same time romanticizing and idealizing native cultures.[16]

Similar to the trend of "psychologization" which occurred with 20th century magic, modern shamanism is often compared to *psychotherapy*, and its techniques are increasingly used by alternative psychotherapists. Dr. Graham Harvey writes: "traditional shamans journey to other worlds, new ones enter their own inner-worlds which are often familiar from Jungian and other therapies." The language of spirits, and journeys to the otherworlds in Neoshamanism often refer to *inner*, psychological realities rather than *outer*, social or empirical ones, according to Harvey.[17] As in psychotherapy, there is an emphasis on "personal growth" and the goal of "self-realization" of the modern shamanic practitioner, rather than service to the community—as in traditional shamanism.

In response to the criticism, it can be argued that westerners must out of necessity adapt shamanistic methods to their own culture and individual needs, which differ from those of indigenous peoples. Ultimately modern forms of shamanism should be judged by whether or not they actually "work". Core Shamanic practitioner Susan Grimaldi insists the techniques have been used for many successful healings which alleviated physical pain and suffering. She writes: "In my own shamanic counseling practice I have witnessed countless recoveries and miracles that have occurred as a result of shamanic healings".[18]

Piers Vitebsky views modern shamanism in the context of the new spiritual movements which have emerged in America and Europe which combine the legacy of the drug culture of the '60's with an interest in non-western religions, environmentalism, strands of the New-Age movement, and various forms of self-help and self-realization. He writes that shamanism's popularity in the western world is the result of it being seen as a "non-institutionalized, undogmatic form of spirituality which offers considerable scope for personal creativity".[19]

Chapter 20 Notes

1. "Tengrism" *Wikapedia*.
2. Sarangarel. *Riding Windhorses: A Journey into the Heart of Mongolian Shamanism*. 2000: 144.
3. Levin, Dan. "Shamans' Spirits Crowd Air of Mongolian Capital". *NYT.com*. published July 10, 2009.
4. "Shamanism Approved as a Religion in Norway". *The Nordic Page*. 15.03.2012. oslo.
5. Sang-Hun, Choe. "In the age of the Internet, Korean shamans regain popularity". *NYT.com*. The New York Times, Asia Pacific, July 6, 2007. 2007.
6. Heinze. *Shamans Of The 20th Century*. 1991:51.
7. Ibid.:203.
8. Grimaldi, Susan. Shi, Kun. "Contemporary Shamanism in China" update October 1, 2000. *Journal for the Foundation of Shamanic Studies*, Issue 23, Dec. 2010. 2010: 16-17.
9. De Mille, Richard. *Castaneda's Journey: The Power and the Allegory*. 1976: 166.
10. Aldred, Lisa. "Plastic Shamans and Astro Turf Sun Dances: New Age Commercialization of Native American Spirituality". *The American Indian Quarterly*. Vol. 24, Number 3, Summer, 2000: 32-352.
11. Grunwell, John N. "Ayahuasca Tourism in South America". *Newsletter of the Multidisciplinary Association for Psychedelic Studies MAPS*- vol. 8 number 3 Autumn. 1998: 59-62.
12. De Rios, Marlene Dobkin. Narby, Jeremy & Huxley, Francis.(ed.) *Shamans Through Time*. 2004: 277.
13. Vitebsky, Piers. *Shamanism*. 2001: 154.
14. Harner, Michael. "Core Shamanism". *Foundation for Shamanic Studies*. 2000-2014.
15. Walter; Fridman,, eds.. *Shamanism: An Encyclopedia of World Beliefs, Practices and Culture*, Vol.1. 2004: 54.
16. Wallis, Robert J. *Shamans/Neo-Shamans: Ecstasies, Alternative Archaeologies & Contemporary Pagans*. 2003 :51.
17. Harvey, Graham. *Animism Respecting the Living World*. 2006: 142.
18. Grimaldi, Susan. "Observations on Daniel Noel's The Soul of Shamanism: A Defense of Contemporary Shamanism and Michael Harner". *Shaman's Drum*. 1997.
19. Vitebsky. *Shamanism*. 2001: 150-151.

The Tree of Visions

Chapter 21: From Root to Branch

"The first prophecies were the words of an oak"
-Plato

Clan generation tree of Namay people, Siberia.

The Revival of Animism
Shamanism and magic represent the oldest spiritual beliefs and practices

of mankind. They have endured for millennia, and continue to thrive in the twenty-first century as they fulfill the needs of individuals and communities for maintaining a living connection with nature and the spiritual dimensions. In the words of the late Nevill Drury: "Why shamanism? Why magic? We need them both."

Magic and shamanism are both rooted in animism—the earliest worldview of humanity. Derived from the Latin word *animus* meaning soul and life, animism is the belief that humans, animals, plants, and even inanimate objects possess a spiritual essence. It is this spiritual force pervading all things that the shaman and magician draw from to empower their work.

Biologist Rupert Sheldrake advocates the revival of animism, insisting that thinking of nature as *alive* not only gives us a renewed sense of relationship to the natural world, but an enriched view of our own human nature.[1] He notes that the vision of humanism, in which mankind achieved peace and prosperity through the technological subjugation and exploitation of nature, has lead to disastrous consequences for the natural ecosystem upon which we depend, and is ultimately unsustainable. He writes:

> "The old dream of progressive humanism is fading fast. There are still those who dream of the conquest of the biosphere by the technosphere, the human control of biological evolution through genetic engineering, and so on. But attitudes are changing around, and within, many of us: there is a shift from humanism to animism, from an intensely man-centered view to a view of a living world. We are not superior to Gaia; we live within her and depend on her".[2]

Sheldrake urges modern people to reconnect with nature through direct intuitive experiences of wilderness, the seaside, forests, plants, animals, or wherever we feel contact with the greater living world. He insists this communion can lead to mystical experiences of illumination, surprise and joy. He believes this reconnection can come from participating with the spirits of natural places—their *genius loci*—during sacred times such as seasonal festivals. We can also learn from traditional societies who have never lost their connection to the living world. Through them we can regain a richer understanding of humanity shaped by tradition and collective memory, as well as the earth, heavens, and all life forms.

While the animistic traditions of indigenous peoples serve as inspirations, we have seen how the belief in a living cosmos is inherent to western esotericism as well. We looked at Plato, the Stoics, and Hermeticists who conceived of the universe as an organism, the *anima mundi* or "world soul" connecting all living creatures. Animism was part of the accepted worldview of western cultures until the Italian renaissance, when the magus and philosopher Giordano Bruno declared: "There is nothing that does not possess a soul..." We are witnessing a revival of animism today. Ethnologist Mihaly Hoppal insists that a new, ecologically conscious animism is essential for the protection and preservation of the environment: "...if everything in nature possesses a soul then we ought to behave in a way so that we avoid hurting, insulting, or polluting them...it is our moral duty to maintain the balance of the natural order".[3]

Thinking Like an Animist

According to psychologist Bruce Charlton, we have never lost the experience of animism—it is the spontaneous and natural way of experience for all human beings. Animism has been with us since we were hunter-gatherers, and is still experienced by children.[4] Charlton insists that modern people experience "animistic thinking" by deliberately inducing altered states of consciousness while in meditation, trance, lucid dreaming, self-hypnosis, hypnogogic states, or through the use of entheogens. He recommends seeking solitude, unstructured time, and direct contact with nature in order to live in the "here and now", to experience this awareness.

Charlton proposes animism as an antidote to our culture's excessive focus on *rationality* and *objectivity* which lead to psychological alienation and a sense of meaninglessness—of not belonging to the world. In his opinion, Neoshamanic techniques can be used to enable people to "think animistically". He writes: "In an ever more rational and objective world it would be ironic, although not altogether surprising, if most people privately practiced some form of Neoshamanism in order to induce a sense of belonging. Recovered animism could become the personal religion of the future." [5]

Revisioning The Future...

Psychologist Roger Walsh insists that for the first time in millions of years of evolution all the major threats to our survival are *human-caused*—resulting from our species' behavior, its fears, phobias, fantasies, desires and delusions. He writes: "The state of the world, in other words, reflects the state of our minds." [6]

The good news is that we as individuals have the power to change our minds—and our dysfunctional attitudes, socially conditioned beliefs, thinking and behavior. Magicians and shamans have always realized the power of the mind and imagination to shape reality. We become what we imagine and believe on individual and societal levels. What is urgently needed at this time are methods for transforming individual and collective consciousness and envisioning new paradigms—ways to re-imagine the world and our role in it—that are more sustainable for humanity and the ecosystem upon which we depend.

Shamanism and the diverse paths of western esotericism offer their own time-tested methods of altering consciousness and living in harmony with the cosmos. They provide powerful tools for healing and self-transformation as well as holistic world-views which can reconnect us to our roots in the natural and spiritual worlds. While grounded in ancient wisdom traditions, they also encourage personal creativity and *gnosis*—direct knowing of spiritual reality.

In search of this essential wisdom, our ancestors endured arduous initiation rites and visionary journeys to the otherworld. We finish by recalling the god Odin's spiritual quest during which he willingly hung himself from the Yggdrasil Tree, vowing to attain knowledge of the magical runes.

> I know that I hung
> on that wind-swept tree,
> through nine long nights,
> pierced by the spear,
> to Odin sacrificed,
> myself to myself,
> on that great tree
> whose roots
> no one knows...

Upon learning the runes, Odin ended his ordeal with a shout of exultation, proclaiming:

> I began to grow,
> thrive and do well,
> and increase in wisdom,
> One word led me
> to other words.
> One work led me
> to other work.[7]

Chapter 21 Notes

1. Sheldrake, Rupert. The Rebirth of Nature: the greening of science and God. 1991: 204.
2. Ibid.: 205-6.
3. Hoppal, Mihaly."Nature Worship in Siberian Shamanism". Folklore, Electronic Journal of Folklore. Vol. 4 1997: 8-9.
4. Charlton, Bruce. "Alienation, Neo-Shamanism and Recovered Animism". Hedweb.com. 2002.
5. Ibid.
6. Walsh, Roger N., M.D., Ph.D. The Spirit of Shamanism. 1990: 254.
7. Metzner. The Well of Remembrance: Rediscovering the Earth Wisdom Myths of Northern Europe. 1994:193-197.

Bibliography

Abercromby, John. *The Pre-and Proto-historic Finns, Both Eastern and Western: with the Magic Songs of the West Finns.* London: David Nutt, 1898.

Achterberg, Jeanne. *Imagery in Healing: Shamanism and Modern Medicine.* Boston and London: New Science Library, Shambala, 1985.

Adler, Margot. *Drawing Down the Moon: Witches, Druids, Goddess-Worshippers, and other Pagans in America.* New York, NY: Penguin Books, 2006.

Agrippa von Nettlesheim, Heinrich Cornelius; (ed.) Tyson, Donald; Freake, James. *Three Books of Occult Philosophy.* St, Paul, MN: Llewellyn 1997.

Agrippa, Henry Cornelius. "Of Occult Philosophy or Magical Ceremonies: The Fourth Book". *www. Hermetics.org.*

Ahlstrom, Dick. "Hundreds of New Discoveries At Stonehenge". *Irish Times,* Wed. Sept. 10, 2014.

Alden, Harold. "Spirit Boat-exploring Finnish shamanism and its relevance for today". "*Shamanism and Sacred Arts in Finland- Part 2*". June 16, 2014.

Aldhouse-Green, Miranda J.; Stephen Aldhouse-Green. *The Quest for the Shaman.* London: Thames & Hudson, 2005.

Aldred, Cyril. *The Egyptians.* London: Thames & Hudson, 1998.

Aldred, Lisa. "Plastic Shamans and Astro Turf Sun Dances: New Age Commercialization of Native American Spirituality". *The American Indian Quarterly.* Vol. 24, Number 3, Summer, 2000. p. 329-352.

Alinei, Mario. "An Introduction in Progress". *The Paleolithic Continuity Paradigm.* May 2012.

Allen, Michael J.B.; Rees, Valery; Davies, Martin; ed. *Marsilio Ficino: His Theology, His Philosophy, His Legacy.* Brill Academic Publishers 2001.

Andreae, Johann Valentin. (1616) "The Chymical Wedding of Christian Rosenkreutz". *The Alchemy Website on Levity.com.* (ed.) Adam McLean; Deirdre Green, 1984.

Andrews, Carol & Faulkner, Raymond Oliver. *The Ancient Egyptian Book of the Dead.* Austin: University of Texas Press 2001.

Anthony, David W. *The Horse, The Wheel, And Language.* Princeton and Oxford: Princeton University Press, 2007.

Antonello, Elio. "The Myths of the Bear". 2011. *Cornell University Library.*

Apuleius. *The Golden Ass, or Metamorphoses.* (trans.) Kenney, E. J. New York: Penguin Classics, 1988.

Asante, Molefi and Mazama, Ama, (ed.) *Encyclopedia of African Religion, vol. 1.* Thousand Oaks, CA.: Sage, 2009.

Ashe, Geoffrey. *Dawn Behind The Dawn: A Search for the Earthly Paradise.* New York: Henry Holt & Co., 1992.

Bakan, David. *Sigmund Freud and the Jewish Mystical Tradition.* Mineola, N.Y.: Dover Publishing, 2004.

Baker, Jean H. *Mary Todd Lincoln: A Biography.* New York: W.W. Norton & Company, 1989.

Ball, Phillip. *The Devil's Doctor- Paracelus and the World of Renaissance Magic and Science.* New York :Farrar, Straus and Giroux, 2006.

Ballasa, Ivan & Ortutay, Gyula. "Hungarian Ethnography and Folklore/ Figures of the World of Beliefs". *Digital Library of Hungarian Studies.* (Trans.) Bales, Kenneth & Maria. 1979.

Balter, Michael. "Mysterious Indo-European homeland may have been in the steppes of Ukraine and Russia". *Science News* 13 Feb. 2015.

Barta, Miroslav, Frouz, Martin. *Swimmers in the Sand.* Dryada: Czech Republic, 2010.

Baukham, Richard. *The Fate of the Dead: Studies on the Jewish and Christian Apocalypses.* Boston: Brill Academic Publishing, 1998.

Bauval, Robert and Gilbert, Adrian. *The Orion Mystery- Unlocking the Secrets of the Pyramids.* New York: Crown Publishers, Inc., 1994.

--------. and Brophy, Thomas. *Black Genesis- The Prehistoric Origins of Ancient Egypt.* Rochester, Vermont, Toronto, Canada: Bear & Company, 2011.

Benjamin, Foster. *From Distant Days: Myths, Tales and Poetry from Ancient Mesopotamia.* Bethesda: Capital Decisions Ltd., 1995.

Beckwith, Christopher, I. *Empires of the Silk Road: A History of Central Eurasia from the Bronze Age to the Present.* Princeton, NJ: Princeton University Books, 2011.

Benko, Stephen. *Pagan Rome and the Early Christians.* Bloomington: Indiana University Press. 1986.

Benz, Ernst. translated by Goodrick- Clarke, Nicholas. *Emanuel Swedenborg Visionary Savant In the Age of Reason.* West Chester, Pennsylvania: Swedenborg Foundation, 2002.

Bergmann, Carlo. "On the origins of the Egyptian Pantheon- part one". *www.carlo-bergman.* 2009.

Betz, Hans Dieter. (ed.) *The Greek Magical Papyri in Translation including the Demiotic Spells.* Second Edition. Chicago & London: The University of Chicago Press, 1992.

Black, Jeremy and Green, Anthony. *Gods, Demons and Symbols of Ancient Mesopotamia.* Austin: University of Texas Press, 1992.

Blavatsky, Helena Petrovna. *Isis Unveiled: A Masterkey to the Mysteries of*

Ancient and Modern Science. Point Loma, Ca: Aryan Theosophical Press, 1919.

Bodi, Daniel. *The Book of Ezekiel and the Poem of Erra*. Freiburg, Schweizi;Universitatsverlag; Gottingen: Vandenhoeck & Ruprecht, 1991.

Boekhoven, Jeroen. *Genealogies of Shamanism: Struggles for Power, Charisma and Authority*. Groningen: Barkhuis, 2012.

Bonewits, Isaac. "Indo-European Paleopaganism and its Clergy". *Druid's Progress #1*, 1984.

--------. "How Many "Pagans" Are There?" *www.neopagan.net*. 2005.

Boudillion, Daniel. "How The Shakers Invented Spiritualism-The Ecstatic Spirits of Holy Hill". *Boudillion Homepage*. 2007, 2009.

Bowden, Hugh. *Mystery Cults of the Ancient World*. Princeton and Oxford: Princeton University Press, 2010.

Boyce, Mary. *Zoroastrians- Their Religious Beliefs and Practices*. London & New York: Routledge, 2001.

Brier, Bob. *Ancient Egyptian Magic*. New York: Quill, 1981.

Brown, Carolyn-Graves. *Dancing For Hathor: Women in Ancient Egypt*. London, New York: Bloomsbury Academic, 2010.

Budge, E.A.Wallis. *Osiris and the Egyptian Resurrection*, vol. 1. London: Phillip Lee Garner, New York: G.P. Putnam's Sons, 1911.

--------.*The Egyptian Book of the Dead (The Papyrus of Ani) Egyptian Text Transliteration and Translation*. New York: Dover Publications, Inc. 1967.

Bunson, Margaret. *Encyclopedia of Ancient Egypt*. New York: Facts on File Books, 2002.

Burkert, Walter. *Greek Religion*. Cambridge, Mass: Harvard University Press, 1985.

--------. *Ancient Mystery Cults*. Cambridge, Mass: Harvard University Press, 1986.

--------. *Babylon, Memphis, Persepolis- Eastern Contexts of Greek Culture*. Harvard: Harvard University Press, 2004.

Burl, Aubrey. *Great Stone Circles*. New Haven & London: Yale University Press, 1999.

Burns, Dylan. "Proclus and the Theurgic Liturgy of Pseudo-Dionysus". *Dionysus*, Vol. XXII. 111-32. Dec. 2004. *www. Academia.edu*.

Campbell, Joseph. *The Masks of God. Occidental Mythology*. New York, NY: Penguin Books,1964.

--------. *The Masks of God: Primitive Mythology*. New York: Penguin Books, 1959.

--------. *The Masks of God: Oriental Mythology*. New York: Penguin Books, 1987.

--------; Kudler, David. *Pathways to Bliss: Mythology and Personal Transformation*. Novato, Calif.: New World Library, 2009.

Carr-Gomm, Phillip. *Druid Mysteries: Ancient Wisdom for the 21st Century*. London: Rider, 2002.

Cauvin, Jacques. *The Birth of the Gods and the Origins of Agriculture*. Cambridge: Cambridge University Press, 2000.

Charlton, Bruce. "Alienation, Neo-Shamanism and Recovered Animism". *Hedweb.com*. 2002.

Chisholm, James Allen. *The Eddas: The Keys to the Mysteries of the North*. Illuminati Books, 2005.

Churton, Tobias. *The Golden Builders- Alchemists, Rosicrucians and the First Freemasons*. York Beach: ME: Weiser Books, 2005.

Circle of Tengerism. "The Different Types of Shamans". *Circle of Tenerism*.

Clarke, Emma C., Dillon, John M., and Hershbell, Jackson P. -translation and introduction and notes. *Iamblichus On the Mysteries*. Atlanta, Ga.: Society of Biblical Literature, 2003.

Clottes, Jean and Lewis-Williams, David. *The Shamans of Prehistory*. New York: Harry N. Abrams Publishers, 1998.

Clottes, Jean. "Paleolithic Cave Art Painting and Rock Art in France". *Adorant Magazine*- 2002.

Collins, Andrew. "Gobekli Tepe: its cosmic blueprint revealed". *www.andrewcollins.com*. 2013.

Collins, Andrew. *Gobekli Tepe Genesis of the Gods*. Rochester Vermont, Toronto, Canada: Bear & Company: 2014.

Collins, Derek. *Magic in the Ancient Greek World*. Malden, MA: Wiley-Blackwell 2008.

Condos, Theony; Eratosthenes. *Star Myths of the Greeks and Romans: A Sourcebook*. Grand Rapids, MI: Phanes Press 1997.

Copenhaver, Brian. *Hermetica, the Greek Corpus Hermeticum and the Latin Asclepius in a new English translation with notes and introduction*. Cambridge (England); New York, N.Y. : Cambridge University Press, 1992.

Copenhaver, Brian, "Giovanni Pico della Mirandola", *The Stanford Encyclopedia of Philosophy* (Summer 2012 Edition), Edward N. Zalta (ed.)

Coppens, Phillip. *Land of the Gods: How a Scottish Landscape Was Sanctified To Become Arthur's Camelot.* Amsterdam: Adventures Unlimited Press, 2007.

--------. "Gobekli Tepe: the world's oldest temple". *Nexus Magazine.* Vol. 16, Number 4 (June-July 2009).

Cosmopoulos, Michael B. (ed.) *Greek Mysteries- The Archaeology and Ritual of Ancient Greek Secret Cults.* London & New York: Routledge, 2003.

Cote', Charlotte. *Spirits of Our Whaling Ancestors.* University of Washington Press: Seattle & London. UBC Press: Vancouver & Toronto. 2010.

Couliano, I.P. *Out of This World.* Boston & London: Shamballa, 1991.

Cox, Robert S. *Body and Soul A Sympathetic History of American Spiritualism.* Charlottsville & London: University of Virginia Press, 2003.

Crowley, Aleister. *Book of the Law.* York Beach, ME: Red Wheel, 2011.

Cumont, Franz. "Astrology and Religion Among the Greeks and Romans". 1912. *Sacred-texts.com.*

"Cuneiform Timeline". *Ancient History Encyclopedia.* http://www.ancient.eu/timeline/cuneiform/

Cunningham, Scott. *Wicca: A Guide for the Solitary Practitioner.* St. Paul, MN: Llewellyn Publications, 2004.

Cunliffe, Barry. *Europe Between The Oceans.* New Haven & London: Yale University Press, 2008.

Daiches, Samuel. *Babylonian Oil Magic in the Talmud and in Later Jewish Literature.* London: (Oxford, printed by H. Hart at the University Press, 1913.

Danielou, Alain. *Gods of Love and Ecstasy: The Traditions of Shiva and Dionysus.* Rochester, VT.:1992.

Daryoush Jahanian, M.D. "The Zoroastrian-Biblical Connections—Influence of Zoroastrianism in Other Religions." *www. zarathustra.com.* 2003.

Davies, Owen. *Grimoires: A History of Magic Books.* New York: Oxford University Press, USA, 2009.

Davidson, H.R. Ellis. *The Lost Beliefs of Northern Europe.* London; New York: Routledge, 1993.

--------. *Gods and Myths of Northern Europe.* Baltimore, Md.: Penguin Books, 1964.

Davila, James R. *Descenders to the Chariot.* Leiden, Boston, Cologne: Brill, 2001.

Davis-Kimball, Jeannine. Ph.D. *Warrior Women.* New York, NY: Warner Books, 2002.

Debus, Allen, G. *Man & Nature in the Renaissance.* Cambridge, New York:

Cambridge University Press, 1978.

De Mille, Richard. *Castaneda's Journey: The Power and the Allegory*. Santa Barbara, CA.: Carla Press, 1976.

Derbeneva, Olga, Starikovskaya, Elena, Wallace, Douglas, Sukernik, Rem. "Traces of Early Eurasians in the Mansi of Northwest Siberia Revealed by Mitochondrial DNA Analysis". *The American Journal of Human Genetics*. April 2002; 70(4) Feb. 13, 2002.

Desoille, Robert. Translated by Haronian, Frank. *The Directed Daydream.*, Princeton: Princeton, N. J. 1965.

Devereux, George. Editor. *Psychoanalysis and the Occult*. Edited by. New York, NY.: International Universities Press, Inc.,1953.

Dickey, Matthew W. *Magic and Magicians In The Greco-Roman World*. London: Routledge, 2001.

Dix, Byron & Mavor, James, Jr. *Manitou*. Rochester, Vermont: Inner Traditions International, Ltd., 1989.

Diogenes Laertus. "Lives of Eminent Philosophers". Book VIII. 8:59 A1. R.D. Hicks ed. *Perseus Digital Library*.

Dobbs, Beth Jo Teeter. *The Foundation of Newton's Alchemy: or,"The hunting of the green lyon"*. Cambridge; New York: Cambridge University Press, 1975.

Dodds, E.R. *The Greeks and the Irrational*. Berkeley: University of California Press, 1968.

--------. *Pagan and Christian in an Age of Anxiety:Some Aspects of Religious Experience from Marcus Aurelius to Constantine*. Cambridge: Cambridge University Press, 1991.

Doyle, Arthur, C. *The History of Spiritualism*. New York: Arno Press, 1975.

Drob, Sanford L., Ph.D. "This Is Gold": Freud, Psychotherapy and the Lurianic Kabbalah". *newkabbalah.com*. Sanford L. Drob. 2001-04.

Drury, Nevill. *The Shaman and the Magician: journeys between the worlds*. London: Arkana, 1987, 1982.

Dumezil, G. *Gods of the Ancient Northmen*. (Ed.) Haugen, E. (trans.) Lindow, J. Berkeley: University of California Press, 1973.

Dunham, Will. "Genetic history of modern Europeans a tangled tale, research finds". *Reuters*, Washington, Wed. Sept. 17, 2014.

Dunn, James D.G. & Rogerson, William John. *Eerdman's Commentary on the Bible*. Grand Rapids, Cambridge.: Wm. B. Eerdman's Pulishing. 2003.

Edmonds, Radcliffe, G. *Myths of the Underworld Journey: Plato, Aristophanes, and the "Orphic" Golden Tablets*. Cambridge: Cambridge University Press, 2004.

Edmonds, Radcliffe Guest. *The "Orphic" Gold Tablets and Greek Religion: Further Along the Path.* Cambridge: Cambridge University Press, 2011.

Edson, Gary. *Shamanism: A Cross-cultural Study of Beliefs and Practices.* Jefferson, N.C. : McFarland & Co. Publishers, 2009.

Ehrenwald, Jan. *The History of Psychotherapy: From Healing Magic to Encounter.* New York: J. Aronson, 1976.

Eliade, Mircea. *The Forge and the Crucible.* Chicago: The University of Chicago Press, 1956.

--------. *Shamanism- Archaic Techniques of Ecstasy.* Princeton: Princeton Bollingen Paperbacks, 1964.

--------. *Myths, Dreams & Mysteries.* New York: Harper & Row, 1975.

--------. *From Primitives to Zen; A Thematic Sourcebook of the History of Religions.* New York: Harper & Row, 1978.

--------. "Shamanism". *Encyclopedia Britannica online.*

--------. *Patterns in Comparative Religion.* Meridian, Paris: 1958.

Erdoes, Richard and Ortiz, Alfonso. *American Indian Myths and Legends.* New York: Pantheon Books, 1985.

Eunapius. *Lives of the Philosophers.* Trans. Wright, W.C. *Philostratus and Eunapius: The Lives of the Sophists.* London: Heinemann, 1922.

Evans-Wentz, W. Y. *Fairy Faith in Celtic Countries.* Mineola, N.Y.: Dover Publications, 2011, 1911.

Falio, Vincent W. *New Developments in Consciousness Research.* New York: Nova Science Publishers, 2006.

Farre, Rowena. *Seal Morning.* New York: Rinehart & Company, Inc., 1956.

Ficino, Marsilio. *Three Books on Life: A Critical Edition and Translation with Introduction and Notes*, by Kaske, Carol V. and Clark, John R. Binghamton, N.Y.: Medieval and Renaissance Texts and Studies, 1989.

Flaherty, Gloria. *Shamanism and the Eighteenth Century.* Princeton, N.J.: Princeton University Press, 1992.

Flavin, Richard D. "The Karanovo Zodiac and Old European Linear". *Epigraphic Society Occasional Papers.* Vol. 23; pp. 86-92.

Flower, Michael. *The Seer in Ancient Greece.* Berkeley, Los Angeles: University of California Press, 2008.

Flowers, Stephen Edred. *Hermetic Magic: the Postmodern Magical Papyrus of Abaris.* York Beach, Maine: S.Weiser, 1995.

Fodor, Nandor. *Freud, Jung, and Occultism.* New Hyde Park, N.Y.: University Books, 1971.

Fortune, Dion. *Applied Magic and Aspects of Occultism.* Wellingborough, Northamptonshire: The Aquarian Press, 1987.

--------. *The Goat Foot God*. Wellingborough, Northamptonshire: The Aquarian Press, 1989.

Fowden, Garth. *The Egyptian Hermes: a historical approach to the late pagan mind/* Cambridge (Cambridgeshire); New York: Cambridge University Press, 1986.

Frank, Roslyn M. "Evidence in Favor of the Paleolithic Continuity Refugium Theory (PCRT) "Hamalu" And Its Linguistic and Cultural Relatives". Part 1. *Insula*, #4. December 2008. p. 91-131.

Frank, Roslyn M. "Hunting the European Sky Bears: German "Straw Bears" and their Relatives as Transformers". *Academia. Edu.* 2010.

Freidel, David, Schele, Linda & Parker, Joy. *Maya Cosmos*. New York: William Morrow and Company, Inc.,1993.

Freke, Timothy; Gandy, Peter. *The Jesus Mysteries: Was the "Original Jesus" a Pagan God?* New York, NY: Random House, Inc., 1999.

Freud, Sigmund. *Moses and Monotheism*. Trans, Katherine Jones. Great Britain.: Hogarth Press, 1939.

Frothingham, A.L. *Babylonian Origin of Hermes the Snake-God, and of the Caduceus*. American Journal of Archaeology- Second Series. Journal of the Archaeological Institute of America, vol. xx (1916) no. 2.

Gilman, Ken. "Twelve Gods & Seven Planets". *C.U.R.A. The International Astrology Research Center.* 1996.

Gimbutas, Marija. *The gods and goddesses of Old Europe: 7000 to 3500 BCE myths, legends and cult images*. Berkeley: University of California Press, 1974.

--------. (Spring–Summer 1985), "Primary and Secondary Homeland of the Indo-Europeans: comments on Gamkrelidze-Ivanov articles", *Journal of Indo-European Studies* 13. (1&2): 185–201

--------. *The Living Goddess*. Berkeley, Los Angeles, London: University of California Press, 1999.

--------.*The Language of the Goddess: Unearthing the Hidden Symbols of Western Civilization.* London: Thames and Hudson, 2001.

Ginzburg, Carlo. *Night Battles: Witchcraft and Agrarian Cults in the Sixteenth and Seventeenth Centuries*. Baltimore: Johns Hopkins University Press, 1983.

--------. *Ecstasies: Deciphering the Witches' Sabbath*. Translated by Rosenthal, Raymond. New York: Pantheon Books, 1991.

Godwin, Joscelyn. *The Golden Thread*. Illinois, India: Quest Books, Theosophical Publishing House, 2007.

Goodman, Ronald. *Lakota Star Knowledge*. Mission South Dakota: Sinte

Gleska University, 1992.

Goodrick-Clarke, Nicholas. *The Western Esoteric Traditions.* Oxford; New York: Oxford University Press. 2008.

Goodrick-Clarke, Clare. *Alchemical Medicine for the 21st Century.* Rochester, Vermont, Toronto, Canada: Healing Arts Press, 2010.

Green, Miranda J. *Symbol & Image in Celtic Religious Art.* London and New York: Routledge, 1989.

--------. *Sun Gods of Ancient Europe.* London: B.T. Batsford, 1992.

Green, Tamara, M. *The City of the Moon God.* New York, Koln: E.J. Brill, Leiden, 1992.

Greene, Elizabeth. *The Celestial Ascent of the Soul- The Morphology of an Enduring Idea.* MA in Cultural Astronomy and Astrology Thesis, Bath Spa University, Sept. 2006.

Greer, John Michael &Warnock, Christopher. (trans.) *Picatrix: The Classic Medieval Handbook of Astrological Magic.*Adocentyn Press, 2010.

Griffith, L.I.; Thompson, Herbert. *The Leyden Papyrus: An Egyptian Magical Book.* New York: Dover Publications, Inc. 1974.

Griffiths, John Gwyn. *The Origins of Osiris and His Cult.* Leiden: E.J.Brill 1980.

Griffiths, Sarah & Newton, Jennifer. "Modern Europe was formed by milk-drinking Russians: Mass migration brought new genetic make-up to continent 5,000 years ago." *Daily Mail.* June 10, 2015.

Grimaldi, Susan. "Observations on Daniel Noel's The Soul of Shamanism: A Defense of Contemporary Shamanism and Michael Harner". *Shaman's Drum.* 1997.

--------. Shi, Kun. "Contemporary Shamanism in China" update October 1, 2000. *Journal for the Foundation of Shamanic Studies,* Issue 23, Dec. 2010.

Grof, Stanislav. *Books of the Dead -Manuals for Living and Dying.* London: Thames & Hudson 1994.

--------. "Spiritual Emergency: Understanding and Treatment of Psychospiritual crises". *Reality sandwich.com.* 2008.

Grunwell, John N. "Ayahuasca Tourism in South America". *Newsletter of the Multidisciplinary Association for Psychedelic Studies* MAPS- vol. 8 number 3 Autumn 1998-pp. 59-62.

Guenon, Rene. *Theosophy: History of a Pseudo-Religion.* Hillsdale, NY: Sophia Perrenis 2004.

Guthrie, W.K.C. *Orpheus and Greek Religion.* W.W. Norton & Company, Inc., 1966.

--------; Chambers, William Keith. *A History of Greek Philosophy: vol. 1, The Earlier Presocratics and the Pythagoreans.* Cambridge: Cambridge University Press, 1979.

Haarman, Harald. *Early Civilization and Literacy in Europe.* Berlin, New York: Mouton de Gruyten, 1995. Cambridge, Mass, London: The Belknap Press of Harvard University Press, 2002.

Halevi, Z'ev ben Shimon. *Adam and the Kabbalistic Tree.* York Beach, ME.: Samuel Weiser, 1990.

Hall, A.R. *The Revolution in Science 1500-1750.* London: Longman, 1983.

Hall, Manly P. *The Secret Teachings of All Ages.* Los Angeles, Ca.: The Philosophical Research Society, Inc., 1988.

--------. *The Story of Astrology: The Belief In The Stars As A Factor in Human Progress.* New York, NY: Cosimo Classics, 2005.

--------. *The Lost Keys of Freemasonry.* New York: Jermemy P. Tarcher/ Penguin, 2006.

Hanegraff, Wouter. *New Age Religion and Western Culture. Esotericism in the Mirror of Secular Thought.* State University of New York, 1996.

--------. "How Magic Survived the Disenchantment of the World". (2003) *Academia.edu.*

Harner, Michael. *The Way of the Shaman.* New York: Bantam New Age Books, 1982.

--------. "Core Shamanism".*Foundation for Shamanic Studies* (website). 2000-2014.

Harris, Elanor L. *Ancient Egyptian Divination and Magic.* York Beach, Maine: Samuel Weiser, Inc.1998.

Harvey, Graham. *Animism Respecting the Living World.* New York: Columbia University Press, 2006.

Haywood, H.L. "Symbolical Masonry". 1923. *Sacredtexts.com.*

Hedrick, Bill. "Athanasius Kircher's Oedipus Aegyptiacus." 1653. *Bill Hedrick's Cross References.*

Heidel, Alexander. *The Babylonian Genesis: The Story of Creation.* Chicago: U of Chicago Press, 1963.

Heinze, Ruth-Inge. *Shamans Of The 20th Century.* NYC, New York: Irvington Publishers, Inc., 1991.

Hermes, Everard, John. (trans.) *Corpus Hermeticum- The Divine Pymander.* San Diego, CA.: Wizard's Bookshelf, 1978, 1884.

Hodder, Ian. *The Leopard's Tale- Revealing the Mysteries of Catalhoyuk.* Thames & Hudson, London. 2006.

Hoeller, Stephen A. "On the Trail of the Winged God—Hermes &

Hermeticism Throughout the Ages". From *Gnosis: A Journal of Western Inner Traditions* (Vol. 40, Summer 1996) *The Gnosis Archive.* 1996.

Holden, James Herschel. *A History of Horoscopic Astrology.* Tempe, AZ: American Federation of Astrologers, Inc., 1996.

Hooper, Lucille, Kroeber, Alfred. Intro by Bean, John Lowell. *Studies in Cahuilla Culture.* Banning: Malki Museum Pr., 1978.

Hoppal, Mihaly. "Nature Worship in Siberian Shamanism". *Folklore, Electronic Journal of Folklore.* Vol. 4 1997.

Hughes, J.D. "Artemis: Goddess of Conservation". *Oxford Journals,* vol. 34, issue 4, pp. 191-197)

Hultkranz, Ake. *The North American Indian Orpheus Tradition: A Contribution to Comparative Religion. Ethnographic Museum of Sweden* 1957.

Humphrey, Caroline & Onon, Urgunge. *Shamans & Elders.* Oxford University Press, Inc., New York: Clarendon Press. 1996.

Hunter, Richard. *Plato and the Traditions of Ancient Literature: The Silent Stream.* Cambridge; New York: Cambridge University Press. 2012.

Hutton, Ronald. *The Pagan Religions of the Ancient British Isles.* Oxford; Malden, Massachusetts : Blackwell Publishers Ltd. 1991.

--------. *Shamans-Siberian Spirituality and the Western Imagination.* London, New York: Hambledon & London, 2001.

Iamblichus. *The Life of Pythagoras.* Trans. Taylor, Thomas. Los Angeles, Ca., 1905.

Iamblichus. *Theology of Arithmetic.* (trans.) Waterfield, Robin. Grand Rapids, MI.: Kairos Books/Phanes Press, 1988.

"Ice Age star map discovered" .World Wide Web. *BBC News/ Sci/Tech.* 9 August, 2000.

Jacobson, Esther. *The Deer Goddess of Ancient Siberia: A Study in the Ecology of Belief.* Leiden, New York: Brill Academic Publishing, 1993.

Jaffe, Aniela. "Details About C.G. Jung's Family". *Spring* (1984): 35-43.

Jaffe, Eric. "Meditate on It- Could ancient campfire rituals have seperated us from Neanderthals?". *Smithsonian.com* /Anthropology and Behavior section. Feb. 1, 2007.

Jahanian, Dr. Jaryoush."The Zoroastrian-Biblical Connections- Influence of Zoroastrianism in other Religions" *Zarathushtra.com.* 2003.

James, Geoffrey. (ed. & trans.) *The Enochian Magic of Dr. John Dee.* San Francisco, CA, Newburyport, MA: Weiser Books. 2009.

James, M.R. "The Testament of Solomon". *Guardian Church Newspaper.* March 15, 1899 p.369. From Ghosts & Scholars 28.

Jaspers, Karl. *The Way To Wisdom.* Translated by Manheim, Ralph. New

Haven & London: Yale University Press, 1951.

Johnsen, Linda. *Lost Masters-Sages of Ancient Greece.* Honesdale, PA: Himalayan Institute Press, 2006.

Johnston, Sarah Iles. *Restless Dead.* Berkeley, Los Angeles, London: University of California Press, 1999.

--------. (ed.) *Religions of the Ancient World: A Guide.* Cambridge, Massachusetts and London, England: The Belknap Press of Harvard University Press, 2004.

Jones, Prudence & Pennick, Nigel. *A History of Pagan Europe.* London; New York: Routledge, 1995.

Joseph, Frank. *Before Atlantis: 20 Million Years of Human and Pre-human Cultures.* Rochester, VT.: Bear & Company, 2013.

Jung, C.G. *Memories, Dreams, Reflections.* edited by Jaffe', Aniela. New York: Vintage Books, 1963.

--------. *Man and His Symbols.* New York: Dell Publishing, 1964.

--------. *The Symbolic Life: Miscellaneous Writing* (The Collected Works of C.G.Jung, vol. 18. Bollingen Series XX. Princeton, NJ.:Princeton University Press, 1977.

--------. *Alchemical Studies.* Vol. 13. Princeton, NJ. Princeton University Press, 1983.

--------. *The Red Book, Liber Novus.* (Ed,& trans.) Shamdasani, Donu, Kyburz, Mark, Peck, John. London, New York: Norton W. W.& Co. Inc., 2009.

Kahn, Charles H. *Pythagoras and the Pythagoreans A Brief History.* Indianapolis/Cambridge: Hackett Publishing Co. Inc. 2001.

Kalweit, Holger. *Dreamtime & Inner Space: the world of the shaman.* Boston; London: Shambala, 1988.

Kaplan, Aryeh. *Sepher Yetzirah.* San Francisco, Ca., Newburyport, MA: Weiser Books,1997.

Kasak, Enn & Veede, Raul. *Understanding Planets in Ancient Mesopotamia.* Folklore Vol. 16, Tartu 2001.

Kaske, Carol V. and Clark, John R. *Marsilio Ficino, Three Books on Life: A Critical Edition and Translation with Introduction and Notes.* Binghamton, N.Y.: Medieval and Renaissance Texts and Studies, 1989.

Kazanas, N. "Plato and the Upanishads". *Department of Philosophy.* (website) Panjab University. 2004.

Kerenyi, Karl. *Eleusis Archetypal Image of Mother and Daughter.* Princeton, New Jersey: Bollingen Series LXV. 4 Princeton University Press, 1960.

Khol, Philip. *Archaeological Transformations. Crossing the Agricultural Pastoral Bridge.* Irana Antiqua. Leiden: E.J.Brill., 2002.

Kieckhefer, Richard. *Magic in the Middle Ages*. Cambridge: Cambridge University Press, 1990.

Kingsley, Peter. *Ancient Philosophy, Mystery and Magic*. Oxford: Clarendon Press, 1995.

--------. *In The Dark Places of Wisdom*. Inverness, CA.: The Golden Sufi Center, 1999.

--------. *A Story Waiting to Pierce You: Mongolia, Tibet and the destiny of the Western world*. Point Reyes Station, Ca.: 2010.

Kirk, G.S., Raven, J.E. & Schofield, Malcolm. *Presocratic Philosophers: a critical history with selection of texts*. Cambridge; New York: Cambridge University Press 1957, 1983.

Koch, Ulla Susanne. "Mesopotamian Astrology". CNI Publications, 1994.

Kraft, John. *The Goddess in the Labyrinth*. Abo: Abo Akademi, 1985.

Kramer, Peter D. *Freud: Inventor of the Modern Mind*. New York: Harper Collins/Atlas Books, 2006.

Kramer, Samuel Noah. *The Sumerians: their history, culture and character*. Chicago; London: University of Chicago Press, 1971, 1963.

--------. *History Begins at Sumer*. Philadelphia: University of Philadelphia Press, 1981.

Krupp, E.C. *Beyond the Blue Horizon: Myths and Legends of the Sun, Moon, Stars, and Planets*. New York: Harper Collins, 1991.

--------. *Skywatchers, Shamans & Kings: Astronomy and the Archaeology of Power*. New York, Chichester, Brisbane, Toronto, Singapore, Weinheim: John Wiley & Sons, Inc. 1997.

-------- *Echoes of Ancient Skies: The Astronomy of Lost Civilizations*. Mineola, N.Y.: Dover Publications, 2003.

Kucich, John J. "Ghostly Communion Cross-Cultural Spiritualism in Nineteenth Century American Literature." *Dartmouth. edu*. Hanover & London, University Press, 2004.

Kuznetsov, Nikolay. "Interview with Hungarian Folklorist and Ethnologist Mihaly Hoppal on the Occasion of his 70th Jubilee". *Folklore, Electronic Journal of Folklore*. Vol. 53, 2013.

Lachman, Gary. *The Quest for Hermes Trismegistus*. Edinburgh: Floris Books, 2001.

--------."Hypnogogia". *Fortean Times*, Oct. 2002.

--------. *Swedenborg: an introduction to his life and ideas*. New York; Jeremy Tarcher/Penguin 2012.

--------..*Jung The Mystic*. New York, NY: Jermeny P. Tarcher/Penguin, 2010.

Lamb, W.R.M. *Plato in twelve Volumes*, vol. #9. trans. Cambridge, Ma.: Harvard U Press; London: William Heinmann Ltd., 1925.

Lecouteux, Claude. *The Book of Grimoires*. Translated by Jon E. Graham. Rochester, Vermont, Toronto, Canada: Inner Traditions, 2013.

Lee, M. Owen. *Virgil as Orpheus: A Study of the Georgics*. Suny Series in Classical Studies. Albany: State University of New York Press., 1996.

Lenderling, Jona. "Alexander and the Chaldeans". *Livius Articles on Ancient History*. 1995-2013.

Lenormant, Francois. *Chaldean Magic: Its Origin and Development*. Kessinger Publishing 1994.

Leitch, Aaron. *Secrets of the Magical Grimoires*. Llewellyn Publications. Woodbury, MN., 2005.

Lethaby, W.R. "Architecture, Mysticism and Myth". 1892. *sacred-texts.com*.

Levi, Eliphas. *Transcendental Magic*. (trans. A.E. Waite) New York: Weiser Books, 1970.

Levin, Dan. "Shamans' Spirits Crowd Air of Mongolian Capital". *NYT.com*. July 10, 2009.

Lewis-Williams, David. *The Mind in the Cave*. London: Thames & Hudson, 2002.

Lewis-Williams, J. David; Pearce, D.G.. *Inside the Neolithic Mind*. London:Thames & Hudson, 2005.

Lewy, Hans. *Chaldean Oracles and Theurgy*. Paris: Institut d'Etudes Augustiniennes, 2011.

Linforth, Ivan M. *The Arts of Orpheus*, New York: Arno Press, 1973.

Lockyer, J. Norman. *The Dawn of Astronomy*. Cambridge, Mass.: M.I.T. Press, 1973.

Long, Charlotte R. *The Twelve Gods of Greece and Rome*. Leiden, New York, Kopenhaven, Cologne: E.J. Brill, 1987.

Colin Low. "The Tree of Life". *Hermetic Kabbalah*. 1995-2015.

Luck, George. *Arcana Mundi -Magic and the Occult in the Greek and Roman Worlds: A Collection of Ancient Texts*. Baltimore: The Johns Hopkins University Press, 2006.

Lyall, Sarah. "Building in Iceland? Better Clear It With the Elves First". *NY Times.com*. July 13, 2005.

MacCulloch, J. A. *The Religion of the Ancient Celts*. London: Constable, 1991, 1911.

Macurdy, Grace Harriet. "Traces of the Influence of Plato's Eschatological Myths in Parts of the Book of Revelation and the Book of Enoch".

Transactions and Proceedings of the American Philological Association, vol. 41 (1910) pp. 65-70.

Maenchen-Helfen, Otto. *The World of the Huns: Studies in Their History and Culture.* Berkeley: University of California Press,1973.

Manco, Jean. *Ancestral Journeys.* London: Thames & Hudson Ltd., 2013.

Magli, Giulio. "Sirius and the project of the megalith enclosures at Gobekli Tepi". *Arxiv.org.*

Mallory, J.P. *"In Search of the Indo-Europeans--Language, Archaeology and Myth".* London, Thames & Hudson.:1989

Malville J.McK, Wendorf, R., Schild, F. & Brenner, R. "Astronomy of Nabta Playa". *African Skies, no. 11, July 2007. The Smithsonian/NASA Astrophysics Data System.*

Mann, Charles C. "Gobekli Tepi- The Birth of Religion". *National Geographic,* June 2011.

Marshall, Peter. *The Mercurial Emperor: The Magic Circle of Rudolph II in Renaissance Prague.* London: Pimlico, 2007.

Marathakis, Ioannis. (trans.) *The Magical Treatise of Solomon or Hygromanteia.* Forward by Stephen Skinner. Singapore: Golden Hoard Press, 2011.

Mathers, MacGregor, S.L.; King, Francis. *Astral Projection, Ritual Magic and Alchemy.* New York, NY, Samuel Weiser: 1972, 1971.

Mathers, MacGregor, S.L.*The Key of Solomon the King (Clivicula Salomonis).* York Beach, Maine. Samuel Weiser, Inc.:1972.

--------. *The Book of the Sacred Magic of Abramelin the Mage.* New York: Dover Publications, Inc., 1975.

-------- (trans.); Crowley, Aleister. (ed.) *The Goetia: The Lesser Key of Solomon the King: Lemegeton — Clavicula Salomonis Regis.* York Beach, ME: Samuel Weiser, 1995.

Matthews, Caitlín; John, Matthews. *The Encyclopedia of Celtic Wisdom.* Shaftesbury, Dorset: Element, 1996.

Matthews, John. *The Druid Source Book: from earliest times to the present day.* London: Blandford Press, 1997.

Mavromantis, Andrea. *Hypnagogia.* London and New York: Rutledge & Kegan Paul,1987.

McGinn, Bernard; Collins, John J.; Stein, Stephen. *The Continuum History of Apocalypticism.* New York: Continuum, 2003.

McEvilley, Thomas. *The Shape of Ancient Thought (Comparative Studies in Greek and Indian Philosophies),* New York : Allworth Press, 2002.

McLean, Adam. "Animal Symbolism in the Alchemical Tradition". *The Alchemy Website.*

McNeill, William, H.; Petheo, Bela. *The Rise of the West: A History of the Human Community*. University of Chicago Press, 2009.

Mead, G.R.S. *Fragments of a Faith Forgotten*. (1900). Kila, MT.: Kessinger Publishing LLC, 1992

--------. Translator. "Stobaei Hermeticum, Libellus VI Of the Decans and the Stars". *The Hermetic Fellowship*. 1999.

--------. *The Doctrine of the Subtle Body in Western Tradition*. 1919. New York, NY: Cosimo Classics, 2005.

Mebane, John S. *Renaissance Magic & the Return of the Golden Age*. Lincoln & London: University of Nebraska Press, 1989.

Menchen-Helfen, Otto. *The World of the Huns: Studies in their History and Culture*. Berkeley: University of California Press, 1973.

Metzner, Ralph. *The Well of Remembrance: Rediscovering the Earth Wisdom Myths of Northern Europe*. Boston; London: Shambhala, 1994.

--------. "Shamanism, Alchemy & Yoga:Traditional Technologies of Transformation". *Green Earth Foundation*. 1987.

Merillat, Herbert Christian. "The Gnostic Apostle Thomas". Chapter 4--"Beyond the Law". *The Gnostic Society Library*. 1997.

Merkur, Dan. *Gnosis: an Esoteric Tradition of Mystical Visions and Unions*. Albany, NY.: State University of New York Press, 1993.

Meyer, Marvin W. *The ancient mysteries: a sourcebook: sacred texts of the mystery religions of the ancient Mediterranean world*. Philadelphia: University of Pennsylvania Press, 1999.

Milstein, Mati. "Oldest Shaman Grave Found; Includes Foot, Animal Parts". *National Geographic News*. Nov. 4, 2008.

Mirandola, Pico della. *On The Dignity of Man*.(trans. Wallis, Charles Glenn; Miller, Paul J.W.; Carmichael, Douglas). Indianapolis, Indiana: Bobbs-Merrill, 1965.

"Modern Behavior Began 40,000 years ago in Africa, Evidence Suggests". *Science Daily*. July 7, 1998. .University of Illinois at Urbana-Champaign.

Monroe, Robert A. *Journeys Out of the Body*. Garden City, New York: Doubleday & Company, Inc., 1971.

--------. *Ultimate Journey*. New York, NY:: Broadway Books, 1994.

--------. *Far Journeys*. New York, NY: Main Street Books, Doubleday & Company, Inc., 1985.

Moody, Raymond A. *Life After Life: the investigation of a phenomenon—survival of bodily death*. New York, NY.: Bantam Books,1975.

Moody, Raymond A.; Perry, Paul. *Reunions*. New York, NY.: Villard Books,

1993.

Munro, Dana Carelton. *Selections From the Laws of Charles the Great.* Kessinger Publishing, 2004.

Mylonas, George F. *Eleusis and the Eleusinian Mysteries.* Princeton: Princeton University Press, 1961.

Nabarz, Payam. *The Mysteries of Mithras.* Rochester, Vermont: Inner Traditions, 2005.

Narby, Jeremy & Huxley, Francis. *Shamans Through Time.* New York: Jeremy P. Tarcher/Penguin, 2004.

"Native Americans and Northern Europeans More Closely Related Than Previously Thought". *Science Daily.* Nov. 30, 2012. Jan. 1, 2014.

Naydler, Jeremy . *Temple of the Cosmos- The Ancient Egyptian Experience of the Sacred.* Rochester, Vermont: Inner Traditions, 1996.

--------. *Shamanic Wisdom of the Pyramid Texts- The Mystical Tradition of Ancient Egypt.* Rochester, Vermont: Inner Traditions, 2005.

--------. *Plato, Shamanism and Ancient Egypt.* Oxford: Abzu Press. 2005.

--------. *The Future of the Ancient World- Essays on the History of Consciousness.* Rochester, Vermont, Toronto, Canada: Inner Traditions, 2009.

Nelson, Geoffrey K. *Spiritualism and Society.* New York, NY. : Routledge & Kegan Paul, Ltd. 1969.

Nichols, Ross. *The Book of Druidry: History, Sites and Wisdom.* London: Aquarian/Thorsons, 1990.

Olcott, William Tyler. *Star Lore Of All Ages (1911) a collection of myths, legends, and facts concerning the constellations of the Northern Hemisphere/.* Kila, MT: Kessinger Publishing Co., 1966, 1911.

"Oldest Astronomical Megalith Alignment Discovered in Southern Egypt by Science Team". *University of Colorado Boulder* website:March 31, 1998.

Oppenheimer, Stephen. *The Real Eve.* New York: Carroll & Graf Publishers, Avalon Publishing Group, Inc., 2003.

Opsopaus, John. "The Ancient Esoteric Doctrine of the Elements: Fire." *Biblioteca Arcana.*1999.

Otto, Bernd-Christian; Stausberg, Michael. (eds.) *Defining Magic: A Reader.* Sheffield, Bristol, CT.: Equinox Publishing, Ltd. 2013.

Pagels, Elaine. *The Gnostic Gospels.* New York: Vintage Books, 1979.

PAP-(Science and Scholarship in Poland."Mesolithic sanctuary reveals constellation riddle". *Past Horizons.* Sept. 23, 2014.

Paracelsus; Turner, Robert; Skinner, Stephen. *The Archidoxes of Magic.* Berwick, Maine: Nicholas-Hays, Ibis Press, 2004.

Parpola, Simo. "The Mesopotamian Soul of Western Culture". Lecture on

Nov.1, 2000 at Harvard University. *Beth Suroyo Assyrian Organization*.

--------. "Sons of God- The Ideology of Assyrian Kingship". *Gateway to Babylon*. 1999.

--------. "The Assyrian Tree of Life: Tracing the Origins of Jewish Monotheism and Greek Philosophy". *Journal of Near Eastern Studies*, volume 52, No. 3. (July 1993) pp. 161-208.

Parry, Donald N.;Ricks, Stephen E. (eds.) Lundquist, John. *What Is A Temple? A Preliminary Typology. (83-118)* in *Temples of the Ancient World*. Salt Lake City: Desert Book and FARMS, 1994.

Pearson, Mike Parker. *Stonehenge A New Understanding*. New York: The Experiment, LLC: 2011.

Pederson, Olaf. *Early Physics and Astronomy: A History*. Cambridge: Cambridge University Press. 1974.

Pegg, Carole. *Mongolian Music, Dance, & Oral Narrative*. University of Washington Press: Seattle & London: 2001.

Pennick, Nigel. *Celtic Sacred Landscapes*. London: Thames and Hudson, 1996.

Peterson, Joseph, H. (trans.) *The Lesser Key of Solomon — Lemegeton Clavicula Salomonis*. York Beach, Maine: Weiser Books, 2001.

--------. "The Testament of Solomon". Trans. Conybeare, F.C. From *Jewish Quarterly Review, Oct. 1898*. Digital edition *Twilit Grotto-Esoteric Archives*. 1997.

Pike, Albert. *Morals and Dogma*. Richmond, Va.: L.H.Jenkins, Inc., 1949.

Pinch, Geraldine. *Magic in Ancient Egypt*. Austin: University of Austin Press, 1994.

Pingree, David. "The Sabians of Harran and the Classical Tradition". *Ebsohost.com*.

Plagels, Elaine H. *The Gnostic Gospels*. New York: Vintage, 1989.

Plato."Phaedrus". Fowler, Harold N. trans. *Plato in Twelve Volumes*.1925. *Perseus Digital Library*.

--------."The Republic- Book X". The Myth of Er. Trans. Jowett, Benjamin. *The Internet Classics Archive*. 1994-2009.

Pliny the Elder. *Natural History*. Books I-II. Trans. Rackham, H. Harvard, Ma.: Harvard University Press, 1938.

Pocs, Eva. *Traces of Indo-European Shamanism in South East Europe*. Tartu: Folk Belief Today, 1995.

Poemandres. "The Shepherd of Men", I. 25. Trans. Mead, G.R.S., *Gnosis. org*.

Poulkouras Iordanis- "The Eleusinian Mysteries". Paper Presented at the

7th Esoteric Quest Conference on The Mysteries and Philosophies of Antiquity, Samothrace. September 2008. *Iordanis.blogspot.com.*

Plutarch. *Plutarch's Moralia* translated by Babbitt, Frank Cole, Helmbold, W.C., and others. Cambridge, Mass: Harvard University Press; London: W. Heinemann, 1927, 1986.

Polo, Marco. *The Travels of Marco Polo.* Based on the Marsden-Wright translation. New York. Orion Press. 1958

Pratt, Christina. *An Encyclopedia of Shamanism.* Vol. 1, A-M. New York. The Rosen Publishing Group, Inc. 2007.

Rasmussen, Knud. *Across Arctic America: Narrative of the Fifth Thule Expedition.* Fairbanks, Alaska: University of Alaska Press, 1999, 1927.

Reale, Giovanni. Edited & translated by Catan, John R. *From the Origins to Socrates: A History of Ancient Philosophy. Vol. I.* Albany: State University of New York Press, 1987.

Reeder, Greg. "A Rite of Passage: The Enigmatic Tekenu in Ancient Egyptian Funerary Ritual". in *KMT: A Modern Journal of Ancient Egypt,* Fall, vol. 5 no. 3. 1994.

Reiner, Erica. *Astral Magic in Babylon.* Philadelphia: The American Philosophical Society, 1995.

Regardie, Israel. *The Golden Dawn.* Vol. 1 & 2. St. Paul, MN.: Llewellyn Publications, 1978.

Regardie, Israel; Cicero, Chic; Cicero Sandra Tabatha. *The Middle Pillar: The Balance Between Mind and Magic.* St. Paul, MN.: Llewellyn Publications, 2002.

Renfrew, Colin. *Archaeology & language: the puzzle of Indo-European origins.* New York: Cambridge University Press, 1987.

Ritner, Robert Kriech. *The Mechanics of Ancient Egyptian Magical Practice.* Chicago, Ill.: Oriental Institute Press, 1993.

Ristic, Radomir. translated by Carter, Michael C. Jr. *Balkan Traditional Witchcraft.* Sunland, CA: Pendraig Publishing, 2009.

Rona-Tas. Andras. *Hungarians and Europe in the Early Middle Ages: An Introduction to Early Hungarian History.* Budapest, New York: Central European University Press, 1999.

Rosano, Matt. "Did Meditating Make Us Human?". *Cambridge Archaeological Journal* 17 (1) : 47-58. 2009.

Roszak, Theodore. *Unfinished Animal: Aquarian Frontier and the Evolution of Consciousness.* New York: Harper & Row, 1977.

Roy, Christian. *Traditional Festivals: A Multicultural Encyclopedia.* Vol. 1. Santa Barbara: ABC-CLIO, 2004.

Rudgley, Richard. *Lost Civilizations of the Stone Age.* New York: NY, The Free Press, 1999.

Rudolph, Kurt; Wilson, R. McL., *Gnosis: The Nature and History of Gnosticism.* San Francisco: Harper & Row, 1983.

Ruggles, Clive. *Astronomy in Prehistoric Britain and Ireland.* New Haven & London: Yale University Press, 1999.

Sabourin, Leopold. *Priesthood: A Comparative Study.* Brill Academic Publishers, 1973.

Salles, Ricardo. *God and Cosmos in Stoicism.* Oxford, New York: Oxford University Press, 2009.

"Sami history". *Wikapedia.* HYPERLINK "https://en.wikipedia.org/wiki/Sami_history" https://en.wikipedia.org/wiki/Sami_history.

Sanders, N.K. "The Epic of Gilgamesh". *Assyrian Int. News Agency Books online.*

Sang-Hun, Choe. "In the age of the Internet, Korean shamans regain popularity". *NYT.com.* The New York Times, Asia Pacific, July 6, 2007.

Sarangerel. *Riding Windhorses: A Journey into the Heart of Mongolian Shamanism.* Rochester, VT: Destiny Books. 2000.

--------.. *Chosen by the Spirits: following your shamanic calling.* Rochester, VT: Destiny Books, 2001.

Saunders, Corinne. *Magic and the Supernatural in Medieval English Romance.* Woodbridge, Suffolk, UK; Rochester, NY: D.S. Brewer publishing, 2010.

Schlesier, Karl H. *The Wolves of Heaven.* Norman & London: University of Oklahoma Press, 1987.

Schmidt, Carl; MacDermot, Violet. *The Books of Jeu and the untitled text in the Bruce Codex.* Leiden: Brill Archive, 1978.

Schmidt, Klaus. *Gobekli Tepi, A Stone Age Sanctuary in South-Eastern Anatolia.* Berlin, Germany: Archae Nova, 2007.

Schneider, Tammi J. *An Introduction to Ancient Mesopotamian Religion.* Grand Rapids, MI./ Cambridge, U.K.: William B. Eerdmans Publishing Company, 2011.

Scholem, Gershom. *Kabbalah.* New York, Scarborough, Ontario: A Meridian Book, 1978.

--------. Werblowsky, R.J. Zwi. *Origins of Kabbalah.* Philadelphia: Jewish Publication Society; (Princeton) : Princeton University Press, 1987.

Schultz., Herbert. *The Prehistory of Germanic Europe.* New Haven, Conn.: Yale University Press, 1983.

Scot, Reginald. *The Discoverie of Witchcraft*. New York, NY: Dover Publications, Inc. 1972.
Grof, Stanislav. "Shamanic Crisis". *Spiritual Emergence Network Australia*. 2013.
Shaw, Gregory. "Containing Ecstasy: The Strategies of Iambichean Theurgy". Academia.edu. *Dionysius Vol XXI*. Dec. 2003, 5-88.
--------. *Theurgy and the Soul: the Neoplatonism of Iamblichus/* University Park, Pa.: Pennsylvania State University Press, Inc., 1995.
Shaw, Ian. *The Oxford History of Ancient Egypt*. Oxford; New York: Oxford University Press. 2000.
Shaltout, M. & Belmonte, M. "Archeoastronomy of Egyptian Temples". *Academia.edu*. Minufiya University, Egypt, Instituto de Astrofisica de Canarius, Spain, 2005.
Sheldrake, Rupert. *The Rebirth of Nature: the greening of science and God*. New York, Toronto, London, Sydney, Auckland: Bantam Books, 1991.
--------. *The Science Delusion: Freeing the Spirit of Enquiry*. London, Coronet Books, 2012.
Silva, Fabio. "Cosmologies in Transition Continuity, Innovation and Transformation in Neolithic Europe". *Academia.edu*. 2012.
Skinner, Stephen; Rankine, David. *The Veritable Key of Solomon: three different texts from those translated by S.L. MacGregor Mathers*. Woodbury, MN.: Llewellyn Publications, 2008.
Skinner, Stephen. *Techniques of Graeco-Egyptian Magic*. Singapore: Golden Hoard Press. 2014.
Smith, Mark S. *The Early History of God. Jahweh and the Other Deities in Ancient Israel*. New York, NY. HarperSanFrancisco, 1987.
Smith, Morton. *Jesus The Magician*. New York, Hagerstown, San Francisco, London: Harper & Row Publishers, 1978.
--------. Cohen, Shaye, J.D. *Studies in the Cult of Yahweh: New Testament, Early Christianity, and Magic (Religions in the Graeco-Roman World, vol. 130/2*. New York: E.J. Brill Academic Publishing, 1996.
--------."Ostanes: Legendary Mage in Classical and Medieval Literature". *Encyclopaedia Iranica*. 2002.
Sophia, Fotopoulou."The Nekromanteio at Acheron". *Newsfinder*. 2003.
Stamatellos, Giannis. *Plotinus and the Presocratics: A Philosophical Study of Presocratic Influences in Plotinus' Enneads*. Albany, NY : State University of New York Press, 2007.
Stanford, Dennis J., Bradley, Bruce A. *Across The Atlantic: The Origin of America's Clovis Culture*. Berkeley & Los Angeles: University of

California Press, 2012.

Stavrianos, Stavros, Leften. *A Global History From Prehistory to the Present.* New Jersey: Prentice, 1991.

Stratton-Kent, Jake. *Geosophia: the argo of magic: from the Greeks to the Grimoires/* Dover: Scarlet Imprint/ Biblioteque Rouge, 2010.

--------. *Necromancy.* Hermetic Tablet Journal of Western Ritual Magic. Winter Solstice, 2015:14.

Strmiska, Michael F. (ed.) *Modern Paganism in World Cultures, Comparative Perspectives.* Santa Barbara, Ca. ABC CLIO, 2005.

Stuckey Johanna. "Spirit Possession and the Goddess Ishtar in Ancient Mesopotamia". *Matrifocus Cross-Quarterly.* Samhain 2008 v. 8-1.

Stutley, Margaret. *Shamanism: An Introduction.* London; New York: Routledge. 2003.

Suzuki, D.T. *Essays in Zen Buddhism.* 1-3 series. London: Rider & Co., 2000.

"Summer Solstice Draws Thousands to Stonehenge". *BBC News Wiltshire-* June 21, 2013.

Swedenborg, Emmanuel. *Heaven and its wonders and hell: drawn from things heard and seen.* (trans.) Dole, George F.; Lang, Bernhard, and others. West Chester, Pa.: Swedenborg Foundation, 2000.

Emanuel Swedenborg. *Life on Other Planets.* West Chester, Pennsylvania, London, England: Swedenborg Foundation, Swedenborg Society, 2006.

Temple, Robert. *Oracles of the Dead- Ancient Techniques for Predicting the Future.* Rochester, Vermont: Destiny Books, 2002.

Thom, Alexander. *Megalithic Sites in Britain.* Oxford: Clarendon Press, 1967.

Thorsson, Eldred. *Futhark: A Handbook of Rune Magic.* York Beach, ME: Red Wheel/Weiser, LLC. 1984.

Thompson, Gary D."Paleolithic European Constellations- Ice-Age star maps? *Members.westnet.com.au* 2013.

Tinh, Tran Tam. Meyer, Ben R. ; Sanders, E.P. editors. *Sarapis and Isis. Jewish and Christian Self-Definition- Vol. Three.* Philadelphia: Fortress Press,1982.

Trithemius, Johannes. "The Art of Drawing Spirits into Crystals". (ed. & trans.) Joseph Peterson. *Twilight Grotto: Archives of Western Esoterica.*

Ulansey, David. *The origins of the Mithraic mysteries: cosmology and salvation in the ancient world.* New York: Oxford University Press, 1989.

Ustanova, Yulia. *The Supreme Gods of the Bosporan Kingdom: Celestial Aphrodite and the Most High God.* Brill Books, 1998.

Uyanik, Muvaffak. *Petroglyphs of South-Eastern Anatolia.* Graz: Akad. Druck-u. Verlaganst, 1974.

Uzdavinys, Algis; Porphyry. *The Heart of Plotinus-The Essential Enneads/* Bloomington, Ind.:World Wisdom, 2009.

--------. *Philosophy & Theurgy In Late Antiquity.* San Rafael, Ca. : Sophia Perennis, 2010.

--------. *Orpheus and the Roots of Platonism.* London: The Matheson Trust, 2011.

Van der Waerden, B.L. *History of the Zodiac.* SA: Archiv fur Orientforschung XVI. 2,5. 216-30, 1953.

Virgil. Translated by Mandelbaum, Allen. *The Aeneid of Virgil.* New York: Bantam Books, 1981.

Vitebsky, Piers. *Shamanism.* Norman: University of Oklahoma Press, 2001.

von Petzinger, Genevieve. "Initial findings from the study of 146 French rock art sites". *Bradshaw Foundation* 2011.

Voss, Angela. "God or the Daemon? A Platonic Astrology in a Christian Cosmos". *Angela Voss.org.*

--------. "Orpheus redivivus: The Musical Magic of Marsilio Ficino".

Wade, Nicholas. "24,000 Year-Old Body Shows Kinship to Europeans and American Indians". *The New York Times. Science.* Nov. 13, 2013.

Waite, Arthur Edward. *The Mysteries of Magic.* Health Research. 1986

Walker, D.P. *Spiritual and demonic magic from Ficino to Campanella.* University Park, Pa.: Pennsylvania State University Press, 2000.

Wallis, Robert J. *Shamans/Neo-Shamans: Ecstasies, Alternative Archaeologies & Contemporary Pagans.* London & New York: RoutledgeTaylor & Francis Group, 2003.

--------. "Re-Enchanting Rock Art Landscapes: Animic Ontologies, Nonhuman Agency and Rhizomic Personhood". *Time and Mind: The Journal of Archaeology, Consciousness and Culture.* 2(1) March 2009, pp.47-70.

Walsh, John. "John Walsh on Monday: Irish road side-tracked by the fairie's right of way". *The Independent,* Sept. 20, 1999.

Walsh, Roger N., M.D., Ph.D. *The Spirit of Shamanism.* Los Angeles: Jeremy P. Tarcher, Inc., 1990.

Walter, Mariko Namba; Fridman, Eva Jane Neumann, editors. *Shamanism: An Encyclopedia of World Beliefs, Practices and Culture,* Vol.1. Santa Barbara, Ca.: ABC-CLIO, 2004.

Warnock, Christopher (ed.) Greer, John Michael (trans.) *De Imaginibus of Thabit Ibn Qurra*. Lulu.com. 2013.

Washington, Peter. *Madame Blavatsky's Baboon*. New York: Schocken Books, 1995.

Wasson, R. Gordon; Hoffman, Albert; Ruck, Carl A.P. *The Road to Eleusis: Unveiling the Secret of the Mysteries*. New York and London: A Harvest/HBJ Book. 1978.

Waters, Frank. *The Book of the Hopi*. New York, NY.: Penguin Group, 1977.

Watkins, Colin. "The Neolithic revolution and the emergence of humanity a cognitive approach to the first comprehensive world-view." Academia. edu.

Webb, James. *The Occult Underground*. La Salle, Illinois: Open Court, 1974.

Wedeck, Harry E. *A Treasury of Witchcraft*. New York: Gramercy, 1989.

West, M.L. *Early Greek Philosophy and the Orient*. Oxford: Oxford University Press, 1971.

--------. *The Orphic Poems*. Oxford: Clarendon Press, 1983.

--------. *Indo-European Poetry and Myth*. Oxford, New York: Oxford University Press, 2007.

"What Does the Bible Say About Demons?". *The Bible Pages*. 2001.

White, Ethan Doyle. *Wicca: History, Belief, and Community In Modern Pagan Witchcraft*. Sussex Academic Press, 2015.

White, Gavin. *Babylonian Star Lore: an illustrated guide to the star-lore and constellations of ancient Babylonia/* London: Solaria Publications 2008.

Whitehouse, Dr. David. "Faces from the Ice Age". *BBC News-world edition*. Science/Nature. Tue. 28 May, 2002.

--------. "Oldest star chart found." *BBC News-world edition*. Science/Nature. Tue. 21 January, 2003.

Wiggerman, F.A.M. *Theologies, Priests, and Worship in Ancient Mesopotamia*. Edited by Sasson, Jack. M. *Civilization of the Ancient Near East*. 1995.

Wilby, Emma. *Cunning Folk and Familiar Spirits: Shamanistic Traditions in Early Modern British Witchcraft and Magic*. Brighton, Portland, Or: Sussex Academic Press, 2006.

--------. *The Visions of Isobel Gowdie: Magic, Witchcraft and Dark Shamanism in Seventeenth-Century Scotland*. Brighton; Portland, Or: Sussex Academic Press, 2011.

Wilford, John Noble. "Traces of Ancient Village Found Near Stonehenge". *New York Times, Science Section-* Jan. 30, 2007.

Wilkinson, Richard H. *The Complete Gods and Goddesses of Ancient Egypt*.

New York: Thames & Hudson, 2003.

Williams, Mike. *Prehistoric belief: shamans, trance and the afterlife.* Stroud: History Press, 2010.

--------."Beyond the Veil: Otherworld Experience as Archaeological Research". *Prehistoric Shamanism.* 2013.

Williamson, Ray, A. *Living the Sky: the Cosmos of the American Indian.* Norman, OK: University of Oklahoma Press, 1987.

Willis, Roy G. *World Mythology.* New York, NY.: H. Holt, 1993.

Winkelman, Dr. Michael. *Shamanism A Biopsychosocial Pardigm of Consciousness and Healing—Second Edition.* Santa Barbara, Ca: Praeger, 2010.

Wisse, Frederik; Walstein, Michael."Apocryphon of John". (trans.) From "The Apocryphon of John: Synopsis on Nag Hammadi Codices".1995. *The Gnostic Society Library.*

Wisse, Frederick. Trans. "Online Text for Apocryphon of John". *Early Christian Writings.* Kirby, Peter. 2014.

Witt, R.E. *Isis in the Ancient World.* Baltimore: Johns Hopkins University Press, 1997.

Witzel, E.J. Michael. *The Origins of the World's Mythologies.* Oxford; New York: Oxford University Press, 2012.

Wolkstein, Diane & Kramer, Samuel Noah. *Inanna Queen of Heaven and Earth.* New York: Harper & Row Publishers, 1983.

--------. "Inanna, Gilgamesh and the Huluppu Tree". Gilgamesh Epic, Tablet 12, *jewishchristianlit.com.* 1983.

Woolley, C.L. *The Sumerians.* New York, NY.: W.W. Norton, 1965.

Worms, Abraham von, compiled by Dehn, Georg. (trans.) Guth, Steven. *The Book of Abramelin- A New Translation.* Lake Worth, Fla: Nicholas-Hays, Inc. Ibis Press, 2006.

Yates, Frances, Amelia. *Giordano Bruno and the Hermetic Tradition.* Routledge, London and New York, 1964.

--------. *The Rosicrucian Enlightenment.* London and New York: Routledge Classics, 1972.

Zimmer, Carl. "DNA Deciphers Roots of Modern Europeans". *NYT Science,* June 10, 2015.

www.ingramcontent.com/pod-product-compliance
Lightning Source LLC
Chambersburg PA
CBHW050158240426
43671CB00013B/2168